Introduction to Program Design and Data Structures

TO THE STUDENT

There is a student solutions manual available with complete, step-by-step solutions to selected end-of-section exercises in this text, as well as complete, documented programs for two programming problems at the end of each chapter. Students can purchase the solutions manual from the local bookstore under the title *Student's Solutions Manual to Accompany Introduction to Program Design and Data Structures* prepared by James Cowles.

Introduction to Program Design and Data Structures

Thomas L. Naps
LAWRENCE UNIVERSITY

WEST PUBLISHING COMPANY
ST. PAUL NEW YORK LOS ANGELES SAN FRANCISCO

To Joseph L. Naps

Copyeditor: Sheryl Rose
Interior design: Paula Schlosser, Lucy Lesiak, and John Rokusek
Illustrations: Miyake Illustration and Design
Cover design: Miyake Illustration and Design
Indexer: Virginia Hobbs
Composition: Carlisle Communications
Production, PrePress, Printing and Binding:
West Publishing Company

WEST'S COMMITMENT TO THE ENVIRONMENT

In 1906, West Publishing Company began recycling materials left over from the production of books. This began a tradition of efficient and responsible use of resources. Today, up to 95 percent of our legal books and 70% of our college texts are printed on recycled, acid-free stock. West also recycles nearly 22 million pounds of scrap paper annually—the equivalent of 181,717 trees. Since the 1960s, West has devised ways to capture and recycle waste inks, solvents, oils, and vapors created in the printing process. We also recycle plastics of all kinds, wood, glass, corrugated cardboard, and batteries, and have eliminated the use of styrofoam book packaging. We at West are proud of the longevity and the scope of our commitment to our environment.

Printed in the United States of America

00 99 98 97 96 95 94 93 8 7 6 5 4 3 2 1 0

Library of Congress Cataloging-in-Publication Data

Naps, Thomas L.
Introduction to program design and data structures / Thomas L. Naps.
p. cm.
Includes index.
ISBN 0-314-93308-5 (soft)
1. Electronic digital computers—Programming. 2. Data Structures (Computer science) I. Title.
QA76.6.N357 1993
005.1—dc20 92-14933

 CIP

Contents

CHAPTER 5 ■ Stacks and Queues 259

CHAPTER 6 ■ More about Recursion 319

CHAPTER 7 ■ Binary Trees, General Trees, and Graphs 373

CHAPTER 8 ■ More Powerful Sorting Methods 449

Preface

In the recently released report, *Computing Curricula 1991,* the Association for Computing Machinery (ACM-IEEE-CS) Joint Curriculum Task Force emphasizes the recurring themes of abstraction, theory, and design in all areas of computer science. A student's second course in computer science is pivotal in emphasizing the importance of these themes. Typically students gain significant exposure to the syntactical details of a programming language in their first computer science course. The second course can then expose students to strategies for developing large, effective programs that solve problems frequently encountered by computer scientists. Students' knowledge of a language such as Pascal thus becomes a necessary tool that is to be used in the second course, analogous to the way that algebra must be used in a calculus course.

Introduction to Program Design and Data Structures begins with the assumption that the reader has a working knowledge of introductory Pascal such as that presented in *Pascal: Understanding Programming and Problem Solving* (third edition or second alternate edition) by Douglas W. Nance. This working knowledge should include familiarity with control structures, procedures and functions (used nonrecursively), parameter passing, arrays, records, sets, text files, and sequential files. From this starting point the text is structured around four objectives.

1. To demonstrate the application of software engineering principles in the design, coding, and testing of large programs.
2. To introduce students to essential data structures such as linked lists, queues, stacks, trees, and (to a lesser extent) graphs. This introduction emphasizes the definition of each structure as an abstract data type before discussing implementations and applications of that structure.
3. To provide a systematic approach to studying algorithms which focuses first on understanding the action of an algorithm and then on analyzing the algorithm from a theoretical time/space perspective. In particular, searching, sorting, and recursive algorithms are covered in detail.

4. To present students with an overview of what lies ahead in their study of computer science.

The first three objectives mesh directly with the themes of design, abstraction, and theory cited in the Joint Curriculum Task Force's report. The fourth objective is intended to stimulate student interest in the discipline of computer science. The student should complete the second course with an exposure to advanced areas and an enthusiasm to explore such areas more deeply.

Organization

Throughout the text, concepts are explained and developed carefully. Frequent examples and diagrams are used to introduce each concept. At the end of each chapter, a Focus on Program Design section uses the concepts presented in the chapter in the design of a complete program. The program designed in this section can often be used as a vehicle for further exploration of the concepts by the student. Throughout the text, emphasis is placed on good writing habits and program documentation. Where appropriate, style tips are offered to help students maintain a high degree of readability in their programs. The opening prologue of the text explicitly states and briefly reviews the Pascal prerequisites assumed in the rest of the text. The prologue should be skimmed before starting Chapter 1. Students should feel confident of their ability to work with all Pascal topics discussed in the prologue before proceeding in the text.

Collectively, Chapters 1–3 present more detailed treatment of software engineering principles. Chapter 1 introduces big-O analysis as the essential tool used by the computer scientist in evaluating alternative strategies from a time/space perspective. Simple sorting and searching algorithms are used as examples for the application of big-O analysis.

Chapter 2 is a critical chapter since it presents the formalism by which ADTs are studied throughout the remainder of the text. This formalism consists of specifying an ADT's operations as a set of language-independent preconditions and postconditions before moving to a Pascal interface for an ADT. Rules for using and implementing ADTs are developed. Strings, two-dimensional tables, and keyed lists are presented as examples of ADTs. Since students have studied big-O analysis in the previous chapter, they are well equipped to compare and contrast the efficiencies of various implementation techniques for these ADTs. These three examples recur frequently throughout the remainder of the text as we explore more advanced techniques for implementing ADTs.

Chapter 3 pulls together and expands upon the software engineering issues that have been introduced in earlier chapters. The first three sections of this chapter are critical in that they present a detailed treatment of the analysis, design, implementation, testing, maintenance, and obsolescence stages of the software system life cycle. The final three sections of the chapter discuss random access file processing, formal verification, and object-oriented programming respectively; these sections are independent of the rest of the text and can be covered at an instructor's discretion.

Chapters 4–7 cover essential data structures and recursion as advanced programming techniques. Each data structure is first defined as an abstract type; various implementations are then discussed and compared using the big-O terminology of Chapter 1. This provides a convincing demonstration of the utility of big-O analysis. Chapter 4, devoted to linked lists and pointers, discusses how linked lists might be used as an alternative implementation strategy for the ADTs that were introduced in Chapter 2. Chapter 5 covers stacks and queues, discussing simulation and parsing respectively as applications of these ADTs. As a follow-up to the discussion of stacks in Chapter 5, Chapter 6 explores recursion in depth. A graduated series of examples is presented, culminating with the use of trial-and-error backtracking as a problem-solving technique. Chapter 7 provides examples of the utility of recursion by using it as the primary technique for processing data in binary trees, general trees, and graphs. The importance of binary search trees as an alternative way of representing keyed lists is also discussed, with comparisons being drawn to the array and linked list implementations previously covered in Chapters 2 and 4. The material on general trees, graphs, and networks in the final two sections of Chapter 7 can be omitted without affecting a student's understanding of the chapters that follow.

The background in software engineering and data structures found in Chapters 1–7 prepares the student for the more complex sort and search algorithms of Chapters 8 and 9. In Chapter 8, sorting methods that break the $O(n^2)$ barrier are investigated. These methods include the shell sort, quick sort, heap sort, and merge sort. Chapter 9 scrutinizes search techniques such as hashing, indexing, indexed sequential search, B-trees, and tries.

T

Throughout this text, algorithms are implemented in standard Pascal. Due to the increasing use of Turbo Pascal with personal computers, Turbo Pascal references are included in the margins to indicate where Turbo differs from standard Pascal.

Features

This text has a number of noteworthy pedagogical features.

- Objectives—a concise list of topics and learning objectives in each section.
- Style tips—suggestions for programming style, intended to enhance readability.
- Exercises—short-answer questions at the end of each section.
- Programming problems and projects—lengthy lists of suggestions for complete programs and projects given at ends of chapters. Many of the projects involve communication skills, as well as programming skills.
- Module specifications for program modules.
- Structure charts to reflect modular development. These include use of data flow arrows to emphasize transmission of data to and/or from each module.
- Notes of Interest—vignettes intended to create awareness of and interest in various aspects of computer science. These provide a vehicle for giving students an overview of what lies ahead in their study of computer science.
- Suggestions for test programs—ideas included in exercises that encourage the student to use the computer to determine answers to questions and to see how to implement concepts in short programs.
- Focus on Program Design—at the end of each chapter, a complete program is designed (and in some cases fully implemented) to illus-

trate the use of concepts developed within the chapter. The Focus sections also introduce students to techniques for laboratory experimentation with complex algorithms.

- Running and debugging tips—these hints precede each end-of-chapter summary section.
- New terms are italicized when first introduced.
- Extensive figures and graphic documentation—these allow students to visualize the effect of algorithms on data. Algorithms are pictorially traced in a way that will bring them to life in the students' minds.
- Tables in chapter-end summaries—these are used frequently to compare and evaluate various Pascal features, data structures, and algorithms. Such compact, side-by-side comparisons emphasize the importance of knowing the relative advantages and disadvantages of the various techniques studied.
- In addition to use of graphic documentation to help students visualize algorithms, run-time trace diagrams are introduced as a means of analyzing recursive algorithms.
- Material emphasizing communication in computer science. This includes text references and exercises in every chapter designed to encourage students to interview people, write reports, give oral reports, and write program specifications without writing code.
- Optional material on formal verification and object-oriented programming is discussed in Chapter 3.

Ancillaries

It is my belief that a broad-based teaching support package is essential for an introductory course in Pascal. Thus, the following ancillary materials are available from West Publishing Company:

1. Laboratory Manuals—In keeping with my intent to provide a modern approach and to meet the growing need for laboratory experience as put forth by the new ACM Curriculum Guidelines, there are two laboratory manuals (one for users of standard Pascal and one for users of Turbo Pascal) that are tied closely to the text's pedagogy. Authored by Carol Wilson and Tom Naps and class-tested with students at two universities, both provide excellent sets of lab exercises to promote students' understanding.
2. A Student's Solutions Manual—This contains solutions to all odd-numbered exercises at the end of each section. These solutions represent more thorough answers than those provided in the Answers to Selected Exercises section in the text. Explanation and development are given for appropriate problems. Complete solutions for two programming problems are included for each chapter.
3. An Instructor's Manual—This manual contains the following for each chapter:
   a. outline
   b. teaching test questions
   c. chapter test questions
   d. answers to test questions
   e. solutions to all even-numbered end-of-section exercises

4. A Set of Transparency Masters—More than 100 transparency masters are available to adopters of the text. These include figures, tables, and selected other material from the text.
5. Software with Machine-Readable Programming Problems—This software contains at least two complete programming problem solutions for each chapter. It also includes the complete Focus on Program Design problem. This software is available for IBM-PCs and compatibles, Apple MacIntoshes, and DEC Vaxes, in both standard and Turbo Pascal.
6. A Computerized Test Bank—Adopters of this edition will receive a computerized test-generation system. This provides a test-bank system that allows you to edit, add, or delete as you wish.
7. West Publishing Company's videotape library—Adopters can choose from a list of relevant computer science videotapes. Contact your West representative for more information.

This text has been designed to mesh with either of two introductory Pascal texts by Douglas W. Nance—*Pascal: Understanding Programming and Problem-Solving* (third edition or second alternate edition). This meshing of texts also allows *Introduction to Program Design and Data Structures* to be used in a class in which other students may be studying from the second half of *Introduction to Computer Science: Programming, Problem-Solving, and Data Structures* (second edition or second alternate edition). The options afforded by the integration of these five texts allows two possible routes for students in a CS1/CS2 sequence. Those students who are initially uncertain about wanting to take CS2 and are using CS1 as an exploratory course for a possible major can use two separate texts for the two courses. Those students who are certain of pursuing a computer science major when enrolling in CS1 can use one text for the entire CS1/CS2 sequence, thereby holding down their book costs. Contact your West representative for details and examination copies of all of these texts.

Acknowledgments

The patient support of my editors at West, Jerry Westby and Denis Ralling, and copyeditor Janet Hunter has been a key ingredient in producing this text. I have now worked with Jerry, Denis, and Janet on a variety of authoring endeavors. In addition to being experts at what they do, they each have become valued long-distance friends. The production staff at West, especially production assistant Lynette D'Amico, have battled a variety of obstacles to keep simultaneous projects on schedule.

As I revised and revised, the wisdom of many reviewers has woven itself into the text. They are:

Stephen J. Allan
Utah State University

Anthony Q. Baxter
University of Kentucky

Sid Bradley
McNeese State University

Robert Christiansen
University of Iowa

Tomothy R. Colburn
University of Minnesota at Duluth

David Cordes
University of Alabama

Lee D. Cornell
Mankato State University

Aija Downing
University of Western Ontario

Linda J. Elliott
LaSalle University

C. Neil Harris
DeAnza College

Gary F. Hasman
Alfred University

Earl Hasz
Metropolitan State College of Denver

Linda Hayden
Elizabeth City State University

Michael Jenkin
York University

William C. Jones, Jr.
Central Connecticut State University

Debbie C. Kaneko
Hampton University

Angela R. Keith
Elizabethtown Community College

S.B. Khleif
Tennessee Technological University

Danny Kopec
University of Maine

Doris K. Lidtke
Towson State University

Antonio M. Lopez
Loyola University

Ronald A. Mann
University of Louisville

William A. Moy
University of Wisconsin-Parkside

Mostafa Nassar
Acadia University

William R. Nico
California State-Hayward

Joshua D. Panar
Ryerson Polytechnical Institute

Sue Pilgreen
McNeese State University

Ingrid F. Russell
University of Hartford

Kay G. Schulze
United States Naval Academy

Patricia A. McQuaid
Auburn University

David J. Thuente
Indiana-Purdue University at Ft. Wayne

Debra Trantina
Arizona State University

Winnie Y. Yu
Southern Connecticut State University

Jim Cowles, Ohio University in Lancaster, has done yeoman's work in preparing many of the ancillaries. Carol Wilson, Western Kentucky University, contributed two Notes of Interest and prepared a Laboratory Manual that can be used with this text. Marilyn Jussell, Kearney State College, revised the Turbo Pascal Notes (Appendix 6) to make this text more practical for classroom use when Turbo is being used by students in the class. George Pothering of the College of Charleston helped with final revisions. Lawrence students Chris Hundhausen, Beth Martinson, and Phoutha Keopanya all contributed solutions to selected exercises for the final section of back matter.

Of course, my greatest debt is to my family. Their contributions go much beyond word processing, proofreading, and making backups. Most importantly they offer continual reminders to put—and keep—computer science in its proper perspective.

Prologue—A Review of Pascal Essentials

This is *not* an introductory programming text. Rather, it assumes that you have acquired basic programming skills and now want to use these skills to explore more advanced problems in computer science. Preferably these skills are in the Pascal language since that is the language in which we will ultimately express the algorithms we develop.

The purpose of this prologue is to review those Pascal tools that are prerequisite to the chapters that follow. These tools are:

- Simple data types: **integer, char, boolean, real**, user-defined subranges, enumerated types
- Selection control structures: **IF-THEN, IF-THEN-ELSE**, and **CASE**
- Iteration control structures: **FOR, WHILE,** and **REPEAT-UNTIL**
- Structured data types including **ARRAYs, RECORDs, SETs**
- Procedures, functions, parameter passing by value and reference (but not including recursive procedures)

If you are confident of your ability to use these tools, feel free to skim the rest of the prologue and begin Chapter 1 in earnest. (However, be sure to read the material on pre- and postconditions and procedural abstraction at the end of the prologue since we establish standards there for our presentation of algorithms throughout the text.) If you feel you need a quick review of these Pascal topics, read the prologue thoroughly. If you are not familiar with some of the topics, read the prologue in conjunction with a more detailed introductory text on Pascal programming, such as *Pascal: Understanding Programming and Problem Solving*, 3rd edition, by Douglas W. Nance (St. Paul, MN: West Publishing, 1992).

Simple Data Types in Pascal Programs

Simple data types are characterized by the fact that the values they admit are *atomic*, that is, they admit no further decomposition. In standard Pascal we have the following simple types:

integer
real
boolean
char
enumerated types
subranges

together with the standard arithmetic (+, −, *, /), logical (**AND, OR, NOT**), and relational (=, <, >, <=, >=, <>) operators that accompany them. Special operations exist for certain types, such as **MOD** and **DIV** for integer.

Recall that TYPE declarations for user-defined enumerated types and subranges are made between the CONST and VAR sections of a Pascal program.

```
CONST
  .
  .
  .
TYPE
  TwentiethCentury = 1900 .. 1999;                     { subrange type    }
  Weather = (Cloudy, Sunny, Rainy, Snowy, Balmy);      { enumerated type }
VAR
  CurrentYear : TwentiethCentury;
  Today, Tomorrow, Yesterday : Weather;
```

Subranges can often be used to build into a program a degree of protection against bad data. If, for example, a data entry operator inadvertently types 1892 instead of 1992 for the current year, execution of a program would halt with the statement

```
readln (CurrentYear);
```

since 1892 is not in the defined subrange. This is not necessarily the best way to avoid bad data with an interactive program, but it is better than allowing bad data to filter through software undetected.

Enumerated types, such as Weather in the previous declarations, allow you to express clearly the logical nature of data and enhance the readability of your program. Typically, enumerated types are used in situations where data admits a relatively small number of values. Without enumerated types, we would have to come up with a numeric coding scheme for these values, for example:

1 corresponds to cloudy weather
2 corresponds to sunny weather
3 corresponds to rainy weather
4 corresponds to snowy weather
5 corresponds to balmy weather

A program working with weather data would then have a large number of statements in this form:

```
IF Today = 2 THEN ...
```

Such statements do not convey program logic as well as a corresponding statement using an enumerated type:

```
IF Today = Sunny THEN ...
```

Enumerated types can also be used as index ranges for arrays. One of our main uses of enumerated types in this text occurs in Chapter 3, where we study a technique known as finite state logic, which can be used to guard a program against faulty input from a user.

■ Selection Control Structures in Pascal

Selection control structures are used to select logical paths through a program. Pascal offers three different means of selecting logical control: **IF-THEN, IF-THEN-ELSE,** and **CASE**. An **IF-THEN** statement selects a particular action upon a condition's evaluating to **true**. No action is taken when the condition is **false**. As an example, consider:

```
VAR
  X, Num : real;
  PostCount : integer;
  .
  .
  .
  IF Num > 0 THEN
    BEGIN
      PosCount := PosCount + 1;
      X := sqrt (Num)
    END;
```

IF-THEN-ELSE logic selects one action upon a condition's evaluating to **true** and a different action upon a **false** evaluation. For instance, to handle negative values in the previous example, we would have:

```
IF Num >= 0 THEN
  BEGIN
    NonNegCount := NonNegCount +1;
    X := sqrt (num)
  END
ELSE
  BEGIN
    NegCount := NegCount + 1;
    X := sqrt (abs (Num))
  END;
```

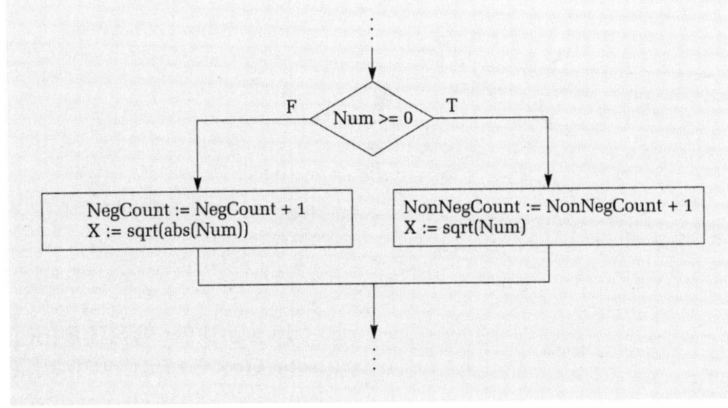

Pascal's **CASE** structure can be used for multiway selection involving ordinal data types such as **integer**, **char**, and enumerated types. For instance, the following **CASE** statement converts an **integer** quiz score between 0 and 100 inclusive to an appropriate letter grade:

```
VAR
  Score, NewScore : integer;
  Grade : char;
  .
  .
  .
  NewScore := Score DIV 10;
  CASE NewScore OF
    10,9            : Grade := 'A';
    8               : Grade := 'B';
    7               : Grade := 'C';
    6, 5            : Grade := 'D';
    4, 3, 2, 1, 0 : Grade := 'F'
  END; { of CASE NewScore }
```

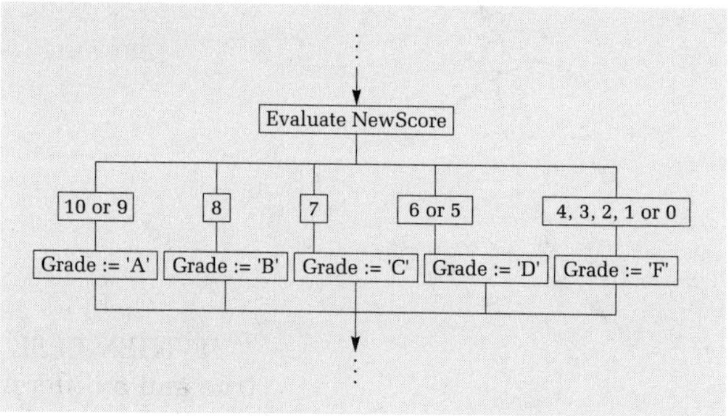

Evaluate NewScore

10 or 9 | 8 | 7 | 6 or 5 | 4, 3, 2, 1 or 0

Grade := 'A' | Grade := 'B' | Grade := 'C' | Grade := 'D' | Grade := 'F'

Iteration Control Structures in Pascal

Fixed repetition of a block of code in Pascal is accomplished by using a **FOR. . .TO. . .DO** loop. For example, the following segment accumulates a total of 30 scores read from standard input:

```
Total := 0;
FOR J := 1 to 30 DO
  BEGIN
    readln (Score);
    writeln (Score:20);
    Total := Total + Score
  END;
```

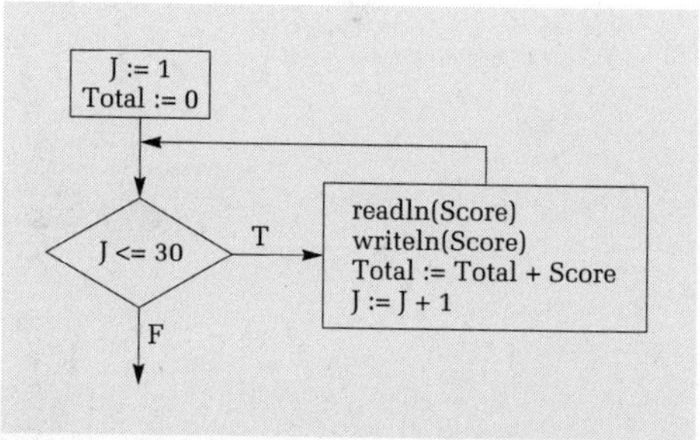

J := 1
Total := 0

J <= 30

T

F

readln(Score)
writeln(Score)
Total := Total + Score
J := J + 1

In a pretest **WHILE** loop, a Boolean condition controls the iteration. Moreover, this condition is checked *before* execution of statements in the body of the loop. This is illustrated in the following code that accumulates a stream of values terminated by a nonpositive sentinel:

```
Total := 0;
readln (Score);
WHILE Score > 0 DO
  BEGIN
    Total := Total + Score;
    readln (Score)
  END;
```


The third iteration control strategy offered in Pascal is a posttest **REPEAT-UNTIL** loop. Again a Boolean condition is used to control the loop. However, unlike a **WHILE** loop, the Boolean condition is not checked until after the body of the loop is executed. The **REPEAT-UNTIL** structure can be conveniently used to accumulate a series of values terminated by a user's response to a query.

```
Total := 0;
REPEAT
  write ('Enter score -->');
  readln (Score);
  Total := Total + Score;
  write ('Another score?');
  readln (Query)
UNTIL (Query = 'N') OR (Query = 'n');
```

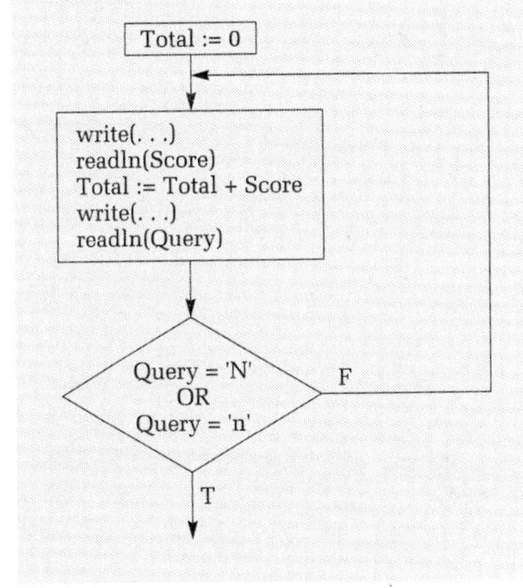

■ Structured ARRAY Types in Pascal

A variable of a structured type uses one identifier to reserve memory capable of holding several individual values. With the array structured type, each individual value within the variable must be the same uniform base type. These base type values are arranged in an indexed order with an accessible first element, second element, third element, and so on. For instance, the following **TYPE** and **VAR** declarations establish an array of 100 integer locations:

```
TYPE
  List100 = ARRAY [1..100] OF integer;
VAR
  Scores : List100;
```

To access individual array entries and determine the largest value in Scores, we have the following segment of code:

```
Max := Score[1];            { Initialize Max to first array value }
FOR J := 2 TO 100 DO
  IF Score[J] > Max THEN    { Compare Max to Jth array entry }
    Max := Score[J];
```

Pascal arrays may be indexed by a subrange of any ordinal type such as **integer**, **char**, or an enumerated type. Strings of characters should be declared to be **PACKED ARRAY OF char**. This allows strings to be written and compared as entire entities without having to refer to individual index positions. Arrays of dimensions higher than one are declared with multiple index subranges, as illustrated by the following:

```
TYPE
  Table4x7 = ARRAY [1..4, 1..7] OF integer;
VAR
  Table : Table4x7;
```

For example, to initialize each Table entry to the sum of its row and column coordinates, a nested loop structure is used in conjunction with double index notation:

```
FOR Row := 1 TO 4 DO               { Row index           }
FOR Col := 1 TO 7 DO               { Col index           }
Table[Row, Col] := Row + Col;      { Double index notation }
```

■ Structured RECORD Types in Pascal

Whereas an array variable forms an aggregate of indexed data items of the same type, a record variable encapsulates data items of potentially different types. Individual items within a record are called fields. Fields may be accessed by using the record name followed by a period (.) and the field name. The following example illustrates this syntax in printing out an array of patient records:

```
TYPE
  String20 = PACKED ARRAY [1..20] OF char;
  PatientInfo = RECORD
                  Name : String20;
                  Age : 0..100;
                  Weight : 0..300
                END;  { of RECORD PatientInfo }
  PatientList = ARRAY [1..100] OF PatientInfo;
VAR
  Patient : PatientList;
.
.
.
FOR J := 1 TO NumPatients DO
  BEGIN
    writeln (Patient[J].Name:30);
    writeln (Patient[J].Age:10, Patient[J].Weight:10)
  END; { of FOR...TO loop }
```

The continual prefacing of a field name by a record name can be eliminated conveniently by using the **WITH** statement. This statement specifies that all field names are to be considered as belonging to the record in the **WITH** clause. The above loop, rewritten using **WITH** syntax, appears as follows:

```
FOR J := 1 TO NumPatients DO
  WITH Patient[J] DO    { Name, Age, Weight now belong to Patient[J] }
    BEGIN
      writeln (Name:30);
      writeln (Age:10, Weight:10)
    END;  { of WITH and FOR }
```

Structured SET Types in Pascal

A set in Pascal consists of a collection of distinct elements from a uniform base type (which must be an ordinal type). A set is defined and used in Pascal in a manner consistent with the use of sets in mathemetics. In particular, this means there is no concept of the position of an element in a set. For example, in a program working with letters of the alphabet, you could declare

```
TYPE
  Alphabet = SET OF 'A'..'Z';
VAR
  Vowels, Consonants : Alphabet;
```

Vowels and Consonants can be initialized to their appropriate contents via assignment statements.

```
Vowels := ['A', 'E', 'I', 'O', 'U'];
Consonants := ['B'..'D', 'F'..'H', 'J'..'N', 'P'..'T', 'V'..'Z']
```

A character that is read could then be examined to see if it was a vowel or consonant using the Pascal reserved word **IN** to test for set membership:

```
VAR
  C : char;
  .
  .
  .
  IF C IN Vowels THEN
    writeln (C, 'is a vowel')
  ELSE IF C IN Consonants THEN
    writeln (C, 'is a consonant')
  ELSE
    writeln (C, 'is not a capital letter');
```

IN tests whether or not a given datum of the base type is a member of a set; other Pascal relational operators can be used to determine whether one set is equal, not equal, subset of, or superset of another set. If A and B are sets, these relational operators between two sets are defined as follows:

Operator	Relational Expression	Definition
= (Equal)	A = B	A equals B; that is, every element in A is contained in B and every element in B is contained in A.
<> (Not equal)	A <> B	A does not equal B; that is, either A or B contains an element that is not contained in the other set.
<= (Subset)	A <= B	A is a subset of B; that is, every element of A is also contained in B.
>= (Superset)	A >= B	A is a superset of B (B is a subset of A); that is, every element of B is contained in A.

Boolean values associated with some set expressions follow.

Set Expression	Boolean Value
`[1,2,3] <= [0..10]`	**true**
`[0..10] <= [1,2,3]`	**false**
`[0..10] = [0..5, 6..10]`	**true**
`[] = ([1,2] - [0..10])`	**true**
`[1..5] <> [1..3, 4, 5]`	**false**

Finally, Pascal provides for the set operations *union, intersection*, and *difference* where, in each case, two sets are combined to produce a single set. If A and B are sets of the same type, these operations are defined as follows:

- The union of A and B is A + B where A + B contains any element that is in A or in B.
- The intersection of A and B is A * B where A * B contains the elements that are in both A and B.
- The difference of A and B is A − B where A − B contains the elements that are in A but not in B.

One caution that must be exercised in using sets is that most implementations of Pascal limit the maximum size of the base type of a set. This limit is such that a base type of **integer** is not allowed. Often the limit is 128 so base types of **char** and subranges of **integer** within 0..127 can usually be used. Later in this text, we shall study ways of implementing set types that are more general than those built into Pascal.

Procedures and Functions in Pascal

Perhaps the most critical skill one acquires in an introductory Pascal course is the ability to solve problems in a structured style. *Structured programming* is the process of developing a program by placing emphasis on the communication between independent modules. Connections between these modules are specified in parameter lists and are usually controlled by the main program. Structured programming is especially suitable to large programs being worked on by teams. By carefully specifying what information is to be received by and returned from the modules, a team of programmers can independently develop their modules and then connect them to the complete program.

To encourage developing programs in a modular, structured style Pascal offers two types of subprograms—procedures and functions. A function is more restricted in its definition in that all of a function's parameters must be value parameters, that is, parameters that are transmitted to the function as copies of values from the program that calls the function. Any altering of a value parameter thus occurs only within the function itself. Upon return from a function, the values of all actual parameters transmitted to the function remain intact. The value computed by a function is returned through the name of the function and must be a simple type such as **integer**, **real**, **char**, **boolean**, or a user-defined enumerated type. The following example illustrates these concepts in a function that computes b^n for any real value b and nonnegative integer exponent n:

```
FUNCTION Power (Base : real;
                Exponent : integer) : real;

  { Given:  Base, a real number, and Exponent, a nonnegative integer.     }
  { Task:   Raise Base to the Exponent power by repeated multiplication.  }
  { Return: Power is Base raised to the Exponent power.                   }

  VAR
    TempPower : Real;
    K : integer;

  BEGIN
    TempPower := 1.0;
    FOR K := 1 TO Exponent DO
      TempPower := TempPower * Base;
    Power := TempPower { Value returned in function name }
  END;  { FUNCTION Power }
```

A call to the Power function from a main program (or any procedure or function whose definition follows that of Power) would appear as:

```
A := Power (3.2, 4);
```

Unlike a function, a Pascal procedure is not limited to returning a single value of a simple type. A procedure's parameter list can include variable parameters as well as value parameters. Variable parameters, also called reference parameters, are denoted by using the reserved word **VAR** to precede the parameter name in the procedure heading. In contrast to a value parameter, the transmission of a datum via a variable parameter allows the procedure to access the actual memory location of the corresponding variable in the calling program. Hence, a procedure can assign or otherwise alter the value of any actual parameter that it receives in a **VAR** parameter slot. To illustrate this difference between value and variable parameters, consider the following complete program. The graphic documentation that accompanies the program highlights the way in which parameters are passed between the main program and **PROCEDURE** VarDemo.

```
PROGRAM ProcDemo (output);

VAR
  X, Y : real;
  Ch : char;

{***********************************************************}

PROCEDURE VarDemo (VAR X1 : real;
                   Y1 : real;
                   VAR Ch1 : char);

  { Given:   Two reals X1, Y1, and a character Ch1                }
  { Task:    Print the values received, change the values,        }
  {                and print the new values                       }
  { Return:  New values for X1 and Ch1                            }

  BEGIN
    writeln (X1:10:2, Y1:10:2, Ch1:5);
    X1 := 2 * X1;
    Y1 := 2 * Y1;
    Ch1 := '*';
    writeln (X1:10:2, Y1:10:2, Ch1:5)
  END;  {  of PROCEDURE VarDemo  }

{***********************************************************}
```

```
BEGIN  {  Main program  }
  X := 3.6;
  Y := 5.2;
  Ch := 'A';
  writeln (X:10:2, Y:10:2, Ch:5);
  VarDemo (X, Y, Ch);
  writeln (X:10:2, Y:10:2, Ch:5)
END.  {  of main program  }
```

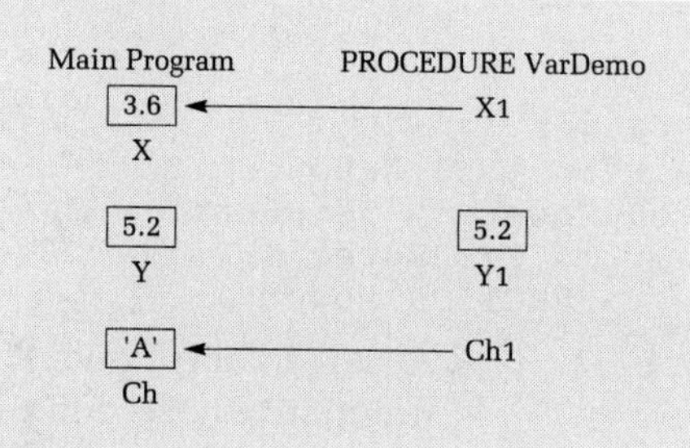

The output from the program is:

```
3.60       5.20    A     (from main program)
3.60       5.20    A     (from procedure)
7.20      10.40    *     (from procedure)
7.20       5.20    *     (from main program)
```

The variables can be depicted as

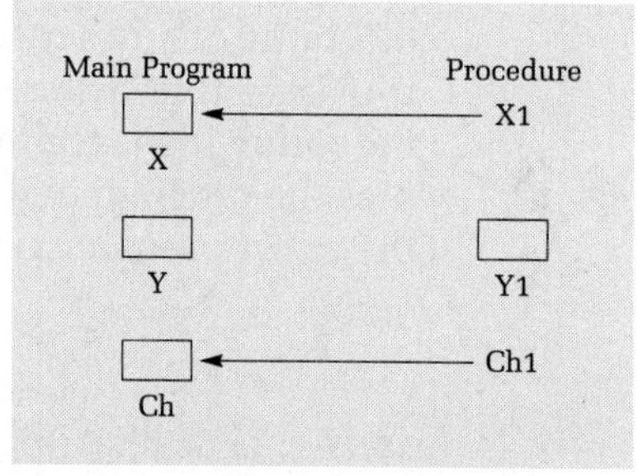

The assignment statements

```
X := 3.6;
Y := 5.2;
Ch := 'A';
```

produce

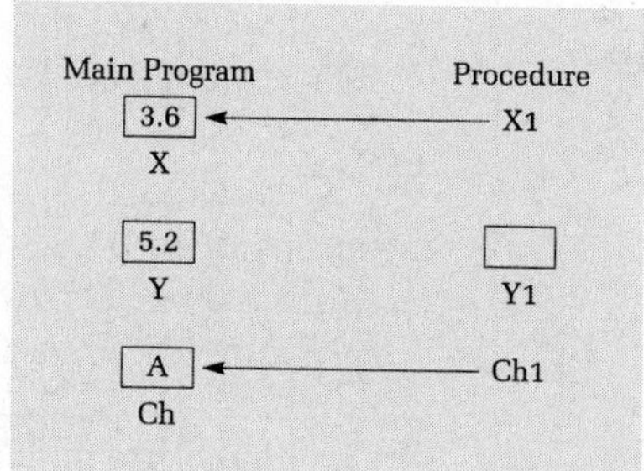

When the procedure is called by

```
VarDemo (X, Y, Ch);
```

the contents can be envisioned as

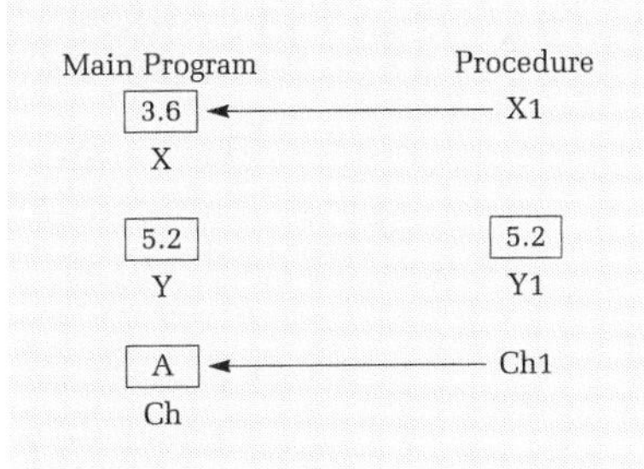

When the procedure assignment statements

```
X1 := 2 * X1;
Y1 := 2 * Y1;
Ch1 :- '*';
```

are executed, the variables become

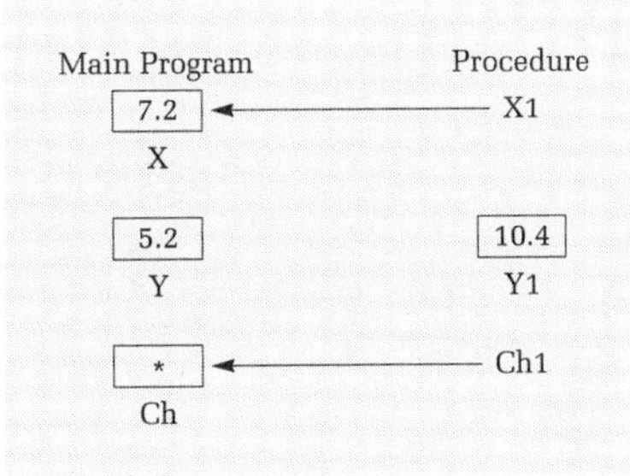

Notice that changes in the variable parameters X1 and Ch1 produce corresponding changes in X and Ch, but a change in the value parameter Y1 does not produce a change in Y.

■ Preconditions and Postconditions

The form of a function's or procedure's definition and its invocation should be familiar from your prior work in Pascal. We wish to emphasize here, however, the role of a function or procedure as an expression of an algorithm in and of itself. The algorithm embodied by the function is completely self-contained in that it makes no use of any global data.

Despite its being self-contained, the utility of a function or procedure depends on the degree to which it can be integrated into larger programs. For this integration to occur, we must have a precise definition of what the function does (though not necessarily the details of how it does it). A convenient way of providing such a definition is to include a block of introductory documentation for the function or procedure that specifies the *preconditions* and *postconditions* for the underlying algorithm. The preconditions for an algorithm specify what can be expected to be true before the algorithm executes; the postconditions specify what can be expected to be true when the algorithm terminates.

Returning to our earlier example of **FUNCTION** Power, the preconditions of the algorithm implemented in this function are:

1. Base is a real number.
2. Exponent is a nonnegative integer.

The sole postcondition is that Power will return Base raised to the Exponent power. The algorithm's preconditions inform us that this particular algorithm will not compute powers for an exponent that is negative or not a whole number.

From the perspective of a Pascal procedure (or function), the pre- and postconditions of the underlying algorithm establish the interface for the procedure. Someone writing a procedure must make sure that the coding inside the procedure adheres to this interface. Anyone incorporating a procedure into a larger program must make sure to use that procedure in a fashion consistent with that interface. Given the paramount importance of interfaces to procedures and functions, it is critical that they be specified consistently and precisely. The style we shall use throughout this text is illustrated in the previous Power and ProcDemo examples. The header for all procedures and functions should be followed by a block of documentation in the following form:

```
{ Given:  The preconditions for the algorithm implemented by the        }
{         procedure. A precise statement of what is true of the values  }
{         given to the algorithm from a calling program.                 }
{ Task:   The computational responsibilities of the algorithm.          }
{ Return: The postconditions for the algorithm. A precise statement of  }
{         what values are returned by the algorithm to the calling      }
{         program.                                                       }
```

Procedural Abstraction

By adopting the view that a procedure or a function is the implementation of a precisely defined interface, we greatly simplify the reasoning needed to write large, complex programs. During the design stage, as a problem is subdivided into tasks, the problem solver (you) should have to consider only what a procedure is to do and not be concerned about details of the procedure. Instead, the procedure name and comments at the beginning of the procedure should be sufficient to inform the user as to what the procedure does. Developing procedures in this manner is referred to as *procedural abstraction.*

Procedural abstraction is the first step in designing and writing a procedure. The list of parameters and comments about the action of the procedure should precede writing the procedure body. This forces clarity of thought and aids design. Using this method might perhaps cause you to discover that your design is not sufficient to solve the task and that redesigning is necessary. Therefore, you could reduce design errors and save time when writing code.

Procedural abstraction becomes especially important when teams work on a project. Each member of the writing team should be able to understand the purpose and use of procedures written by other team members without having to analyze the body of each procedure. This is analogous to the situation in which you use a predefined function without really understanding how the function works.

The theme of abstraction is one we shall often return to in this text. In general terms, wherever this theme emerges, it refers to a layer of separation between the formal definition of a concept and its eventual implementation in a programming language (for us, Pascal). For procedures and functions, this layer of separation is an interface provided in terms of pre- and postconditions. We will soon see how abstraction can also enhance our ability to define complex data structures as well as procedures and functions.

Nothing puzzles me more than time and space.
Charles Lamb 1775–1834

Algorithm Analysis—Space and Time Considerations

In this chapter, we will introduce a technique for analyzing the efficiency of algorithms. We can then use this technique, known as *big-O analysis,* to categorize algorithms with respect to the length of time and the amount of storage they require for their execution. In Sections 1.2 and 1.3, we will use big-O analysis to examine the time efficiency of some simple sorting algorithms. In Section 1.4, we will use big-O analysis to describe the interplay between the time and storage requirements of an algorithm. In Section 1.5, we will analyze the time efficiency of simple *search algorithms*. Finally, in the Focus on Program Design section, we will discuss a scheme for developing programs to measure empirically the efficiency of an algorithm.

1.1 Designing Programs—A Look Back and a Look Ahead

OBJECTIVES

- to develop a prespective on the study of computer science beyond the learning of a particular programming language, such as Pascal
- to be able to identify criteria by which complex software is evaluated

You are embarking upon an important step in your exploration of computer science. Up to this point, it has been difficult to divorce your study of computer science from the learning of Pascal. You have developed problem-solving skills, but the problems encountered have been very focused. That is, the problems were chosen specifically to illustrate a particular feature of Pascal. This is the way that problem-solving skills must be developed: starting with small problems and working toward large ones.

By now you know almost all features of the Pascal programming language. You are ready to direct your attention toward larger, more complex problems that require integrating many of the particular skills you have developed. Now our attention will be directed more toward issues of software design and less toward describing Pascal. If we need a particular feature of Pascal that has not yet been discussed, we will introduce it when appropriate. But our primary objective is to study more complex problems and the software design issues that arise out of them. From here on, we view Pascal primarily as the vehicle to implement, test, and experiment with our solutions to problems. The techniques of software design we are about to explore will enable us to write programs that are

- Large. Actually our programs could properly be called systems since they typically involve numerous modules that interact to solve one complex problem.
- Reliable. The measure of the reliability of a system is that it anticipate and handle all types of exceptional circumstances.
- Flexible. The system should be easily modified to handle circumstances that may change in the future.
- Expandable. If the system is successful, it will frequently spawn new computing needs. We should be able to incorporate solutions to these new needs into the original system with relative ease.
- Efficient. The system should make optimal use of time and space resources.
- Structured. The system should be divided into compact modules, each of which is responsible for a specific, well-defined task.
- User-friendly. The system should be clearly documented so that it is easy to use.

In designing software to meet these criteria, one of the key skills you must develop is the ability to choose the appropriate tools for the job. You should not have to rediscover algorithms and techniques for information storage and retrieval each time you write a new program. As a computer scientist, you must have a detailed knowledge of algorithms and data storage techniques at your fingertips and be able to apply this knowledge when designing software to solve a variety of problems. You should be able to look into your storehouse of algorithms and data storage strategies, choose the most appropriate methods, and then tailor them to the application at hand.

As you expand your knowledge of computer science, you will find that a given problem frequently lends itself to more than one method of solution. Hence, in addition to knowing the individual principles, you must also be able to evaluate them comparatively. This comparative evaluation must be conducted in as systematic and quantitative a fashion as possible. That is, you must be able to justify your choice of a method by presenting cogent arguments based on facts and figures pertinent to the problem. Given this perspective on computer science, we must turn our attention to a twofold task:

1. Stocking our algorithmic toolbox with methods that have become standards in computer science.
2. Developing criteria for knowing which tool to choose in a particular situation.

To begin this task, we reach back to the sorting and searching algorithms that you probably encountered in your first computer science course. We also consider some new techniques for sorting and searching. We then evaluate these techniques for their efficiency in terms of execution time and use of space (memory) resources. To conduct such a time/space analysis, we introduce what has come to be known as big-O notation. In effect, big-O notation is the mathematical measuring stick by which computer scientists quantitatively evaluate algorithms. It allows us to place algorithms into categories based on their efficiency. Such categorization helps us determine whether or not a proposed solution is practical in terms of the real world requirements and constraints dictated by the problem.

1.2 Simple Sorting Algorithms

Our discussion in this section will use an array of records that we want to sort in ascending order according to a given field within each record. The field on which the sort is based is known as the key field. For instance, we may wish to arrange a list of student records in alphabetical order according to student last name or a list of inventory records in order according to product identification numbers. Hence the following Pascal declarations provide a suitable setting for our coming discussion of the sorting problem.

```
CONST
  MaxIndex = 100;       {  Easily adjusted  }

TYPE
  SortRecord = RECORD
                 Key : KeyType;  {  Any type that can be ordered  }
                 OtherData : WhateverType {  Data associated with the Key  }
               END;
  SortArray = ARRAY [1..MaxIndex] OF SortRecord;
```

We wish to write a sort procedure that meets the following specifications:

```
PROCEDURE Sort (N : integer; VAR List : SortArray);

  {  Given:   Array List containing entries in locations 1 through N.       }
  {  Task:    Apply appropriate sorting algorithm to these entries.         }
  {  Return:  Array List with first N entries arranged in ascending order.  }
```

OBJECTIVES

- to develop a procedural interface that can be used with a variety of sorting algorithms
- to understand the potential difference in efficiency between the computer operations of comparing data items and interchanging them
- to be able to trace in detail the comparisons and interchanges of data items that occur during execution of the bubble sort algorithm
- to be able to trace in detail the comparisons and interchanges of data items that occur during execution of the selection sort algorithm
- to be able to trace in detail the comparisons and interchanges of data items that occur during execution of the insertion sort algorithm

Two aspects of these declarations are worth noting. First, the fashion in which we have made our **CONST** and **TYPE** declarations allows this procedure to eventually sort an array of any size and base type provided that the definitions of MaxIndex, KeyType, WhateverType, and SortRecord are appropriately altered. This method of declaration represents an attempt to make the Pascal procedure abstract: it embodies an algorithm that can sort a variety of data types.

Second, the measure of an algorithm's run-time efficiency is in direct proportion to the number of elementary machine operations that must be performed as the algorithm is executed. With sorting algorithms, these elementary machine operations compare and interchange two data items. Depending upon the amount of data in the OtherData field in the preceding declarations, it is entirely possible that interchanging two data items could be considerably more costly in machine time than comparing two items. Why? An interchange of large data items will generate a loop that moves a significant number of bytes at the machine language level.

Our analysis of run-time efficiency should take this into account. It may well be more important to minimize data interchanges at the expense of comparisons. This complication did not enter into our earlier discussion of sorting because, at that stage, we were concerned with sorting arrays of simple, unstructured data items only.

EXAMPLE 1.1

Given arrays A and B of type NameList as follows,

```
TYPE
  NameData = PACKED ARRAY [1..40] OF char;
  NameList = ARRAY [1..1000] OF NameData;
```

consider the following two code fragments that act upon them.

Fragment 1

```
StartWithX := 0;
FOR J := 1 TO 1000 DO
  IF A[J,1] = 'X' THEN
    StartWithX := StartWithX + 1;
```

Fragment 2

```
B := A;
```

In this instance, an assignment statement can be misleading in its efficiency. The assignment statement in Fragment 2 results in 1,000 names being copied from A to B. Moreover, each name consists of 40 characters, so 40,000 elementary machine operations may be involved. In Fragment 1, each of the 1,000 comparisons and the potential incrementing of StartWithX represents a faster sequence of operations than the internal copying of 40 characters from one location to another. Hence Fragment 1 illustrates how repeated comparisons can be considerably less costly than seemingly simple assignment statements that manipulate large data aggregates.

Bubble Sort

The first sorting algorithm we will scrutinize is the *bubble sort.* The motivation behind this algorithm may be described as follows. Given a list of data records stored in an array, pass through the array and compare adjacent pairs of keys. Whenever two keys are out of order with respect to each other, interchange the associated records. The effect of such a pass through a list of names is traced in Figure 1.1, where a "snapshot" of the array after each comparison is given. Notice that after such a pass, we are assured that the list will have the name that comes last in alphabetical order in the final array position. That is, the last name will "sink" to the bottom of the array, and preceding names will gradually "percolate" to the top.

If one pass through an array of N records can guarantee that the record with the key that comes last in order is in the appropriate position, then slicing off the last element and passing through the remaining $N - 1$ entries using the same logic will guarantee that the record with the key second to last in order is in its appropriate position. Repeating the process for a total of $N - 1$ passes eventually insures that all records are in their appropriate positions. In general, on the Kth pass through the array, $N - K$ comparisons of pairs must be made.

Thus, the bubble sort algorithm involves two nested loops. The outer loop controls the number of (successively smaller) passes through the array. The inner loop controls the pairs of adjacent entries being compared.

FIGURE 1.1
Trace of bubble sort on an array with four names

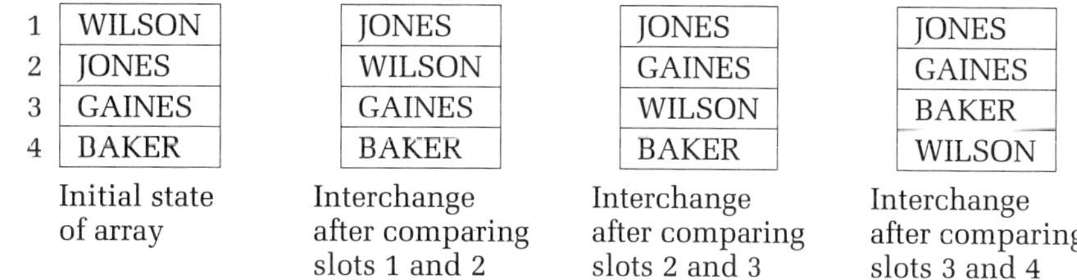

If we ever make a complete pass through the inner loop without having to make an interchange, we can declare the array sorted and avoid all future passes through the array. A top-level pseudocode development of the algorithm is

1. Initialize counter K to zero.
2. Initialize Boolean ExchangeMade to **true.**
3. **WHILE** (K < N − 1) **AND** ExchangeMade
    - 3.1. set ExchangeMade to **false**
    - 3.2. increment counter K
    - 3.3. **FOR** J := 1 **TO** N − K
        - 3.3.1. **IF** Key field of entry in Jth slot > Key field of entry in (J + 1)st slot **THEN**
            - 3.3.1.1. exchange these entries
            - 3.3.1.2. set ExchangeMade to **true**

The complete Pascal procedure to implement this algorithm for an arbitrary array of records follows. The procedure assumes the existence of appropriate **CONST** and **TYPE** declarations.

```
PROCEDURE BubbleSort (N : integer; VAR List : SortArray);

  {  Given:   Array List containing entries in locations 1   }
  {           through N.                                     }
  {  Task:    Apply bubble sort logic to List.               }
  {  Return:  Array List with first N entries arranged in    }
  {           ascending order.                               }

  VAR
    K, J : integer;
    ExchangeMade : boolean;
    Temp : SortRecord;

  BEGIN
    K := 0;
    ExchangeMade := true;
    { Make up to N - 1 passes through array, exit early if no exchanges }
    { are made on previous pass.                                        }
    WHILE (K < N - 1) AND ExchangeMade DO { K  counts passes  }
      BEGIN
        ExchangeMade := false;
        K := K + 1;
        { Compare N - K adjacent pairs of array entries.            }
        FOR J := 1 TO N - K DO {  Number of comparisons on Kth pass  }
          IF List[J].Key > List[J + 1].Key THEN {  Must interchange  }
            BEGIN
              Temp := List[J];
              List[J] := List[J+1];
              List[J+1] := Temp;
              ExchangeMade := true
            END
      END
  END; {  of PROCEDURE BubbleSort  }
```

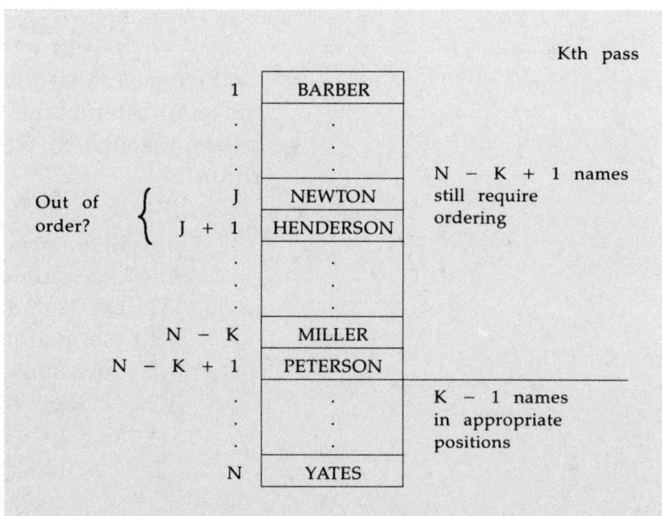

EXAMPLE 1.2

Trace the action of the **PROCEDURE** BubbleSort if N is 5 and the array List initially contains

1	43
2	20
3	24
4	31
5	36

First pass through array

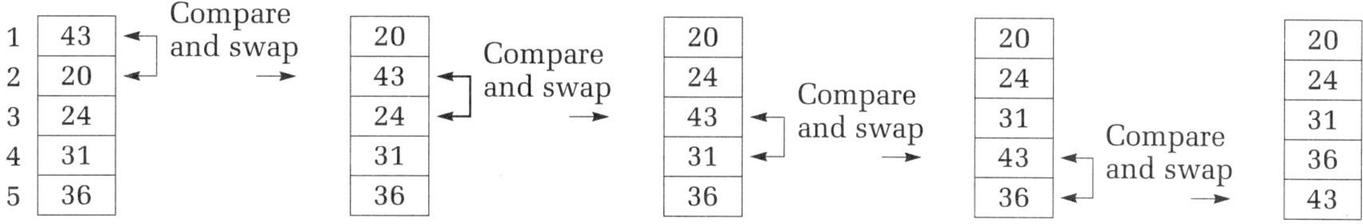

Second pass through array

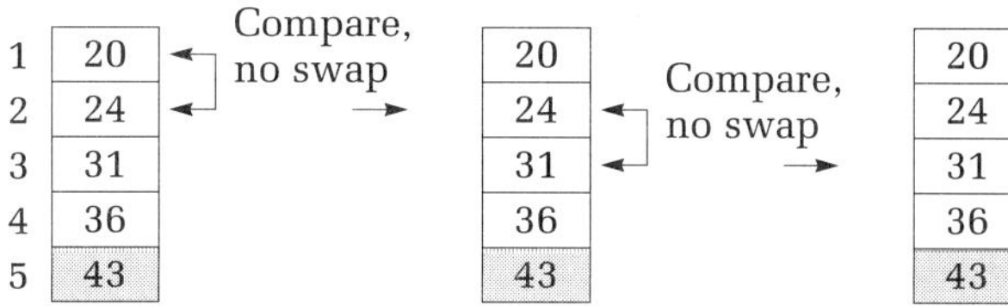

ExchangeMade remained false throughout inner loop, so algorithm is done.

■ ■

In the next section we analyze in detail the run-time efficiency of the bubble sort. But we should first consider two other sorting algorithms to which the efficiency of bubble sort may be compared: *selection sort* and *insertion sort*.

Selection Sort

The motivation of the bubble sort is to place the (current) largest array value in the (current) last array slot, then seal off that slot from future consideration, and repeat the process. The selection sort algorithm is somewhat similarly motivated, but it attempts to avoid the multitude of interchanges of adjacent entries. To do this, on the Kth pass through the array, it determines the position of the smallest entry among

```
List[K].Key, List[K+1].Key, ..., List[N].Key
```

Then this smallest entry is swapped with the Kth entry, K is incremented by 1, and the process is repeated. Figure 1.2 illustrates how this algorithm works on repeated passes through an array with six entries. Asterisks are used to indicate the successively smallest (alphabetically) entries as they are being correctly located in the array.

As we see next, the Pascal procedure for selection sort uses, as its inner loop, a simple algorithm to find the minimum entry and store its position in a variable MinPosition. This inner loop avoids the potentially frequent interchange of array elements that is necessary in the inner loop of BubbleSort.

FIGURE 1.2
Trace of selection sort logic

Original order of Keys	K = 1	K = 2	K = 3	K = 4	K = 5
DAVE	ARON*	ARON*	ARON*	ARON*	ARON*
TOM	TOM	BEV*	BEV*	BEV*	BEV*
PAM	PAM	PAM	DAVE*	DAVE*	DAVE*
ARON	DAVE	DAVE	PAM	PAM*	PAM*
BEV	BEV	TOM	TOM	TOM	SAM*
SAM	SAM	SAM	SAM	SAM	TOM*

```
PROCEDURE SelectionSort (N : integer; VAR List : SortArray);

  {  Given:   Array List containing entries in locations 1   }
  {           through N.                                     }
  {  Task:    Apply selection sort logic to List.            }
  {  Return:  Array List with first N entries arranged in    }
  {           ascending order.                               }

  VAR
    K,  J,  MinPosition : integer;
    Temp :  SortRecord;

  BEGIN
    { Make N - 1 passes through successively smaller segments  }
    { of the array.                                            }
    FOR K := 1 TO N - 1 DO {  Number of passes  }
      BEGIN
        { The following loop will find the position of the     }
        { Kth smallest array entry.                            }
        MinPosition := K; {  Initially assume Kth is smallest  }
        FOR J := K + 1 TO N DO  {  Test previous smallest  }
          IF List[J].Key < List[MinPosition].Key THEN
            MinPosition := J;
            {  Note index, not array element, assigned here.  }
        Temp := List[K];  {  Now swap smallest outside the inner loop  }
        List[K] := List[MinPosition];
        List[MinPosition] := Temp
      END
  END;  {  of PROCEDURE SelectionSort  }
```

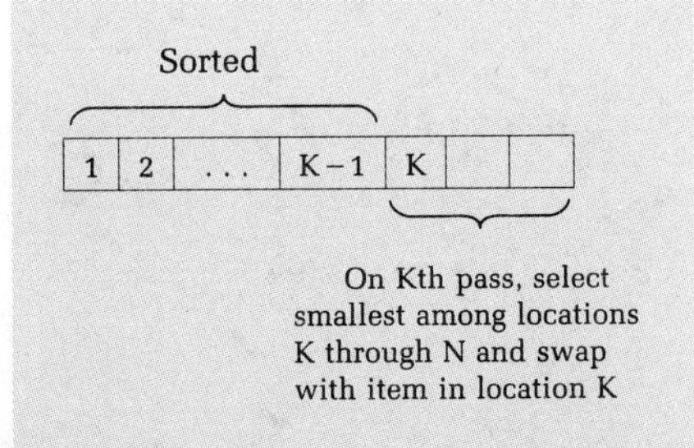

Example 1.3 indicates that the selection sort algorithm swaps no data values until exiting the inner loop. This apparently reduces the number of data interchanges and makes the selection sort more efficient than the bubble sort. Is this a significant improvement? Or have other subtle inefficiencies been introduced to offset this apparent gain? These are difficult questions to answer unless we have a better grasp of how to measure program efficiency. We'll explore efficiency in the next section; but first, let's see one more sorting algorithm for comparison purposes.

EXAMPLE 1.3

Trace the action of the **PROCEDURE** SelectionSort if N is 5 and the array List initially contains

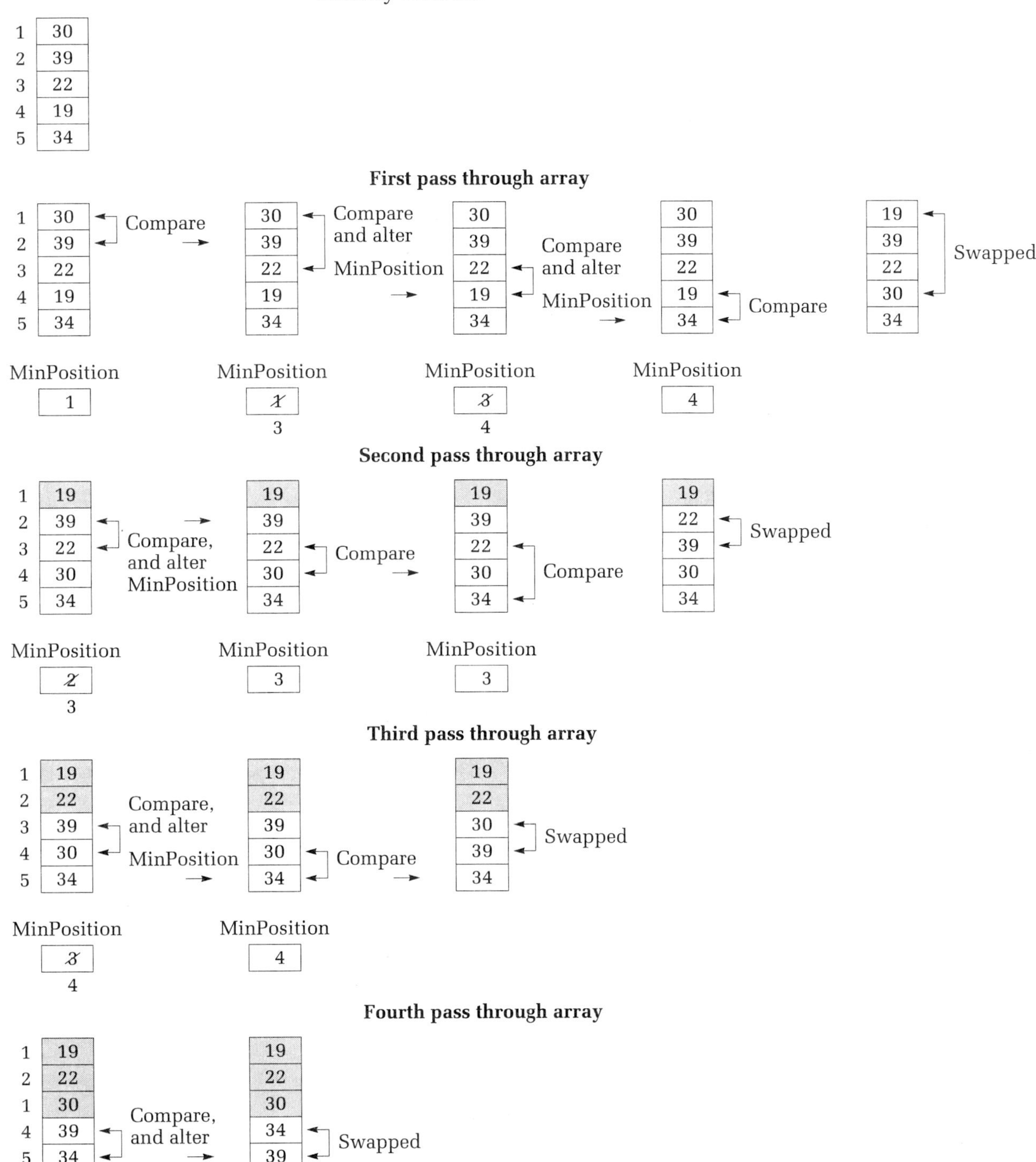

Insertion Sort

Although it reduces the number of data interchanges, the selection sort apparently will not allow an effective—and automatic—loop exit if the array becomes ordered during an early pass. In this regard, bubble sort is more efficient than selection sort for an array that is nearly ordered to begin with. However, even with just one entry out of order, bubble sort's early loop exit can fail to reduce the number of comparisons that are made.

The insertion sort attempts to take greater advantage of an array's partial ordering. The goal is that on the Kth pass through, the Kth element among

```
List[1].Key, List[2].Key, ... List[K].Key
```

should be inserted into its rightful place among the first K entries in the array. Thus, after the Kth pass (K starting at 2), the first K elements of the array should be in sorted order. This is analogous to the fashion in which many people pick up playing cards and arrange them in order in their hands. Holding the first (K − 1) cards in order, a person will pick up the Kth card and compare it with cards already held until its appropriate spot is found. The following steps will achieve this logic:

1. **FOR** K := 2 **TO** N { K index of array element to insert }
   1.1 ItemToInsert := List[K].Key
   1.2 J := K − 1 { J starts at K − 1 and is decremented until insertion position is found }
   1.3 **WHILE** (insertion position not found) **AND** (not beginning of array) **DO**
      1.3.1 **IF** ItemToInsert < List[J].Key **THEN**
         1.3.1.1 Move List[J] to index position J + 1
         1.3.1.2 Reduce J by 1
      1.3.2 **ELSE**
         1.3.2.1 The insertion position has been found
   1.4 ItemToInsert should be positioned at index J + 1

In effect, for each pass, the index J begins at the (K − 1)st element and moves that element to position J + 1 until we find the insertion point for what was originally the Kth element.

Insertion sort for each value of K is traced in Figure 1.3. In each column of this diagram the data items are sorted in alphabetical order relative to each other above the item with the asterisk; below this item the data are not affected.

FIGURE 1.3
Trace of repeated passes from insertion sort

Original order of Keys	First pass K = 2	Second pass K = 3	Third pass K = 4	Fourth pass K = 5	Fifth pass K = 6
PAM	PAM	DAVE	ARON	ARON	ARON
SAM	SAM*	PAM	DAVE	DAVE	BEV
DAVE	DAVE	SAM*	PAM	PAM	DAVE
ARON	ARON	ARON	SAM*	SAM	PAM
TOM	TOM	TOM	TOM	TOM*	SAM
BEV	BEV	BEV	BEV	BEV	TOM*

To implement the insertion sort algorithm in Pascal we have the following code:

```
PROCEDURE  InsertionSort (N : integer; VAR List : SortArray);

  {  Given:   Array List with entries in locations 1          }
  {           through N.                                       }
  {  Task:    Apply insertion sort logic to List.              }
  {  Return:  Array List with first N entries arranged in      }
  {           ascending order.                                 }

  VAR K, J : integer;
      ItemToInsert : SortRecord;
      StillLooking : boolean;

  BEGIN
    { On the Kth pass, insert item K into its correct position among   }
    { the first K entries in array.                                    }
    FOR K := 2 TO N DO
      BEGIN
        { Walk backwards through list, looking for slot to insert A[K] }
        ItemToInsert := List[K];
        J := K - 1;
        StillLooking := true;
        WHILE (J >= 1) AND StillLooking DO
          { ItemToInsert is compared to List[J] }
          IF ItemToInsert.Key < List[J].Key THEN
            BEGIN
              List[J + 1] := List[J];
              J := J - 1
            END
          ELSE
            StillLooking := false;
        { Upon leaving loop, J + 1 is the index where ItemToInsert belongs }
        List[J + 1] := ItemToInsert
      END  { FOR }
  END;  { of PROCEDURE InsertionSort }
```

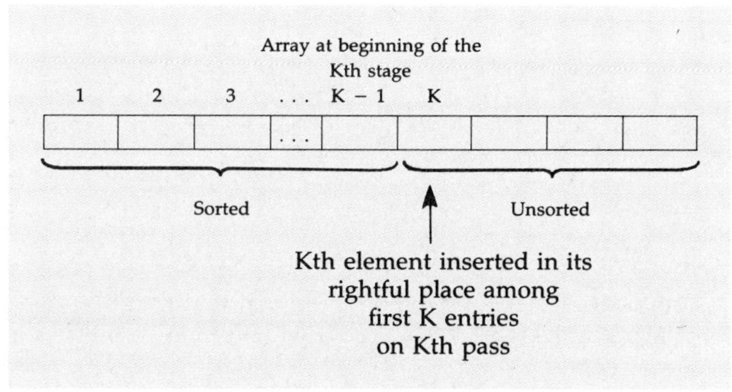

■ EXAMPLE 1.4

Trace the action of the **PROCEDURE** InsertionSort if N is 5 and the array List initially contains

1	80
2	40
3	32
4	54
5	61

First pass (K=2)

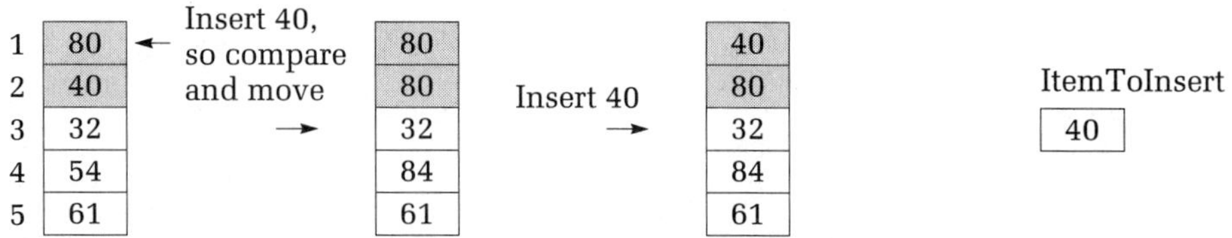

Second pass (K=3)

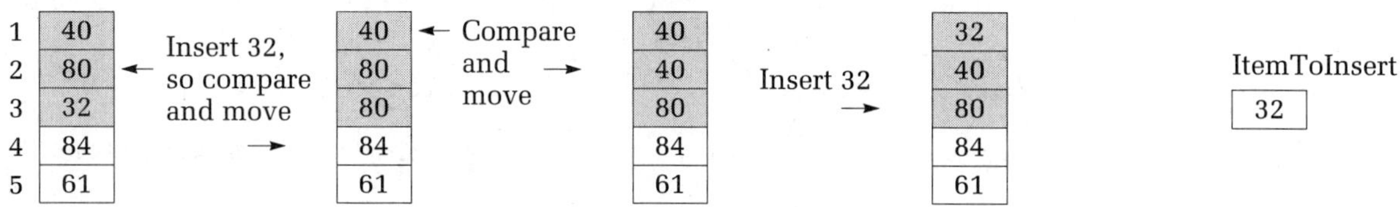

Third pass (K=4)

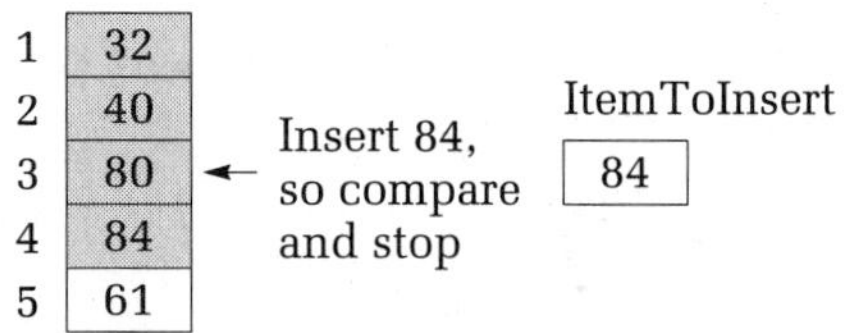

Fourth pass (K=5)

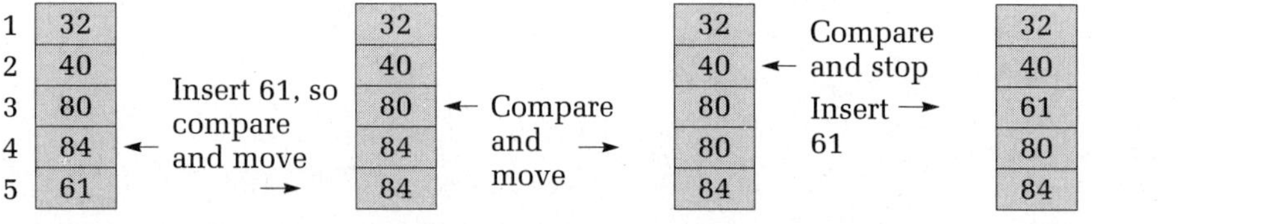

■

Exercises 1.2

1. Which of the sorting methods studied in this section allows a possible early exit from its inner loop? What is the potential advantage in using this early exit?
2. Which of the sorting methods studied in this section allows a possible early exit from its outer loop? What is the potential advantage in using this early exit?
3. Which of the sorting methods studied in this section does not allow the possibility of an early exit from its inner or outer loops? What potential advantage does this method have over the other two methods that were presented?
4. Suppose that, intially, an array contains seven integer entries arranged in the following order:

1	43
2	40
3	18
4	24
5	39
6	60
7	12

Trace the order of the array entries after each successive pass of the bubble sort.

5. Repeat Exercise 4 for the selection sort.

6. Repeat Exercise 4 for the insertion sort.

7. Consider the following sort algorithm. Which of the methods studied in this section does this new algorithm most closely resemble? In what ways is it different from that method? Trace the action of this new sort algorithm on the array from Exercise 4.

```
PROCEDURE Sort (N : integer; VAR List : SortArray);

  {  Given:    Array List containing entries in locations 1   }
  {            through N.                                     }
  {  Task:     Apply sort logic to List.                      }
  {  Return:   Array List with first N entries arranged in    }
  {            ascending order.                               }

  VAR
    K, J : integer;
    ExchangeMade : boolean;
    Temp : SortRecord;

  BEGIN
    K := 0;
    ExchangeMade := true;
    WHILE (K < N - 1) AND ExchangeMade DO
      BEGIN
        ExchangeMade := false;
        K := K + 1;
        FOR J := N DOWNTO K + 1  DO
          IF List[J].Key < List[J - 1].Key THEN
            BEGIN
              Temp := List[J];
              List[J] := List[J - 1];
              List[J - 1] := Temp;
              ExchangeMade := true
            END
      END
  END; {  of PROCEDURE Sort  }
```

8. Consider the following sort algorithm. Which of the methods studied in this section does this new algorithm most closely resemble? In what ways is it different from that method? Trace the action of this new sort algorithm on the array from Exercise 4.

```
PROCEDURE Sort (N : integer; VAR List : SortArray);

  {  Given:    Array List containing entries in locations 1   }
  {            through N.                                     }
  {  Task:     Apply sort logic to List.                      }
  {  Return:   Array List with first N entries arranged in    }
  {            ascending order.                               }
```

```
VAR
  K, J, Position : integer;
  Temp :  SortRecord;

BEGIN
  FOR K := 1 TO N - 1 DO
    BEGIN
      Position := 1;
      FOR J := 2 TO N - K + 1 DO
        IF List[J].Key > List[Position].Key THEN
          Position := J;
      Temp := List[N - K + 1];
      List[N - K + 1] := List[Position];
      List[Position] := Temp
    END
END;  {  of PROCEDURE Sort  }
```

9. Consider the following sort algorithm. Which of the methods studied in this section does this new algorithm most closely resemble? In what ways is it different from that method? Trace the action of this new sort algorithm on the array from Exercise 4.

```
PROCEDURE  Sort (N : integer; VAR List : SortArray);

  {  Given:   Array List with entries in locations 1        }
  {           through N.                                    }
  {  Task:    Apply sort logic to List.                     }
  {  Return:  Array List with first N entries arranged in   }
  {           ascending order.                              }

  VAR
    K, J : integer;
    Done : boolean;
    Temp : SortRecord;

  BEGIN
    FOR K := N - 1 DOWNTO 1 DO
      BEGIN
        J := K;
        Done := false;
        WHILE (J <= N - 1) AND NOT Done DO
          IF List[J].Key > List[J + 1].Key THEN
            BEGIN
              Temp := List[J];
              List[J] := List[J + 1];
              List[J + 1] := Temp;
              J := J + 1
            END
          ELSE
            Done := true
      END  {  of FOR loop  }
  END;  {  of PROCEDURE Sort  }
```

10. Devise sample data sets to demonstrate the *best-case* and *worst-case* behavior of the bubble sort, insertion sort, and selection sort. That is, for each sorting algorithm, construct data sets that illustrate the minimum and maximum number of comparisons required for that particular algorithm.

11. Construct a data set in which just one value is out of order and yet the Boolean test of the ExchangeMode variable never allows an early exit from the outer loop of bubble sort. How does the insertion sort perform on this same data set? Better, worse, or the same? Explain why.

12. Modify the sorting algorithms of this section so that they receive an additional argument indicating whether the sort should be in ascending or descending order.

13. The inner loop of an insertion sort can be modified to merely find the appropriate position for the Kth array entry instead of actually shifting items to make room for this entry. The shifting of items and placement of the original Kth entry can then be achieved in a separate loop. Write a new insertion sort procedure that implements this modification. Intuitively, is your new version more or less efficient than the old version? Why?

14. Modify all of the sorting algorithms presented in this chapter to include counters for the number of comparisons and data interchanges that are made. Then run those sorting algorithms on a variety of data sets, maintaining a chart of the counters for each algorithm. Prepare a written statement to summarize your conclusions about the relative efficiencies of the algorithms.

1.3 Which Sort Is Best? A Big-O Analysis

OBJECTIVES

- to understand the formal definition of big-O notation
- to be able to use big-O notation in classifying the time efficiency of algorithms involving nonrecursive, iterative control constructs
- to see the relationship between an algorithm's big-O classification and its expected run-time on a computer
- to recognize often-used big-O categories
- to apply big-O notation in analyzing the time efficiencies of the bubble sort, selection sort, and insertion sort algorithms

Computers do their work in terms of certain fundamental operations: comparing two numbers, moving the contents of one memory word to another, and so on. It should come as no surprise to you that a simple instruction in a high-level language such as Pascal may be translated (via a compiler) into many of these fundamental machine-level instructions. On most modern computers the speeds of these fundamental operations are measured in microseconds—that is, millionths of a second—although some larger supercomputers are beginning to break the nanosecond (billionth of a second) barrier. Let's assume, for the sake of argument, that we are working with a hypothetical computer that requires one microsecond to perform one of its fundamental operations.

With execution speeds of this kind, it makes little sense to analyze the efficiency of those portions of a program that perform only initializations and final reporting of summary results. The key to analyzing a procedure's efficiency is to scrutinize its loops and, even more importantly, its nested loops. Consider the following two examples of nested loops intended to sum each of the rows of an $N \times N$ two-dimensional array A, storing the row sums in a one-dimensional array Sum and the overall total in GrandTotal.

EXAMPLE 1.5

```
GrandTotal := 0;
FOR K := 1 TO N DO
  BEGIN
    Sum[K] := 0;
    FOR J := 1 TO N DO
      BEGIN
        Sum[K] := Sum[K] + A[K,J];
        GrandTotal := GrandTotal + A[K,J]
      END
  END
```

EXAMPLE 1.6

```
GrandTotal := 0;
FOR K := 1 TO N DO
  BEGIN
    Sum[K] := 0;
    FOR J := 1 TO N DO
      Sum[K] := Sum[K] + A[K,J];
    Grandtotal := GrandTotal + Sum[K]
  END
```

If we analyze the number of addition operations required by these two examples, it should be immediately obvious that Example 1.6 is better in this respect. Because Example 1.5 incorporates the accumulating of GrandTotal into its inner loop, it requires $2N^2$ additions. That is, the additions Sum[K] + A[K,J] and GrandTotal + A[K,J] are each executed N^2 times, for a total of $2N^2$. Example 1.6, on the other hand, accumulates GrandTotal after the inner loop; hence it requires only $N^2 + N$ additions, which is less than $2N^2$ for any N after 1. Example 1.6 is seemingly guaranteed to execute faster than Example 1.5 for any nontrivial value of N.

But note that "faster" here may not have much significance in the real world of computing. Assuming that our hypothetical computer allows us to declare an array that is 1,000 by 1,000, Example 1.5 would require two seconds to perform its additions; Example 1.6 would require just over one second. On a larger 100,000 by 100,000 array, Example 1.5 would crunch numbers for slightly under six hours and Example 1.6 would take about three hours.

Although Example 1.6 is certainly better from an aesthetic perspective, it is not good enough to be appreciably different from a user's perspective. That is, in situations where one version will respond within seconds, so will the other. Conversely, when one is annoyingly slow, the other will be also. In terms of the *order of magnitude* of run-time involved, these versions should not be considered significantly different. For the 1,000 by 1,000 array, both versions would be fast enough to allow their use in an interactive environment. For the 100,000 by 100,000 array, both versions would dictate an overnight run in batch mode since an interactive user will be no more willing to wait three hours than six hours for a response.

Thus, because of the phenomenal execution speeds and very large amounts of available memory on modern computers, proportionally small differences between algorithms often have little practical impact. Such considerations have led computer scientists toward devising a method of algorithm classification that makes more precise the notion of order of magnitude as it applies to time and space considerations. This method of classification, typically referred to as *big-O notation* (in reference to "on the order of"), hinges on the following definition:

Big-O notation. Suppose there exists a function $f(n)$ defined on the nonnegative integers such that the number of operations required by an algorithm for an input of size n is less than some constant C times $f(n)$ for all but finitely many n. That is, the number of operations is *proportional* to $f(n)$ for all large values of n. Such an algorithm is said to be an $O(f(n))$ algorithm relative to the number of operations it requires to execute. Similarly, we could classify an algorithm as $O(f(n))$ relative to the number of memory locations it requires to execute.

Figure 1.4 provides a graphical aid to understanding this formal definition of big-O notation. In general, we expect an algorithm's run-time to increase as it must manipulate an increasing number of data items, that is, as n increases. This increasing run-time is depicted by the somewhat irregular, wavy curve in Figure 1.4. Now compare the wavy curve representing actual run-time to the smoother curve of $C*f(n)$. Note that, for some small values of n, the actual number of operations for the algorithm may exceed $C*f(n)$.

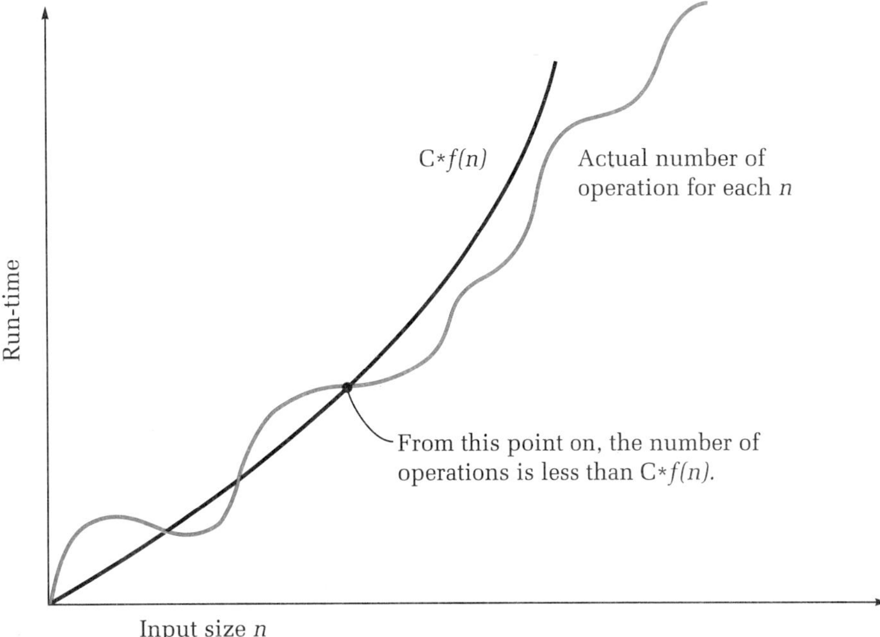

FIGURE 1.4
Graphical representation of $O(f(n))$

However, the graph indicates that there is a point on the horizontal axis beyond which $C*f(n)$ is always greater than the number of operations required for n data items. This is precisely the criterion that defines an algorithm's being $O(f(n))$.

To say that an algorithm is $O(f(n))$ thus indicates that the function $f(n)$ may be useful in characterizing how the algorithm is performing for large n. For such n, we are assured that the operations required by the algorithm will be bounded by a constant times $f(n)$. The phrasing "for all large values of n" in the definition highlights the fact that there is little difference in the choice of an algorithm if n is reasonably small. For example, almost any sorting algorithm would sort 100 integers instantly.

We should also note that a given algorithm may be $O(f(n))$ for many different functions f. As Figure 1.5 depicts, any algorithm that is $O(n^2)$ will also be $O(n^3)$.

Our main interest in classifying an algorithm with big-O notation is to find a relatively simple function $f(n)$ such that $C*f(n)$ parallels the number of operations as closely as possible. Hence, saying that an algorithm is $O(n^2)$ is considered a better characterization of its efficiency than saying it is $O(n^3)$.

The importance of the constant C, known as the constant of proportionality, lies in comparing algorithms that share the same function $f(n)$; it makes almost no difference in the comparison of algorithms for which $f(n)$ is of different magnitude. It is therefore appropriate to say that the function $f(n)$ dominates the run-time performance of an algorithm and characterizes it in its big-O analysis. The following example should help clarify this situation.

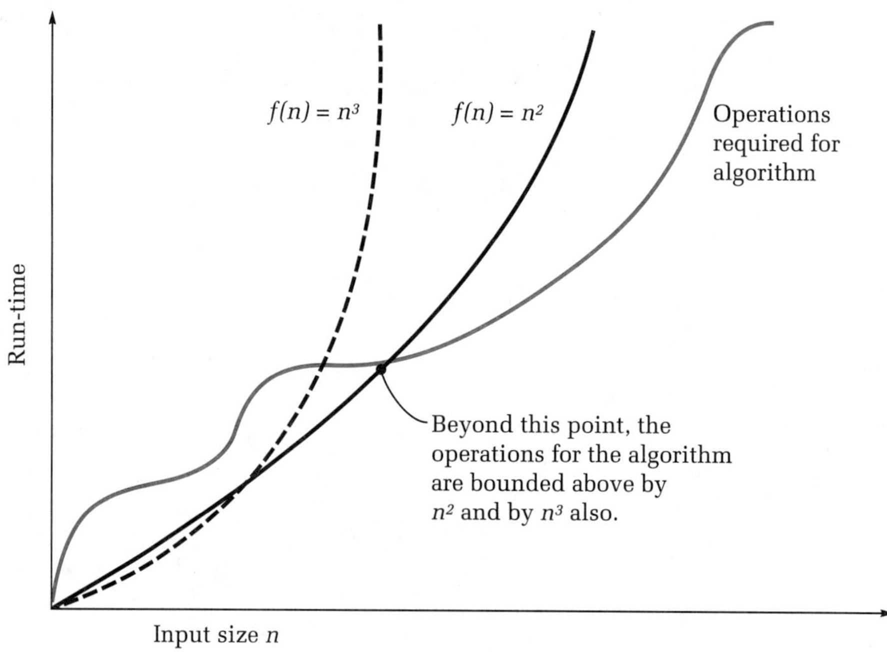

FIGURE 1.5
Any algorithm which is $O(n^2)$ is also $O(n^3)$

Consider two algorithms L_1 and L_2 with run-times equal to $2n^2$ and n^2 respectively. The constants of proportionality of L_1 and L_2 are 2 and 1 respectively. The dominating function $f(n)$ for both of these algorithms is n^2, but L_2 runs twice as fast as L_1 for a data set of n values. The different sizes of the two constants of proportionality indicate that L_2 is faster than L_1. Now suppose that the function $f(n)$ for L_2 is n^3. Then, even though its constant of proportionality is half of what it is for L_1, L_2 will be frustratingly slower than L_1 for large n. This latter comparison is shown in Figure 1.6.

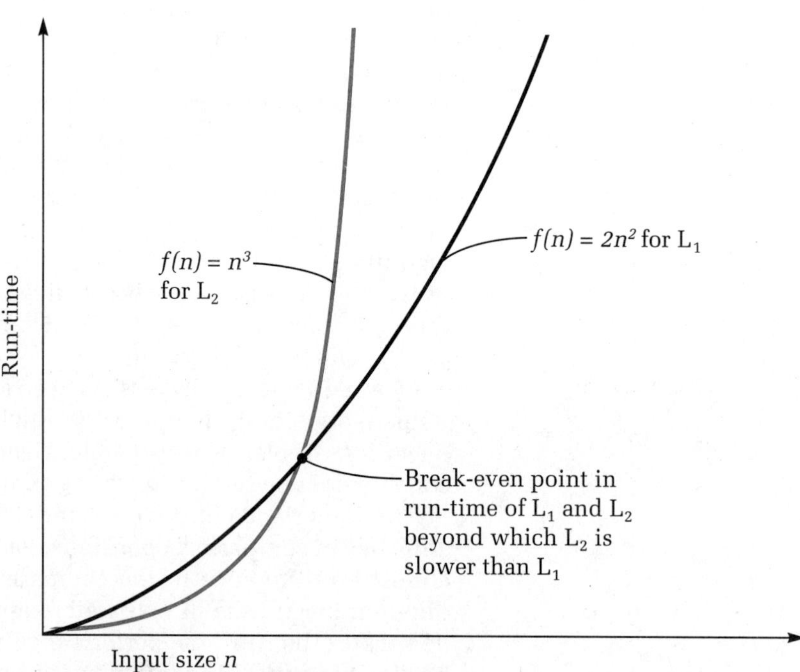

FIGURE 1.6
Graphical comparison of two run-times

EXAMPLE 1.7

Use big-O analysis to characterize the two code segments from Examples 1.5 and 1.6 respectively.

Because the algorithm of Example 1.5 performs $2N^2$ additions, it is characterized as $O(N^2)$ with 2 as a constant of proportionality. We previously determined that the code of Example 1.6 performs $N^2 + N$ additions. However, $N^2 + N \leq 1.1N^2$ for any $N \geq 10$. Hence, we can characterize Example 1.6 as an $O(N^2)$ algorithm using 1.1 as a constant of proportionality. These two characterizations demonstrate that, although Example 1.6 is almost twice as fast as Example 1.5, they are in the same big-O category. Coupled with our earlier analysis of these two examples, this is an indication that algorithms in the same big-O category may be expected to have the same orders of magnitude in their run-time.

How Well Does the Big-O Notation Provide a Way of Classifying Algorithms from a Real World Perspective? To answer this question, consider Table 1.1. This table presents some typical $f(n)$ functions we will use to classify algorithms and their order of magnitude run-time for inputs of various sizes on a hypothetical computer. From this table, we can see that an $O(n^2)$ algorithm will take hours to execute for an input of size 10^5. How many hours is dependent upon the constant of proportionality in the definition of the big-O notation.

TABLE 1.1
Some typical $f(n)$ functions and associated run-times

	Assuming proportionality constant K = 1 and one operation per microsecond, approximate run-times for input of size		
$f(n)$	10^3	10^5	10^6
$log_2 n$	0.000010 seconds	0.000017 seconds	0.000020 seconds
n	0.001 seconds	0.1 seconds	1 second
$n\ log_2 n$	0.01 seconds	1.7 seconds	20 seconds
n^2	1 second	3 hours	12 days
n^3	17 minutes	32 centuries	3×10^4 centuries
2^n	10^{285} centuries	10^{10^4} years	10^{10^5} years

Regardless of the value of this constant of proportionality, a categorization of an algorithm as an $O(n^2)$ algorithm has thus achieved a very practical goal. We now know that, for an input of size 10^5, we cannot expect an immediate response for such an algorithm. Moreover, we also know that, for a reasonably small constant of proportionality, we have an algorithm for which submission as an overnight job would not be impractical. That is, unlike an $O(n^3)$ algorithm, we could expect the computer to finish executing our algorithm in a time frame that would be acceptable if it could be scheduled to not interfere with other uses of the machine. On the other hand, an $O(n^3)$ algorithm applied to a data set of this size would be completely impractical.

How Does One Determine the Function $f(n)$ That Categorizes a Particular Algorithm? We give an overview of that process here and illustrate it by doing actual analyses for our three sorting algorithms. It is generally the case that, by analyzing the loop structure of an algorithm, we can estimate the number of run-time operations (or amount of memory units) required by the algorithm as a sum of several terms, each dependent on n, the number of items being processed by the algorithm. That is, typically we are able to express the number of run-time operations (or amount of memory) as a sum of the form

$$f_1(n) + f_2(n) + \ldots f_k(n)$$

Moreover, it is also typical that we identify one of the terms in this expression as the *dominant term.* A dominant term is one which, for bigger values of n, becomes so large that it allows us to ignore all the other terms from a big-O perspective. For instance, suppose that we had an expression involving two terms such as

$$n^2 + 6n$$

Here, the n^2 term dominates the $6n$ term since, for $n \geq 6$, we have

$$n^2 + 6n \leq n^2 + n^2 = 2n^2$$

Thus, $n^2 + 6n$ would lead to an $O(n^2)$ categorization because of the dominance of the n^2 term.

In general, the problem of big-O categorization reduces to finding the dominant term in an expression representing the number of operations or amount of memory required by an algorithm.

■ EXAMPLE 1.8

Use big-O notation to analyze the time efficiency of the following fragment of Pascal code.

```
FOR K := 1 TO N DIV 2 DO
  BEGIN
    .
    .
    .
    FOR J := 1 TO N * N DO
      BEGIN
        .
        .
        .
      END;
    .
    .
    .
  END;
```

Since these loops are nested, the number of times statements within the innermost loop are executed is the product of the number of repetitions of the two individual loops. Hence the efficiency is $N^3/2$, or $O(N^3)$ in big-O terms, with a constant of proportionality equal to ½.

Note that the important principle illustrated by this example is that, for two loops with $O(f_1(n))$ and $O(f_2(n))$ efficiencies, the efficiency of the nesting of these two loops (in any order) is $O(f_1(n) * f_2(n))$.

■ ■

■ EXAMPLE 1.9

Use big-O notation to analyze the time efficiency of the following fragment of Pascal code.

```
FOR K := 1 TO N DIV 2 DO
  BEGIN
    .
    .
    .
  END;
FOR J := 1 TO N * N DO
  BEGIN
    .
    .
    .
  END;
```

Since one loop follows the other the number of operations executed by both of them is the sum of the individual loop efficiencies. Hence the efficiency is $N/2 + N^2$, or $O(N^2)$ in big-O terms.

The important principle illustrated by Example 1.9 is that, for two loops with $O(f_1(n))$ and $O(f_2(n))$ efficiencies, the efficiency of the sequencing of these two loops (in any order) is $O(f_D(n))$ where $f_D(n)$ is the dominant of the functions $f_1(n)$ and $f_2(n)$.

EXAMPLE 1.10

Use big-O notation to analyze the time efficiency of the following fragment of Pascal code.

```
K := N;
WHILE K > 1 DO
  BEGIN
    .
    .
    .
    K := K DIV 2
  END;
```

Since the loop control variable is cut in half each time through the loop, the number of times that statements inside the loop will be executed is $\log_2 N$. Note that the halving of a loop is central to the binary search algorithm, which you may have encountered in an earlier course and which will be explored further in Section 1.5.

The principle emerging from Example 1.10 is that an algorithm that halves the data remaining to be processed on each iteration of a loop will be an $O(\log_2 n)$ algorithm.

Table 1.2, which lists frequently occurring dominant terms, will prove helpful in our future big-O analyses of algorithms.

TABLE 1.2
Common dominant terms in expressions for algorithmic efficiency based on the variable n

n dominates $\log_a n$, a is often 2
$n \log_a n$ dominates n, a is often 2
n^2 dominates $n \log_a n$
n^m dominates n^k when $m > k$
a^n dominates n^m for any $a > 1$ and $m \geq 0$

It is worthwhile to briefly characterize some of the classes of algorithms that arise due to the dominant terms listed in Table 1.2. Algorithms whose efficiency is dominated by a $\log_a n$ term (and hence are categorized as

$O(\log_a n)$) are often called *logarithmic algorithms.* Since $\log_a n$ will increase much more slowly than n itself, logarithmic algorithms are generally very efficient.

Algorithms whose efficiency can be expressed in terms of a polynomial of the form

$$a_m n^m + a_{m-1} n^{m-1} + \ldots + a_2 n^2 + a_1 n + a_0$$

are called *polynomial algorithms.* Since the highest power of n will dominate such a polynomial, such algorithms are $O(n^m)$. The only polynomial algorithms we will discuss in this book have $m = 1, 2,$ or 3; they are called *linear, quadratic,* or *cubic algorithms* respectively.

Algorithms with efficiency dominated by a term of the form a^n are called *exponential algorithms.* Exponential algorithms are of more theoretical than practical interest because they cannot reasonably be run on typical computers for moderate values of n. (However, to see why this last statement may have to change in the future, be sure to read this section's Note of Interest, which discusses *parallel processing.*)

Big-O Analysis of Bubble Sort

We are now ready to carry out some real comparisons between the three sorting methods we have discussed so far—bubble, insertion, and selection. To do so, we must determine functions $f(n)$ that allow us to make statements like "Sorting algorithm X requires $O(f(n))$ comparisons." If it turns out that all three sorts share the same $f(n)$ function, then we can conclude that the differences between them are not approaching an order of magnitude scale. Rather, they would be more subtle distinctions, which would not appear as dramatic run-time differences.

We also realize that the key to doing a big-O analysis is to focus our attention on the loops in the algorithm. We do that first for the bubble sort. Recall the loop structure of the bubble sort.

```
K := 0;
ExchangeMade := true;
WHILE (K < N - 1) AND ExchangeMade DO
  BEGIN
    ExchangeMade := false;
    K  := K + 1;
    FOR J := 1 TO N - K DO
      IF List[J].Key > List[J+1].Key THEN
      .
      . {Swap}
      .
```

Inner Loop

Outer Loop

Assume that we have a worst case possible for bubble sort, in which the ExchangeMade variable is always set to **true** so that an early exit is never made from the outer loop. If we then consider the comparison at the top of the inner loop, we note that it will be executed first $n - 1$ times, then $n - 2$ times, and so on down to one time for the final execution of the inner loop. Hence, the number of comparisons will be the sum of the sequence of numbers

$$\begin{array}{c} n - 1 \\ n - 2 \\ \cdot \\ \cdot \\ \cdot \\ 1 \end{array}$$

A NOTE OF INTEREST

Artificial Intelligence, the Complexity of Algorithms, and Parallel Processing

Perhaps no area of computer science demands as much in terms of efficient algorithms as does *artificial intelligence* (AI). Those engaged in research in this field are concerned with writing programs that have the computer mimic intelligent human behavior in limited domains such as natural language understanding, theorem proving, and game playing. Why is efficiency so important in such programs? Typically the strategy behind such a system is to have the computer search an enormous number of possibilities for the solution to the problem it is given. These possibilities comprise what is typically called the *state space* for the problem. For instance, for a computer program that plays a game like checkers or chess, the state space would be a suitable representation of all game board configurations that could eventually be generated from the current state of the game. The computer's goal is to search through the state space, looking for a state in which it would win the game. The state space determined by the initial configuration of a chess game has been computed to be about 10^{120} different possible moves. The time required for a computer to examine each of these different moves, assuming it could examine one every microsecond, would be 10^{95} years. Even for a simpler game such as checkers, the time required for a computer to search all states in the game would require 10^{23} years.

The reason for these extraordinarily large and impractical time frames is that a "brute force" strategy of searching all states in such AI applications leads to exponential algorithms. To avoid exponential algorithms, researchers in artificial intelligence have attempted to follow the lead of human reasoning. That is, the human mind seems able to eliminate many of the possibilities in a search space without ever examining them. Similarly AI programmers attempt to weed out large sections of the state space to be searched using what are known as *heuristics*. Heuristics are rules of thumb that enable one to rule out a vast number of possible states by doing some relatively simple computations. For instance, in a game like checkers or chess, a heuristic might involve a mathematical formula that attached a positive or negative weight to a particular state of the game. Those states for which the heuristic value indicates a probable lack of success in future searching are simply eliminated from the state space. Since a heuristic is the computational equivalent of an educated guess, it runs the risk of making an error. However, it is often viewed as a worthwhile risk if it can enhance the efficiency of the search algorithm to a category that is no longer exponential.

In addition to the use of heuristics to increase algorithmic efficiency, there is another ray of hope on the horizon for those presently working in AI research and other fields where exponential algorithms are often encountered. That ray of hope is *parallel processing*. A parallel processing computer has a network of processors that allow many operations (such as those involved in searching a state space) to be performed simultaneously, that is, in parallel. From a theoretical perspective, if a sufficient number of processors can be linked into such a parallel processing network and if the logic of a particular algorithm allows many operations to be performed in parallel, then it is conceivable that—in the future—some exponential algorithms may run in a reasonable time frame on larger data sets than can be accommodated on single-processor machines.

The success or failure of parallel processing computers will definitely play an instrumental role in the future of artificial intelligence and other areas of computer science in which exponential algorithms are frequently encountered. If parallel processing succeeds, we may find ourselves in the exciting position of having to reconsider what makes an algorithm practical or impractical.

A formula from algebra will show this sum to be

$$n(n - 1) / 2$$

Thus we conclude that the bubble sort is an $O(n^2)$ algorithm in those situations for which the ExchangeMade test does not allow an early loop exit.

Big-O Analysis of Insertion Sort

Recall that the loop structure of the insertion sort is given by

```
FOR K := 2 TO N DO                                            ┐
  BEGIN                                                       │
    ItemToInsert := List[K];                                  │
    J := K - 1;                                               │
    StillLooking := true;                                     │
    WHILE (J >= 1) AND StillLooking Do               ┐        │
      IF ItemToInsert.Key < List[J].Key THEN         │        │ Outer
        BEGIN                                        │        │ Loop
        .                                            │        │
        .  {  Move List[J]  }                        │        │
        .                                            │        │
          J := J - 1                                 │ Inner  │
        END                                          │ Loop   │
      ELSE                                           │        │
        StillLooking := false                        │        │
        .                                            │        │
        .                                            │        │
        .                                            ┘        ┘
```

Here, if the inner loop is never short-circuited by Done, the comparison appearing as its first statement will be executed once for the first execution of the outer loop, then twice, and so on, reaching $n - 1$ executions on the final pass. We have a situation virtually identical to our preliminary analysis of the bubble sort. That is, the number of comparisons can be bounded by $n^2/2$ and the algorithm is therefore $O(n^2)$. Of course, with the insertion sort, the hope is that setting the Boolean variable Done in the **ELSE** clause can reduce the number of comparisons made by the inner loop. However, it is clear that we can concoct many data sets for which this will have little or no effect. So, as with bubble sort, we are forced into concluding that insertion sort cannot guarantee better than $O(n^2)$ comparisons.

Big-O Analysis of Selection Sort

The loop structure of this algorithm was given by

```
FOR K := 1 TO N - 1 DO                                   ┐
  BEGIN                                                  │
    MinPosition := K;                                    │
    FOR J := K + 1 TO N DO                       ┐       │
      IF List[J].Key < List[MinPosition].Key THEN│       │ Outer
        MinPosition := J;                        │       │ Loop
    .                                            │ Inner │
    .                                            │ Loop  │
    .                                            ┘       ┘
```

A little investigation uncovers a familiar pattern to the nested loops of the selection sort. Observe that the first time the inner loop is executed, the comparison in the **IF** statement will be made $n - 1$ times. Then it will be made $n - 2$ times; $n - 3$ times; . . . ; and finally, just one time. This is precisely the way the **IF** statement in the bubble sort was executed in repeated passes. Thus, like the bubble and insertion sorts, the selection sort is an $O(n^2)$ algorithm in terms of number of comparisons. The area in which the selection sort potentially offers better efficiency is that the number of interchanges of data in array locations is guaranteed to be $O(n)$ because the swap in selection sort occurs in the outer loop. In both of the other sorts, the swap occurs in the inner loop but is subject to a conditional test. This means that, in their worst cases, both of the other algorithms require $O(n^2)$ swaps as well as $O(n^2)$ comparisons.

Despite the fact that selection sort will usually fare better in the number of data interchanges required to sort an array, it has a drawback not found in the other two. It is apparently impossible to short-circuit either of the nested loops in selection sort when it is given a list in nearly sorted order. So, for such data sets, the selection sort may be an order of magnitude worse than the other two. This is initially rather disheartening news. It seems as if it is impossible to declare any sort a decisive winner. Indeed, our big-O analyses indicate that there is little to choose from the bubble, insertion, and selection algorithms.

The fact that we were able to reach such a conclusion, systematically however, is significant. It reveals the value of a big-O analysis. After all, even knowledge of a negative variety can be valuable in choosing appropriate algorithms under certain circumstances. For instance, if a particular application usually involved adding a small amount of data at the end of an already sorted list and then re-sorting, we now know to avoid selection sort. Moreover, when we study more powerful sorting techniques in the next section (and again in Chapter 8), we will see that it is indeed possible to break the $O(n^2)$ barrier limiting each of our three methods.

Exercises 1.3

1. Do a big-O analysis for those statements inside each of the following nested loop constructs.

a.
```
FOR K := 1 TO N DO
  FOR J := 6 TO M DO
    .
    .
    .
```

b.
```
FOR K := 1 TO N DO
  BEGIN
    J := N;
    WHILE J > 0 DO
      BEGIN
        .
        .
        .
        J := J DIV 2
      END
  END
```

c.
```
K := 1;
REPEAT
  J := 1;
  REPEAT
    .
    .
    .
    J := 2 * J
  UNTIL J >= N;
  K := K + 1
UNTIL K >= N
```

2. Suppose we have an algorithm that requires precisely

$$6 * \log_2 n + 34 * n^2 + 12$$

operations for an input of n data items. Indicate which of the following are valid big-O classifications of the algorithm.

a. $O(n^3)$
b. $O(n^2)$
c. $O(n)$
d. $O(n^2 * \log_2 n)$
e. $O(n * \log_2 n)$
f. $O(\log_2 n)$
g. $O(1)$

Of those that you have indicated are valid, which is the best big-O classification? Why?

3. A certain algorithm always requires 32 operations, regardless of the amount of data input. Provide a big-O classification of the algorithm that reflects the efficiency of the algorithm as accurately as possible.

4. An algorithm has an efficiency $O(n^2 \text{ Sin}(n))$. Is it any better than $O(n^2)$ for large integer n?

5. Suppose that each of the following expressions represents the number of logical operations in an algorithm as a function of n, the size of the list being manipulated. For each expression, determine the dominant term and then classify the algorithm in big-O terms.

   a. $n^3 + n^2\log_2 n + n^3\log_2 n$

   b. $n + 4n^2 + 4^n$

   c. $48n^4 + 16n^2 + \log_8 n + 2^n$

6. Consider the following nested loop construct. Categorize its efficiency in terms of the variable N using big-O notation. Finally, suppose the statements indicated by the ellipses required four main memory accesses (each requiring one microsecond) and two disk file accesses (each requiring one millisecond). Express in milliseconds the amount of time this construct would require to execute if N were 1,000.

```
X := 1;
REPEAT
  Y := N;
  WHILE Y > 0 DO
    BEGIN
     .
     .
     .
     Y := Y - 1
    END;
  X := X + X
UNTIL X > N * N;
```

7. Look back to the data set you constructed for Exercise 11 in Section 1.2. Evaluate the performance of insertion sort on that data set in terms of a big-O analysis.

8. You and a friend are engaged in an argument. She claims that a certain algorithm is $O(n^2 * \log_2 n)$ in its efficiency. You claim that it is $O(n^2)$. Consider and answer the following questions.

   a. Are there circumstances under which both of you could be correct? If so, explain what such circumstances are.

   b. Are there circumstances under which both of you could be wrong? If so, explain what such circumstances are.

   c. Are there circumstances under which she could be right and you could be wrong? If so, explain what such circumstances are.

   d. Are there circumstances under which she could be wrong and you could be right? If so, explain what such circumstances are.

9. You and your friend are engaged in another argument. She claims that a certain algorithm is $O(n^2 + \log_2 n)$ in its efficiency. You claim that it is $O(n^2)$. Consider and answer the following questions.

   a. Are there circumstances under which both of you could be correct? If so, explain what such circumstances are.

   b. Are there circumstances under which both of you could be wrong? If so, explain what such circumstances are.

   c. Are there circumstances under which she could be right and you could be wrong? If so, explain what such circumstances are.

d. Are there circumstances under which she could be wrong and you could be right? If so, explain what such circumstances are.

10. Is an $O(n^2)$ algorithm also an $O(n^3)$ algorithm? Justify your answer in a carefully written paragraph.

■ ■ ■ ■

1.4 The Space/Time Trade-off: Pointer Sort and Radix Sort

OBJECTIVES

- to understand the concept of a pointer
- to understand the difference between physically sorting and logically sorting
- to be able to apply pointers in logically sorting an array without interchanging data items
- to understand what is meant by the time/space trade-off
- to understand the radix sort algorithm and be able to trace its action on appropriate data sets
- to analyze the time and space efficiency of the radix sort algorithm
- to understand why the radix sort algorithm is not as generally applicable as other sorting algorithms we have studied

Early in our discussion of efficiency considerations, we noted that true run-time efficiency was best measured in fundamental machine operations and that one instruction in a high-level language may actually translate into many such primitive operations. To illustrate this, suppose that the data being sorted by one of our algorithms are records, each of which require 100 bytes of internal storage. Then, depending on your computer, it is entirely conceivable that one comparison or assignment statement in a high-level language could generate a machine language loop with 100 repetitions of such fundamental operations: one for each of the bytes that must be swapped. Those seemingly innocent portions of code, which swap two records using a temporary storage location, actually lead to the movement of 300 bytes inside the machine.

The first question we address in this section is whether, in such a situation, we can replace this large-scale internal transfer of entire records with the much swifter operation of swapping two integers. Although the solution we discuss does not achieve an order of magnitude speed increase in the big-O sense, it nonetheless reduces the number of actual machine-level swaps by a factor proportional to the record length involved, a factor that could produce a noticeable improvement in the procedure's run-time.

Bubble Sort Implemented with Pointers

So far our algorithms to sort data have implicitly assumed that the data are to be *physically sorted,* that is, the data are to be arranged in order within the array being sorted. Hence, the data in the first index of our List array are the data that come first in order according to the Key field; the data in the second index, second in order; and so on. However, if we are only interested in processing the data of List in order by Key field, is it really necessary that the data be arranged in physically ordered fashion in computer memory? No. It is possible to step logically through the data in order by Key without physically arranging it that way in memory. To do so we must use another array of *pointers.*

> **Pointer.** A pointer is a memory location in which we store the location of a data item as opposed to the data item itself.

Pointers can keep track of the *logical order* of the data without requiring it to be physically moved. At the end of our sorting routine, Pointer[1] tells us the location of the data that should come first in our alphabetical listing; Pointer[2] contains the location of the data that should come second; and so on. The sorting algorithm itself uses the logic of the bubble sort to interchange pointers instead of interchanging actual data. The actual data never move, remaining precisely where they were stored upon initial input. Instead of the expensive, time-consuming swapping of potentially large records, we are able to swap integer pointers quickly.

A Pascal procedure to implement this *pointer sort* technique follows. In addition to the declarations we have already been using in this chapter, this procedure assumes an external declaration of the form

```
TYPE
  .
  .
  .
  PointerArray = ARRAY [1..MaxIndex] OF integer;
```

Besides the List array, the procedure receives an array Pointer of type PointerArray. The procedure initializes the Pointer array to the state pictured in the "Before" snapshot of Figure 1.7. Then, via repeated swaps of integer pointers, the array is returned as shown in the "After" snapshot.

FIGURE 1.7
"Before" (left) and "After" (right) snapshots of pointer sort

	Key field of List	Pointer
1	MAXWELL	1
2	BUCKNER	2
3	LANIER	3
4	AARON	4

Snapshot of List and Pointer immediately after initializaion

Key field of List	Pointer
MAXWELL	4
BUCKNER	2
LANIER	3
AARON	1

Snapshot of List and Pointer returned by PointerBubbleSort

As the figure indicates, the List array itself is never altered.

```
PROCEDURE  PointerBubbleSort (N : integer;
                              List : SortArray;
                              VAR Pointer : PointerArray);

  {  Given:   Array List containing entries in locations 1    }
              through N.                                      }
  {  Task:    Use bubble sort logic to arrange an array of    }
  {           pointers that yield logical ordering of List.   }
  {  Return:  Appropriately arranged Pointer array.           }

  VAR
    K, J, Temp : integer;
    ExchangeMade : boolean;

  BEGIN
    {  Begin by initializing Pointer array  }
    FOR K := 1 TO N DO
      Pointer[K] := K;
    K := 0;
    ExchangeMade := true;
    { Make up to N - 1 passes through array, exit early if no exchanges }
    { are made on previous pass.                                         }
    WHILE (K < N - 1) AND ExchangeMade DO
      BEGIN
        K := K + 1;
        ExchangeMade := false;
        { Via pointers, compare N - K adjacent pairs of array entries. }
        FOR J := 1 TO N - K DO
          {  Compare values referenced by Pointer  }
          IF List[Pointer[J]].Key > List[Pointer[J+1]].Key THEN
            {  If necessary, swap pointers but not data  }
```

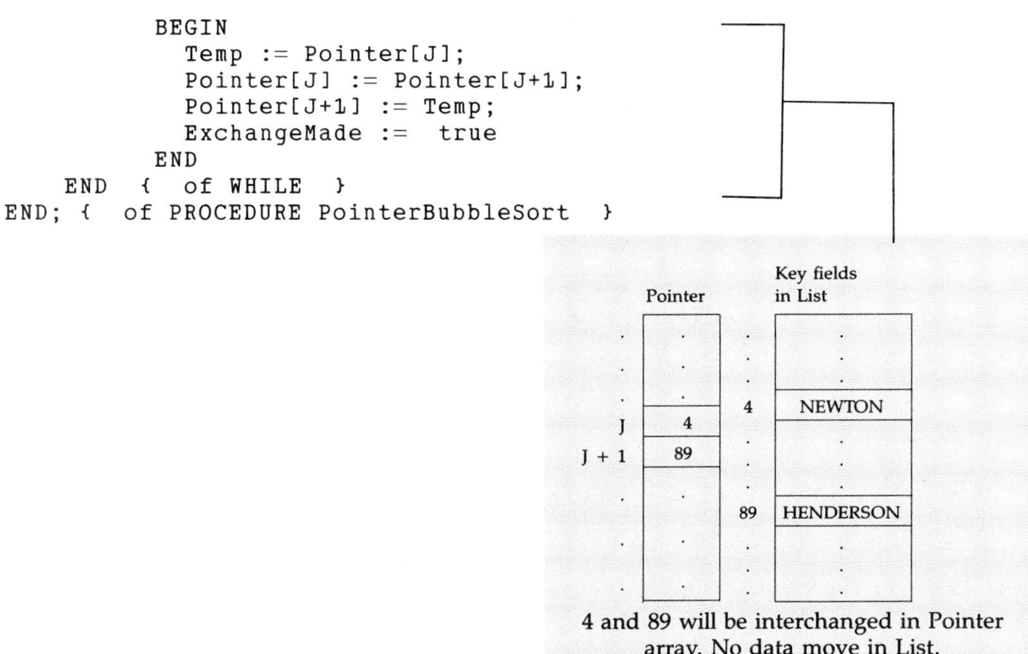

```
          BEGIN
            Temp := Pointer[J];
            Pointer[J] := Pointer[J+1];
            Pointer[J+1] := Temp;
            ExchangeMade :=  true
          END
      END  {  of WHILE  }
   END; {  of PROCEDURE PointerBubbleSort  }
```


■ EXAMPLE 1.11

Given the physically ordered List of Figure 1.7, trace the action of **PROCEDURE** PointerBubbleSort on the array of pointers during each pass through the algorithm.

List	Pointer
MAXWELL	1
BUCKNER	2
LANIER	3
AARON	4

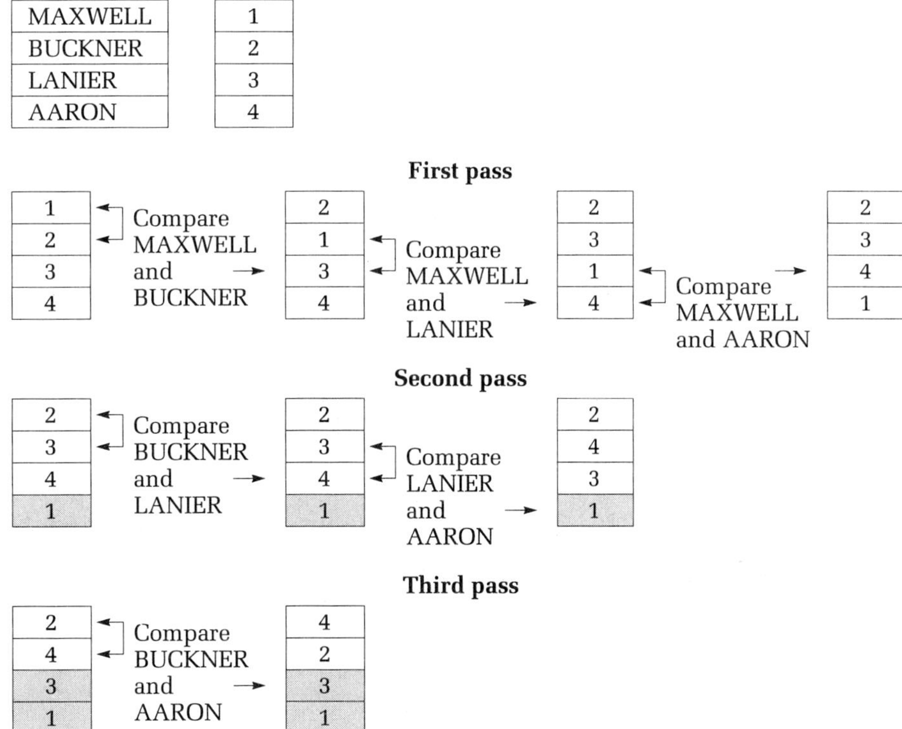

■

EXAMPLE 1.12

Suppose that PointerBubbleSort was invoked from a main program or another procedure via the call

```
PointerBubbleSort (NumberOfStudents, StudentList, Pointer);
```

where NumberOfStudents, StudentList, and Pointer are of appropriate types. If the logical order established by the Pointer array is alphabetical by student name, explain how a report that listed students alphabetically could be printed after this invocation. Assume the existence of a procedure PrintHeading to print column headings for the report and a procedure PrintStudent to receive an individual student record and print it in formatted form as one detail line of the report.

After the call to PointerBubbleSort, Pointer[1] contains the position of the record that is first in alphabetical order, Pointer[2] contains the position of the record that is second, and so on. Hence the following loop will step through all of the entries in the desired order.

```
PrintHeading;
FOR K := 1 TO NumberOfStudents DO
  PrintStudent (StudentList[Pointer[K]]);
```

Efficiency Analysis for Sorts Implemented with Pointers. The pointer technique illustrated here for the bubble sort may also be used with the insertion and selection algorithms. In any of these cases, the mere introduction of the pointer strategy will not reduce the big-O categorization of the sort. However, in cases where the data items being sorted use enough internal storage to substantially slow down swapping times, the pointer sort can attain a considerable savings in run-time.

Is this run-time savings achieved without any sacrifice? An old saying that has been passed down by computer people since the days of the early vacuum tube machines is "You get nothing for nothing." We have not escaped the consequences of that adage by using pointers to increase run-time efficiency. The pointers store *data about data;* this requires additional memory. If your application is not approaching the limits of memory, this cost may not be crucial. In certain situations, however, it could be the last straw for a program running short of memory. Thus, the pointer sort is essentially a trade-off; by using more memory, we get a program that runs faster.

This *time/space trade-off* continually recurs in the analysis of computer algorithms. Many sophisticated techniques to increase speed will need to store substantial data about data to do so. Those algorithms that solve a problem in a fashion that saves space *and* decreases run-time are indeed worthy of special praise. We will be sure to note them.

Finally, the notion of a pointer, as defined and introduced here, plays an important role in our study of data structures beginning in Chapter 4. The time you spend exploring the details of the pointer sort technique will prove very valuable in your understanding of this topic in the future.

Radix Sort

The *radix sort* algorithm is also called the *bin sort,* a name derived from its origin as a technique used on (now obsolete) machines called card sorters.

A NOTE OF INTEREST

Computer Graphics, Visualization, and Virtual Reality

In *computer graphics,* the efficiency of algorithms and the speed of processing hardware are of vital importance. Recent hardware developments now enable scientists to transform numeric data into computer images approaching the quality of photographs in their realism. The essential principle behind such graphics is to develop a numerical model of a physical phenomenon and then, via sophisticated mathematical algorithms, transform the model into a picture on the screen of a high-resolution graphics workstation. With faster computers and algorithms, more considerations of physical laws can be built into such models. The result of being able to incorporate more such laws is to produce images that appear very realistic.

The computational cost of such photorealism remains steep, however, progress is being made. Each year the Association of Computing Machinery's Special Interest Group on Computer Graphics (ACM SIGGRAPH) sponsors an art show at their annual meeting. The best of the digital imagery displayed at these shows is typically highlighted in the July issue of *Communications of the ACM.* For example, "Digital Image—Digital Cinema" (*Communications of the ACM* 33, No. 7 (July 1990): 30–39) and "Art & Design & Computer Graphics Technology" (*Communications of the ACM* 34, No. 7 (July 1991): 30–39) present full-color portfolios that demonstrate the degree to which the computer is influencing art and graphic design.

Who knows? Might we someday achieve the situation described by Robert Heinlein in his science-fiction novel *The Moon Is a Harsh Mistress.* In this story the president of the United States, Adam Selene, appears only on television, never in person. Why? Because he is not a human being, but solely the product of computer-generated graphic images. Such animation may soon be possible as faster hardware merges with the more efficient rendering algorithms that experts in computer graphics are now developing. Such techniques are giving rise to a new area of research known as virtual reality, in which the computer is used to view ideas without having to build a physical model.

Though it's unlikely that virtual reality will create a simulated president such as Adam Selene, it is already having a dramatic effect in design-intensive fields such as architecture. Donald Greenberg of Cornell University described such virtual reality systems in "Computers and Architecture" (*Scientific American* 264, No. 8 (February 1991). According to Greenberg, "advanced modeling and rendering algorithms allow designers and clients to walk visually through buildings long before construction . . . seeing results of their design decisions immediately and revising them interactively."

These machines would sort a deck of keypunched cards by shuffling the cards into small bins, then collecting the cards from the bins into a newly arranged deck, and repeating this shuffling-collection process until the deck was magically sorted. There was, as we shall see, a very clever algorithm behind this rapid shuffling.

For integer data, the repeated passes of radix sort focus first on the ones digit of each number, then on the tens digit, the hundreds digit, and so on until the highest order digit of the largest number is reached. For string data, the first pass hinges on the rightmost character in each string with successive passes always shifting their attention one character position to the left. To illustrate the algorithm, we will trace it on the following list of nine integers:

459 254 472 534 649 239 432 654 477

On each pass through this data, radix sort will arrange it into ten sublists (bins)—one sublist for each of the digits 0 through 9. Hence, on the first pass, all the numbers with ones digit equal to zero are grouped in one sublist, all those with ones digit equal to one are grouped in another sublist, and so on. The resulting sublists follow.

First pass of radix sort

Digit	Sublist
0	
1	
2	472 432
3	
4	254 534 654
5	
6	
7	477
8	
9	459 649 239

The sublists are then collected into one large list with the numbers in the sublist for 0 coming first, then those in the sublist for 1, and so on up to the sublist for 9. Hence we would have a newly arranged list:

472 432 254 534 654 477 459 649 239

This new list is again partitioned into sublists, this time keying on the tens digit. The result is shown below.

Second pass of radix sort

Digit	Sublist
0	
1	
2	
3	432 534 239
4	649
5	654 254 459
6	
7	472 477
8	
9	

Note that in each sublist the data are arranged in order relative to their last two digits. The sublists would now be collected into a new master list:

432 534 239 649 654 254 459 472 477

Now, focusing on the hundreds digit, the master list would be classified into ten sublists one more time. These final sublists are shown below. When the sublists are collected from this final partitioning, the data are arranged in ascending order.

Third (final) pass of radix sort

Digit	Sublist
0	
1	
2	239 254
3	
4	432 459 472 477
5	534
6	649 654
7	
8	
9	

A pseudocode statement of the radix sort algorithm follows.

1. Begin with the current digit as the one's digit
2. **WHILE** there is still a digit on which to classify data **DO**
   - 2.1 **FOR** each number in the master list **DO**
     - 2.1.1 add that number to appropriate sublist, keying on current digit
   - 2.2 **FOR** each sublist (from 0 through 9) **DO**
     - 2.2.1 append that sublist to a newly arranged master list
   - 2.3 Advance the current digit one place to the left

If the radix sort is being applied to character strings instead of integers, this algorithm would have to proceed from the rightmost character to the leftmost character instead of from the ones digit to the highest order digit.

Efficiency of Radix Sort. An analysis of the loop structure in the preceding pseudocode for radix sort indicates that, for each pass through the outer **WHILE** loop, $O(n)$ operations must be performed. These $O(n)$ operations consist of the arithmetic necessary to isolate a particular digit within a number, appending that number to the proper sublist, and then collecting it again into a new master list. Since the outer **WHILE** loop will only be executed C times—where C is the number of digits (or characters) in the integer (or string)—the radix sort is an $O(n)$ sorting algorithm.

Although the radix sort is significantly faster than the other $O(n^2)$ algorithms we have studied in this chapter, there are again trade-off factors to consider. It is potentially much less space efficient than the other sorting algorithms we have studied. This is due to the need for storing sublists for each of the possible digits in the number or characters in the string. Using arrays to store the sublists and without any prior knowledge about the distribution of the data, we would be forced to allocate an additional $10n$ storage locations when sorting an array of n integers and $27n$ storage locations when sorting n strings of letters and blanks. We shall alleviate this memory crunch somewhat when we study linked lists in Chapter 4, but even then the radix sort will remain a space inefficient algorithm compared to other sorting algorithms. Other criteria negating the very good time efficiency of the radix sort are its inflexibility for data of varying size and the fact that, although $O(n)$ in time, its constant of proportionality in this regard is often large enough to often make it less time efficient than the more sophisticated sorting algorithms we will study in Chapter 8.

EXAMPLE 1.13

Assume the existence of the following declarations and procedure to perform radix sort on an array of four-digit numbers.

```
CONST
  MaxIndex = 100;
TYPE
  SingleDigit = 0..9;
  FourDigitNumbers = 0..9999;
  SortArray = ARRAY [1..MaxIndex] OF FourDigitNumbers;
  BinStructure = ARRAY [SingleDigit] OF SortArray;
  BinCounters = ARRAY [SingleDigit] OF integer;
  .
  .
  .
FUNCTION Digit(Number, K : integer) : SingleDigit;
```

```
  {  Given:   Integers Number and K.                                    }
  {  Task:    Determine Kth digit in Number, with one's digit being     }
  {           viewed as first.                                          }
  {  Return:  The Kth digit in Number.                                  }
  .
  .
  .
PROCEDURE InitializeCtrs (VAR S : BinCounters);

  {  Given:   S, an array of bin counters.                              }
  {  Task:    Initialize all counters in array to zero.                 }
  {  Return:  The array initialized to zero.                            }
  .
  .
  .
PROCEDURE AddToBin (VAR Bins : BinStructure;
                    VAR S : BinCounters;
                    Number, Place : integer);

  {  Given:   Bins, an array of bins, along with counters               }
  {           indicating number of values currently in each             }
  {           individual bin.                                           }
  {  Task:    Insert Number in bin indicated by Place.                  }
  {  Return:  Bins with Number added and updated counter array S.       }
  .
  .
  .
PROCEDURE CollectBins (VAR A : SortArray;
                       Bins : BinStructure;
                       S : BinCounters);

  {  Given:   Bins, with each bin containing number of values           }
  {           indicated by BinCounter array S.                          }
  {  Task:    Append Bins to each other starting with bin indexed       }
  {           by zero.                                                  }
  {  Return:  Appended Bins in array A.                                 }
```

Then the Pascal code for radix sort would be

```
PROCEDURE RadixSort (N : integer; VAR List : SortArray);

  {  Given:   Array List containing entries in locations 1 through N. }
  {  Task:    Apply radix sort algorithm.                              }
  {  Return:  Array List with first N entries arranged in ascending    }
  {           order.                                                   }

  VAR
    K, J : integer;
    Bins : BinStructure;
    BinCtr : BinCounters;

  BEGIN
    InitializeCtrs (BinCtr);
    {  For K loop controls digit used to classify data.  }
    FOR K := 1 TO 4 DO
      BEGIN
        {  For J loop iterates through all numbers, putting them into }
        {  bin determined by Kth digit.                               }
        FOR J := 1 TO N DO
          AddToBin (Bins, BinCtr, List[J], Digit(List[J], K));
        CollectBins (List, Bins, BinCtr);
        InitializeCtrs(BinCtr)
      END
  END;  {  of PROCEDURE RadixSort  }
```

■ ■

Exercises 1.4

1. Suppose that you are given the following list of keys

1	9438
2	3216
3	416
4	9021
5	1142
6	3316
7	94

   Show what the contents of the Pointer array would be after each pass through the outer loop of **PROCEDURE** PointerBubbleSort discussed in this section.

2. Consider again the data set given in Exercise 1. How many passes would be made through the outer loop of the radix sort algorithm for this data? Trace the contents of the array after each of these passes.

3. Consider the following list of strings:

1	CHOCOLATE
2	VANILLA
3	CARAMEL
4	PEACH
5	STRAWBERRY
6	CHERRY

   How many passes would be made through the outer loop of the radix sort algorithm for these data? Trace the contents of the list after each of these passes.

4. Explain the difference between physical and logical ordering.

5. Cite an application in which the mere logical ordering of data, as achieved by the pointer sort technique, would not be sufficient; that is, give an application in which physical ordering of data is required.

6. What is the time/space trade-off? Define and discuss various contexts in which it may arise.

7. When the bubble sort was modified with an array of pointers, did it improve its $O(n^2)$ run-time efficiency in a significant sense? Under what circumstances would you call the improvement in efficiency significant? Provide your answer to this question in a short essay in which you define "significant" and then explain why the circumstance you describe would lead to a significant improvement.

8. The bubble, insertion, and selection sort algorithms are all $O(n)$ in their space requirements. That is, each algorithm requires memory proportional to n to sort the items in an array of n items. From a big-O perspective, what are the space requirements of these algorithms when the pointer sort technique is incorporated into their logic?

9. Would you expect that the pointer strategy would have least effect on the run-time efficiency of bubble, selection, or insertion sort? Provide a rationale for your answer in a short essay.

10. Suppose you have 1,000 records to be sorted. Would the run-time efficiency of the pointer sort increase significantly if the 1,000 records were broken into four groups, each group sorted, and then merged together as one large sorted array as compared to sorting the initial unsegmented array? Why or why not?

11. Incorporate the pointer sort technique into the selection sort algorithm.

12. Incorporate the pointer sort technique into the insertion sort algorithm.

13. Write the procedures and functions assumed to exist in the version of RadixSort given in Example 1.13.

14. Write a radix sort procedure to sort an arbitrary array of integers. Analyze the space efficiency of your procedure.

15. Write a radix sort procedure to sort an array of strings. Analyze the space efficiency of your procedure. Be sure to carefully state the assumptions you make about strings in performing your analysis of space efficiency.

16. Describe the complications in implementing the radix sort algorithm for an array of real numbers. Discuss a strategy that could be used to overcome these complications.

■ ■ ■ ■

1.5 Simple Search Algorithms

OBJECTIVES

- to formalize a context in which search algorithms may be applied
- to understand the logic of the sequential search algorithm
- to analyze the efficiency of the sequential search algorithm
- to understand the logic of the binary search algorithm
- to recognize situations in which a key-to-address transformation may be used as an O(1) search method.

Many programs extensively employ algorithms that find a particular data item in a large collection of such items. Such algorithms, typically called *search algorithms,* are given the value of a key field that identifies the item being sought; they then return either all the data associated with that particular key or a flag indicating that it could not be found. You have probably encountered such algorithms in an earlier computer science course. We now explore search algorithms and subject them to an efficiency analysis using the big-O notation we have developed.

The general setup for the search algorithms we discuss in this chapter is given by the following skeletal declarations:

```
CONST
  MaxIndex = 100; {  Easily adjusted  }
  .
  .
  .
TYPE
  KeyType = {  Appropriate data type for key field in record  };
  DataRec = RECORD
               Key : KeyType;
               OtherData : {  Appropriate Type  }
            END;
  DataArray = ARRAY [1..MaxIndex] OF DataRec;
  .
  .
  .
PROCEDURE   Search (Target : KeyType;
                    SearchList : DataArray;
                    VAR InfoWanted : DataRec;
                    VAR Found : boolean);

  {  Given:    A collection of records in SearchList and Target storing key  }
  {            value of record being sought.                                 }
  {  Task:     Find the record associated with Target.                       }
  {  Return:   All data associated with Target in InfoWanted and Found set   }
  {            to true or false indicating whether or not the search         }
  {            was successful.                                               }
```

Figure 1.8 graphically portrays this setup. Specific search algorithms may require some additional information for their implementation; for example,

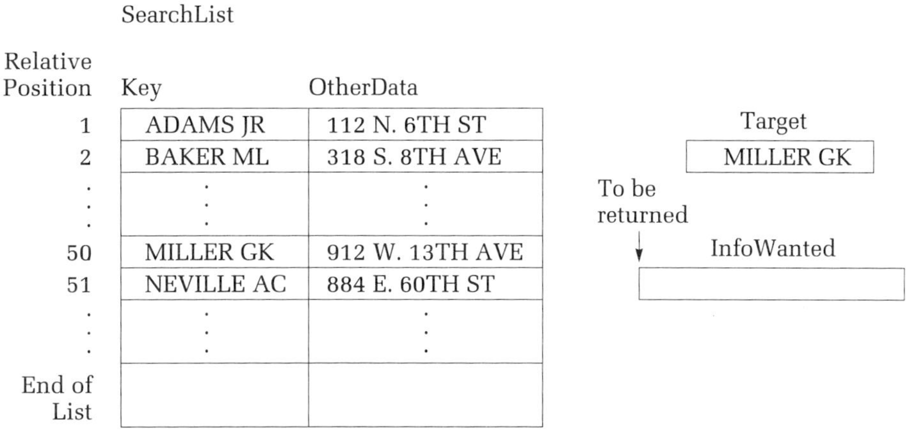

FIGURE 1.8
General setup for search algorithm

SearchList

Relative Position	Key	OtherData
1	ADAMS JR	112 N. 6TH ST
2	BAKER ML	318 S. 8TH AVE
⋮	⋮	⋮
50	MILLER GK	912 W. 13TH AVE
51	NEVILLE AC	884 E. 60TH ST
⋮	⋮	⋮
End of List		

a particular sentinel value that marks the end of the list or knowledge of the number of entries in the list. We will discuss these particulars with the individual algorithms themselves.

Sequential Search Algorithm

The task of a computer scientist working with search algorithms may be compared to that of a librarian. Just as the librarian must devise a method of storing books on shelves in a fashion that allows patrons to easily find the books they want, so must a computer scientist devise methods of organizing large collections of electronic data so that records within that data can always be quickly found. Imagine the plight of the librarian who just throws books upon shelves as they are unpacked from shipping boxes, without any consideration toward organizing the chaos! Unless the library had an artificially small collection, it would take patrons an impractical length of time to find their reading material. Because of the lack of any organizational order imposed on the books, the only search strategy available would be to pull books from the shelves in some arbitrary sequence until the desired book was found.

As a programmer given a completely unordered set of data, this is the same strategy you would have to follow. The logic of such a *sequential search* strategy is extremely simple and appears in the following **PROCEDURE** SequentialSearch. This procedure assumes that the final record in the list is flagged by a special Sentinel value in its Key field.

```
PROCEDURE SequentialSearch  (Target : KeyType;
                             Sentinel : KeyType;
                             SearchList : DataArray;
                             VAR InfoWanted : DataRec;
                             VAR Found : boolean);

  {  Given:   List of records in SearchList, Target storing  }
  {           key value being sought, and Sentinel value     }
  {           marking end of list.                           }
  {  Task:    Sequentially pass through SearchList seeking   }
  {           Target.                                        }
  {  Return:  DataRec associated with Target in InfoWanted.  }
  {           If not found, return false in boolean          }
  {           variable Found.                                }
```

```
VAR
  K : integer;

BEGIN
  Found := false; {  Initially set to false and not changed  }
                  {  unless find Target.                     }
  K := 1;
  {  From position 1, advance sequentially through SearchList  }
  {  until encounter Sentinel or Target.                       }
  WHILE (SearchList[K].Key <> Sentinel) AND NOT Found DO
    IF SearchList[K].Key = Target THEN
      BEGIN
        Found := true;
        InfoWanted := SearchList[K]
      END
    ELSE
      K := K + 1
END; {  of PROCEDURE SequentialSearch  }
```

Efficiency of Sequential Search. Unfortunately, the simplicity of the sequential search is offset by its inefficiency as a search strategy. Obviously, the average number of probes into the list before the target key is found will be $n/2$, where n is the number of records in the list. For unsuccessful invocations of the procedure, all n records must be checked before we can conclude failure. Thus, in terms of a big-O classification, the method is clearly $O(n)$. This may not seem bad when compared to the $O(n^2)$ efficiency of our sorting methods, but searching is conceptually a much simpler operation than sorting: it should be significantly faster. Moreover, though $O(n)$ may seem fast enough at microsecond speeds, there are many applications where an $O(n)$ time factor can be unacceptably slow.

For instance, when a compiler processes your source program in Pascal, it must continually search a list of identifiers that have been previously declared. (This list is typically called a *symbol table.*) Hence, in such an application, the search operation merely represents the inner loop within a much more complex outer loop that is repeating until it reaches the end of your source file: an inner loop which, repeated at $O(n)$ speeds, would make your compiler intolerably slow.

Another situation in which $O(n)$ is not good enough for searching occurs when the list being searched is stored in a *disk file* instead of a main memory array. Now, because accessing data on disk is a much slower operation than accessing data in main memory, each probe into the list might conceivably require approximately one millisecond (one-thousandth of a second) instead of a microsecond. Searching such a list of one million records at $O(n)$ speed would hence require one thousand seconds instead of just one second. That long a wait for one record is certain to generate angry users. We conclude that, although the sequential search may be fast enough for small and infrequently accessed lists stored in main memory, we need something that is better by an order of magnitude for many practical applications.

Binary Search Algorithm

By paying what may initially seem like a small price, we can dramatically increase the efficiency of our search effort using the *binary search* algorithm. The price we must pay is threefold.

1. The list of records with keys must be maintained in physically sorted order unless we are willing to use an additional list of pointers similar to that used in the PointerBubbleSort algorithm. (See the Exercises at the end of this section.)
2. The number of records in the list must be maintained in a separate variable.
3. We must be able to randomly access, by relative position, records in the list. This is the type of access you have in Pascal arrays, but which is lacking in standard Pascal files.

For instance, suppose that the list of integer keys appearing in Figure 1.9 has the access facility of the third point just cited and that we wish to locate

FIGURE 1.9
Physically ordered random access list of keys for binary search

Position	Key
1	1119
2	1203
3	1212
4	1519
5	1604
6	1649
7	1821
8	2312
9	2409
10	3612

Number of Records $n = 10$
Target = 1649

the randomly accessible data associated with the Target key 1649. The strategy of the binary search is to begin the search in the middle of the list. In the case of Figure 1.9, this would mean beginning the search with the key found at position 5. Since the Target we are seeking is greater than the key found at position 5, we are able to conclude that the key we want will be found among positions 6 through 10—if at all.

We will split those positions that remain viable candidates for finding the Target by accessing the middle position:

(6 + 10) / 2 = 8

Since the key at position 8 is greater than Target, we are able to conclude that the key being sought will be found in positions 6 or 7—if it is to be found at all. Notice that, after only two accesses into the list, our list of remaining viable candidates for a match has shrunk to 2. (Compare this figure to a sequential search after two accesses into the same list.) We now split the distance between positions 6 and 7, arriving (by integer arithmetic) at position 6. Here we find the key being sought after a mere three probes into the list.

Crucial to the entire binary search algorithm are two pointers, Low and High, to the bottom and top respectively of the current list of viable candidates. We must repeatedly compute the Middle index of that portion of the list between Low and High and compare the data at that Middle index to the Target using the following logic.

```
IF Target < SearchList[Middle].Key THEN
  High must be reduced to Middle - 1
ELSE IF Target > SearchList[Middle].Key THEN
  Low must be increased to Middle + 1
ELSE
  Search is done
  Target has been found in SearchList
```

Should these pointers ever cross, that is, if High were to become less than Low, we would conclude that the Target does not appear in the list. The entire algorithm is formalized in the following Pascal procedure:

```
PROCEDURE  BinarySearch (Target : KeyType;
                         N : integer;
                         SearchList : DataArray;
                         VAR InfoWanted : DataRec;
                         VAR Found : boolean);

  {  Given:   List of sorted records in SearchList, Target    }
  {           storing key value being sought, and N storing   }
  {           number of records in the list.                  }
  {  Task:    Apply binary search algorithm.                  }
  {  Return:  DataRec associated with Target in InfoWanted.   }
  {           If not found, return false in Boolean           }
  {           variable Found.                                 }

  VAR
    High, Low, Middle : integer;

  BEGIN
    Found := false;
    Low := 1;
    High := N;
    {  Indices between Low and High inclusive represent positions  }
    {  where Target could possibly located.                        }
    WHILE NOT Found AND (Low <= High) DO
      BEGIN
        Middle := (Low + High) DIV 2;
        IF Target < SearchList[Middle].Key THEN {  Work with low end  }
          High := Middle - 1
```

	Key	
1	102	Initial Low
2	183	
.	219	
.	264	If Target > 351, then
Middle	351	Low must be reset to
.	499	point at 499
.	506	
	530	
N	642	Initial High

	Key	
1	102	Initial Low
2	183	
.	219	
.	264	If Target < 351, then
Middle	351	High must be reset to
.	499	point at 264
.	506	
	530	
N	642	Initial High

```
        ELSE IF Target > SearchList[Middle].Key THEN {  Work with high end  }
          Low := Middle + 1
        ELSE  {  Success!  }
          BEGIN
            Found := true;
            InfoWanted := SearchList[Middle]
          END
      END
  END; {  of PROCEDURE BinarySearch  }
```

EXAMPLE 1.14

Trace the action of **PROCEDURE** BinarySearch as it locates the record associated with Target 1519 in the array of Figure 1.9.

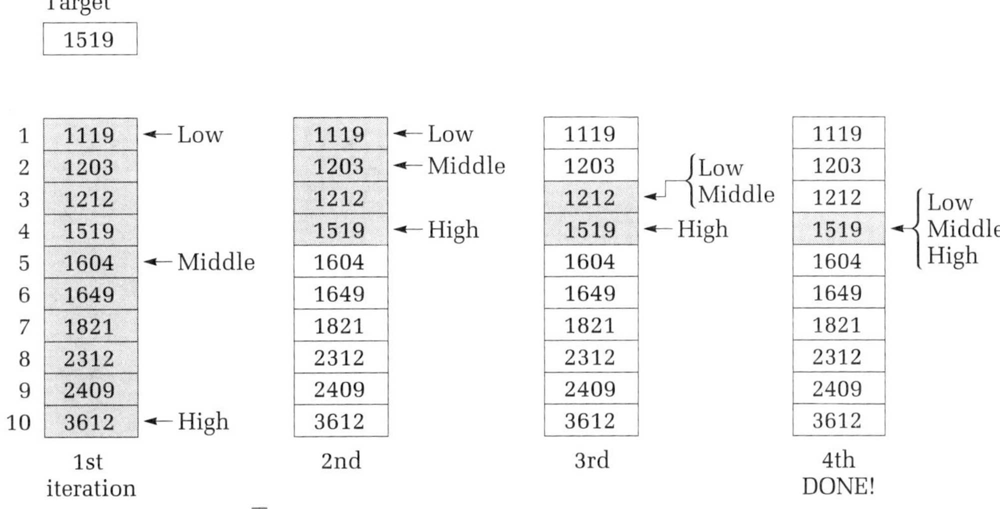

EXAMPLE 1.15

Trace the action of **PROCEDURE** BinarySearch as it reports that target 2392 cannot be found in the array of Figure 1.9.

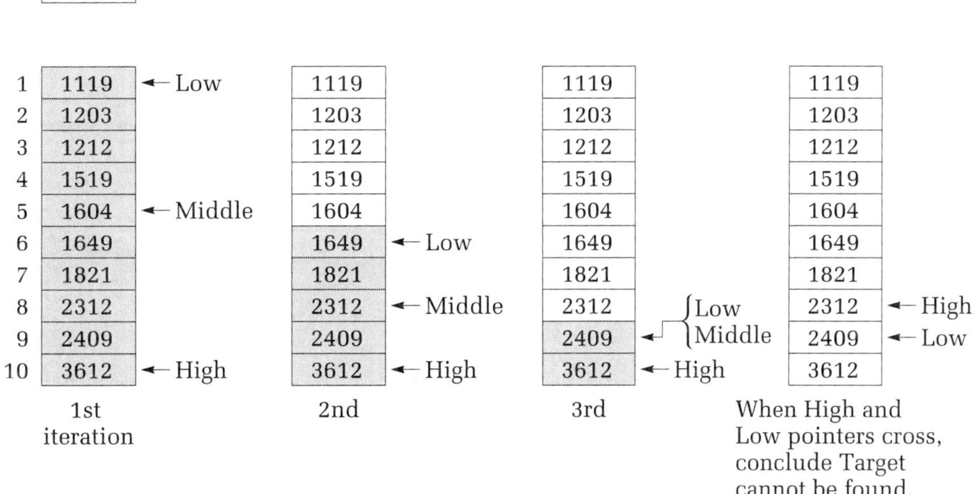

Efficiency of Binary Search. As indicated by the shaded portions of the lists in the preceding examples, the binary search continually halves the size of the list that must still be searched. This continual halving is critical to the effectiveness of the algorithm. When applied to the list of keys in Figure 1.9, the method in the worst case would require four different accesses. For an ordered list of 50,000 keys, the worst-case efficiency is a mere sixteen different accesses. (In case you do not believe this dramatic increase in efficiency as the list gets larger, try plugging 50,000 into a handheld calculator and count how many times you must halve the displayed number to reduce it to 1.) The same list of 1,000,000 records stored on disk that would require approximately 1,000 seconds to search sequentially will result in a virtually instantaneous response with the binary search strategy.

More formally, for a list of n items, the maximum number of times we would cut the list in half before finding the target item or declaring the search unsuccessful is

$$(\log_2 n) + 1$$

Thus, the binary search is the first $O(\log_2 n)$ algorithm we have studied. (See Example 1.10.) In terms of the categorizations discussed in Section 1.3, it is a logarithmic algorithm. Expressions involving a $\log_2 n$ factor will arise frequently as we analyze other algorithms. They are extremely fast when compared to $O(n)$ algorithms, particularly for large values of n.

The drawback of the binary search lies not in any consideration of its processing speed but rather in a reexamination of the price that must be paid for being able to use it. For a volatile list (that is, one undergoing frequent additions and deletions), the requirement of maintaining the list in physical order can be quite costly. For large lists, it makes the operations of adding and deleting records so inefficient that the very fast search speed is all but negated. We will analyze this problem of list maintenance more deeply in future chapters.

Key-to-Address Transformations

A search technique so simple that it is often overlooked presents itself in certain situations where a record's key value can be transformed conveniently into a position within a list by applying a function to the key value. For instance, suppose that a school assigns its students five-digit identification numbers in which the first two digits indicate the student's year of matriculation and the last three digits are simply assigned in a sequential fashion among students matriculating in a given year. Hence the fourteenth student admitted in the class of 1992 would have the identification number

9 2 0 1 4

year of matriculation (9 2) — sequence number within that year (0 1 4)

In such a situation, student records could be stored in a two-dimensional table in which rows were indexed by year of matriculation and columns indexed by sequence number within a given year. Then the integer arithmetic operations

Key **DIV** 1000

and

Key **MOD** 1000

would yield a given student's row and column index respectively. The address of a student's record could therefore be obtained from the student's identification number using a mere two operations.

In such situations, the search efficiency to locate a student's record is O(1) in its big-O classification. The apparent restriction that must apply for this technique to work is that the transformation applied to a key to yield an address cannot yield the same address for two different students. As we shall see in Chapter 9, even this restriction can be relaxed somewhat if slightly more sophisticated search techniques are employed. Another drawback of the key-to-address transformation technique is its potentially inefficient use of space. You will perform such a space analysis for this strategy in this section's Exercises.

Exercises 1.5

1. Suppose that an array contains key values

   18 40 46 50 52 58 63 70 77 90

   in index locations 1 through 10. Trace the index values for the Low, High, and Middle pointers in the binary search algorithm if the Target 43 is being sought. Repeat for Target values 40 and 90.

2. In Exercise 10 of Section 1.2 we defined the notions of best-case and worst-case behavior of an algorithm. Devise sample data sets to demonstrate the best-case and worst-case behavior of the binary search algorithm.

3. What is a compiler symbol table? Explain why a sequential search applied to such a table is not a practical strategy.

4. Explain the difference in run-time efficiency considerations for a program that manipulates data in a main memory array versus one that accesses data stored in a disk file.

5. How many times would the **WHILE** loop in **PROCEDURE** BinarySearch be executed if $n = 1{,}000{,}000$?

6. Consider the following modified version of the binary search algorithm. (Modifications are indicated by a comment highlighted by asterisks.) Will this new version of the binary search algorithm work correctly for all data? If not, specify a situation in which this version will fail.

```
PROCEDURE  BinarySearch (Target : KeyType;
                         N : integer;
                         SearchList : DataArray;
                         VAR InfoWanted : DataRec;
                         VAR Found : boolean);

  {  Given:   List of sorted records in SearchList, Target   }
  {           storing key value being sought, and N storing  }
  {           number of records in the list.                 }
  {  Task:    Apply binary search algorithm.                 }
  {  Return:  DataRec associated with Target in InfoWanted.  }
  {           If not found, return false in Boolean          }
  {           variable Found.                                }

  VAR
    High, Low, Middle : integer;

  BEGIN
    Found := false;
    Low := 1;
    High := N;
    WHILE NOT Found AND (Low <= High) DO
```

```
      BEGIN
        Middle := (Low + High) DIV 2;
        IF Target < SearchList[Middle].Key THEN {  Work with low end  }
          High := Middle    { ******  Modification here ****** }
        ELSE IF Target > SearchList[Middle].Key THEN {  Work with high end  }
          Low := Middle      { ****** Modification here ****** }
        ELSE  {  Success!  }
          BEGIN
            Found := true;
            InfoWanted := SearchList[Middle]
          END
      END
  END; {  of PROCEDURE BinarySearch  }
```

7. Consider the following modified version of the binary search algorithm. (Modifications are indicated by a comment highlighted by asterisks.) Will this new version of the binary search algorithm work correctly for all data? If not, specify a situation in which this version will fail.

```
PROCEDURE  BinarySearch (Target : KeyType;
                         N : integer;
                         SearchList : DataArray;
                         VAR InfoWanted : DataRec;
                         VAR Found : boolean);
  {  Given:   List of sorted records in SearchList, Target    }
  {           storing key value being sought, and N storing   }
  {           number of records in the list.                  }
  {  Task:    Apply binary search algorithm.                  }
  {  Return:  DataRec associated with Target in InfoWanted.   }
  {           If not found, return false in Boolean           }
  {           variable Found.                                 }

  VAR
    High, Low, Middle : integer;

  BEGIN
    Found := false;
    Low := 1;
    High := N;
    REPEAT    { ***** Use REPEAT instead of WHILE ***** }
      Middle := (Low + High) DIV 2;
      IF Target < SearchList[Middle].Key THEN {  Work with low end  }
        High := Middle - 1
      ELSE IF Target > SearchList[Middle].Key THEN {  Work with high end  }
        Low := Middle + 1
      ELSE  {  Success!  }
        BEGIN
          Found := true;
          InfoWanted := SearchList[Middle]
        END
    UNTIL Found OR ( Low > High )    { ****** Loop exit condition ****** }
  END; {  of PROCEDURE BinarySearch  }
```

8. Consider the example of a key-to-address transformation for student identification numbers given in this section. Discuss the space efficiency of this strategy. Upon what factor is the space efficiency dependent?

9. Devise a key-to-address transformation to locate records in a data structure for employees of the East Publishing Company. Departments in the company are identified by a one-letter code A–Z. An employee's payroll identification number consists of a department code followed by another one-letter code representing the employee's pay rate classification, and a two-digit number assigned in sequential fashion to employees within a given department. Hence, the identification number DX40 is assigned to the 40th employee in department D; the X indicates the employee's pay rate category.

10. The requirement for the binary search that the data in an array be physically ordered can actually be circumvented by keeping track of the logical order of the data via a pointer array analogous to that used in the pointer sort. Rewrite the binary search algorithm under such an assumption. Explain why it might be advantageous to use this technique.

11. Implement the following modification to the sequential search algorithm. Temporarily insert the key for which you are searching at the end of the list. Search sequentially until you find this key; then examine the position where you found it to determine whether or not the search was successful. Note that this strategy requires your knowing the number of items in the list rather than a sentinel value stored at the end of the list. Comment on the run-time efficiency of this new strategy versus the sequential search algorithm discussed in this chapter.

12. Modify the insertion sort algorithm of Section 1.2 so that it finds the insertion point for the next array entry using an appropriate modification of the halving strategy employed by the binary search algorithm. Once this insertion point is determined, other array entries must be moved accordingly to make room for the entry being inserted. After completing this modified version of the insertion sort, perform a big-O analysis of its efficiency.

13. In a search procedure such as sequential or binary search, the array to be searched is passed as a value parameter to the procedure because we do not want the array altered during execution of the procedure. Write a short essay in which you explain why, from a time efficiency perspective, it would be wiser to pass large arrays as **VAR** parameters to such procedure—even though this violates dictates of program style that we have previously established. *Remember:* Your answer to this question should be based on efficiency rather than on style considerations. Check with your instructor about whether you should incorporate such a change in philosophy into future programming efforts. *Hint:* Think about what must be done by a compiler to provide a procedure with a copy of a data item passed as a value parameter. Compare this to what must be done when a parameter is passed by reference.

14. Imagine that you have been hired to write an information retrieval program for a company or organization. You must interview people within the organization to determine exactly what their information retrieval needs are. Construct questions that you could ask in such an interview to enable you to determine which search strategy would be most appropriate for the program you must write. Then, in an essay explain how answers to these questions would dictate your choice of search strategy.

■ ■ ■ ■

FOCUS ON PROGRAM DESIGN

We will close each chapter with a special section that focuses on the design issues that have arisen in the chapter. In the Focus section of this first chapter we examine how we can augment a program to help us analyze its own efficiency. This technique, known as *profiling,* consists of inserting counters that accumulate the total number of times that certain critical operations are performed as an algorithm executes.

We will illustrate the technique on a program that determines all prime numbers less than or equal to a specified positive integer NUMBER. For purposes of this program, we will use the mathematical property that a number is prime if it has no divisors other than 1 and itself. For example, 37 is such a number. Also, note that 1 is not prime by definition.

For the moment, let us consider a first-level pseudocode development for the problem of finding primes *apart* from the profiling technique mentioned earlier. This pseudocode is

```
1. Get a number
WHILE MoreData Do
    2. Examine the number
    3. Get a number
```

A structure chart for this problem is shown in Figure 1.10.

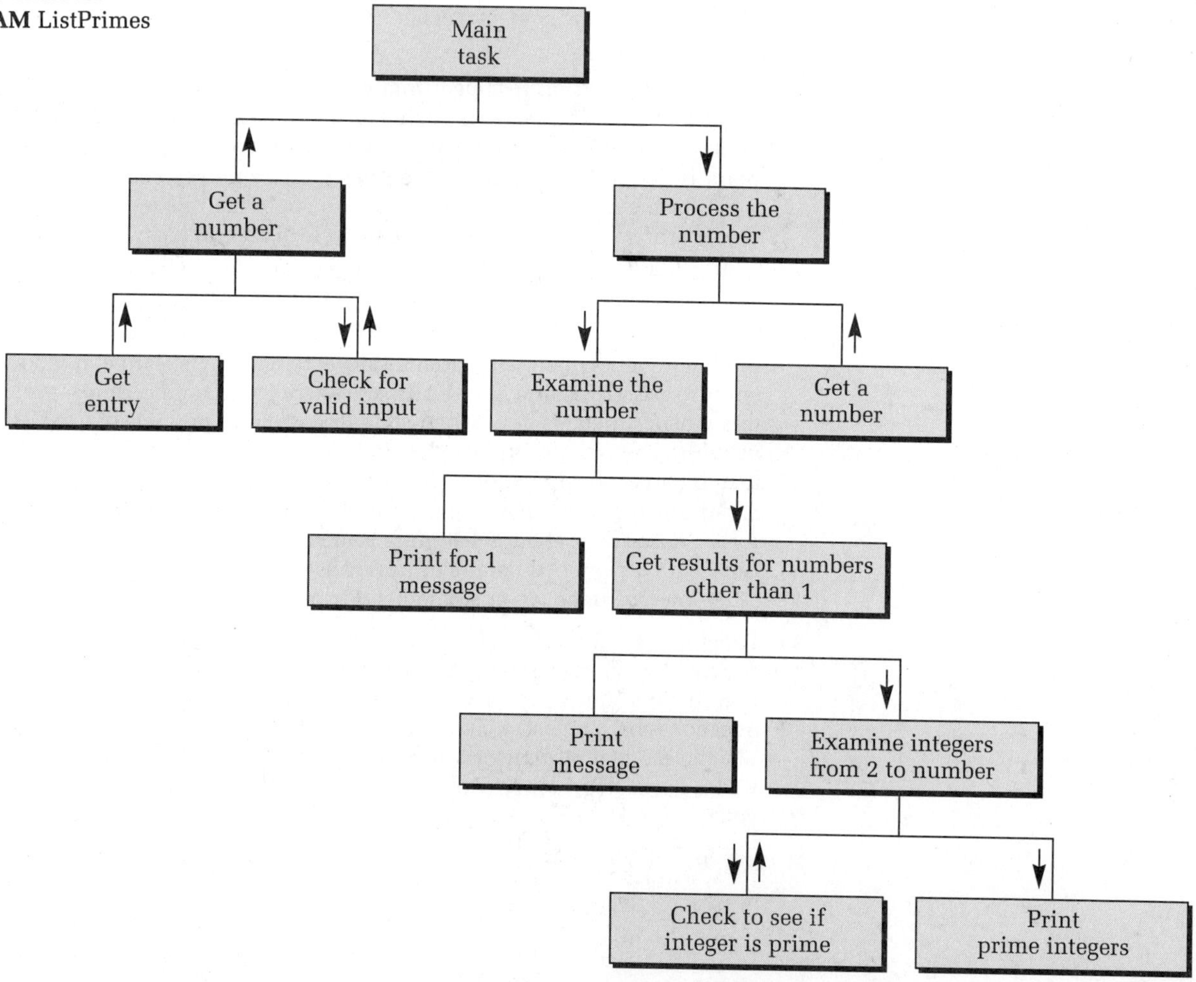

FIGURE 1.10
Structure chart for **PROGRAM** ListPrimes

The module specifications for the main modules are

1. <u>GetANumber Module</u>
   Data received: None
   Information returned: Number
   Boolean flag MoreData
   Logic: Get an entry from the keyboard.
   Make sure it is a valid entry or the sentinel value for terminating the process.
   If it is the sentinel value, set the **boolean** variable MoreData to **false.**

```
2. ExamineTheNumber Module
   Data received: The integer read
   Information returned: None
   Logic: IF the number is 1 THEN print a message
          ELSE
            Print a heading.
            FOR K := 2 TO Number DO
              Check K for a prime number.
              IF K is prime THEN print it.
```

A second-level development is

```
1. Get a number
   1.1 Get entry from the keyboard
   1.2 Check for valid entry
WHILE MoreData DO
2. Examine the number
   IF Number is 1 THEN
      2.1 print a message for one
   ELSE list the primes
      2.2 print a message
      2.3 check for primes less than or equal to Number
3. Get a number
   3.1 Get entry from the keyboard
   3.2 Check for valid entry
```

Step 2.3 can be refined to

```
      2.3 check for primes less than or equal to Number
          FOR K := 2 TO Number DO
             2.3.1 check to see if K is prime
             2.3.2 IF K is prime THEN
                      print K in list of primes
```

Thus, the complete pseudocode development is

```
1. Get a number
   1.1 Get entry from the keyboard
   1.2 Check for valid entry
WHILE MoreData DO
2. Examine the number
   IF Number is 1 THEN
      2.1 print a message for one
   ELSE list the primes
      2.2 print a message
      2.3 check for primes less than or equal to Number
          FOR K := 2 TO Number DO
             2.3.1 check to see if K is prime
             2.3.2 IF K is prime THEN
                      print K in a list of primes
3. Get a number
   3.1 Get entry from the keyboard
   3.2 Check for valid entry
```

With this pseudocode development, the main program to solve the problem of finding primes would be

```
BEGIN  {  Main program  }
  GetANumber (Number, MoreData);
  WHILE MoreData DO
    BEGIN
      ExamineTheNumber (Number);
      GetANumber (Number, MoreData)
    END  {  of WHILE loop  }
END.  {  of main program  }
```

The complete program is given below. Those portions of the program which are shaded represent additions necessary to implement the profiling of the program. We will return to a discussion of these additions after you've had a chance to read the program. Pay particular attention to the ListAll-Primes procedure since it is central to analyzing the efficiency of the program.

```
PROGRAM ListPrimes (input, output);

CONST
  Skip = ' ';
  Dashes = '---------------------------------------------------';
  Profile = true;

VAR
  Number : integer;
  MoreData : boolean;
  ProfiledOperations : integer;

{****************************************************************}

PROCEDURE GetANumber (VAR Number : integer;
                      VAR MoreData : boolean);

  {  Given:   Nothing                                          }
  {  Task:    Read an integer entered from the keyboard        }
  {  Return:  The integer read                                 }

  BEGIN
    REPEAT
      writeln;
      writeln ('Enter a positive integer, <-999> to quit.');
      readln (Number);
      MoreData := Number <> -999
    UNTIL (Number > 0) OR (Number = -999)  { assumes valid data }
  END;  {  of PROCEDURE GetANumber  }

{****************************************************************}

PROCEDURE PrintOneMessage;

  {  Given:   Nothing                                          }
  {  Task:    Print a message for 1                            }
  {  Return:  Nothing                                          }

    BEGIN
      writeln;
      writeln (Skip:10, Dashes);
      writeln;
      writeln (Skip:20, '1 is not prime by definition.')
  END;  {  of PROCEDURE PrintOneMessage  }

{****************************************************************}
```

```
PROCEDURE PrintMessage (Number : integer);

  {  Given:  The integer read                                     }
  {  Task:   Print a heading for the output                       }
  {  Return: Nothing                                              }

  BEGIN
    writeln;
    writeln (Skip:10, Dashes);
    writeln;
    writeln (Skip:20, 'The number is  ', Number,
             '.  The prime numbers');
    writeln (Skip:20, 'less than or equal to ', Number, ' are:');
    writeln
  END;  {  of PROCEDURE PrintMessage  }

{***************************************************************}


PROCEDURE ListAllPrimes (Number : integer);

  {  Given:   The integer read                                    }
  {  Task:    List all primes less than or equal to the integer }
  {           read                                                }
  {  Return:  Nothing                                             }

  VAR
    Prime : boolean;
    Candidate, Divisor : integer;
    LimitForCheck : real;

  BEGIN
    IF Profile THEN
      ProfiledOperations := 0;
    FOR Candidate := 2 TO Number DO
      BEGIN
        Prime := true;
        Divisor := 2;
        LimitForCheck := Candidate - 1;
        WHILE (Divisor <= LimitForCheck) AND Prime DO
          BEGIN
            IF Candidate MOD Divisor = 0 THEN
              Prime := false        {  Candidate has a divisor   }
            ELSE
              Divisor := Divisor + 1;
            IF Profile THEN
              ProfiledOperations := ProfiledOperations + 1
          END;
        IF Prime THEN               {  Print in list of primes   }
          writeln (Candidate:35)
      END  {  of FOR loop  }
  END;  {  of PROCEDURE ListAllPrimes  }

{***************************************************************}


PROCEDURE ProfileReport (Number : integer);

  {  Given:  The count of profiled operations (global)           }
  {          and Number being profiled                           }
  {  Task:   Report a comparison of the number of profiled       }
  {          operations to O(N^2)                                }
```

```
  BEGIN
    writeln;
    writeln('     For N: ', Number : 3);
    writeln;
    writeln('     Number of profiled operations: ', ProfiledOperations : 6);
    writeln('     Compare to O(N^2):              ', Number * Number : 6);
    writeln
  END;  { of PROCEDURE ProfileReport }

{*************************************************************}

PROCEDURE ExamineTheNumber (Number : integer);

  {  Given:   The integer read (Number)                        }
  {  Task:    Print primes less than or equal to Number        }
  {  Return:  Nothing                                          }

  BEGIN
    If Number = 1 THEN
      PrintOneMessage
    ELSE
      BEGIN
        PrintMessage (Number);
        ListAllPrimes (Number);
        IF Profile THEN
          ProfileReport (Number)
      END  {  of ELSE option  }
  END;  {  of PROCEDURE ExamineTheNumber  }

{*************************************************************}

BEGIN  {  Main Program  }
  GetANumber (Number, MoreData);
  WHILE MoreData DO
    BEGIN
      ExamineTheNumber (Number);
      GetANumber (Number, MoreData)
    END  {  of WHILE loop  }
END.  {  of main program  }
```

To analyze the time efficiency of this program we will turn our attention to the ListAllPrimes procedure. The nested loop structure of this procedure is given by the following schematic

```
FOR Candidate := 2 TO Number
  :
  WHILE
    :
```

Inner **WHILE** loop executed Candidate - 2 or fewer times

Outer **FOR** loop executed Number − 1 times

Certainly the schematic indicates that we are safe in saying that **PROCEDURE** ListAllPrimes is O(Number^2) in its time efficiency. However, the early exit condition from the inner loop will be reached quite often. This leads us to believe that the algorithm may actually be substantially faster than O(Number^2).

Unfortunately, determining how much faster it is than O(Number^2) by using a purely mathematical analysis may be impossible or at least require a knowledge of mathematical number theory beyond our present means. We propose instead to use the computer to help us analyze the algorithm from an empirical perspective. An examination of the shaded code in the program listing indicates that profiling the ListAllPrimes algorithm is achieved by

- Declaring a global Boolean constant that is set to **true** to "turn on" profiling. All executable statements related to profiling are conditionally qualified by

  ```
  IF Profile THEN . . .
  ```

  Thus, to turn off profiling in the program, you would merely set this constant to **false**.
- A global variable ProfiledOperations is initialized to zero upon entry to ListAllPrimes and then increased by 1 each time an addition or **MOD** operation is performed.
- A ProfileReport procedure is called conditionally by the main program to report a comparison between N^2 and the actual number of operations performed during execution of the algorithm.

We should justify the use of globally declared data within the procedure ListAllPrimes. The alternative would be to add extra parameters to the formal parameter list of ListAllPrimes—parameters that are concerned with profiling instead of the actual algorithm implemented by ListAllPrimes. That is, the profiling data items are completely extraneous to the logic of the procedure; they are there only to measure empirically the performance of the algorithm. As such, adding them to the formal parameter list would make the interface to the procedure considerably more confusing than necessary.

We emphasize that the use of globals in such profiling applications is an exceptional circumstance. In general, the maxim that procedures and functions should only use locally declared data remains true.

The results of a few sample runs of this program, with profiled output, are:

```
Enter a positive integer, <-999> to quit. 17

          ------------------------------------------------
                    The number is 17.  The prime numbers
                    less than or equal to 17 are:

                                 2
                                 3
                                 5
                                 7
                                11
                                13
                                17

    For N:  17

    Number of profiled operations:      55
    Compare to O(N^2):                 289

Enter a positive integer, <-999> to quit.  45
    .
    . (primes listed here)
    .
    For N:  45

    Number of profiled operations:    296
    Compare to O(N^2):               2025
```

```
Enter a positive integer, <-999> to quit.   100
     .
     . (primes listed here)
     .
     For N: 100

     Number of profiled operations:   1133
     Compare to O(N^2):              10000

Enter a positive integer, <-999> to quit.   150
     .
     . (primes listed here)
     .
     For N: 150

     Number of profiled operations:   2414
     Compare to O(N^2):              22500

Enter a positive integer, <-999> to quit.  -999
```

What have we learned from the runs of this profiled program? The observed number of operations that are reported by the program offers empirical evidence that we are well within the bounds of an $O(N^2)$ algorithm. They indicate that we can perhaps even place the algorithm into a more efficient big-O category. What category? This could be explored by fine-tuning the ProfileReport procedure to compare the actual number of performed operations with N^r for values of r less than 2 or with $N * \log_2 N$.

We can now suggest a number of ways to improve the algorithm and evaluate the efficiency of each succeeding version of the algorithm by a combination of formal big-O analysis and empirical profiling. Our series of refinements is illustrative of a process that can often be applied to the first version of an algorithm. That is, reflection upon how a given algorithm works can often lead to a new algorithm, which achieves the same end in a much more efficient manner.

Observation 1
The greatest divisor of a number, other than itself, cannot exceed one-half of the number.

Observation 2
Divisors of a number come in pairs. For instance, 36 is divided evenly by 4 since $4 * 9 = 36$. Here the divisor 4 is paired with the divisor 9. The search for divisors in the inner loop of our algorithm need not consider the larger value in such a divisor pair. Why? Because it cannot find such a larger divisor without first finding the smaller value in the divisor pair.

Observation 3
The Greek mathematician Eratosthenes devised a "sieve" technique for finding all prime numbers between 2 and Number. The *sieve of Eratosthenes* can be viewed as a Boolean array indexed from 2 to Number and initialized to **true** in all of its locations. Successive array indices that are

Multiples of 2 greater than 2 are set to false.
Multiples of 3 greater than 3 are set to false.
Multiples of 4 can be ignored. Why?
Multiples of 5 greater than 5 are set to false.

Multiples of 6 can be ignored. Why?
Multiples of 7 greater than 7 are set to false.

and so on. The prime numbers are those array indices where a true value remains.

You will be asked to continue exploration of such prime number algorithms in the problems. Profiling can be a valuable aide in such exploration. It provides statistical evidence of an algorithm's performance in cases where pure mathematical analysis may be inconclusive.

RUNNING AND DEBUGGING TIPS

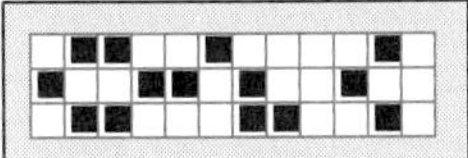

1. Procedures with an array as a value parameter in their formal parameter list will run faster if the array parameter is converted into a **VAR** parameter. Making such a change will eliminate the machine instructions involved in copying an actual parameter that is passed to the procedure. However, making such a change for the sake of efficiency should be carefully weighed against the consideration that the procedure's actual parameter list will now not reflect whether the role of an array parameter is to serve only as input to the procedure.
2. When profiling an algorithm, use a Boolean constant that can be set to **true** or **false** to turn profiling on or off respectively.
3. When using integer counters in profiling a program, be careful that the number of operations executed by the algorithm does not overflow the capacity of integer storage. Most Pascal implementations offer additional integer data types that can accommodate values too large for standard integers. Consult local system reference materials to find out what your version of Pascal may offer in this regard.

■ Summary

Key Terms

artificial intelligence
best case
big-O analysis
big-O notation
binary search
bin sort
bubble sort
compiler symbol table
computer graphics
cubic algorithm
data about data
disk file
dominant term
exponential algorithm
heuristics
insertion sort
linear algorithm
logarithmic algorithm
logical order
$\log_2 n$ search algorithm
order of magnitude
parallel processing
permutation
physically sorted
pointers
pointer sort
polynomial algorithm
profile
proportional
quadratic algorithm
radix sort
search algorithm
selection sort
sequential search
shaker sort
sieve of Eratosthenes
state space
symbol table
time/space trade-off
worst case

Key Concepts

- An integral part of designing efficient software is the selection of appropriate algorithms to perform the task at hand.
- Two of the criteria used in selecting algorithms for a given task are time and space efficiency. An algorithm's time efficiency determines how long it requires to run. An algorithm's space efficiency is a measure of how much primary and secondary memory it consumes.
- Three simple sorting algorithms are the bubble sort, insertion sort, and selection sort. The latter minimizes the number of data interchanges that must be made at

the expense of not being more efficient for data that are already partially ordered.

- Pointer sort and radix sort are techniques to enhance the time efficiency of a sort at the expense of increased space requirements.
- Three simple search algorithms are the sequential search, binary search, and key-to-address transformation technique.
- Profiling is an empirical technique that can be used to measure an algorithm's efficiency when a big-O analysis is inconclusive.
- Big-O analyses of sort and search algorithms discussed in this chapter are summarized in the following table, which is continued on the next page.

Algorithms	Time Efficiency	Additional Comments
Bubble sort	$O(n^2)$ comparisons and interchanges in worst case	Can be faster if input data already almost sorted.
Insertion sort	$O(n^2)$ comparisons and interchanges in worst case	Also can be faster if input data already almost sorted.
Selection sort	$O(n^2)$ comparisons, $O(n)$ interchanges in worst case	Not significantly faster if input data already almost sorted.
Pointer sort	Reflects number of comparisons of method upon which it is layered	Though number of interchanges not reduced, amount of data swapped for each interchange is potentially less. Drawback is the additional memory required for pointers.
Radix sort	$O(n)$ comparisons and interchanges	Limited in the types of data upon which it works. Though $O(n)$, may have a large constant of proportionality, which can make the $O(n)$ rating a misleading one. For arrays, a large space requirement for storing sublists.
Sequential search	$O(n)$ probes into list in worst case	Most inefficient of search algorithms we will study, but still appropriate for small lists stored in main memory.
Binary search	$O(\log_2 n)$ probes in worst case	Drawbacks are that we must continually maintain a count of number of records in list and that the list must be maintained in sorted order.
Key-to-address transformation	$O(1)$ list probes	Not applicable for many types of keys. Potential space inefficiencies.

■ Programming Problems and Projects

1. Incorporate each of the observations cited in the Focus on Program Design section into the ListAllPrimes algorithm. For each successive modification to the algorithm, run a series of tests in which you use profiling to measure the efficiency of the resulting algorithm. Write up the results of your experimentation, addressing such issues as:
   a. Which technique produces the fastest runs?
   b. Does any technique appear to be an order of magnitude better in its time efficiency? Cite results from profiling to back up your claims in this regard.
   c. What trade-offs are involved in using these techniques to achieve a faster run-time?
2. Suppose that you know the keys in a list are arranged in increasing order. How could the sequential search algorithm presented in this chapter be improved with this knowledge? Rewrite the Pascal procedure to incorporate this improvement and then test your new procedure in a complete program.
3. Rewrite the binary search algorithm presented in this chapter with a splitting strategy other than halving. One possibility would be to use an interpolation strategy that would examine the target's distance from the current low and high pointers. This is more analogous to the way in which we look up names in a phone book. That is, for a name beginning with *S*, we do not open the phone book to the middle page but rather to a point approximately two-thirds of the way from the beginning of the book. Test run your program against a pure binary search and, through tracing the performance of each algorithm, determine whether there is any significant difference between the two techniques.
4. Repeat Problem 3, but change your algorithm so that, after the initial interpolative guess as to the location of the target, data locations are examined sequentially in an appropriate direction until the key is found or until it can be determined that the key is not in the list.
5. Consider a list of records for students at a university. The list includes fields for student name, credits taken, credits earned, and total grade points. Write a program that, based upon a user's request, will sort the list of records in ascending or descending order keying on one of the four fields within the record. For instance, the user might specify that the sort should proceed in descending order according to credits earned. As much as possible, try to refrain from having to write a separate sort procedure for each particular ordering and field. Experiment by developing different procedures based on each of the five sorting strategies discussed in this chapter.
6. Consider the same list of records as in Problem 5. Now write a procedure to sort the records in descending order by credits earned. Records having the same number of credits earned should be arranged in descending order by total grade points. Those with the same number of credits earned and total grade points should be arranged alphabetically by name. Incorporate this procedure into the complete program that you wrote for Problem 5. Experiment by developing different procedures based on each of the five sorting strategies discussed in this chapter.

7. Rewrite the pointer sort with the pointer array as a local variable instead of as a global variable. How would this affect a higher level procedure that calls upon the pointer sort? Illustrate by calling your new version of the pointer sort from a sample main program.

8. Merge the segmenting strategy described in Exercise 10 from Section 1.4 with the insertion sort, bubble sort, and selection sort algorithms. Empirically test how this affects the run-time of the sort on a file of 1,000 records. Does altering the number of segments affect the run-time?

9. Implement the binary search algorithm for a disk file containing approximately 1,000 records of the structure described in Problem 5.

10. Design a complete program to load information into the data base for employees of East Publishing Company described in Exercise 9 of Section 1.5. Then repeatedly call on a search procedure to retrieve the information associated with a given employee's identification key.

11. A *permutation* of the integers from 1 to N is an arrangement of these integers in which no repetition occurs. For example,

    3 1 4 5 2
    and
    5 3 2 4 1

    are two permutations of the integers from 1 to 5.

    Write a procedure to load an array indexed from 1 . . N with a randomly generated permutation of the integers from 1 to N. (If your version of Pascal does not have a random number generator, see Appendix 9, in which an algorithm for generating random numbers in standard Pascal is discussed.) This procedure should be an O(N) algorithm. [T]

    Once you have written this procedure, use it to repeatedly load an array that is then passed to a sorting algorithm such as bubble, selection, or insertion sort. Add profiling counters to the sort algorithm to keep track of the number of comparisons and data interchanges performed by the algorithm. Average out these profiling counters over repeated invocations of the sort procedure and describe how these averages fit into the big-O analyses that were done in this chapter. Do you observe any discrepancies between your averages and the predictions of the big-O analyses? If so, attempt to explain them.

For any or all of Problems 12–16, design a program to answer the question posed. Then analyze the time efficiency of your program by using an appropriate combination of big-O analysis and profiling. Run your program to try to see the relationship between big-O classification and actual run-time as measured by a clock. Finally, for each program you implement, attempt to refine its run-time efficiency by making observations similar to those described in the Focus on Program Design section for this chapter.

12. In the first century A.D. the numbers were separated into "abundant" (such as 12, whose divisors have a sum greater than 12), "deficient" (such as 9, whose divisors have a sum less than 9), and "perfect" (such as 6, whose divisors add up to 6).

In all cases, you do not include the number itself. For example, the only numbers that divide evenly into 6 are 1, 2, 3, and 6, and $6 = 1 + 2 + 3$.

Write a program to list all numbers between 2 and N and classify each as abundant, deficient, or perfect and keep track of the numbers in each class.

13. In the first century A.D., Nicomachus wrote a book entitled *Introduction Arithmetica*. In it, the question "How can the cubes be represented in terms of the natural numbers?" was answered by the statement that "Cubical numbers are always equal to the sum of successive odd numbers and can be represented this way." For example,

$$1^3 = 1 = 1$$
$$2^3 = 8 = 3 + 5$$
$$3^3 = 27 = 7 + 9 + 11$$
$$4^3 = 64 = 13 + 15 + 17 + 19$$

Write a program to find the successive odd numbers whose sum equals K^3 for K having the values from 1 to N.

14. A conjecture, first made by the mathematician Goldbach, whose proof has defied all attempts, is that "every even number larger than two can be written as the sum of two prime numbers." For example,

$$4 = 2 + 2$$
$$6 = 3 + 3$$
$$8 = 3 + 5$$
$$10 = 3 + 7$$
$$100 = 89 + 11$$

Write a program that determines for every even integer N with $2 \leq N$ two prime numbers P and Q such that $N = P + Q$.

15. A pair of numbers M and N are called "friendly" (or they are referred to as an "amicable pair") if the sum of all the divisors of M (excluding M) is equal to the number N and the sum of all the divisors of the number N (excluding N) is equal to M ($M \neq N$). For example, the numbers 220 and 284 are an amicable pair because the only numbers that divide evenly into 220 (1, 2, 4, 5, 10, 11, 20, 22, 44, 55, and 110) add up to 284, and the only numbers that divide evenly into 284 (1, 2, 4, 71, and 142) add up to 220.

Write a program to find at least one other pair of amicable numbers. Be prepared to let your program search for some time.

16. A consequence of a famous theorem (of the mathematician Fermat) is the fact that

$$2^{(P-1)} \textbf{ MOD } P = 1$$

for every odd prime number P. An odd positive integer K satisfying

$$2^{(K-1)} \textbf{ MOD } K = 1$$

is called a pseudoprime. Write a program to determine a table of pseudoprimes and primes between 2 and N. How many pseudoprimes occur that are not prime numbers?

17. The importance of communication skills in "selling" a program to those who will eventually use it should not be underestimated. Keep-

ing this in mind, write a user's guide for the program you developed in Problem 5. You should assume that the user is able to log-on to (or boot) the system, but beyond that has no other knowledge of how to run this or any other program. Remember that unless the user's guide is very, very clear *and* very, very concise, it will probably be thrown in a file drawer—and your program never used.

18. (For the mathematically inclined) In this chapter's Note of Interest on "Artificial Intelligence, the Complexity of Algorithms, and Parallel Processing," the claim is made that parallel processing may allow some exponential algorithms to run "in a reasonable time frame on larger data sets than can be accommodated on single-processor machines." Note that no claim is made that exponential algorithms will, *in general,* become practical on parallel processing machines.

    Provide a carefully constructed argument in which you show that adding more processors to a machine can never result in an exponential algorithm's becoming practical for a wide variety of data sets. Your argument should explain the relationship between the number of processors used and the size of the data set that can be accommodated in reasonable time by the exponential algorithm. In essay form, justify the claim that the only real mathematical answer to solving a problem with an exponential algorithm in reasonable time is to discover a non-exponential algorithm that solves the same problem.

19. One of the drawbacks to the bubble sort algorithm is that a data set with just one item out of order can lead to worst-case performance for the algorithm. First, explain how this can happen.

    Because of this phenomenon, a variation on the bubble sort called a *shaker sort* will, on alternative passes through the array, put the largest entry into the last index and then the smallest entry into the first index. Explain how this idea can eliminate the worst-case performance of bubble sort on an array with just one item out of order. Then implement the shaker sort algorithm. Profile the number of comparisons and data interchanges in both the shaker sort and the bubble sort for a variety of data sets. Keep track of the empirical results you obtain from profiling these two algorithms. Finally, in a written report, compare the performance of these two algorithms based upon your empirical data. Be sure that your report addresses situations in which the shaker sort will actually perform worse than the plain bubble sort.

Our life is frittered away by detail . . . Simplify, simplify.
Henry David Thoreau
1817–1862

Data: From Abstraction to Implementation

Typically a first course in computer science focuses on the control structures used in developing algorithms. Before you code an algorithm in Pascal, there are various techniques that allow you to describe such control structures at a more abstract level. For instance, pseudocode is often used to depict iterative and decisional considerations involved in algorithms. Similarly, modular structure charts model the stepwise refinement process that subdivides a complex problem into smaller, more manageable problems.

Usually a first course does not develop similar techniques to conceptualize the data being manipulated by our algorithms. Instead, increasingly complex structured data types such as arrays, records, and sets are often described directly by their declarations in Pascal. In this respect, our perspective on structured data has been somewhat restricted by considerations of what Pascal conveniently provides for us. We now wish to consider the problem of data (and particularly data structures) from a more abstract, conceptual perspective.

In Section 2.1, we discuss the importance of building abstract models of data and draw analogies to the model-building often done by engineers. In Section 2.2, we introduce the notion of an *abstract data type,* using strings as our initial example. The two-dimensional table and keyed list abstract data types are discussed in Sections 2.3 and 2.4 respectively. Each of these abstract data types is presented first as a conceptual object, equipped with formal properties and operations; various implementations of these abstractions are also discussed and evaluated. As we pursue our study of data structures in later chapters, the three abstract data types introduced in this chapter will continue to appear in applications.

Recall the goals that we have set for ourselves in Section 1.1: designing software systems that are large, reliable, flexible, expandable, and efficient.

2.1 The Computer Scientist as a Builder of Models

OBJECTIVES

- to understand the importance of abstraction in design processes
- to recognize parallels between the modeling done by a design engineer and that done by a software system designer
- to view the process of developing a software system as an evolutionary process, which begins at a highly abstract level of design and culminates in a complete implementation of the system on a particular computer

Clearly, these are nontrivial. How can we have a reasonable chance of attaining them? The evolution of the answer to this question is an indication of how far the young discipline of computer science has progressed. In the late 1950s and early 1960s, there was a widely held belief that designing effective software systems was something akin to an occult art. That is, those who succeeded in designing such systems did so for a variety of mysterious reasons that could not be discerned. Their success, as opposed to the high percentage of software designers who failed, was somewhat mystical—similar to the spark of unfathomable inspiration that separates a great painter from a doodler.

Software Engineering

This view of successful software designers began to change in the latter part of the 1960s. It became increasingly evident that their methodology is typical of an engineer's approach to problem solving. What characterizes this engineering approach? To answer the question, consider the various phases involved in the successful development of a complex structure such as a bridge. First, the engineer gets together with the (often nontechnical) people who want the bridge built to learn about the function of the bridge: is it to be part of a heavily traveled urban freeway or a one-lane country road? From such meetings, the engineer develops a conceptual picture of the bridge. This picture exists as an abstract entity in the engineer's mind and perhaps in very rough form as an initial drawing. At this stage the engineer is working with ideas and ignoring most physical construction details; that is, the engineer is working with *abstractions.*

The next steps allow the engineer to come successively closer to the tangible implementation of the bridge as a physical structure. A miniature prototype of the bridge will be built. This model will allow the engineer to come face-to-face with many potential construction problems. It also provides a way to check whether the bridge will serve the needs specified by those who originally wanted the bridge built. This prototype will be followed by the development of detailed plans in blueprint form. Again this represents a step away from the purely abstract view of the bridge toward its actual implementation. These blueprints provide the essential details to the contractor who will eventually build the bridge. This contractor completes the entire process by implementing the engineer's plans in the physical structure of the bridge.

As we review the engineering approach, two important points should be made.

1. The entire process that culminates in the building of the bridge is a series of refinements from an abstract view of the bridge to its very tangible implementation. This process parallels very closely the phases in the development of a successful software system, beginning with a purely conceptual view of the problem to be solved and culminating with the implementation of a solution to that problem in (Pascal) program code.
2. This engineering approach truly places the emphasis on design issues. The design process is a very creative endeavor. Typically, during the design process, engineers will want to try out various combinations of possible options and will frequently change their minds about many significant aspects of the overall design. The time for such experimentation is when the design exists only in abstract form. That is when such creative considerations are possible—even encouraged—because of the openness of the conceptual model. As

the model draws nearer to actual implementation, a myriad of details specific to the chosen implementation make similar "what-if" reasoning expensive and often impossible for all practical purposes.

As early software developers analyzed frequent programming failures, they looked to the already established field of engineering for a paradigm. The engineering methodology of successively refining abstract models toward an eventual implementation made sense as an approach to developing programs also. A system designer who moves too quickly into the detailed coding phase of a programming project is analogous to an engineer who allows construction of a bridge to begin before adequate planning has been done. Both are heading for final results that are inelegant and riddled with serious flaws. However, because of the more rigorous design methodology embedded for years in their profession, engineers did not find themselves in this predicament as often as did programmers.

The solution seemed obvious: attempt to embed a similarly rigorous methodology into the discipline of computer science. Hence software engineering has developed into an important area of study within computer science. It represents an attempt to apply the structured methods of engineering to

A NOTE OF INTEREST

FORTRAN 53, 66, 77, 90: Keeping Pace with the Trends

In 1953 John Backus, now a fellow at the IBM Almaden Research Center and a winner of the prestigious Turing Award, invented FORTRAN (FORmula TRANslation), the first high-level programming language. It is interesting that, in an industry whose products typically become obsolete in three to five years, FORTRAN still remains the most widely used language for scientific and engineering applications. Part of the reason for this longevity is FORTRAN's reputation for generating extremely efficient machine code. Another ingredient is the fact that so much is invested in already written and optimized FORTRAN code; it would cost a fortune to redo all that work in another language.

Another important factor in the continuing saga of FORTRAN is its ability to keep pace with current trends in programming methodology. For instance, the first standards document for FORTRAN was written in 1966. The so-called FORTRAN 66 language emphasized modular program development by providing a fairly comprehensive facility for developing subroutines with parameter lists. Those subroutines could be compiled separately and then linked into a variety of applications. This led to the development of a large number of well-designed FORTRAN libraries for number-crunching tasks; these libraries are still used by a large core of programmers.

The trade press began to sound the death knell for FORTRAN when the structured programming "revolution" occurred in the late 1960s and early 1970s. FORTRAN 66 did not provide the necessary decisional and iterative control constructs to perform truly structured programming. The reaction of the FORTRAN community was to develop a new set of standards: FORTRAN 77. FORTRAN 77 remained upward compatible with FORTRAN 66, thereby ensuring that existing programs would continue to work in the new language. However, it also introduced a variety of structured control constructs to answer its critics. The results? Most scientists and engineers chose to stick with FORTRAN instead of converting to upstart languages such as Pascal and C.

In the 1980s, data abstraction replaced structured programming as the computer science trend of the decade. As early as 1979, those who defined FORTRAN standards had begun to react. After 13 years of bitter negotiations, the new standard—FORTRAN 90—has emerged. Among the features of FORTRAN 90 are

- IN and OUT subroutine parameters, a device that encourages the definition of an algorithm by formal preconditions and postconditions.
- Modules that allow PUBLIC and PRIVATE access to data types. In particular, implementors may use these access facilities to hide the details of the data structures they are implementing in a module.
- Recursive procedures.
- New data types, including pointers.

Computer scientists (including the authors of this text) may continue to look upon FORTRAN with disdain, but that doesn't mean the language won't continue to be a survivor in the faddish computer industry. Though FORTRAN may not be a trendsetter, those who define this language have shown a knack for recognizing which trends will endure and then building these trends into the next set of standards for the language.

software development. At the same time, it fosters creativity by freeing the system designer from the details of program code and allowing work at a higher level of abstraction. Its goal is to assure that software is produced in a way that is cost-effective and reliable enough to deserve the increasing trust we are placing in it. We will follow its dictates as we begin our excursion into more advanced programming methodology.

Exercises 2.1

1. What are the characteristics of the software engineering approach to system development?
2. From a software design perspective, explain why it is less costly to consider changes in design when the system is being modeled abstractly instead of when it is being implemented. Be sure to specify what factors enter into your consideration of the term *costly*.
3. You are working on a large software project as part of a development team. Another member of the team maintains that doing a conceptual design for the software will only result in getting a late start in writing Pascal code and will make the project fall behind schedule. Write a tactful memorandum to this team member in which you provide a convincing argument against the team member's position.

■ ■ ■ ■

2.2 The String Abstract Data Type

OBJECTIVES

- to understand what is involved in defining an abstract data type (ADT)
- to understand what is meant by data abstraction
- to see how ADTs facilitate conceptual model-building
- to understand what is meant by the implementation of an ADT
- to formally define and be able to use the string ADT
- to compare and contrast several implementations of the string ADT
- to see the motivation for three guidelines that govern the definition and implementation of all ADTs: the encapsulation principle, the ADT use rule, and the ADT implementation rule

The best way to clarify the conceptual, model-building approach is to provide an example. We wish to write a program to solve the problem involving strings that is presented in Example 2.1.

The high-level solution presented in Example 2.1 is totally independent of considerations regarding how the strings will be declared in Pascal. Such considerations are details of the eventual implementation of strings and must be completely avoided at this early stage of design. To consider them now would place severe restrictions on the design endeavor.

Instead, the high-level pseudocode takes the perspective that strings are abstract entities that are manipulated by abstract operations such as search, length, and delete. As we begin to refine this pseudocode, it is necessary to pin down exactly what we mean by these abstractions. That is, we must define the notion of a string precisely enough to insure that our pseudocode algorithm is unambiguous. Yet, our definition must be entirely conceptual: it must be free from specifics about how a string will be implemented in a programming language. Such a definition will allow us to refine our algorithm without worrying about details of how a string will eventually be declared.

To define a string, or any other data type, at such a conceptual level is to define it as an abstract data type (ADT).

> **Abstract data type (ADT).** An ADT is a collection of data objects that share a defined set of properties and operations for processing the objects.

In providing a definition for an ADT such as a string, we must specify both the properties and operations shared by all strings. Typically the properties are specified by describing the individual elements composing an object *and* the relationships among those individual elements. The operations may be specified using preconditions and postconditions. A precondition for an ADT operation must indicate what can be expected to be true before the operation is performed. A postcondition indicates what can be expected to be true after the operation is performed.

EXAMPLE 2.1

The program will read pairs of strings. The first string in a pair is designated the master string; the second is the target string. All occurrences of the target string in the master string should be removed from the master string, and the modified master string should then be written out. Thus, if the master string were "BAA-BAA BLACK SHEEP" and the target string were "BAA", the modified master string should be "- BLACK SHEEP".

We begin to design our solution to this problem by describing an algorithm in high-level pseudocode.

1. Read the MasterString
2. Read the TargetString
3. Search the MasterString from its beginning for an occurrence of the TargetString
4. **WHILE** an occurrence of TargetString is found
   4.1 Delete characters from the MasterString, beginning at the position where TargetString was found. Delete as many characters from the MasterString as there are characters in the length of TargetString
   4.2 Search the MasterString for an occurrence of the TargetString beginning at the position where the last match occurred
5. Write the (modified) MasterString

To illustrate defining ADTs, here is a definition of the string ADT. You will find Table 2.1 helpful in visualizing the effects of the operations described in the definition.

String. A string is a finite sequence of characters excluding a specially-designated null character. (Hence non-null characters are the individual elements in a string.) By *sequence*, we mean that the characters in a string are related in linear fashion with an identifiable first element, second element, and so on. The *null character* is the character whose ordinal value is zero.

The operations associated with the string ADT are

Create operation	
Preconditions:	*S* is an arbitrary string in an unknown state.
Postconditions:	*S* is an initialized empty string.
ReadAString operation	
Preconditions:	*S* is a previously created string.
Postconditions:	*S* contains a sequence of characters read from standard input.
WriteAString operation	
Preconditions:	*S* is a previously created string with arbitrary contents.
Postconditions:	*S* is unchanged and its contents have been written to standard output.

Assign operation	
Preconditions:	*Source* and *Destination* are previously created strings with arbitrary contents.
Postconditions:	*Destination* contains a copy of the string in *Source*.
Length operation	
Preconditions:	*S* is a previously created string with arbitrary contents.
Postconditions:	*Length* returns the number of characters in *S*.
Concatenate operation	
Preconditions:	*S* and *T* are two arbitrary, previously created strings.
Postconditions:	*S* has contents of *T* appended to it. *T* is left unchanged.
Substring operation	
Preconditions:	*S* is an arbitrary, previously created string. *Start* and *Stop* represent positions within *S*, with *Start* <= *Stop*.
Postconditions:	*T* contains a copy of that portion of *S* beginning at *Start* and ending at *Stop*. If *Stop* > *Length*(*S*), then *T* terminates with the last character in *S*. If *Start* > *Length*(*S*), then *T* is empty.
Search operation	
Preconditions:	*Master* and *Target* are two previously created strings with *Target* potentially contained in *Master*. *Start* represents a character position in *Master*.
Postconditions:	*Search* returns the position of the first occurrence of *Target* in *Master* at position *Start* or after. Zero is returned if *Target* is not found in this portion of *Master*.
Insert operation	
Preconditions:	*S* and *T* are two arbitrary, previously created strings. *Place* represents the position where a copy of *T* is to be inserted in *S*.
Postconditions:	*S* has a copy of *T* inserted at position *Place*. If *Place* is greater than *Length*(*S*), *S* is not altered.
Delete operation	
Preconditions:	*S* is an arbitrary, previously created string. *Start* and *Number* represent a starting position in *S* and a number of characters to delete from *S*, beginning at that position.
Postconditions:	*S* is returned with the designated characters removed. If the number of characters specified extends beyond the length of *S*, delete only through the end of the string.
Equal operation	
Preconditions:	*S* and *T* are two arbitrary, previously created strings.
Postconditions:	*Equal* returns true if *S* and *T* match, character for character; otherwise it returns false.
LessThan operation	
Preconditions:	*S* and *T* are two arbitrary, previously created strings.
Postconditions:	*LessThan* returns true if *S* precedes *T* in lexicographic order. Otherwise it returns false.
GreaterThan operation	
Preconditions:	*S* and *T* are two arbitrary, previously created strings.
Postconditions:	*GreaterThan* returns true if *S* follows *T* in lexicographic order; otherwise false is returned.

Several comments are now in order. First, note that a string is described from a completely conceptual perspective: there is no hint of a realization of strings in a particular programming language. Second, the Create operation will be a standard operation for every ADT we discuss. It represents an initialization process which any object must undergo before it can be reliably acted upon by other operations. We have tried to emphasize this point in the definition of the string ADT by frequently mentioning the need for a "previously created" string in the precondition for an operation. In future ADT definitions we shall frequently leave this unsaid. Remember that the assumption is that no object is ever acted upon by any operation until it has been created.

Table 2.1 provides visual examples of the effect of the various string operations. You should study this table carefully before proceeding. Use it to make sure that you have a precise understanding of each string operation. To make this real; you may find it helps to think of operations you typically perform on text when editing with your favorite word processor.

TABLE 2.1
Examples of string operations

Create					
S		yields →	S		
???			"" (An empty string)		
Assign					
Source	Destination	yields →	Source	Destination	
"BIRD"	"DOG"		"BIRD"	"BIRD"	
Length					
S		yields →			
"BIRDS OF A FEATHER"			18		
Concatenate					
S	T	yields →	S		
"BIRD"	"DOG"		"BIRDDOG"		
Substring					
S		Start	Stop	yields →	T
"TALE OF TWO CITIES"		4	7		"E OF"
Search					
Master			Target	yields →	
"MODERN BASEBALL HISTORY"			"BASEBALL"		8
Insert					
S		T	Place	yields →	S
"SALT PEPPER"		" AND"	5		"SALT AND PEPPER"
Delete					
S		Start	Number	yields	S
"SALT AND PEPPER"		5	9		"SALTER"

TABLE 2.1
Examples of string operations (*continued*)

Equal			
S	T	yields →	
"WIG"	"WAG"		**false** since S and T differ in second position
LessThan			
S	T	yields →	
"WIG"	"WAG"		**true** since S precedes T in lexicographic ordering
GreaterThan			
S	T	yields →	
"WIG"	"WAG"		**false**

The separation of an ADT's specification from declarations and instructions that implement the data type in a particular language is called *data abstraction.* It turns out that some abstract data types will have very easy implementations in Pascal. The Pascal implementations of other abstract data types will be much less direct. At early stages of problem analysis, we don't want language considerations to influence our solution to the problem. Such considerations should come later, after we have accurately described the problem.

An abstract data type may be viewed as a formal description of data elements and relationships that are envisioned by the software engineer; it is thus a conceptual model. Ultimately, however, this model will be implemented in an appropriate computer language via declarations for the elements and relationships and instructions (often in the form of procedure/function calls) for the operations. At an even deeper level, the implementation of the abstract data type in a computer language is translated by the compiler into a physical, electronic representation on a particular computer.

This hierarchy of levels of abstraction is illustrated in Figure 2.1.

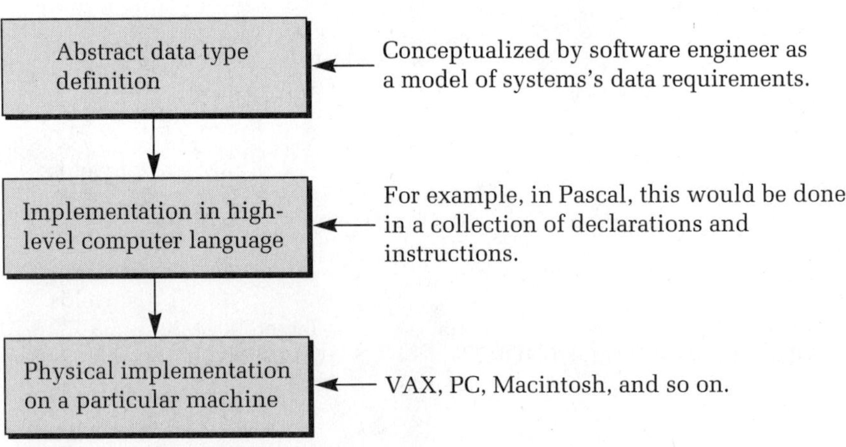

FIGURE 2.1
Levels of abstraction in specifying data

T Pascal Interface for String Operations

The first step in moving toward an implementation of an ADT in a particular computer language such as Pascal is to restate the operations that act on ADT objects as procedure and function headers. We shall call such a collection of procedure and function headers the Pascal *interface for an ADT.* Such an interface for the string ADT is given here. The

```
{ Given:                                    }
{ Task:                                     }
{ Return:                                   }
```

style of documentation that we have used throughout the text is used to describe the preconditions and postconditions of each operation.

```
PROCEDURE Create (VAR S : String);

  {  Given:   An arbitrary string variable S in an unknown state       }
  {  Task:    Initialize S                                             }
  {  Return:  S as an initialized empty string.                        }

PROCEDURE ReadAString (VAR S : String);

  {  Given:   A previously created string S with arbitrary contents    }
  {  Task:    Read a line of characters from the standard input source }
  {           into S                                                   }
  {  Return:  S contains the characters read from standard input.      }

PROCEDURE WriteAString (S : String);

  {  Given:   A previously created string S with arbitrary contents    }
  {  Task:    Write the contents of S to standard output               }
  {  Return:  Nothing.                                                 }

PROCEDURE Assign (Source : String;
                  VAR Destination : String);

  {  Given:   Source, a string with arbitrary contents                 }
  {  Task:    Copy the contents of Source to Destination               }
  {  Return:  Destination contains copy of Source.                     }

FUNCTION Length (S : String) : integer;

  {  Given:   An arbitrary string S                                    }
  {  Task:    Count the number of non-null characters in S             }
  {  Return:  The counted number of characters in S.                   }

PROCEDURE Concatenate (VAR S : String;
                           T : String);

  {  Given:   S and T, two arbitrary strings                           }
  {  Task:    Append the contents of T to S                            }
  {  Return:  S, with T appended to it.                                }

PROCEDURE Substring (S : String;
                     Start, Stop : integer;
                     VAR T : String);

  {  Given:   S -- an arbitrary string                                 }
  {           Start and Stop representing positions within S           }
  {           Assume Start <= Stop                                     }
  {  Task:    Copy the characters between positions Start and Stop in S }
  {           into T                                                   }
  {  Return:  T contains that portion of S beginning at Start and      }
  {           ending at Stop.  If Stop > Length(S), then stop at last  }
  {           character in S.  If Start > Length(S), then T is empty.  }
```

```
FUNCTION Search (Master, Target : String;
                 Start : integer) : integer;

  {  Given:    Master, Target --  two strings with Target potentially         }
  {            contained in Master                                            }
  {            Start -- representing a character position in Master           }
  {  Task:     Master is to be searched for Target from the Start             }
  {            position onward                                                }
  {  Return:   The position of the first occurrence of Target in              }
  {            Master at position Start or after.  Zero returned              }
  {            if Target is not found in this portion of Master.              }

PROCEDURE Insert (VAR S : String;
                  Place : integer;
                  T : String);

  {  Given:    S and T -- two arbitrary strings                               }
  {            Place -- the position where T is to be inserted in S           }
  {  Task:     Insert T into S                                                }
  {  Return:   S with T inserted at position Place.  If Place is greater      }
  {            than Length(S), S is not altered.                              }

PROCEDURE Delete (VAR S : String;
                  Start, Number : integer);

  {  Given:    S --  an arbitrary string                                      }
  {            Start, Number -- a starting position in S and a number         }
  {            of characters to delete from S, beginning at that position     }
  {  Task:     Delete the designated characters from S                        }
  {  Return:   S with the designated characters removed.  If the number of    }
  {            characters specified extends beyond Length(S), delete only     }
  {            through the end of the string.                                 }

FUNCTION Equal (S, T : String) : boolean;

  {  Given:    S and T -- two arbitrary strings                               }
  {  Task:     Test the two strings for equality                              }
  {  Return:   True if S and T match, character for character;                }
               false otherwise.                                               }

FUNCTION LessThan (S, T : String) : boolean;

  {  Given:    S and T -- two arbitrary strings                               }
  {  Task:     Test if S precedes T in alphabetical order                     }
  {  Return:   True if S precedes T in alphabetical order;                    }
  {            false otherwise.                                               }

FUNCTION GreaterThan (S, T : String) : boolean;

  {  Given:    S and T, two arbitrary strings                                 }
  {  Task:     Test if S follows T in alphabetical order                      }
  {  Return:   True if S follows T in alphabetical order;                     }
  {            false otherwise.                                               }
```

The interface for an ADT provides the means by which we are allowed to use an ADT when programming in a particular language. The interface should parallel the formal operations of an ADT as closely as the programming language will allow. It is the view of the ADT given to those who want to use it. The implementor of an ADT must provide a package of procedures and functions that adheres to the interface.

Note that neither our definition nor our Pascal interface provides any clue about how the string ADT will be implemented. (You may be thinking that strings are packed arrays of characters. We will soon see that there are more efficient alternatives.) In effect both the definition and the interface tell us *what* a string is and *what* we can do with strings, but shield us from the detail of *how* the various operations are actually achieved. Drawing a distinction between *what* and *how* is a critical test of a good ADT definition and an interface to that ADT in a particular language. Both the definition and interface should be crystal clear in regard to the former and offer no insight with respect to the latter.

EXAMPLE 2.2

Refine the high-level pseudocode of Example 2.1 into a Pascal main program to remove all occurrences of a target string from a substring. Use only the operations provided by the Pascal interface for the string ADT; assume nothing about how strings will be implemented.

```
TYPE
  String = { The hidden implementation of string is put here };

VAR
  MasterString, TargetString : String;
  Continue : char;
  Pos : integer;
  .
  :
BEGIN { Main program }
  { Remember to "create" all strings before using them }
  Create (MasterString);
  Create (TargetString);
  { Allow user to run until 'N' is entered }
  REPEAT
    writeln ('Enter master string');
    ReadAString (MasterString);
    writeln ('Enter target string');
    ReadAString (TargetString);
    { Pos is index of first occurrence of Target in Master }
    Pos := Search (MasterString, TargetString, 1);
    WHILE Pos <> 0 DO
      BEGIN
        Delete (MasterString, Pos, Length (TargetString));
        { Set Pos to index of next occurrence }
        Pos := Search (MasterString, TargetString, Pos)
      END;
    { Pos is 0 when there are no more occurrences of Target in Master }
    WriteAString (MasterString);
    writeln;
    write ('Again? ');
    readln (Continue)
  UNTIL (Continue = 'N') OR (Continue = 'n')
END.
```

Example 2.2 indicates that an algorithm that manipulates strings will not necessarily use all string operations. This is because an ADT is intended to be a general, reusable component. The string operations we have defined can be used in a wide variety of applications. Our goal in implementing the string ADT will be to insure this high degree of generality. If we can do that, we will no longer need to reinvent code for strings each time we need them in an application. This is the power of abstraction.

Implementations of the String ADT

We already have developed a main program that uses the string ADT at a high level of abstraction. We are now ready to switch gears, move to a lower level, and discuss how to implement this abstraction. It is critically important that our implementation does not force any change upon the logic at the higher level of abstraction.

Packed Array Implementation of the String ADT. Your prior study of Pascal may lead you to declare the type string as a packed array of **char.**

```
CONST
  MaxStringLength = 132;     { Or other appropriate size limit  }
TYPE
  String = PACKED ARRAY [1..MaxStringLength] of char;
```

If the length of a given string is less than MaxStringLength, then the null character **chr**(0) can be used to fill an array location marking the end of the string. Under this implementation, a string cannot have more than MaxStringLength characters; this recognizes the fact that implementations of ADTs may introduce limitations due to a particular programming language construct.

Given this **TYPE** declaration, we must now provide complete procedures or functions for each of the string operations. As illustrated in the following examples, the implementations must adhere precisely to the Pascal interface we have specified in our ADT definition.

■ EXAMPLE 2.3

Implement the Create operation for the packed array implementation of the string ADT.

```
PROCEDURE Create (VAR S : String);

  {  Given:   An arbitrary string variable S in an unknown state        }
  {  Task:    Initialize S                                              }
  {  Return:  S as an initialized empty string                          }

  VAR
    K : integer;

  BEGIN
    { Since Length will rely on a null character at the end of a string  }
    { that is less than MaxStringLength characters, we will initialize   }
    { S[1] to chr(0).                                                    }
    S[1] := chr(0)
  END; { of PROCEDURE Create }
```

■ ■

EXAMPLE 2.4

Implement the ReadAString operation for the packed array implementation of the string ADT.

```
PROCEDURE ReadAString (VAR S : String);

  {  Given:   A previously created string S with arbitrary contents      }
  {  Task:    Read a line of characters from the standard input source   }
  {           into S                                                     }
  {  Return:  S contains the characters read from standard input         }

  VAR
    K, L : integer;

  BEGIN
    K := 0;
    WHILE NOT eoln AND ( K < MaxStringLength ) DO
      BEGIN
        K := K + 1;
        { K references the position to store the next character }
        read (S[K])
      END;
    readln;
    { Now put a null character at the end of a string containing less than}
    { MaxStringLength characters.                                          }
    IF K < MaxStringLength THEN
      S[K + 1] := chr(0)
  END;  { of PROCEDURE ReadAString }
```

EXAMPLE 2.5

Implement the Length operation for the packed array implementation of the string ADT.

```
FUNCTION Length (S : String) : integer;

  {  Given:   An arbitrary string S                                          }
  {  Task:    Count the number of characters in S                            }
  {  Return:  The counted number of characters in S                          }

  VAR
    K : integer;
    FoundNull : boolean;

  BEGIN
    { Search through the string until encounter null character or reach   }
    { MaxStringLength                                                      }
    K := 1;
    FoundNull := false;
    { Initially, K references first character in the string               }
    WHILE (K <= MaxStringLength) AND NOT FoundNull DO
      IF S[K] = chr(0) THEN
        FoundNull := true
      ELSE
        K := K + 1;
    { If null character encountered, K is 1 more than length of string    }
    IF FoundNull THEN
      Length := K - 1
    ELSE
      Length := MaxStringLength
  END; { of FUNCTION Length }
```

In this implementation of the Length operation, it is tempting to try to control the **WHILE** loop with a condition that doesn't require a Boolean:

```
WHILE (K <= MaxStringLength) AND (S[K] <> chr(0)) DO
```

Unfortunately, this fails in Pascal when K reaches (MaxStringLength + 1). Instead of exiting the loop, the (S[K] <> chr(0)) test will generate an "index out of range" error.

■ ■

■ EXAMPLE 2.6

Implement the Search operation for the packed array implementation of the string ADT.

The logic of this algorithm is somewhat more difficult than that of the operations we have implemented in earlier examples. It can be described in skeletal pseudocode as follows.

1. Initially, align the Target string against the leftmost portion of the Master string
2. **WHILE** a match can still be found **AND** a match has not yet been found **DO**
   - 2.1 Do a character-by-character comparison of Target against Master until you can conclude match or no match;
   - 2.2 **IF** no match **THEN** realign Target one position to the right against new portion of Master

Figure 2.2 depicts how this search would proceed for a particular example. In the first snapshot of that figure, we see the three-character string "KOM" aligned against the first three characters of "KOKOMO" with a mismatch occurring in position 3. In the second snapshot (the next time through the **WHILE** loop), "KOM" is aligned against "OKO" in "KOKOMO"; a mismatch occurs immediately. On the next iteration of the **WHILE** loop, a match is found, starting at position 3.

FIGURE 2.2
Trace of Search ("KOKOMO", "KOM", 1)

```
                                      1 2 3 4 5 6
Snapshot 1          Master         :  K O K O M O
                    Target         :  K O M
                                          ↑
                                   Mismatch in
                                   position 3

                                      1 2 3 4 5 6
Snapshot 2          Master         :  K O K O M O
                    Target         :    K O M
                                        ↑
                                    Mismatch in
                                    position 2

                                      1 2 3 4 5 6
Snapshot 3          Master         :  K O K O M O
                    Target         :      K O M

                                   Successful match,
                                   return position 3
```

The refinement of the pseudocode into a full Pascal implementation yields the following function.

```
FUNCTION Search (Master, Target : String;
                 Start : integer) : integer;

  {  Given:    Master, Target --  two strings with Target potentially      }
  {            contained in Master                                         }
  {            Start -- representing a character position in Master        }
  {  Task:     Master is to be searched for Target from the Start          }
  {            position onward                                             }
  {  Return:   The position of the first occurrence of Target in           }
  {            Master at position Start or after.  Zero returned           }
  {            if Target is not found in this portion of Master.           }

  VAR
    M, T : integer;

  BEGIN
    { M references position in Master, T in Target }
    M := Start;
    T := 1;
    WHILE (T <= Length(Target)) AND
          (Length(Target) <= Length(Master) - Start  + 1) DO
      IF Master[M] = Target[T] THEN  {  Current characters match }
        BEGIN
          M := M + 1;
          T := T + 1
        END
      ELSE                           { No match, so realign }
        BEGIN
          Start := Start + 1;
          M := Start;
          T := 1
        END;
```

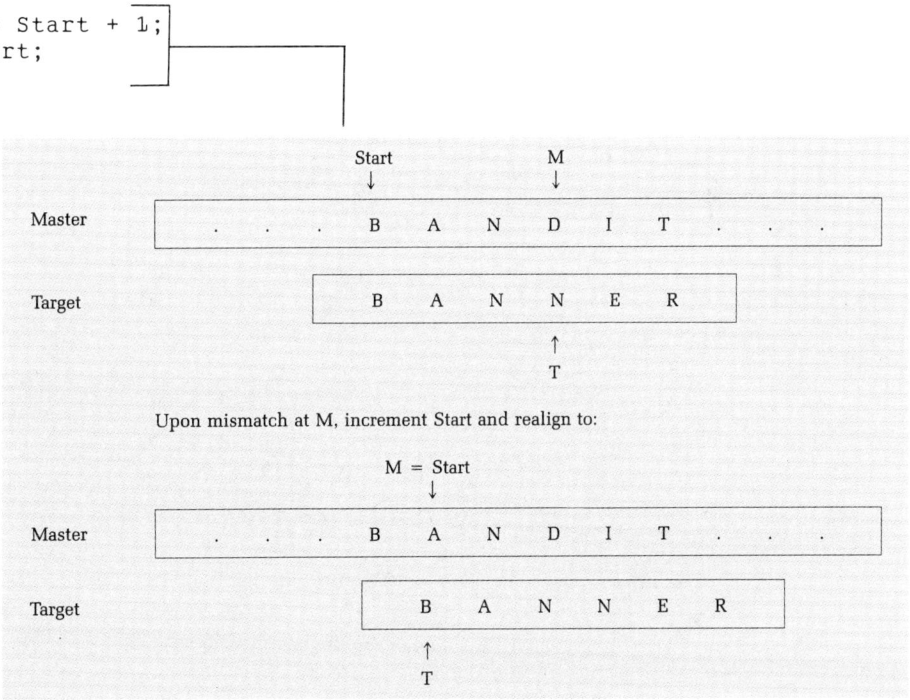

```
    { If T incremented beyond Length(Target), a match was found. }
    IF T > Length(Target) THEN
      Search := Start
    ELSE
      Search := 0
  END; { of FUNCTION Search }
```

The average performance of the implementation of the Search operation in Example 2.6 is worth analyzing. It is highly dependent on the nature of the text being processed. In normal English text, we would not expect to proceed very far into Target before determining that realignment is necessary. In the worst case, however, we may have to proceed all the way up to the last character of Target before determining that realignment is necessary. In such a case, the efficiency of Search deteriorates to O(Length(Master) * Length(Target)). This worst case is illustrated in Figures 2.3 and 2.4.

FIGURE 2.3
Worst case for Search

```
Master  :  AAAAAAAAAAAAH
Target  :  AAAAAAH
```

We must repeatedly compare characters all the way up to H before realigning

FIGURE 2.4
Action of Search for data of Figure 2.3

```
Snapshot 1     Master  :   AAAAAAAAAAAAH
               Target  :   AAAAAAH
                                 ↑
```

The first pass through Target ends here with a mismatch of A and H

```
Snapshot 2     Master  :   AAAAAAAAAAAAH
               Target  :    AAAAAAH
                            ↑
```

The second pass through Target starts here

```
Snapshot 3     Master  :   AAAAAAAAAAAAH
               Target  :    AAAAAAH
                                  ↑
```

The second pass ends here after 6 matches of the A character followed by a mismatch of A and H

■ EXAMPLE 2.7

Implement the Delete operation for the packed array implementation of the string ADT.

```
PROCEDURE Delete (VAR S : String;
                  Start, Number : integer);

  {  Given:   S --  an arbitrary string                                }
  {           Start, Number -- a starting position in S and a number   }
  {           of characters to delete from S, beginning at that position }
  {  Task:    Delete the designated characters from S                  }
  {  Return:  S with the designated characters removed.  If the number of }
  {           characters specified extends beyond Length(S), delete only }
  {           through the end of the string.                           }

  VAR
    J, EndOfString : integer;

  BEGIN
    EndOfString := Length (S);
    IF (Number > 0) AND (Start <= EndOfString) THEN  { there is something to do }
      BEGIN
        { Adjust Number in case it takes us beyond end of string }
        IF Start + Number > EndOfString THEN
          Number := EndOfString - Start + 1;
        { First, shift text at end of string }
        FOR J := Start + Number TO EndOfString DO
          S[J - Number] := S[J];
        { Then, add the null character to mark end of string }
        S[EndOfString - Number + 1] := chr(0)
      END
  END; { of PROCEDURE Delete }
```

Examples 2.3–2.7 have provided a start toward a full implementation of the string ADT using a **PACKED ARRAY OF char.** Notice how all of these procedures and functions must be coordinated with each other. Also notice that the limit on a string's length imposed by the constant MaxStringLength keeps this implementation from being a perfect model of the ADT. When you complete the implementation in the Exercises, you will have to be careful to point out how this limitation can affect the result of certain operations.

Now, consider efficiency. Why might the packed array implementation of strings not be appropriate for certain applications? The Length operation in this implementation is O(MaxStringLength). This means that higher-level applications that repeatedly invoke the Length function (such as that in Example 2.2) might be slowed considerably by using this implementation. We will now examine another implementation of strings that can provide O(1) efficiency for the Length operation.

Embedded Length Implementation of the String ADT. Our strategy in this implementation will be to associate an integer with each packed array of **char.** The integer will be used to maintain the current length of the string. Thus, a string will now be implemented as two data items: an **integer** length and a **PACKED ARRAY OF char.** However, it is imperative that high-level logic using the string ADT still be able to view a string as a single abstract entity. Toward this end, we will encapsulate the data items comprising a string into a record.

```
CONST
  MaxStringLength = 132;
TYPE
  String = RECORD
             StringText : PACKED ARRAY [1..MaxStringLength] OF char;
             Length     : integer
           END;
```

Such encapsulation is relatively simple and is extremely important to programming with abstract data types. Without it, high-level procedures would not be able to identify the ADT as a single, unified entity. To stress the critical role played by encapsulation of ADTs, we formalize it in the following principle.

> **Encapsulation principle.** Whenever the implementation of an ADT involves several data items, these data items should be grouped into a record by which the ADT is identified to high-level logic.

Adhering to this principle, we can now carry out this new implementation of the string ADT. Implementations of five operations are provided in Examples 2.8–2.12; the rest are left for you in the Exercises.

EXAMPLE 2.8

Implement the Create operation for the embedded length implementation of the string ADT.

```
PROCEDURE Create (VAR S : String);

  {  Given:    An arbitrary string variable S in an unknown state      }
  {  Task:     Initialize S                                            }
  {  Return:   S as an initialized empty string.                       }

  BEGIN
    S.Length := 0
  END;  { of PROCEDURE Create  }
```

EXAMPLE 2.9

Implement the ReadAString operation for the embedded length implementation of the string ADT.

```
PROCEDURE ReadAString (VAR S : String);

  {  Given:    A previously created string S with arbitrary contents       }
  {  Task:     Read a line of characters from the standard input source    }
  {            into S                                                      }
  {  Return:   S contains the characters read from standard input.         }

  VAR
    K : integer;
```

```
  BEGIN
    K := 0;
    WHILE NOT eoln AND (K < MaxStringLength) DO
      BEGIN
        K := K + 1;
        { K references the position to store the next character }
        read (S.StringText[K])
      END;
    { K has recorded the length of the string }
    readln;
    S.Length := K
  END;  { of PROCEDURE ReadAString }
```

■ ■

■ EXAMPLE 2.10

Implement the Length operation for the embedded length implementation of the string ADT.

```
FUNCTION Length (S : String) : integer;

  {  Given:   An arbitrary string S                                     }
  {  Task:    Count the number of characters in S, up to and including  }
  {           the last nonblank character                               }
  {  Return:  The counted number of characters in S.                    }

  BEGIN
    Length := S.Length
  END;  {  of FUNCTION Length  }
```

It is particularly noteworthy that the embedded length implementation achieves an O(1) efficiency for this operation. Compare this to the efficiency of Example 2.5, in which a packed array implementation was used.

■ ■

■ EXAMPLE 2.11

Implement the Search operation for the embedded length implementation of the string ADT.

```
FUNCTION Search (Master, Target : String;
                 Start : integer) : integer;

  {  Given:   Master, Target --  two strings with Target potentially     }
  {           contained in Master                                        }
  {           Start -- representing a character position in Master       }
  {  Task:    Master is to be searched for Target from the Start         }
  {           position onward                                            }
  {  Return:  The position of the first occurrence of Target in          }
  {           Master at position Start or after.  Zero returned          }
  {           if Target is not found in this portion of Master.          }

  VAR
    M, T : integer;
```

```
BEGIN
  {M references position in Master, T in Target }
  M := Start;
  T := 1;
  WHILE (T <= Target.Length) AND
        (Target.Length <= Master.Length - Start  + 1) DO
    IF Master.StringText[M] = Target.StringText[T] THEN { Current characters
                                                          match }
      BEGIN
        M := M + 1;
        T := T + 1
      END
    ELSE                        { No match, so realign }
      BEGIN
        Start := Start + 1;
        M := Start;
        T := 1
      END;
  { If T is incremented beyond Length(Target), a match was found }
  IF T > Target.Length THEN
    Search := Start
  ELSE
    Search := 0
END; { of FUNCTION Search }
```

■ ■

■ EXAMPLE 2.12

Implement the Delete operation for the embedded length implementation of the string ADT.

```
PROCEDURE Delete (VAR S : String;
                  Start, Number : integer);

  {  Given:   S --  an arbitrary string                                 }
  {           Start, Number -- a starting position in S and a number    }
  {           of characters to delete from S, beginning at that position  }
  {  Task:    Delete the designated characters from S                   }
  {  Return:  S with the designated characters removed.  If the number of }
  {           characters specified extends beyond Length(S), delete only  }
  {           through the end of the string.                            }

  VAR
    J  : integer;

  BEGIN
    IF (Number > 0) AND (Start <= S.Length) THEN { there is something to do }
      BEGIN
        { Adjust Number in case it takes us beyond end of string }
        IF Start + Number > S.Length THEN
          Number := S.Length - Start + 1;
        { Shift text at end of string }
        FOR J := Start + Number TO S.Length DO
          S.StringText[J - Number] := S.StringText[J];
        { Compute the new length }
        S.Length := S.Length - Number
      END
  END; { of PROCEDURE Delete }
```

■ ■

Compare the collection of operations implemented in Examples 2.8–2.12 to the corresponding operations implemented for the packed array string implementation in Examples 2.3–2.7. It should be apparent that the embedded length implementation offers greater overall elegance and time efficiency—at the expense of the space associated with the embedded integer length field.

Observations on ADTs and Their Implementations

We can now make some observations about the relationship between ADTs and their various implementations. These observations represent general conclusions that may be applied to all of the ADTs we will study. Here, we illustrate them with the string ADT and its two implementations.

First, high-level logic, such as that presented in Example 2.2, cannot distinguish between different implementations of an ADT. We should be able to plug any implementation of an ADT into high-level logic without changing that logic. This shielding of high-level logic from any implementation details is summarized in the following two rules.

ADT use rule. Algorithms that use an abstract data type should only access variables of that ADT through the operations provided in the ADT definition.

ADT implementation rule. An implementation of an abstract data type must provide an interface that is entirely consistent with the operations specified in the ADT's definition.

If users and implementors of ADTs comply fully with these rules, all high-level logic will be plug-compatible with all possible implementations of an ADT. The implementation is said to exhibit *information hiding:* it hides information from higher level logic. This is the ideal. In some situations, the syntax of Pascal will force us into compromising the ideal. We will be careful to point those out and hold such compromises to a minimum.

Second, if high-level logic cannot tell the difference between two implementations, then why would we ever want more than one implementation of an ADT? Part of the answer lies in the different time and space efficiencies that various implementations provide. For instance, the high-level logic of Example 2.2 iteratively calls the string Length function. Because this function has O(1) time efficiency in the embedded length implementation and O(MaxStringLength) time efficiency in the packed array implementation, the former implementation represents a more efficient choice for this application.

Another aspect of the answer to this question is the limitations that an implementation may impose as it attempts to model an abstraction. For instance, both the packed array and embedded length implementations of the string ADT impose a maximum string length limitation. When we study linked lists in Chapter 4, we will be able to provide an implementation of the string ADT that does not have this maximum length restriction. You may also explore a more flexible implementation of strings, the *workspace-index method,* in the problems at the end of the chapter.

The availability of different implementations of an ADT—all compatible from their outward interface—gives rise to some very exciting prospects for the software design endeavor we have been describing in this chapter. The implication is that, at a high level, we design complex software by constructing a model that operates only on abstract data types. Once we have a high-level model with which we are satisfied, we can plug in the best implementation of the ADT for our particular application.

If formalized big-O analysis is inconclusive about which is the best implementation, it is relatively painless to experiment with several implementations. Different implementations can be plugged in, we can empirically profile their performance, and then choose the best. With the ADT approach, all this experimentation can be done without any modification of the high-level model.

Exercises 2.2

1. Using only the operations provided by the string ADT, write a high-level algorithm in Pascal to scan a master string and replace all occurrences of a given target string by a specified replacement string. For example, if the master string is

   "MARY MARY QUITE CONTRARY"

   and the target and replacement string are "ARY" and "ARTHA", then the resulting master string would be

   "MARTHA MARTHA QUITE CONTRARTHA"

2. Consider the following version of the Pascal code that appeared in Example 2.2. The shaded line has been modified. From an ADT perspective, what is wrong with this version of the code?

```
TYPE
  String = { The hidden implementation of string is put here };

VAR
  MasterString, TargetString: String;
  Continue: char;
  Pos: integer;
  .
  .
  .

BEGIN { Main program }
  Create (MasterString);
  Create (TargetString);
  REPEAT
    writeln ('Enter master string');
    ReadAString (MasterString);
    writeln ('Enter target string');
    ReadAString (TargetString);
    Pos := Search (MasterString, TargetString, 1);
    WHILE Pos <> 0 DO
      BEGIN
        Delete (MasterString, Pos, TargetString.Length);
        Pos := Search (MasterString, TargetString, Pos)
      END;
    WriteAString (MasterString);
    writeln;
    write ('Again? ');
    readln (Continue)
  UNTIL (Continue = 'N') OR (Continue = 'n')
END.
```

3. The algorithm of Example 2.2 will work for both the packed array and embedded length implementations of the string ADT without the two initial calls to

TABLE 2.2
Flight/pilot data base for Wing-and-a-Prayer Airlines

	Flight Number					
Pilot Number	**3000**	**3001**	**3002**	...	**4498**	**4499**
1000	**true**	**false**	**false**	...	**true**	**false**
1001	**false**	**false**	**false**	...	**true**	**true**
1002	**true**	**true**	**false**	...	**false**	**false**
.	.	.	.	...	.	.
.	.	.	.	...	.	.
.	.	.	.	...	.	.
2398	**false**	**true**	**false**	...	**false**	**false**
2399	**false**	**false**	**true**	...	**false**	**true**

1. Initialize the table to all **false**s
2. Load the table by reading pairs of numbers representing a pilot and a flight for which the pilot is qualified. Assign **true** to these locations.
3. **REPEAT**
   3.1 Read a Query
   3.2 **CASE** Query **OF**
      3.2.1 Query is a flight number:
         3.2.1.1 Travel along corresponding column, writing out number of each qualified pilot
      3.2.2 Query is a pilot number
         3.2.2.1 Travel along corresponding row, writing out each flight for which the pilot is qualified
      3.2.3 Query is flight and pilot number
         3.2.3.1 Access information at that row and column
         3.2.3.2 **IF true THEN**
            write ('QUALIFIED')
            ELSE
            write ('NOT QUALIFIED')

■ ■

To refine the algorithm presented in Example 2.13, we must provide a formal definition for the two-dimensional table ADT.

> **Two-dimensional table.** A two-dimensional table is a collection of data of the same type arranged as a rectangular grid. Any entry in the grid may be specified by giving its row and column position. The rows and columns themselves are each indexed by a separate contiguous range of some ordinal data type, such as the integers.

The operations performed on a table are

> *Create operation*
> Preconditions: T is a two-dimensional table in an unreliable state.
> Postconditions: T is a two-dimensional table with all row and column entries initialized to a designated default value.

Retrieve operation	
Preconditions:	*T* is an arbitrary two-dimensional table that has been previously created. *R* is a particular row index within the contiguous range of valid row indices for the table. *C* is similarly a particular column index.
Postconditions:	Retrieve returns the value stored in row *R*, column *C* of table *T* without affecting the table at all.
Assign operation	
Preconditions:	*T* is a previously created two-dimensional table. *R* and *C* are row and column indices respectively for table *T*. *V* is a value of the type stored at each table location.
Postconditions:	The value *V* is stored at row *R*, column *C* of table *T*.

The effect of each of these operations may be illustrated using the pilot-flight table of Table 2.2. Here the data at each grid location is Boolean. The Create operation for this table returns a table with all **false** entries—the default value for a particular pilot and flight. The Assign operation is then used to place the value **true** at specified table locations. The Assign operation also can be used to place a **false** value in a particular row and column of the table. Finally, the Retrieve operation returns the Boolean value stored at a given location in the grid. For instance, Retrieve for row index 1001 and column index 4498 yields **true** in Table 2.2. For row 2398 and column 3000 this operation yields **false.**

Although Table 2.2 illustrates a two-dimensional table with Boolean data stored at each grid location, you should recognize that not all two-dimensional tables will store Boolean data. The only requirements are that data items at each grid location in a given table are of the same type and that there is a well-defined default value to which all grid locations are set as a result of the Create operation.

To move toward an implementation of the two-dimensional table ADT in Pascal we must translate the precondition and postcondition specifications for table operations into Pascal procedure and function headers. Such a Pascal interface for the two-dimensional table ADT is provided next.

Pascal Interface for Two-Dimensional Table

```
PROCEDURE Create (VAR T: TwoDTable);

  {  Given:    T, a two-dimensional table in an unreliable state          }
  {  Task:     Initialize the table to the default value for table entries }
  {  Return:   T, an initialized table                                     }

FUNCTION Retrieve (T : TwoDTable;
                   R, C : integer) : TableData;

  {  Given:    T, an arbitrary two-dimensional table, which as been        }
  {            previously created                                          }
  {  Task:     Retrieve the value at row R and column C of the table       }
  {  Return:   The value retrieved                                         }
```

```
PROCEDURE Assign (VAR T : TwoDTable;
                  R, C : integer;
                  V : TableData);

  {  Given:   T, an arbitrary two-dimensional table, which has been        }
  {           previously created                                           }
  {  Task:    Assign value V to row R, column C of the table               }
  {  Return:  T, with value V assigned to the designated row and column    }
```

EXAMPLE 2.14

Given this formal definition and Pascal interface for the two-dimensional table ADT, refine the algorithm of Example 2.13 into a Pascal main program. Be sure to follow the ADT use rule.

```
CONST
  LowFlight = 3000;
  HighFlight = 4499;
  LowPilot = 1000;
  HighPilot = 2399;

TYPE
  FlightRange = LowFlight..HighFlight;
  PilotRange = LowPilot..HightPilot;
  TableData = boolean;
  TwoDTable = { The hidden implementation of two-dimensional table would
                appear here }

VAR
  Pilot : PilotRange;
  Flight : FlightRange;
  PFInfo : TwoDTable;
  Query : Char;
  PFFile : text;

BEGIN { Main program }
  Create (PFInfo);
  reset(PFFile);

  { The next loop reads in all pilot/flight pairs from the file and "loads"
    them in the table by calling on the Assign operation. }

  WHILE NOT eof(PFData) DO
    BEGIN
      readln(PFFile, Pilot, Flight);
      Assign(PFInfo, Pilot, Flight, true)
    END;

  { Then enter the loop that fields the three types of queries.  Note that
    the Retrieve operation is used extensively to process these queries }

  REPEAT
    write('Query type [F]light, [P]ilot, [B]oth, or [Q]uit-->');
    readln(Query);
    CASE Query OF
      'F', 'f':
        BEGIN
          write('Enter flight number-->');
          readln(Flight);
          writeln('Qualified pilots are:');
```

```
          FOR Pilot := LowPilot TO HighPilot DO
            IF Retrieve (PFInfo, Pilot, Flight) THEN
              writeln(Pilot)
        END;
      'P', 'p':
        BEGIN
          write('Enter pilot number-->');
          readln(Pilot);
          writeln('(S)he may pilot flights');
          FOR Flight := LowFlight TO HighFlight DO
            IF Retrieve (PFInfo, Pilot, Flight) THEN
              writeln(Flight)
        END;
      'B', 'b':
        BEGIN
          write('Enter pilot and flight number-->');
          readln(Pilot, Flight);
          IF Retrieve (PFInfo, Pilot, Flight) THEN
            writeln('QUALIFIED')
          ELSE
            writeln('NOT QUALIFIED')
        END;
      'Q', 'q':
        BEGIN
        END { Quit Option }
    END { Case }
  UNTIL (Query = 'Q') OR (Query = 'q')
END.
```

Implementations of the Two-Dimensional Table ADT

Example 2.14 has provided a complete main program that makes no assumptions about the implementation of the underlying ADT. Only after completing such high-level logic is it appropriate to begin thinking about implementation details. In the case of the two-dimensional table ADT, it is tempting to use the implementation that is provided directly by Pascal arrays. In particular, the following declarations would be suitable for Table 2.2.

```
CONST
  LowFlight = 3000;
  HighFlight = 4499;
  LowPilot = 1000;
  HighPilot = 2399;
  .
  .
  .
TYPE
  FlightRange = LowFlight..HighFlight;
  PilotRange = LowPilot..HighPilot;
  TwoDTable = ARRAY [PilotRange,FlightRange] OF boolean;
  .
  .
  .
VAR
  PFInfo : TwoDTable;
```

We wish to discuss two issues with respect to this implementation of Wing-and-a-Prayer's table. First, when Pascal provides an obvious and direct implementation of the abstract data type, how does Pascal itself implement your declarations? The designers of your Pascal compiler must translate the declarations and instructions in your Pascal programs into a suitable representation in the internal machine code of your computer. Recall that this deeper level implementation issue was alluded to in Figure 2.1 though not discussed in detail. We now more fully realize that the designers of a compiler are concerned with implementing abstractions from a perspective that is different than that of the users of the compiler. In the case of a two-dimensional table, the implementation issue facing designers of a compiler is how to represent a two-dimensional structure on a machine in which units of computer memory are inevitably arranged as a one-dimensional sequence of cells.

Second, after discussing the compiler's implementation of your declaration for a two-dimensional table, we will want to evaluate that implementation. How efficient is the compiler's implementation of your structure with respect to time and space considerations? This is a particularly important question for exceedingly large tables such as the one we need in our current Wing-and-a-Prayer application. We will see that the compiler's implementation of a two-dimensional table may be, at best, inefficient and, at worst, totally impractical for our application.

Row-Major Implementation of Two-Dimensional Arrays

To simplify the discussion that follows, instead of working with the huge amount of information in Table 2.2, let's work with the following more manageable declaration:

```
VAR
  Numbers : ARRAY [1..6,1..5] OF integer;
```

A sample assignment of values to the table Numbers is pictured in Figure 2.5.

FIGURE 2.5
Values in the ARRAY Numbers

Row \ Column	1	2	3	4	5
1	10	18	42	6	14
2	13	19	8	1	44
3	63	80	12	90	51
4	16	13	9	8	4
5	12	11	12	14	83
6	1	4	18	99	90

From the perspective of the compiler writer, a two-dimensional array declaration represents a level of abstraction because internally computer memory is not arranged as a rectangular grid. Instead, computer memory locations are arranged in a linear sequence beginning with location 1, and then 2, 3, 4, and so on. Because of this, there must be manipulations behind the scenes when a program requests the entry in the 5th row and 4th column of a two-dimensional array (as highlighted in Figure 2.5). Essentially, the coordinates of the 5th row and the 4th column must be transformed into an address within this linear sequence of memory locations. The nature of the transformation is dependent upon how the designers of the compiler have chosen to implement the application programmer's mental image of rows and columns within the linear sequence of memory locations.

Suppose that our compiler has chosen to store the 30 entries in the two-dimensional array Numbers as indicated in Figure 2.6.

FIGURE 2.6
Linear storage of data from Figure 2.5

10	18	42	6	14	13	19	8	1	44	63	80	12	90	51	16	13	9	8	4	12	11	12	14	83	1	4	18	99	90

According to this arrangement, the first row would take up the first five locations in the list allocated for the array; the second row, the second five locations; and so on. The entry in the 5th row and 4th column would in fact be located in the 24th position within the list.

In this array the Kth row and the Jth column must be transformed into the

(5 * (K − 1) + J)th

position in the list. In even more general terms, if NCol is the number of columns in the array, then the entry in the Kth row and Jth column is given as the

(NCol * (K − 1) + J)th

entry in the linear list corresponding to the two-dimensional array. Most high-level computer languages implement two-dimensional arrays (and higher) in such a *row-major* fashion and do so in a way that is largely hidden from the applications programmer. However, all programmers should be aware that multidimensional arrays are inherently less efficient than one-dimensional arrays because of the computations required by the transformation from row/column coordinates to linear address each time an entry in the array is accessed. Such a transformation is often called a *mapping function.*

If you've programmed in FORTRAN, you will recall that, when initializing a two-dimensional array via a data statement, the entries for the array must be listed by column; that is, first column, second column, and so on. This is because FORTRAN is one of the few high-level languages to store a multidimensional array in *column-major* order, as indicated in Figure 2.7.

FIGURE 2.7
Column-major storage of data from Figure 2.5

10	13	63	16	12	1	18	19	80	13	11	4	42	8	12	9	12	18	6	1	90	8	14	99	14	44	51	4	83	90

To access the entry in the Kth row and the Jth column of a two-dimensional array stored in column-major order, the transformation

NRow * (J − 1) + K

is required; NRow represents the number of rows in the array. The fact that this transformation requires the number of rows but not the number of columns also explains why many FORTRAN compilers insist that a subroutine be informed of the number of rows in an array passed down from a calling program but not the number of columns.

The Sparse Table Problem

From what has been said about the compiler's possible implementation strategy for a two-dimensional array, it should be clear that we might be paying a very high price in memory for the flight-pilot table of Wing-and-a-Prayer Airlines. In general, for a two-dimensional table with NRow rows and NCol columns, the space efficiency of a row-major implementation is O(NRow * NCol).

In particular, we would be charged for 2,100,000 (1,500 × 1,400) Boolean memory locations if our Pascal compiler implemented the array in row-major fashion. Since many Pascal compilers allocate one byte of storage for each Boolean location, your seemingly simple declaration of a two-dimensional table may require over two megabytes (two million bytes) of memory. Depending on your computer, this is quite likely to exceed the amount of memory a program is allowed to consume. Thus, we have a real space-efficiency problem. Our Pascal declarations for the Wing-and-a-Prayer table may be nothing more than a wishful pipe dream that is not remotely realizable on our machine.

Does this mean that you cannot implement the conceptual flight/pilot table? For the sake of your job (as computer operations manager), we hope not! Rather, this illustrates that designers must be acutely aware of how the compiler may "automatically" implement certain concepts for them and then they must be prepared to implement them differently when the compiler's strategy fails. In this instance, we propose to take advantage of an additional fact given to us in the specifications. That is, any given pilot qualifies to fly on only a relatively small percentage of flights. This means that relatively few entries in Table 2.2 will be **true.** A table such as this, in which a high percentage of the data storage locations will be one uniform value (**false** in this case), is called a *sparse table.* We can use the sparseness of **true** values in the table to implement it by strategies other than row-major or column-major form (and hence save your job). However, note that, regardless of the implementation we choose, we are still working with a table at the abstract level.

An Alternative Implementation for a Sparse Table

We are seeking an implementation that will conserve memory by not actually storing the high percentage of **false** entries that appear in the conceptual table. One possibility is simply to store a list of ordered pairs of integers: the first entry in the pair is a pilot number and the second is a flight number. One of those pairs is on the list for each **true** entry in the conceptual table. Conversely, a **false** entry in the conceptual table does not get a (pilot, flight) pair on the ordered list. Hence, a probe into the Kth row and the Jth column of the conceptual table returns **true** if an appropriate search algorithm can find the pair (K, J) on the list implementation of the table; it returns **false** otherwise.

What have we gained? For each **true** value in the conceptual table, we now must store two integers—so there is actually a loss in this regard. However, for the much higher percentage of **false** values, we now store absolutely nothing on the list.

The Example, Exercises, and Problems that follow have you explore this suggested implementation for a sparse table. In designing a system based on this implementation, you will discover certain run-time inefficiencies that can be at least partially overcome by using the more sophisticated implementation strategies to be introduced in Chapters 4 and 9.

A NOTE OF INTEREST

Sparse Tables and Language Compilers

Two-dimensional tables play a crucial role in many language compilers. To see why, consider a problem substantially easier than writing a compiler. Suppose that you are reading a stream of characters intended to identify one of the twelve months. You are to read these characters until you have read enough to uniquely identify a month or until you can conclude that the stream of characters will not identify any month. Thus, upon reading 'D', you could declare the month to be DECEMBER. However, you would have to read the three characters 'JUL' before you could declare the month to be JULY. Moreover, if you read the three characters 'JUK', you could declare that the input stream cannot possibly identify any month. (Note that the problem we are describing does not demand that the input stream be a completely correct spelling of some month, only that the input stream begin with characters that uniquely define a month. Thus, both 'DECEMBER' and 'DIZZY' would be viewed as input streams that uniquely identify the month DECEMBER because you could quit processing characters as soon as the leading 'D' is read.)

The driving force behind an algorithm that would allow you to process an input stream in the fashion just described is a two-dimensional table such as that pictured here. The columns of this table are indexed by the letters of the alphabet, and the rows are indexed by the various "frames of mind" (officially called states) in which you may find yourself after having read a portion of the input stream. For instance, this table indicates that, if you begin processing characters in the *start* state and read the character 'J', then you switch to the *j* state. One in the *j* state, you expect to encounter either 'A' or 'U' as the next character, which will respectively cause you to switch to the *jan* state or the *ju* State. In addition to the states that index the rows of this table, we also have the states

jan, feb, mar, apr, may, jun, jul, aug, sept, oct, nov, dec

which correspond to your having recognized a uniquely defined month. The state *error* is indicated by the vacant entries in the table.

Given this table, the algorithm to recognize a month is extremely compact. It follows in pseudocode form.

	Letter																									
State	**A**	**B**	**C**	**D**	**E**	**F**	**G**	**H**	**I**	**J**	**K**	**L**	**M**	**N**	**O**	**P**	**Q**	**R**	**S**	**T**	**U**	**V**	**W**	**X**	**Y**	**Z**
start	a			dec		feb				j			m	nov	oct				sep							
j	jan																				ju					
m	ma																									
a																apr					aug					
ju												jul		jun												
ma																		mar							may	

1. state := start
2. **REPEAT**
   2.1 read(c)
   2.2 state := table [state,c]
3. **UNTIL eoln**
   OR state = error
   OR state is one of months jan..dec

Why is our month-recognition algorithm a relevant issue with respect to the topics we have discussed in this chapter? First note that our two-dimensional table clearly embodies the sparse table concept. In this particular sparse table, the vast majority of entries are the error state. Hence, our algorithm to recognize a month from an incoming stream of characters is dependent on our ability to implement a sparse table.

Second, this particular example is representative, on a small scale, of an entire class of algorithms for recognizing a valid sequence of symbols arriving on an input stream. In fact, this is precisely what must be done by a compiler for a high-level language such as Pascal. That is, it must successfully read the symbols in the source program that serves as its input stream and declare the sequence of symbols valid or invalid according to the rules of the language. Many compilers are actually driven by a table similar to the one we used for our month recognition algorithm. One of the major differences in such a compiler table is the increased size of the table due to the relative complexity of the language (versus our simple month recognition example). Hence, an efficient representation of a sparse matrix can be crucial to determining whether or not a compiler can process source programs at a reasonable rate of speed.

Algorithms that are driven by a table such as the one we have discussed here are known as finite state machines, or finite state automata. We will examine another application of finite state machines in Chapter 3. For a more general treatment, we encourage you to consult Chapter 10 of *Discrete Mathematics* (second edition) by Richard Johnsonbaugh (New York: Macmillan, 1990).

EXAMPLE 2.15

The following declarations would provide a suitable basis for implementing Wing-and-a-Prayer's sparse pilot/flight table in the fashion just discussed.

```
CONST
  LowFlight = 3000;
  HighFlight = 4499;
  LowPilot = 1000;
  HighPilot = 2399;
  MaxPairs = 6000;      {  Or other appropriate constant indicating the  }
                        {  maximum overall number of pilot/flight        }
                        {  qualification pairs.                          }

  HighPilotPlus1 = 2400;  {  Used as sentinel.  }

TYPE
  FlightRange = LowFlight .. HighFlight;
  PilotRange = LowPilot .. HighPilot;
  PilotRangePlus1 = LowPilot .. HighPilotPlus1;
  PFSparseTableRec = RECORD
                       PilotNum : PilotRangePlus1;
                       FlightNum : FlightRange
                     END;
  TwoDTable = ARRAY [1..MaxPairs] OF PFSparseTableRec;
  TableData = boolean;
```

The following function could be used to implement the retrieve operation for the sparse table.

```
FUNCTION Retrieve (T : TwoDTable;
                  R, C : integer) : TableData;

  {  Given:   T, an arbitrary two-dimensional table                         }
  {  Task:    Retrieve the value at row R and column C of the table         }
  {  Return:  The value retrieved                                           }

  { In this implementation of TwoDTable for the Wing-and-a-Prayer pilot-    }
  { flight data base, an array of (pilot, flight) pairs with HighPilotPlus1  }
  { in the PilotNum field of the last record of the array is used to        }
  { implement the conceptual table of boolean values.                       }

  VAR
    K : integer;
    Found : boolean;

  BEGIN
    Found := false;
    K := 1;
    WHILE NOT Found AND (T[K].PilotNum <> HighPilotPlus1) DO
      { K proceeds sequentially through the list of pilot/flight pairs }
      IF (T[K].PilotNum = R) AND (T[K].FlightNum = C) THEN
        Found := true
      ELSE
        K := K + 1;
    { If loop exited because T[K].PilotNum = HighPilotPlus1, Found will be false }
    Retrieve := Found
  END;  { of FUNCTION Retrieve }
```

In Section 1.4, we introduced the notion of the time/space trade-off. The Retrieve operation implemented in Example 2.15 clearly illustrates this trade-off. To avoid storage of a multitude of default **false** values, we are paying the price of a sequential search each time the Retrieve operation is invoked. In the Exercises, you will use big-O notation to analyze more formally the efficiency of the two-dimensional table implementation we have suggested here. You will also explore using the binary search as an alternate means of searching the list of pilot/flight pairs used in this implementation. More efficient implementations will be presented in future chapters as we examine more sophisticated data structures.

Exercises 2.3

1. Show by an example how the row-major and column-major implementations for a two-dimensional array would differ.
2. What would the mapping function be for a three-dimensional table implemented in row-major form? Can you generalize this to tables of even higher dimensions?
3. Give some examples (besides the flight/pilot data base) of applications that, at the abstract level, call for a sparse table.
4. Is a two-dimensional M by M array more or less efficient than a one-dimensional array of extent M^2? Explain your answer.
5. Many languages, such as Pascal, allow subscripts for an arbitrary range of ordinal values, not necessarily always integers starting at 1. Specify how this would affect the mapping functions discussed in this chapter to translate two-dimensional table coordinates into linear list positions.
6. The two-dimensional array in Pascal is an obvious, built-in implementation of the two-dimensional table ADT. Write full versions of the Create, Retrieve, and Assign operations for this implementation. Assume that TableData is of **TYPE** integer with a default value of zero. Be sure that you follow the dictates of the ADT implementation rule introduced in Section 2.2.

Exercises 7–12 refer to the alternate implementation for a sparse table discussed at the end of this section and in Example 2.15.

7. Given the declarations and implementation of the Retrieve operation in Example 2.15, write the **PROCEDURE** for the corresponding Create operation.
8. Given the declarations and implementation of the Retrieve operation in Example 2.15, write the **PROCEDURE** for the corresponding Assign operation.
9. Rewrite the implementation of the retrieve operation in Example 2.15 to use a modified version of the binary search algorithm. How must your answers to Exercises 7 and 8 change to accommodate this?
10. Using big-O notation, analyze the time efficiency of the retrieve and assign operations you have implemented in Exercise 9.
11. Analyze the space efficiency of the sparse table implementation you have provided in your answers to Exercise 9 versus a row-major implementation of the same table. What percentage of values would have to be false for your implementation to be more space efficient than a row-major implementation?
12. Discuss why the binary search technique you employed in Exercise 9 would be a poor strategy for a two-dimensional table that is frequently changed by the Assign operation. Compare and contrast the effectiveness of the binary search strategy versus the sequential search strategy used in Example 2.15. Which of the strategies would you use for the pilot/flight table needed by Wing-and-a-Prayer Airlines? Defend you choice in a short essay.
13. Implementations of ADTs may not achieve a perfect representation of the abstraction they embody. The definition of a two-dimensional table ADT por-

trays a rectangular grid with no inherent limit on the number of rows and number of columns. In what sense are the implementations of the two-dimensional table ADT discussed in this section (row-major, column-major, and Example 2.15) imperfect representations of this concept?

14. How would the sparse table implementation discussed at the end of this section have to be adjusted for non-Boolean data?

15. In what sense does the radix sort algorithm discussed in Section 1.4 require a sparse table?

16. In the Pascal interface for a two-dimensional table, the table T is given as a value parameter. From an efficiency perspective, explain why it would be better to have T be a **VAR** parameter. What are the arguments against T being a **VAR** parameter?

■ ■ ■ ■

2.4 The Keyed List Abstract Data Type

OBJECTIVES

- to understand and be able to use the definition of the keyed list ADT
- to understand how procedures can be used as parameters to other procedures
- to consider several different implementations of the keyed list ADT
- to recognize the shortcomings of each of these implementations and recognize the need for more sophisticated implementations to be studied in future chapters.

In Chapter 1, we approached sorting and searching from the perspective of manipulating an array of records, each of which had a designated key field. So many data processing activities organize records by key fields that it would seem worth our while to view a list of such records from an abstract perspective. Doing so may allow us to bring the power of abstraction to bear in a variety of applications. Toward that end, we introduce the following definition of the *keyed list* ADT.

> **Keyed list.** A keyed list is a collection of records, each of which is the same type. The records in the list are organized around a designated key field in each record. This key field must take on a unique value for each record and have a well-defined ordering in the sense that, for two different values a and b, we can determine whether $a < b$ or $a > b$. Clearly, data types such as integer, real, and string meet this ordering criterion. The records are to be viewed as arranged in logical order by this key field.

The operations for a keyed list are

Create operation	
Preconditions:	L is an arbitrary keyed list in an unreliable state.
Postconditions:	L is initialized to the empty list.
Add operation	
Preconditions:	L is a keyed list. *Item* is a record to be inserted in L. *Success* is a Boolean variable.
Postconditions:	If possible, L has *Item* inserted with respect to the ordering on the key field. *Success* is returned as **true** to signal this insertion. If *Item* cannot be inserted in L, *Success* is returned as **false,** and the list is left unchanged.

Delete operation	
Preconditions:	*L* is a keyed list. *Target* is a key value associated with a record to be removed from the list *L*. *Success* is a Boolean variable.
Postconditions:	If the record with the *Target* key can be found in *L*, it is removed from *L* and *Success* is set to **true.** Otherwise, *Success* is set to **false** and *L* is left unchanged.
Retrieve operation	
Preconditions:	*L* is a keyed list, *Target* is a key value to be found in *L*, *Success* is a Boolean variable.
Postconditions:	If the *Target* can be found in *L*, then *Item* contains the record associated with *Target* and *Success* is set to **true.** Otherwise, *Success* is set to **false,** and *Item's* contents are unreliable. In either case, the keyed list *L* is left unchanged.
TraverseInOrder operation	
Preconditions:	*L* is a keyed list and *ProcessNode* is an algorithmic process which can be applied to each data node on the list *L*.
Postconditions:	Each data node in *L* is visited in the order determined by the key field. As each node is visited, *ProcessNode* is applied to it.

The effect of each list operation is highlighted in Figure 2.8 for a list in which the key field is a string representing a last name. For such a keyed list, the natural ordering would be alphabetical by last name. Note from the figure that all list operations preserve this order. It is also apparent from this figure that the TraverseInOrder operation is a bit different than other ADT opera-

FIGURE 2.8
Keyed List Operations

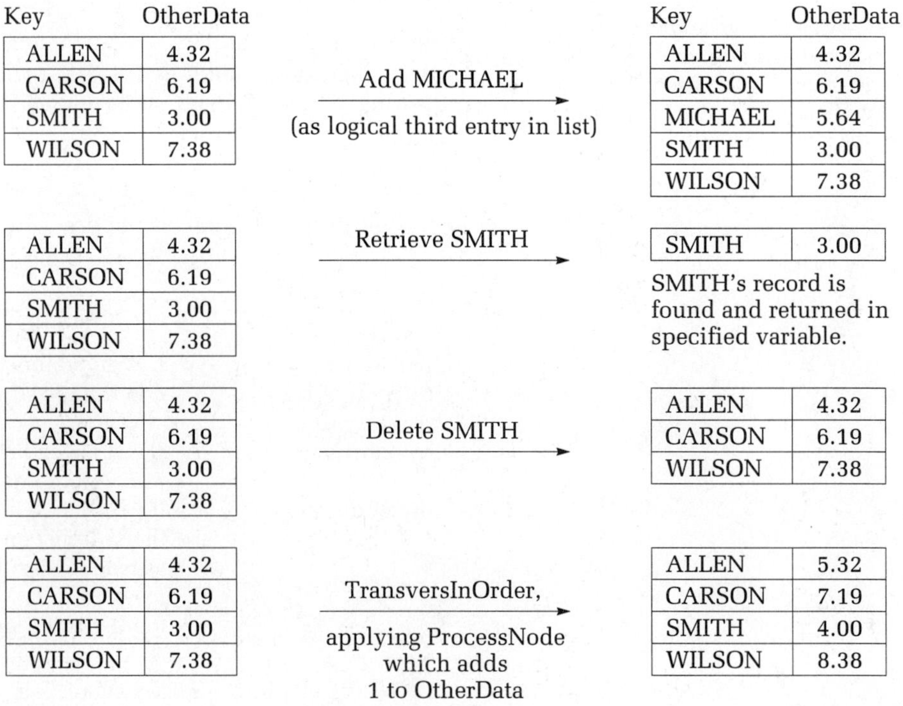

Key	OtherData
ALLEN	4.32
CARSON	6.19
SMITH	3.00
WILSON	7.38

Add MICHAEL → (as logical third entry in list)

Key	OtherData
ALLEN	4.32
CARSON	6.19
MICHAEL	5.64
SMITH	3.00
WILSON	7.38

ALLEN	4.32
CARSON	6.19
SMITH	3.00
WILSON	7.38

Retrieve SMITH →

SMITH	3.00

SMITH's record is found and returned in specified variable.

ALLEN	4.32
CARSON	6.19
SMITH	3.00
WILSON	7.38

Delete SMITH →

ALLEN	4.32
CARSON	6.19
WILSON	7.38

ALLEN	4.32
CARSON	6.19
SMITH	3.00
WILSON	7.38

TransversInOrder, → applying ProcessNode which adds 1 to OtherData

ALLEN	5.32
CARSON	7.19
SMITH	4.00
WILSON	8.38

tions we have discussed. Not only is this operation given a data structure to act upon, but it is also given a process that acts upon each node in the data structure. In the figure, this process adds 1 to the OtherData field in each list node. If, however, we wanted an alphabetical listing of each record in the list, we could also achieve this by using the TraverseInOrder operation—providing it with a ProcessNode algorithm that printed each record in an appropriate format.

Pascal Interface for Keyed List ADT

The ability of the TraverseInOrder operation to receive not only data in the form of a keyed list but also an algorithmic process that can be applied to each node in the list will complicate the translation of keyed list operations into Pascal procedure headers. This complication is reflected in the following Pascal interface. The **PROCEDURE** TraverseInOrder in this interface must have a parameter which is itself a procedure. The syntax for doing this in Pascal is discussed after the interface.

```
TYPE
  KeyType = { An appropriate type for the key field in list records       }
  OtherDataType = { An appropriate type for the other data associated with  }
                  { each key field                                          }
  ListNode = RECORD
               Key : KeyType;
               OtherData : OtherDataType
             END;
  KeyedList = { The hidden implementation }

PROCEDURE Create(VAR L : KeyedList);

  {  Given:    An arbitrary keyed list variable L           }
  {  Task:     Initialize the list                          }
  {  Return:   L initialized to the empty list.             }

PROCEDURE Add (VAR L : KeyedList;
               Item : ListNode;
               VAR Success : boolean);

  {  Given:    A keyed list L ordered by Key field          }
  {            and an Item to be inserted in that list      }
  {  Task:     Insert the item into the list                }
  {  Return:   L with Item inserted with respect to the     }
  {            ordering on the key field.  If L cannot be   }
  {            inserted, Success is returned as false, and  }
  {            the list is left unchanged.  Otherwise,      }
  {            Success returned as true.                    }

PROCEDURE Delete (VAR L : KeyedList;
                  Target : KeyType;
                  VAR Success : boolean);

  {  Given:    A keyed list L ordered by Key field          }
  {            and a Target key to be removed from          }
  {            that list                                    }
  {  Task:     Remove the record with key field matching    }
  {            Target from the list                         }
  {  Return:   L with the Target key removed.  If the Target }
  {            cannot be found, Success is returned as      }
  {            false.  Otherwise, it is returned as true.   }
```

```
PROCEDURE Retrieve (L : KeyedList;
                    Target : KeyType;
                    VAR Item : ListNode;
                    VAR Success : boolean);

  {  Given:   A keyed list L ordered by Key field          }
  {           and a Target key to be found in that list.   }
  {  Task:    Find the record with key field matching      }
  {           Target's value                               }
  {  Return:  The data associated with Target in Item.  If }
  {           the Target cannot be found, then Success is  }
  {           returned as false; otherwise true.           }

PROCEDURE TraverseInOrder (VAR L : KeyedList;
                           PROCEDURE ProcessNode (VAR Item : ListNode));

  {  Given:   Keyed list L                                 }
  {  Task:    Traverse the list in the order determined by }
  {           the key field, applying the procedure        }
  {           ProcessNode to each record in the list       }
  {  Return:  L with each node affected by ProcessNode.    }
```

Procedures and Functions as Parameters

T The TraverseInOrder operation in the preceding interface employs a Pascal technique that we have not seen before. Notice that one of the formal parameters in the interface for **PROCEDURE** TraverseInOrder is a procedure. The formal parameter

```
PROCEDURE ProcessNode(VAR Item: ListNode)
```

will allow us to pass to TraverseInOrder an actual parameter which is itself a procedure. This actual parameter is the one that is applied to each item in the keyed list L. By passing in different procedures in this parameter slot, we may have different processes applied to each item in the list. The following example should help clarify this usage.

EXAMPLE 2.16

Write procedures to print an item in a keyed list and add 1 to a real OtherData field in a keyed list. Then pass these procedures to the TraverseInOrder operation to print each item in a list, add 1 to the OtherData field of each item, and finally print each item again with its updated OtherData field.

```
CONST
  StringLength = 15;

TYPE
  String = PACKED ARRAY [1..StringLength] OF char;
  KeyType = String;
  OtherDataType = real;
  ListNode = RECORD
               Key : KeyType;
               OtherData : OtherDataType
             END;
  KeyedList = { The hidden implementation }

VAR
  L : KeyedList;
```

```
PROCEDURE PrintNode (VAR Item : ListNode);

  {  Given:   One node's data to be printed  }
  {  Return:  The node with its data printed }

  BEGIN
    writeln (Item.Key:20, Item.OtherData:5)
  END;

PROCEDURE AddOne (VAR Item : ListNode);

  {  Given:   One node in a keyed list       }
  {  Task:    Add one to the OtherData field }
  {           in that node                   }
  {  Return:  The list node with an updated  }
  {           OtherData field                }

  BEGIN
    Item.OtherData := Item.OtherData + 1.0
  END;
    .
    .
    .
{ In main program }
TraverseInOrder (L, PrintNode);
TraverseInOrder (L, AddOne);
TraverseInOrder (L, PrintNode);
```

A procedure passed as a parameter to another procedure must have a formal parameter list that matches, in number and type of arguments, the declaration in the formal parameter list of the receiving procedure. For instance, in Example 2.16, the formal parameter lists of PrintNode and AddOne must match that of the formal procedure parameter ProcessNode.

Judicious use of procedural parameters can enhance a procedure's ability to be of general use. For instance, the procedural parameter in the TraverseInOrder operation allows this single procedure to perform a variety of actions on each item in a keyed list. Which action is invoked on a particular call to TraverseInOrder is determined by the actual parameter passed in the ProcessNode slot.

Example 2.16 illustrated how you call a procedure with another procedure as parameter, but it did not show the details of writing the procedure that is invoked. These details are uncovered in the next example.

EXAMPLE 2.17

Write a sorting procedure that makes its comparison using a general Precedes relationship passed in as a parameter. No specific < or > comparison should appear in the sort procedure's definition. Then use this procedure in a program to sort an array of integers first in descending order and then in ascending order.

```
PROGRAM ProcedureParameter(input,output);

  { Demonstrate the use of procedure parameters in Pascal.          }
  { A sort procedure is written which sorts values in the order     }
  { determined by a function parameter passed to the Sort procedure. }
```

```
CONST
  IndexLimit = 100;

TYPE
  ElementType = integer;
  SortArray = ARRAY [1..IndexLimit] of ElementType;

VAR
  Size, J : integer;
  Data : SortArray;

FUNCTION GreaterThan (A, B : ElementType) : boolean;
  { Used as the actual parameter for Precedes }

  {  Given:   Two values to compare                                       }
  {  Task:    Compare the two values using a "greater than"               }
  {           relation appropriate for ElementType                        }
  {  Return:  True if A is greater than B and false otherwise             }

  BEGIN
    GreaterThan := (A > B)
  END; {  of FUNCTION GreaterThan  }

FUNCTION LessThan (A, B : ElementType) : boolean;
  { Used as the actual parameter for Precedes }

  {  Given:   Two values to compare                                       }
  {  Task:    Compare the two values using a "less than"                  }
  {           relation appropriate for ElementType                        }
  {  Return:  True if A is less than B and false otherwise                }

  BEGIN
    LessThan := (A < B)
  END; {  of FUNCTION LessThan  }

{ Insertion sort algorithm }
PROCEDURE Sort ( VAR A : SortArray;
                 N : integer;
                 Precedes : FUNCTION (A, B: ElementType) : boolean );

  {  Given:   Array of values to be returned in order          }
  {           according to Precedes relation and N, the        }
  {           number of values in array                        }
  {  Task:    Sort the array using the insertion sort          }
  {           algorithm                                        }
  {  Return:  The array arranged in order by the Precedes      }
  {           relation that is passed in as a parameter        }

  VAR
    K, J : integer;
    ItemToInsert : ElementType;
    StillLooking : boolean;

  BEGIN  { Sort }
    FOR K := 2 TO N DO
      BEGIN
        { Walk backwards through list, looking for slot to insert A[K] }
        ItemToInsert := A[K];
        J := K - 1;
        StillLooking := true;
        WHILE (J >= 1) AND StillLooking DO
          { ItemToInsert is compared to A[J] }
          IF Precedes(ItemToInsert, A[J]) THEN  { Here use Precedes parameter }
```

```
            BEGIN
              A[J + 1] := A[J];
              J := J - 1
            END
          ELSE
            StillLooking := false;
        { Upon leaving loop, J + 1 is the index where ItemToInsert belongs }
        A[J + 1] := ItemToInsert
      END  { FOR }
  END;  { of PROCEDURE Sort }

BEGIN { Main program to demonstrate procedure call to sort in descending order }
  write('How many values to sort? ');
  readln(Size);
  FOR J := 1 TO Size DO
    read(Data[J]);
  readln;
  { Sample call to produce a sort of integers in descending order }
  Sort (Data, Size, GreaterThan);
  writeln ('Descending Order');
  FOR J := 1 TO Size DO
    writeln(Data[J]:6);
  { Sample call to produce a sort of integers in ascending order }
  Sort (Data, Size, LessThan);
  writeln ('Ascending Order');
  FOR J := 1 TO Size DO
    writeln(Data[J]:6)
END.
```

The shaded lines in the previous code indicate how the function parameter is used in the definition of **PROCEDURE** Sort and, then, how Sort is invoked with actual GreaterThan and LessThan relationships.

A sample run of this program would appear as:

```
How many values to sort?  4
12
70
34
88
Descending Order
    88
    70
    34
    12
Ascending Order
    12
    34
    70
    88
```

Don't underestimate the generality of the Sort procedure in Example 2.17. It can be used for much more than merely sorting integers in ascending or descending order. For instance, if ElementType were a more complex record structure, we could define suitable actual parameters for the Precedes relationship to sort an array of records in ascending order based on one field and in descending order based on another field. You will explore these more general uses on the Sort procedure in the Exercises.

Implementations of the Keyed List ADT

We needed the preceding digression on procedure and function parameters because of the operations presented in the definition of the keyed list ADT. Now that we understand the use of such parameters, it is time to again direct our attention to this ADT and its implementations. We will consider two implementations in this section; each will have major shortcomings from an efficiency perspective. In future chapters, we will explore more sophisticated implementations that can improve these inefficiencies.

Implementation 1: Physically Ordered Array with Binary Search. The strategy of this implementation is to maintain an array of records in physical order by key field. Bundled with the array is a count of the number of records in the structure. Hence, the declaration for the encapsulated implementation of the keyed list is

```
CONST
  MaxListSize =  {  An appropriate choice for the maximum number of records
                    that can be stored in the list at any one time  }

TYPE
  KeyType =  {  An appropriate type for the key field in list records  }
  OtherDataType =  {  An appropriate type for the other data associated with
                      each key field  }
  ListNode = RECORD
               Key : KeyType;
               OtherData : OtherDataType
             END;
  KeyedList = RECORD
                DataRec : ARRAY [1..MaxListSize] OF ListNode;
                NumberRec : integer
              END;
```

A keyed list L with four records in it is depicted in Figure 2.9.

FIGURE 2.9
Implementation of keyed list by physically ordered array

KeyedList

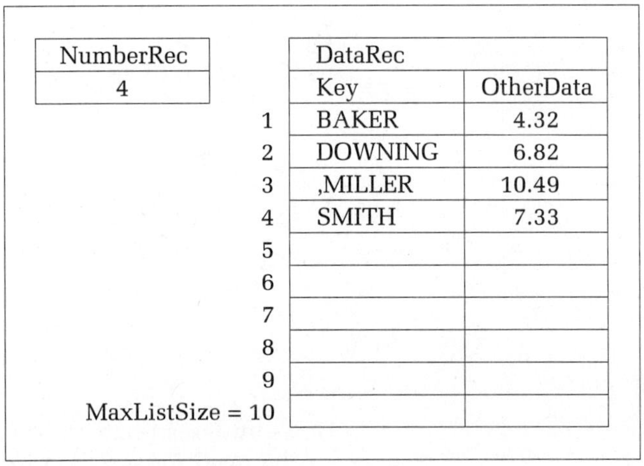

NumberRec
4

	DataRec	
	Key	OtherData
1	BAKER	4.32
2	DOWNING	6.82
3	,MILLER	10.49
4	SMITH	7.33
5		
6		
7		
8		
9		
MaxListSize = 10		

To add a record to the list in this figure, we must

1. Search for the first record in the list that has a key field value greater than that of the item we are adding.

2. Then, beginning with that record, move all records down one slot in the array.
3. Finally, insert the new item into the array slot that has been vacated and increase by 1 the number of records.

These actions are highlighted in Figure 2.10. Carefully study that figure in conjunction with examining the code in Example 2.18.

FIGURE 2.10
Add PATRICK to list of Figure 2.9

NumberRec
4

	DataRec	
	Key	OtherData
1	BAKER	4.32
2	DOWNING	6.82
3	MILLER	10.49
4	SMITH	7.33
5		
6		
7		
8		
9		
10		

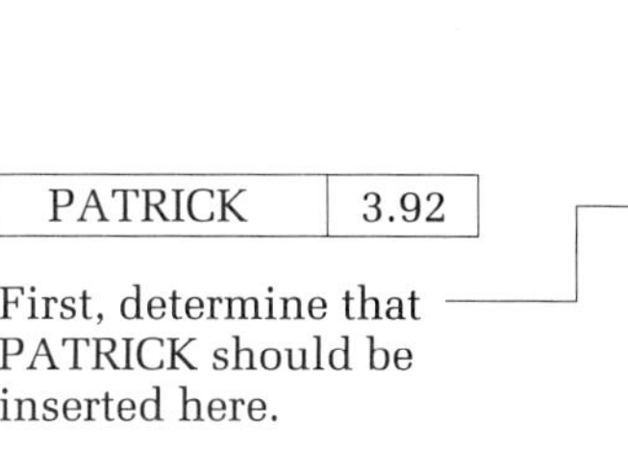

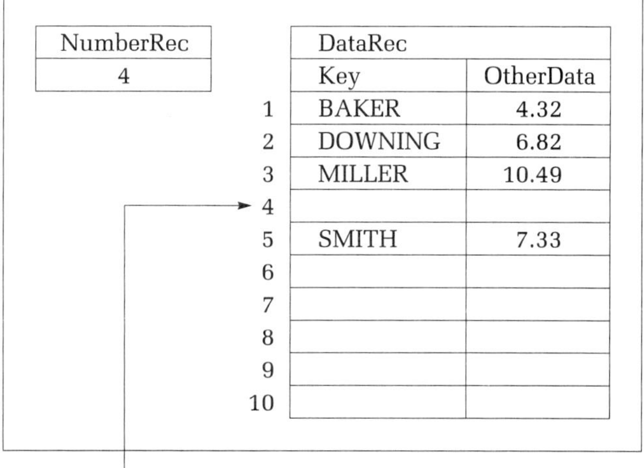

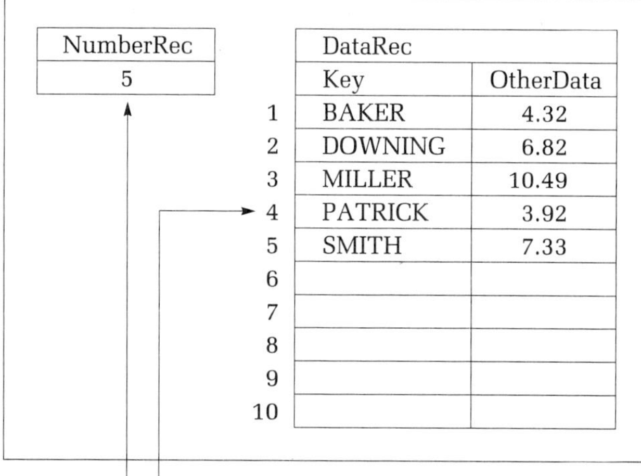

EXAMPLE 2.18

Write complete Pascal code for the Add operation. Be sure to follow the ADT implementation rule.

```
PROCEDURE Add (VAR L : KeyedList;
               Item : ListNode;
               VAR Success : boolean);
```

```
{  Given:   A keyed list L ordered by Key field          }
{           and an Item to be inserted in that list      }
{  Task:    Insert the item into the list                }
{  Return:  L with Item inserted with respect to the     }
{           ordering on the key field.  If L cannot be   }
{           inserted, Success is returned as false, and  }
{           the list is left unchanged.  Otherwise,      }
{           Success returned as true.                    }

VAR
  J, K : integer;
  Done : boolean;

BEGIN
  IF L.NumberRec = MaxListSize THEN
    Success := false
  ELSE
    BEGIN
      Success := true;
      { Find insertion slot for Item in physically ordered list }
      K := 1;
      Done := false;
      WHILE (K <= L.NumberRec) AND NOT Done DO
        { Compare Item's Key to that at index K }
        IF L.DataRec[K].Key > Item.Key THEN
          Done := true   { K is insertion slot }
        ELSE
          K := K + 1;
      { From insertion slot down, each record must be moved down one slot }
      FOR J := L.NumberRec DOWNTO K DO
        L.DataRec[J + 1] := L.DataRec[J];
      L.DataRec[K] := Item;
      L.NumberRec := L.NumberRec + 1
    END
END; { of PROCEDURE Add }
```

Because the implementation of Add always maintains the array in physical order by key field, the Retrieve operation can be implemented using the binary search algorithm. (Note that a variation of the binary search algorithm could also be used to find the insertion slot in **PROCEDURE** Add; you will develop this variation in the Exercises.)

We complete our discussion of this implementation by illustrating how the TraverseInOrder procedure would use its procedure parameter.

EXAMPLE 2.19

Write complete Pascal code for the TraverseInOrder operation. Be sure to obey the ADT implementation rule.

```
PROCEDURE TraverseInOrder (VAR L : KeyedList;
                           PROCEDURE ProcessNode (VAR Item : List-
                           Node));
  {  Given:   Keyed list L                                 }
  {  Task:    Traverse the list in the order determined by }
  {           the key field, applying the procedure        }
  {           ProcessNode to each record in the list       }
  {  Return:  L with each node affected by ProcessNode     }

  VAR
    J : integer;
```

```
BEGIN
  FOR J := 1 TO L.NumberRec DO
    ProcessNode (L.DataRec[J])
END;  {  of PROCEDURE TraverseInOrder  }
```

Implementation 2: Unordered Array with Sequential Search and Pointer Sort. Our second implementation attempts to eliminate the inefficiency involved in moving a potentially large number of records each time an Add or Delete is performed. The encapsulation of the keyed list ADT still includes an array of records and a counter. However, now when a record is added, it is merely added at the end of the list. Figure 2.11 illustrates this strategy.

FIGURE 2.11
Addition of records using unordered array implementation

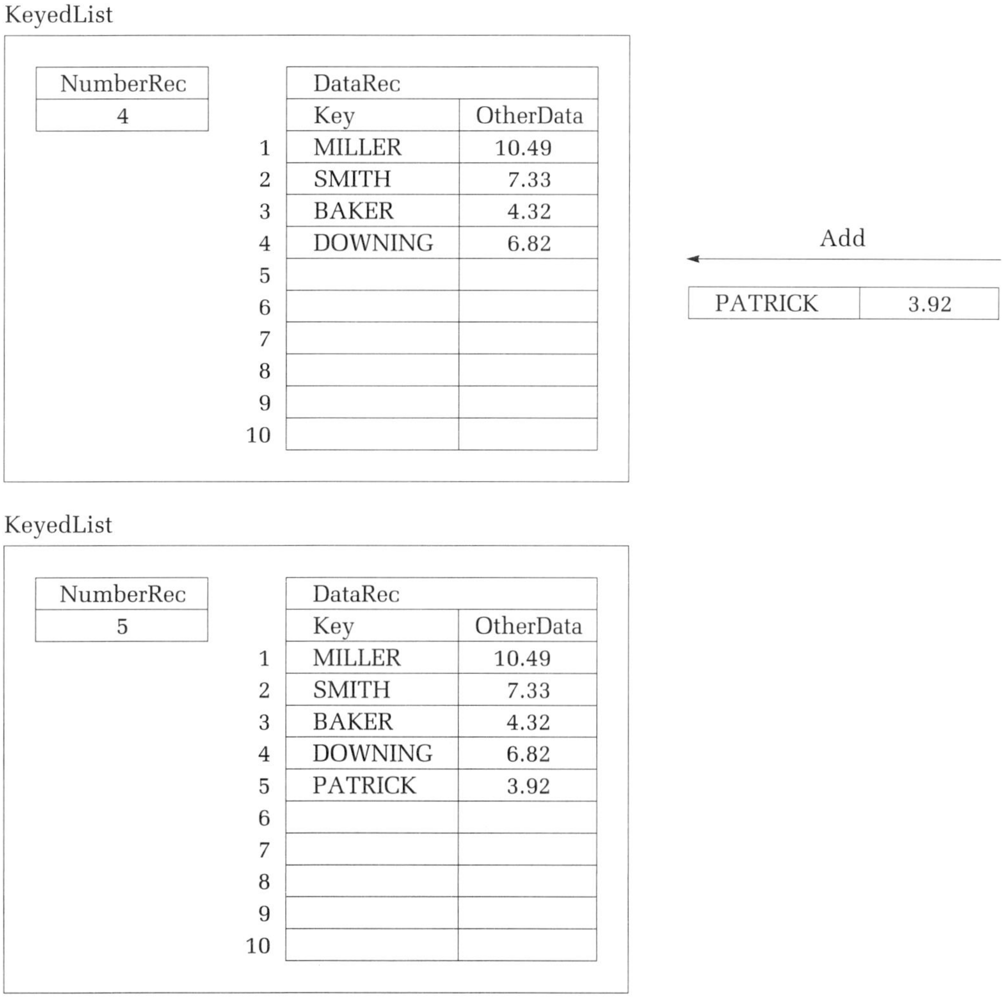

KeyedList

NumberRec
4

	DataRec	
	Key	OtherData
1	MILLER	10.49
2	SMITH	7.33
3	BAKER	4.32
4	DOWNING	6.82
5		
6		
7		
8		
9		
10		

Add ←

PATRICK	3.92

KeyedList

NumberRec
5

	DataRec	
	Key	OtherData
1	MILLER	10.49
2	SMITH	7.33
3	BAKER	4.32
4	DOWNING	6.82
5	PATRICK	3.92
6		
7		
8		
9		
10		

As you can see, the increase in efficiency of the Add operation is being bargained for a decrease in efficiency for other operations. For instance, the Retrieve operation would now require a sequential search. Also, implementation of the TraverseInOrder operation would require initially performing a pointer sort (Section 1.4) so that the list could be accessed in order by key field. The details of this implementation are left for you in the Exercises.

These trade-offs in efficiency for various operations are what make the keyed list ADT a particularly interesting one to study. We will return to it often in future chapters.

Exercises 2.4

1. What is wrong with the following **PROCEDURE** PrintNode and its use in a call to the TraverseInOrder operation for the keyed list ADT?

```
CONST
StringLength = 15;

TYPE
  String = PACKED ARRAY [1..StringLength] OF char;
  KeyType = String;
  OtherDataType = real;
  ListNode = RECORD
               Key : KeyType;
               OtherData : OtherDataType
             END;
  KeyedList = { The hidden implementation }

VAR
  L : KeyedList;

PROCEDURE PrintNode (Item : ListNode);

  {  Given:   One node's data to be printed    }
  {  Return:  The node with its data printed.  }

  BEGIN
    writeln (Item.Key:20, Item.OtherData:5)
  END;
   .
   .
   .
{ In main program }
TraverseInOrder (L, PrintNode);
```

2. What is wrong with the following **PROCEDURE** Increase and its use in a call to the TraverseInOrder operation for the keyed list ADT?

```
CONST
StringLength = 15;

TYPE
  String = PACKED ARRAY [1..StringLength] OF char;
  KeyType = String;
  OtherDataType = real;
  ListNode = RECORD
               Key : KeyType;
               OtherData : OtherDataType;
             END;
  KeyedList = { The hidden implementation }

VAR
  L : KeyedList;

PROCEDURE Increase (VAR Item : ListNode
                    X : real);
```

```
{  Given:    One node in a keyed list,                  }
{            and a value to add to the                  }
{            OtherData field in that node               }
{  Task:     Add X to the OtherData field               }
{            in that node                               }
{  Return:   The list node with an updated              }
{            OtherData field.                           }

BEGIN
  Item.OtherData := Item.OtherData + X
END;
  .
  .
  .
{ In main program }
TraverseInOrder (L, Increase (Item, 3.0) );
```

3. Given the following declaration for the data nodes in a keyed list,

```
CONST
StringLength = 15;

TYPE
  String = PACKED ARRAY [1..StringLength] OF char;
  KeyType = String;
  OtherDataType = real;
  ListNode = RECORD
               Key : KeyType;
               OtherData : OtherDataType;
             END;
  KeyedList = {  The hidden implementation  }
```

write a procedure that can be used as an actual parameter passed to the TraverseInOrder operation. This procedure should change to zero the OtherData field in those nodes that have a negative OtherData field; other nodes should be left unchanged. Finally indicate how you would call on TraverseInOrder using the procedure you have written.

4. Consider the problem given in Example 2.17. Suppose that ElementType in this program was not integer but instead defined by the following declaration.

```
TYPE
  ElementType = RECORD
                  Field1 : PACKED ARRAY [1..20] OF char;
                  Field2 : real
                END;
```

Define procedures that may be passed as actual parameters for the Precedes argument in **PROCEDURE** Sort to achieve the following orderings:

a. Array arranged alphabetically by Field1.
b. Array arranged in descending order by Field2.
c. Array arranged in descending order by Field2; those array elements which have the same value for Field2 should be arranged alphabetically.

Then indicate how you would invoke Sort with each of these procedures to achieve the desired ordering.

Exercises 5–8 refer to Implementation 1 of a keyed list, that is, physically ordered array with binary search to retrieve data.

5. Consider the following modification to the **FOR** loop to move records down in the code for the Add operation of Example 2.18.

```
{  From insertion slot down, each record must be moved down one slot  }
FOR J := K TO L.NumberRec DO
  L.DataRec[J + 1] := L.DataRec[J];
```

Will the procedure still work with this change to the loop? If not, describe what will go wrong.

6. Complete the implementation of the keyed list by developing code for the Create, Delete, and Retrieve operations. Be sure to obey the ADT implementation rule.

7. Given the implementations of operations in Examples 2.18, 2.19, and Exercise 6, provide a big-O efficiency analysis of each operation. You should consider both the number of comparisons and data interchanges in this analysis.

8. Modify the implementation of the Add operation in Example 2.18 so that a variation of the binary search algorithm is used to find the insertion slot. How does this new implementation affect your efficiency analysis from Exercise 7?

Exercises 9–10 refer to Implementation 2 of a keyed list, that is, an unordered array with sequential search to retrieve data and pointer sort to traverse in order.

9. Write data declarations and Pascal code for all keyed list operations under this implementation.

10. Given the implementations of operations in Exercise 9, provide a big-O efficiency analysis of each operation. You should consider both the number of comparisons and data interchanges in this analysis.

11. You have been assigned the task of developing an application that uses a keyed list in which the key field is a postal zip code. There is to be a record in the list for each zip code in the United States. Given this list, users of the application you develop will often want to see the information associated with a particular zip code and print reports in zip code order.
    Which of the two implementations of a keyed list that were presented in this section would you choose for your application? Write a memo to your supervisor defending your choice.

12. In the keyed list ADT, there is no operation that allows changing a record's key field. Show how one could, however, change a record's key field by using the Delete and Add operations.

13. In a written statement discuss various reasons why the Success Boolean parameter for the Add operation might return a **false** value.

■ ■ ■ ■

FOCUS ON PROGRAM DESIGN

To illustrate how approaching a design at an abstract level can make a hard problem easier, consider the task specified in the following memorandum.

Approaching a solution to this problem from an abstract data type perspective means that we essentially need not worry about how to handle an individual transaction on the keyed list of employees. This keyed list will be the computer embodiment of the stack of index cards presently maintained by the payroll director. These individual transactions are viewed as provided operations. Our logic is instead focused at a higher level, reflected in the modularstructure chart of Figure 2.12.

Similarly the module specifications need not specify details of the list because we will access the list only through the allowable, defined operations.

1. LoadEmployeeList Module
   Data received: None
   Information returned: A keyed list of employee records is read in from a text file

MEMORANDUM
FlyByNight Credit Card Company

TO: Computer Operations Manager
FROM: Director of Payroll
DATE: November 18, 1996
RE: Hourly employee payroll system

The number of hourly employees we have is growing so fast that we *must* computerize record keeping for them *immediately.* Here is a description of the process as we presently do it by hand. As much as possible, the essence of this process should be preserved in the automated system you will develop.

A record for each employee is kept on an index card. There are two items of information on that index card: an employee's name (in "lastname, firstname" form) and hourly pay rate. These index cards are kept in alphabetical order by employee name.

Each Friday, I go through the stack of index cards and perform three tasks. First, I add cards (in alphabetical order, of course) of new employees. Second, I go through the entire stack and write a paycheck for each employee. The information on this paycheck consists of the employee's name and salary. The salary is determined by multiplying the employee's hourly rate times the number of hours worked during that week. Finally, after all paychecks have been produced, I remove from the stack the index cards belonging to those employees who have been released or who have quit.

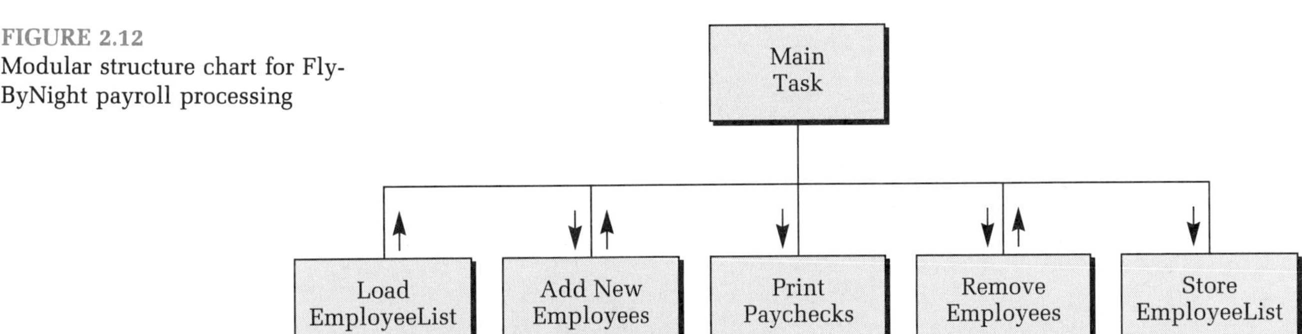

FIGURE 2.12
Modular structure chart for FlyByNight payroll processing

Logic: Repeatedly get a record from the text file and Add it to the employee list

2. AddNewEmployee Module
   Data received: List of previous employees
   Information returned: List of previous employees augmented with records of new employees
   Logic: While there is a new employee to add, obtain information on new employee and Add record to employee list

3. PrintPaychecks Module
   Data received: List of Employees
   Information returned: None
   Logic: Traverse the list, applying to each record a procedure that obtains the hours worked for a given employee and then prints a paycheck for that employee

4. RemoveEmployees Module
   Data received: List of employees
   Information returned: List with departing employees removed
   Logic: While there is another departing employee, obtain the employee's name and delete that record

5. StoreEmployeeList Module
   Data received: List of employees
   Information returned: None
   Logic: Traverse the List, applying to each record a procedure that writes the record to a text file

The program itself is derived immediately from these specifications. Since we are assuming the basic operations on keyed lists, those procedures and the details of their implementation are omitted in the following listing. Any implementation of the keyed list data type could be plugged into this program, and it would function correctly. By providing an abstract definition of a data type that may be used in this and other applications, we have been able to separate our solution to this problem from the details of implementing that data type.

```
PROGRAM FlyByNightPayroll (input, output, EmployeeFile, NewEmployeeFile);

  { The following is a partial program to solve the problem posed in the     }
  { memo from FlyByNight's payroll director.  The implementations of the     }
  { keyed list are hidden.  Also, the implementations of the operations on   }
  { the keyed list ADT are not provided.  The portion of the program that    }
  { is given accesses the keyed list ADT only through its abstract           }
  { definition.                                                              }

CONST
  NameLength = 30;  { Maximum length for name }

TYPE
  KeyType = PACKED ARRAY [1..NameLength] of char;  { Employee name }
  OtherDataType = real;  { Hourly salary rate }
  ListNode = RECORD
               Key : KeyType;
               OtherData : OtherDataType
             END;
  KeyedList =         { The hidden implementation }

VAR
  EmployeeFile, NewEmployeeFile : text;
  EmployeeList : KeyedList;

  { The implementation of keyed list operations would appear here in      }
  { complete program.                                                     }

PROCEDURE LoadEmployeeList (VAR EmployeeList : KeyedList);

  {  Given:   An empty keyed list                                          }
  {  Task:    Load list from text file EmployeeFile                        }
  {  Return:  EmployeeList containing data on all employees in file.  If data }
  {           on all employees in file will not fit in EmployeeList,       }
  {           EmployeeList contains as many records as possible.           }

  VAR
    K : integer;
    Item : ListNode;
    Success : boolean;
```

```
  BEGIN
    reset (EmployeeFile);
    Success := true;
    { Read until end of file or cannot add more to list }
    WHILE (NOT eof (EmployeeFile)) AND Success DO
      BEGIN
        FOR K := 1 TO NameLength DO
          read (EmployeeFile, Item.Key[K]);
        readln (EmployeeFile, Item.OtherData);
        Add (EmployeeList, Item, Success)
      END;
    { If Success is false, could not add all records from file }
    IF NOT Success THEN
      writeln ('Warning -- not able to load entire file');
    close (EmployeeFile)
  END; { of PROCEDURE LoadEmployeeList }

PROCEDURE ReadAKey (VAR Name : KeyType);

  {  Given:   Nothing                                                  }
  {  Task:    Read an employee name from standard input                }
  {  Return:  Employee name in Name, with spaces appended in character }
  {           positions beyond end of name.                            }

  VAR
    K, L : integer;

  BEGIN
    K := 0;
    WHILE NOT eoln DO
      BEGIN
        K := K + 1;
        read (Name[K])
      END;
    readln;
    { Pad with spaces from index K + 1 onward }
    FOR L := K + 1 TO NameLength DO
      Name[L] := ' '
  END; { of PROCEDURE ReadAKey }

PROCEDURE AddNewEmployees (VAR EmployeeList : KeyedList);

  {  Given:   List of previous employees                               }
  {  Task:    Add records of new employees to the list                 }
  {  Return:  Original list augmented by new employees.  If no room in }
  {           list for new employee, warn user and quit.               }

  VAR
    Item : ListNode;
    Success : boolean;

  BEGIN
    write ('Enter new employee name (* to quit) ');
    ReadAKey (Item.Key);
    Success := true;
    { Continue adding new employees until * entered or Success returned as false }
    WHILE (Item.Key[1] <> '*') AND Success DO
      BEGIN
        write ('Enter pay rate ');
        readln (Item.OtherData);
        Add (EmployeeList, Item, Success);
        IF Success THEN
```

```
        BEGIN
          write ('Enter employee name (* to quit) ');
          ReadAKey (Item.Key)
        END
      ELSE
        writeln ('Warning -- unable to add this record')
    END
  END; { of PROCEDURE AddNewEmployees }

PROCEDURE PrintPayChecks (EmployeeList : KeyedList);

  { Given:   List of all employee records                              }
  { Task:    Print paycheck for each employee                          }
  { Return:  Employee list unchanged.                                  }

  PROCEDURE PrintOneCheck (VAR Item : ListNode); { Used as procedure para-    }
                                                 { meter to TraverseInOrder   }

  {  Given:   Data on one employee in Item                                    }
  {  Task:    Inquire about that employee's hours worked, and use this        }
  {           information to print paycheck for employee                      }
  {  Return:  Employee's data unchanged.                                      }

    VAR
      HrsWorked : integer;

    BEGIN
      writeln;
      write ('Hours worked for ',Item.Key);
      readln (HrsWorked);
      writeln;
      writeln ('************************************************************')
      writeln ('            FlyByNight Credit Co. Payroll');
      writeln (Item.Key);
      writeln ('Pay is: ', Item.OtherData * HrsWorked : 10 : 2);
      writeln ('************************************************************')
    END; { of PROCEDURE PrintOneCheck }

  BEGIN
    TraverseInOrder (EmployeeList, PrintOneCheck)
  END; { of PROCEDURE PrintPayChecks }

PROCEDURE RemoveEmployees (VAR EmployeeList : KeyedList);

  {  Given:   Keyed list of employee records                                  }
  {  Task:    Determine which records must be removed and delete them         }
  {  Return:  EmployeeList with those records deleted                         }

  VAR
    Target : KeyType;
    Success : boolean;

  BEGIN
    write ('Enter employee name to delete (* to quit) ');
    ReadAKey (Target);
    WHILE Target[1] <> '*' DO
      BEGIN
        Delete (EmployeeList, Target, Success);
        IF NOT Success THEN
          writeln ('Warning -- cannot find ', Target);
        write ('Enter employee name to delete (* to quit) ');
        ReadAKey (Target)
      END
  END; { of PROCEDURE RemoveEmployees }
```

```
PROCEDURE StoreEmployeeList (EmployeeList : KeyedList);

  {  Given:   Keyed list of employee records                                   }
  {  Task:    Write those records, alphabetically, to new employee file         }
  {  Return:  Permanent file with all employee records.                        }

  PROCEDURE StoreOneRecord (VAR Item : ListNode);  { Used as procedure          }
                                                   { parameter to               }
                                                   { TraverseInOrder            }

    {  Given:   One employee record                                            }
    {  Task:    Write those records, alphabetically, to new employee file      }
    {  Return:  Permanent file with all employee records.                      }

    BEGIN
      writeln (NewEmployeeFile, Item.Key, Item.OtherData : 8 : 2)
    END;  { of PROCEDURE StoreOneRecord }

  BEGIN
    rewrite (NewEmployeeFile);
    TraverseInOrder (EmployeeList, StoreOneRecord);
    close (NewEmployeeFile)
  END; { of PROCEDURE StoreEmployeeList }

BEGIN  { main program                                                          }
  Create (EmployeeList);
  LoadEmployeeList (EmployeeList);
  AddNewEmployees (EmployeeList);
  PrintPayChecks (EmployeeList);
  RemoveEmployees (EmployeeList);
  StoreEmployeeList (EmployeeList)
END.

Sample input file:
BENTON,GRACE                 6.92
HARRISON,DAVID               5.98
TAYLOR,EDNA                  7.23

Sample run
Enter new employee name (* to quit) MILLER,JAMES
Enter pay rate 9.10
Enter employee name (* to quit) *

Hours worked for BENTON,GRACE                    40
************************************************************
            FlyByNight Credit Co. Payroll
BENTON,GRACE
Pay is:     276.80
************************************************************

Hours worked for HARRISON,DAVID                  10
************************************************************
            FlyByNight Credit Co. Payroll
HARRISON,DAVID
Pay is:      59.80
************************************************************

Hours worked for MILLER,JAMES                    25
************************************************************
            FlyByNight Credit Co. Payroll
MILLER,JAMES
Pay is:     227.50
************************************************************
```

```
Hours worked for TAYLOR,EDNA                   50
*****************************************************
           FlyByNight Credit Co. Payroll
TAYLOR,EDNA
Pay is:     361.50
*****************************************************
Enter employee name to delete (* to quit) HARRISON,DAVID
Enter employee name to delete (* to quit) *

The new employee file created by this run is

BENTON,GRACE                    6.92
MILLER,JAMES                    9.10
TAYLOR,EDNA                     7.23
```

RUNNING AND DEBUGGING TIPS

When accessing an ADT, be sure that you only use those operations specified in the ADT definition. This is the ADT use rule. For instance, it would be wrong to access a record in a keyed list by referring to its array index. This would be assuming that the implementor of the ADT is storing data in an array. Such an assumption is not warranted according to the definition of this ADT.

When writing the implementation of an ADT, be sure that the procedures and functions you develop obey the interface established by the ADT's definition. This is the ADT implementation rule. For instance, if you, as implementor, need a counter to keep track of the number of records in a keyed list, don't add the counter as an extra parameter in procedure calls. Instead, encapsulate it in a record containing all data items needed for the implementation.

When providing the implementation of an ADT, be sure that each individual operation is thoroughly tested and debugged before it is used by higher level logic. Then if errors occur when higher level modules execute, you can be assured that these errors are the result of the algorithms that use the ADT and are not in the implementation of the ADT.

The importance of the Create operation for an ADT should not be underestimated. From the implementor's perspective, here is where crucial initializations occur that will insure the smooth functioning of other operations. From the prospective of the user of the ADT, you must be sure to call the Create operation for each instance of a variable of that type. Failing to do so will usually lead to very bizarre program behavior.

■ Summary

Key Terms

abstract data type
abstraction
ADT implementation rule
ADT use rule
column major
data abstraction
embedded length implementation
encapsulation principle
implementation
information hiding
interface for an ADT
keyed list
mapping function
packed array implementation
physically ordered array implementation
row major
sparse table
string ADT
two-dimensional table
unordered array implementation
workspace-index method

Key Concepts

- Computer scientists engage in a modeling process as they develop software to satisfy users' needs. In this respect, the way in which a computer scientist works parallels the engineering profession. Consequently, this systematic approach towards the development of successful software is often called software engineering.

- Abstract data types are defined apart from considerations of their implementation in a particular programming language. A complete definition for an abstract data type must include a description of the individual elements, the relationship between these individual elements, and the operations that can be performed upon them. These operations are conveniently specified as procedure and function interfaces.
- The string is an example of an abstract data type. Two implementations for this ADT are the packed array implementation and the embedded length implementation.
- The encapsulation principle, the ADT use rule, and the ADT implementation rule are guidelines governing the relationship between implementations of an ADT and higher level algorithms using that implementation.
- We must often determine which of a variety of implementations is best in terms of time and space efficiency for a particular application.
- Another abstract data type, the two-dimensional table, can consume a large amount of memory.
- When most entries in a two-dimensional table are the same value, the table is said to be sparse. We must often devise implementations for sparse tables that are more space efficient than the row-major implementation used by most Pascal compilers.
- The keyed list is an ADT characterized by operations that add, retrieve, delete, and traverse in order. All of these operations are performed relative to a particular key field.
- A physically ordered array with binary search and an unordered array with pointer sort are two ways of implementing a keyed list.

Programming Problems and Projects

Many of the problems in this chapter require that you write the implementation for an ADT and then use that ADT in a program. It is often interesting to work on such a problem with a classmate. One of you provides the implementation of the ADT; the other writes the higher level algorithm that uses the ADT. If you both obey the ADT use implementation rules, you should be able to work independently of each other and develop an elegant solution to the problem.

In other Problems (5, 6, 7, 10, and 11) you are asked to write an ADT definition as part of your answer to the problem. Your definition should be presented first in formal precondition and postcondition form and then translated into an appropriate Pascal interface. Be sure you are not ambiguous in your presentation of the definition and interface. This aspect of these problems will serve to test the precision with which you write and document.

1. Complete the program in the Focus on Program Design section by providing an implementation of the keyed list ADT.
2. Write a small-scale text editor system by loading lines of text from a file into an array of strings.
   a. Allow the user of your program to appropriately modify the text in this array of strings. These modifications should be performed by accessing the strings in the array only through string ADT operations.
   b. Once the text has been modified, write the array of strings out to a new text file.

c. Test your text editor by using it to create and then modify a modest Pascal program, which you then provide as input to your compiler.

3. Write a program to solve the following problem that is often faced by designers of word processors. Read several lines of text as input. Then print the message with each line starting in column 10 and no line exceeding column 70. No word should be separated at the end of a line. Your program should only access the strings it manipulates by calling on appropriate string ADT operations. Do you need to define any new operations for the string ADT to solve this problem? If so, be sure to document their interfaces very carefully.

4. Write a program to solve the following problem. The transpose of a matrix is a new matrix with the row and column positions reversed. That is, the transpose of matrix A, an M by N matrix, is an N by M matrix B, with each element $A[m,n]$ stored in $B[n,m]$. Given a 3×5 matrix of integers, create a matrix that is its transpose. Print both the original matrix and the new matrix. Your program should access the matrix only through defined operations on the two-dimensional table ADT. Then, provide an implementation of the two-dimensional table other than the standard row-major implementation provided by Pascal. Use this new implementation in your program.

5. Consider a rational number as an abstract data type. (Recall that a rational number is one that can be expressed as the quotient of two integers.) Write a definition for this ADT that includes operations such as

   - Add two rational numbers.
   - Subtract two rational numbers.
   - Multiply two rational numbers.
   - Divide two rational numbers.
   - Reduce a rational number to lowest terms.

   Finally, by using an implementation of your defined ADT, develop a program that will add, subtract, multiply, and divide fractions. Input will consist of a single line representing a fraction arithmetic problem as follows:

   integer/integer operation integer/integer

   For example, a line of input might be

   ```
   2/3 + 1/2
   ```

   Your program should
   a. check for division by zero.
   b. check for proper operation symbols.
   c. print the problem in its original form.
   d. print the answer reduced to lowest terms.
   e. print all fractions in vertical form.

   For the sample input

   ```
   2/3 + 1/2
   ```

   sample output is

   ```
   2   1   7
   - + - = -
   3   2   6
   ```

Be sure that you access the fractions manipulated in that program only by provided ADT operations.

6. Begin this problem by providing a definition of a complex number as an abstract data type. Recall that complex numbers are numbers of the form $a + bi$ where a and b are real and i represents $\sqrt{-1}$. Complex number arithmetic is defined by

Sum	$(a + bi) + (c + di) = (a + c) + (b + d)i$
Difference	$(a + bi) - (c + di) = (a - c) + (b - d)i$
Product	$(a + bi)(c + di) = (ac - bd) + (ad + bc)i$
Quotient	$(a + bi)/(c + di) = \frac{ac+bd}{c^2+d^2} + \frac{bc-ad}{c^2+d^2}i$

Next provide an implementation for your definition of the complex number ADT. Finally, use your implementation to write a main program to perform calculations on two complex numbers. Each line of data consists of a single character designator (S, D, P, or Q) followed by four reals representing two complex numbers. For example, $(2 + 3i) + (5 - 2i)$ is represented by

```
S2 3 5 -2
```

The output should be in the form $a + bi$.

Be sure that you access the complex number ADT only through the provided operations.

7. If you are now familiar with the notion of a set from your previous work in mathematics, formalize the definition of a set as an abstract data type. Be sure to minimally include the following operations in your definition:

- Given a value V and a set S, determine whether or not V is **IN** S.
- Given two sets S_1 and S_2, determine whether or not S_1 is equal to S_2.
- Given two sets S_1 and S_2, determine whether or not S_1 is a subset of S_2.
- Given a value V and a set S, add the value V to the set S.
- Given a value V and a set S, remove the value V from the set S.
- Given two sets S_1 and S_2, return their set intersection.
- Given two sets S_1 and S_2, return their set difference.
- Given two sets S_1 and S_2, return their union.

Pascal offers its users a predefined set type. Browse in your local reference material and find out how your version of Pascal implements sets. What are the limitations of this particular implementation? Give some examples of applications where this compiler-provided implementation would be insufficient. Develop your own implementation for the set ADT that you have defined.

One idea for such an implementation is to use a Boolean array indexed by the values that could be in a set. Then you can determine whether or not a value X is in a set by examining the Boolean value stored in index position X of the associated array. If this Boolean value is **true**, view X as being in the set. Otherwise X is not considered a member of the set.

Finally, use your implementation of sets in a program to solve the following problem. Typists often complain that the standard QWERTY keyboard

Q W E R T Y U I O P
A S D F G H J K L ;
Z X C V B N M , . /
space bar

is not efficient. As you can see, many frequently used letters (E, T, N, R, and I) are not on the middle row. A new keyboard, the Maltron keyboard, has been proposed. Its design is

Q P Y C B V M U Z L
A N I S F E D T H O R ; : .
J G W K X
space bar

Your program should analyze a text file to see how many jumps are required by each keyboard. For purposes of this program, a jump will be any valid symbol not on the middle row. Output should include the number of valid symbols read and the number of jumps for each keyboard.

Be sure that your program obeys the ADT use rule.

8. Invented by mathematician John H. Conway (*Scientific American,* October 1970, p. 120), The Game of Life models the growth and changes in a complex collection of living organisms. The model can be interpreted as applying to a collection of microorganisms, an ecologically closed system of animals or plants, or an urban development.

Start with a checkerboard of size N by N on which "markers" are to be placed. Each location that is not on a border has eight neighbors. The markers are born, survive, or die during a "generation" according to the following rules:

- *Survival:* Markers with two or three neighboring markers survive to the next generation.
- *Death:* Markers with four or more neighbors die from overcrowding and are removed for the next generation. Markers with zero or one neighbors die from isolation and are removed for the next generation.
- *Birth:* Each empty location that has exactly three markers in the eight neighboring locations is a birth location. A marker is placed in the location for the next generation.

For example, on a 6 × 6 space the following pattern

		X			
	X	X			
				X	
	X			X	

would look as follows in the next generation:

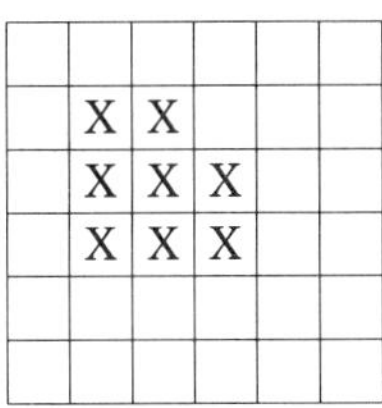

Certain patterns are stable; for example,

Other patterns repeat a sequence:

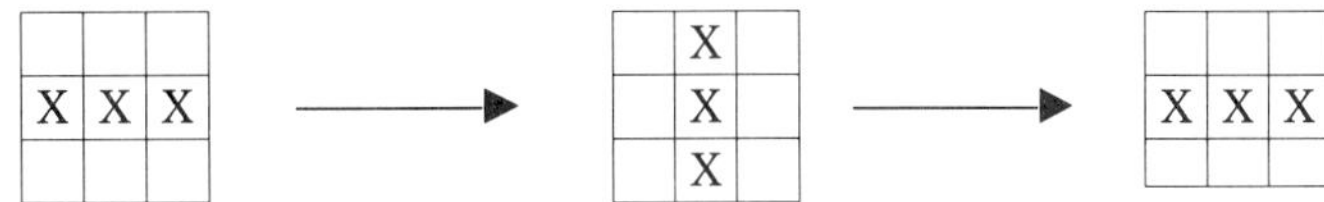

Because, conceptually, two N × N matrices are required to implement The Game of Life, it is clear that memory limitations could easily become a problem for a large N.

After initializing the first generation, print it out. Then calculate the next generation in another array and print this too. Repeat for a specified number of generations. Your output should be an "X" for live cells and a blank otherwise.

Develop the high-level logic of your program by employing the fundamental Assign/Retrieve operations for matrices. First use your compiler's implementation of these operations. Then, switch to the implementation of sparse matrices described in Section 2.3. Your high-level logic should not need to change at all. In a written statement, describe the performance differences you observe with these two implementations. Explain why these differences occur.

9. Though the packed array and embedded length method for strings are very easy to implement, they lead to two potential problems. First, what about the string longer than MaxStringLength characters? These methods simply cannot accommodate such a string. Second, since most strings will be considerably shorter than MaxStringLength characters, these methods will waste a sizable amount of memory. This memory waste is shown in Figure 2.13.

FIGURE 2.13
Memory wasted by fixed length implementations of string

1 2 3 4 5 6 7 8 9 . . . 39 40 = MaxStringLength

S M I T H J O E

Approximately 75 percent wasted

We'll look at another possible implementation for strings in the next chapter when we discuss linked lists. The alternate implementation method we propose here is known as the *workspace-index method.* The idea behind the workspace-index method is that one large memory workspace is allocated to storing all strings. Additionally an index table of records with two fields for each string is maintained. One field in the record for a string contains the address in the workspace at which that particular string starts, and the other contains the length of each string. This principle is illustrated in Figure 2.14.

FIGURE 2.14
Workspace-index method of handling strings

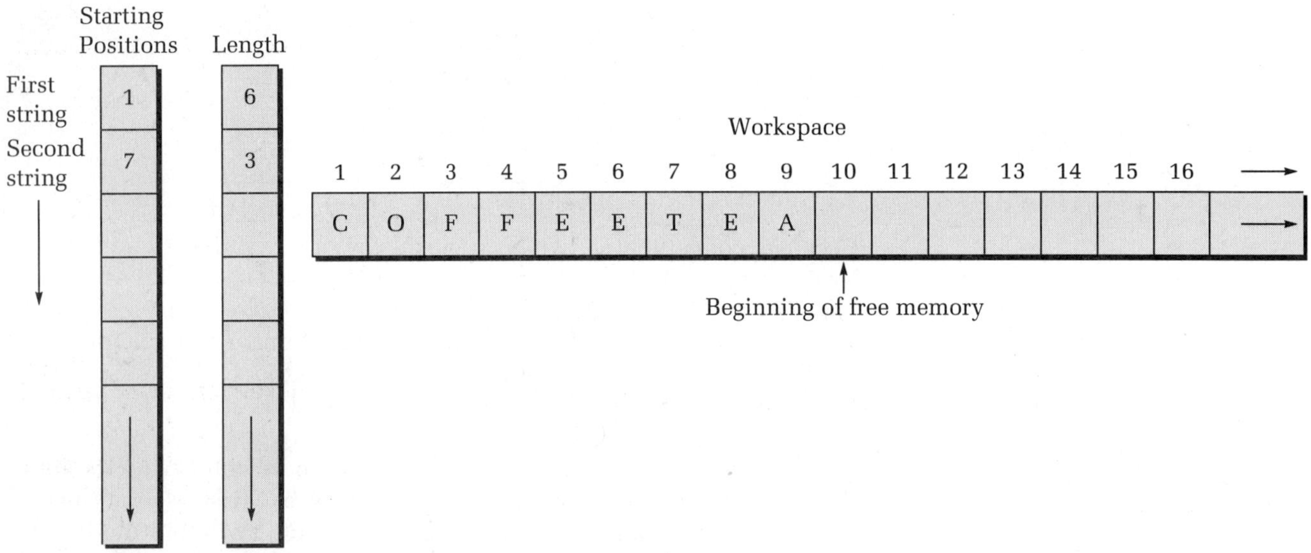

Suppose now that we were to add a third string to the collection in Figure 2.14. All that we need to know is where the free portion of the workspace begins (in this case it begins at location 10). We place the string starting at that location, add appropriate entries to our index table, and adjust the pointer to the beginning of the free memory. This threefold process is illustrated in Figure 2.15 for the addition of the string 'CREAM'.

The storage advantages of the workspace-index method should be evident. By associating two indexing integers with each string, we are trading off the storage required for two integers against the potentially large number of wasted characters that pad strings in the fixed length method. Moreover, the only restraint on maximum string length is the amount of storage left in the workspace.

Begin your work on this problem by a workspace-index implementation of all string operations. Then, plug this new implementation into a program like the high-level text editor you developed for Problem 2.

10. The radix sort algorithm, presented in Section 1.4, uses the notion of bins: data repositories that contain numbers or strings in a particular category as the algorithm progresses. Formalize the concept of a bin for the radix sort algorithm by providing an ADT definition for it.

FIGURE 2.15
String 'CREAM' added to workspace-index storage of Figure 2.14

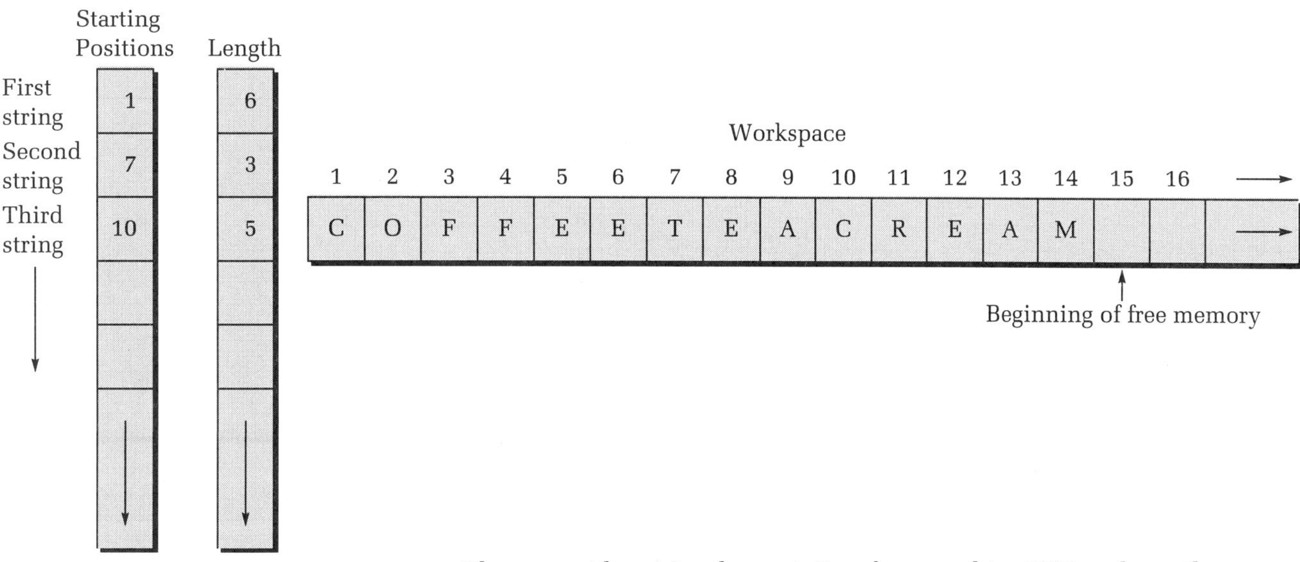

Then provide an implementation for your bin ADT and use the operations provided by the bin ADT to write a high-level version of radix sort.

11. The definition of the keyed list ADT in Section 2.4 specifies that each record in the list must have a unique key value, that is, a key value shared by no other value in the list. Consider a variation on this ADT in which we allow multiple records to share the same key value (for example, several people may have identical names). Call this ADT a keyed list with duplicate keys.
    a. Provide a complete definition for this ADT. Be very precise about what happens for each of the Add, Delete, Retrieve, and Traverse-InOrder operations. Do you need to add any new operations because of the possibility of duplicate keys?
    b. Translate your definition from Part **a** into a Pascal interface for a keyed list with duplicate keys.
    c. Develop an implementation for this ADT. Discuss in a written statement any limitations of your implementation relative to the definition and interface of Parts **a** and **b.**
    d. Test your implementation by plugging it into a program like that of this chapter's Focus on Program Design section. In a program such as this one, how can you distinguish between employees who have the same name?

Before working Problems 12 and 13, reread the Note of Interest on Sparse Tables and Language Compilers in Section 2.3.

12. Write a program that will appropriately recognize a month from an input stream of characters. Implement that sparse two-dimensional table as a Pascal function that uses **CASE** and/or **IF . . . THEN . . . ELSE** statements. This function should receive a current state and a character and return the next state given by that table.

13. (This problem is especially appropriate for a class of 15 or more students.) Write a program that appropriately recognizes a first name of a member of your computer science class.

    Use the following strategy. Obtain a list of first names of all class members; discard any duplicates from this list. Then develop a two-dimensional table analogous to the table developed for month names in the Note of Interest. The same algorithm (used to recognize month names in the Note of Interest section) may now be used to recognize names from members of your class. Implement the sparse two-dimensional table needed for this algorithm as a Pascal function that uses **CASE** and/or **IF . . . THEN . . . ELSE** statements. This function should receive a current state and a character and return the next state given by the table.

I believe in Michelangelo, Velázquez, and Rembrandt; in the might of design.
George Bernard Shaw
(1856–1950)

Software Engineering and the System Life Cycle

In Chapter 2 we reviewed briefly a philosophy of software design called software engineering. This philosophy emphasizes an evolutionary progression from the building of a conceptual model of the system to the eventual implementation of that model in a programming language such as Pascal. At the heart of this progression lies the abstract data type as a means of conceptualizing the data needs of the system before considering how those needs are to be implemented.

In Chapter 1, we described some relatively simple algorithms to perform operations on arrays and illustrated how to evaluate such algorithms using big-O notation. The purpose of this description was twofold. First, as software designers, we need to be aware of the variety of algorithms available to perform a particular task such as sorting or searching. Chapter 1 began to equip us with this knowledge in a systematic, organized fashion. Second, along with an understanding of various algorithms, we must be able to evaluate and select the best of all possible algorithms for a particular application. Big-O analysis provides us with a guide for such evaluation and selection.

It is now time to put these methods into the context of large-scale systems development. In so doing, we will describe a series of phases known as the software system life cycle. As we walk through these phases, we hope you begin to appreciate the enormous complexity involved in the development of successful software systems. It is not uncommon that a problem which appears simple spawns a variety of complications. Handling such complications in a graceful and efficient fashion is an essential ingredient to succeeding in computer science.

In Section 3.1, we examine the initial analysis phase of the system life cycle. This phase is followed by the design and implementation phases, as described in Section 3.2. Section 3.3 treats the testing, maintenance, and obsolescence stages. Section 3.4 touches upon the pragmatic issues of file processing. We examine its importance in certain types of software systems and discuss the inadequacies of standard Pascal for such systems.

Sections 3.5 and 3.6 provide a brief glimpse of some future directions in software engineering. In Section 3.5, we discuss formal verification as an alternative to testing. In Section 3.6, we investigate a programming paradigm called *object-oriented programming.*

■ 3.1 The Analysis Phase of the System Life Cycle

OBJECTIVES

- to understand what is done during the analysis phase of systems development
- to be able to define the responsibilities of a systems analyst
- to gain additional familiarity with the use of data flow diagrams as a tool for modeling user needs
- to recognize the importance of oral and written communication skills in the analysis phase

It has been said that the only simple problems in computing are those defined in textbooks. Perhaps a key to the truth of this statement is its use of the word *defined.* Once a problem is specifically defined, the most difficult obstacle to solving that problem effectively may well have been surmounted. In the analysis phase you must define in detail the problem that you are charged with solving.

It is important to remember that in trying to provide such a definition, you are typically working with a problem originally posed by someone other than yourself. We have tried to emphasize this fact in the preceding chapter by introducing problems in the form of memoranda from computer users. This is done to emphasize that programs are written not for computer scientists but for computer users, users who often know virtually nothing about the computer other than a vague (and often inaccurate) notion that it can magically take care of all of their recordkeeping and computational needs. Bridging the gap between potentially naive users and the computer-oriented people who eventually are responsible for implementing the software system constitutes the first phase of the system life cycle.

Though many people are aware that *systems analysts* work with computers in some way, few know specifically what a systems analyst does. More than anything else, the systems analyst is responsible for the *analysis* phase of the system life cycle. A systems analyst talks to the users who initally request the system to learn exactly what these users need. This is done not only by talking to users, but also by studying in detail what these users do. For instance, a systems analyst working for a bank on an automated teller system would have to become an expert on the various duties and responsibilities of a teller. Having learned what the automated system is supposed to do, the systems analyst must then develop formal specifications describing the system and its requirements. The technical people who design and code the software will work from these specifications.

FIGURE 3.1
Data flow diagram for payroll department

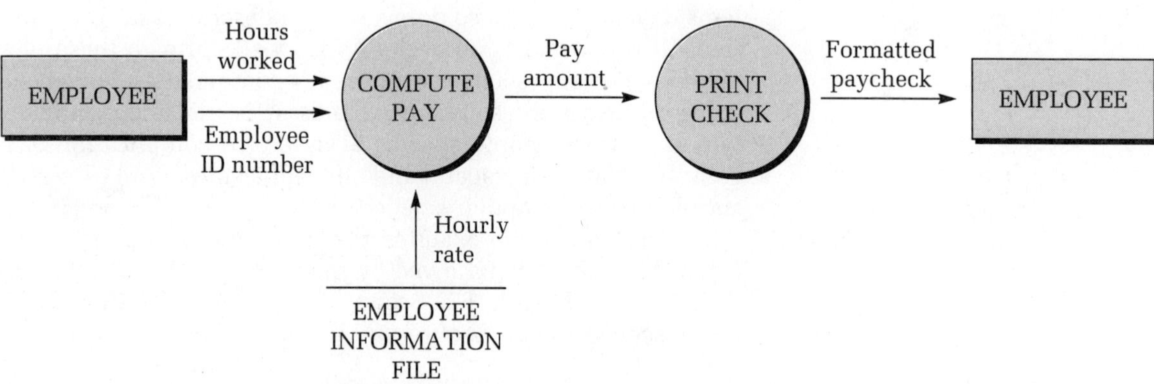

Using Data Flow Diagrams

A *data flow diagram* is a graphic specification technique often used by systems analysts to provide a clear picture of a user's requirements. On the surface, a data flow diagram could be viewed as a collection of circular "bubbles" joined together by strings. (In fact, data flow diagrams are sometimes referred to as bubble diagrams.) The strings connecting the bubbles are officially called data flows and are named in a way that reflects the information they carry. The circular bubbles represent processes that transform incoming data flows into outgoing data flows, which may in turn be acted upon by another process.

Figure 3.1 depicts a portion of a data flow diagram that describes how a payroll department might operate. Rectangular boxes in a data flow diagram indicate initial sources and final destinations of data flows. In Figure 3.1, the EMPLOYEE is both an initial source (of hours worked and ID number) and a final destination (of a formatted paycheck). Parallel lines highlight a data base that must be accessed to do the required processing. For instance, in Figure 3.1, the hourly rate must be retrieved from the EMPLOYEE INFORMATION FILE by the COMPUTE PAY process.

EXAMPLE 3.1

You receive the following memorandum from the registrar at the University of Hard Knocks. In it she requests the automation of the university's recordkeeping on its students. Provide a data flow diagram to depict the information processing done by the registrar.

MEMORANDUM
University of Hard Knocks

TO: Director of Data Processing
FROM: Head Registrar
DATE: July 29, 1995
RE: Automation of recordkeeping on students

As you know, we presently maintain our student records by manual methods. We believe the time has come to computerize this operation and request that you do so for us.

Here is what we need. Each student's record consists of his or her name, the number of credits that student has taken, the number of credits earned, and the total grade points for that student. We maintain these records by student's last name. Of course, at numerous times, we must add new students to our records and remove those who have graduated or withdrawn from school. Students often come into our office and request to see their current record, so we must be able to quickly find that information. At the end of each semester we print a grade report for each student. This report consists of the four items cited plus the student's GPA. At the end of the year, the Dean of Students requests two lists of graduating seniors. One of these lists is to be printed in alphabetical order by student name. The other is printed in order by student grade point average.

Certainly the situation described in this memo is an oversimplification of any real college registrar's office. However, even this relatively unsophisticated situation can offer us some interesting food for thought. For one thing, the memo demonstrates the fact that your first contact with a user requesting the system will often leave gaps in your knowledge about the system she wants. The head registrar's memo leaves unanswered the following questions.

1. What is the university's definition of grade points?
2. When grade reports are printed for each student, is it important that they be printed in any particular order?
3. Since grade reports are printed at the end of each semester, do you need some means of updating a student's record at the end of a semester?
4. What is the method used to compute a student's GPA?
5. What separates seniors who graduate from those seniors who don't graduate?
6. Is the list printed in order by student GPA arranged from best student to worst student or vice versa?

You would have to communicate those questions to the registrar before the specifics of the system could be modeled in a data flow diagram. Suppose that you do that and receive the following reply.

MEMORANDUM
University of Hard Knocks

TO: Director of Data Processing
FROM: Head Registrar
DATE: August 2, 1995
RE : Responses to your questions

Question 1: Four grade points are assigned for a one-credit A grade, three for a B, two for a C, one for a D, and zero for an F. Courses worth more than one credit have their corresponding grade points multiplied accordingly.

Question 2: Grade reports should be printed in alphabetical order by student last name.

Question 3: At the end of each semester, faculty turn in grades for each class they teach. We use the grades on these class rosters to update a student's academic information before printing a grade report.

Question 4: GPA is computed as the quotient of total grade points divided by credits taken.

Question 5: A graduating senior must have earned at least 120 credits.

Question 6: The list is to be printed from best student to worst student.

This sort of diaglogue with the registrar allows you, a systems analyst, to generate the data flow diagram in Figure 3.2. In this figure, the process PrintGradeReport transforms a student academic record into an appropri-

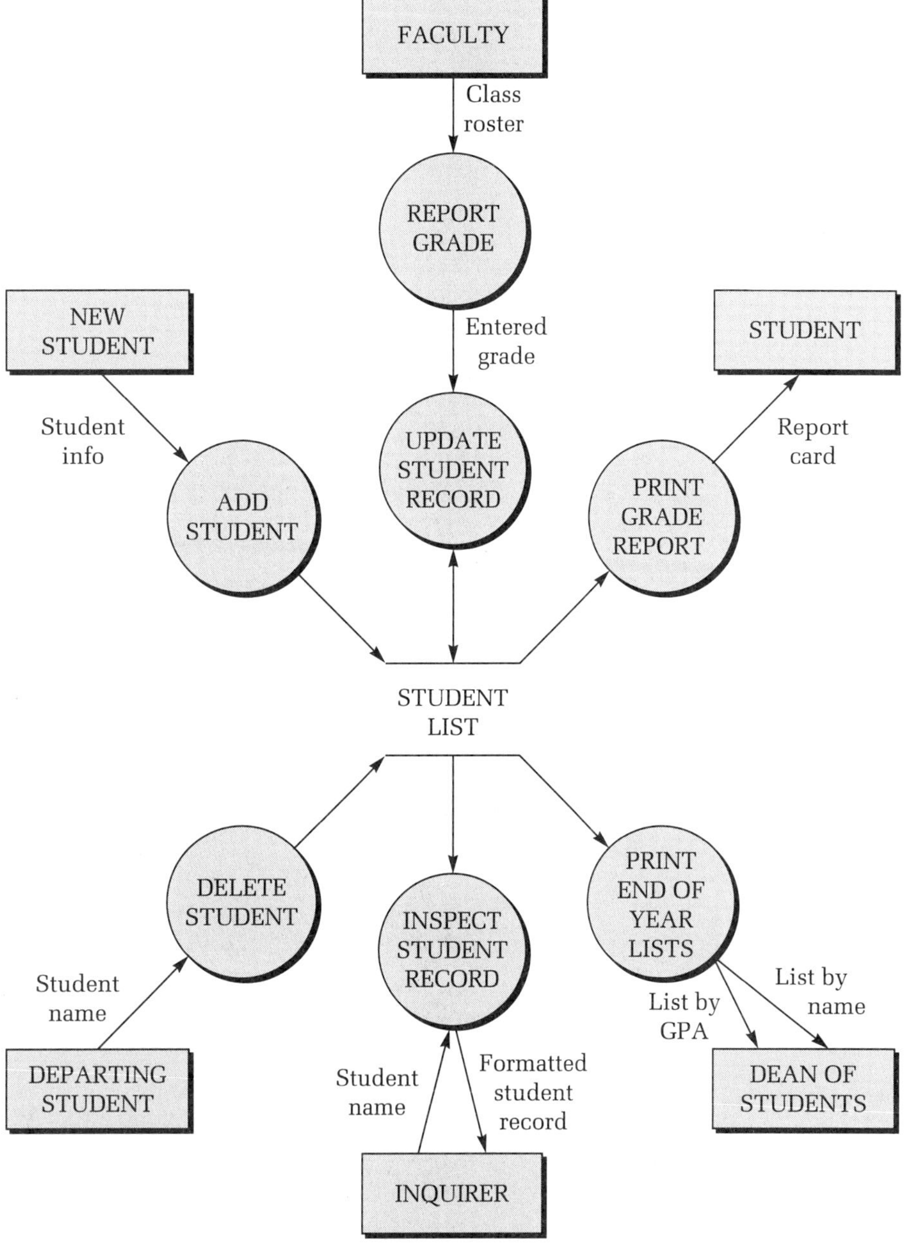

FIGURE 3.2
Data flow diagram of information to be processed in registrar's system

ately formatted report card. Similarly, the process ChangeStudent transforms newly reported grades for a student into an appropriately updated student record in the StudentList data base.

Perfecting the Model

The role of the data flow diagram in the various phases of modeling that occur in the development of a system is to provide an initial overview of the fashion in which a user processes information. Data flow diagrams for a system would be developed before any decisions are made regarding the modular structure and abstract data types upon which the eventual program will be based. In this sense, they represent the first step in the progression of structured techniques used to insure that a software system adequately meets the needs of its end users.

For more complex systems, data flow diagrams such as that appearing in Figure 17.2 may have to be refined into a collection of more detailed subordinate diagrams. Additionally, the systems analyst may have to provide written specifications for each process represented in the diagram. A more detailed discussion of these aspects of the analysis phase may be found in *Modern Structured Analysis* by Edward Yourdon (Englewood Cliffs, N.J.: Prentice-Hall, 1989).

The systems analyst serves as a liaison and translator between the users and the implementors of the system. Depending on the size and structure of the organization, the systems analyst may or may not become involved in the design and coding of the system. Typically, such involvement will occur in smaller organizations where the analyst may wear many hats, but not in larger organizations where staff sizes allow a greater degree of specialization.

Since an exact assessment of the end user's needs is vital for the most satisfactory design of the system, the systems analyst must have excellent interpersonal communication skills as well as a strong computer background.

It is beyond the scope of this text to present any detailed treatment of systems analysis strategies. Instead, we will occasionally present specifications for programs in the form of memoranda from hypothetical users. These memoranda will serve as realistic reminders of the role of the user in the software development process. Yet they will be simplistic enough to avoid the massive headaches often connected with the analysis phase of a project. Instead, we will concentrate on the next phases of the software system life cycle.

Exercises 3.1

1. Consider the memorandum from Wing-and-a-Prayer's vice president in charge of scheduling (see Section 2.3). Draw a data flow diagram to model the information processing that it describes.

2. Draw a data flow diagram to model the information processing activities that you do each month in maintaining your checking account at a local bank.

3. BugFree Incorporated sells software for personal computers. Most orders that BugFree receives come from subscribers to computer magazines who respond to BugFree's advertisement by filling out forms in the ads and then mailing them to the company. BugFree also uses a toll-free phone number to accept orders, answer inquiries, and handle payments and cancellations of orders. Software ordered from BugFree is either sent directly to the customer or to local computer stores, which then distribute the product to the customer. This rapidly expanding business must keep records on its customers, product inventory, and billing information. Draw a data flow diagram to depict the flow of information at BugFree.

4. Develop a data flow diagram to depict the flow of information described in the memorandum that accompanied the Focus on Program Design section in Chapter 2.

5. For this task, you'll work with another student. Each of you should develop a memorandum to specify what you view as the information-processing needs of an administrative office at your school (or any other office environment with which you may be familiar). Your memorandum should provide information

similar to that provided by the registrar at the University of Hard Knocks (see Example 3.1).

Exchange your memoranda and draw a data flow diagram to model the activity described in the other person's memo. Then get together with the other person to resolve any questions you might have and to critique the accuracy and completeness of the other's data flow diagram.

6. Consider the following memorandum from the registrar at the renowned American Basket Weaving University—one of the main competitors of the University of Hard Knocks.

MEMORANDUM
American Basket Weaving University

TO: Director of Data Processing
FROM: Head Registrar
DATE: July 29, 1996
RE: Automation of record keeping on students

Records for students at our school consist of a University identification number, a last name, a first name, a middle initial, a Social Security number, a list of courses the student has taken along with the grade received in each course, and a list of extracurricular activities in which the student has indicated an interest. A university identification number for a student consists of a six-digit number: the first two digits represent the year a student entered the university. The remaining four digits are simply assigned on a sequential basis as students are admitted to the school. For instance, the student with ID number 930023 is the 23rd student admitted in the class that entered A.B.W.U. in 1993.

Given this data base, we frequently need to work with it in the following ways:

- Find and display all data for a particular student, as identified by university ID number.
- Add and delete student records from the data base.
- Print records for all students in Social Security number order, starting with the most recent class and working backwards.
- Add, change, or delete the information on a course for a particular student. For instance, change the grade received by student 930023 in CompSci2 from C to B.
- Find all students with an extracurricular interest that matches a particular target interest. Students' extracurricular interests are viewed as arbitrarily long strings. These strings are entered into our records directly from information provided by students on their registration forms. For instance, a given student may have indicated PLAYING BASKETBALL and GOING TO PLAYS as her two interests. We would want to be able to find this student (as well as students who indicated an interest such as WATCHING BASKETBALL or SHOOTING BASKETBALLS) if we were to search our data base for students who had an interest matching BASKETBALL.

Develop a data flow diagram to model the information processing that occurs in the registrar's office at A.B.W.U.

7. Write an essay in which you defend or attack the following position: To prepare for a career as a systems analyst, it is more important to develop interpersonal communication skills than it is to acquire a mass of technical knowledge about specific computer systems.

3.2 The Design and Implementation Phases of the System Life Cycle

OBJECTIVES

- to understand the responsibilities of the design phase of the software system life cycle
- to see the relationship between the analysis and design phases
- to reiterate the importance of modular structure charts as a design tool
- to understand what is meant by top-down design (as opposed to bottom-up design)
- to develop criteria that separate good designs (and their modular structure charts) from poor ones
- to see how a data flow diagram from the analysis phase may be transformed into a modular structure chart for the design phase
- to realize that writing code in a programming language represents only a small part of the overall implementation of a system
- to realize the importance of the role played by documentation in the implementation of a system

Given specifications for the user's requirements, the next phase in the system's development is the construction of a relatively detailed design plan. This will guide future work on the implementation of the system. Note that, during the design phase, emphasis switches from understanding and specifying user needs to specifying how we will develop a software system to meet those needs. As such, we begin to consider, from a technical perspective, the data structures that will be needed to process information in the system. This processing of information must be achieved in a fashion consistent with the data flow diagrams and other documents produced during the analysis phase.

Design

The key feature of design plan is that it must effectively divide the overall problem into a collection of smaller, more manageable problems. Each of these smaller units will be handled by a separate program module in the implementation phase. These modules should be tested, verified, and debugged individually before being integrated into the entire system.

We can draw certain analogies between this modular structuring of a program and the boss-worker relationships that typically exist in any large corporation. Just as any effective boss must be able to delegate responsibilities, program modules that control the major logical decisions in a software system must be able to rely on lower level modules to reliably preform subordinate tasks.

Modular structure charts, which we have been using throughout this text, represent one of the most important graphic tools used by software designers to reflect the relationships between the modules comprising the entire software system. Given a comprehensive data flow diagram from the analysis phase, the software designer can transform this into an initial structure chart by roughly equating each process in the data flow diagram with a module in the structure chart (see Figure 3.3). This initial structure chart can then be refined into a more detailed design by establishing hierarchical relationships between modules and by adding lower level modules.

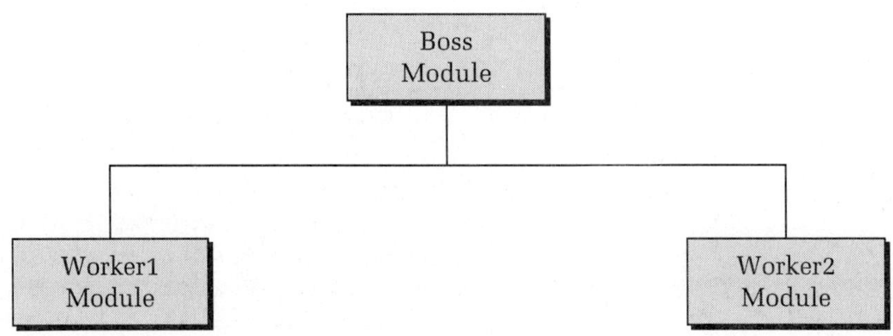

FIGURE 3.3
Modular structure chart for three-module system

What distinguishes a good modular structure from a poor one? To answer this question we may again draw some apt comparisons between software structure and corporate boss-worker relationships. First, we note that such a structure should be developed in a *top-down* fashion. The overriding principle of top-down design is that we make decisions about the responsibilities of top-level bosses before deciding what the lower-level workers are to do. If such decisions are made in a way which progresses downward on a level-by-level basis in the structure chart, we find that boss modules truly will control the major logic of a program, just as corporate bosses should be in control of the most important aspects of their company's policy.

To proceed in an opposite, bottom-up fashion is to court organizational disaster. That is, if we decide what worker modules are to do before considering the responsibilities of boss modules, we frequently run into situations where a boss module is forced into some very clumsy program logic. By proceeding bottom-up, we are not able to see the full range of subordinate tasks that a boss may require. The end result is that the boss will have to take care of minor details—a situation comparable to a corporate executive's having to momentarily leave his or her desk to go out on the assembly line and fasten a bolt that everyone else had forgotten. Such distraction can only result in the boss's doing a poorer job in more important areas of responsibility.

A second criterion to be used in judging the modular structure of a system is the degree to which individual modules are *functionally cohesive.* That is, each module should focus on achieving one particular predefined task without having unexpected side effects on the performance of other modules in the same system. For instance, a module responsible for formatting an output line in a report should not also be updating a field within a customer's record. This could potentially cause great confusion for the module whose assigned task was to guarantee updating of the entire customer record. Thus, as a system designer, you must insure that you break down the system into its component modules following the "natural" lines of decomposition. The case studies presented in our Focus on Program Design sections will help you develop a feel for what such natural lines are. This talent will be further honed as you take more advanced courses in software engineering.

A third criterion used to evaluate the modular structure of a system is the way in which the modules within the system interact with each other. This interface between a pair of modules is often referred to as *coupling.* In drawing modular structure charts, we have used unlabeled arrows to indicate whether a given module receives data from its calling module, returns information to its calling module, or both. These data flow arrows have thus given some sense of the coupling between two modules.

Ideally, a given module in a system works independently of the others. Yet we can never attain this ideal because modules must interact with each other in any meaningful system. Hence the goal is to hold this interaction to a minimum. That is, there should be no more coupling between modules than necessary to allow them to perform their respective tasks within the framework of the overall system.

Consider the following example of a situation in which an excess of coupling could exist between two modules. Suppose we have a module to update a customer record for a business. One of the tasks subordinate to updating this record is to read new transactions in which the customer has taken part and update the balance owed field within the customer record. Schematically, the relationship between these two modules is given in Figure 3.4.

The coupling question that arises from this figure is: How do the data flow arrows between the modules UpdateCustomerRecord and UpdateBalanceOwed eventually resolve themselves as parameters? One possibility would

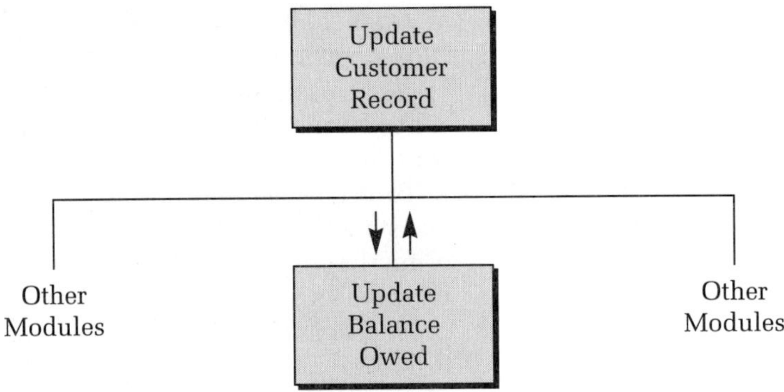

FIGURE 3.4
Portion of modular structure chart for coupling example

be for UpdateCustomerRecord to pass the entire customer record to UpdateBalanceOwed as a **VAR** parameter. A second possibility is for UpdateCustomerRecord to merely pass the balance owed field within the customer record to UpdateBalanceOwed. From a data coupling perspective, the second alternative is much better. In the first alternative, more coupling than necessary exists between the modules because UpdateBalanceOwed is given access to more than it requires to do its specific task. A careless error in UpdateBalanceOwed could inadvertently alter another field such as an address or name within the customer record. Hence, the UpdateBalanceOwed module could have erroneous side effects which might corrupt the entire system. The second alternative, on the other hand, completely eliminates the chance of this happening by simply not allowing UpdateBalanceOwed to access fields it does not specifically need. Thus, minimizing coupling has guarded the system against any inadvertent side effects of a low-level module.

Having generated a structure chart in which modules are functionally cohesive and minimally coupled, the designer must then describe the general data structures to be manipulated by the system and the logic to be followed by each module. In an ideal world, the former could be done simply by specifying the abstract data types that the system will need. This ideal situation occurred in the Focus on Program Design section of Chapter 2. There we had a payroll application for which the keyed list ADT provided a perfect fit.

In more complex situations, an ADT may provide only a starting point in describing the data structures required by the system. For example, we may need the operations provided by the keyed list ADT plus a few more operations that are not included in the ADT's definition. This situation occurs in the registrar's system we analyzed in Example 3.1. This application requires everything offered by the keyed list ADT plus:

- The ability to alter a record that already exists in the list
- The ability to traverse the list in decreasing GPA order as well as alphabetically by name

Because applications frequently require variations upon off-the-shelf ADTs, it is not inappropriate for the designer to give some indication of how such variations might be accomplished. This is illustrated in the following example.

EXAMPLE 3.2

Design a modular structure chart along with the data structures for the registrar's system analyzed in Example 3.1.

As a designer presented with a data flow diagram from the analysis phase (Figure 3.2), your task is to transform it into an appropriate modular structure chart for the system. To a certain extent, the processes specified in the data flow diagram have already provided an initial breakdown of the problem facing the registrar. This initial breakdown can be represented in what is frequently called a first-cut (or first-level) structure chart, an early, relatively rough modular structure for a system. It's called first-cut because we intend to modify and expand upon its structure as we go through a stepwise refinement of the system's design.

The first-cut structure chart for the registrar's system is presented in Figure 3.5.

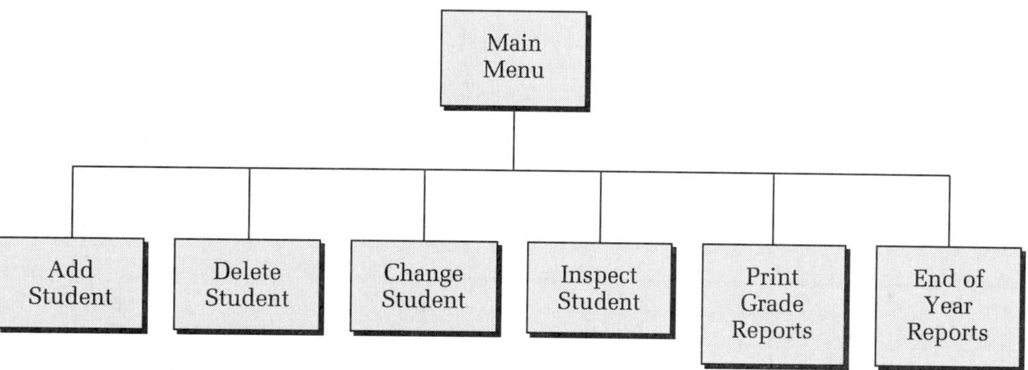

FIGURE 3.5
First-cut structure chart for registrar's system

Transforming this first-cut structure chart into a final modular structure that completely specifies the system's design will require careful consideration of such issues as the user interface presented by our program and the implementation of data structures needed by the system. First, we want our top-level program to interact with users through a menu of choices. We want the user to be able to select a particular operation; the program should then dispatch processing to the appropriate subordinate module. Hence, we will need a GetSelection module assigned the task of handling this interface between the user and the menu of choices. Second, we must begin to consider the pertinent data structures, their implementation, and the subordinate modules necessary to access these data structures.

For the registrar's system, the crucial data structure is the keyed list of student records. As we have already indicated, the keyed list used in this system must be extended to allow for changes to records and traversing in GPA order. In this design of the registrar's system, we will use an array implementation of the list. We will maintain the array in physical order using student name as a key, hence allowing a binary search of the list when we wish to inspect a student by name. We therefore need to add the following modules to the system's design:

- A FindStudent module to implement the binary search so that records can be inspected, changed, and deleted.
- A FindSlot module to determine the position where a new student record will be added.
- Modules to produce formatted lists in name order and GPA order. Since the list is being maintained in name order, producing a list in GPA order will require a subordinate sorting algorithm. The pointer sort algorithm discussed in Section 1.4 will be ideal for this GPA sort since it will not disturb the physical order of the records.

With these considerations taken into account, a refined structure chart emerges. This final structure chart (Figure 3.6) now provides us with a detailed blueprint of the system's design.

FIGURE 3.6
Modular structure for registrar's system

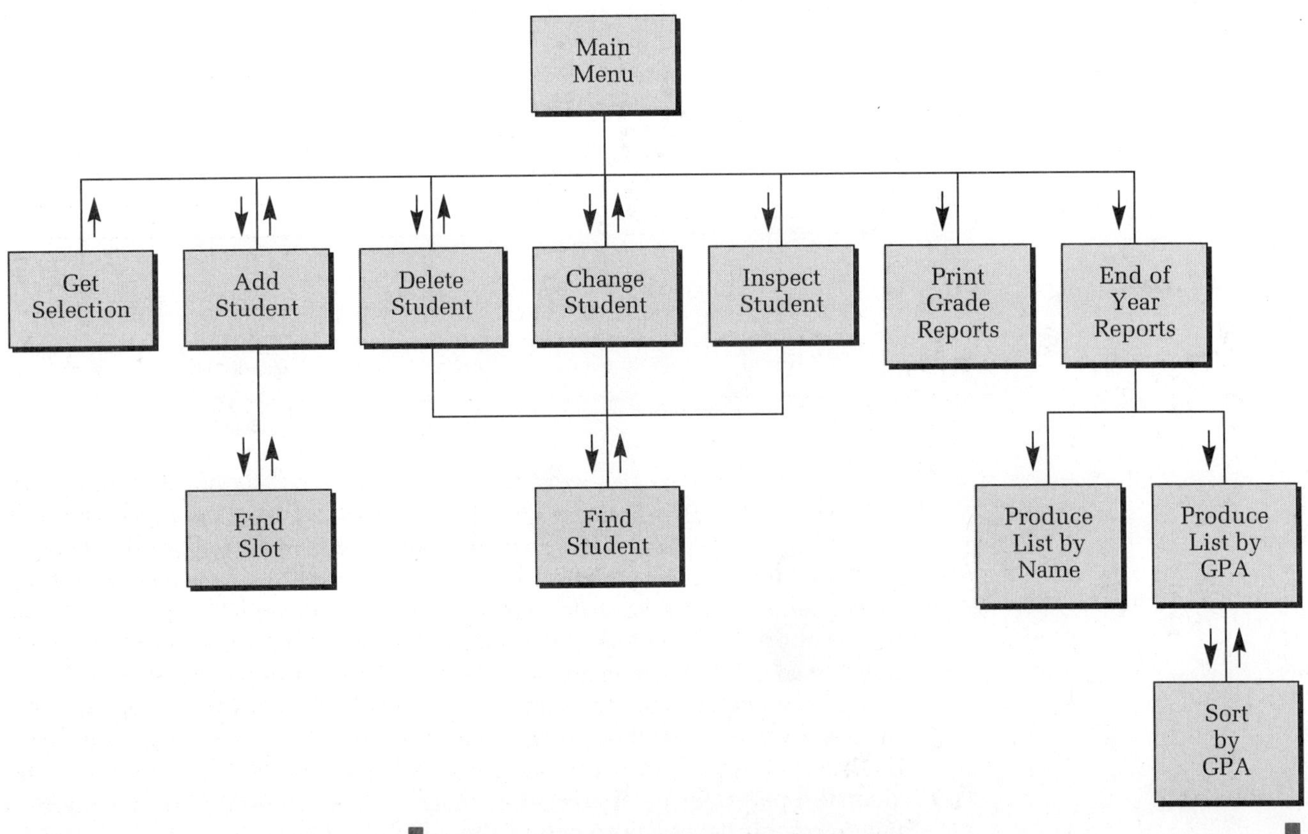

Two comments are in order regarding the design that evolved in Example 3.2. First, what are the ramifications of our having to extend the notion of a keyed list by adding ChangeStudent and SortByGPA operations? Conceptually, this is a fairly simple extension. However, from a coding perspective, it means that we will not be able to plug directly into a provided implementation of the keyed list ADT. Instead, we will have to tinker with the code of such an implementation, in effect reinventing and then extending the wheel.

This will be a nuisance, but it is a nuisance necessitated by Pascal language syntax—not by any flaw in the design process. A newer class of languages, called object-oriented languages, offer features that make it much easier for programmers to extend ADTs to meet the needs of a particular implementation. We will briefly discuss object-oriented languages in Section 3.6.

Second, in Example 3.2, we made the design decision that we would maintain an array in physical order by student name to allow use of the binary search algorithm when a particular student's record is being retrieved. Like many design decisions, this carries with it a trade-off. The price we will pay for being able to use the binary search algorithm in the InspectStudent module will be a potentially excessive amount of data movement in the AddStudent and DeleteStudent modules. To see why this excessive data movement will occur, consider the add situation pictured in Figure 3.7.

FIGURE 3.7
Possible add situation for array implementation of student list

To be inserted: BAKER FRANK → (between 1 and 2)

	Name	Other Fields
1	ALLEN ELIZABETH	
2	BOWEN CHARLES	
3	COOPER PAMELA	
4	DAVIS WARREN	
.	.	.
.	.	.
.	.	.
NumberOfStudents	WARDEL EVE	
MaxStudents		

NumberOfStudents = current number of students
MaxStudents = maximum students possible

Here the addition of BAKER FRANK will force all records beginning at the second index to be moved down one slot. In a realistic situation where the school may have 10,000 students, each with a record consisting of 500 bytes, this will mean shuffling 5,000,000 bytes of data around in computer storage. If the storage involved is a magnetic disk instead of primary memory, this "pushing down" of all records starting with the second one could well leave the system in a loop that would require several minutes to execute.

An analogous problem occurs when a record near the top of the list is deleted. All the records below it must rise one slot to maintain the list in physical order. Thus, the design proposed in Example 3.2 will not fare particularly well with respect to add and delete performance. Nonetheless, in this chapter, we will live with these inefficiencies so that we may illustrate an actual implementation with the techniques we presently know. As we develop more powerful methods later in the text, we'll consider implementation strategies that circumvent these problems.

After determining the modular structure chart and major data structures for a system, the final step in the design process is to develop logic specifications for each module in the system. There are a variety of techniques for doing this; our preference is to follow the three-step approach we have used consistently throughout the text.

1. Specify the data received by the module. This serves to specify the preconditions for the module; that is, what we know to be true upon entry to the module.
2. Specify the information returned from the module. This serves to specify the postconditions for the module; that is, what we know to be true upon leaving the module.
3. Specify the logic to be followed by the module. Pseudocode is a convenient vehicle for doing this. The amount of detail given in the specifications is dependent on the degree to which you view the design of the system as dictating the implementation phase that follows. For instance, if you as designer have a great deal of confidence in the programmers who will implement the system, you will not need to specify logic in minute detail.

EXAMPLE 3.3

Provide a modular specification for the AddStudent module in the design of the registrar's system from Example 3.2.

Because that design specified a physically ordered array as an implementation technique for the student list, our modular specification should take this into account.

AddStudent Module

Data Received: List of students (with encapsulated number of students)

Information Returned: Transformed list with appropriate addition
Updated number of students

Logic: Obtain data for new student.
Call on FindSlot module to find array location to insert student.
Roll down all entries in array below this location.
Insert new student at vacated location.
Update total number of students.

EXAMPLE 3.4

Provide a modular logic specification for the FindStudent module in the design of the registrar's system from Example 3.2.

Here, because a well-known algorithm (binary search) is to be used, we may choose to provide minimal logical detail. Our assumption is that the eventual implementor of this module will be familiar with the code for the binary search.

FindStudent Module

Data Received: List of students (with encapsulated number of students)
Target name

Information Returned: Record containing data associated with target name
Array location of that record
Boolean flag indicating whether record found

Logic: Binary search algorithm.

In summary, the design phase of the system life cycle includes developing specifications for

1. The modular structure of the program.
2. The major data structures to be used by the program.
3. The logic needed by individual modules.

The system designer thus produces a set of documents that are then used by programmers who begin the actual coding of the system in an appropriate computer language. As we shall see, an effective design will facilitate this coding effort and will lead to a rather natural way of testing and verifying the correctness of the software that is written.

Implementation

In the implementation phase, you must churn out the Pascal code (or other appropriate language) necessary to put into effect the blueprint developed in the design phase. Although the terminology "churn out" may seem a bit degrading considering the amount of effort that must go into the writing of a program, we use it to stress the importance of the design phase. Given an appropriate set of formal specifications from the design phase, coding the programs really can be an easy task. The completeness of the design phase is the key to determining how easy coding is. Time spent in the design phase will be more than repaid by time gained in coding. This point cannot be overemphasized! The most common mistake made by most beginning programmers is jumping almost immediately into the *coding phase,* thereby digging themselves into holes they could have avoided by more thorough consideration of design issues.

A side issue of the coding phase is *documentation:* the insertion of explanatory remarks into your program so that it makes sense when read by someone else (or by yourself at some time in the distant future). Few computer scientists like to do documentation. However, that does not eliminate the absolute necessity of doing it.

In the real world, programs are worked on by teams of programmers, not just one individual. In such an environment, you must explain what your code is doing to the other people who will have to work with it. Moreover, should your code have to undergo revisions in the future (often termed *program maintenance*), your documentation will be vitally important. Without it, those programmers doing the revisions will have to waste days or even weeks trying to decipher logic that the passage of time has made cryptic. Computer lore is filled with horror stories of programmers who were assigned the unenviable task of maintaining poorly documented code. Edward Yourdon has presented this problem by saying,

> *Virtually every major organization that began computerizing 20 years ago is now faced with 20-year-old systems whose implementation is a mystery, and, far worse, whose user requirements are a mystery. The only solution to this crisis in the future is to maintain accurate, up-to-date documentation for as long as the system itself survives* (Modern Structured Analysis *(Englewood Cliffs, N.J.: Prentice-Hall, 1989), 448*).

Minimally, each module you write should include documentation stating its general purpose, identifying all parameters and major local variables, and clarifying any obscure code segments. So, get into the habit of documenting all procedures via the "Given:, Task:, Return:" style that we have been using throughout the text. When combined with other written specifications from the analysis and design phases, well-documented code will help insure that your software system has a long and productive lifetime.

Exercises 3.2

1. What is meant by the term *functionally cohesive* in reference to modular structure charts?
2. What is meant by the term *coupling* in reference to modular structure charts?
3. Explain why the following portion of a modular structure chart for a payroll system is not functionally cohesive.

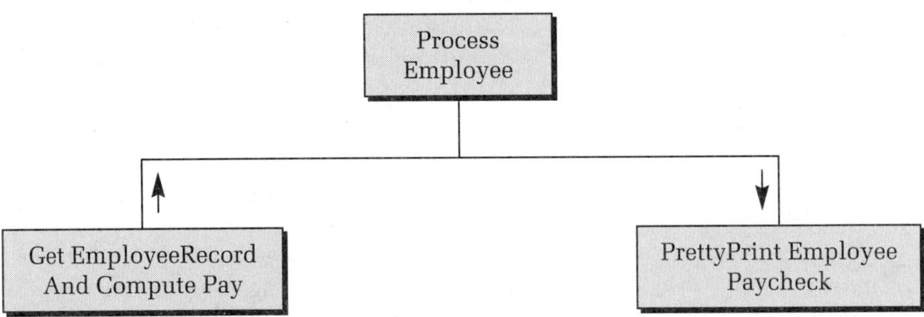

   Correct the modular structure to make it more functionally cohesive.
4. Suppose that we have a search module that receives a customer identification key and then searches for that customer's record in a list of records, returning it to the calling module. Suppose also that this search module prints a "CANNOT FIND CUSTOMER" message if the record associated with this key cannot be located. From the perspective of functional cohesion, why is the printing of this message a poor strategy?
5. Explain why using global variables is a poor strategy from a data coupling perspective.
6. Suppose that a student record at the University of Hard Knocks contains information about the student's grades in courses the student has taken and about the tuition that the student owes the university. Why should a module that computes a student's grade point average not be passed the entire student record as a parameter?
7. Data flow diagrams and modular structure charts are graphic modeling tools related to the development cycle of a software system. Discuss similarities and differences between these two tools.
8. In Exercise 6 of Section 3.1 you analyzed a system requested by the registrar at American Basket Weaving University. Now follow up this analysis by doing a design for the system. Include a complete set of module specifications in your design.

■ ■ ■ ■

3.3 Testing, Maintenance, and Obsolescence Phases of the System Life Cycle

OBJECTIVES

- to realize that we must develop well-conceived strategies for testing software if we are to insure its reliability
- to understand the differences between modular, system, and acceptance testing
- to understand the difference between white-box and black-box testing
- to know what is meant by the robustness of a module
- to be able to use the finite state machine paradigm as a means of guarding against invalid input
- to gain insight into developing test cases for modules
- to realize the importance of being able to maintain a software system over its lifetime of use

A program's usefulness is ultimately demonstrated in the final three phases—testing, maintenance, and obsolescence—of the system life cycle.

Testing

An endeavor far more creative than coding and documentation is the testing that must be coordinated with a system's implementation. This chapter's Notes of Interest will attest to the importance of software reliability; it has become a moral and ethical issue as well as a technical one. Given this importance, how do we systematically verify the correctness of the software we develop?

First, we must realize that testing and verification is a critical and full-fledged phase of the system life cycle. As such, time must be allocated for it. A common mistake beginning programmers make is to assume the correctness of their program after one or two successful test runs. Though you should feel confident that your software will be error-free if it has been carefully designed, even well-designed systems must be thoroughly tested and verified before being released to users.

As an example, consider the following statistics, which summarize the percentages of total project time (not including maintenance) devoted to testing in several computerized systems developed for Air Force space missions.

SAGE	47%
NAVAL TACTICAL DATA SYSTEM	50%
GEMINI	47%
SATURN V	49%

(See R. W. Jensen and C. C. Tonies, *Software Engineering* (Englewood Cliffs, N.J.: Prentice-Hall, 1979), 330.)

Such statistics are amazingly consistent across a wide variety of large system development projects. "In examining conventionally scheduled projects," Frederick P. Brooks "found few that allowed one-half of the projected schedule for testing, but that most did indeed spend half of the actual schedule for that purpose. Many of these were on schedule until and except in system testing" (*The Mythical Man-Month* (Reading, Mass.: Addison-Wesley, 1982)).

The general rule of thumb is that the *testing phase* of a large project can (and should) consume roughly half of the time scheduled for the project. Of course, assignments in a programming course may not be of the same magnitude as an Air Force space mission, but the message is clear. If you fail to schedule a considerable amount of time to verify the correctness of your program, your users (or instructor) will inevitably find bugs in it.

How exactly does one verify the correctness of a large program? One way is to construct formal mathematical proofs of your algorithm's correctness. Though progress is being made in applying this type of formal mathematical approach (see Section 3.5), the complex problems of most real-world systems do not allow this method to be used efficiently. Consequently, the most often employed method of verifying a program's correctness is to test it thoroughly.

Modular Testing. If testing is important enough to take 50 percent of your time, it must clearly require more than a haphazard approach. Hence, we

A NOTE OF INTEREST

Software Reliability and Defense Systems

The issue of software testing takes on great importance as we begin to increasingly rely on the computer as an aide in the decision-making process.

In "Computer System Reliability and Nuclear War" (*Communications of the ACM* 30, No. 2 (February 1987): 112–131), Alan Borning of the University of Washington evaluates the problems of software testing for the Strategic Defense Initiative, popularly known as Star Wars:

> *The SDI envisions a multilayer defense against nuclear ballistic missiles. The computer software to run such a defense would be the most complex ever built. A report by the Defensive Technologies Study Team, commissioned by the Department of Defense to study the feasibility of such a system, estimates a system with 6–10 million lines of code. Enemy missiles would first be attacked in their boost phase, requiring action within 90 seconds or so of a detected launch. This time interval is so short that the human role in the system could be minimal at best, with virtually no possibility of decision making by national leaders. Although pieces of the system could be tested and simulation tests performed, it would be impossible to test the entire system under actual battle conditions short of fighting a nuclear war. It has been the universal experience in large computer systems that there is no substitute for testing under actual conditions of use. The SDI is the most extreme example so far of an untestable system.*

Such systems are somewhat unique in that (we hope) many of them will never actually be used. If they ever are used, it may be too late to engage in the repair of minor flaws that normally arise in the maintenance phase of the system life cycle. It is not an understatement to say that the future of the human race may be riding on the thoroughness with which the systems have been tested. Is there any testing strategy that can be convincing enough under these circumstances? The apparent success of American Patriot missiles in destroying Iraqi Scud missiles in the Persian Gulf War has refueled speculation about the role of computer-controlled defense systems. Of the 43 Scud missiles launched against coalition forces in Saudi Arabia and Kuwait, Patriot systems intercepted 29, while 11 others were allowed to land in the ocean or remote areas of the desert. However, mere numbers can be somewhat deceiving. In his article "Lessons from the Patriot Missile Software Effort" (*IEEE Software* 8, No. 3 (May 1991): 105–108), Galen Gruman points out:

> *In one case, an Iraqi missile intercepted by a Patriot system stationed in Israel was merely knocked off target. In several other cases, debris from the intercepted Scuds damaged homes and injured people. Tougher for any interceptor are missiles that fall apart in flight, since the Patriot at best will hit only one piece, which may not be the warhead. For example, of the Scuds launched against Saudi Arabia and Kuwait, seven (including some that were allowed to fall) broke up during flight and could not be targeted—including one missile whose debris fell on a military barracks near Dhahran, Saudi Arabia, killing 28 soldiers. The Scuds fell apart because they were apparently old and poorly maintained, but both the U.S. and Soviet Union have multiple-warhead missiles designed just to avoid total destruction by antimissile systems.*

counsel against strategies such as creating your test data "on the fly" or creating test data by random techniques. Testing must be planned to be convincing. The plan that we shall briefly describe here begins with *modular testing.* Modular testing is the natural outgrowth of the principles of modular design.

The key to modular testing is to test each individual module as it is developed. Do not wait until the entire system has been coded to begin your testing. Thus, testing on the modular level involves

1. Developing short *driver modules* that artificially call modules you wish to test. A driver module normally contains only the minimum declarations and value assignments needed to invoke the modules being tested. When a module is to return values to its caller, the driver module will report the values returned.
2. Developing short *stub modules* that (again artificially) are called by a module that you wish to test. A stub has the same interface as the

actual module that will later eventually replace it, but its code is usually simpler. Stubs typically report any intermediate values they are sent and return appropriate values so the module being tested can continue executing. When a version of a module that invokes stubs runs correctly you know that its logic is correct and that values are being passed to and from modules correctly.

3. Designing *test cases* that exercise all the logical possibilities the module may encounter. Be aware that such test cases consist of more than just strategically chosen input data. Each set of input data must also include its expected result (sometimes called the *test oracle*) if it is truly to convince anyone of the module's correctness.

Normally, techniques for writing drivers and stubs are covered in an introductory programming course, and hence we assume you are familiar with them. It is the third point, about testing on the modular level, to which we now turn our attention.

In designing test cases, programmers begin to mix methods of science and art. Every mathematician knows that we can never actually prove anything by testing examples (that is, input data). So, how can we verify a module's correctness by merely concocting examples? One proposed answer is to classify input data according to possible testing conditions. Hence, a finite set of well-chosen equivalence classes of test cases can be sufficient to cover an infinite number of possible inputs. Deciding what such equivalence classes should be is the point at which the process becomes more of an art than a science.

EXAMPLE 3.5

To illustrate these principles, consider the fee structure at the E-Z Park parking lot. Parking fees for vehicles are based on the following rules:

The module is given two data items: a character, which may be 'C' or 'T' indicating whether the vehicle is a car or truck; and an integer number indicating the number of hours the vehicle spent in the parking lot. Cars are charged \$1.00 for each of the first three hours they are in the lot and \$0.50 for each hour after that. Trucks are charged \$2.00 for each of the first four hours they are in the lot and \$0.75 per hour thereafter.

After computing the appropriate charge, a new module (ComputeParkingFee) is to call on another new module (PrettyPrintTicket), which appropriately formats a parking fee ticket showing the vehicle type, hours parked, and resulting fee. The ComputeParkingFee module is given here.

```
PROCEDURE ComputeParkingFee (VehicleCategory : char;
                             Hours : integer);

  {  Given:   Vehicle type in VehicleCategory and time spent in lot in Hours.    }
  {           Assume both parameters checked for validity outside this module.   }
  {  Task:    Compute charge for parking and call on PrettyPrintTicket           }
  {           to output ticket.                                                  }
  {  Return:  Nothing.                                                           }

  VAR
    Charge : real;
```

```
BEGIN
  CASE VehicleCategory OF
    'C' : IF Hours <= 3 THEN
            Charge := Hours
          ELSE
            Charge := 3 + (Hours - 3) * 0.5;
    'T' : IF Hours <= 4 THEN
            Charge := Hours * 2
          ELSE
            Charge := 8 + (Hours - 4) * 0.75
  END; { of CASE VehicleCategory }
  PrettyPrintTicket (VehicleCategory, Hours, Charge)
END; { of PROCEDURE ComputeParkingFee }
```

An appropriate driver main program would simply allow us to repeatedly send data to the ComputeParkingFee module to check its behavior in a variety of situations. An appropriate stub for the call to PrettyPrintTicket would merely inform us that we reached this subordinate module and print the values received so that we could be sure they had been transmitted correctly. At this stage, the stub need not concern itself with detailed, formatted output; we are at the moment interested only in testing ComputeParkingFee.

In testing this module, we can begin by identifying the following six *equivalence classes:*

1. A car in the lot less than three hours.
2. A car in the lot exactly three hours.
3. A car in the lot more than three hours.
4. A truck in the lot less than four hours.
5. A truck in the lot exactly four hours.
6. A truck in the lot more than four hours.

Choosing one test case for each equivalence class, we arrive at the following set of test cases.

VehicleCategory	Hours	Expected Results
'C'	2	Charge = 2.00
'C'	3	Charge = 3.00
'C'	5	Charge = 4.00
'T'	3	Charge = 6.00
'T'	4	Charge = 8.00
'T'	8	Charge = 11.00

The test cases for exactly three hours for a car and exactly four hours for a truck are particularly important since they represent *boundary conditions* at which a carelessly constructed conditional check could easily produce a wrong result.

■ ■

This parking lot example, though illustrative of the method we wish to employ, is artificially simple. The next example presents a more complex testing situation.

EXAMPLE 3.6

Consider developing a strategy to test the sorting algorithms we discussed in Chapter 1. Recall that each of these algorithms—bubble sort, insertion sort, and selection sort—received an array of physical size MaxIndex and an integer N to indicate the logical size of the array, that is, the number of items currently stored in the array.

Our criterion for choosing equivalence classes of test data for such a sorting algorithm is based on two factors:

1. The size of N: the number of items to be sorted.
2. The ordering of the original data.

The following table presents a partitioning of test data into equivalence classes for this example.

Size of N	Order of Original Data	Expected Results
N = 1	Not applicable	Array to be arranged in ascending order for all cases.
N = 2	Ascending	
N = 2	Descending	
N midsize and even	Descending	
N midsize and even	Ascending	
N midsize and even	Randomized	
N midsize and odd	Ascending	
N midsize and odd	Descending	
N midsize and odd	Randomized	
N = physical array size	Ascending	
N = physical array size	Descending	
N = physical array size	Randomized	

The module should be run for a minimum of 12 cases, one for each of the classes dictated by our table. Ideally, a few subcases should be run for each of the randomized cases. We cannot overemphasize the importance of testing seemingly trivial cases such as N = 1 and N = 2. These lower boundary conditions are typical examples of data that may cause an otherwise perfectly functioning loop to be incorrectly skipped. Similarly, it is important to test the upper boundary condition in which N reaches the physical array size.

Testing for Robustness. Yet another issue in modular testing is the question of how a module will react when it receives invalid data. For instance, in our current version of the ComputeParkingFee module in Example 3.5, there is a potentially disastrous side effect that occurs when the module receives a vehicle type other than 'C' or 'T.' (What is it?)

Similar reasoning dictates that the sort test data of Example 3.6 should perhaps contain test cases for N = 0 and N greater than the physical array size even though such cases should not arise in normal use of the sort module. A *robust* module is one that guards against harmful side effects when it receives invalid or unexpected data.

It is particularly critical that any modules with which the user is to interact be robust. Inadvertent wrong keystrokes by a user can crash a program or, even worse, result in a program performing its computations with incorrect data. Robustness may be so critical in some systems that you may have to improve upon the interaction capabilities provided by your programming language. Consider, for instance, what your version of Pascal will do when a user enters

```
l.15 (first character is a lowercase L)
```

instead of

```
1.15
```

in response to **read** (X) where X is a real. The accidentally typed lowercase 'l' can crash the **read** procedure offered by many versions of Pascal.

One way to avoid these problems is to write your own procedure to read a real number. In this procedure, read the input a character at a time and convert the incoming stream of characters to its corresponding real value. Because you are reading characters instead of reals, nothing the user types can crash your procedure. If a character that is not expected as part of a real is read, your procedure can take corrective action and warn the user of the problem.

A paradigm known as a *finite state machine* is often used by software engineers to perform such robustness checks on user input. (See the Note of Interest in Chapter 2 entitled "Sparse Tables and Language Compilers.") A finite state machine is best described by a diagram referred to as a *state-transition diagram.* A state-transition diagram for the problem of reading a real number entered in decimal form appears in Figure 3.8.

Interpret the circles in this diagram as the states of the machine. Hence the machine of Figure 3.8 can be in a LeadingSpaces state, a LeftOfDecimal state, a RightOfDecimal state, a Done state, or an Error state. In a particular state, the machine is expecting certain characters as valid input for that state.

FIGURE 3.8
State-transition diagram for reading a real number in decimal form

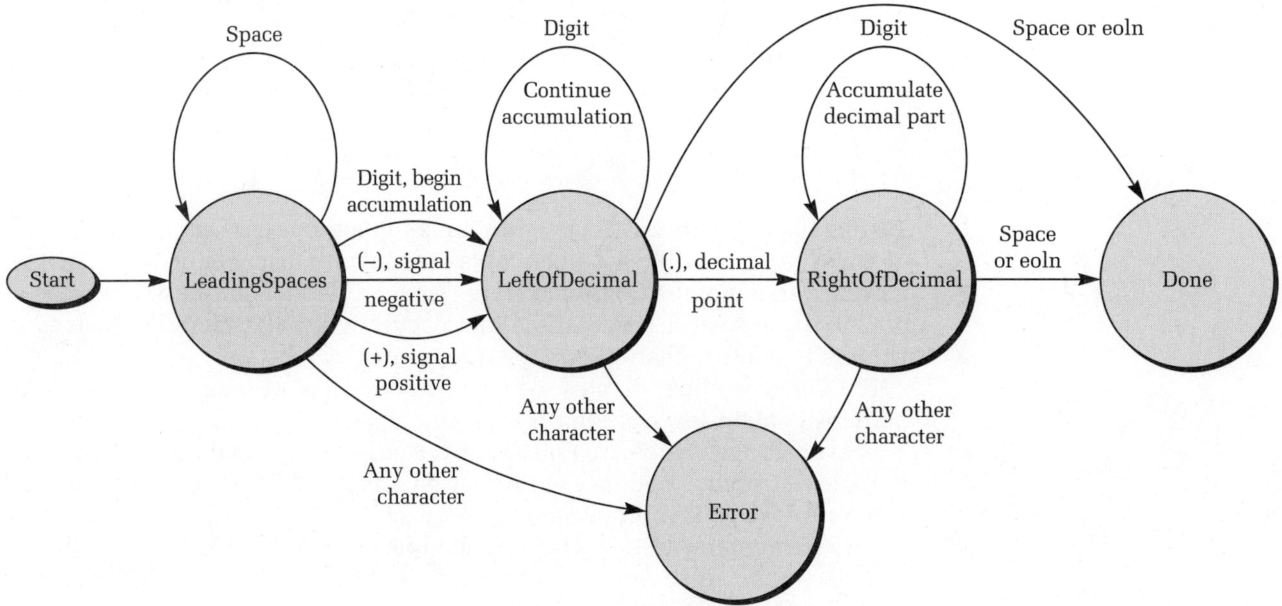

The arrows leading from the states are called *transitions*. Transitions indicate what the machine will do when it encounters a particular character in its current state. Each transition is labeled with one or more characters and, potentially, an action to take upon reading such a character. For instance, when the machine of Figure 3.8 is in the LeadingSpaces state and it reads a space, it remains in the LeadingSpaces state. Consistent with Pascal syntax for entering a real in decimal form, the machine must read a '+', '−', or digit before it can begin the accumulation of a real value and switch to the LeftOfDecimal state. Any other character read in the LeadingSpaces state results in an error.

While in the LeftOfDecimal state, the machine reads digits on a character-by-character basis. As each digit is read, its value must be added to a running total that will be returned from the procedure. The only valid transitions from the LeftOfDecimal state occur when a space, **eoln,** or decimal point is encountered. In a similar fashion, the RightOfDecimal state must read characters until the machine reaches the Done or Error state. You should trace the action of the machine in Figure 3.8 on a variety of input sequences to convince yourself that it correctly handles all possibilities.

The following example illustrates that using Pascal's enumerated type makes it relatively easy to translate a finite state machine into a Pascal procedure.

EXAMPLE 3.7

Write a robust Pascal procedure to read a real number employing the logic of the finite state machine in Figure 3.8.

The strategy of the procedure is to repeatedly read a character which is then analyzed in a **CASE** statement driven by the current state of the machine.

```
PROCEDURE ReadReal(VAR Val : real);

  { Given:    Nothing                                              }
  { Task:     Read one real value in decimal form from the current }
  {           line of input characters.  Assume at least one digit }
  {           to the left of a decimal point. If the current line of }
  {           input characters  does not constitute a valid real,  }
  {           force the user to  retype the offending sequence of  }
  {           characters.                                          }
  { Return:   The real value read in Val.                          }

  TYPE
    { This enumerated type captures the states of Figure 3.8       }
    Possibilities = (LeadingSpaces, LeftOfDecimal, RightOfDecimal, Error,
                     Done);

  VAR
    Ch : char;
    State : Possibilities;
    Negative : boolean; { To signal negative numbers }
    Multiplier : real; { For digits to right of decimal }

  BEGIN
    REPEAT { Stay in the outer REPEAT until read a valid real }
      { The inner loop embodies the logic of the finite state machine }
      { in Figure 3.8                                                 }
```

```
    Negative := false; { Initially assume positive, toggle to signal negative }
    Multiplier := 0.1;
    Val := 0;
    State := LeadingSpaces; { Initial state to consume any leading spaces }
    REPEAT
      READ(Ch);
      CASE State OF
        LeadingSpaces:
          IF ('0' <= Ch) AND (Ch <= '9') THEN { Have read a digit }
            BEGIN
              State := LeftOfDecimal;
              Val := 10 * Val + (ord(Ch) - ord('0')) { Use ord to convert   }
                                                      { character to number }
            END
          ELSE IF Ch = '-' THEN { Signal negative number }
            BEGIN
              Negative := true;
              State := LeftOfDecimal
            END
          ELSE IF Ch = '+' THEN { Leading positive sign }
            State := LeftOfDecimal
          ELSE IF Ch <> ' ' THEN
            State := Error;
        LeftOfDecimal:
          IF ('0' <= Ch) AND (Ch <= '9') THEN { Have read a digit }
            Val := 10 * Val + (ord(Ch) - ord('0'))
          ELSE IF Ch = '.' THEN { Decimal point }
            State := RightOfDecimal
          ELSE IF (Ch = ' ') THEN { End of current number }
            State := Done
          ELSE
            State := Error;
        RightOfDecimal:
          IF ('0' <= Ch) AND (Ch <= '9') THEN { Have read a digit }
            BEGIN
              Val := Val + Multiplier * (ord(Ch) - ord('0'));
              Multiplier := Multiplier * 0.1
            END
          ELSE IF (Ch = ' ') THEN { End of current number }
            State := Done
          ELSE
            State := Error
        END {CASE}
     UNTIL (State = Error) OR (State = Done) OR eoln;
     { If there was bad input, force the user to reenter until get valid real }
     IF State = Error THEN
       BEGIN
         writeln ('Bad Number - Please reenter this number ');
         readln
       END
     ELSE IF Negative THEN
       Val := - Val
   UNTIL (State = Done) OR eoln
END; { ReadReal }
```

To illustrate the use of the **PROCEDURE** ReadReal, consider the following driver program and the results of the sample run.

```
BEGIN {  Driver program  }
  REPEAT
    ReadReal (Number);
    IF eoln THEN
      readln;
```

```
      writeln (Number : 10 : 2)
    UNTIL Number = 0.0
  END.
```

A sample run is as follows:

```
45.61
     45.61
11.2 34.8
     11.20
     34.80
19.6            <—— Note that lowercase L typed instead of digit 1
Bad Number - Please reenter this number
19.6
     19.60
0.0
     0.00
```

It is probably safe to say that no module of reasonable complexity can be guaranteed to be 100 percent robust. For each safeguard against invalid data, a user will no doubt find some way of inadvertently bypassing that safeguard. How robust an individual module must be is a reflection of how it fits into the overall modular structure of the system. It is not reasonable to expect every module in a system to guard itself against every potential kind of invalid data. Such a strategy would have the vast majority of modules more preoccupied with this issue than with their assigned responsibility within the system. A better strategy is to have a few modules whose only responsibility is to screen incoming data against invalid values. In this way we can assure that other modules will be called only when we have valid data to give them. The degree to which an individual module should be robust is thus intimately tied to the overall system design and should be stated as part of the specifications for that module.

White Box/Black Box Testing. One factor that can influence the design of test cases is the knowledge you have of the design and implementation of the module being tested. If you have detailed knowledge of the design and implementation, you can engage in *white box testing.* That is, the module represents a "white box" because you are aware of the internal logic and data structure implementations in the module. In white box testing, test cases can be partitioned into equivalence classes which specifically exercise each logical path through a module. In *black box testing,* the module is approached without knowledge of its internal structure. You know what the module is supposed to do but not how it does it.

For instance, in Examples 3.2 and 3.4, we made the design decision to implement the list of students in the registrar's system with an array maintained in physical order by student name. This decision allowed us to use the binary search algorithm in the specifications for the FindStudent module. We'll work with this module again in the next examples.

EXAMPLE 3.8

Provide Pascal code for implementing the list of students and the FindStudent module described in Examples 3.2 and 3.4.

```
CONST
  MaxStudents   = 10;   { Small for testing purposes }
  StringLength = 40;

TYPE
  StudentRec = RECORD
                Name : String;  { Assume appropriate implementation of     }
                                { the String ADT                           }
                CredTaken : integer;
                CredEarned : integer;
                TotalGradePts : integer
              END;
  StudentList = RECORD  { Encapsulated list }
                 List : ARRAY [1..MaxStudents] OF StudentRec;
                 NumberOfStudents : integer
               END;
  .
  .
  .

  PROCEDURE FindStudent (Target : String;
                         Students : StudentList;
                         VAR InfoWanted : StudentRec;
                         VAR Mid : integer;
                         VAR Found : boolean);

    {  Given:   List of student records, each identified by a unique Name field. }
    {           A name to search for in Target.                                  }
    {  Task:    Apply binary search algorithm to find Target.                    }
    {  Return:  If Target found, return associated record in InfoWanted,         }
    {           associated position in Mid, and Found as true.                    }
    {           Otherwise return Found as false.                                  }

    VAR
      High, Low : integer;

    BEGIN
      Found := false;
      Low := 1;
      High := Students.NumberOfStudents;
      WHILE NOT Found AND (Low <= High) DO
        BEGIN
          Mid := (Low + High) DIV 2;
          IF LessThan (Target, Students.List[Mid].Name) THEN
            High := Mid - 1
          ELSE IF GreaterThan (Target, Students.List[Mid].Name) THEN
            Low := Mid + 1
          ELSE
            BEGIN
              Found := true;
              InfoWanted := Students.List[Mid]
            END
        END
    END; {  of PROCEDURE FindStudent  }
```

■ ■

■ EXAMPLE 3.9

To design a complete set of test cases for **PROCEDURE** FindStudent in Example 3.8, we use the following table. The seven cases presented in the table exercise all logical paths through the binary search algorithm.

Test Case	NumberOf-Students	List	Target	Expected Results	Rationale
I	10	ALLEN BAKER DAVIS GREEN HUFF MILLER NOLAN PAYTON SMITH TAYLOR	Try each name in the Students list	Found **true.** InfoWanted contains associated record. Mid contains associated position	Can we find everything in the full list?
II	10	Same as test case I	Try AARON, NATHAN, ZEBRA	Found **false.**	Is Found correctly returned as **False** for Target data items that precede all list elements, follow all list elements, and are interspersed in the middle of the list? This case tests the full list.
III	5	ALLEN DAVIS HUFF NOLAN SMITH	Same as test case I	Same as test case I	Can we find everything in a mid-sized list?
IV	5	Same as test case III	Same as test case II	Same as test case II	Same as test case II but for mid-sized list.
V	1	HUFF	HUFF	Same as test case I	Can we handle successful search in a one-element list?
VI	1	HUFF	Same as test case II	Same as test case II	Can we handle unsuccessful searches in a one-element list?
VII	0		HUFF	Same as test case II	Robustness check. What if we call on FindStudent with the empty list?

■ ■

Note that, in Example 3.9, our test cases are sure to exercise the situation in which the array is completely full. This represents a boundary condition for the algorithm; we are aware of this condition because we are testing from a white box perspective. Were we testing instead from a black box perspective, it might not be possible to exercise all such boundary conditions.

System and Acceptance Testing. In practice, testing at the modular level tends to be white box testing since a well-designed module will be compact and focused. Hence it is relatively easy to explore the internal structure of a module and create test cases geared toward that internal structure. As modules merge together into a full-fledged software system, the testing of the entire system takes on more of a black box perspective.

In *system testing,* you exercise the interfaces between modules instead of the logic of a particular module. System testing should not occur until each module has been individually tested by white box methods. In larger systems you may find it advantageous to test related subcollections of modules before jumping to a test of the entire system. This will allow you more easily to localize the location of any errors that are found.

Ultimately, the system is tested not only by technical people but by the end users who must work with the system on a regular basis. This final phase of *acceptance testing* carried out by end users is totally black box in nature. Typically end users neither want nor need detailed knowledge of *how* a system is implemented; instead, they have a very substantial interest in *what* the system does. Does it successfully meet the specifications that were described very early in the analysis phase of the project? Consequently, end users will test and ultimately accept or reject the system based upon how it meets these specifications.

Debugging Errors Found During Testing. The main goal of all testing we have discussed is to find errors. Though at first glance this statement may seem counterproductive, remember that it is better for errors to be detected at the testing stage than when the software is in use (or when your instructor is assigning a grade). Given this negative premise of testing, you must also know how to debug your programs when testing achieves its goal of finding errors. If testing can be categorized as an art, debugging could facetiously be described as bordering on the occult.

The following general guidelines apply to the debugging of all programs.

1. Typing is no substitute for thinking. Don't be too quick to make changes in your source program. Instead, when an error occurs, take your test cases and trace them by hand through the logic currently present in your module. Here the advantage of modular testing becomes apparent. Such hand tracing is nearly impossible if you are working with an entire system; with merely one module it is quite manageable.
2. Make use of the various debugging tools provided with most compilers. These tools allow you to scatter tracer output (to display the value of key variables at various stages of an algorithm) and breakpoints (to halt program execution at a key step so that you can examine the values contained in variables) throughout your program in a conveniently interactive fashion. The time you spend learning how to use such tools will be repaid many times over.
3. Don't assume that once you've repaired your program for the test case which generated the error, all previous tests cases will still work correctly. You now have a new program, and all of your carefully designed test cases need to be applied again.
4. Leave time to debug. This avoids "band-aid" corrections (often called patches) and encourages alternatives that may actually improve the design of your program. There is nothing wrong with completely scrapping an approach that has been shown, by testing, to be ill-conceived. Indeed, to try to make such an approach work by in-

A NOTE OF INTEREST

The (Lack of) Responsibility of Software Developers

If you have ever purchased software such as a word processor or spreadsheet for a microcomputer you have probably signed a license agreement in which you agree not to copy the software except for your own backup protection. The fineprint in such software licenses also typically contains disclaimers about the responsibility of the software developer should you eventually do something such as underpay your income tax because of a bug in the spreadsheet you used to keep your tax records.

For instance, the second page of the user's guide of a popular spreadsheet program provides the following disclaimer of warranties. The actual company name (designated here as X) is not given. This disclaimer is typical of that used by virtually all software companies.

The software and user manuals are provided "as is" and without express or limited warranty of any kind by either X or anyone who has been involved in the creation, production, or distribution of the software, including, but not limited to, the implied warranties of merchantability and fitness for a particular purpose. The entire risk as to the quality and performance of the software and user manuals is with you. Should the software and user manuals prove defective, you (and not X or anyone else who has been involved in the creation, production, or distribution of the software) assume the entire cost of all necessary servicing, repair or correction.

Compare such a disclaimer to the claims that appear in the software ads that adorn all popular computing magazines and you will see a real contradiction. Products that profess to do virtually everything guarantee absolutely nothing.

Perhaps the reservations that software developers have about guaranteeing the reliability of their products should not be surprising given what we have learned about the software system life cycle. The complexity of software design and testing makes it virtually impossible to develop software that is 100 percent free of bugs. To customers in the software marketplace, the message is clear: Caveat emptor (Let the buyer beware)!

stalling repeated and intricate fixes can only lead to a system doomed to a very short life.

5. Keep your test cases in a file so that as you make future modifications you can use them again conveniently.

Maintenance

What follows acceptance testing of your system? Once your program has been thoroughly tested, it is ready to be released to the users who originally requested it. In theory, you are done; these users will live happily ever after using the program that you so painstakingly developed. In practice, unfortunately, it rarely works out this way. Instead, users begin to find flaws with your program. (Nobody is perfect!) These flaws typically are due to such factors as

- Your misunderstanding the users' exact needs during the analysis phase.
- Your system's slow performance when it encounters large volumes of user data.
- User needs that have changed since you initially did your analysis.
- Changes in computer hardware and operating system software.

When flaws like these arise, you must maintain your system. That is, you must make the necessary changes to correct the flaws. Here is where good program design and documentation pay off again. It is absolutely essential that you (or someone else assigned to *maintenance*) be able to understand your code after months or perhaps years away from it. Moreover, if your modules are functionally cohesive and minimally coupled, then you should be able to make the appropriate changes in them without causing problems in other modules of the system. That a program must be maintained is not an indication of poor design; it is rather a fact of the software life cycle. That a program can be easily maintained is actually an indication that it was soundly designed from its conception.

Obsolescence

In spite of all your best efforts and no matter how good your program may be, it will almost certainly become obsolete. At that point, the system life cycle must begin anew. You may then be asked to develop a new program to meet the changed needs of the user and to make use of any expanded software capabilities.

Dynamic Nature of the System Life Cycle

Let us recap the phases of the system life cycle: analysis, design, implementation (coding), testing and verification, maintenance, and obsolescence. Though we have discussed each as a separate entity, they are all interwoven into a dynamic, iterative process. The process is dynamic because the dividing lines between the phases are always changing. That is, as you are doing analysis, you are probably already beginning to consider many design and coding issues. The process is iterative in that, from one phase, you may frequently have to return to an earlier phase. For instance, though you may be designing your system, if a question arises about what the user wants, you will have to temporarily return to analysis before completing the design. Similarly, during implementation, you may find it necessary to alter certain design considerations. The fact that many people are usually involved in the system life cycle—users, analysts, designers, and programmers—also contributes to the volatile nature of systems development.

Perhaps one of the worst misconceptions about those of us who work in the computer field is that we deal with problems that have very rigid, well-defined solutions. We hope our discussion of the system life cycle has convinced you that nothing could be further from the truth. To truly contribute over the span of the entire life cycle, you must be skilled at communicating with people, thinking abstractly, and then following through on the details of a plan. The effective computer scientist must truly be a person for all seasons.

Exercises 3.3

1. Summarize what is involved in each of the phases of the system life cycle. If you were to specialize your career in one of these phases, which one would it be? Why? Provide your answer in essay form.
2. What is meant by the term *boundary conditions* for an algorithm?
3. What is a robust module? Should every module in a system be completely robust? Justify your answer in a written essay.
4. Consider the ComputeParkingFee procedure discussed in this section (Example 3.5). Is it robust? What does it do if it does not receive a 'C' or 'T' for its Category parameter? Rewrite this module to make it more robust.
5. Employees at the University of Hard Knocks are paid by the following rules.
   - Employees who sign a contract for a total annual wage are paid 1/52 of that amount each week.

- Hourly employees receive a paycheck based on the number of hours they w in a given week and their hourly rate. They are paid this hourly rate for each the first 40 hours they work. After 40 hours, they are paid time-and-a-half for each additional hour of work. Moreover, work on a holiday is a special case for hourly employees. They get paid double-time for all holiday work.

Write a procedure to compute the pay for an employee of the University of Hard Knocks and then dispatch the appropriate information to a check printing module. Completely test the procedure you write by integrating it with appropriate driver and stub modules and by designing a complete set of test data for the module.

6. Develop test data for the AddStudent module of Example 3.3.
7. Design test data for **PROCEDURE** ReadReal of Example 3.7. Remember that robustness is a high priority for this module, so your test data should be designed with that in mind. If your test data detect any flaws in the algorithm, fix them.
8. Extend the finite state machine of Figure 3.8 to accept reals entered with Pascal's "E" exponential notation. Then incorporate this extended finite state machine into the **PROCEDURE** ReadReal of Example 3.7. Finally, design test data for the extended procedure.
9. Extend the **PROCEDURE** ReadReal of Example 3.7 so that it rejects any number outside of a certain range (to be specified by additional parameters). Illustrate the use of your new procedure in a driver program.
10. Develop modular test data for the implementation of each string operation defined in Section 2.2. Then carry out system testing for the main program of Example 2.2.
11. Each type of computer has its own particular syntax for what it allows as a valid file name. Often such a file name may include an optional disk and directory specifier. Along the lines of Figure 3.8, develop a finite state machine to validate an input stream of characters intended to represent a file name on the computer system you use. Then translate your finite state machine into a robust procedure which returns in a string a file name entered by a user. Design test data for this procedure and create a driver program to test it.
12. This section has presented modular testing as the design of equivalence classes of test cases that exercise all the logical possibilities a module may encounter. You are working on a software system with a friend who claims that such comprehensive testing is impossible. As evidence, the friend cites a module she has written with 20 **IF . . . THEN . . . ELSE** statements in it. Your friend points out that there are approximately 2^{20} logical paths through this module, and that comprehensive modular testing is therefore impossible. In a written essay, refute your friend's claim. (*Hint:* Consider the cohesion of the module used as an example by your friend.)

3.4 Pragmatics: Random Access File Implementations of Lists (Optional)

In the Focus on Program Design section of Chapter 2, we used an array as a means of implementing a keyed list. In Example 3.2, the array again emerged as a strategy for implementing an extended form of the keyed list ADT to be used by a university registrar. In both of these situations, an array does not represent a realistic solution to the problem posed. Why? Array storage is not permanent; when we quit a program, data in an array are lost.

We can try to overcome this limitation by loading the array from a text file at the beginning of a program and then writing it out to another text file when we quit the program. This is the strategy we used in Chapter 2's Focus on Program Design section. However, then we often run into another problem: the limited amount of main memory storage that an array may claim. Since arrays reside in main memory, the amount of data they may contain at any one time is dependent on the amount of memory available on your computer system. In many practical situations, loading an entire employee payroll list or student registration list into an array for processing isn't remotely possible. The size of the list exceeds by far the main memory at your disposal. In such situations, there is no choice but to store and process the data using a file.

You have no doubt processed files sequentially in the course of your Pascal programming experience, perhaps using files with structured components. For example, the declarations

```
TYPE
   .
   .
   .
   StudentRec = RECORD
                   Name : String;
                   CredTaken : integer;
                   CredEarned : integer;
                   TotalGradePts : integer
                END;
   StudentList = FILE OF StudentRec;
   .
   .
   .
VAR
   .
   .
   .
   NextStudent : StudentRec;
   Students : StudentList;
```

allow you to process sequentially the records in the disk file Students, where Pascal's caret notation, Students^, lets you access the contents of the *file buffer.* Essentially, the buffer for the file Students is an area in main memory capable of storing precisely one record from the file (which may have arbitrarily many records stored on a permanent basis). The standard Pascal statement

```
NextStudent := Students^;
```

assigns the contents of the buffer to the record variable NextStudent. Similarly

```
Students^ := NextStudent;
```

copies the contents of NextStudent into the buffer. The standard Pascal statement **put**(Students) transfers the contents of the buffer to the currently accessed record in the file Students, whereas **get**(Students) moves data in the opposite direction, that is, from the currently accessed file record to the buffer. These Pascal file concepts are highlighted in Figure 3.9.

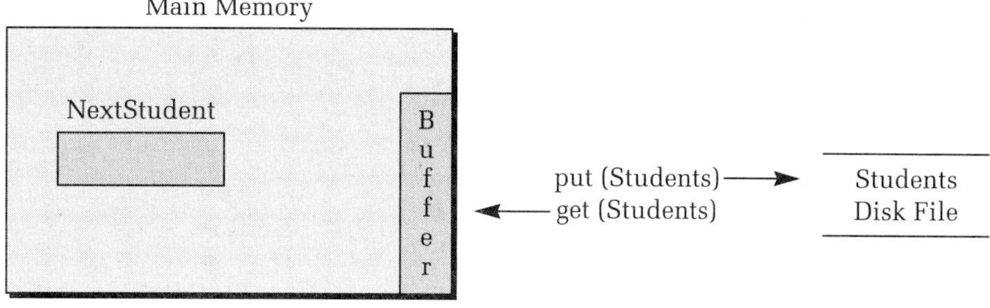

FIGURE 3.9
File operations in standard Pascal

EXAMPLE 3.10

A typical loop to process every record in an already existing Students file is

```
reset (Students);
WHILE NOT eof (Students) DO
  BEGIN
    NextStudent := Students^;
    ProcessRecord (NextStudent);  {  Assume procedure exists  }
    get (Students)
  END;
```

Note that **reset** retrieves the first record into the buffer; hence the **get** appears at the end of the loop.

EXAMPLE 3.11

To create a file, the following loop is used.

```
rewrite (Students);
CreateRecord (NextStudent);  {  Assume procedure exists  }
WHILE  {  NextStudent to be added to file  }  DO
  BEGIN
    Student^ := NextStudent;
    put (Students);
    CreateRecord (NextStudent)
  END;
```

In practice, most Pascal implementations also allow **read** and **write** to access files that are not text files. In such implementations, the single statement

```
read (Students, NextStudent);
```

is equivalent to the two statements

```
NextStudent := Students^;
get (Students);
```

Similarly, the single statement

```
write (Students, NextStudent);
```

is equivalent to

```
Students^ := NextStudent;
put (Students);
```

T Turbo Pascal supports only **read** and **write** in this fashion, hence eliminating the standard **get** and **put** from its repertoire.

The problem with the Pascal file processing statements we have reviewed is that they perform only sequential file processing, that is, processing in which the records in a file are accessed in the order first record, second record, third record, and so on. Hence, to access the 40th record, you first have to access records 1 through 39. This type of processing is simply not suitable if we are to use a permanent disk file to implement a keyed list.

List operations and algorithms such as the binary search require that we be able to randomly access any record by specifying its relative position in the list. One approach to overcoming this limitation is to load all the components of a file into an array at the beginning of a program and then write out the (perhaps updated) components to a new file when the program terminates. This strategy will work with small files, but it is not adequate for large files since such files typically consume too much space if loaded entirely into an array in main memory.

T Although random file processing is not part of standard Pascal, it is so essential to file processing algorithms that most Pascal compilers include nonstandard extensions that allow you to perform direct access file operations. For instance, using the Turbo Pascal compiler, the statements

```
seek (Students, K);
read (Students, NewStudent);
```

will directly retrieve the Kth file record into the record variable NewStudent, with the first file record referenced by K = 0. Similarly, the statements

```
seek (Students, K);
write (Students, NewStudent);
```

will send the contents of the record variable NewStudent to the Kth record position in the file Students.

If you are not using Turbo Pascal, you should consult local system documentation to find out what nonstandard statements will perform similar *random access file* operations for your compiler. (Appendix 10 provides a summary of such statements for many popular Pascal compilers.) The point is that, as long as your version of Pascal supports random file access, our array implementation of a list can be easily converted to a random access file implementation. For instance, again using Turbo Pascal for illustration purposes, the array-based statement

```
Students[K] := NewStudent;
```

becomes

```
seek (Students, K);
write (Students, NewStudent);
```

in a file-based implementation. You will be asked to convert the registrar's system to such a random access file implementation in the Problems at the end of the chapter.

The practical importance of file-oriented implementations of abstract data types versus array implementations cannot be overstated. The permanent nature of data stored in files makes such implementations essential in many data processing applications. Files have the additional advantage of being almost limitless in size (arrays are bounded by the restraints of main memory). Of course, what we already have learned about the trade-off computer scientists often face should warn you that these advantages do not come without a price. With random access files, that price is slower access. Whereas array entries can be accessed at microsecond speeds, random file access is at millisecond speed: slower by a factor of 1,000. This becomes crucial in the more powerful search algorithms we'll discuss in later chapters.

Despite the importance of random access files, the case studies we present in this text will typically be written using arrays. We do this for two main reasons. First, the code for arrays tends to be cleaner, usually involving fewer statements to get the same conceptual operation done. Second, the system-dependent aspect of random access file processing in Pascal tends to make such presentations less worthwhile for those of you using different versions of Pascal than we are. However, given what we have already said about the conceptual similarities between arrays and random access files, conversion from the former to the latter should always be a relatively easy matter.

Exercises 3.4

1. Discuss the advantages and disadvantages of an array implementation of a list versus an implementation using a random access file.
2. Using Appendix 10 or local system reference material, determine the statements used for random access file processing in the version of Pascal you use. Use the statements to write instruction sequences that will
   a. Assign to a main memory variable the Kth component of a random access file.
   b. Assign to the Kth component of a random access file the contents of a main memory variable of the same type as a file component.
3. Discuss how the instruction sequences you developed for Exercise 2 could be used to convert an array implementation of a list into a random file implementation.
4. Explain why a pointer sort that uses an array of pointers in main memory would be particularly appropriate for a list implemented via a random access file.
5. Recall from your experiences with sequential file processing that altering just one component of a sequential file would require copying all the records in the file into a new file. Explain why this is not practical for many applications and how random access files provide a more efficient means of updating an individual component of the file. Illustrate by using appropriate random file instructions from your version of Pascal.
6. Explain why loading a sequential file into an array at the beginning of a program and then writing the array to a sequential file at the end of a program is often not a viable alternative to random file processing. Under what conditions would it be a viable alternative?
7. You are implementing a keyed list (Section 2.4) as a physically ordered random access file with the binary search algorithm used for the Retrieve operation. From an efficiency perspective, discuss the implications of this implementation strategy with respect to the Add and Delete operations.

■ ■ ■ ■

■ 3.5 Formal Verification (Optional)

The approach we have taken in Section 3.3 to insuring software reliability is to emphasize the construction of thorough and convincing test data as a means of verifying program/module correctness. However, this strategy of verification cannot be construed as a formal proof of the algorithm's correctness. We have attempted to show that an algorithm is correct by showing that it works for a comprehensive set of examples. But, from a mathematical perspective, a theorem cannot be proven by example. This is because there are infinitely many possibilities for such examples, hence making it impossible to test every one. Instead of testing, a formal approach to algorithm verification demands an airtight proof using the basic axioms and principles of logic.

Formal Algorithm Verification by the Method of Inductive Assertions

Some work has been done in this area of formal algorithm verification. We shall attempt to summarize one of the more frequently used techniques, known as the *method of inductive assertions,* by formally proving the correctness of the following algorithm. The algorithm is to compute N^M for N a real and M a nonnegative integer. Our correctness proof will use the principle of mathematical induction. (This principle is covered extensively in most discrete mathematics texts; be sure to review it before proceeding if you are not familiar with it.)

```
PROCEDURE Power (N : real;
                M : integer;
                VAR R : real);

  {  Given:    N, a real number, and M, a nonnegative integer.  }
  {  Task:     Compute N raised to power M.                     }
  {  Return:   The computed value in R.                         }

  BEGIN
    R := 1;
    WHILE M > 0 DO
      BEGIN
        R := R * N;
        M := M - 1
      END
  END;  {  of PROCEDURE Power  }
```

A formal proof of such an algorithm involves appropriately identifying the input assertions, output assertions, and loop invariants of the algorithm. All three of these are statements about the algorithm expressed in formal mathematical terms. The input assertions represent all necessary input conditions to the algorithm. For our example, the input assertions would be

$N \in$ reals

$M \in$ integers

$M \geq 0$

The output assertions represent in formal terms the desired result. Here we would have

$R = N^M$

as the lone output assertion for our algorithm.

Finally, we must identify the loop invariants of our algorithm. A loop invariant may be thought of as a special type of assertion that expresses a relationship between variables and remains constant through all iterations of a loop. Note that it is not the variables that remain fixed but rather the relationship between them. This is a key distinction to make. As we shall see, correctly identifying loop invariants is often the most crucial and difficult step in setting the stage for a proof (by induction) of an algorithm's correctness.

For the Power algorithm under consideration, let R_k and M_k be the respective values of R and M after k times through the **WHILE** loop. Both R and M change each time the loop is executed while N remains fixed throughout the algorithm. The loop invariant relationship we wish to prove is then given by

$$R_k \times N^{M_k} = N^M$$

If we can prove this loop invariant, then it follows immediately that the algorithm is correct. Why? If the looping ends after j times through the loop, M_j will be zero because of the conditional test in the **WHILE.** Hence, because of the loop invariant relationship, we will have

$$R_j \times N^{M_j} = N^M$$

$$\downarrow$$

$$R_j \times N^0 = N^M$$

$$\downarrow$$

$$R_j = N^M$$

Therefore, when the loop terminates after j iterations, R will contain the value N^M and thereby satisfy the output assertion. The entire problem of proving the algorithm's correctness has thus been reduced to achieving an inductive proof of the loop invariant relationship.

Inductive Proof

Now we will work through the inductive proof of

$$R_k \times N^{M_k} = N^M$$

Basis Step with $k = 0$. Before looping begins, $R_0 = 1$ and $M_0 = M$ since these are the values of the variable established by the input assertions. Hence the loop invariant relationship for $k = 0$ becomes

$$1 \times N^M = N^M$$

which is trivially true.

Inductive Step. By the standard inductive assumption, we assume

$$R_k \times N^{M_k} = N^M$$

and attempt to show

$$R_{k+1} \times N^{M_{k+1}} = N^M$$

In going from the kth pass through the **WHILE** loop to the $(k + 1)$st pass through the loop we have

$$R_{k+1} = R_k \times N$$

and

$$M_{k+1} = M_k - 1$$

Hence

$$\begin{aligned} R_{k+1} \times N^{M_{k+1}} & \\ &= (R_k \times N) \times N^{(M_k - 1)} \\ &= R_k \times N^{M_k} \\ &= N^M \end{aligned}$$

by the inductive assumption.

The inductive step thus completes the formal proof of the algorithm's correctness. Note how the pivotal point in the entire proof was the determination of the loop invariant. This determination drives the rest of the proof. We can summarize the steps involved in the overall proof as follows:

1. Specification of input assertions.
2. Specification of output assertions.
3. Specification of loop invariants, from which the output assertions follows.
4. Proof (via induction) of the loop invariants.

What Do Proofs Really Prove?

One of the valid criticisms of our proof is that it proves correct an algorithm which is obviously correct to start with. This criticism can often be made of formal correctness proofs as they presently stand. That is, the present state of the art in *formal verification* methods has not advanced to the point where they are of value in most realistically complex situations. Other criticisms of the method include:

1. The proof method assumes the correctness of the input and output assertions. If they are wrong, a proof of the program could be done but the program could still contain errors.
2. The proof method says nothing about how the program will act when exceptional conditions occur which deviate from the input assertions.
3. The proof method focuses only on the logic within an individual module. It verifies nothing with respect to how the modules of a system will interact.
4. The proof method relies upon a completely accurate interpretation of the action dictated by a given algorithmic statement. This action is often called the *semantics* of the statement. If our interpretation of a statement's semantics does not match what actually happens when the program runs, the program may result in an error even though it has been proved correct.
5. Practical machine limitations such as round-off and overflow are usually not considered in formal correctness proofs.
6. Proof techniques ignore the problem of unwanted side effects caused by an algorithm. Such side effects may result in an error in the overall system even though each module has been proved correct.
7. Proofs of nonnumerical algorithms such as searching and sorting are much more difficult than proofs of numerical algorithms. (These

criticisms are set forth in more expanded form in Glenford Myer, *Software Reliability* (New York: Wiley & Sons, 1976), 319–320.)

Formal correctness proofs must currently be considered as a technique that is mostly of theoretical importance. They simply are not sophisticated enough to find practical application in programs that solve realistically complex problems. However, a technique should not be rejected because it presently has little practical value. Many useful methods in computer science had their roots in pure theory. Perhaps the ultimate hope for the formal correctness methods we have discussed is that they can be automated. That is, in the future we may have software that receives input/output assertions as its input, generates the code to satisfy these assertions, and then proves the correctness of the code. Though it is obviously a long way from happening, such automatic program synthesis does not seem to be impossible in principle. (The potential of formal methods in algorithm verification is the feature topic in the September 1990 issues of *IEEE Computer* and *IEEE Software.*)

A NOTE OF INTEREST

Program Verification: Possible or Not?

According to mathematical logician Jon Barwise, an article by University of Minnesota, Duluth philosopher James Fetzer has touched off a debate that could be "just as exciting and just as acrimonious" as the debates about the nature of mathematics that raged in the early twentieth century. Fetzer's article, entitled "Program Verification: The Very Idea" appears in the September, 1988 issue of the *Communications of the ACM* (Vol. 31, No. 8: 1048–1063). In it, Fetzer argues that computer programs, as "encodings of algorithms that can be compiled and executed by a machine," defy formal proofs of correctness in the sense discussed in Section 3.5 of this text. Arguing from the premise that "the function of a program is to satisfy the constraints imposed by an abstract machine for which there is an intended interpretation with respect to a physical system," Fetzer argues that "the behavior of that system cannot be subject to conclusive absolute verification but requires instead empirical inductive investigation to support inconclusive relative verifications."

To a degree, Fetzer's article can be viewed as an attack upon much of the research being done in formally proving the correctness of programs. As such, it has been the subject of heated criticism from many computer scientists. For instance, one letter of response signed by 10 computer scientists from institutions including the University of Maryland, Cornell University, and Stanford University blasted the *Communications* for even publishing Fetzer's article:

> *However, by publishing the ill-informed, irresponsible, and dangerous article by Fetzer, the editors of* Communications *have abrogated their responsibility, to both the ACM membership and to the public at large, to engage in serious enquiry into techniques that may justify the practice of computer science as a socially responsible engineering endeavor. The article is ill-informed and irresponsible because it attacks a parody of both the intent and the practice of formal verification. It is dangerous because its pretentious and ponderous style may lead the uninformed to take it seriously* (Communications of the ACM *32, No. 3 (March 1989): 287–288).*

The war of letters and responses over Fetzer's article raged on in the April, 1989 *Communications of the ACM.* At issue appears to be the role of abstract reasoning about algorithms in ensuring the correctness of software that runs on real-world machines. Like many philosophical questions, those raised by Fetzer will probably never be answered to the satisfaction of everyone involved in the debate. Nonetheless, as pointed out by Michael Evangelist, a senior researcher in software technology at MCC in Austin, Texas, "Fetzer has helped to draw the distinction better between reasoning about physical objects and about abstractions of those objects."

Exercises 3.5

1. Use the method of inductive assertions to prove the correctness of the following algorithm.

```
PROCEDURE Difference (X, Y : integer;
                      VAR Z : integer);

  {  Given:    Integers X and Y.                }
  {  Task:     Compute the difference X - Y.    }
  {  Return:   Computed difference in Z.        }

  VAR W : integer;

  BEGIN
    Z := X;
    W := Y;
    WHILE W > 0 DO
      BEGIN
        Z := Z - 1;
        W := W - 1
      END
  END; { of PROCEDURE Difference  }
```

2. Use the method of inductive assertions to prove the correctness of the following algorithm.

```
PROCEDURE Cube (X : integer;
                VAR Z : integer);

  {  Given:    Integer X.                   }
  {  Task:     Compute X cubed.             }
  {  Return:   The computed value in Z.     }

  VAR A, B, C : integer;

  BEGIN
    A := 1;
    B := 0;
    C := X;
    Z := 0;
    WHILE C > 0 DO
      BEGIN
        Z := Z + A + B;
        B := B + 2 * A + 1;
        A := A + 3;
        C := C - 1
      END
  END; { of PROCEDURE Cube  }
```

3. Could an algorithm that has been proven correct by formal verification methods still produce a "wrong answer" when it is implemented in a particular programming language on a particular machine? Provide a written rationale for your answer.

■ ■ ■ ■

■ 3.6 Object-Oriented Programming (Optional)

In Chapter 2 we introduced the notion of abstract data types. That chapter's Focus on Program Design section illustrated that using abstract data types by invoking their operations without making assumptions about their implementations can be a powerful aide in controlling the complexity of a program. Then, in Example 3.2, we carried out a system design which illustrated a shortcoming of abstract data types. In that example, we needed a data structure that resembled a keyed list ADT but that required a bit more. The rigidity of the ADT's definition makes it difficult for the code resulting from that design (see this chapter's Focus on Program Design) to plug directly into the operations provided with the keyed list. Instead, we are forced to reinvent the wheel: we can borrow many ideas from the keyed list ADT but must start our coding efforts from scratch. We have lost the timesaving advantage of being able to reuse code provided by an ADT's implementation.

System developers using the ADT approach frequently found themselves restricted in this fashion by the inflexibility of ADT definitions. They needed a way of making an ADT's definition more malleable. This would allow a developer to redefine certain ADT operations, extend the ADT by defining new operations, and yet still reuse much of an ADT's implementation. What has emerged from this need to fine-tune ADTs to particular applications is a new paradigm called *object-oriented programming.*

A detailed discussion of object-oriented programming is certainly beyond the scope of this text, in part because the Pascal language does not support this paradigm. Object-oriented programming will, however, certainly play a major role in the future of software engineering. Many implementors of Pascal compilers, aware of this coming trend, are beginning to offer object-oriented extensions to their versions of Pascal. Other languages, such as Smalltalk and C++, have incorporated object-oriented features as part of their standards. To provide you with a base of information, we will provide a brief description of some of the key components of the object-oriented paradigm.

Object-Oriented Encapsulation

The object-oriented paradigm carries encapsulation one step further than we were able to do in Chapter 2 by bundling both the data fields and the operations for an ADT into the ADT's declaration. Such a ADT declaration creates what is called a *class object.* Think of it as a "super" **TYPE** declaration. Using a hypothetical Pascal-like syntax, the declaration of a class object for the keyed list ADT might appear as follows.

```
TYPE
  KeyType = { An appropriate type for the key field in list records }
  OtherDataType = { An appropriate type for the other data associated with }
                  { each key field                                          }
  ListNode = RECORD
               Key : KeyType;
               OtherData : OtherDataType
             END;
  KeyedList = OBJECT { Hypothetical syntax only }
                { The next two items are data fields used for an array }
                { implementation                                        }
                List : ARRAY [1..MaxListSize] OF ListNode;
                NumberOfNodes : integer;
                { Then come the operations owned by an object of       }
                { type KeyedList                                        }
                PROCEDURE Create;
                PROCEDURE Add (Item : ListNode;
                               VAR Success : Boolean);
                PROCEDURE Delete (Target : KeyType;
                                  VAR Success : boolean);
                PROCEDURE Retrieve (Target : KeyType;
                                    VAR Item : ListNode;
                                    VAR Success : boolean);
                PROCEDURE TraverseInOrder (PROCEDURE ProcessNode
                                              (VAR Item : ListNode))
              END; { of definition of class object KeyedList }
```

We could then declare *instances* of the class KeyedList. Instances are themselves objects that could be thought of as variables of **TYPE** KeyedList.

```
VAR  { Hypothetical syntax only  }
  List1, List2 : KeyedList;
```

Because the operations have been encapsulated within the definition of the KeyedList class, the instances List1 and List2 are viewed as owning these operations. Hence we invoke an operation not by passing List1 or List2 as an argument to the operation but rather by "telling" List1 or List2 to perform that operation. For example, again using a hypothetical Pascal-like syntax, we would have

```
List1.Create;  { Tell List1 to create itself }
readln (Item);
List1.Add (Item,Success);  { Tell List1 to add Item to itself }
```

One interesting perspective that emerges from object-oriented encapsulation is called *programming by personification.* Objects take on a person-like quality, and we invoke operations by telling an object to perform an operation that is part of its encapsulation. Object-oriented disciples often use the term *message-passing;* for example, "send the Create message to object List1."

Clearly, object-oriented programming requires a slightly different view of algorithms and data structures. Feeling at ease with that view only comes with much experience. Our intent here is not to provide that experience, but only to present an overview of what the object-oriented paradigm has to offer.

Object-Oriented Inheritance

One of the key features of object-oriented programming is the ability to extend previously defined class objects. Such extension is termed *inheritance.* The newly defined class object automatically inherits everything the original class had, but it also can provide new operations specific to a particular application. Recall this was exactly the obstacle we faced in designing the student list for the registrar's system in Example 3.2. An object-oriented language allows us to define a new class object StudentList by inheriting from and extending the KeyedList class object.

```
TYPE
  .
  .
  .
  StudentList = OBJECT (KeyedList)   { Hypothetical inheritance syntax }
                  GPAPointerArray : ARRAY [1..MaxListSize] OF integer;
                                     {used to apply pointer sort algorithm
                                      for ordering by GPA }
                  PROCEDURE PrintGPAOrderedList
                END;
  .
  .
  .
VAR
  Students : StudentList;
```

In this sample code, Students is a KeyedList because it is an instance of a class object that inherits KeyedList. Hence, we could invoke all the operations that come with KeyedList. For instance,

```
Students.Create;
ReadNewStudent (Item);
Students.Add (Item,Success);
```

However, we also have the ability to define operations beyond a plain KeyedList. In our sample code segment, we could provide our own implementation of operation PrintGPAOrderedList and invoke it by

```
Students.PrintGPAOrderedList
```

Inheritance is thus a powerful, object-oriented mechanism. It allows you to reuse code already developed for a class object and yet extend the capabilities of that original class in ways particularly suited to your needs.

Object-Oriented Polymorphism

Polymorphism (which is Greek for "many shapes") is a feature of object-oriented programming that allows one operation to have different meaning for different kinds of objects. For instance, continuing from the previous sample code, suppose that the Create operation had to perform different tasks for objects belonging to class StudentList than it did for objects belonging to class KeyedList. Then, we could add an overriding definition of the Create operation to the declaration of class StudentList.

```
TYPE
  .
  .
  .
  StudentList = OBJECT (KeyedList)    { Hypothetical inheritance syntax }
                  PROCEDURE Create;   { Overrides KeyedList Create }
                  GPA PointerArray : ARRAY [1..MaxListSize] OF integer;
                                       { used to apply pointer sort algorithm }
                                       { for ordering by GPA                  }
                  PROCEDURE PrintGPAOrderedList
                END;
  .
  .
  .
VAR
  PlainList : KeyedList;
  Students : StudentList;
```

Polymorphism now implies that an object-oriented language would use KeyedList's Create when PlainList.Create is invoked and StudentList's Create when Students.Create is called. Our simple example belies the importance of polymorphism in developing large object-oriented systems. It allows the design of complex hierarchies of object classes, many of which inherit behavior from other classes. Polymorphism eliminates name clashes among the operations that may be defined for these various classes. In effect, it allows one name to take "many shapes" in the form of operations appropriate to differing data types.

We hope this brief excursion into object-oriented programming has whetted your appetite. There seems little doubt that the next decade will find this paradigm playing an increasingly active role in accelerating the software system life cycle. An excellent source to continue your exploration of this topic is *Object-Oriented Programming: An Evolutionary Approach* by Brad J. Cox (Reading, Mass.: Addison-Wesley, 1986).

A NOTE OF INTEREST

IBM and Apple = Pinstripes and T-Shirts

After signing the Treaty of Amiens in 1802, Napoleon said, "What a beautiful fix we are in now; peace has been declared." In July 1991, representatives of IBM and Apple announced an alliance that similarly shocked many industry analysts. IBM has long been positioned in the mainstream of the computer industry, gaining its reputation more from selling the reliability of its corporate image than from technological innovation. Apple, on the other hand, has based its claim to fame on bold new technologies developed by computer enthusiasts with a distinct bent toward "hacking." For instance, the window-based environment of the first Apple Macintosh in 1983 established a new and exciting mode of human-computer interaction. When IBM and Microsoft later "copied" the "look and feel" of the Mac environment to an IBM-compatible operating system, Apple promptly took them to court in a case whose effects on the software industry are still being debated.

Small wonder that eyebrows have been raised by the agreement between these two corporate antagonists. What are the underlying reasons for the move? According to joint press releases, the companies will cooperate on four fronts:

1. IBM will take steps to better integrate the Mac into IBM-based computer networks.
2. Apple will build future machines using IBM's RISC architecture chip technology.
3. The companies will work together on developing data standards for multimedia.
4. There will be a joint endeavor to produce a new, object-oriented operating system that will eventually be marketed for both IBM and Apple computers.

The last of these ventures is the one that seems to be generating the most excitement on an industry-wide basis. The two companies had been working individually on object-oriented operating systems. Apple had been calling their exploratory system Pink; IBM had called theirs Metaphor. It now appears that the Pink and Metaphor research groups will combine their efforts, with the long-range goal that users and third-party software developers will only have to deal with one common interface for a variety of different machines from the two companies. By taking advantage of the abstraction emphasized by the object-oriented approach, the details of the particular machine will be completely hidden.

It all sounds good in theory, but can researchers from two such historically different companies really define a common set of goals? If they can, will it destroy their own individual initiatives? Only time will tell.

Exercises 3.6

1. Consult local reference documents for the version of Pascal that you are using to see if it offers object-oriented extensions to the standard. If it does, use these extensions to develop an object-oriented, encapsulated implementation of the string or keyed list ADT. Then incorporate your implementation into a higher level algorithm that uses this ADT. See the Problems at the end of Chapter 2 for some ideas regarding such higher level algorithms.
2. Read the first chapter of the text by Cox cited at the end of this section. Then, in your own words, explain how the object-oriented approach can often eliminate complex **CASE** constructs from a program.

FOCUS ON PROGRAM DESIGN

In this section, we complete the design of the registrar's system as begun in Example 3.2. In particular, we must develop modular specifications for the structure chart of Figure 3.6. Once we complete this design, we will code the system, using an array physically ordered by student name to implement the list of student records. The program presented here assumes an appropriate implementation of the string ADT that we defined in Chapter 2. Testing and fine-tuning the robustness of the system is left for you to carry out in the Problems.

1. <u>MainMenu Module</u>
   Data Received: None
   Information Returned: None
   Logic: Perform necessary initializations.
   Repeatedly call on GetSelection module to obtain user choice of operation and dispatch to appropriate subordinate module.
2. <u>GetSelection Module</u>
   Data Received: None
   Information Returned: User choice of operation in form of character
   Logic: Print menu of possible operations.
   Read user choice from terminal.
3. <u>AddStudent Module</u>
   Data Received: List of students (with encapsulated number of students)
   Information Returned: Transformed list with appropriate addition
   Updated number of students
   Logic: Obtain data for new student.
   Call on FindSlot module to find array location to insert student.
   Roll down all entries in array below this location.
   Insert new student at vacated location.
   Update total number of students.
4. <u>FindSlot Module</u>
   Data Received: List of students (with encapsulated number of students)
   Name of student to add
   Information Returned: Array location to insert student
   Logic: Repeatedly examine array location beginning with first until we encounter a student whose name alphabetically follows that of new student.
5. <u>DeleteStudent Module</u>
   Data Received: List of students (with encapsulated number of students)
   Information Returned: Transformed list with appropriate deletion
   Updated number of students
   Logic: Obtain name of student to be deleted.
   Call on FindStudent module to get the array location of this student.
   Provided that the student was found in the array, move all students following the one to be deleted up one slot in the array, hence destroying data for deleted student.
   Update total number of students.
6. <u>ChangeStudent Module</u>
   Data Received: List of students (with encapsulated number of students)
   Information Returned: Transformed list with appropriate record change
   Logic: Obtain name of student whose records are to be altered.
   Call on FindStudent module to get array location of this student.

Provided that the student was found in the list, determine field to be changed and assign the appropriate new value to that field in the located record.

7. InspectStudent Module
   Data Received: List of students (with encapsulated number of students)
   Information Returned: None
   Logic: Obtain name of student to inspect.
   Call on FindStudent module to return that student's complete record.
   Provided the student was found, display the record in an appropriate format.
8. FindStudent Module
   Data Received: List of students (with encapsulated number of students)
   Target name
   Information Returned: Record containing data associated with target name
   Array location of that record
   Boolean flag indicating whether record found
   Logic: Binary search algorithm.
9. PrintGradeReports Module
   Data Received: List of students (with encapsulated number of students)
   Information Returned: None
   Logic: For each student, access record in list and print out appropriately formatted report card including grade point average
10. EndOfYearReports Module
    Data Received: List of students (with encapsulated number of students)
    Information Returned: None
    Logic: Print appropriate headings for report in alphabetical order by name.
    Call on PrintListByName module to print detail lines in appropriate order.
    Print appropriate headings for report in order by GPA.
    Call on PrintListByGPA module to print detail lines in appropriate order.
11. PrintListByName Module
    Data Received: List of students (with encapsulated number of students)
    Information Returned: None
    Logic: Proceed through list in the physical order in which it has been maintained, printing out each student's record in appropriate format.
12. PrintListByGPA Module
    Data Received: List of students (with encapsulated number of students)
    Information Returned: None
    Logic: Call on SortByGPA to establish pointers that will lead through list in descending GPA order.
    Use these pointers to proceed through list in logical order, printing each record in appropriate format.

13. SortByGPA Module
Data Received: List of students (with encapsulated number of students)
Information Returned: Array of pointers to lead through list in descending GPA order
Logic: Pointer bubble sort algorithm.

```
PROGRAM RegistrarSystem (input, output);

  {  Array implementation of registrar's system at U. of Hard    }
  {  Knocks.  Allows all needed list operations, including grade }
  {  reports and end of year reports sorted by name and end of   }
  {  year reports sorted by grade point average.                 }

  CONST
    MaxStudents = 10;     {  Maximum number of students          }
    CredToGrad = 120;     {  Credits to graduate                 }

  TYPE
    StudentRec = RECORD
                   Name : String;  { Assume appropriate implementation of the
                                     string ADT }
                   CredTaken : integer;
                   CredEarned : integer;
                   TotalGradePts : integer
                 END;
    StudentList = RECORD  {  Encapsulated implementation of list }
                    List : ARRAY [1..MaxStudents] OF StudentRec;
                    NumberOfStudents : integer  { Current number of students }
                  END;

  VAR
    Choice : char;              {  User's choice of menu option  }
    Students : StudentList;     {  Array implementation of list  }

{*****************************************************************}

  PROCEDURE GetSelection (VAR Choice : char);

    {  Given:   Nothing.                                         }
    {  Task:    Print menu and read user's response.             }
    {  Return:  User's response in Choice.                       }

    BEGIN
      writeln;
      writeln ('A)dd Student');
      writeln ('C)hange Student Record');
      writeln ('I)nspect Student Record');
      writeln ('D)elete Student Record');
      writeln ('G)rade Reports');
      writeln ('E)nd of Year Reports');
      writeln ('Q)uit');
      write ('Choose by entering first letter of selection-->');
      readln (Choice)
    END;  {  of PROCEDURE GetSelection  }

{*****************************************************************}

  PROCEDURE CreateStudentList (VAR Students : StudentList);

    {  Given:   Uninitialized list of students                   }
    {  Task:    Initialize the list to the empty list            }
    {  Return:  Students initialized to the empty list           }

    VAR K : integer;
```

```
      BEGIN
        Students.NumberOfStudents := 0;
        { Initialize all strings in the list  }
        FOR K := 1 TO MaxStudents DO
          Create (Students.List[K].Name)
      END;

  {****************************************************************}

    PROCEDURE AddStudent (VAR Students : StudentList);

      {  Given:   List of students.                                }
      {  Task:    Prompt user for student to add, find             }
      {           appropriate slot for that student, and insert    }
      {           new student in that slot.                        }
      {  Return:  List and NumberOfStudents in updated form.       }

      VAR
        NewStudent : StudentRec;
        K, LocationOfAdd : integer;

      PROCEDURE FindSlot (Students : StudentList;
                          NewName : String;
                          VAR LocationOfAdd : integer);

        {  Given:   List of student records in Students and name   }
        {           of student to add in NewStudent.               }
        {  Task:    Search Students sequentially for slot to       }
        {           locate NewName.                                }
        {  Return:  Index location for NewName in LocationOfAdd.   }

        VAR
          Found : boolean;

        BEGIN {  PROCEDURE FindSlot  }
          LocationOfAdd := 1;
          Found := false;
          WHILE (LocationOfAdd <= Students.NumberOfStudents) AND NOT Found DO
            IF GreaterThan (Students.List[LocationOfAdd].Name, NewName) THEN
              Found := true
            ELSE
              LocationOfAdd := LocationOfAdd + 1
        END; {  of PROCEDURE FindSlot  }

      BEGIN {  PROCEDURE AddStudent  }
        WITH NewStudent DO

          BEGIN
            Create (Name);
            write ('Enter new student name-->');
            ReadAString (Name);
            write ('Enter credits taken, earned, and total grade points-->');
            readln (CredTaken, CredEarned, TotalGradePts);
            {  Find slot where new student belongs  }
            FindSlot (Students, Name, LocationOfAdd)
          END;

        {  From that slot on, move down rest of records  }
        FOR K := Students.NumberOfStudents DOWNTO LocationOfAdd DO
          Students.List[K + 1] := Students.List[K];
        Students.NumberOfStudents := Students.NumberOfStudents + 1;
        Students.List[LocationOfAdd] := NewStudent
      END;  {  of PROCEDURE AddStudent  }

  {****************************************************************}
```

```
PROCEDURE FindStudent(Target : String;
                      Students : StudentList;
                      VAR InfoWanted : StudentRec;
                      VAR Mid : integer;
                      VAR Found : boolean);

  {  Given:   List of student records in Students and          }
  {           to search for in Target.                         }
  {  Task:    Apply binary search algorithm to find Target.    }
  {  Return:  If Target found, return associated record in     }
  {           InfoWanted, associated position in Mid, and      }
  {           Found as true.  Otherwise return Found as        }
  {           false.                                           }

  VAR
    High, Low : integer;

  BEGIN
    Found := false;
    Low := 1;
    High := Students.NumberOfStudents;
    WHILE NOT Found AND (Low <= High) DO
      BEGIN
        Mid := (Low + High) DIV 2;
        IF LessThan (Target, Students.List[Mid].Name) THEN
          High := Mid - 1
        ELSE IF GreaterThan (Target, Students.List[Mid].Name) THEN
          Low := Mid + 1
        ELSE
          BEGIN
            Found := true;
            InfoWanted := Students.List[Mid]
          END
      END
  END; {  of PROCEDURE FindStudent  }

{*****************************************************************}

PROCEDURE DeleteStudent (VAR Students : StudentList);

  {  Given:   List of student records in Students.             }
  {  Task:    Prompts user for name to delete.  If this name   }
  {           is in list, remove it.  Otherwise print error    }
  {           message.                                         }
  {  Return:  Updated List and NumberOfStudents  if name       }
  {           is found.                                        }

  VAR
    DeleteName : String;
    K, LocationOfDelete : integer;
    Found : boolean;
    DeleteRec : StudentRec;

  BEGIN
    Create (DeleteName);
    write ('Student to delete-->');
    ReadAString (DeleteName);

    {  Call on binary search to locate student  }
    FindStudent (DeleteName, Students, DeleteRec,
                 LocationOfDelete, Found);
    IF NOT Found THEN
      writeln ('Error in delete')
    ELSE
      BEGIN
```

```
        {  Move up all records below delete location  }
        FOR K := LocationOfDelete TO Students.NumberOfStudents - 1 DO
          Students.List[K] := Students.List[K + 1];
        Students.NumberOfStudents := Students.NumberOfStudents - 1
      END
    END;  {  of PROCEDURE DeleteStudent  }


{*************************************************************}


  PROCEDURE ChangeStudent(VAR Students : StudentList);

    {  Given:   List of student records in Students.              }
    {  Task:    Prompt user for change desired if record can be   }
    {           found, make appropriate change.  Otherwise,       }
    {           print error message.                              }
    {  Return:  Students list with updated record.                }

    VAR
      ChangeName : String;
      ChangeField : integer;
      Found : boolean;
      ChangeRec : StudentRec;
      ChangeLoc : integer;

    BEGIN
      Create(ChangeName);
      writeln ('Enter name of student to change-->');
      ReadAString (ChangeName);

      {  Call on binary search to find record wanted  }
      FindStudent (ChangeName, Students, ChangeRec,
                   ChangeLoc, Found);
      IF NOT Found THEN
        BEGIN
          WriteAString (ChangeName);
          writeln (' not found.')
        END
      ELSE
        BEGIN
          write ('Field to change--> 1-Taken,2-Earned,3-Points');
          readln (ChangeField);

          {  Obtain new value for appropriate field  }
          WITH Students.List[ChangeLoc] DO
            CASE ChangeField OF
              1 : BEGIN
                    write ('New value for credits taken-->');
                    readln (CredTaken)
                  END;
              2 : BEGIN
                    write('New value for credits earned-->');
                    readln(CredEarned)
                  END;
              3 : BEGIN
                    write('New value for total grade points-->');
                    readln(TotalGradePts)
                  END
          END   {  of CASE ChangeField  }
        END   {  of ELSE statement  }
    END;  {  of PROCEDURE ChangeStudent  }


{*************************************************************}
```

```
  PROCEDURE InspectStudent (Students : StudentList);

    {  Given:   List of student records in Students and current  }
    {           number of students in NumberOfStudents.          }
    {  Task:    Prompts user for name to inspect and calls on    }
    {           binary search to find it.                        }
    {  Return:  Nothing.                                         }

    CONST
      Skip = ' ';

    VAR
      InspectName : String;
      InspectLoc : integer;
      InspectRec : StudentRec;
      Found : boolean;

    BEGIN
      Create(InspectName);
      write ('Name of student to inspect-->');
      ReadAString (InspectName);

      {  Call on binary search to obtain desired record  }
      FindStudent (InspectName, Students, InspectRec,
                   InspectLoc, Found);
      IF NOT Found THEN
        BEGIN
          WriteAString (InspectName);
          writeln (' not found.')
        END
      ELSE
        WITH InspectRec DO
          BEGIN
            WriteAString (Name);
            writeln (Skip:2, CredTaken, CredEarned, TotalGradePts)
          END
    END;  {  of PROCEDURE InspectStudent  }

{**************************************************************}

  PROCEDURE PrintGradeReports (Students : StudentList);

    {  Given:   List of student records in Students.            }
    {  Task:    Proceed sequentially through list, computing    }
    {           and printing report card for each student.      }
    {  Return:  Nothing.                                        }

    VAR
      K : integer;
      GPA : real;

    BEGIN
      FOR K := 1 TO Students.NumberOfStudents DO
        WITH Students.List[K] DO
          BEGIN
            GPA := TotalGradePts / CredTaken;
            write ('Student ');
            WriteAString (Name);
            writeln;
            writeln ('Taken ', CredTaken : 10 );
            writeln ('Earned ', CredEarned : 9 );
            writeln ('GPA ', GPA: 6 : 2);
            writeln
          END {of WITH...DO }
    END;  {  of PROCEDURE PrintGradeReports  }
```

```
{*****************************************************************}

 PROCEDURE EndOfYearReports (Students : StudentList);

   {  Given:   List of student records in Students.            }
   {  Task:    Oversees printing of end of year reports for     }
   {           graduating seniors.                              }
   {  Return:  Nothing.                                         }

   CONST
     Skip = '';

   PROCEDURE PrintListByName (Students : StudentList);

     {  Given:   List of student records in Students.          }
     {  Task:    Sequentially print detail lines in             }
     {           alphabetical order by name, which is also the  }
     {           physical order of the list.                    }
     {  Return:  Nothing.                                       }

     VAR
       K : integer;

     BEGIN {  PROCEDURE PrintListByName  }
       FOR K := 1 TO Students.NumberOfStudents DO
         WITH Students.List[K] DO
           IF CredEarned >= CredToGrad THEN
             BEGIN
               WriteAString (Name);
               writeln (Skip : 40 - Length (Name), CredTaken : 10, CredEarned : 10,
                         TotalGradePts : 10)
             END
     END;  {  of PROCEDURE PrintListByName  }

   PROCEDURE PrintListByGPA (Students : StudentList);

     {  Given:   List of student records in Students.          }
     {  Task:    Establishes GPA order in Pointer array and     }
     {           then prints detail lines in this GPA order.    }
     {  Return:  Nothing.                                       }

     TYPE
       PointerArray = ARRAY [1..MaxStudents] OF integer;

     VAR
       K : integer;
       GPA : real;
       Pointer : PointerArray;

     PROCEDURE SortByGPA (Students : StudentList;
                          VAR Pointer : PointerArray);

       {  Given:   List of student records in Students.        }
       {  Task:    Apply pointer bubble sort algorithm to       }
       {           determine GPA descending order.              }
       {  Return:  Pointer array indicating GPA order.          }

       VAR
         K, J, Temp : integer;
         ExchangeMade : boolean;

       BEGIN  {  PROCEDURE SortByGPA  }
         FOR K := 1 TO Students.NumberOfStudents DO
           Pointer[K] := K;
```

```
        K := 0;
        ExchangeMade := true;
        WHILE (K <= Students.NumberOfStudents - 1) AND ExchangeMade DO
          BEGIN
            ExchangeMade := false;
            K := K + 1;
            FOR J := 1 TO Students.NumberOfStudents - K DO

              {  Sort algorithm keys on grade point average  }
              IF Students.List[Pointer[J]].TotalGradePts /
                 Students.List[Pointer[J]].CredTaken <
                 Students.List[Pointer[J + 1]].TotalGradePts /
                 Students.List[Pointer[J + 1]].CredTaken THEN
                BEGIN
                  Temp := Pointer[J];
                  Pointer[J] := Pointer[J + 1];
                  Pointer[J + 1] := Temp;
                  ExchangeMade := true
                END  {  of IF...THEN  }
          END  { of WHILE }
      END;  {  of PROCEDURE SortByGPA  }

    BEGIN  {  PROCEDURE PrintListByGPA  }
      SortByGPA (Students, Pointer);
      FOR K := 1 TO Students.NumberOfStudents DO
        WITH Students.List[Pointer[K]] DO
          IF CredEarned >= CredToGrad THEN
            BEGIN
              GPA := TotalGradePts / CredTaken;
              WriteAString (Name);
              writeln (Skip: 40 - Length (Name), CredTaken: 10, CredEarned: 10,
                       GPA: 10: 2)
            END {  of IF...THEN  }
    END;  {  of PROCEDURE PrintListByGPA  }

  BEGIN  {  PROCEDURE EndOfYearReports  }
    writeln ('                    REPORT BY NAME ');
    writeln ('NAME', Skip : 36, 'TAKEN': 10, 'EARNED': 10, 'POINTS': 10);
    PrintListByName (Students);
    writeln;
    writeln ('                    REPORT BY GPA ');
    writeln ('NAME', Skip : 36, 'TAKEN': 10, 'EARNED': 10, 'GPA': 10);
    PrintListByGPA (Students);
  END;  {  of PROCEDURE EndOfYearReports  }


{*****************************************************************}


 BEGIN  {  Main  }
   writeln ('Welcome to Registrar System at U. of Hard Knocks');
   CreateStudentList (Students);
   REPEAT
     GetSelection (Choice);
     CASE Choice OF
       'A': AddStudent(Students);
       'C': ChangeStudent(Students);
       'I': InspectStudent(Students);
       'D': DeleteStudent(Students);
       'G': PrintGradeReports(Students);
       'E': EndOfYearReports(Students);
       'Q': BEGIN END
     END {  of CASE Choice  }
   UNTIL Choice = 'Q'  {  Q is quit option  }
 END.  {  of main program  }
```

Sample runs for a few of the menu options follow. These are included to give you a feel for the functioning of the system once all the pieces have been tied together. However, these sample runs should by no means be considered complete in terms of testing the system. In the Problems, you will develop a testing strategy for this system.

```
Welcome to Registrar System at U. of Hard Knocks

A)dd Student
C)hange Student Record
I)nspect Student Record
D)elete Student Record
G)rade Reports
E)nd of Year Reports
Q)uit
Choose by entering first letter of selection-->A
Enter new student name-->SMART, LES
Enter credits taken, earned, and total grade points-->80 60 120

A)dd Student
C)hange Student Record
I)nspect Student Record
D)elete Student Record
G)rade Reports
E)nd of Year Reports
Q)uit
Choose by entering first letter of selection-->A
Enter new student name-->WOOD, HOLLY
Enter credits taken, earned, and total grade points-->123 120 357

A)dd Student
C)hange Student Record
I)nspect Student Record
D)elete Student Record
G)rade Reports
E)nd of Year Reports
Q)uit
Choose by entering first letter of selection-->A
Enter new student name-->AVREG, JOE
Enter credits taken, earned, and total grade points-->96 93 208

A)dd Student
C)hange Student Record
I)nspect Student Record
D)elete Student Record
G)rade Reports
E)nd of Year Reports
Q)uit
Choose by entering first letter of selection-->A

Enter new student name-->CLEAR, BEA
Enter credits taken, earned, and total grade points-->120 120 436

A)dd Student
C)hange Student Record
I)nspect Student Record
D)elete Student Record
G)rade Reports
E)nd of Year Reports
Q)uit
Choose by entering first letter of selection-->G
```

```
Student AVREG, JOE
Taken          96
Earned         93
GPA          2.17

Student CLEAR, BEA
Taken         120
Earned        120
GPA          3.63

Student SMART, LES
Taken          80
Earned         60
GPA          1.50

Student WOOD, HOLLY
Taken          123
Earned         120
GPA           2.90

A)dd Student
C)hange Student Record
I)nspect Student Record
D)elete Student Record
G)rade Reports
E)nd of Year Reports
Q)uit
Choose by entering first letter of selection-->E
                            REPORT BY NAME
NAME                                    TAKEN    EARNED    POINTS
CLEAR, BEA                                120       120       436
WOOD, HOLLY                               123       120       357
                            REPORT BY GPA
NAME                                    TAKEN    EARNED    POINTS
CLEAR, BEA                                120       120      3.63
WOOD, HOLLY                               123       120      2.90

A)dd Student
C)hange Student Record
I)nspect Student Record
D)elete Student Record
G)rade Reports
E)nd of Year Reports
Q)uit
Choose by entering first letter of selection-->Q
```

RUNNING AND DEBUGGING TIPS

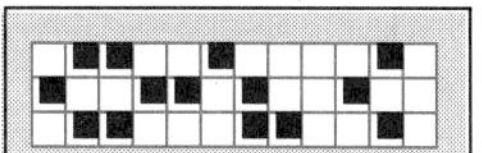

1. When testing a large program, always test modules individually before testing the entire system.
2. When developing test cases, keep them in a file so that they can be used again easily after fixing errors.
3. The finite state machine paradigm is a systematic way of insuring that users enter valid input to your program.
4. Be sure to design test data that exercises the boundary conditions of a module: this is where an error is most likely to occur.

Summary

Key Terms

acceptance testing
analysis
black box testing
boundary conditions
coding phase
coupling
data flow diagram
documentation
driver module
encapsulation
equivalence classes
finite state machine
fixed length method
functionally cohesive
maintenance
modular specification
modular testing
robust
state-transition diagram
strings
structured English
stub module
systems analyst
system testing
test cases
testing phase
test oracle
transitions
white box testing

Key Terms (Optional)

class object
file buffer
formal verification
inheritance
instances
inductive assertions
loop invariant
message-passing
method of inductive assertions
object-oriented programming
polymorphism
programming by personification
random access file
semantics
sequential access files

Key Concepts

- During the analysis phase of the software system life cycle you must determine the users' requirements. Typically, this involves considerable interaction between the systems analyst and end users. A data flow diagram is one example of a document that would be developed during this phase. Ultimately, the users' requirements must be described in a form suitable to pass on to the design phase.
- During the design phase, the users' requirements are examined, and the system that will ultimately meet these requirements begins to take shape. Software designers must turn out a blueprint of the eventual software system that can then be translated into program code. Typical of the documents produced during the design phase are modular structure charts, layout of data structures, and modular logic specifications.
- A good design is developed in a top-down fashion. Individual modules within the design should be functionally cohesive: they should focus on one particular task. Modules within the design should be minimally coupled; they should not transfer more information than necessary between themselves. This avoids the possibility of one module's inadvertently affecting data being used by another.
- Testing and verification can consume up to 50 percent of the time spent in developing a software system. Each module should be tested as it is finished. Use drivers to feed inputs into the module and stubs to check the module's interactions with subordinate modules.
- System and acceptance testing follows modular testing.
- The maintenance phase of a system follows its release to users. During this phase, adjustments must be made to the system in response to bugs and changes in user requirements.
- Obsolescence is the sixth, and ultimately inevitable, phase of the software system life cycle.

Key Concepts (Optional)

- Though not part of standard Pascal, random access files provide a useful means of implementing a list in situations where the data must be stored permanently. The price one pays for this permanent storage is a longer time to access one list entry.

- Formal algorithm verification by such methods as inductive assertions is of theoretical interest now and offers promise of more reliable software in the future.
- Object-oriented programming allows systems developers to reuse and extend implementations of ADTs in a more flexible fashion than traditional languages.

Programming Problems and Projects

1. Design a complete set of modular test cases for the system in the Focus on Program Design section. Be as thorough as possible in your testing; pay particular attention to robustness issues. Wherever your testing locates an error, modify the code to fix it. (An interesting class experiment for this program is to turn it into a contest. The student who finds and fixes the most errors wins.)
2. If your instructor assigned Section 3.4, modify the program in the Focus on Program Design so that the student list is implemented with a random access file.
3. Invite the registrar of your university to your class to discuss the type of data processing operations in which the registrar's office is typically engaged. After this discussion (which should no doubt include time for questions), describe the data involved in the operations of your registrar's office in terms of abstract data types. Develop a data flow diagram to picture the way in which the registrar's office processes information.
4. Consider the following data declaration and function header.

```
TYPE
  KindOfTriangle = (Scalene, Isosceles, Equilateral, Impossible);
  .
  .
  .
FUNCTION TriangleType (Side1, Side2, Side3 : Integer) : KindOfTriangle;

{ This function receives three positive integers representing the     }
{ length of sides of a possible triangle. It is to return the         }
{ type of triangle with those lengths as sides:                       }
{                                                                     }
{         Equilateral--all sides equal                                }
{         Isosceles--two sides equal                                  }
{         Scalene--no sides equal                                     }
{                                                                     }
{ Additionally, the function should return the value Impossible if    }
{ the three positive integers do not constitute a valid set of        }
{ triangle sides.                                                     }
```

   For this problem, work with another student. Each of you should develop independently, first, a robust version of the function just described and, second, a complete set of test data (including robustness checks) for the function. Next, jointly develop a driver program and test your functions. Have your partner use his or her test data on the function you developed. Then use your test data on your partner's function. The winner is the one whose function fails for the fewer number of test cases.

5. In Exercise 8 of Section 3.2 you designed a system for the registrar at American Basket Weaving University. Implement and fully test that system.
6. In Exercise 11 of Section 3.3 you developed and tested a module to read strings that are valid file names on your particular computer sys-

tem. Incorporate this module into a larger program that could be used to backup text files. The user should enter two file names: a source file and a destination file. Your program should then copy from the source to the destination. If your file name module does its job correctly, your program should never crash because it tries to access an "invalid file name."

7. For Problem 5 of Chapter 2, you developed a program that allowed its user to enter rational numbers and then perform operations upon them. Now make your program more user-friendly and robust by reading all rational numbers entered by the user in a module ReadRational. The logic of this module should be driven by a finite-state machine that filters out erroneous input. Submit a diagram of the finite-state machine as part of the documentation accompanying your program.

8. For Problem 6 of Chapter 2, you developed a program that allowed its user to enter complex numbers and then perform operations upon them. Now make your program more user-friendly and robust by reading all complex numbers entered by the user in a module ReadComplex. The logic of this module should be driven by a finite-state machine that filters out erroneous input. Submit a diagram of the finite-state machine as part of the documentation accompanying your program.

9. Assume that you would like to make some extra cash by writing a program to facilitate some activity for a particular business, organization, or school. Write a proposal that clearly explains what your program will do, how much it would cost, why the purchase of this program would be beneficial to the institution, and how soon you could complete this project. Be sure to limit your project so that it does not exceed your ability as a programmer.

10. Research the topic of formal methods in algorithm verification, using the September 1990 issues of *IEEE Computer* and *IEEE Software* as initial references. Then write a paper in which you discuss the role that formal algorithm verification may play in future software development. Your paper should address such issues as how formal verification can reduce the amount of time spent in testing software and how it can be used to insure a degree of software reliability exceeding what can be achieved by testing alone. Be sure to respond to the criticisms of formal verification summarized in Section 3.5.

11. Interview a systems analyst at a local company or organization. Then, write a paper or prepare a presentation in which you describe the techniques used by that systems analyst to determine user needs and to document these user needs in written or diagrammatic form.

12. The September 1990 issue of *Communications of the ACM* was dedicated to the topic of object-oriented programming. Using the articles in this issue as a starting point, write a research paper in which you describe how software development will be affected by the object-oriented paradigm. Your paper should discuss such issues as building software libraries that are usable in a variety of contexts and building software systems that are easily extended when the need to do so arises.

These are the ties which, though light as air, are strong as links of iron.

Edmund Burke
1729–1797

Linked Lists and Pointers

In the previous chapters we discovered that an array implementation (with binary search) of a keyed list requires $O(n)$ data interchanges for the add and delete operations. Attempting to maintain such an array-implemented list in order parallels the dynamics of waiting in a long line. When someone cuts into the middle of the line, there is a domino-like effect that forces everyone behind that person to move back. When someone in the middle of the line decides to leave the line, the reverse effect occurs; everyone behind the departed person is able to move ahead one slot. It is possible to draw an analogy between people waiting in a line and data items stored next to each other in computer memory. If the data items are arranged in some type of order and it becomes necessary to insert into or delete from the middle of the line, a considerable amount of data movement is involved. This data movement requires computer time and decreases program efficiency. The central motivation behind the linked list data structure is to eliminate the data movement associated with insertions into and deletions from the middle of the list. Of course, by now we might suspect that efficiency in eliminating such data movement can only come by trading off other efficiency factors. One of the crucial questions to ask yourself as we study linked lists is "What price are we paying to handle additions and deletions effectively?"

One way of conceptually picturing a linked list is to think of a game some parents use to make the opening of holiday gifts particularly exciting for their children. One feature of the game that helps to build children's anticipation insures that minor gifts are opened first, gradually building up to the most substantial gift. (Recall from your own childhood experience the partial letdown that occurred when you opened a gift package containing a mere pair of socks after having already unwrapped something significantly more exciting such as a baseball glove or new doll.) Thus, the premises of this gift-giving game are that gifts may be ranked according to their desirability and that the game is more fun when the most desirable gifts are opened last.

To achieve this end, parents will hide their child's wrapped gifts at various locations throughout the home. For instance, let us suppose a scenario in which parents have the following four gifts for their child, ranked and hidden as indicated.

Ranking	Gift	Hiding Place
Least desirable	Pair of socks	Under Bed
↓	Box of candy	Kitchen drawer
	Video game	Basement cabinet
Most desirable	Bicycle	Garage

The parents will then tell the child *only* the location of the least desirable gift; here, for instance, they would give instructions to look under a bed for the first gift. Upon opening that gift, the child will find the uninspiring pair of socks *plus* a more intriguing note with the information that the child's next gift will be in a kitchen drawer. The pattern should now be obvious. From the box of candy, the child follows an informational pointer to a basement cabinet, where the video game is discovered along with a similar informational link to the garage as a location where something bigger and better may be found. Here the now-eager child will uncover a bike along with a final (and no doubt disappointing) note indicating that the end of the chain of gifts has been reached.

A conceptual picture of this chain of gifts is presented in Figure 4.1.

FIGURE 4.1
A linked chain of gifts

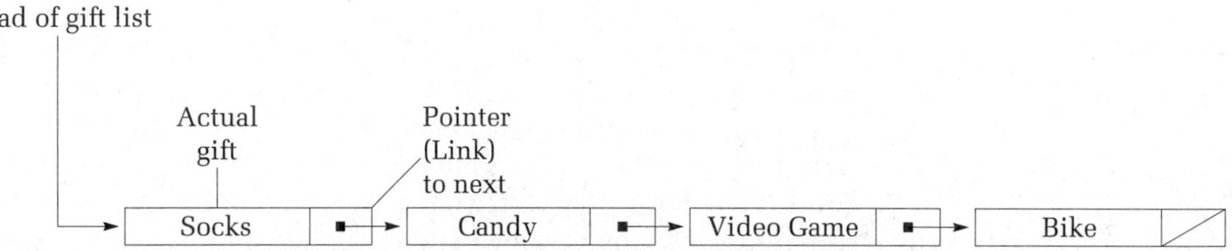

This same conceptual picture applies to the *linked list* abstract data structure we are about to study. In this figure, the arrows connecting packages represent the informational note in each package which tells us the location of the next package. Conceptually, the form taken by this informational pointer is not important. However, it is crucial that we have a reliable *pointer* to the leading gift (often called a *head pointer*) and, thereafter, a reliable pointer in each package (often called a *node*) to the next package. Should any pointer be flawed, the remaining gifts on the chain become essentially inaccessible (much to the dismay of the child who wanted that bike so desperately).

In addition to introducing us to much of the vernacular that comes with linked lists, this review of a simple childhood game can also give us a hint of the ease with which such a linked chain of nodes can handle additions and deletions. For instance, suppose that a sudden windfall allows the parents of the child in our example to buy a baseball glove in addition to the four gifts they had already purchased. Assuming that this new gift is ranked between the video game and the bicycle in desirability, consider what must be done to link it into the gift chain. We must do as follows:

1. Find a place to hide it; for example, the attic.
2. Take the informational linking note from the video game package and put it in the baseball glove package. (Why?)
3. Insert a new informational pointer in the video game package, indicating the attic as the location of the next node. (Why?)

Figure 4.2 portrays such an addition with circled numbers corresponding to the three steps just described. The important aspect to note in this series of moves is that no gift that was already in place had to be moved to accommodate adding the new gift. From a conceptual perspective, this is why linked lists will be able to avoid the movement of data that was associated with an insertion into an array-implemented list.

FIGURE 4.2
Adding a baseball glove to the chain of Figure 4.1

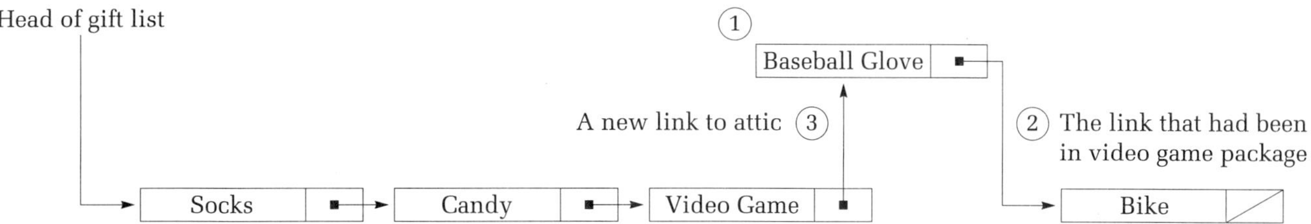

Along the same lines, let us now suppose that our shameless parents devour all of their child's candy before the holiday arrives. Clearly they must remove this package from the chain to hide this disgusting behavior from their child. Using Figure 4.3, convince yourself that the following steps will accomplish this deletion:

1. Remove the now-empty candy package from the kitchen drawer.
2. Before throwing away the empty package, remove the linking note from it and put this note in the package containing the socks.
3. Dispose of the incriminating candy container and the linking note that originally was in the package with the socks.

FIGURE 4.3
Removing candy from the chain of Figure 4.2

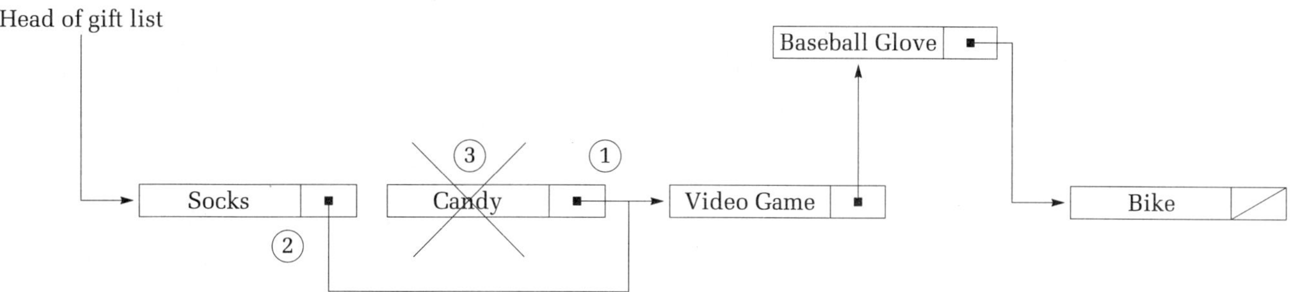

It is important to note again that no package remaining on the chain had to be physically moved to a new location: a situation much different from what happened when we removed a name from an array-implemented list in the last chapter.

Have we strayed too far from computer science in using such a nontechnical, elementary example to introduce our chapter on linked lists? Not at all! In fact, we've achieved two very important goals. First, if you understand all the details of the gift-giving game, then you essentially understand the important concepts involved in the linked list data structure. Second, this is just another illustration of the fact that computer techniques are often just formalizations in a logic machine of the way we, as human beings, have been doing things for many years. Consequently, you should never feel intimidated by such a computer technique; merely try to relate it to an analogous—and familiar—manual method. Doing this will help give substance to the more formal computer science method.

4.1 The Linked List as an Abstract Data Type

OBJECTIVES

- to formalize the notion of a linked list as an ADT
- to understand, at an abstract level, why a linked list allows additions and deletions of nodes with minimal data movement
- to realize, at an abstract level, the price paid in search efficiency for the efficiency gained in adding and deleting nodes.
- to realize that, although a linked list may be viewed as an ADT, it is also a data structure that can be used to implement other ADTs, such as keyed lists

Recall from Chapter 2 that to formally specify an abstract data type (ADT), we must describe the individual elements of the structure, the relationship(s) between these elements, and the logical operations to be performed on the structure.

A formalization for the intuitive notion of a linked list follows. This formalization uses the terminology *linear ordering*. By linear ordering, we mean any ordering of data in which there is an identifiable first element, second element, and so forth. For instance, a string could be viewed as a linear ordering of characters. Also, a keyed list has a linear ordering determined by its key field. It is important to realize that linear ordering is a logical concept; it need not coincide with physical ordering of data.

Linked list. A linked list is a collection of elements called nodes. Each node contains a data portion and a pointer. The data portions in all nodes are of the same type. The pointer in a given node contains the location of the node that follows the given node in the linear ordering of the list. The entire list is referenced by a separate head pointer to the first element in the linear ordering. The head pointer is simply the location of this first element. It is not a linked list node and hence has no data associated with it. A special value designated as *Null* is assigned to a pointer that references an empty linked list.

The operations that can be performed on a linked list are:

Create operation

Preconditions:	*Head* is a pointer whose value is arbitrary.
Postconditions:	*Head* pointer is initialized to *Null*, thereby referencing the empty list.

Empty operation

Preconditions:	*Head* is a pointer that references a linked list.
Postconditions:	*Empty* returns **true** if the linked list referenced by *Head* is empty and **false** otherwise.

Next operation

Preconditions:	*P* is a pointer to a node in a linked list. Assume that *P* is not *Null*.
Postconditions:	*Next* returns a pointer to the node following that referenced by *P*. If no node follows *P* in the list, then *Next* returns *Null*.

InsertNode operation

Preconditions:	*Head* pointer references a linked list. *P* and *Prev* are also pointers. *P* references a node to be inserted in the linked list after the list node referenced by *Prev*. *Prev* is equal to *Null* if the insertion is to occur at the front of the list.
Postconditions:	Node referenced by *P* is inserted into list referenced by *Head* after the node referenced by *Prev*.

DeleteNode operation

Preconditions:	*Head* pointer references a linked list. *P* and *Prev* are also pointers. *P* references a node to be deleted from the linked list. *Prev* references the list node preceding that referenced by *P*. *Prev* is equal to *Null* if *P* references the first node in the list.
Postconditions:	Node referenced by *P* is removed from the list referenced by *Head*.

LinkedTraverse operation

Preconditions:	*Head* is a pointer referencing a linked list, and *ProcessNode* is an algorithmic process which can be applied to the data portion of each node on the list.
Postconditions:	Each node in the list referenced by *Head* is visited in the linear order determined by the pointers in the list. As each node is visited, *ProcessNode* is applied to it.

Figure 4.4 depicts the action of the Create, Next, InsertNode, DeleteNode, and LinkedTraverse operations on a linked list of integers. Study this figure carefully and observe that every linked list will have one *Null* pointer associated with it. After the Create operation, the Head pointer for the resulting empty list is *Null*. For a non-empty list, the pointer in the final node on the list is *Null*. Note the distinction between a pointer that is *Null* and a pointer that is undefined. The former reliably indicates a reference to an empty structure through a specific flagging value. The latter is completely unreliable in terms of what it references.

The figure also indicates that insertion into and deletion from a linked list require a pointer to the node to be acted upon and a pointer to the node which precedes this node in the linear ordering of the list. For both of these operations, the pointer to the preceding node is necessary since the pointer within that node must be altered as part of the operation. For example, in Figure 4.4, when we insert 46 after the node containing 19, the node containing 19 is altered by having its pointer reference the node containing 46 instead of the node containing 63. This alteration of the node containing 19 requires that we have a pointer (*Prev*) that references it. In the event that the insertion or deletion occurs at the front of the list, the *Prev* pointer is set to *Null* to signal this special condition.

Finally, Figure 4.4 illustrates that the linear ordering of the linked list may not necessarily coincide with the natural ordering of data in the list. In this figure, the linear ordering of the list is not in correspondence with either ascending or descending order by integer value. What defines the linear ordering will vary from application to application.

FIGURE 4.4
Actions of some linked list operations

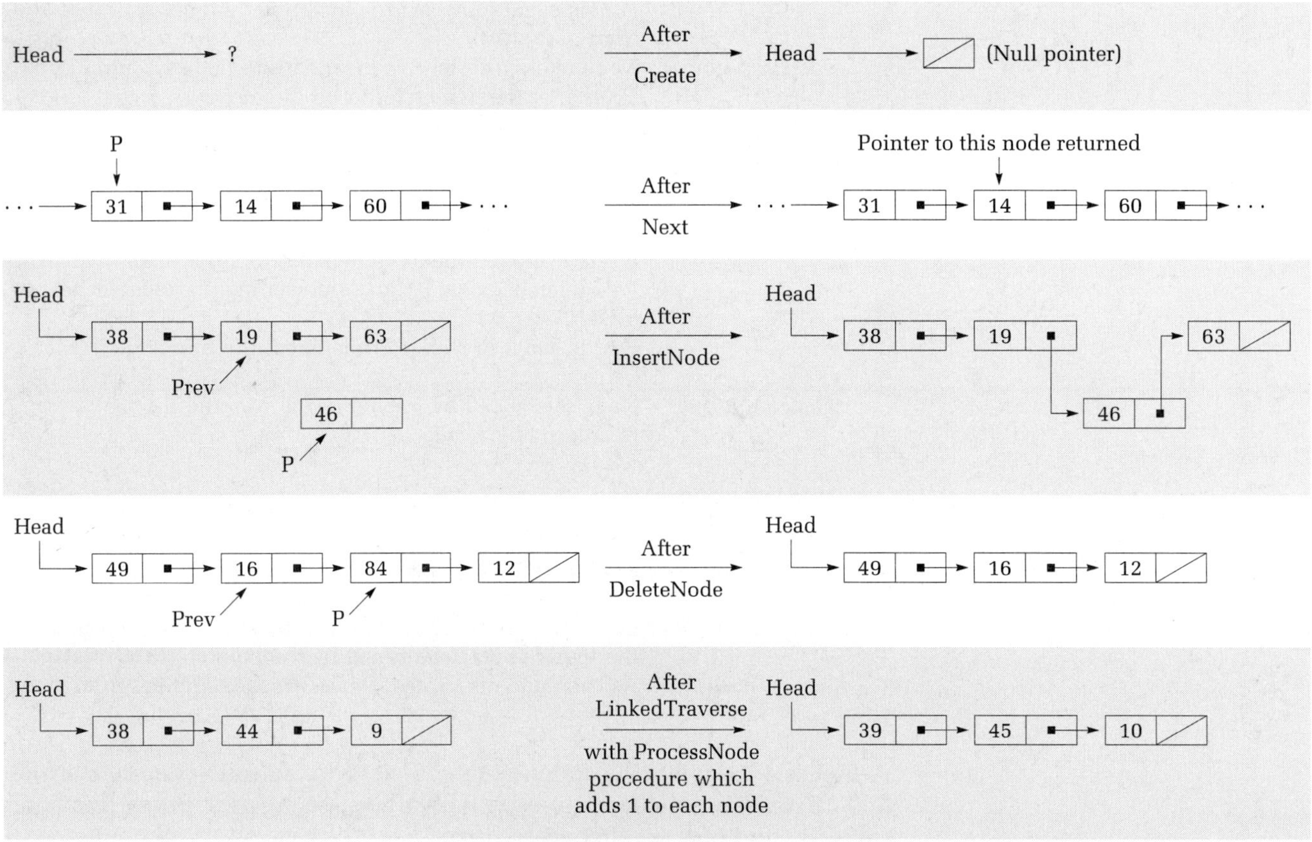

One application we can immediately envision is to use a linked list as an implementation technique for the keyed list ADT. The linear ordering established by the links would mirror the order determined by the key fields in the nodes. For instance, Figure 4.5 depicts a linked list in which the links establish an alphabetical ordering according to key field.

FIGURE 4.5
Alphabetically ordered linked list with four nodes

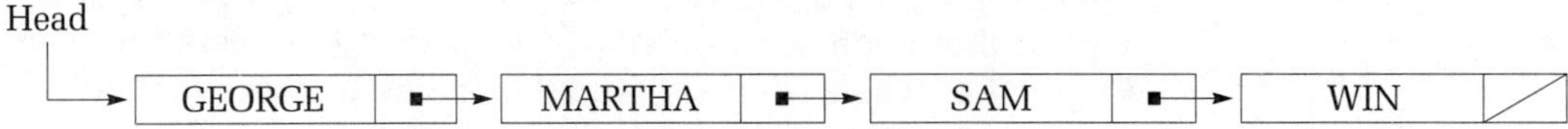

The operations of adding a node and deleting a node from such a list may also be conveniently represented in such a schematic form. In fact, you will soon discover that the best way to conceive algorithms that manipulate linked lists is to draw what you want to happen via such logical pictures. Such a picture of a linked list is completely at the abstract level; it implies nothing about how the linked list will finally be implemented. Once you understand the concept from such a graphic representation, it is usually a straightforward matter to actually implement it.

For instance, we now wish to add a node containing PRIM to the list shown in Figure 4.5; then all we need to do is to store PRIM in an available memory location outside of the list, such as the one pointed to by P in Figure 4.6. We then reset the pointer link of the node containing MARTHA to point to the node containing PRIM, and the pointer link of the node containing PRIM to point to the node containing SAM. This logically maintains the alphabetical order of the data in the nodes without physically moving any of the existing nodes.

FIGURE 4.6
Insertion of node containing PRIM into linked list of Figure 4.5

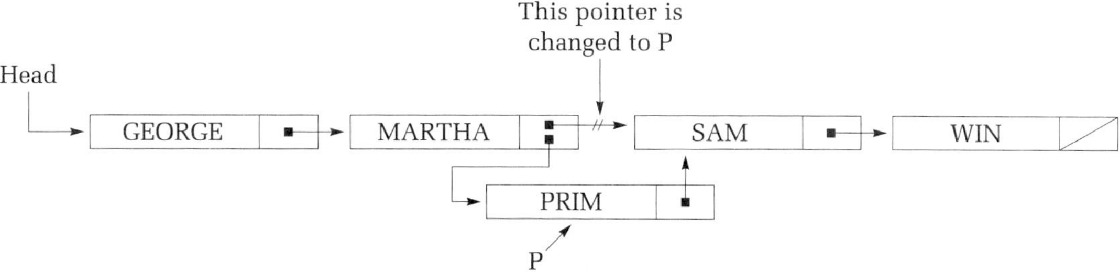

Similarly, should you then wish to delete an existing node from the linked list, a graphic representation of the list can again indicate how the pointers should be altered to reflect such a change. For example, given the list of Figure 4.6, the diagram of Figure 4.7 pictorially outlines what must be done if we want to delete the node containing MARTHA. Notice in this figure that, as was the case for insertion, only pointers must be changed to delete a node. Again, no movement of data occurs.

FIGURE 4.7
Deletion of node containing MARTHA from linked list of Figure 4.6

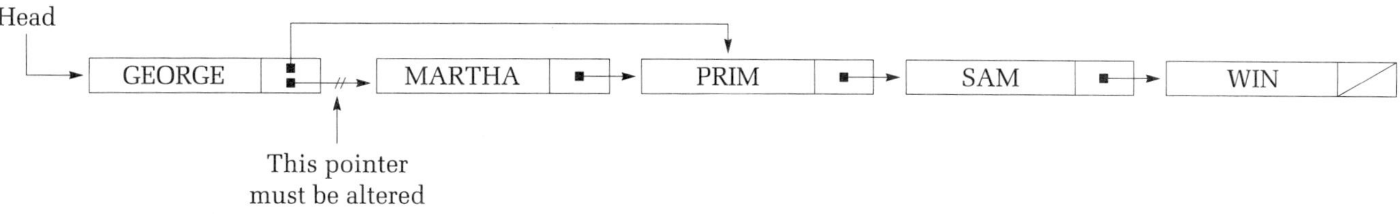

Efficiency Considerations for Linked Lists

These addition/deletion considerations may make a linked list an attractive alternative to an array implementation of a keyed list. The diagrams of Figures 4.6 and 4.7 indicate that adds and deletes merely require the exchange of two pointers. Since pointers are merely locations of other nodes, this means that we are usually manipulating mere integers or similarly simple data in doing such pointer operations. Hence, both additions and deletions would appear to be O(1) operations in terms of data movement for linked lists. This compares very favorably to the massive movement of entire records which was forced by an addition or deletion on an array implementation of a list. In general, such insertion and removal operations will be $O(n)$ in terms of data movement in an array implementation of a list.

Despite this substantive advantage, you should proceed cautiously and not be too quick to adopt the linked list as a cure for all the ills involved with list-oriented systems. The experience you have already gained should make you suspicious that there has to be a trade-off involved to get this superior efficiency for add and delete operations. Here the price we pay is to give up random access on the nodes in the list. For example, to access the fourth node, we must follow the head pointer to the first node, the first node's pointer to the second, and so on, until we reach the fourth node. Hence, any operation that requires finding a particular node on the list will essentially have to invoke a sequential search algorithm.

The superb $O(\log_2 n)$ search efficiency that was possible with an array implementation of a list cannot be approached with a linked implementation of the same list because the binary search algorithm we used to achieve this efficiency requires random access into the list. Instead we must settle for the $O(n)$ efficiency of the sequential search. Note that this is even a deterring factor in add and delete operations because, typically, an appropriate spot in the list must be found before the add or delete can occur. Although the add or delete itself may require only O(1) data movements, an $O(n)$ search must usually precede it.

Despite this search inefficiency, linked lists can be used to tremendous advantage when implementing lists that are highly *volatile;* that is, frequently undergoing insertions and deletions. If the percentage of these operations is sufficiently high in relation to requests for finding and inspecting nodes, then the linked implementation will probably pay off.

Before proceeding, we should clarify one point regarding linked lists as an ADT. That is, although a linked list may be viewed from this abstract perspective, it also represents an implementation strategy for more general linear structures such as the keyed list ADT. In that sense, we can compare the linked list to the array implementation of a keyed list, which we have already studied, and to several other list implementation schemes, which we will present in future chapters.

Thus, a linked list is, from one perspective, an implementation strategy; from another, it's an abstract structure. This is entirely consistent with what we have said regarding the progression from abstraction to implementation that you go through as a designer of software. The linked list provides another implementation option for the representation of more general linear structures. But it remains itself an abstraction because we have not yet described how we shall implement a linked list. It is to these implementation considerations that we shall turn our attention in the next section.

Pascal Interface for the Linked List ADT

To develop an implementation of the linked list ADT, we must establish a **PROCEDURE** and **FUNCTION** interfaces for the operations we have defined.

```
CONST
  Null =  { A special flagging value for the TYPE Pointer below.  A pointer   }
          { with the value Null is to be viewed as pointing at an             }
          { empty linked list.  This is significantly different from          }
          { a pointer's being undefined, in which case it may be              }
          { unreliably pointing at "garbage."                                 }

TYPE
  Pointer = { Still an abstract notion, to be regarded as capable of          }
            { storing the location in memory of a linked list node            }
  LinkedListNode = RECORD
                     Data : LinkedListData { Any appropriate type   };
                     Link : Pointer
                   END;

PROCEDURE Create (VAR Head : Pointer);

  {  Given:   A pointer Head whose value is arbitrary          }
  {  Task:    Initialize linked list referenced by Head        }
  {           to the empty list                                }
  {  Return:  Head pointer referencing the empty list.         }

FUNCTION Empty (Head : Pointer) : boolean;

  {  Given:   A linked list referenced by the pointer Head     }
  {  Task:    Determine if the linked list is empty            }
  {  Return:  True if the linked list is empty and             }
  {           false otherwise.                                 }

FUNCTION Next (P : Pointer) : Pointer;

  {  Given:   A pointer P to a node in a linked list.          }
  {           Assume that P is not Null.                       }
  {  Task:    Determine the node which follows the node        }
  {           referenced by P                                  }
  {  Return:  A pointer to the node following that             }
  {           referenced by P. If no node follows P, then      }
  {           return Null.                                     }

PROCEDURE InsertNode (VAR Head : Pointer;
                      P, Prev : Pointer);

  {  Given:   Linked list referenced by Head pointer.          }
  {           Node referenced by P to be inserted in the       }
  {           list after node referenced by Prev, with         }
  {           Prev equal to Null if insertion is to            }
  {           occur at front of list.                          }
  {  Task:    Set pointers to link node P into list            }
  {  Return:  Appropriately updated linked list.               }

PROCEDURE DeleteNode (VAR Head : Pointer;
                      P, Prev : Pointer);

  {  Given:   Linked list referenced by pointer Head.          }
  {           Pointer P to node to be removed from this        }
  {           list and pointer Prev to node preceding P.       }
  {           Prev is Null if node referenced by P is at       }
```

```
  {           front of list.                                 }
  {  Task:    Remove node P from list                        }
  {  Return:  Appropriately altered list.                    }

PROCEDURE LinkedTraverse (VAR Head : Pointer;
                          PROCEDURE ProcessNode (VAR Item : LinkedListData));

  {  Given:   Linked list referenced by Head pointer         }
  {  Task:    Traverse the list in the linear order          }
  {           determined by the links, applying the          }
  {           procedure ProcessNode to each record           }
  {           in the list                                    }
  {  Return:  The list referenced by Head with each node     }
  {           affected by ProcessNode.                       }
```

Exercises 4.1

1. In what way is the data structure involved with the PointerSort in Chapter 1 not a linked list?
2. What are the advantages and the disadvantages of a linked list implementation of a keyed list compared to a physically ordered array implementation?
3. What are the advantages and disadvantages of a linked list implementation of a keyed list compared to an implementation that uses an unordered array with sequential search?

For Exercises 4–6, use the Pascal interface to the linked list ADT to write appropriate program segments.

4. Given that the **TYPE** LinkedListData is **char**, use LinkedTraverse with a ProcessNode parameter that will print the **ord** value of each character in a linked list.
5. Given that the **TYPE** LinkedListData is **real**, use LinkedTraverse with a ProcessNode parameter that will print the value of each positive number in a linked list. Numbers in the list that are not positive should not be printed.
6. Given that the **TYPE** LinkedListData is **integer**, write a loop that starts at the beginning of a linked list and returns a pointer to the first list node with the value zero in its Data field. If no such node exists in the list, a Null pointer should be returned. (*Hint*: Use the Next operation.)

■ ■ ■ ■

■ 4.2 Array Implementation of a Linked List

OBJECTIVES

- to reiterate that a linked list is an ADT which may itself be used to implement more general linear ADTs such as a keyed list
- to develop an implementation of the linked list ADT in which linked list nodes are embedded in an array
- to develop a scheme for efficiently managing the nodes that are inserted into and deleted from linked lists

Objectives continued.

Our previous remarks on the layers between pure abstraction and pure implementation should be heeded here so that you do not confuse the previously presented array implementations of a keyed list (Section 2.4) with the array implementation of a linked list which we are about to describe. Figure 4.8 makes this distinction more apparent. By using an array to now implement a linked list, we will be providing a different implementation of a keyed list than the straightforward array schemes presented in Section 2.4. This different implementation will carry with it all of the advantages and disadvantages that come with using linked lists; that is, efficient additions and deletions but slow sequential searching.

The technique for implementing a linked list using an array should already be evident from our earlier discussion of the chain of gifts. We merely need to declare an array of records—each with an appropriate Data field and a Link field—to serve as a pointer to the next record on the list. Since the location of this next record can be specified as an array position, it is clear

- to be able to write programs that use the linked list ADT in a fashion consistent with the ADT use rule; that is, in a fashion that is shielded from the underlying implementation

that this Link field need only be an ordinary integer. Figure 4.9 portrays such an array implementation of a simple linked list of five alphabetically ordered names.

In order to implement a procedure for inserting a node into such a linked list, we must first consider where such nodes are to come from. That is, we need a procedure that supplies an unused node from the pool of available unused locations. We call this procedure GetNode. Similarly, when a node in the linked list is deleted, we should be able to return it to the pool of available nodes. ReturnNode will be our procedure to do this.

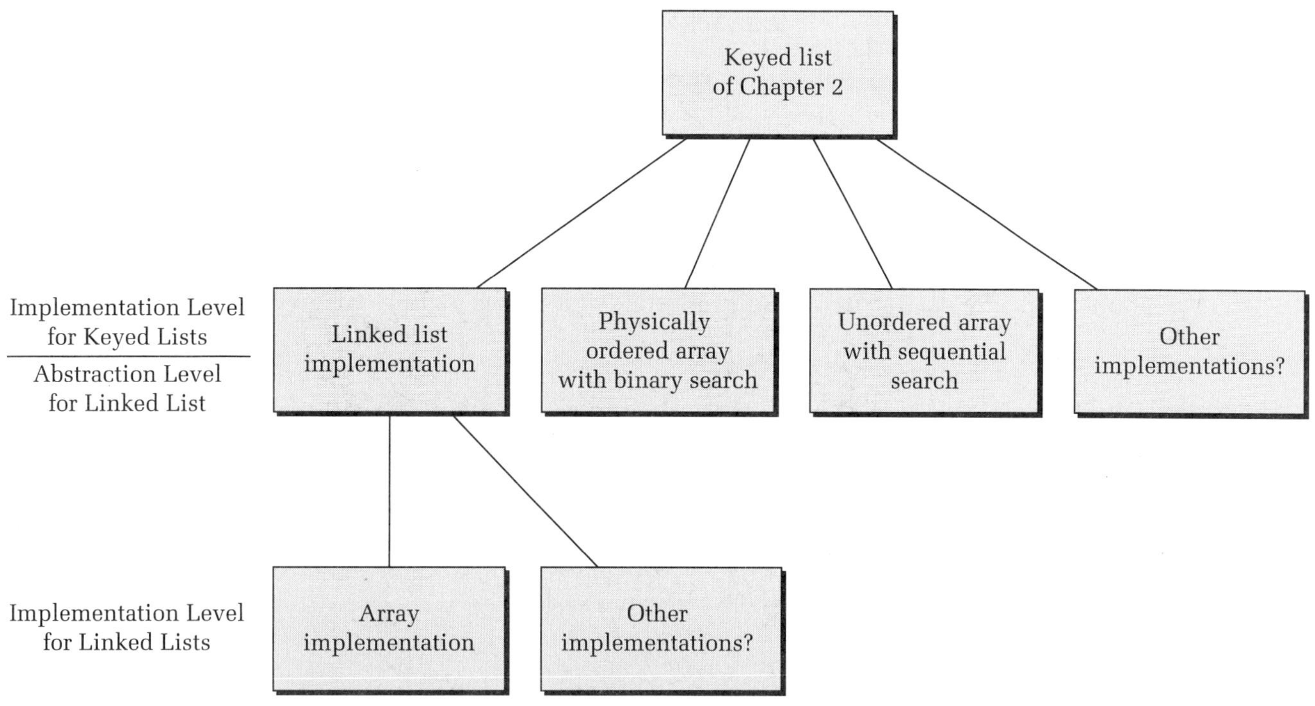

FIGURE 4.8
Levels of abstraction in implementing lists

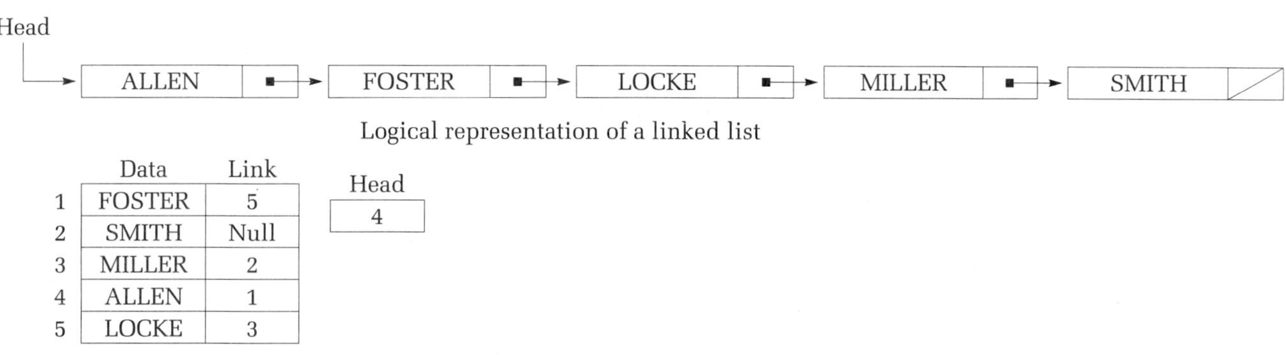

	Data	Link
1	FOSTER	5
2	SMITH	Null
3	MILLER	2
4	ALLEN	1
5	LOCKE	3

FIGURE 4.9
Logical representation versus array implementation

The most convenient way of viewing this available pool of nodes is as a special linked list with its own head pointer, Avail, which is woven into the same array used by the active nodes on other lists. Because the order of nodes is not important in this available space list, all insertions and deletions can occur at its head.

■ EXAMPLE 4.1

Write a package of procedures to manage the pool of available nodes that are accessed by linked list operations.

We will call these procedures InitializeSpace, GetNode, and ReturnNode. The pool of available nodes is identified by the global variable Space. Because this pool is used by all linked list operations, we will access it as a global variable when implementing these operations. The less attractive alternative is to include it as an extra parameter for all operations. This latter alternative would force users of the linked list ADT to include an additional Space parameter whenever they invoke a linked list operation. That additional parameter would *decrease* the degree to which the linked list's implementation was hidden from users.

The InitializeSpace procedure activates the available space list by intially linking all array locations into the available chain. The graphic documentation that accompanies the procedures highlights how this available node list is then manipulated by GetNode and ReturnNode.

```
{ Global declarations }

CONST
  TotalSpace = {  Set to the number of nodes in available space pool };
  Null = 0;     {  To flag end of list                                }

TYPE
  Pointer = integer;  { Pointers will just reference array indices }
  LinkedListNode = RECORD
                     Data : LinkedListData;
                     Link : Pointer
                   END;
  SpaceStructure = RECORD
                     Nodes : ARRAY [1..TotalSpace] OF LinkedListNode;
                     Avail : Pointer  { References first available node }
                   END;

VAR
  Space : SpaceStructure;  { The global pool of available nodes }

PROCEDURE InitializeSpace;

  {  Given:   Collection of nodes in Space for available      }
  {           space list and pointer Avail for that list.     }
  {  Task:    Set Avail to point at first one and link        }
  {           rest of nodes together.                         }
  {  Return:  Initialized available space pool with           }
  {           pointer Avail to first available node.          }

  VAR
    K : integer;
```

```
BEGIN
  WITH Space DO
    BEGIN
      { Initially, a node in available space is linked to  }
      { node in the immediately adjacent array position.   }
      FOR K := 1 TO TotalSpace - 1 DO
        Nodes[K].Link := K + 1;
      Nodes[TotalSpace].Link := Null;
      Avail := 1
    END
END; {  of PROCEDURE Initialize  }
```

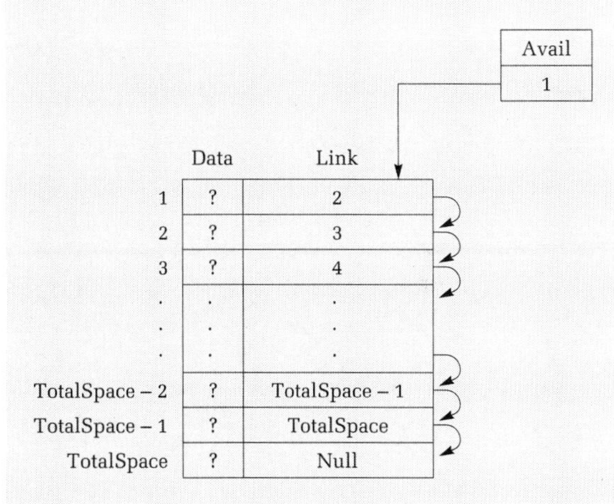


```
PROCEDURE GetNode (VAR P : Pointer);

  {  Given:   Global list of available nodes in Space with    }
  {           pointer Avail to first available node.          }
  {  Task:    Determine first available node.                 }
  {  Return:  Pointer P to that available node and new        }
  {           available space list with that node removed.    }

  BEGIN
    WITH Space DO
      IF Avail = Null THEN
        writeln ('No space available.')
      ELSE
        BEGIN
          P := Avail;
          Avail := Nodes[Avail].Link
        END
  END; {  of PROCEDURE GetNode  }
```

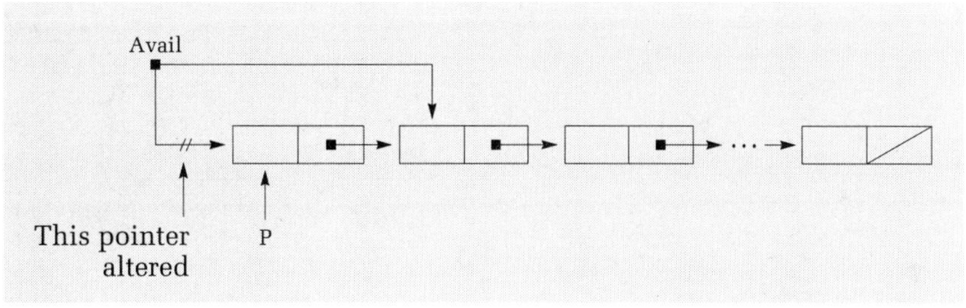

```
PROCEDURE ReturnNode (P :  Pointer);

  {  Given:    Global list of available nodes in Space with    }
  {            pointer Avail to first available node, and a    }
  {            pointer P to a node to be returned to           }
  {            available space.                                }
  {  Task:     Return node referenced by P to list of          }
  {            available nodes.                                }
  {  Return:   Appropriately updated list of available nodes.  }

   BEGIN
     Space.Nodes[P].Link := Space.Avail;
     Space.Avail := P
   END; {  of PROCEDURE ReturnNode  }
```

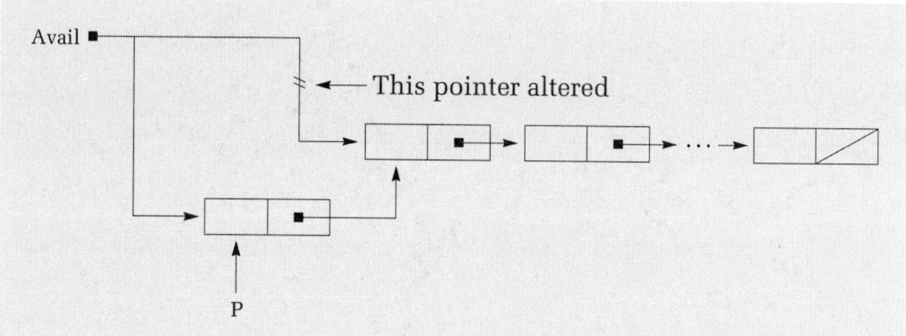

We are now ready to implement the Create, Next, and InsertNode operations for the linked list ADT. The linked lists that these operations manipulate are assumed to reside in the global structure Space defined in Example 4.1.

EXAMPLE 4.2

Implement the Create operation for the linked list ADT.

```
{  Assume global declarations from Example 4.1  }

PROCEDURE Create (VAR Head : Pointer);

  {  Given:   A pointer Head whose value is arbitrary      }
  {  Task:    Initialize linked list referenced by Head    }
  {           to the empty list                            }
  {  Return:  Head pointer referencing the empty list.     }

  BEGIN
    Head := Null
  END;  {  of PROCEDURE Create  }
```

EXAMPLE 4.3

Implement the Next operation for the linked list ADT.

```
FUNCTION Next (P : Pointer) : Pointer;

  {  Given:   A pointer P to a node in a linked list.          }
  {           Assume that P is not Null.                        }
  {  Task:    Determined the node that follows the node         }
  {           referenced by P.                                  }
  {  Return:  A pointer to the node following that              }
  {           referenced by P. If no node follows P, then       }
  {           return Null.                                      }

  BEGIN
    Next := Space.Nodes[P].Link
  END;
```

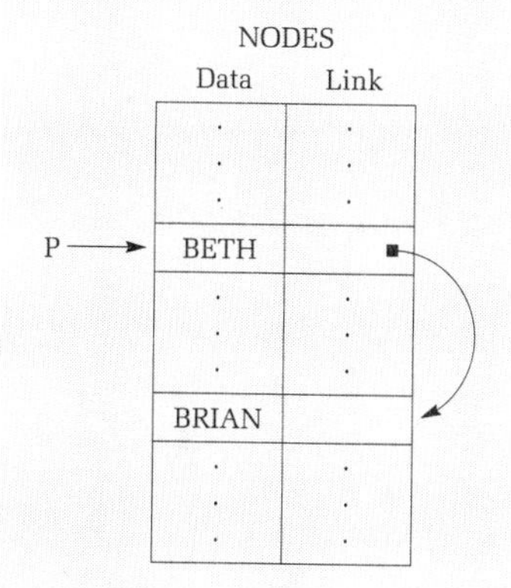

Although the code for the Next operation is only one instruction, it is not trivial. You should ponder it and the accompanying graphic documentation until you are convinced of its correctness. It may well be one of the most powerful single-line procedures you will ever see.

EXAMPLE 4.4

Implement the InsertNode operation for the linked list ADT.

```
PROCEDURE InsertNode (VAR Head : Pointer;
                      P, Prev : Pointer);

  {  Given:    Linked list referenced by Head pointer.          }
  {            Node referenced by P to be inserted in the       }
  {            list after node referenced by Prev, with         }
  {            Prev equal to Null if insertion is to            }
  {            occur at front of list.                          }
  {  Task:     Set pointers to link node P into list.           }
  {  Return:   Appropriately updated linked list.               }
```

```
BEGIN
  WITH Space DO
    IF Prev = Null THEN {  Insert at front  }
      BEGIN
        Nodes[P].Link := Head;
        Head := P
      END
    ELSE
      BEGIN
        Nodes[P].Link := Nodes[Prev].Link;
        Nodes[Prev].Link := P
      END {  IF  }
END;  {  of PROCEDURE InsertNode  }
```

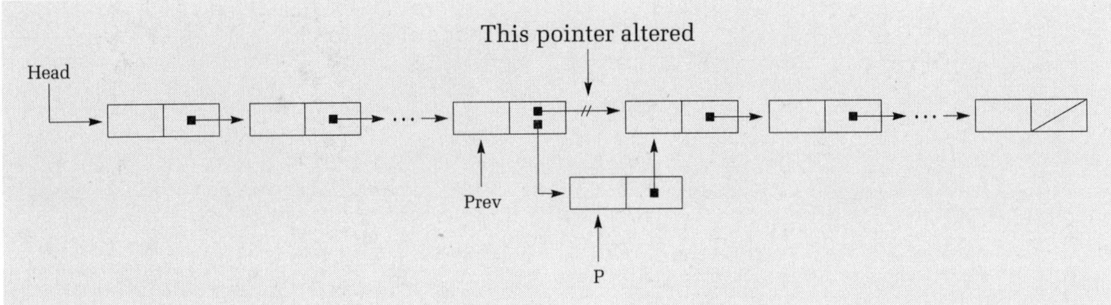

As with code for the Next operation in Example 4.3, the brevity of InsertNode's implementation in Example 4.4 belies its complexity. You should convince yourself that the present version of InsertNode is sufficient to handle all cases: insertion in an empty list and insertion at the front, middle, and end of a nonempty list. The best way to do this is to draw an abstract picture of the list for each of these conditions and trace the action of the procedure's statements on that picture. (See Figure 4.10.)

FIGURE 4.10
Tracing of four possibilities in InsertNode procedure

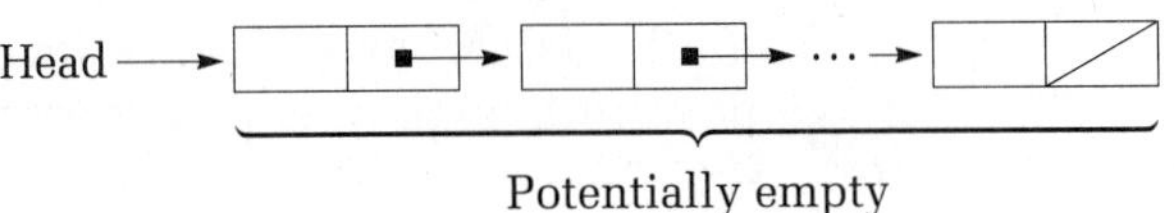

If list is nonempty, P's link field is appropriately set to point at current head of list by statement Nodes[P].Link := Head. If empty, P's link field is set to Null by the same statement. Then Head altered to point at P.

Condition Prev = Null takes care of insertion into empty list or at head of nonempty list

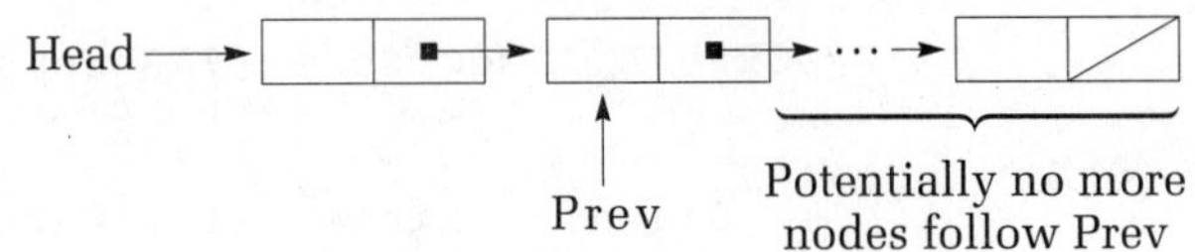

If insertion at end of list, the statement Nodes[P].Link := Nodes[Prev].Link will appropriately set P's link field to Null. Otherwise the same statement will set P's link field to point at the node currently following Prev.

ELSE clause takes care of insertion in middle or at end of nonempty list

The InsertNode operation alone is not sufficient to load data into a meaningful linked list. First, InsertNode assumes that the pointer P, which references the node to be inserted, has already been obtained via a call to GetNode and filled with appropriate data. Thus, InsertNode is concerned only with the pointer manipulations that link the node into the list, not with finding the insertion point. Second, InsertNode assumes that the location in the list where the insertion is to occur has already been found and stored in Prev.

We now consider how to find the pointer Prev that InsertNode requires. For this discussion, we assume that the list is to be maintained in ascending order. To determine Prev, we must therefore compare the data in the node referenced by P (the node to be inserted) to the data in successive nodes along the list. We know that we have found the spot to insert the node referenced by P when we come to the first node on the list containing data greater than (or equal to) that in P. That is, a loop to find the node that should follow P may be roughly given as

```
Start pointer Q at head of list
WHILE (data referenced by P > data referenced by Q)
    AND NOT at end of list DO
        Advance Q to next node
```

Unfortunately this loop will not find the node after which P belongs but rather the node before which it belongs. This can be easily remedied by adding Prev as a "tag-along" pointer in the loop.

```
Start Prev at Null
Start Q at head of list
WHILE (data referenced by P > data referenced by Q)
    AND NOT at end of list DO
        Set Prev to Q {  Prev tagging along  }
        Advance Q to next node
```

EXAMPLE 4.5

Provide a Pascal implementation of the logic described in the preceding pseudocode.

```
{  Assume same global declarations used in Example 4.1 }

PROCEDURE  FindInsertionSlot (Head, P : Pointer;
                              VAR Prev : Pointer);

  {  Given:    Linked list referenced by Head and node to be    }
  {            inserted referenced by P.  Assume that the       }
  {            linear order of the list matches ascending       }
  {            order by Data field.                             }
  {  Task:     Find node in list after which node referenced    }
  {            by P is to be located.                           }
  {  Return:   Pointer Prev to that node.  Prev is Null if      }
  {            node referenced by P belongs at front of list.   }

  VAR  Q : Pointer; {  Pointer used to advance through loop     }
       SlotFound : boolean;

  BEGIN
    Prev := Null;
    Q := Head;
    SlotFound := false;
```

```
  {  Q advances until end of list is reached or until data referenced  }
  {  by Q is greater than or equal to that referenced by P.            }
  WHILE (Q <> Null) AND NOT SlotFound DO
    IF Space.Nodes[P].Data > Space.Nodes[Q].Data THEN
      BEGIN
        Prev := Q; {  Prev tags along behind Q  }
        Q := Next (Q) {  Q advances  }
      END
    ELSE
      SlotFound := true
END; {  of PROCEDURE FindInsertionSlot  }
```

The Boolean variable SlotFound is required in FindInsertionSlot because of the way in which Pascal may determine the Boolean result of an **AND** conditional. It is tempting to try to avoid using this Boolean and instead rewrite the **WHILE** condition as

```
WHILE (Q <> Null) AND (Space.Nodes[P].Data > Space.Nodes[Q].Data) DO
  BEGIN
    Prev := Q;
    Q := Next (Q)
  END;
```

This will work fine as long as the node referenced by P does not belong at the end of the list. However, when P does belong at the end of the list, the conditional test

```
Space.Nodes[P].Data > Space.Nodes[Q].Data
```

may result in a run-time "Index out of range" error because Q is Null. Thus, the SlotFound Boolean variable is necessary to avoid Q's becoming an invalid index reference for the Space array.

With the procedures InsertNode and FindInsertionSlot that we have developed, it is now clear how we could build up a linked list. Assuming appropriate variable declarations, the following sequence will create a linked list referenced by Head and then successively add nodes to it until SentinelValue is entered.

```
InitializeSpace;  {  Initialize available space.  }
Create (Head);    {  Initialize linked list referenced by Head.  }
GetNode (P);
ReadInData (Space.Nodes[P].Data);  {  Call procedure which fills  }
                                   {  data portion of node.       }

WHILE Space.Nodes[P].Data <> SentinelValue DO
  BEGIN
    FindInsertionSlot (Head, P, Prev);
    InsertNode (Head, P, Prev);
    GetNode (P);
    ReadInData (Space.Nodes[P].Data)
  END;
ReturnNode (P);  {  Return last node entered since  }
                 {  it was not linked into list.    }
```

EXAMPLE 4.6

Given the Initialize, GetNode, and insertion procedures we have discussed, trace the status of the Data and Link fields in the Nodes array and the Avail and Head pointers as the following items arrive for insertion into an alphabetically arranged linked list.

WAGNER
ELLIS
GORDON
NIEMAN
HILLER

Before first insertion

	Data	Link
1		2
2		3
3		4
4		5
5		6
6		7
7		8
8		Null

TotalSpace

Avail
1

Head
Null

After first insertion

	Data	Link
1	WAGNER	Null
2		3
3		4
4		5
5		6
6		7
7		8
8		Null

TotalSpace

Avail
2

Head
1

After second insertion

	Data	Link
1	WAGNER	Null
2	ELLIS	1
3		4
4		5
5		6
6		7
7		8
8		Null

TotalSpace

Avail
3

Head
2

After third insertion

	Data	Link
1	WAGNER	Null
2	ELLIS	3
3	GORDON	1
4		5
5		6
6		7
7		8
8		Null

TotalSpace

Avail
4

Head
2

After fourth insertion

	Data	Link
1	WAGNER	Null
2	ELLIS	3
3	GORDON	4
4	NIEMAN	1
5		6
6		7
7		8
8		Null TotalSpace

Avail
5

Head
2

After fifth insertion

	Data	Link
1	WAGNER	Null
2	ELLIS	3
3	GORDON	5
4	NIEMAN	1
5	HILLER	4
6		7
7		8
8		Null TotalSpace

Avail
6

Head
2

The DeleteNode operation can be implemented in a fashion similar to InsertNode. Using the logic outlined in Figure 4.7, the node is first unchained from the list. Then a call to ReturnNode restores this node to the pool of available nodes. As in the InsertNode procedure, DeleteNode presupposes that P and Prev have been determined. This determination could be done in a FindNodeToDelete procedure similar to (though slightly different from) the FindInsertionSlot procedure we developed.

EXAMPLE 4.7

Implement the DeleteNode operation.

```
{  Assume same global declarations used for Example 4.1 }

PROCEDURE DeleteNode (VAR Head: Pointer;
                      P, Prev : Pointer);

  {  Given:   Linked list referenced by pointer Head.          }
  {           Pointer P to node  to be removed from this       }
  {           list and pointer Prev to node preceding P.       }
  {           Prev is Null  if node referenced by P is at      }
  {           front of list.                                   }
  {  Task:    Remove node P from list.                         }
  {  Return:  Appropriately altered list.                      }
```

```
BEGIN
  IF Prev = Null THEN  {  Delete first node  }
    Head := Space.Nodes[Head].Link
  ELSE
    Space.Nodes[Prev].Link := Space.Nodes[P].Link;
  ReturnNode (P)   {  Return the deleted node  }
END;  {  of PROCEDURE DeleteNode  }
```

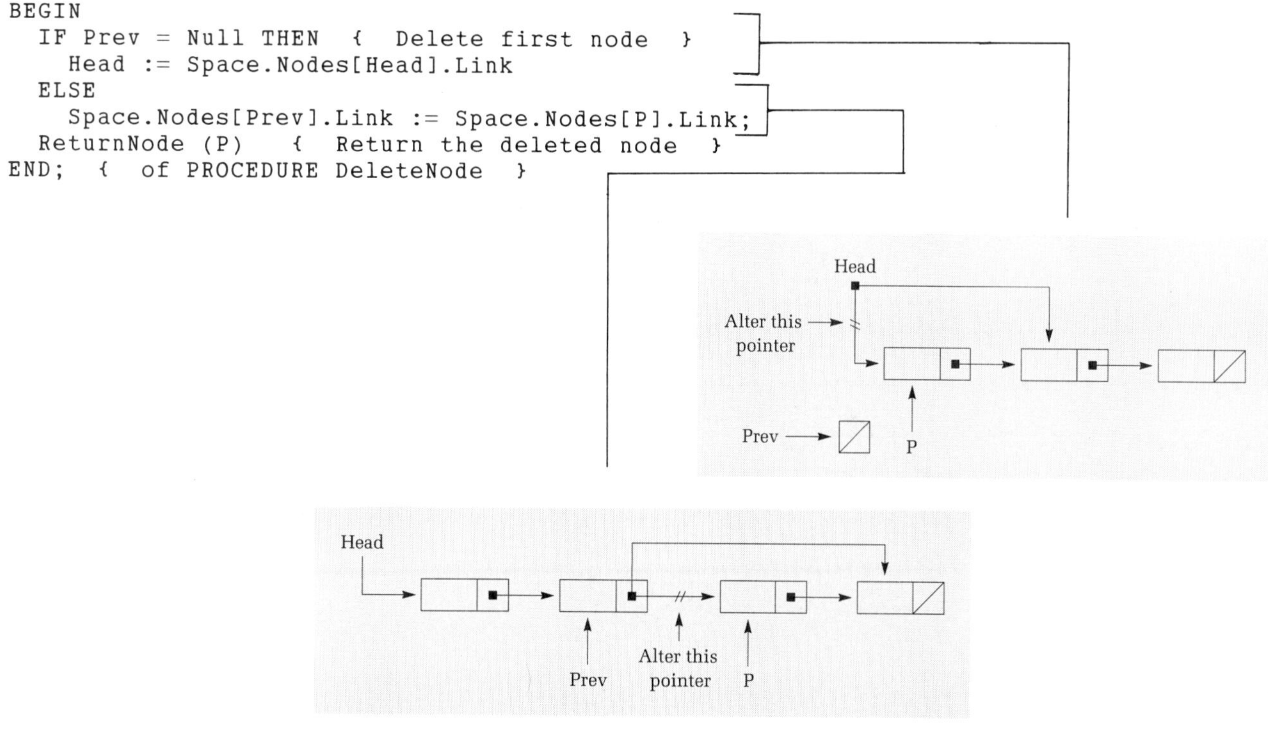

EXAMPLE 4.8

Assume that the following operations occur in sequence on the list developed in Example 4.6.

Delete WAGNER
Delete NIEMAN
Insert ZARDA

Trace the status of the Space array and the Avail and Head pointers as these operations occur.

After first deletion

	Data	Link	
1	WAGNER	6	
2	ELLIS	3	
3	GORDON	5	
4	NIEMAN	Null	
5	HILLER	4	
6		7	
7		8	
8		Null	TotalSpace

Avail
1

Head
2

After second deletion

	Data	Link
1	WAGNER	6
2	ELLIS	3
3	GORDON	5
4	NIEMAN	1
5	HILLER	Null
6		7
7		8
8		Null

TotalSpace

Avail	Head
4	2

After insertion of ZARDA

	Data	Link
1	WAGNER	6
2	ELLIS	3
3	GORDON	5
4	ZARDA	Null
5	HILLER	4
6		7
7		8
8		Null

TotalSpace

Avail	Head
1	2

Note that data contained in nodes that are returned to the available space pool are not actually destroyed until the nodes are reused via a call to GetNode.

We have begun to develop a package of procedures that may be used to process linked lists implemented by arrays. These procedures are low-level in the sense that they would appear deep in the modular structure chart of a software system that used linked lists. They represent essential linked list operations. Note that more such primitive procedures would need to be developed to complete a linked list package; for example, finding a particular node and traversing the list in a specified order. You will be developing these additional procedures in the Exercises. The following example indicates how this package of procedures could be used to maintain a list of strings in alphabetical order.

EXAMPLE 4.9

Use a linked list implemented by an array to maintain a list of strings in alphabetical order. The modular structure chart for such a program is given by Modular specifications are not given here because logic for most of the mod-

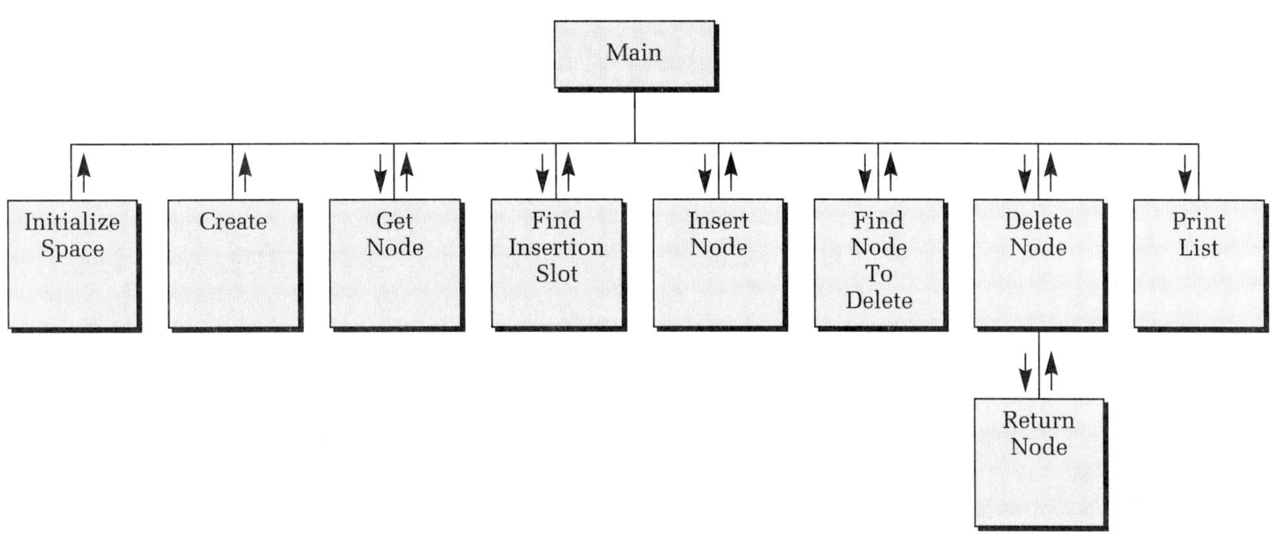

ules has already been developed in the preceding discussion. Rather, the following main program indicates how these individual modules may be used in concert with each other. To avoid a name conflict between the Create operations for linked lists and strings, the program uses a call of the form CreateString for the string ADT.

```
PROGRAM ArrayImpOfLinkedList (input, output);

{  Demonstrate use of essential operations for array              }
{  implementation of a linked list by maintaining a list          }
{  of strings in alphabetical order.                              }

{  Global declarations of Example 4.1 augmented for the particular  }
{  needs of this program.                                          }

CONST
  TotalSpace = 100;
  Null = 0;    {  to flag end of list  }

TYPE
  Pointer = integer;  { Since pointers will just reference array indices }
  LinkedListData = String;  { Assume appropriate implementation of string ADT }
  LinkedListNode = RECORD
                     Data : LinkedListData;
                     Link : Pointer
                   END;
  SpaceStructure = RECORD
                     Nodes : ARRAY [1..TotalSpace] OF LinkedListNode;
                     Avail : Pointer  { References first available node }
                   END;

VAR
  Space : SpaceStructure;  { The global pool of available nodes }
  Head, P : Pointer;
```

```
  DeleteData : LinkedListData;
  Command : char;

  .
  .  { Procedures for linked list and string operations here }
  .

{ PrintOneNode is passed as parameter to LinkedTraverse }
PROCEDURE PrintOneNode (VAR Item : LinkedListData);

  {  Given:    Item, one data item on a linked list          }
  {  Task:     Print the item                                }
  {  Return:   Nothing                                       }

  BEGIN
    WriteAString (Item);
    writeln
  END; { of PROCEDURE PrintOneNode }

BEGIN {  Main program  }
  InitializeSpace;
  Create (Head);
  REPEAT
    write('[A]dd node, [D]elete node, [P]rint list, or [Q]uit --> ');
    readln(Command);
    CASE Command OF
      'A', 'a':
        BEGIN
          GetNode (P);
          write ('Enter data --> ');
          CreateString (Space.Nodes[P].Data);  {  Create for string  }
          ReadAString (Space.Nodes[P].Data);
          FindInsertionSlot(Head, P, Prev);
          InsertNode(Head, P, Prev)
        END;
      'D', 'd':
        BEGIN
          write ('Enter node to delete --> ');
          CreateString (DeleteData);  {  Create for string  }
          ReadAString (DeleteData);
          FindNodeToDelete (Head, P, Prev, DeleteData, Found);
          IF Found THEN
            DeleteNode(Head, P, Prev)
          ELSE
            BEGIN
              WriteAString (DeleteData);
              writeln (' not found')
            END
        END;
      'P', 'p':
        LinkedTraverse (Head, PrintOneNode)
      'Q', 'q':
        BEGIN
        END
      END {  CASE  }
  UNTIL (Command = 'q') OR (Command = 'Q')
END.
```

A sample run of this program would appear as

```
[A]dd node, [D]elete node, [P]rint list, or [Q]uit --> A
Enter data --> SMITH
[A]dd node, [D]elete node, [P]rint list, or [Q]uit --> A
Enter data --> JONES
```

```
[A]dd node, [D]elete node, [P]rint list; or [Q]uit --> A
Enter data > MILLER
[A]dd node, [D]elete node, [P]rint list, or [Q]uit --> P
JONES
MILLER
SMITH
[A]dd node, [D]elete node, [P]rint list, or [Q]uit --> D
Enter node to delete --> MILLER
[A]dd node, [D]elete node, [P]rint list, or [Q]uit --> P
JONES
SMITH
[A]dd node, [D]elete node, [P]rint list, or [Q]uit --> Q
```

The particular package we have started upon here represents only one of two possible implementation strategies we will discuss for linked lists. In the next section we shall describe a similar package of procedures for an alternate strategy using a special feature of Pascal called a pointer variable. These two implementation strategies will prove to be interchangeable to a degree. Since you've learned the details of the array implementation, understanding how Pascal pointer variables are manipulated should be relatively easy. As you'll see, each implementation has inherent advantages and disadvantages. We'll contrast these advantages and disadvantages as we present the pointer variable scheme.

Exercises 4.2

1. Suppose that you are given the following initial state of an array implementation of a linked list.

	Data	Link
1	47	3
2	89	5
3	66	7
4	100	2
5	13	10
6	55	2
7	112	4
8	178	0
9	79	6
10	19	8

   a. Indicate the nodes on the list if the head pointer is 9 and 0 is used to indicate the Null pointer.

   b. Indicate the final state of the Data and Link fields after the following program segment is executed.

```
WITH Space DO
  BEGIN
    J := 4;
    Nodes[J].Data := 883;
    J := Nodes[J].Link;
    WHILE Nodes[J].Link <> 0 DO
      BEGIN
        J := Nodes[J].Link;
        Nodes[J].Data := 912
      END
  END;
```

2. Consider the array implementation of a linked list of names that appears in Figure 4.9. Suppose that the physical order of the five names in that list was given by

Data	Link
LOCKE	?
MILLER	?
SMITH	?
FOSTER	?
ALLEN	?

Head
?

Fill in the Head and Link fields so that the list could be traversed in logical alphabetical order.

3. Indicate the changes in the Link and Head fields from Exercise 2 if MILLER is deleted from the list.

4. Indicate the changes in the Link and Head fields from Exercise 2 if ALLEN is deleted from the list.

5. Consider an array implementation of a linked list of names which is to be maintained in alphabetical order. Trace the status of the Data and Link fields and the Head and Avail pointers as the following operations are performed on the list:

Insert JAMES
Insert CHILTON
Insert SEFTON
Insert LEE
Delete CHILTON
Insert WAGNER
Delete JAMES
Insert AARON

6. Consider the following slightly modified version of **PROCEDURE** InsertNode.

```
PROCEDURE InsertNode (VAR Head : Pointer;
                      P, Prev : Pointer);

  {  Given:    Linked list referenced by Head pointer.          }
  {            Node referenced by P to be inserted in the       }
  {            list after node referenced by Prev, with         }
  {            Prev equal to Null if insertion is to            }
  {            occur at front of list.                          }
  {  Task:     Set pointers to link node P into list.           }
  {  Return:   Appropriately updated linked list.               }

  BEGIN
    WITH Space DO
      IF Prev = Null THEN {  Insert at front  }
        BEGIN
          Nodes[P].Link := Head;
          Head := P
        END
      ELSE
        BEGIN
          Nodes[Prev].Link := P;
          Nodes[P].Link := Nodes[Prev].Link
        END {  IF  }
  END;  {  of PROCEDURE InsertNode  }
```

Will this version of the procedure still perform the InsertNode operation correctly? If not, explain what it will do to a linked list when called; use diagrams of a linked list before and after the procedure is called to clarify your explanation.

7. Assuming an array implementation of a linked list, write **PROCEDURE** LinkedTraverse as specified in the definition of the linked list ADT in Section 4.1.

8. Assuming an array implementation of a linked list, write **FUNCTION** Empty as specified in the definition of the linked list ADT in Section 4.1.

9. Write the **PROCEDURE** FindNodeToDelete that is invoked in the main program of Example 4.9.

10. The main program of Example 4.9 doesn't completely obey the ADT use rule in that it fails to hide completely the array implementation of a linked list that it is using. How does it fail in this regard? How would you correct it? (*Hint*: Think about adding an operation to our definition of the linked list ADT in Section 4.1.)

11. Use an array implementation of a linked list to develop implementations of each of the keyed list ADT operations specified in Section 2.4.

12. Write a procedure to reverse a linked list referenced by the pointer Head.

13. Suppose you sort a list of input values by reading them in one at a time and inserting them into a linked list arranged in ascending order. Clearly, after you have read all of the input values you will have a sorted list. Let's call this algorithm the *linked list sort*. Analyze the time efficiency of this algorithm in terms of number of comparisons and number of data interchanges. Compare its efficiency to that of the other sort algorithms we have studied—insertion, bubble, selection and radix sort.

14. Your friend claims that nodes in the available space list are always linked to nodes in the next physical array location; that is, an available node at location P is always linked to the node at location P + 1. Is your friend right or wrong? If your friend is wrong, write a statement explaining the error in your friend's logic.

■ ■ ■ ■

■ 4.3 Pascal Pointer Variable Implementation of a Linked List: Dynamic Memory Management in Pascal

OBJECTIVES

- to realize the static limitations of the array implementation of a linked list
- to gain familiarity with the syntax of Pascal pointer variables
- to understand the use of Pascal's **new** and **dispose** procedures in managing that segment of memory known as the heap
- to be able to develop an implementation of the linked list ADT using Pascal pointer variables

Objectives continued.

Perhaps the biggest drawback of the array method of implementing a linked list is the static nature of the memory storage associated with an array. Suppose, for example, we declare an array Nodes of size 100. Then the storage in the Space structure is static in the sense that it is allocated at the time the program is compiled, not when it actually runs. Because of this, we are charged for 100 locations whether or not they are all used. When we have only 50 records to process in the array, 50 percent of the memory allocation is being wasted. Even more serious is the limitation that, if we have over 100 records to process, we must edit and recompile the program using a larger array size.

Pascal pointer variables, on the other hand, are an example of a technique known as *dynamic memory management*. A feature that is not available in many older languages such as FORTRAN, COBOL, and BASIC, dynamic memory management is used by Pascal to allow the programmer to claim only that amount of memory which is actually needed at run-time.

To understand dynamic memory management, we must first understand the configuration of memory when your program is loaded into it from an external file. As indicated in Figure 4.11, there are memory costs that must

- to understand the difference between static and dynamic memory management
- to compare the two implementations of linked list we have studied—array and pointer variables

be paid in addition to the storage space required for the object code of your program. In particular, memory must have room to accommodate:

- Various operating system requirements.
- A stack used by the operating system for procedure and function processing (to be explained in Chapter 5).
- The object code of your program; that is, the machine-language version of your program's instructions.
- Static data areas; that is, the globally declared variables in your program.

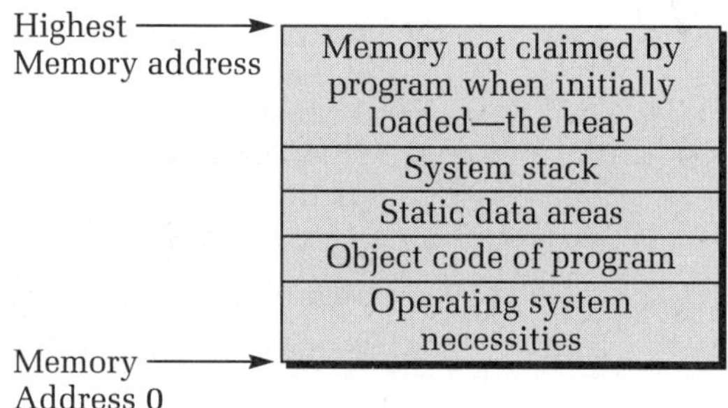

FIGURE 4.11
Computer memory configuration for typical program

Notice that the four memory components listed generally will not consume all of the available computer memory. What remains is called the *heap*. Unless you have already used the dynamic memory allocation scheme of a language like Pascal, your programs have never been able to get at the heap and take advantage of it. With Pascal's pointer variables, all this changes.

Suppose we have a record declaration, such as that for LinkedListNode in our definition of the linked list ADT. Then, by using a caret (^) character, we can declare a **TYPE** for variables that are pointers to such a record. Syntactically, the declarations would appear as

```
TYPE
  .
  .
  .
  Pointer = ^LinkedListNode;
  LinkedListNode = RECORD
                     Data : LinkedListData {  Any appropriate type  };
                     Link : Pointer
                   END;
  .
  .
  .
VAR
  P : Pointer;
```

These declarations establish P as a variable of user-defined **TYPE** Pointer. A variable of **TYPE** Pointer references ("points at") records of **TYPE** LinkedListNode. Note there is a hint of circularity here in that Pointer uses LinkedListNode in its declaration, and there is a field of **TYPE** Pointer in the declaration of LinkedListNode. Syntactically, Pascal requires the declaration of the **TYPE** Pointer before the declaration of a record (or other structure) that incorporates elements of **TYPE** Pointer.

With Pascal pointer variables, you are able to call upon Pascal's memory management system—a high-powered parallel to the GetNode and ReturnNode operations that we developed in Section 4.2. The key is a supplied

A NOTE OF INTEREST

Storage of Disk Files and Computer Security

Operating systems typically grant their users disk storage in units called blocks. On the magnetic disk itself, a block is a contiguous area capable of storing a fixed amount of data. For example, a block in DEC's well-known VAX/VMS time-sharing system is 512 bytes. As a user enters data into a disk file, the system must grant additional blocks of storage as they are needed. In such a time-sharing environment, although each block represents a physically contiguous storage area on the disk, it may not be possible for the operating system to give a user blocks that are physically next to each other. Instead, when a user needs an additional storage block, the operating system may put information into the current block about where the next block is located. In effect, a link is established from the current block to the next block. By the time a naive user has completed entering a four-block file, it may be scattered over the entire disk surface, as indicated in the following diagram:

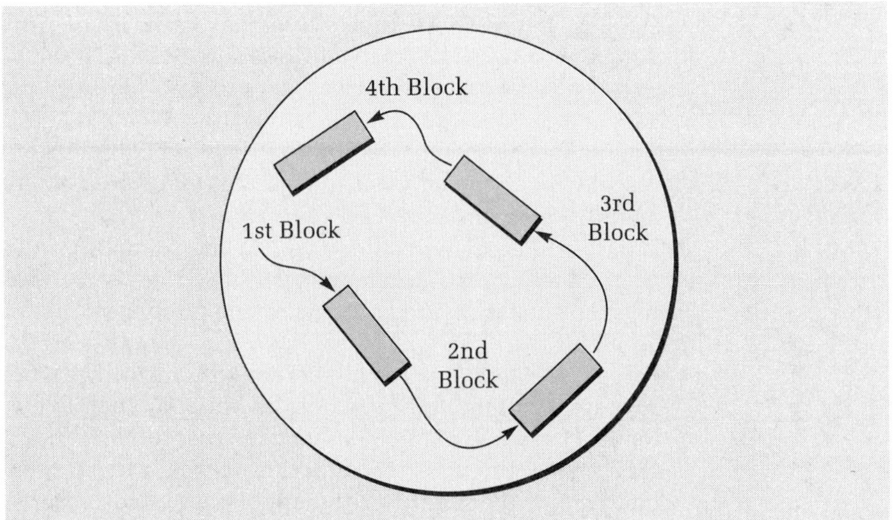

Although this may seem like an ingenious way of extending files indefinitely, one pays in several ways for such scattered blocks. Namely, the read-write head that seeks and puts data on the disk surface is forced to move greater distances, thereby slowing system performance. To combat such inefficiencies, shrewd users can often take advantage of options that allow them to preallocate the contiguous disk storage that will be required for a file. Moreover, system managers may occasionally shut down the entire system to rebuild disks, a process that entails copying all files that are presently scattered over the disk onto a new disk in physically contiguous form.

Yet another more serious price which may be paid for storing disk files in this fashion revolves around the issue of data security and what the operating system does with blocks that are no longer needed by a user. From what we have discussed in this chapter, it is clear that the disk blocks used to store a file are returned to some type of available block list when a user deletes that file from his or her directory. When these blocks are returned to that available space list, the data in them may remain intact until another user's request to extend a file results in the blocks' being reallocated to that new user. This means that, if clever users ("hackers") know how to access the available space list, they may be able to scavenge through data that other users once owned and then released (assuming it was destroyed upon being released).

One of the authors was actually involved in an incident in which such a clever student was able to "find" old versions of a test that a professor had typed in on the computer and then discarded into this available block list. Needless to say, the professor whose tests were being explored by the student was somewhat alarmed upon discovering what had happened. As a protection against this type of scavenging, many operating systems will, by default or as an option, actually destroy data that is returned to the available block list.

procedure **new**, which takes as its only argument a pointer variable such as P and returns in P a pointer; that is, a memory address indicating the location within the heap where the heap manager has allocated space for the currently requested record. Thus, **new** is essentially a Pascal-supplied dynamic version of the GetNode procedure which we developed ourselves for the array implementation of a linked list.

Several facts about the **new** procedure should be emphasized at this point.

- **new** is a run-time request for memory. Unlike an array, you are not charged for the memory requested until you actually have something to store in it. Moreover, unlike static array declarations, you are not charged for an excess of memory that you may not even need for this particular run of the program.
- After a call to **new**(P) for a suitably declared pointer variable P, P is a memory address. As such, its actual value is of little concern to you. Suffice it to say that it is an address somewhere in the heap. How the heap manager was able to arrive at such an address involves a system-dependent, more sophisticated version of our own GetNode algorithm. Note that, as a memory address, P's actual value is not important. In fact, Pascal won't even let you see what it is since a statement like **write**(P) will result in a syntax error.
- However, Pascal will allow you to manipulate pointer variables in the ways necessary to implement a variety of data structures, including linked lists. For instance, the contents of one pointer variable may be assigned to another.
- Pascal also lets you get at the contents of records that are stored at an address "pointed to" by a pointer variable such as P. To access the contents of such a dynamically allocated record, the caret (^) notation (also referred to as the up-arrow notation) is again used. Hence P^ refers to the contents of the record at the address pointed to by P. That is, P^ is the actual data and P is where the data are stored. Figure 4.12 illustrates this crucial difference between the adress stored in a pointer variable P and the contents of the record stored at that address. Given P, fields within such a record may be examined by the usual dot qualification; for example, P^.Name or P^.Address. (In this figure, P itself is 22706, a memory address. P^ is the contents of the record at address 22706. Hence P^.Name is BURTON JB and P^.Address is 194 E MAPLE ST. NY NY.)
- Should you request space from the heap manager when none is available, a run-time error will result.

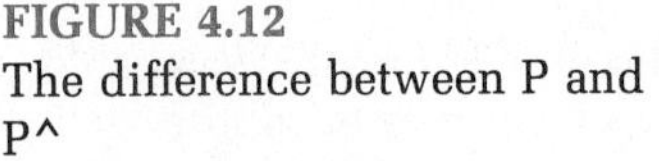

FIGURE 4.12
The difference between P and P^

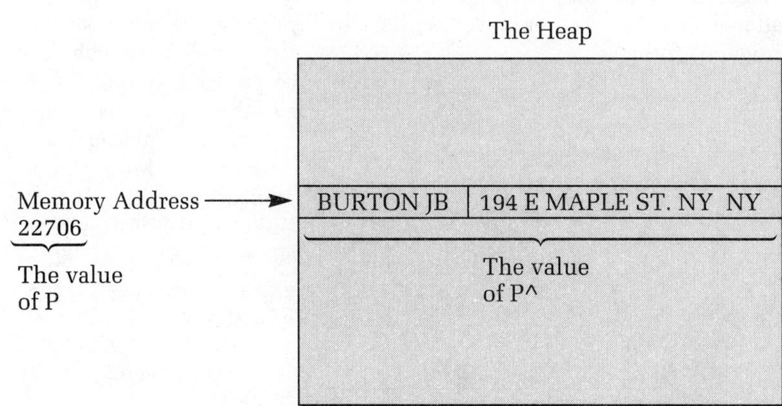

Just as **new** provides an alternative to the GetNode procedure from our earlier array implementation, Pascal also provides a **dispose** procedure as a dynamic alternative to our ReturnNode procedure. If P is appropriately declared as a pointer variable, then the statement

```
dispose (P)
```

will return the memory space being referenced by P to the Pascal memory management system for later use. The amount of space obtained by **new**(P) or returned by **dispose**(P) is always equal to the size of the record associated with P.

Pascal uses the reserved word **NIL** as a special flagging value for pointer variables. **NIL** is essentially the analogue of the defined constant Null in our array-based implementation. When a pointer variable in Pascal has the value **NIL**, it is well-defined, but it is not pointing to any node in memory. Thus, it is valid to check whether P = **NIL**, but it is not valid to refer to P^ when P is **NIL**. The latter type of reference will usually cause a run-time error. Typically the **NIL** value is assigned to the Head pointer before any nodes are added to the list and to the link field pointer in the last node on the list.

Consider now some sample statements that could be used to manipulate variables of the **TYPE** Pointer we defined in our previous declarations. To assign a value to the Data field, of a node referenced by P, a statement of the form

```
P^.Data := X
```

would suffice where X is of the appropriate type. The Link field in the node referenced by P could be "aimed at" another node referenced by a pointer Q via the statement

```
P^.Link := Q
```

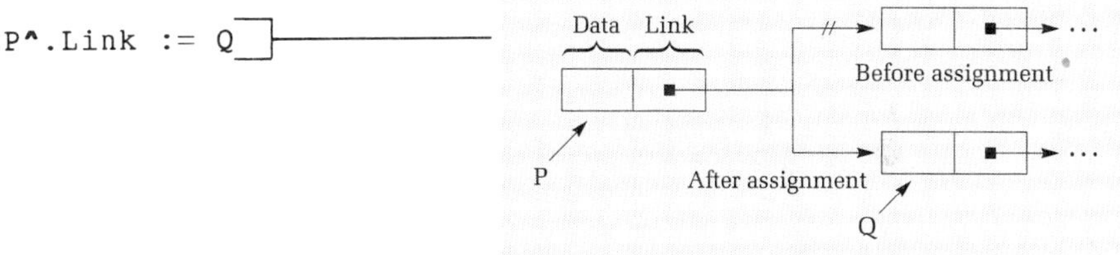

Finally, if the node referenced by P has been appropriately chained into an existing linked list, then P can be advanced to the next node on the list by the statement

```
P := P^.Link
```

Note that this statement is the direct analogue of the statement

```
P := Space.Nodes[P].Link
```

from our array implementation of a linked list.

Some additional examples will serve to clarify the logic involving pointer variables.

EXAMPLE 4.10

Suppose we have a pointer type established by the following declarations:

```
TYPE
  PtrToNode = ^Node;
  Node = RECORD
           Info : integer;
           FollowedBy : PtrToNode
         END;
```

```
VAR
  P, Q, : PtrToNode;
```

Describe the effect of the following sequence of instructions:

```
new(P);                    {1}
new(Q);                    {2}
P^.Info := 5;              {3}
Q^.Info := 3;              {4}
P^.FollowedBy := Q;        {5}
Q^.FollowedBy := NIL;      {6}
```

The easiest way to describe such code is to visualize its effect. Consequently, we provide an answer in the form of a series of snapshots, identified by the bracketed number that marks each line of code.

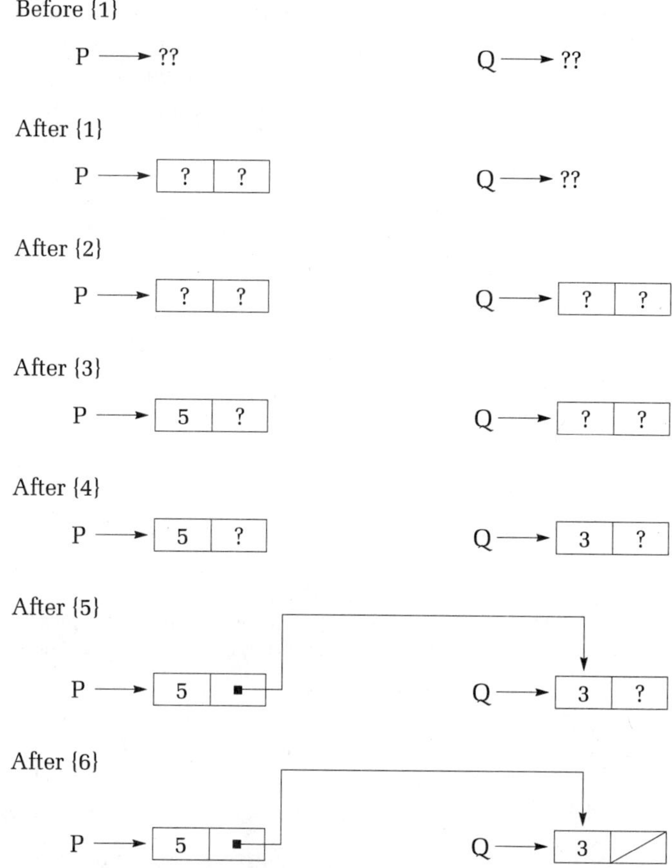

EXAMPLE 4.11

Given the declarations of Example 4.10, write a code segment specifically designed to add a node containing Info value 12 to the following list referenced by P:

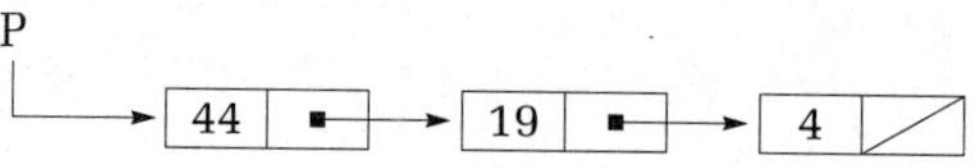

```
new(Q);                                      {  Grab a node in the heap     }
Q^.Info := 12;                               {  Assign its Info value       }
Q^.FollowedBy := NIL;                        {  Q will be at end of list    }
P^.FollowedBy^.FollowedBy^.FollowedBy := Q;  {  Chain it into list at end   }
```

■ ■

Clearly, programming with Pascal pointer variables requires your having an accurate mental image of the effects of each instruction. You can never actually grasp the value of the pointer itself—as you can with array-based pointers. In one sense, this allows Pascal pointer variables to be dynamic and hence more powerful than their array-based counterparts. However, because you cannot effectively trace the value of a Pascal pointer variable, you must exercise extreme care when programming with them. The debugging technique of inserting tracer **writeln** instructions no longer will allow you to examine the value of an unreliable pointer variable. Faced with a bug, you must carefully draw linked list pictures and manually execute your code against those pictures until you find the instruction that is going awry.

Implementing the Linked List ADT with Pascal Pointer Variables

Now that we have covered the syntax of Pascal pointer variables, we are ready to use them to provide an alternate implementation for the linked list ADT. Doing so will be relatively easy because the detailed logic of each operation parallels exactly what we have already done for the array implementation. In the following four examples, we provide Pascal pointer variable versions of the Create, Next, InsertNode, and DeleteNode operations. You should compare them to their array-based analogues in Examples 4.2, 4.3, 4.4, and 4.7 respectively.

■ **EXAMPLE 4.12**

Consider the following **TYPE** declarations for a Pascal pointer variable implementation of the linked list ADT.

```
TYPE
  Pointer = ^LinkedListNode;
  LinkedListNode = RECORD
                     Data : LinkedListData;
                     Link : Pointer
                   END;
```

Using these declarations, implement the Create operation for the linked list ADT.

```
PROCEDURE Create (VAR Head : Pointer);

  {  Given:  A pointer Head whose value is arbitrary       }
  {  Task:   Initialize linked list referenced by Head     }
  {          to the empty list                             }
  {  Return: Head pointer referencing the empty list       }

  BEGIN
    Head := NIL
  END; {  of PROCEDURE Create  }
```

■ ■

■ EXAMPLE 4.13

Implement the Next operation for the Pascal pointer version of the linked list ADT.

```
FUNCTION Next (P : Pointer) : Pointer;

  {  Given:  A pointer P to a node in a linked list.     }
  {          Assume that P is not NIL.                   }
  {  Task:   Determine the Node which follows the node   }
  {          referenced by P.                            }
  {  Return: A pointer to the node following that        }
  {          referenced by P. If no node follows P, then }
  {          return NIL.                                 }

  BEGIN
    Next := P^.Link  {  Note that a function may return a pointer type  }
  END;
```

■ ■

■ EXAMPLE 4.14

Implement the InsertNode operation for a Pascal pointer linked list.

```
PROCEDURE InsertNode (VAR Head : Pointer;
                      P, Prev : Pointer);

  {  Given:    Linked list referenced by Head pointer.          }
  {            Node referenced by P to be inserted in the       }
  {            list after node referenced by Prev, with         }
  {            Prev equal to NIL if insertion is to             }
  {            occur at front of list.                          }
  {  Task:     Set pointers to link node P into list.           }
  {  Return:   Appropriately updated linked list.               }

  BEGIN
    IF Prev = NIL THEN {  Insert at front  }
      BEGIN
        P^.Link := Head;
        Head := P
      END
    ELSE
      BEGIN
        P^.Link := Prev^.Link;
        Prev^.Link := P
      END {  IF  }
  END;  {  of PROCEDURE InsertNode  }
```

■ ■

■ EXAMPLE 4.15

Implement the DeleteNode operation for a Pascal pointer variable implementation.

```
PROCEDURE DeleteNode (VAR Head : Pointer;
                      P, Prev : Pointer);

  {  Given:    Linked list referenced by pointer Head.          }
  {            Pointer P to node to be removed from this        }
  {            list and pointer Prev to node preceding P.       }
```

```
{           Prev is NIL if node referenced by P is at      }
{           front of list.                                 }
{  Task:    Remove node P from list.                       }
{  Return:  Appropriately altered list.                    }

BEGIN
  IF Prev = NIL THEN  {  Delete first node  }
    Head := Head^.Link
  ELSE
    Prev^.Link := P^.Link;
  dispose (P)  {  Return the deleted node  }
END;  {  of PROCEDURE DeleteNode  }
```

Since both the InsertNode and DeleteNode procedures assume that the pointers P and Prev have been appropriately set prior to calling, we should describe how this would be done for a pointer variable implementation. The following procedure, FindNodeToDelete, is based on a pointer variable implementation. You should carefully compare it to the FindInsertionSlot procedure we developed for an array implementation in Example 4.5. Note the similarities in the way the procedures' loops are controlled. Just as we had to use a Boolean variable to avoid a potential Null index reference in the array procedure, so must we use a Boolean variable to avoid a potential reference through a **NIL**-valued pointer in the pointer variable version.

EXAMPLE 4.16

Develop a procedure that could be called prior to DeleteNode to find the node to remove from a linked list and establish the P and Prev parameters for DeleteNode.

```
{  Assume same declarations used in previous examples }

PROCEDURE  FindNodeToDelete (Head : Pointer;
                             VAR P, Prev : Pointer;
                             Target : LinkListData;
                             VAR Found : boolean);

  {  Given:   Linked list referenced by pointer variable      }
  {           Head and Target data to be found in that list.  }
  {  Task:    Search list for Target.                         }
  {  Return:  Pointers P and Prev to node containing Target   }
  {           data and the preceding node respectively.       }
  {           Prev set to NIL if Target occurs at the front   }
  {           of the list.  Found set to true or false        }
  {           depending upon whether or not Target was found. }

  BEGIN
    Prev := NIL;
    P := Head;
    Found := false;
    {  P advances until end of list or Target value is        }
    {  reached.                                               }
    WHILE (P <> NIL) AND NOT Found DO
      IF P^.Data = Target THEN
        Found := true
      ELSE { Still looking }
```

```
                BEGIN
                  Prev := P;   {  Prev tags along   }
                  P := P^.Link {   P advances   }
                END
          END;  {  of PROCEDURE FindNodeToDelete  }
```

■ **EXAMPLE 4.17**

In Example 4.9 we provided a complete main program to maintain a list of strings in alphabetical order using an array implementation of a linked list. Here we change the underlying implementation of the linked list structure in that program to a Pascal pointer variable implementation. Other than that change, the design and logic of the program parallels exactly that of Example 4.9.

```
PROGRAM PointerVarImpOfLinkedList (input, output);

{  Demonstrate use of essential operations for Pascal pointer        }
{  implementation of a linked list by maintaining a list             }
{  of strings in alphabetical order.                                 }

TYPE
  Pointer = ^LinkedListNode;
  LinkedListData = String;  { Assume appropriate implementation of string ADT }
  LinkedListNode = RECORD
                     Data : LinkedListData;
                     Link : Pointer
                   END;

VAR
  Head, P : Pointer;
  DeleteData : LinkedListData;
  Command : char;

  .
  .  { Procedures for linked list and string operations here }
  .

{ PrintOneNode is passed as parameter to LinkedTraverse }
PROCEDURE PrintOneNode (VAR Item : LinkedListData);

  {  Given:    Item, one data item on a linked list          }
  {  Task:     Print the item                                }
  {  Return:   Nothing                                       }

  BEGIN
    WriteAString (Item);
    writeln
  END; { of PROCEDURE PrintOneNode }

BEGIN {  Main program  }
  Create (Head);
  REPEAT
    write('[A]dd node, [D]elete node, [P]rint list, or [Q]uit --> ');
    readln(Command);
    CASE Command OF
      'A', 'a':
        BEGIN
          new (P);
          write ('Enter data --> ');
          CreateString (P^.Data);  {  Create for String  }
```

```
          ReadAString (P^.Data);
          FindInsertionSlot(Head, P, Prev);
          InsertNode(Head, P, Prev)
        END;
      'D', 'd':
        BEGIN
          write ('Enter node to delete --> ');
          CreateString (DeleteData);  {  Create for string  }
          ReadAString (DeleteData);
          FindNodeToDelete (Head, P, Prev, DeleteData, Found);
          IF Found THEN
            DeleteNode(Head, P, Prev)
          ELSE
            BEGIN
              WriteAString (DeleteData);
              writeln (' not found')
            END
        END;
      'P', 'p':
        LinkedTraverse (Head, PrintOneNode)
      'Q', 'q':
        BEGIN
        END
      END {  CASE  }
  UNTIL (Command = 'q') OR (Command = 'Q')
END.
```

The sample run for this program would appear *exactly* as that given in Example 4.9. This is not surprising since we have changed only the underlying implementation of the list structure. At the user level, this change should be completely hidden. Also note that the main programs of the two examples are nearly identical. You will consider how to make them identical in the Exercises.

Now let's compare the two linked list implementations we have discussed. From an efficiency perspective, there is little difference because the algorithms behind Pascal's **new** and **dispose** procedures mirror very closely the logic of their counterparts GetNode and ReturnNode in the array implementation. The array implementation has the advantage of not being specifically tied to Pascal or a similar language that directly supports dynamic memory management. Moreover, the array implementation can be directly converted to a random access file implementation using the strategy we discussed in Chapter 3.

The array implementation also allows for easier program tracing when debugging is needed since the values of the links may be directly printed via **write** statements. However, this advantage is somewhat tempered by the fact that most Pascal compilers come with debugging tools that allow you to actually see the values of pointer variables even though Pascal itself will not let you **write** them.

From a convenience perspective, pointer variables emerge a clear winner—totally eliminating your worries about managing available nodes. Pascal's dynamic memory management also allows your linked list (or other data structure) to expand into all of the memory available at run-time. Array implementations, on the other hand, are bounded by the size of an array declared at compile time. In this book, we tend to use pointer variable implementations for data structures where possible because of the convenience. However, in certain situations where a concept can be more clearly illustrated by giving some tangible numbers for pointer values, we occasionally resort to array implementations.

Exercises 4.3

Exercises 1–6 refer to the following **TYPE** and **VAR** declarations:

```
TYPE
  Ptr = ^Node;
  Node = RECORD
           Num : integer;
           Next : Ptr
         END;

  VAR
    A, B, C : Ptr;
```

1. Specify which of the following statements are syntactically correct. For those that are wrong, explain why they are wrong.
   a. `A := B;`
   b. `A := A^.Num;`
   c. `A := A^.Ptr;`
   d. `dispose (B^);`
   e. `dispose (B^.Num);`
   f. `dispose (B);`
   g. `writeln (B);`
   h. `writeln (B^);`
   i. `writeln (B^.Num);`
2. Show how the schematic

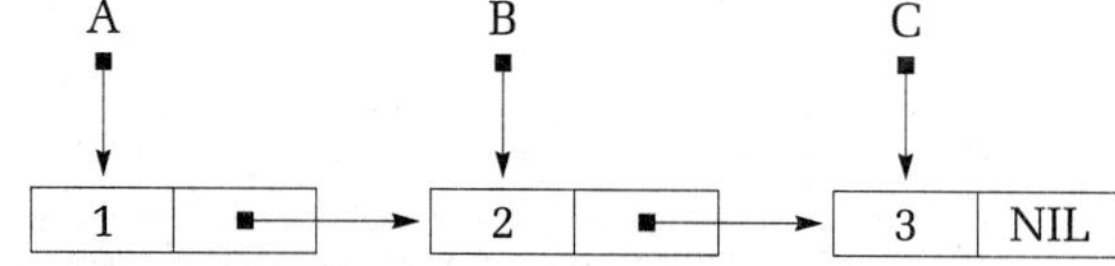

   would be changed by each of the following:
   a. `A := A^.Next;`
   b. `B := A;`
   c. `C := A^.Next;`
   d. `B^.Num := C^.Num;`
   e. `A^.Num := B^.Next^.Num;`
   f. `C^.Next := A;`
3. Write one statement to change

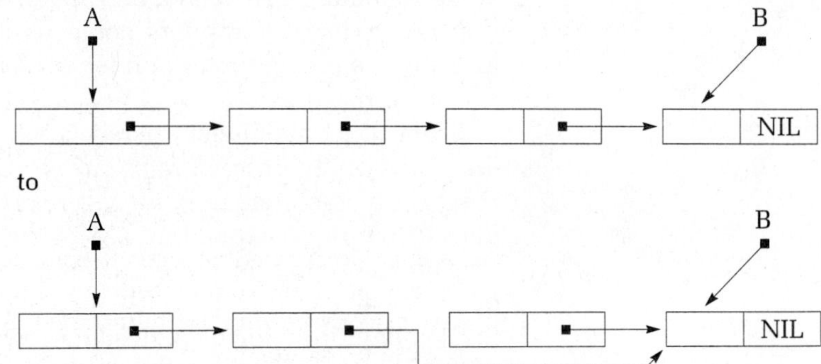

4. Consider the list

Write code to create a new linked list element with value 12 and insert it at the beginning of the list headed by A.

5. Consider the list

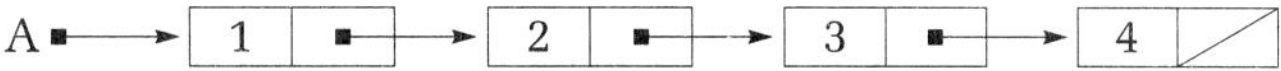

Write code to remove the element at the head of the list and then add this element at the end of the list.

6. Indicate the output for each of the following:

a.
```
new (A);
new (B);
A^.Num := 10;
B^.Num := 20;
B := A;
A^.Num := 5;
writeln (A^.Num, B^.Num);
```

b.
```
new (C);
C^.Num := 100;
new (B);
B^.Num := C^.Num MOD 8;
new (A);
A^.Num := B^.Num + C^.Num;
writeln (A^.Num, B^.Num, C^.Num);
```

c.
```
new (A);
new (B);
A^.Num := 10;
A^.Next := B;
A^.Next^.Num := 100;
writeln (A^.Num, B^.Num);
```

7. The statement

```
P := P + 1
```

advances a pointer to the next node for an array implementation of a keyed list. What corresponding statement advances a pointer to the next node for an array implementation of a linked list? For a pointer variable implementation of a linked list? Qualify your answers by providing the record description from which you are working.

8. Implement the LinkedTraverse operation for a Pascal pointer linked list.

9. Write a procedure to reverse a linked list referenced by a Pascal pointer variable.

10. Write a function Sum to sum the integers in a linked list of integers. Show how it is called from the main program.

11. Write a procedure to dispose of all nodes in a linked list referenced by the Pascal pointer variable Head. Why can't it be done by simply passing the **dispose** procedure as an actual parameter to the LinkedTraverse operation?

12. Write a procedure that receives head pointers to two linked lists arranged in ascending order. Your procedure should merge these two lists into a single list, also arranged in ascending order. A head pointer to the merged list should be returned.

13. In what ways are the main programs of Examples 4.9 and 4.17 not identical? How would you adjust the definition of the LinkedList ADT so that the two programs could be identical?
14. Discuss ways in which Pascal's **new** and **dispose** are more powerful than the GetNode and ReturnNode operations that were developed in Section 4.2.
15. Suppose that you have a program that manipulates a dynamic structure using Pascal pointer variables. At the end of this program you wish to save this data structure to a file so that it may be reloaded upon the next run of the program. One strategy is to simply traverse the data structure, writing each node (including its pointer values) to a disk file. Although this approach is legal in Pascal, it will not work. Explain why. Then describe an alternate strategy that will allow saving a data structure from one run of the program to the next.
16. You are writing a program that requires two linked lists, each with a different data type in its nodes. Would you use array implementations for the linked lists or Pascal pointer variable implementations? Explain why.

■ ■ ■ ■

■ 4.4 Variations on Linked List Structures

Linked lists provide a tremendously useful tool in situations where a highly volatile general list must be maintained in some prescribed logical order. Their widespread use has led to the development of several "tricks of the trade" particularly suitable in certain applications. These are ways of fine-tuning the basic linked list structure to tailor it to the needs of particular situations. Four such variations on the linked list are presented in this section: dummy headers, circular lists, doubly linked lists, and multilinked lists.

Dummy Headers

A *dummy header* node in the list before the first actual data node can often contain useful information about the structure (for example, the number of nodes). If such information is of a different type than other list nodes, a variant record can be used to store it. A query algorithm can then determine the status of the list by examining the contents of the dummy header node without having to traverse the entire list. This amounts to adding one more node to the list. Figure 4.13 illustrates this concept.
Additions to and deletions from the list require changing this information-keeping field in the dummy header node of the list.

FIGURE 4.13
Linked list with dummy header indicating the length of the list

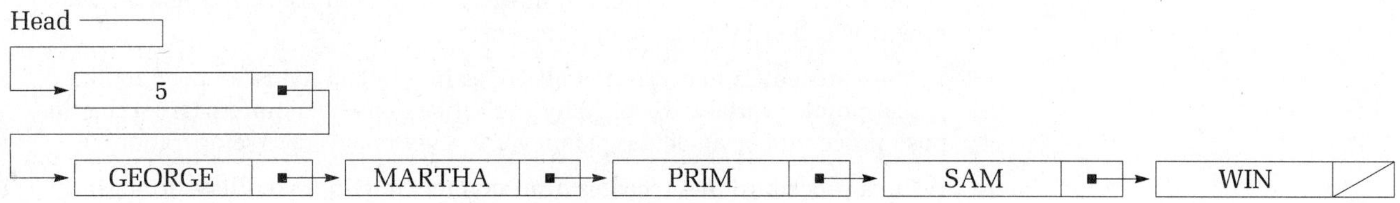

There is another distinct advantage of the dummy header node. If the list becomes empty and a dummy header node is not used, then the Head pointer for the list must be made **NIL.** But if the dummy header node is present, then the Head pointer never needs to be changed to **NIL** because it always points to this dummy header. That is, the empty list is only empty in a logical sense. Physically, it still contains the dummy header. This convention can serve to simplify the coding involved in procedures InsertNode and DeleteNode by removing the special handling previously required for inserts and deletes at the beginning of the list. (You will write these simplified procedures as an exercise at the end of this section.) This convenience factor alone provides substantial practical motivation for always using dummy headers.

Circular Linked Lists

Although linked lists are as we have described them are satisfactory in many instances, some applications must continuously cycle through the data in a list. After completing one cycle through the list, another is immediately begun. For such applications, the existence of a **NIL** pointer in the final node of a list represents an inconvenience. It would be desirable to be able to enter the list anywhere and process it efficiently independent of the entry point. In other words, we need a linked list that has no beginning or end.

Circular linked lists are precisely such data structures. A singly linked circular list is a linked list in which the last node of the list points to the first node in the list. Notice that in circular list structures, there are no **NIL** links. Figure 4.14 depicts a singly linked circular list.

FIGURE 4.14
Singly linked circular list

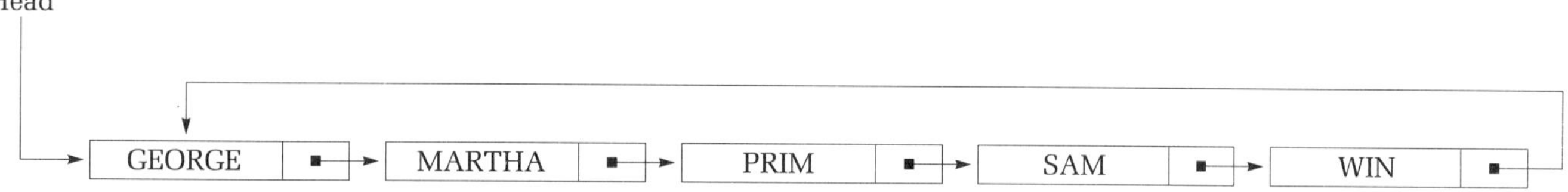

As an example of the utility of such a circular list in the area of operating systems, suppose the nodes in Figure 4.14 represent current users on a time-sharing computer. In such an environment, the operating system schedules each user for a small time slice on the central processing unit (CPU) and then proceeds to devote its momentary attention to the next user. When the final user has completed his or her time slice, ownership of the CPU must again revert to the first user, and the scheduling cycle starts again. Because of the speed of the CPU, this cyclic scheduling creates the illusion for each user that the computer is dedicated to his or her particular process. Clearly, a circular linked list is made to order for this type of scheduling. The circularity insures no unnecessary interruptions in restarting the scheduling cycle when the end of the user list is reached. The linked nature of the structure enables the operating system to quickly process new users who log on and users who then complete their work and log off.

Doubly Linked Circular Lists

In the previously developed procedures InsertNode and DeleteNode, we had prior knowledge about where in the list insertions and deletions were to be performed. In general, this information may have to be determined through a routine that searches the entire list. Because search algorithms require time proportional to the length of the list, run-time can be substantial if the list is very long. As an example, suppose we have a singly linked list in which we wish to insert a node A pointed to by Point1 just before a node B pointed to by Point2. We can change the link field of A to point to B, but we do not know the address of (that is, a pointer to) the node preceding B. If we are to depend upon the current structure of the list, then we must search the list for B—an inefficient procedure we wish to avoid. In other words, even in situations where we may be able to locate B by other means (such as a hashing strategy to be studied in Chapter 9), we must traverse the list up to B to find the previous node.

Inserting node A before node B is shown in Figure 4.15. In a singly linked structure, time-consuming sequential searching is required to determine the address of the node preceding B.

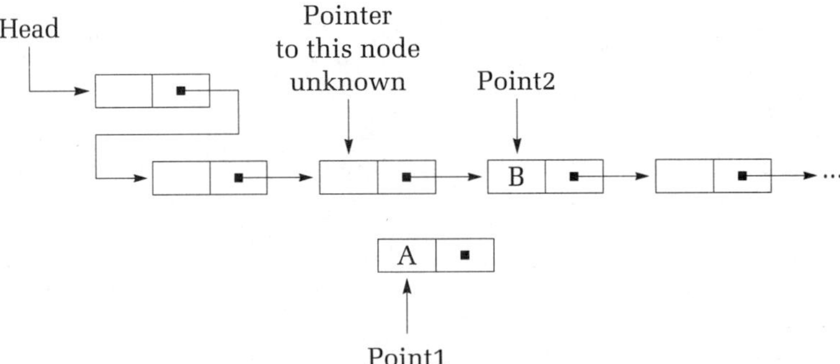

FIGURE 4.15
Inserting node A before node B

A satisfactory way of getting around the difficulty presented in Figure 4.15 is a *doubly linked circular list* in which each node has two pointers: a forward link and a backward link. The forward link is a pointer to the next node in the list; the backward link points to the preceding node. The circular nature of the list, along with a special dummy header node, can be used to conveniently avoid special conditional checking when adding to or deleting from the beginning or end of the list.

Figure 4.16 illustrates a doubly linked circular list. This list has five nodes (plus a dummy header), each having a forward link (FLink) and a backward link (BLink). FLink points to the successor node, whereas BLink points to the predecessor node. Because the list is circular, BLink of the first node must point to the last node, and FLink of the last node must point to the first node.

FIGURE 4.16
Doubly linked circular list

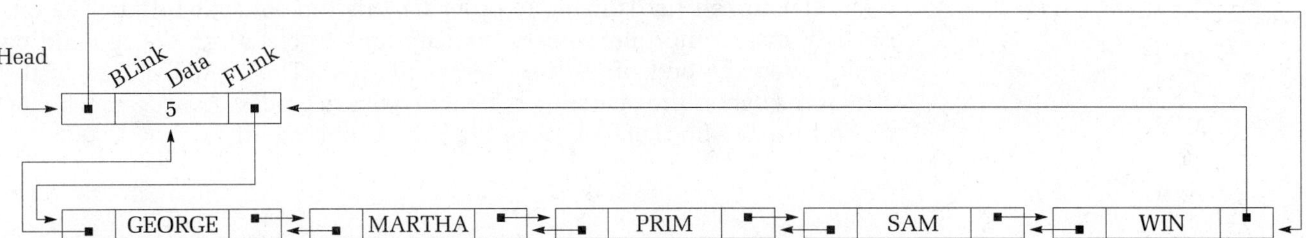

Inserting a node into a doubly linked list, or deleting one from it, is potentially a much easier task because we do not need a separate pointer to a preceding node. Hence we may be able to avoid the time inefficiency inherent in finding such a pointer in situations where the insertion or deletion point can be found by means faster than traversing the list.

EXAMPLE 4.18

Develop a procedure to insert a node into a doubly linked circular list with a dummy header. As with the InsertNode operation for singly linked lists, assume that the point for insertion has already been found according to criteria suitable for the particular list.

```
{  Global declarations  }

TYPE
  Pointer = ^LinkedListNode;
  LinkedListNode = RECORD
                Data  : LinkedListData;
                FLink : Pointer;
                BLink : Pointer
              END;

PROCEDURE InsertNodeDouble (Point1, Point2 : Pointer);

  {  Given:   Doubly linked circular list with a dummy header  }
  {           and a node within that list referenced by       }
  {           Point2. Point1 referencing a node to be         }
  {           inserted in that list prior to node referenced  }
  {           by Point2.                                      }
  {  Task:    Adjust pointers to link node referenced by      }
  {           Point1 into the list.                           }
  {  Return:  Appropriately altered list.                     }

 VAR
    Prev : Pointer;

  BEGIN
    Prev := Point2^.BLink;
    Point1^.FLink := Point2;
    Point1^.BLink := Prev;
    Prev^.FLink := Point1;
    Point2^.BLink := Point1
  END; {  of PROCEDURE InsertNodeDouble  }
```

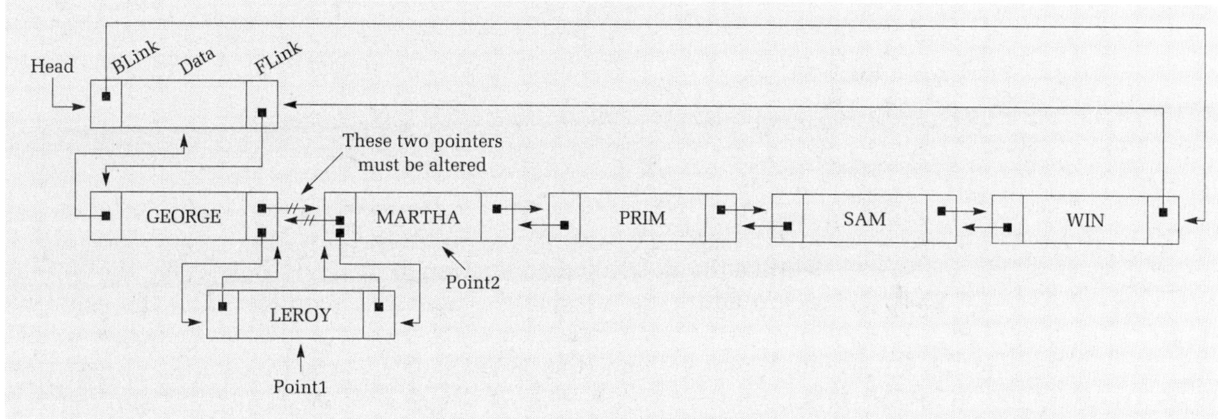

Note that the procedure InsertNodeDouble illustrates how streamlined insert and delete procedures become when a dummy header is used. In particular, because the empty list appears as

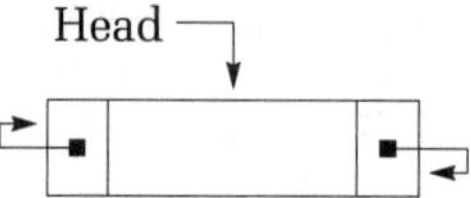

the procedure works without any awkward checking of whether the list is empty or whether the insertion is being made at the front of the list. Clearly a dummy header simplifies procedures in this situation.

EXAMPLE 4.19

Develop a procedure to delete a node from a doubly linked list consistent with the declarations in Example 4.18.

```
PROCEDURE DeleteNodeDouble (Point1 : Pointer);

  {  Given:    Node referenced by Point1 in a circular      }
  {            doubly linked list with a dummy header.      }
  {  Task:     Adjust pointers to remove node Point1 from   }
  {            the list.                                    }
  {  Return:   Appropriately altered list with Point1       }
  {            removed.                                     }

VAR
  Save : Pointer;

  BEGIN
  Save := Point1^.Blink;
  Save^.Flink := Point1^.Flink;
  Save := Point1^.Flink;
  Save^.Blink := Point1^.Blink;
  dispose (Point1)
END; {  of PROCEDURE DeleteNodeDouble  }
```

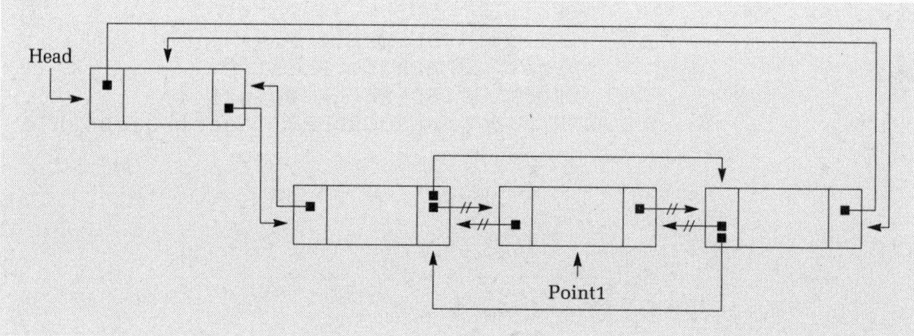

Unlike the DeleteNode operation for a singly linked list, the corresponding procedure for a doubly linked list requires only one parameter—a pointer to the node to be removed. The critical pointer to the preceding node is built into the node that is deleted.

A NOTE OF INTEREST

Computer Viruses

Many computer installations are now confronted with a threat akin to germ warfare, which could disable their largest machines. A computer "virus" attacks a computer system in essentially the same way a biological virus attacks the human body.

A computer virus is actually a small undetected program that, over time, infects other programs and eventually disables the entire system. A typical virus in a host program might contain the following instructions:

1. Temporarily suspend execution of host program
2. Search the computer's memory for other likely uninfected programs.
3. If found, insert a copy of these instructions.
4. Return control of computer back to host program.

This virus would take less than a second to execute, would be virtually undetected, and could attack indefinetely. It can even spread to other computers, when an infected program is swapped or copied for another user.

Adding to the problem is the fact that the saboteur can add instructions to delay the signal for the virus to attack. As researcher Fred Cohen explains, a disgruntled employee instructed the program to remain dormant until his personal password was removed from the system. Once the employee was fired, and his password removed, the virus shut down the entire system.

The Pentagon addresses this problem by isolating its top-secret computers. The military's most sensitive computers are kept in electronically shielded rooms and, when necessary, connected with wire that runs through pipes filled with gas under pressure. The gas pressure would drop if someone attempted to penetrate the pipes to tap into the wires. Marvin Shaefer, chief scientist at the Pentagon computer security center, admits that computers without good access controls are vulnerable to virus attacks.

Computer scientists differ as to whether or not public discussion of computer viruses should even be encouraged. Jerry Lobel, manager of computer security at Honeywell International in Phoenix expresses concern because "it only takes a half-way decent programmer about half a day of thinking to figure out how to do it. If you tell enough people about it there's going to be one crazy out there who's going to try."

Cohen disagrees, insisting that ignorance is always more dangerous than knowledge. "It's better to have somebody friendly do the experiments, tell you how bad it is, show you how it works, and help you counteract it, than to have somebody vicious come along and do it." If you wait, it might be too late.

If your curiosity is aroused, you can find more detailed accounts of the evolution of the computer virus problem in "Attack of the Computer Virus" by Lee Dembart (*Discover*, November 1984), "Is Your Computer Infected?" by William D. Marbach (*Newsweek*, February 1, 1988), and *Computer Viruses, Worms, Data Diddlers, Killer Programs, and Other Threats to Your System* by John McAfee and Colin Haynes (New York, N.Y.: St. Martin's Press, 1989).

Multilinked Lists

We shall end this discussion of variations on the linked list theme by noting that a doubly linked list is a special case of a structure known as a *multilinked list.* Because each link field determines an order in which the nodes of a list are to be processed, we can in fact establish a different link field for every different order in which we wish to process the nodes in a list. Figure 4.17 illustrates such a multilinked list. By following the IDLink fields, we traverse the list in IDNumber order; by following the NameLink fields, we traverse the list in alphabetical order by Name.

FIGURE 4.17
Link fields for processing nodes

IDHead: 4 NameHead: 3

	Name	IDNumber	NameLink	IDLink
1	SAM	8316	4	Null
2	MARTHA	4212	5	5
3	GEORGE	6490	2	1
4	WIN	1330	Null	2
5	PRIM	5560	1	3

Multilink List

In the problems at the end of the chapter, you will consider how a multilinked list could have been used as an alternative implementation for the list of student records in Chapter 3's Focus on Program Design section.

Exercises 4.4

1. Repeat Exercise 5 from Section 4.2, this time using a linked list with a dummy header.
2. Repeat Exercise 5 from Section 4.2 with a circular linked list and a dummy header.
3. Repeat Exercise 5 from Section 4.2 for a doubly linked circular list with a dummy header.
4. Suppose that we also wish to be able to go through the list of Exercise 5 from Section 4.2 in zip code order where:

   JAMES has zip code 54952
   CHILTON has zip code 48649
   SEFTON has zip code 22111
   LEE has zip code 84682
   WAGNER has zip code 11843
   AARON has zip code 99218

   Trace the status of all fields (including headers and available space pointer) in an array-based, multilinked implementation of this list of names and zip codes.
5. In Examples 4.18 and 4.19 we provided procedures for insertion into and deletion from a doubly linked circular list with dummy header. Each of those procedures used a locally declared pointer variable. Rewrite each of those procedures without using such a locally declared pointer.
6. Examples 4.18 and 4.19 provided implementations for the Insert and Delete operations for a doubly linked list. Complete the implementation of a package of operations for this data structure by writing procedures/functions for the Create, Empty, Next, and LinkedTraverse operations. Be sure that your implementations of these operations are consistent with those presented in Examples 4.18 and 4.19.
7. Rewrite the InsertNodeDouble and DeleteNodeDouble procedures of Example 4.18 and 4.19 under the assumption that the doubly linked list is *not* circular and does *not* have a dummy header. (Doing this should make you appreciate the elegance of dummy headers.)
8. Write a package of procedures and functions to implement the Create, Next, Empty, InsertNode, DeleteNode, and Linked Traverse operations for a singly linked list with a dummy header. Be sure that your LinkedTraverse procedure doesn't process the dummy header.
9. Write a package of procedures and functions to implement the Create, Next, Empty, InsertNode, DeleteNode, and LinkedTraverse operations for a singly linked circular list with no dummy header. Be sure that your LinkedTraverse procedure does not loop infinitely.
10. Write a package of procedures to implement the Create, Next, Empty, InsertNode, DeleteNode, FindInsertionSlot (see Example 4.5), and FindNodeToDelete (see Example 4.16) for a multilinked list that maintains a list in alphabetical order by name (a string) and also in order by integer identification number (like the list in Figure 4.17). Finally, develop traversal operations for each possible ordering of the list.

■ ■ ■ ■

■ 4.5 An Implementation of Strings Using Linked Lists

OBJECTIVES

- to understand how linked lists could be used to implement the string ADT
- to be able to write implementations of string operations using linked lists of characters
- to analyze the efficiency of using linked lists of characters to implement strings, particularly from a space perspective
- to see how character clusters can enhance the space efficiency of a linked list implementation of strings

Thus far our discussion of linked lists has focused upon their application as an implementation technique for the keyed list ADT. However, linked lists provide means of implementing a wide variety of higher-level ADTs. In this section, we shall give some indication of how linked lists could be used to implement the string ADT introduced in Section 2.2.

Recall that we have already presented two implementation strategies for strings: the **PACKED ARRAY** and embedded length implementations. Both of these strategies imposed a static limit on the maximum length of a string. This static limit poses a twofold disadvantage. First, short strings waste much of the static array storage. Second, strings longer than the statically declared maximum length simply cannot be accommodated. Yet another drawback of both of these implementation techniques is that a tremendous amount of data movement would occur if the Insert and Delete operations for strings are frequently invoked.

Linked lists of characters stored in the heap (*linked list implementations of strings*) could improve upon these inefficiencies. The virtually "infinite" size of the heap would allow strings to attain arbitrary length, and the Insert and Delete operations would be handled swiftly by pointer manipulations. By using a doubly linked circular list, we would even have a conveniently accessible pointer to the last character in the string. This pointer will prove necessary in implementing the Insert and Delete operations. Under this implementation, the three strings 'COFFEE', 'TEA', and 'CREAM' would appear as depicted in Figure 4.18.

FIGURE 4.18
'COFFEE', 'TEA', and 'CREAM', each in a circular doubly linked list

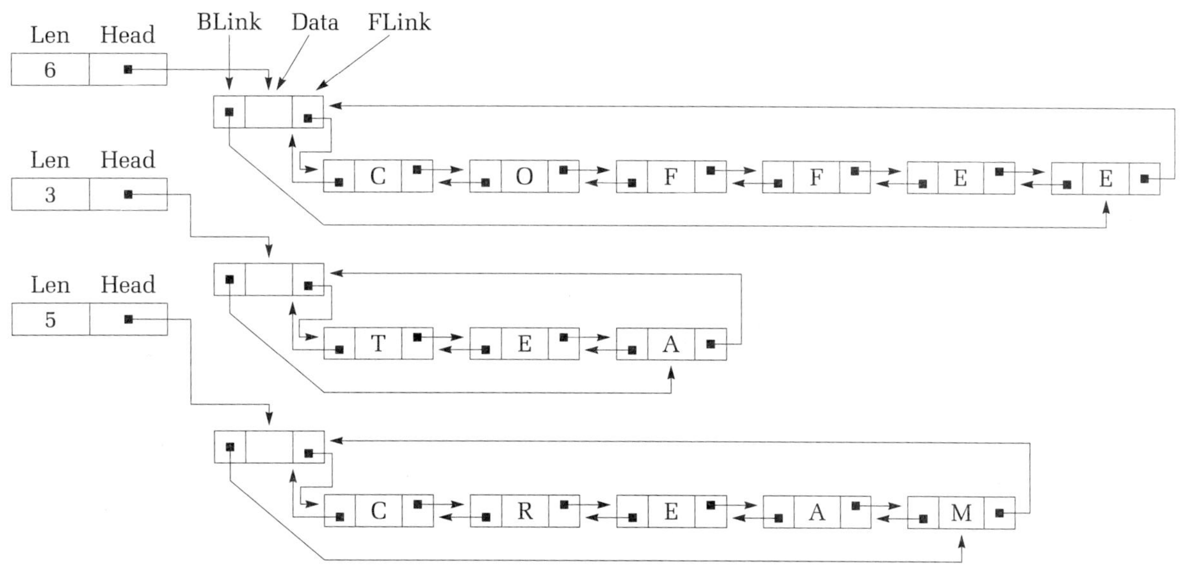

A Pascal declaration to match the snapshots in Figure 4.18 declares a string in the following fashion:

```
TYPE
  StringPtr  = ^StringNode;
  StringNode = RECORD
                 BLink : StringPtr;
                 Data  : char;
                 FLink : StringPtr
               END;
  String     = RECORD
                 Head : StringPtr;
                 Len  : integer
               END
```

Thus, the String type is an encapsulation of a head pointer to a doubly linked list of characters and a length field. Including the latter field will make the Length operation O(1) in its efficiency. Although this field could be avoided by using the dummy header as a record variant, there are reasons for not doing so in this particular application. You will discover these reasons in the Exercises.

Let us consider how some of the string operations we have specified would be performed in such an implementation. The assignment of one string to another could be achieved in very slick and efficient (though perhaps somewhat deceptive) fashion. That is, instead of physically creating two identical strings, we will simply have two separate Head pointers referencing the same string. This particular strategy does have some potential repercussions which might have to be avoided in certain applications (as we'll see in the Exercises). The Search operation for strings presents no real problem and is examined in an exercise at the end of the chapter. The Substring operation does present a problem and will be discussed in greater detail later in this section. Insertion, deletion, and concatenation (which may be viewed as a special case of insertion) can be handled elegantly and efficiently using the linked list method, as the following example indicates.

EXAMPLE 4.20

Implement the Insert operation for strings using the encapsulation of the preceding declarations.

```
PROCEDURE Insert (VAR S : String;
                  Place : integer;
                  T : String);

  { Given:       S and T--two arbitrary strings                        }
  {              Place--the position where T is to be inserted in S    }
  { Task:        Insert T into S                                        }
  { Return:      S with T inserted at position Place.  If Place is greater  }
  {              than Length(S), S is not altered.                      }

  VAR
    K : integer;
    FirstInT, LastInT, P : StringPtr;

  BEGIN
    IF Place <= S.Len THEN
      BEGIN
        P := S.Head;
        {    First find position by traversing list  }
        FOR K := 1 TO Place DO
          P := P^.FLink;
```

```
        {  Now link it in  }
        FirstInT := T.Head^.FLink;
        LastInT := T.Head^.BLink;
        FirstInT^.BLink := P^.BLink;
        LastInT^.FLink := P;
        P^.BLink^.FLink := FirstInT;
        P^.BLink := LastInT;
        {  Finally update length  }
        S.Len := S.Len + T.Len
      END
  END; {  of PROCEDURE Insert  }
```

Note that this procedure is doing a task slightly more complicated than our previous insertion algorithm for a linked list. Earlier, we were concerned only with inserting one node. Here we are inserting an entire collection of nodes; we are inserting one linked list within another (see Figure 4.19). This is done with relative ease because our implementation of a doubly linked list gives us convenient pointers to both the first and last nodes in the list. Hence, our linked list implementation of strings has provided a rather neat illustration of the utility of double linking.

FIGURE 4.19
Two strings from Figure 4.18 after Insert (S, 4, T)

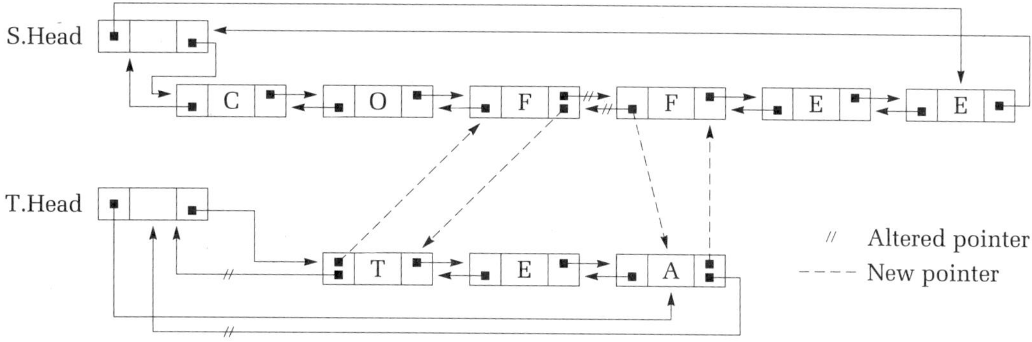

Efficiency Considerations for the Linked List Method

In this string-handling application we have seen that the linked list method allows both dynamic string allocation with no practical limit on string length and extremely efficient insertion and deletion operations. However, there are also some potentially steep costs in using this method.

Three general problem areas exist. First, you may have already noticed that, although the procedure Insert achieves a very efficient insertion, it renders string T thereafter inaccessible as a separate entity. This is because the pointers within string T had to be altered to chain it into string S. (See Figure 4.19).

Second, consider an application in which operating with substrings is of more importance than insertion and deletion. With both the **PACKED ARRAY** and embedded length, the substring consisting of the Jth through the Kth characters could be directly accessed because the characters within any given string are physically next to each other. Accessing the same substring via the linked list implementation requires beginning at the initial character in the string and traversing the entire string until the Jth character is reached. Our implementation of a string as a doubly linked list allows this process to be made somewhat more efficient. In particular, the length of the string from which we want to extract a substring could be checked to determine if the substring occurs in the front or back half. If it is in the back half, the pointer to the last character in the string could be used to begin a traversal from the rear of the list until we reach the desired substring. However, this would still require a sequential processing of the list until the desired substring is found. Hence, for substring operations, the linked list method does not stack up to either of the other two methods.

A third problem arises in the efficiency of memory utilization for the linked list method as we have described it here. If the data portion of a node in the linked list contains only one character, then the two pointers associated with that node could require four to eight times more memory than the data. That is, only 11 to 20 percent of memory is being utilized to store the data in which we are really interested; the rest of the memory is storing data about data.

This memory utilization problem may be somewhat alleviated by making the data portion of a node a *cluster* of characters. Suppose, for instance, we choose a cluster size of four characters. Then the same strings given in Figure 4.18 would appear as shown in Figure 4.20. Here we have used the symbol (~) to represent a null character, that is, a character that is always ignored when the string is processed.

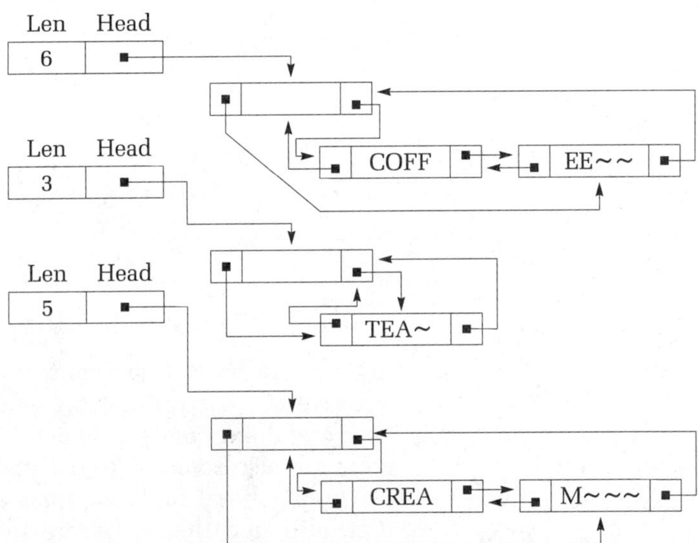

FIGURE 4.20
Strings from Figure 4.18 with a cluster size of four

Notice that, although this technique has enabled us to devote a greater percentage of memory for storage of data, a significant complication has been added: our code must now always account for null characters. For example, if we wish to insert the second string from Figure 4.19 in the first string beginning at position 4, the scheme pictured in Figure 4.21 emerges.

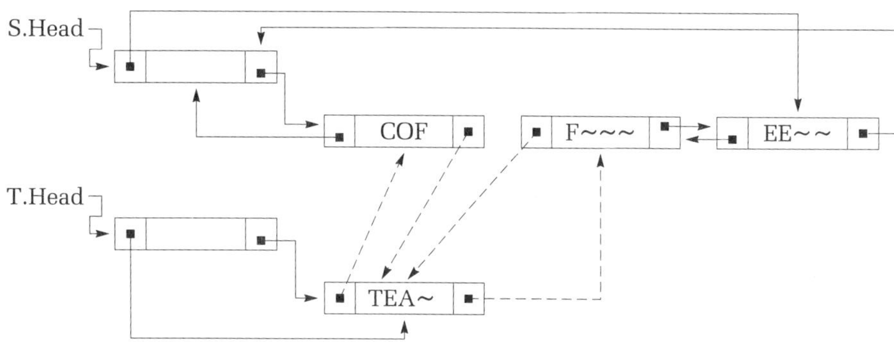

FIGURE 4.21
After insertion of T into S beginning at position 4

Here the node containing 'COFF' had to be split into the two nodes 'COF~' and 'F~~~' to achieve an effective insertion. As you might expect, we have had to trade-off one feature for another. To gain more effective memory utilization, we have had to make our program code more cumbersome and less efficient in its execution time.

Exercises 4.5

1. Discuss some of the potential unsuspected results that might occur if the string assignment strategy discussed in this section were actually used. In particular, consider what might happen in the following situation:

```
Create (S1);
Create (S2);
ReadAString (S1);
Assign (S1, S2);   { ADT operation for S2 := S1 }
ReadAString (S1);
WriteAString (S2);
```

   Now suppose that a user enters the string 'COFFEE' for the first ReadAString and 'TEA' for the second ReadAString. What's the output?

2. Hou would you correct the problem identified in Exercise 1? Implement this correction by providing code for the Assign operation.

3. Write implementations for each operation of the string ADT using the doubly linked list method described in this section. Then analyze the time efficiency of each implemented operation.

4. Repeat Exercise 3 except now use a singly linked list of characters with a head pointer and no dummy header.

5. Exercises 3 and 4 provide two alternative linked list methods of implementing strings.

   a. For each method, develop a formula that expresses the percentage of memory devoted to storing overhead data (as opposed to actual character data). Each of these formulas should be expressed as a function of the following general parameters:

      P—The number of bytes to store a pointer/integer.
      S—The number of bytes to store one character (usually S = 1).
      C—The cluster size.
      A—The average string length in your application.

      For each formula you develop, explain how you derive it.

b. Your answer to Exercise 5a should indicate that the singly linked method is generally more space efficient than the doubly linked list. However, suppose your application calls for frequently inserting one string in another. For this application, the doubly linked list method is more time efficient. Explain why. If it will help, include diagrams in your explanation.

6. How would you rewrite the declarations for the doubly linked list implementation of string to incorporate the storage of a string's length into the dummy header for the list? Would your declarations be more or less space efficient than those given in this section? Explain your answer.

■ ■ ■ ■

4.6 A Linked List Implementation of a Sparse Table

OBJECTIVES

- to understand how linked lists could be used to implement a sparse table
- to be able to write implementations of sparse table operations using linked lists
- to analyze the efficiency of linked lists as an implementation technique for sparse tables

In previous sections we have seen how a linked list or variation thereof may be used to efficiently implement keyed lists and strings. To further emphasize the utility of linked lists, we will now show how linked lists may be used to implement a two-dimensional sparse table (as defined in Chapter 2); we call this a *linked list implementation of a sparse table.*

Consider the sparse table of integers pictured in Table 4.1. In Section 2.3, we described a strategy for implementing such a table which would have us store a list of those row and column coordinates that do not resolve to zero. Along with each such coordinate pair we would store its associated nontrivial value. The drawback of this approach stems from the implementation of the list of nonzero coordinates via an array. The array implementation will result in a solution that is extremely inefficient for any volatile table of data. The reasons for this inefficiency parallel those that often make an array implementation of the keyed list ADT inadequate. That is, if we somehow order the data to enable use of the binary search, adds and deletes (in this case assigning a nonzero value to a location which was previously zero or vice versa) will involve the shifting of large amounts of data. Conversely, if we neglect to order the data, adding new nonzero values can be done efficiently but search efficiency will deteriorate.

TABLE 4.1
Sparse table of integer data

	1	2	3	4	5	6	7	8	9	10	11	12	13	14
1	0	83	19	40	0	0	0	0	0	0	0	0	0	0
2	0	0	0	91	0	42	12	0	0	0	0	0	0	0
3	0	0	0	0	0	18	4	0	0	0	0	0	0	0
4	0	0	0	0	0	0	0	0	71	64	0	13	0	0
5	0	0	0	0	0	0	0	0	0	0	0	0	21	40

The implementation method we now propose uses linked lists to insure no data shifting occurs when a zero value is changed to nonzero (or vice versa). Moreover, by employing many linked lists (one for each row), it reduces the length of sequential searches to the number of nonzero column coordinates in a particular targeted row instead of all nonzero row-column coordinates for the entire table. The method requires an array of pointers, each leading to a linked list storing the nonzero data in a given row of the sparse table. Each node in one of these linked lists would need to contain not only an entry from the table but also an indication of which column within that particular row is occupied by the data in this node. We further stipulate that, for efficiency in processing, each linked list be arranged in ascending order of column numbers within that row. Given these conventions, the 5 × 14 table from Table 4.1 would be represented by Figure 4.22.

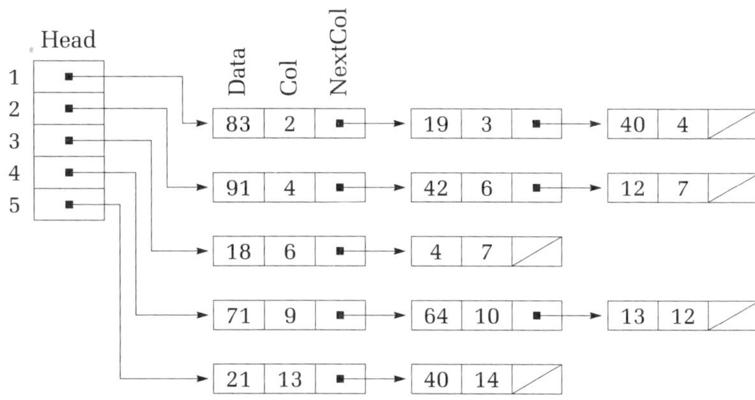

FIGURE 4.22
Linked list representation of sparse table from Table 4.1

■ **EXAMPLE 4.21**

Given the implementation scheme depicted in Figure 4.22, provide declarations for the two-dimensional table ADT. Then write code for the Retrieve operation (see Section 2.3).

```
CONST
  NumberRows = { This constant sets number of rows in the sparse table. }
               { There is no limit on number of columns in this         }
               { implementation.                                         }

TYPE
  SparsePointer = ^SparseNode;
  SparseNode = RECORD
                 Data : TableData;  { Any appropriate numeric type }
                 Col : integer;
                 NextCol : SparsePointer
               END;
  TwoDTable = ARRAY [1..NumberRows] OF SparsePointer;

FUNCTION Retrieve (T : TwoDTable;
                   R, C : integer) : TableData;

  { Given:       T, an arbitrary two-dimensional table                  }
  { Task:        Retrieve the value at row R and column C of the table  }
  { Return:      The value retrieved                                     }

  { A limitation--R must not be greater than NumberRows.  We will later }
  { discuss a way of overcoming this limitation.                         }

  VAR
    P : SparsePointer;
    Exit : boolean;
```

```
BEGIN
  Exit := false;
  P := T[R];
  { P advances through list, searching for column index greater than or    }
  { equal to C.                                                             }
  WHILE (P <> NIL) AND NOT Exit DO
    IF P^.Col < C THEN
      P := P^.NextCol
    ELSE
      Exit := true;
  IF P = NIL THEN
    Retrieve := 0
  ELSE IF P^.Col > C THEN
    Retrieve := 0
  ELSE
    Retrieve := P^.Data
END; { of FUNCTION Retrieve }
```

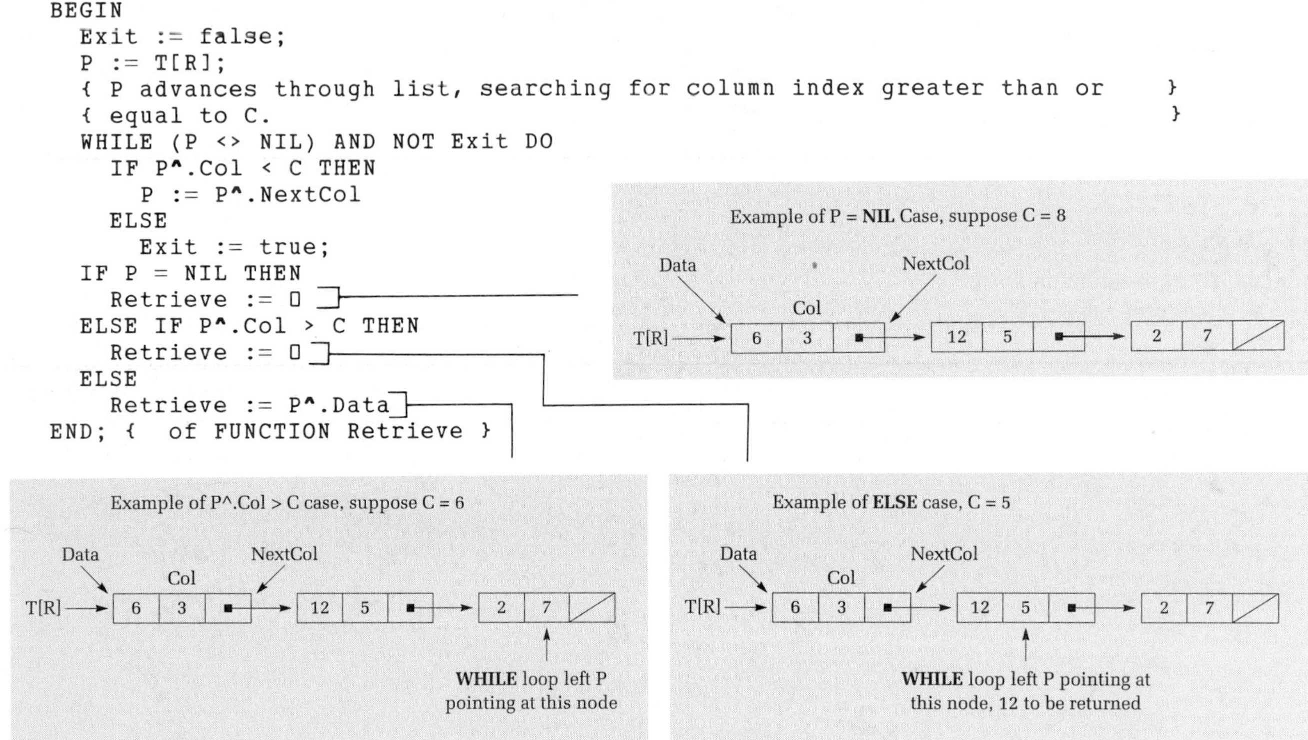

Efficiency Considerations for the Sparse Table

Our comments preceding Example 4.21 indicated that, with respect to run-time, the efficiency of this implementation of a sparse table will require no wholesale data movement when values are assigned to the array. Moreover, since accessing a particular value in the table requires a sequential search along one of the many linked lists which contain a row, we essentially have a retrieval time of O(NumberOfColumns).

Since the main motivation for an implementation of a sparse table is to save memory space, a more important efficiency consideration is exactly how much space we have saved. To determine this, we define the efficiency ratio of a sparse table implementation by the fraction

$$\frac{\text{Number of storage locations used by particular sparse table implementation method}}{\text{Number of storage locations used by standard row-major form}}$$

Clearly, the smaller we can make this ratio, the better our implementation is with respect to memory utilization. Moreover, this ratio must drop below 1 before a particular method can even begin to surpass standard row-major form. In the case of Table 4.1, if we assume that a pointer takes as much memory as one integer, the *efficiency ratio* of our linked list method is given by

5 locations for head-of-list pointers
3 locations for each of 13 nonzero values

This yields a total of 44 storage locations, compared to 70 for a row-major implementation, hence giving a desirable efficiency ratio of 44/70.

However, our simple example of a 5 × 14 table is so small that it is hardly worth considering. A more interesting question is attempting to determine, in general, when a linked list implementation as described here achieves a savings in memory over the standard row-major method. We claim that, assuming that the data in a sparse table are of integer type, the efficiency ratio for this linked list implementation of a sparse matrix drops below 1 only when the number of nonzero locations in the table is less than

$$NRow * (NCol - 1) / 3$$

where NRow is the number of rows in the original table and NCol is the number of columns. To see this, note that each nonzero matrix entry requires three integers to represent it in the linked list implementation. Moreover, each row requires an integer head pointer. Thus the total number of integers required to store N nonzero entries via the linked list method is

$$NRow + N * 3$$

Since we want to force the efficiency ratio

$$\frac{NRow + N * 3}{NRow * NCol}$$

to be less than 1, we conclude that

$$\begin{aligned} NRow + N * 3 &< NRow * NCol \\ N * 3 &< NRow * NCol - NRow \\ N &< NRow * (NCol - 1) / 3 \end{aligned}$$

Similar types of efficiency analyses can be carried out for different base data types and implementation schemes.

Two limitations of the implementation that we have devised in Example 4.21 should be noted. First, from a conceptual standpoint, there sould be no static limit on the number of rows or number of colums in a two-dimensional table. The declarations in Example 4.21, however, place such a static limit on the number of rows because an array of head pointers is used. Using a linked list of row head pointers would remove this limitation, as indicated in Figure 4.23. You will analyze the cost of removing it in the Exercises.

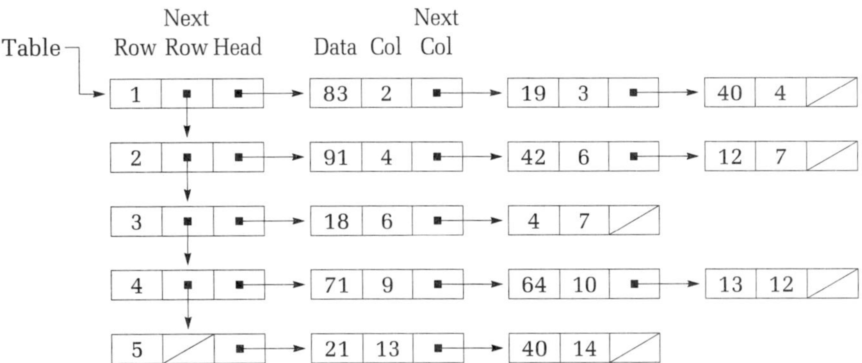

FIGURE 4.23
A linked list implementation of a two-dimensional table with no limitation on the number of rows or number of columns

Second, for many higher-level algorithms that manipulate two-dimensional tables, it is important to traverse a row or column of the table, applying a certain process to each element along that row or column. The high-level algorithm expressed in Example 2.14 provided an illustration of the need for such row and column traversals. In such applications, it would be convonient to extend the basic operations on a two-dimensional table with the two additional operations defined by

```
PROCEDURE TraverseRow (VAR T : TwoDTable;
                       R : integer;
                       PROCEDURE ProcessElement (VAR Element : TableData) );

  { Given:   A two-dimensional table T, R representing a row within the    }
  {          table, and a procedure that can be applied to any data        }
  {          element in the table                                          }
  { Task:    Apply procedure ProcessElement to each table element in row R }
  { Return:  Table T with each element in row R affected by ProcessNode    }

PROCEDURE TraverseColumn (VAR T : TwoDTable;
                          C : integer;
                          PROCEDURE ProcessElement (VAR Element : TableData) );

  { Given:   A two-dimensional table T, C representing a column within     }
  {          that table, and a procedure that can be applied to any data   }
  {          element in the table                                          }
  { Task:    Apply procedure ProcessElement to each table element in       }
  {          column C                                                      }
  { Return:  Table T with each element in column C affected by ProcessNode }
```

The representations suggested by Figures 4.22 and 4.23 will provide a very efficient means of implementing the TraverseRow operation but will bog down in TraverseColumn. This is because, to move from table position T[J, K] to T[J, K+1] we need only follow one link in Figures 4.22 and 4.23. However, to move from T[J, K] to T[J+1,K] we must potentially search the entire linked list representing row J + 1.

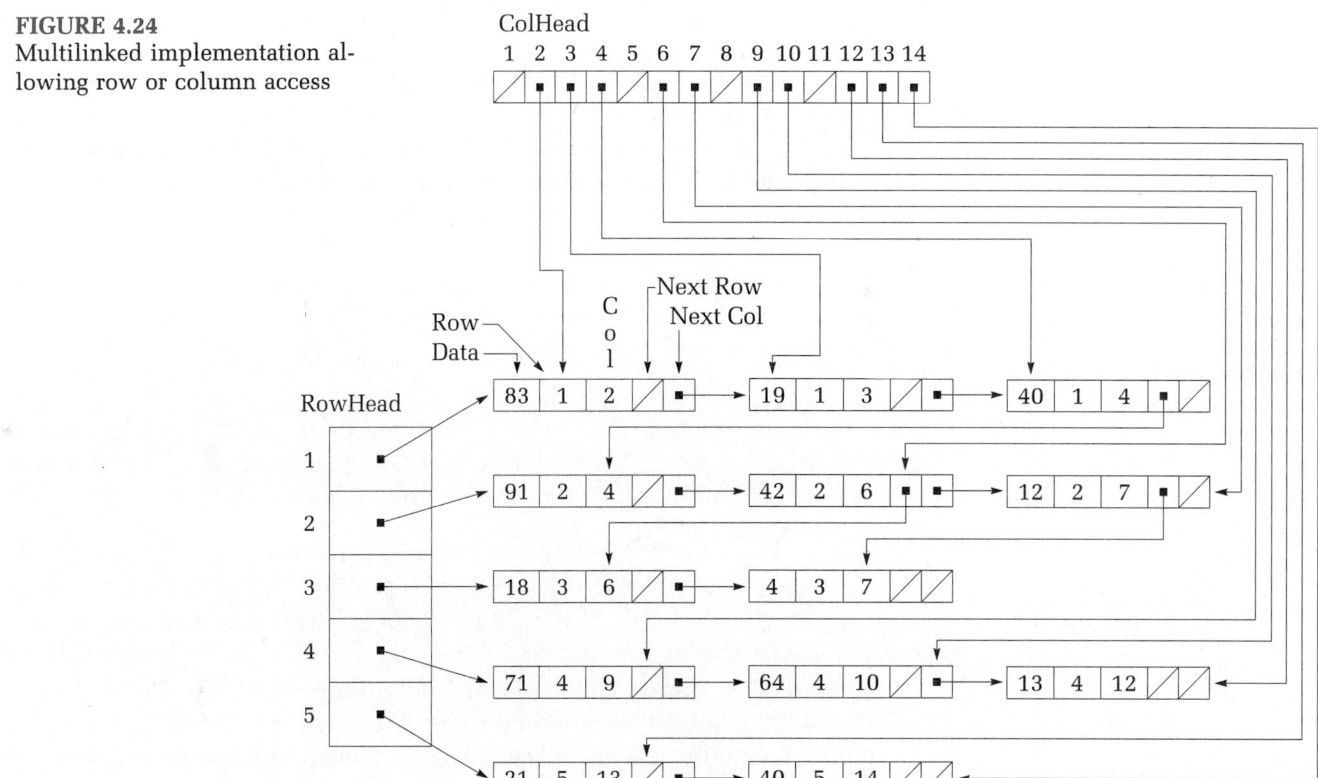

FIGURE 4.24
Multilinked implementation allowing row or column access

By employing a multilinked representation, we can eliminate this bias toward row traversals in our representation schemes. That is, not only must we link the nodes representing nontrivial data along a given row, but also along each column. The picture of such a structure that emerges from Table 4.1 is given in Figure 4.24.

Exercises 4.6

1. Complete the implementation of the two-dimensional table that was begun in Example 4.21. That is, provide code for the Create and Assign operations consistent with the Retrieve operation in that example.
2. Analyze the time efficiency of the Assign operation that you wrote for Exercise 1.
3. Implement the Create, Assign, and Retrieve operations for the representation of a two-dimensional table suggested by Figure 4.23.
4. Analyze the efficiency of each operation you implemented in Exercise 3.
5. Look back to the high-level algorithm that appeared in Example 2.14. Rewrite this algorithm using the TraverseRow and TraverseColumn operations introduced in Section 4.6.
6. Extend your implementation of the two-dimensional table from Exercise 3 by coding the TraverseRow and TaverseColumn operations. What are the respective time efficiencies of each of these operations?
7. Implement the two-dimensional table operations, including TraverseRow and TraverseColumn, using the representation suggested by Figure 4.24. Analyze the efficiencies of the two traversal operations, and compare those efficiencies to your results from Exercise 6.
8. In this section we carried out a space efficiency analysis for the two-dimensional table representation suggested by Figure 4.22. We found that, for a table with integer data, this scheme become space efficient when

   $$N < NRow * (NCol - 1) / 3$$

   where N is the number of nontrivial values in a sparse table. Carry out a similar space efficiency analysis for the representation of Figure 4.23.
9. Repeat Exercise 8 for the two-dimensional table implementation suggested by Figure 4.24. In a written statement, discuss the price that is paid for the faster column access allowed by this representation.

■ ■ ■ ■

FOCUS ON PROGRAM DESIGN

Although we can define the linked list as an ADT, a key theme of this chapter has been that the linked list is of great value when viewed as an implementation technique for other higher-level ADTs and their logic. We have seen linked lists used to implement the keyed list, string, and two-dimensional table ADTs.

Now, in this section, we will use the linked list to implement a very space-efficient version of the radix sort algorithm (see Section 1.4). Moreover, this will be one of those rare instances in which a space-efficient version is also more time-efficient. To achieve this, we will specify that the sort algorithm receive a linked list of integers to be sorted, rather than an array. A top-level pseudocode description of radix sort is then given by

1. Set NumberOfDigits to the number of digits in largest number in the list

2. **FOR** K := 1 **TO** NumberOfDigits **DO**
   2.1 **WHILE** the list to sort is not empty **DO**
      2.1.1 Transfer the first number in the sort list to the appropriate bin, keying on the Kth digit (1 corresponding to ones digit, 2 to tens digit, and so forth).
   2.2 **FOR** J := 0 **TO** 9 **DO**
      2.2.1 Append the numbers in Jth bin to the list to sort

In our discussion of the radix sort in Section 1.4, we were somewhat shackled by approaches that employed static allocation of the bins used to classify numbers. For instance, we determined that sorting n numbers by this algorithm would require $11n$ storage locations—n for the numbers being sorted and an additional $10n$ locations for the bins associated with the 10 possible digits.

Pascal pointer variables provide a new implementation strategy for the bins needed by radix sort. The dynamic allocation associated with these pointer variables will allow each bin to claim only the storage that it needs as the algorithm runs. We propose the following implementation for bins.

```
TYPE
  BinPointer = ^BinNode;
  BinNode = RECORD
              Data : integer;  {  or other data type for sorting  }
              Link : BinPointer
            END;

  Bin  = RECORD
           Head : BinPointer;
           Tail : BinPointer
         END;
  BinStructure  = ARRAY [0. .9] OF Bin;

VAR
  Bins : BinStructure;
```

Unlike other instances of linked lists we have studied in this chapter, a list of **TYPE** Bin will include a Tail pointer to the last node on the list as well as a Head pointer to the first node. This additional pointer will enable us to be particularly efficient during that phase of the algorithm that collects the bins associated with particular digits into a new master bin. Figure 4.25 depicts how this efficiency can be achieved. To append Bins[K] (the Kth bin in a BinStructure) to the ListToSort, we must:

1. Aim the Link field in the last node of the ListToSort at the first node in Bins[K]. See [1] in Figure 4.25.
2. Aim the Tail pointer for the ListToSort at the last node in Bins[K]. See [2] in Figure 4.25.

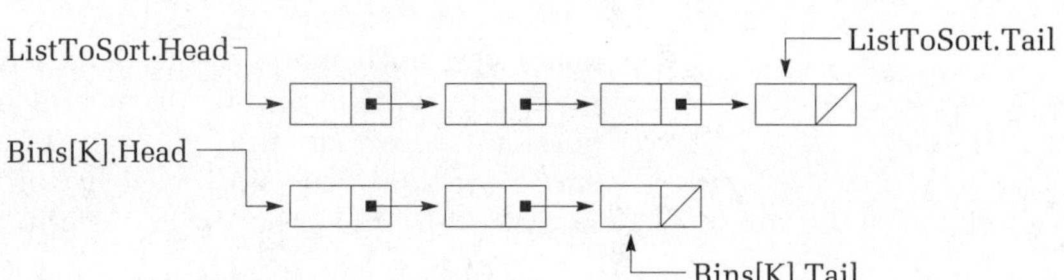

FIGURE 4.25
Appending one bin to another

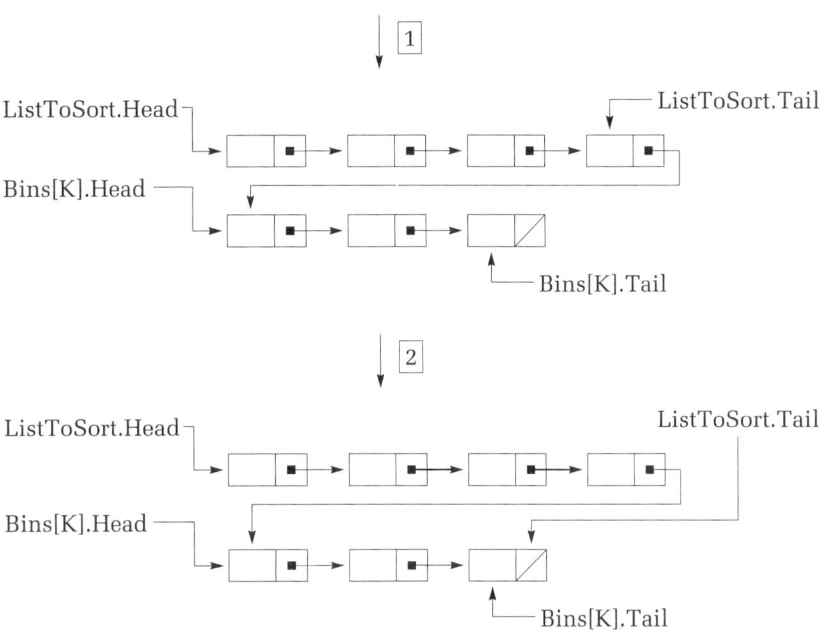

The entire process of appending one bin to the list to sort is thus achieved by resetting two pointers. Compare this to our implementation of bins by arrays in Section 1.4. There the process of appending a bin required physically moving each item in the bin to the array being sorted.

We can now refine our high-level pseudocode for this new version of radix sort. It will require the subordinate modules indicated in the structure chart shown in Figure 4.26.

FIGURE 4.26
Structure chart for RadixSort

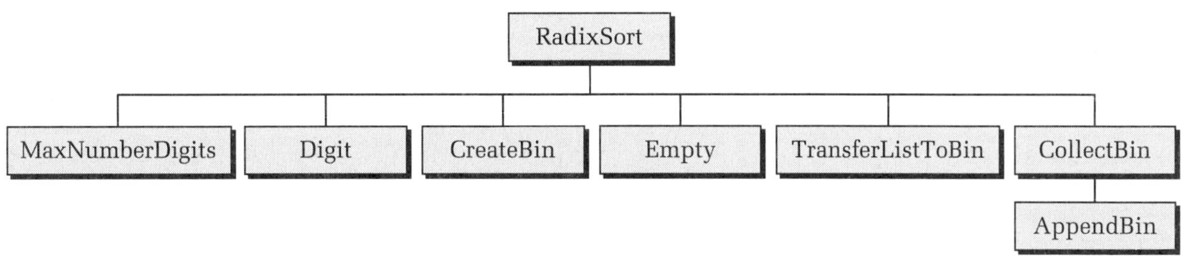

The specifications for each subordinate module are

1. MaxNumberDigits Module
   Data Received: List of integers (assumed to be non-negative)
   Information Returned: The number of digits in the largest integer in list
   Logic: Make one pass through list to determine largest
2. Digit module
   Data Received: Nonnegative integer Number
   K representing a digit position in Number, with
   K = 1 corresponding to ones digit, 2 to tens digit, and so on

Information return: Digit in position K of Number
Logic: Use modular arithmetic functions of Pascal

3. Createbin Module
   Data Received: One list of type Bin in arbitrary state
   Information Returned: Bin intialized to emtpy list
   Logic: Set Head and Tail pointers appropriately
4. TransferListToBin Module
   Data Received: List to sort
   A bin
   Information Returned: First number in list to sort has been removed and appended to bin
   Logic: Only involves pointer exchanges
5. Empty Module
   Data Received: List of type Bin
   Information Returned: **true** if list empty, **false** otherwise
   Logic: Check head and tail pointers
6. CollectBins Module
   Data Received: BinStructure Array
   List to sort (empty when received)
   Information Returned: Sublists in BinStructure have been successively
   appended to sort list
   Logic: Order of appending runs from bin 0 to bin 9
   Repeatedly call on AppendBin
7. AppendBin Module
   Data Received: List to sort
   A bin
   Information Returned: List to sort has bin appended to it
   Logic: See Figure 4.25

These module specifications give rise to the following Pascal procedure for the radix sort algorithm. We present only the top-level sort procedure; the subordinate modules are left for you to implement in the problems. You will also formally analyze the time and space efficiency of this new implementation of radix sort in the problems.

```
TYPE
  BinPointer = ^BinNode;
  BinNode = RECORD
              Data : integer;   { or other appropriate type }
              Link : BinPointer
            END;
  Bin = RECORD
          Head : BinPointer;
          Tail : BinPointer
        END;

PROCEDURE RadixSort (VAR List : Bin);

  {  Given:   List containing entries to sort                  }
  {  Task:    Apply radix sort algorithm to list               }
  {  Return:  List with entries arranged in                    }
  {           ascending order.                                 }

  TYPE BinStructure = ARRAY [0..9] OF Bin; { index subrange must change if  }
                                           { sorting data other than        }
                                           { integers                       }
```

```
VAR
  K, J, NumberOfDigits, WhichBin : integer;
  Bins : BinStructure;

.
.   { Subordinate procedures would appear here }
.
BEGIN
  NumberOfDigits := MaxNumberDigits (List);
  FOR K := 1 TO NumberOfDigits DO
    BEGIN
      FOR J := 0 TO 9 DO
        Create (Bins[J]);
      { Go through the list to sort, continuially removing the first      }
      { number in the list and transferring it to the appropriate bin.    }
      WHILE NOT Empty (List) DO
        BEGIN
          WhichBin := Digit (List.Head^.Data, K); { Which bin to transfer to? }
          TransferListToBin (List, Bins[WhichBin])
        END;
      CollectBins (List, Bins)
    END
END; { of PROCEDURE RadixSort }
```

RUNNING AND DEBUGGING TIPS

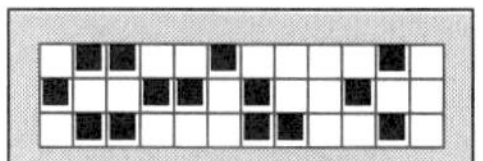

1. You must be very careful when programming with pointers; one misplaced pointer can "lose" an entire data structure. Consequently, modular testing is more important than ever. Test the reliability of each module before releasing it for use in a large program.

2. Be sure that you consider the boundary conditions when developing linked list algorithms. Are you sure that your logic covers the empty list, the first node on the list, the last node on the list? For instance, if your insertion algorithm works for all lists but the empty list, it might as well not work at all since you'll never be able to get any data on the list.

3. Never reference P^ when P is a **NIL** pointer. The following loop control structure

   ```
   WHILE (P <> NIL) AND (P^.Data <> Target) DO
   ```

   is asking for trouble because when P is **NIL**, the reference to P^.Data may cause a run-time error before the loop is exited. The test for (P^.Data <> Target) should be in the loop body and flagged with a Boolean variable.

4. Programming with pointers is programming with logical pictures of linked lists. Draw a picture of what you want to do with a pointer and then write the code to make it happen. When debugging, verify and trace your code by drawing pictures of what it does with your data. For instance, an assignment to a pointer in your code corresponds to aiming an arrow somewhere in your corresponding snapshot of the data structure.

5. An array implementation of linked lists will allow you to insert tracer **writeln**s to see the actual values of pointers. Design your algorithms so that an array implementation can be conveniently plugged in. Then, if you're in deep enough trouble, you can always resort to tracing pointers values via the array implementation.

6. If your Pascal compiler comes with a software debugger, learn how to use it. Most compilers do, and most debuggers will allow you to step through your program one instruction at a time, actually examining the contents of pointer variables that may have gone astray. The hour you spend learning how to use the debugger will be repaid many times over in the time you save debugging this and future programs involving pointers.

■ Summary

Key Terms

circular linked list
cluster
concatenation
data movement
doubly linked circular list
dummy header
dynamic memory management
efficiency ratio
head pointer
heap
linear ordering
link
linked list
linked list implementation of sparse table
linked list implementation of strings
list traversal
multilinked list
node
Pascal pointer variable
pointer
volatile list

Keywords

dispose **new** **NIL**

Key Concepts

- The linked list structure is especially convenient for implementing a variety of higher-level list ADTs in situations where add and delete operations dominate search operations.
- The linked list allows adds and deletes to occur by mere pointer manipulation instead of large-scale data movement. The price paid for this gain is the inefficiency of a sequential search strategy.
- An overview of the advantages and disadvantages of a linked list versus an array implementation of a keyed list is given in the following table.

	Implementation of keyed list using array maintained in physical order so that binary search may be used	**Implementation of keyed list using linked list**
Add	$O(\log_2 n)$ comparisons to find location where addition should occur. $O(n)$ data interchanges to rearrange list.	$O(n)$ comparisons to find location where addition should occur. O(1) pointer interchanges to rearrange list.
Retrieve	$O(\log_2 n)$ comparisons to find data item.	$O(n)$ comparisons to find data item.
Delete	$O(\log_2 n)$ comparisons to find data item to delete. $O(n)$ data interchanges to rearrange list.	$O(n)$ comparisons to find data item to delete. O(1) pointer interchanges to rearrange list.
TraverseInOrder	Immediate if the logical order of the traversal matches the physical order of the list. Otherwise a pointer sort algorithm must be used.	If more than one logical ordering desired, a multilinked list must be used. That is, a series of links for each ordering must be maintained.
Other considerations	Number of items in list must be maintained. Size of list is bounded by physical size of array.	If Pascal pointers are used to implement, size of list is bounded only by available space in heap.

- A linked list can be implemented by an array or by Pascal pointer variables. The following table summarizes the advantages and disadvantages of each implementation strategy.

	Dynamic versus static	Ease of use	Random access file applicability	Debugging	Other languages
Array implementation of linked list	Static. Size of array declared at compile time and limits number of linked list nodes.	Must write your own available space routines.	Easily generalized to random access files.	Values of pointers are merely integers and thus can be easily traced.	Easily adaptable to any languages that have arrays.
Pascal pointer variable implementation	Dynamic. Request memory as needed from Pascal heap.	Pascal's **new** and **dispose** take care of heap management for you.	Pascal's pointer variables exist only in main memory.	Pascal will not let you see, via **write** statements, the values of pointers. You can examine only the contents of what the pointer variables are referencing.	Not available in older languages such as BASIC, FORTRAN, and COBOL.

- Four variations on the basic linked list structure are dummy headers, circular linking, double linking, and multilinking.
- Dummy headers are used to store special information about a list (such as number of nodes) and to simplify the logic of insertion and deletion algorithms.
- Double linking avoids the necessity of having a tag-along pointer to the node prior to the one to be deleted. This is particularly important if we can find a node for deletion by means other than sequential searching of the list.
- Multilinking allows traversal of the list in logical order according to more than one key field.

Programming Problems and Projects

1. Complete the development of a linked list radix sort (see the Focus on Program Design section) in stages.
   a. Write the necessary subordinate modules.
   b. Write a main program so that you can thoroughly test the algorithm.
   c. Design test data that are sure to exercise the various boundary conditions of the subordinate modules.
   d. Do a big-O analysis of the time and space requirements of this version of radix sort. If you also implemented an array version of radix sort in Chapter 1, profile both versions by counting the number of operations that each must perform (see the Focus on Program Design section in Chapter 1). Prepare a written report in which you compare the empirical performance of both versions.

2. Wing-and-a-Prayer Airlines maintains four scheduled flights per day which they identify by the numbers 1, 2, 3, and 4. For each of these flights, they keep an alphabetized list of passengers. The data base for the entire airline could hence be viewed as four linked lists. Write a program that sets up and maintains this data base by handling commands of the following form:

   Command→Add
   Flight number→3
   Passenger name→BROWN

   Command→Delete
   From flight number→1
   Passenger name→JONES

   Command→ List
   Flight number→2
   (List alphabetically all passengers for the specified flight)

   Use an appropriate string storage strategy for the passenger names.

3. In order to take care of their growing business, the Fly-by-Night credit card company would like to update their customer data file. Write a program in a high-level language that sets up a doubly linked list into which a record is
   a. Inserted into the list in the correct place, sorted according to the social security number of the customer.
   b. Updated if the customer record exists.
   c. Deleted if the customer no longer wishes to patronize the company.

   In the preceding data manipulation activities, the list should always remain in order sorted by the social security number.

4. As a struggling professional football team, the Bay Area Brawlers have a highly volatile player roster. Write a program that allows the team to maintain its roster as a linked list in alphabetical order by player last name. Other data items stored for each player are
   - Height
   - Weight
   - Age
   - University affiliation

   As an added option, allow your program to access players in descending order of weight and age.

5. Develop a line-oriented text editor that assigns a number to each line of text and then maintains the lines in a linked list by line number order (similar to the fashion in which BASIC programs are maintained on many systems). Your program should be able to process the following commands:

   I-line number 'text'
   (instruction to insert text at specified line number)
   L-line1-line2
   (instruction to list line1 through line2)
   D-line1-line2
   (Instruction to delete line1 through line2)

If you feel really ambitious, incorporate into your program a string storage strategy which will allow the user to perform editing operations such as inserting and deleting characters within a given line.

6. Write a program that, given a file of text, will add to an index those words in the text that are marked by special delimiting brackets []. The words in the index will be printed after the text itself has been formatted and printed. Words in this index should be listed in alphabetical order with a page number reference for each page of text on which they are delimited by the special brackets. Note that this program would be part of a word processing system an author could use when developing a book with an index of terms.

7. Write a program that allows input of an arbitrary number of polynomials as coefficient and exponent pairs. Store each polynomial as a linked list of coefficient-exponent pairs arranged in descending order by exponent. Note that the coefficient-exponent pairs need not be input in descending order; it is the responsibility of your program to put them in that order. Your program should then be able to evaluate each of the polynomials for an arbitrary argument X and be able to output each of the polynomials in the appropriate descending exponent order. Be sure that your program works for all "unusual" polynomials such as the zero polynomial, polynomials of degree one, and constant polynomials.

8. Implement the registrar's system (see the Focus on Program Design section of Chapter 3) using a multilinked list structure.

9. Develop a sparse table solution for Wing-and-a-Prayer's pilot/flight data base (see Section 2.3) using a multilinked list to implement the sparse table.

10. Redo Problem 3 from Chapter 2, except now use linked lists to implement the string ADT required in that program.

11. Redo Problem 4 from Chapter 2, except now use linked lists to implement the two-dimensional table ADT.

12. Redo Problem 7 from Chapter 2, except now use linked lists to implement the set ADT that you defined for that problem.

13. Redo the Game of Life program that you developed for Problem 8 in Chapter 2, except now use linked lists to implement the two-dimensional table ADT.

14. Use a linked list implementation of a keyed list to compete the partial program presented in the Focus on Program Design in Chapter 2.

15. Redo Problem 5 of Chapter 3, for the registrar of American Basket Weaving University, except now use linked lists to implement the ADTs that you designed for that program.

16. In Example 4.17, we developed main program to maintain a list of strings in alphabetical order. Now extend that main program to a multilinked list structure in which you maintain records in alphabetical order by a string field and in descending order by another integer field. Besides allowing additions and deletions, your program should provide traversals based on the string or integer field.

17. Consider the following problem, often referred to as the Josephus problem. Imagine that N people have decided to commit mass suicide by arranging themselves in a circle and killing the Mth person around the circle, with the size of the circle being reduced by one each time a person is killed. The problem is to find out which person is the last to die, or more generally, to find the order in which the people are executed. For example, if $N = 9$ and $M = 5$, then the people are killed in the order 5, 1, 7, 4, 3, 6, 9, 2, and 8.

    To solve the Josephus problem, write a program that inserts people 1 through N into a list and then appropriately deletes people from the list until only one is left.

18. Computers can store and do arithmetic only with integers of limited size. When integers surpass that limiting value, overflow occurs and the results will either be unreliable or cause your program to die with a run-time error. However, by altering the implementation of an integer, you can develop algorithms to do virtually limitless integer arithmetic. The basis of such an implementation is to store each digit of an integer in a list. That is, represent an integer as a list of digits. Then develop algorithms to do integer arithmetic operations on a digit-by-digit basis, taking carries, borrows, and so forth into account as you do when performing these operations by hand.

    After carefully considering which list implementation best suits the problem, develop procedures to perform extended integer addition, subtraction, multiplication, and division (quotient and remainder). As one test case, add the following integers and print the sum.

    $$\begin{array}{r} 5643127821 \\ +9276577159 \\ \hline \end{array}$$

19. By consulting reference manuals for your version of Pascal and by writing a variety of experimental programs, attempt to discover the details of how your Pascal compiler manages the allocation of memory in the heap. Prepare a written report in which you describe your findings. Be sure to compare the array-based implementation of pointers presented in Section 4.2 of this chapter with the techniques used by your Pascal compiler.

20. Your friend offers the following criticism of linked lists: "The problem with linked lists is that they cannot be used with large data bases stored in files since pointers represent locations in main memory."

    Explain the fallacy in your friend's criticism. Then, in a detailed statement, discuss how linked lists could be implemented for data stored in random access files.

Stacks and Queues

Achilles: What would happen if you took some popping-tonic without having previously pushed yourself into a picture?
Tortoise: I don't precisely know, Achilles, but I would be rather wary of horsing around with these strange pushing and popping liquids.
Douglas Hofstadtler

The other line always moves faster.
Barbara Ettore

In the last chapter we introduced the linked list as a data structure designed to handle conveniently the insertion and deletion of entries in a linearly ordered list. In this chapter we shall study two special types of linearly ordered lists: the stack and the queue. These lists are special because of the restrictions imposed upon the way in which entries may be inserted and removed. Both structures may be implemented by arrays or dynamically allocated linked lists.

The linear order of a stack is often described as *last-in, first-out (LIFO).* Consider, for example, the order in which a smart traveler will pack a suitcase. To minimize shuffling, the last item packed should be the first worn. Another familiar example of such a storage strategy is that of the pop-up mechanism used to store trays for a cafeteria line. The first trays loaded into the mechanism may well have a long wait before they escape to a passing diner.

A list of data items processed via a last-in, first-out scheduling strategy is called a *stack.* As we shall see in this and later chapters, stacks are an extremely useful data structure. They find extensive applications in the processing of subroutine calls, the syntactical checking and translation of programming languages by compilers, and the powerful programming technique of recursion (see Chapter 6).

In contrast to the linear order of a stack, a *queue* is a *first-in, first-out (FIFO)* list. This latter name comes close to completely characterizing the restricted types of adds and deletes that can be performed on a queue. Insertions are limited to one end of the list, whereas deletions may occur only at the other end. The conceptual picture that emerges from the notion of a queue is that of a waiting line; for example, jobs waiting to be serviced by a computer, or cars forming a long line at a busy toll booth.

■ 5.1 The Stack Abstract Data Type and Its Implementation

OBJECTIVES

- to define a stack as an ADT
- to understand conceptually the role played by a stack in processing procedure and function calls
- to be able to implement a stack using a static array
- to be able to implement a stack using a dynamically allocated linked list

The last-in, first-out nature of the stack implies that all additions and deletions occur at one designated end of the stack. That designated end is called the *top,* and the operations of adding to or deleting from the stack are referred to as *pushing* and *popping* respectively. More formally, we define the stack ADT as follows.

Stack. A stack is a restricted list in which entries are added to and removed from one designated end called the top.

The operations to be performed on a stack are specified by the following pre- and postconditions.

Create operation
Preconditions: *S* is an arbitrary stack in an unknown state.
Postconditions: *S* is initialized to the empty stack.

Empty operation
Preconditions: *S* is a previously created stack.
Postconditions: *Empty* returns **true** if *S* is empty, **false** otherwise.

Full operation
Preconditions: *S* is a previously created stack.
Postconditions: *Full* returns **true** if *S* is full, **false** otherwise.

Push operation
Preconditions: *S* is a previously created stack. *Item* is a value to be added to the top of the stack.
Postconditions: *S* is returned with *Item* added to the top of the stack. If *S* is full, it is left unchanged.

Pop operation
Preconditions: *S* is a previously created stack.
Postconditions: *S* has its top value removed. *Item* contains the value that was on the top of the stack *S*. If *S* is empty, contents of *Item* are unreliable and *S* is unchanged.

OnTop operation
Preconditions: *S* is a previously created stack.
Postconditions: *OnTop* returns the value on the top of the stack *S*. Unlike *Pop*, the stack is left unchanged. If the stack *S* is empty, the value returned by *OnTop* is unreliable.

Figure 5.1 depicts the critical push and pop operations for the stack ADT. Conceptually, it is easiest to develop a mental image of the push and pop operations if you picture a stack as a vertical list with the first entry at the bottom and the last at the top. Then, as indicated in Figure 5.1, adding to the stack—that is, pushing—essentially makes this stack become taller, and removing from the stack—that is, popping—results in a shorter stack.

Stacks and Procedure Calls

Before we discuss methods of implementing a stack, we shall give some hint of their importance in the processing of procedure (and function) calls. Of key importance to the processing of procedures in any language is that the return from a procedure must be to the instruction immediately following the call that originally transferred control to the procedure. For example, in the partial coding that follows:

```
PROGRAM Main;
      .
      .
      .
```

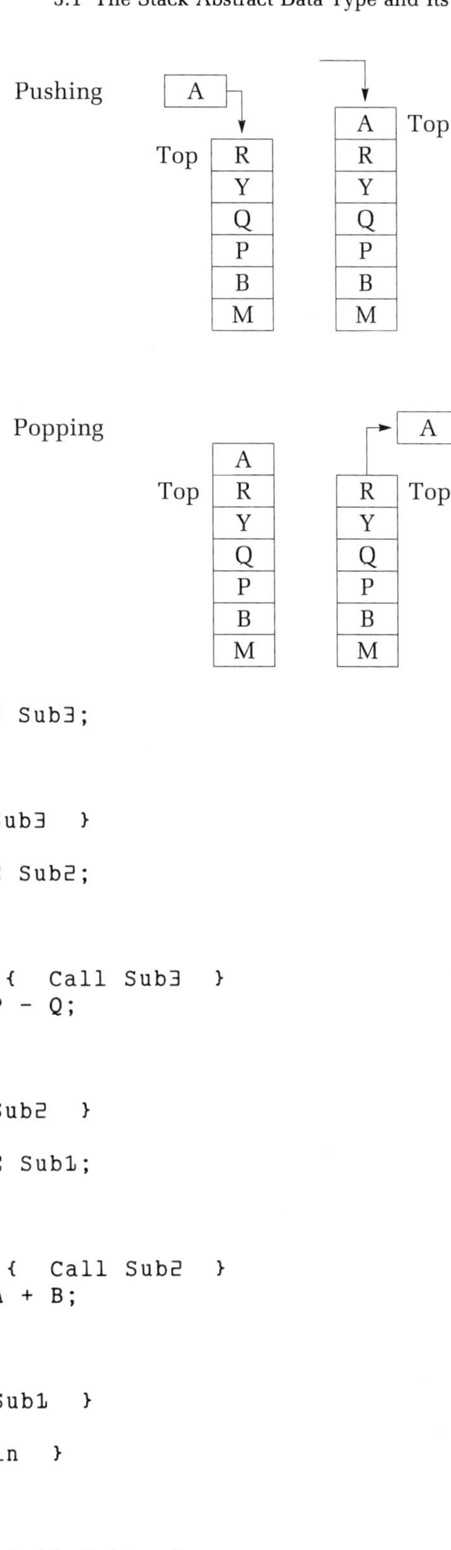

FIGURE 5.1
Pushing onto and popping from the stack

```
   PROCEDURE Sub3;
     .
     .
     .
   END; {  Sub3  }

   PROCEDURE Sub2;
     .
     .
     .
      Sub3; {  Call Sub3  }
      P := P - Q;
     .
     .
     .
   END; {  Sub2  }

   PROCEDURE Sub1;
     .
     .
     .
      Sub2; {  Call Sub2  }
      A := A + B;
     .
     .
     .
   END; {  Sub1  }

BEGIN {  Main  }
  .
  .
  .
   Sub1; {  Call Sub1  }
   writeln(Q);
  .
  .
  .
END. {  Main  }
```

the order of operations would be

1. Leave Main and transfer to Sub1.
2. Leave Sub1 and transfer to Sub2.
3. Leave Sub2 and transfer to Sub3.
4. Return from Sub3 to the instruction P := P − Q in Sub2.
5. Return from Sub2 to the instruction A := A + B in Sub1.
6. Return from Sub1 to the instruction writeln(Q) in Main.
7. End of Main.

Each time a call is made, the machine must remember where to return upon completion of that procedure.

A stack is precisely the structure capable of storing the data necessary to handle calls and returns in this sequence. Hence the preceding partial coding would generate a stack that develops as illustrated in Figure 5.2. (The numbers in the figure correspond to the order of operations just shown.)

FIGURE 5.2
Memory stack generated by previous partial coding

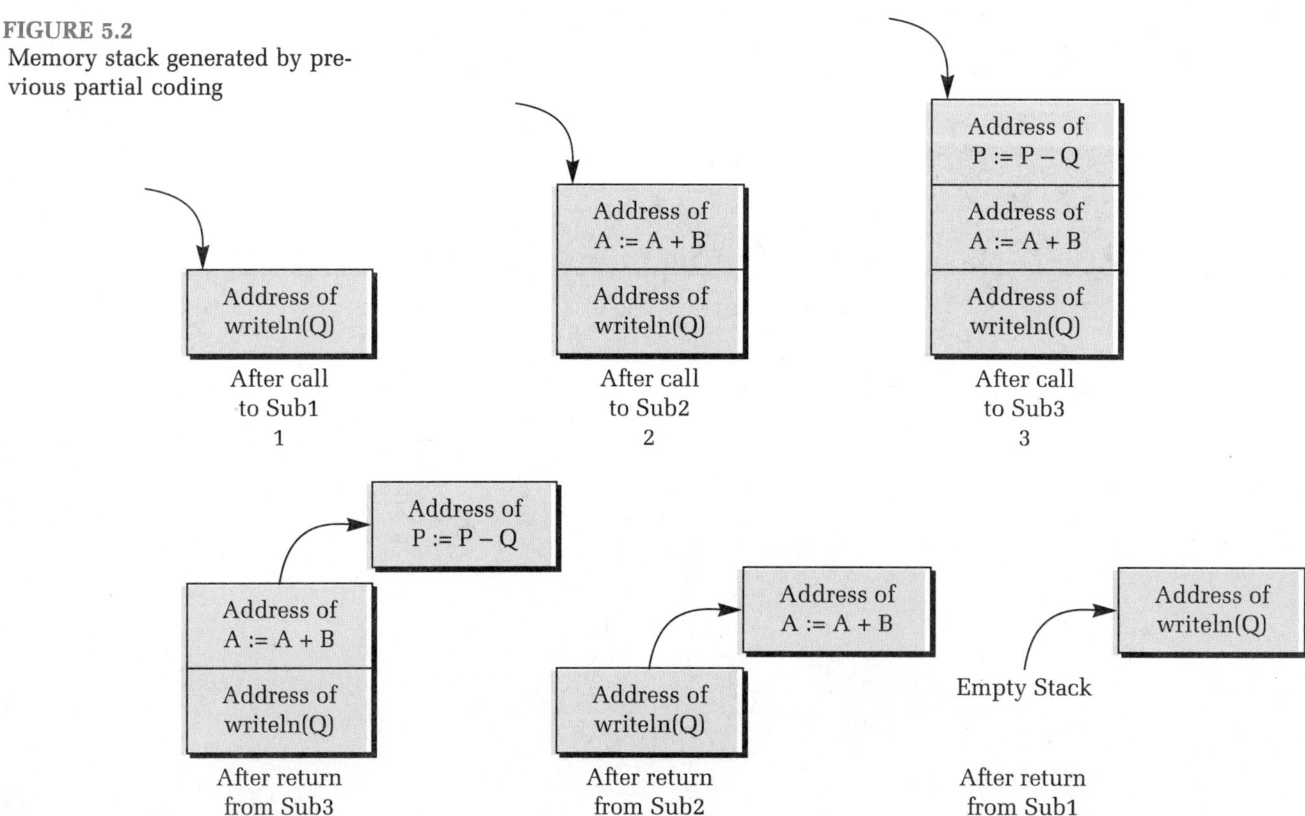

Each time a call to a procedure is made, a return address is pushed on top of the stack. Each time a procedure is completed, the top item on the stack is popped to determine the memory address to which the return operation should be made. The nature of the leave-return sequence for procedures makes it crucial that the first return address accessed be the last one that was remembered by the computer. Because there is only one point, the top, at which data may enter or exit a stack, it is the ideal data structure to be used for this "last-stored, first-recalled" type of operation.

This description of the method by which a compiler actually implements procedure calls is just one illustration of the utility of stacks. In Chapter 6, we'll discuss a different type of procedure usage called recursion, and examine in detail the role of the stack in handling such a recursive call.

Pascal Interface for the Stack Abstract Data Type

The transition from defining a stack as an ADT to implementing this structure in a computer language requires, as usual, an interface to the ADT's operations. A Pascal interface for the stack ADT follows.

```
TYPE
  StackData = {  The type of each data item in the stack  };

PROCEDURE Create (VAR S : Stack);

  {  Given:    An arbitrary stack variable S in unknown state.          }
  {  Task:     Initialize S to the empty stack.                         }
  {  Return:   S initialized to the empty stack.                        }

FUNCTION Empty (S : Stack) : boolean;

  {  Given:    A previously created stack S.                            }
  {  Task:     Check if S is empty.                                     }
  {  Return:   True if S is empty, false otherwise.                     }

FUNCTION Full (S : Stack) : boolean;

  {  Given:    A previously created stack S.                            }
  {  Task:     Check if S is full.                                      }
  {  Return:   True if S is full, false otherwise.                      }

PROCEDURE Push (VAR S : Stack;
                Item : StackData);

  {  Given:    A previously created stack S.  An item to be added to    }
  {            the top of the stack.                                    }
  {  Task:     Add the item to the stack if possible.                   }
  {  Return:   S with Item added to the top of the stack.  If S is      }
  {            full, it is left unchanged.                              }

PROCEDURE Pop (VAR S : Stack;
               VAR Item : StackData);

  {  Given:    A previously created stack S.                            }
  {  Task:     Remove the item from the top of the stack if possible.   }
  {  Return:   S with its top value removed.  Item contains the value   }
  {            that was on the top of the stack S.  If S is empty,      }
  {            contents of Item are unreliable and S is unchanged.      }

FUNCTION OnTop (S : Stack) : StackData;  { Only valid if StackData is   }
                                         { a valid return value for     }
                                         { a function.                  }

  {  Given:    A previously created stack S.                            }
  {  Task:     Determine the value on top of the stack without changing }
  {            the stack.                                               }
  {  Return:   The value on the top of the stack.  Unlike Pop,          }
  {            the stack is left unchanged.  If the stack S is          }
  {            empty, the value returned by OnTop is unreliable.        }
```

We will discuss two implementations of these procedural interfaces in Pascal. The first uses an array and, consequently, limits the size to which a stack may grow. The second employs a linked list with pointer variables, thereby allowing the stack to become as large as the free space in the Pascal heap.

Array Implementation of a Stack

Using an array to implement a stack is relatively straightforward. Because insertions and deletions occur at the same end of a stack, only one pointer will be needed. We call that pointer Top. In Figure 5.3, we trace it through the procedure example from Figure 5.2.

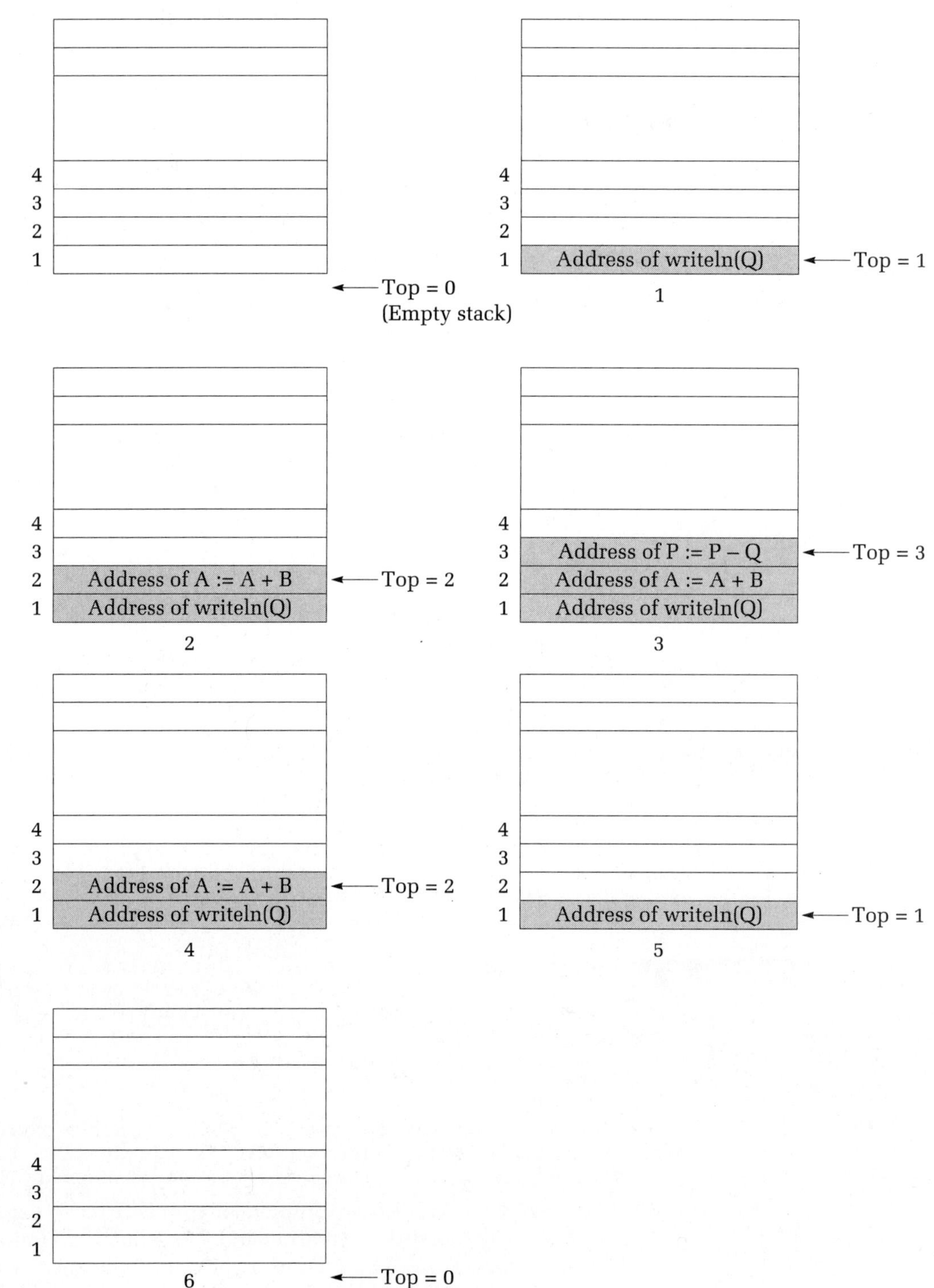

FIGURE 5.3
Array implementation of stack from Figure 5.2

As in Figure 5.2, the numbers below each array correspond to the operations performed in our previous sequence of procedure calls and returns. The empty stack is signaled by the condition Top = 0. If we think of Top as pointing to the last entry pushed, then the two instructions

```
Top := Top + 1;
S[Top] := Item;
```

will push the contents of Item onto the stack. Popping an entry from the stack into Item requires

```
Item := S[Top];
Top := Top - 1;
```

Complete procedures for the Push and Pop operations follow in Example 5.1. These procedures use a record to encapsulate the top pointer and data array into one unified Stack type. These procedures also assume the existence of Empty and Full functions to test for these special boundary conditions. You will be asked to write these functions in the Exercises at the end of this section.

EXAMPLE 5.1

Implement the Push and Pop operations for an array implementation of a stack.

```
CONST
  StackSize = { Maximum number of elements allowed in stack at any time };

TYPE
  StackData = { The type of each data item in the stack };
  Stack = RECORD
            List : ARRAY [1..StackSize] OF StackData;
            Top : integer
          END;

PROCEDURE Push (VAR S : Stack;
                Item : StackData);

  {  Given:   A previously created stack S.  An item to be added to     }
  {           the top of the stack.                                     }
  {  Task:    Add the item to the stack if possible.                    }
  {  Return:  S with Item added to the top of the stack.  If S is       }
  {           full, it is left unchanged.                               }

  BEGIN
    IF NOT Full (S) THEN
      BEGIN
        S.Top := S.Top + 1;
        S.List[S.Top] := Item
      END
  END;  { of PROCEDURE Push }
```

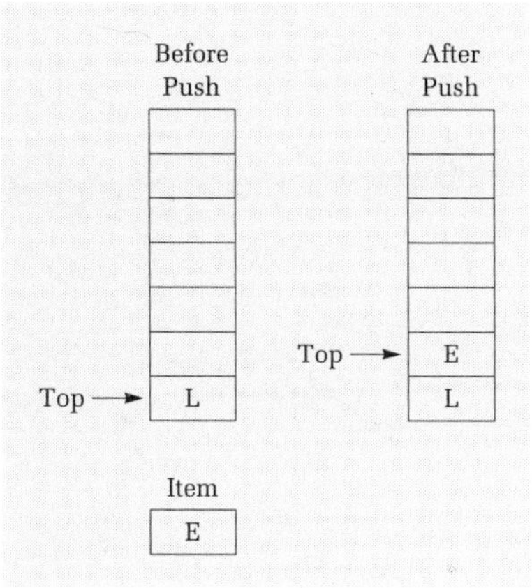

```
PROCEDURE Pop (VAR S : Stack;
               VAR Item : StackData);

  {  Given:    A previously created stack S.                          }
  {  Task:     Remove the item from the top of the stack if possible. }
  {  Return:   S with its top value removed.  Item contains the value }
  {            that was on the top of the stack S.  If S is empty,    }
  {            contents of Item are unreliable and S is unchanged.    }

  BEGIN
    IF NOT Empty (S) THEN
      BEGIN
        Item := S.List[S.Top];
        S.Top := S.Top - 1
      END
  END;  { of PROCEDURE Pop }
```

Linked List Implementation of a Stack

When we choose a linked list implementation of a stack, we are paying the price of a relatively small amount of memory space needed to maintain linking pointers for the dynamic allocation of stack space. Assuming that we do not use a dummy header for the linked list, a stack with the three integer entries 18, 40, and 31 would appear as follows:

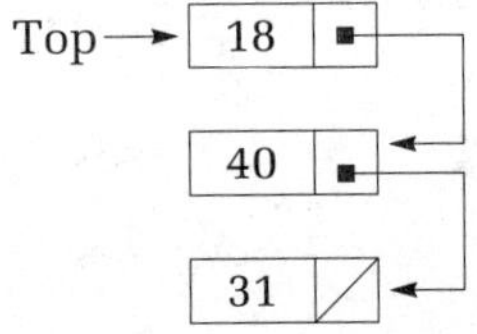

The Top pointer must be initialized to **NIL,** and, thereafter, the condition

```
Top = NIL
```

could be used to test for an empty stack. A full stack occurs only when Pascal's **new** procedure reports that there is no available space—a condition that standard Pascal does not allow you to check.

Full procedures to push and pop the stack now become nothing more than insertions to and deletions from the beginning of a linked list. As such, they are special cases of the procedures already developed in Chapter 4. You will write them as exercises at the end of this section.

EXAMPLE 5.2

To illustrate the use of stack operations in a program, let's consider a program that will check an arithmetic expression to make sure that parentheses are correctly matched (nested). Our program considers

(3 + 4 * (5 **MOD** 3))

to make sure that each left parenthesis is paired with a following right parenthesis in the expression.

A first-level pseudocode for this problem is

1. **WHILE NOT eoln DO**
   1.1 Read a character
   1.2 **IF** it is a "(" **THEN**
   Push it onto the stack
   1.3 **IF** it is a ")" **THEN**
   Check for empty stack before popping previous "("
2. Check for empty stack

The growing and shrinking of the stack is illustrated in Figure 5.4.

FIGURE 5.4
Using a stack to check for balanced parentheses

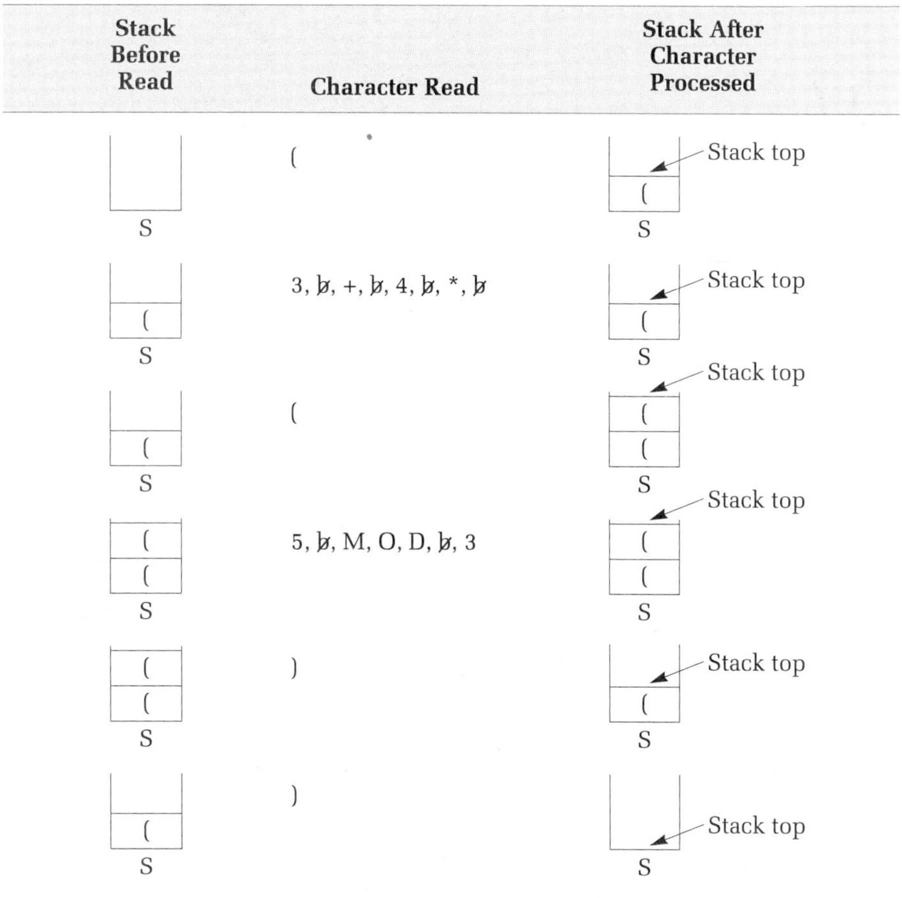

Stack Before Read	Character Read	Stack After Character Processed
S: (empty)	(	S: (← Stack top
S: (	3, b̸, +, b̸, 4, b̸, *, b̸	S: (← Stack top
S: (	(	S: (, (← Stack top
S: (, (	5, b̸, M, O, D, b̸, 3	S: (, (← Stack top
S: (, (	)	S: (← Stack top
S: (	)	S: (empty) ← Stack top

*b̸ represents a blank space

Assuming the existence of procedures and functions for the basic stack operations, the main body of a program that examines an expression for correct use of parenthesis is

```
BEGIN  {  Main program  }
  Create (S);
  WHILE not eoln DO
    BEGIN
      read (Symbol);
      IF Symbol = '(' THEN
        Push (S, Symbol)
      ELSE IF Symbol = ')' THEN
        IF Empty (S) THEN
          writeln ('The parentheses are not correct.')
        ELSE
          Pop (S, Symbol)
    END; {  of WHILE  }

  {  Now check for empty stack  }
  IF NOT Empty (S) THEN
    writeln ('The parentheses are not correct.'
END.  {  of main program  }
```

This program will print an error message for an invalid expression and nothing for a valid expression. Several modifications of this short program are available and are suggested in the Exercises at the end of this section.

■ ■

Exercises 5.1

1. Draw a picture of the stack of integers S after each one of the following operations is performed:

```
Create (S);
Pus (S, 4);
Push (S, 10);
Push (S, 12);
Pop (S, Item);
Push (S, 3*Item);
Item := OnTop (S);
Push (S, 3*Item);
```

2. The OnTop operation described in the definition of the stack as an abstract data type is actually unnecessary since it can be defined in terms of other stack operations. Provide such a definition of the OnTop operation.

3. Write procedures to implement each of the following operations for an array implementation of a stack. Be consistent with the operations already implemented in Example 5.1.

   a. Create(S)
   b. Full(S)
   c. Empty(S)
   d. OnTop(S)

4. Write procedures to implement each of the following stack operations for a linked list implementation of a stack.

   a. Create(S)
   b. Full(S)
   c. Empty(S)
   d. Push(S, Item)
   e. Pop(S, Item)
   f. OnTop(S)

5. Using the program for checking parentheses (Example 5.2), illustrate how the stack grows and shrinks when the following expression is examined.

```
(5/(3 - 2 * (4 + 3) - (8 DIV 2)))
```

6. Modify the program in Example 5.2 so that several expressions may be examined. Also provide more descriptive error messages.

7. Write a program that utilizes a stack to print a line of text in reverse order.
8. Consider an additional stack operation called Destroy. Destroy is the opposite of Create. That is, it disposes of a stack and recovers whatever memory space can be recovered.
   a. Write a formal Pascal interface for the Destroy operation. Be sure the interface is completely documented.
   b. For which of the stack implementations discussed in Section 5.1 would this operation have no real effect? Explain why.
   c. Develop a complete version of the Destroy operation for the stack implementation that you did not identify as your answer to (b).

■ ■ ■ ■

5.2 An Application of Stacks: Parsing and Evaluating Arithmetic Expressions

OBJECTIVES

- to understand the differences between infix, postfix, and prefix forms of algebraic expressions
- to see why the postfix and prefix forms of expressions never need parentheses to override operator hierarchy
- to be able to convert infix expressions to their postfix and prefix equivalents using manual methods
- to understand the computer algorithm that relies on a stack to convert infix expressions to their postfix equivalents
- to be aware of the role of infix and in-stack priority functions in driving the algorithm to convert infix expressions to postfix
- to understand the algorithm that uses a stack to evaluate a postfix expression

Often the logic of problems for which stacks are a suitable data structure involves the necessity to backtrack, to return to a previous state. For instance, consider the problem of finding your way out of a maze. One approach to take would be to probe a given path in the maze as deeply as possible. Upon finding a dead end, you would need to backtrack to previously visited maze locations in order to try other paths. Such backtracking would require recalling these previous locations in the reverse order from which you visited them.

Not many of us need to find our way out of a maze. However, the designers of compilers are faced with an analogous backtracking situation in the evaluation of arithmetic expressions. As you scan the expression

A + B/C + D

in left-to-right order, it is impossible to tell upon initially encountering the plus sign whether or not you should apply the indicated addition operation to A and the immediately following operand. Instead, you must probe further into the expression to determine whether an operation with a higher priority occurs. While you undertake this probing of the expression, you must stack previously encountered operation symbols until you are certain of the operands to which they can be applied.

Compounding the backtracking problem just described, there are often many different ways of representing the same algebraic expression. For example, the assignment statements

```
Z := A * B/C + D;
Z := (A * B)/C + D;
Z := ((A * B)/C) + D;
```

should all result in the same order of arithmetic operations even though the expressions involved are written in distinctly different form. The process of checking the syntax of such an expression and representing it in one unique form is called *parsing* the expression. One frequently used method of parsing relies heavily upon stacks.

Infix, Postfix, and Prefix Notation

Usual algebraic notation is often termed *infix* notation; the arithmetic operator appears between the two operands to which it is being applied. Infix notation may require parentheses to specify a desired order of operations.

For example, in the expression A/B + C, the division will occur first. If we want the addition to occur first, the expression must be parenthesized as A/(B + C).

Using *postfix* notation (also called reverse Polish notation after the nationality of its originator, the Polish logician Jan Lukasiewicz), the need for parentheses is eliminated because the operator is placed directly after the two operands to which it applies. Hence, A/B + C would be written as AB/C+ in postfix form. This says:

1. Apply the division operator to A and B.
2. To that result, add C.

The infix expression A/(B + C) would be written as ABC+/ in postfix notation. Reading this postfix expression from left to right, we are told to

1. Apply the addition operator to B and C.
2. Then divide that result into A.

Although relatively short expressions such as the preceding ones can be converted from infix to postfix via an intuitive process, a more systematic method is required for complicated expressions. We propose the following algorithm for humans (and will soon consider a different one for computers):

1. Completely parenthesize the infix expression to specify the order of all operations.
2. Move each operator to the space held by its corresponding right parenthesis.
3. Remove all parentheses.

Consider this three-step method as it applies to the following expression in which ^ is used to indicate exponentiation:

A/B^C + D*E − A*C

Completely parenthesizing this expression yields

(((A/(B^C)) + (D*E)) − (A*C))

Moving each operator to its corresponding right parenthesis, we obtain

(((A/(B^C)) + (D*E)) − (A*C))

Removing all parentheses, we are left with

ABC^/DE*+AC*−

Had we started out with

A/B^C − (D*E − A*C)

our three-step procedure would have resulted in

((A/(B^C)) − ((D*E) − (A*C)))

Removing the parentheses would then yield

ABC^/DE*AC*− −

In a similar way, an expression can be converted into *prefix* form, in which an operator immediately precedes its two operands. The conversion algorithm for infix to prefix specifies that, after completely parenthesizing the infix expression according to order of priority, we move each operator to its corresponding left parenthesis. Applying the method to

A/B^C + D*E − A*C

gives us

((A/(B^C)) + ((D*E) − (A*C)))

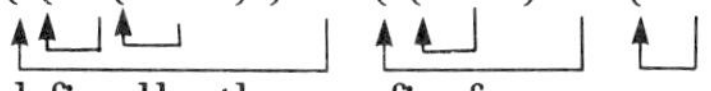

and finally the prefix form

+/A^BC−*DE*AC

The importance of postfix and prefix notation in parsing arithmetic expressions is that these notations are completely free of parentheses. Consequently, an expression in postfix (or prefix) form is in unique form. In the design of compilers, this parsing of an expression into postfix form is crucial because having a unique form for an expression greatly simplifies its eventual evaluation. Thus, in handling an expression, a compiler must

1. Parse into postfix form.
2. Apply an evaluation algorithm to the postfix form.

We limit our discussion here to postfix notation. The techniques we cover are easily adaptable to the functionally equivalent prefix form.

Converting Infix Expressions to Postfix

First consider the problem of parsing an expression from infix to postfix form. Our three-step procedure is not easily adaptable to machine coding. Instead, we will use an algorithm that has as its essential data structures:

1. A stream of characters containing the infix expression and terminated by the special delimiter '#'.
2. A stack OpStack which may contain
   a. Arithmetic operators: '+', '−', '*', and '/'
   b. The left parenthesis '('. The right parenthesis ')' is processed by the algorithm but never stored in the stack.
   c. The special delimiter: '#'
3. A string Postfix containing the final postfix expression.

To eliminate details that would only clutter the main logic of the algorithm, we will assume that the string representing the infix expression contains *tokens* (that is, incoming symbols) consisting only of the arithmetic operators '+', '−', '*', and '/'; parentheses; the delimiting character '#'; and operands that each consist of a single uppercase alphabetic character. We will also assume that these tokens may be read from a line without any intervening spaces. Later, we will consider some of the complications introduced by tokens of varying size and type and by the exponentiation operator '^'. Thus, for the present, the algorithm we discuss will convert infix expressions of the form

A*B+(C−D/E)

into their corresponding postfix notation.

The description of the algorithm is as follows:

1. Define a function InfixPriority, which takes an operator, parenthesis, or # as its argument and returns an integer as

Character	*	/	+	−	(	)	#
Returned Value	2	2	1	1	3	0	0

This function reflects the relative position of an operator in the arithmetic hierarchy and is used with the function StackPriority (defined in step 2) to determine how long an operator waits in the stack before being appended to the postfix string.

2. Define another function StackPriority, which takes the same possibilities for an argument and returns an integer as

Character	*	/	+	−	(	)	#
Returned Value	2	2	1	1	0	undefined	0

This function applies to operators in the operator stack as their priority in the arithmetic hierarchy is compared to that of incoming operators from the infix string. The result of this comparison determines whether or not an operator waits in the stack or is appended to the postfix string.

3. Initialize OpStack by pushing #.
4. Read the next character Ch from the infix expression.
5. Test Ch and
   - **5.1** If Ch is an operand, append it to the Postfix string.
   - **5.2** If Ch is a right parenthesis, then pop entries from stack and append them to Postfix until a left parenthesis is popped. Doing this insures that operators within a parenthesized portion of an infix expression will be applied first, regardless of their priority in the usual arithmetic hierarchy. Discard both left and right parentheses.
   - **5.3** If Ch is a #, pop all entries that remain on the stack and append them to Postfix string.
   - **5.4** Otherwise, pop from the stack and append to the Postfix string operators whose StackPriority is greater than or equal to the InfixPriority of Ch. Stop this series of popping operations when you reach a stack element whose StackPriority is less than the InfixPriority of Ch. This comparison, keying on the priority of Ch from the infix string and operators that have previously been pushed onto the operator stack, insures that operators are applied in the right order in the resulting postfix string. After popping these operators, push Ch.
6. Repeat steps 4 and 5 until Ch is the delimiter #.

The key to the algorithm is the use of the stack to hold operators from the infix expression that appear to the left of another given operator even though that latter operator must be applied first. The defined functions InfixPriority and StackPriority are used to specify this priority of operators and the asso-

A NOTE OF INTEREST

Hypertext

The recent introduction of HyperCard software by Apple Computer Company has enabled thousands of microcomputer users to have at their fingertips a medium known as hypertext. Apple's description of the HyperCard software revolves around the notion of a stack of computerized cards on which almost any type of information may be stored in a very free format. However, this stack of hypertext cards differs somewhat from the formal stack data structure that we are studying in this chapter.

A stack of hypertext cards may be viewed as a collection of data nodes through which one may browse, normally in sequence from top card to bottom card. One difference between hypertext nodes and conventional documents is that, in addition to text and computer graphics, hypertext nodes may consist of sound, video sequences, and animation. Moreover, hypertext stacks are associative. That is, at any card in the stack, the user is allowed to follow a variety of links which may lead to other stacks. For instance, a card that was playing a Beethoven symphony could allow us to follow a link to a musical history stack where the importance of that symphony from a historical perspective could be explored.

According to John B. Smith and Stephen F. Weiss (in "Hypertext," *Communications of the ACM* 31, No. 7 (July 1988)), this unrestricted associativity between hypertext stacks parallels the flexibility of human memory. Smith and Weiss cite the following quotation from Vannevar Bush, a well-known electrical engineer who speculated as early as the 1940s about the way in which humans think:

> *The human mind . . . operates by association. With one item in its grasp, it snaps instantly to the next that is suggested by the association of thoughts, in accordance with some intricate web of trails carried by the cells of the brain.*
>
> *Selection by association, rather than indexing may yet be mechanized. One cannot hope . . . to equal the speed and flexibility with which the mind follows an associative trail, but it should be possible to beat the mind decisively in regard to the permanence and clarity of the items resurrected from storage.*

If the notion of electronic hypertext intrigues you, consult the *Communications of the ACM* issue cited here and *Communications of the ACM* 33, No. 3 (March 1990). Both of these issues are dedicated to this revolutionary and rapidly growing field.

ciated pushing and popping operations. This entire process is best understood by carefully tracing through an example.

EXAMPLE 5.3

Parse the infix expression

```
A*B+(C-D/E)#
```

into its equivalent postfix form. Trace the contents of the operator stack and the postfix string as each character is read.

The solution to this problem is presented in Table 5.1. In this table, the parenthesized numbers in the "Commentary" column refer to subcases of step 5 in the preceding algorithm.

The following Pascal procedure implements our algorithm for converting infix expressions of the form we have specified. You should study and thoroughly understand this algorithm before moving on to this chapter's Focus on Program Design section. There, the infix-to-postfix algorithm will be the focal point for an entire program that works with expressions of a slightly more complicated form.

TABLE 5.1
Parsing of infix expression
A*B+(C−D/E)#

Ch	OpStack	Postfix	Commentary
	#		Push #
A			Read Ch
		A	Append Ch to Postfix (5.1)
*			Read Ch
	* #		Push Ch (5.4)
B			Read Ch
		AB	Append Ch to Postfix (5.1)
+			Read Ch
	+ #	AB*	Pop *, append * to Postfix, push Ch (5.4)
(			Read Ch
	(+ #		Push Ch (5.4)
C			Read Ch
		AB*C	Append Ch to Postfix (5.1)
−			Read Ch
	− (+ #		Push Ch (5.4)
D			Read Ch
		AB*CD	Append Ch to Postfix (5.1)
/			Read Ch
	/ − (+ #		Push Ch (5.4)
E			Read Ch
		AB*CDE	Append Ch to Postfix (5.1)
)			Read Ch
	+ #	AB*CDE/−	Pop and append to Postfix until (reached (5.2)
#			Read Ch
		AB*CDE/− +#	Pop and append rest of stack to Postfix (5.3)

```
TYPE
  PostfixString = { Assume a suitable implementation of the string ADT, }
                  { augmented by an Append operation.  Append (S, C) is }
                  { invoked to append a character C to the end of a     }
                  { string S.                                           }
  StackData = char;
  Stack = { Assume a suitable ADT implementation }

PROCEDURE Convert (VAR Postfix : PostFixString);

  {  Given:   Infix expression being read from standard input.          }
  {           The expression consists of single-letter variable         }
  {           names; operators +, *, -, /; parentheses; and the         }
  {           special end token #.  Assume that no spaces are           }
  {           embedded in expression.                                   }
  {  Task:    Convert this input into postfix expression.               }
  {  Return:  The postfix expression in Postfix.                        }

  VAR
    Item, Ch : char;
    OpStack : Stack;

  BEGIN {  Convert  }
    CreateString (Postfix);  { CreateString avoids name clash with      }
                             { Create operation for stack               }
    Create (OpStack);
    Push (OpStack,'#');
    { Read character tokens until eoln encountered                      }
    REPEAT
      read (Ch);
      IF ('A' <= Ch) AND (Ch <= 'Z') THEN
        {  Single character operand  }
        Append (Postfix, Ch)
      ELSE IF Ch = ')' THEN
        BEGIN
          Pop (OpStack, Item);
          WHILE Item <> '(' DO
            BEGIN
              Append (Postfix, Item);
              Pop (Opstack, Item)
            END
        END
      ELSE IF Ch = '#'
        BEGIN
          WHILE NOT Empty (OpStack) DO
            BEGIN
              Pop(Opstack, Item);
              Append (Postfix, Item)
            END
        END
```

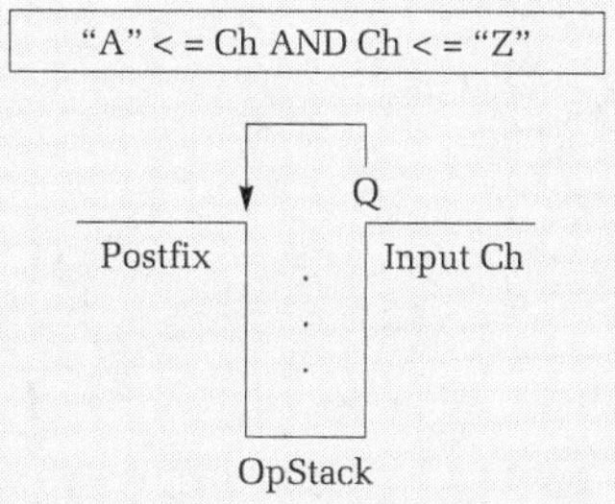

In this case, transfer Ch to Postfix.

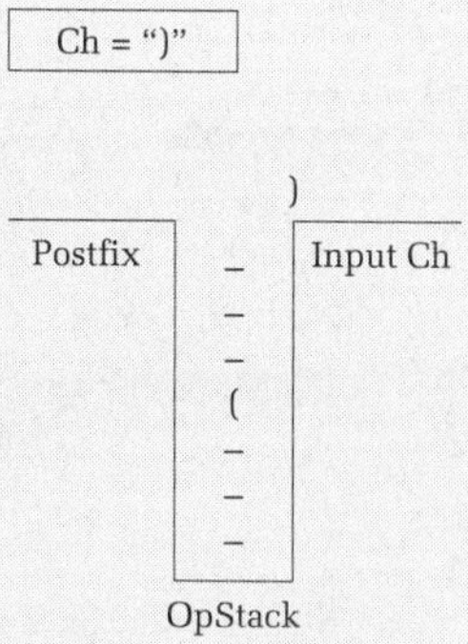

In this case, pop stack until encounter matching left parenthesis.

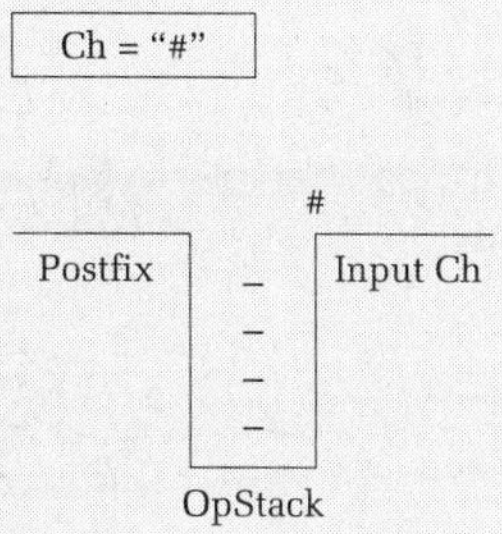

In this case, pop rest of stack to Postfix.

```
    ELSE { Operator +, -, *, / or left parenthesis }
      BEGIN
        Pop (OpStack, Item);
        WHILE StackPriority (Item) >= InfixPriority (Ch) DO
          BEGIN
            Append (Postfix, Item);
            Pop (OpStack, Item)
          END;
        Push (Opstack, Item);
        Push (Opstack, Ch)
      END
  UNTIL Ch = '#';
  readln    { So standard input is ready for next call to Convert }
END; {  of PROCEDURE Convert  }
```

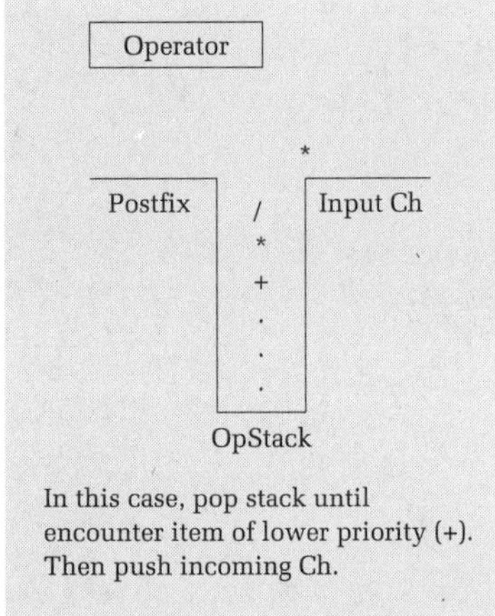

In this case, pop stack until encounter item of lower priority (+). Then push incoming Ch.

Evaluating Postfix Expressions

Once an expression has been parsed and represented in postfix form, another stack plays an essential role in its final evaluation. To evaluate a postfix expression, we repeatedly read characters from the postfix expression. If the character read is an operand, push the value associated with it onto the stack. If it is an operator, pop two values from the stack, apply the operator to them, and push the result back onto the stack. After the last operand in the postfix expression has been processed, the value of the expression is the one entry on the stack. The technique is illustrated in the following example.

EXAMPLE 5.4

Consider the postfix expression from Example 5.3.

AB*CDE/− +#

Let us suppose that the symbols A, B, C, D, and E had associated with them the following values:

Symbol	Value
A	5
B	3
C	6
D	8
E	2

The evaluation of the expression under this assignment of values proceeds as indicated in Figure 5.5.

■ ■

FIGURE 5.5
Evaluation of AB*CDE/−+#

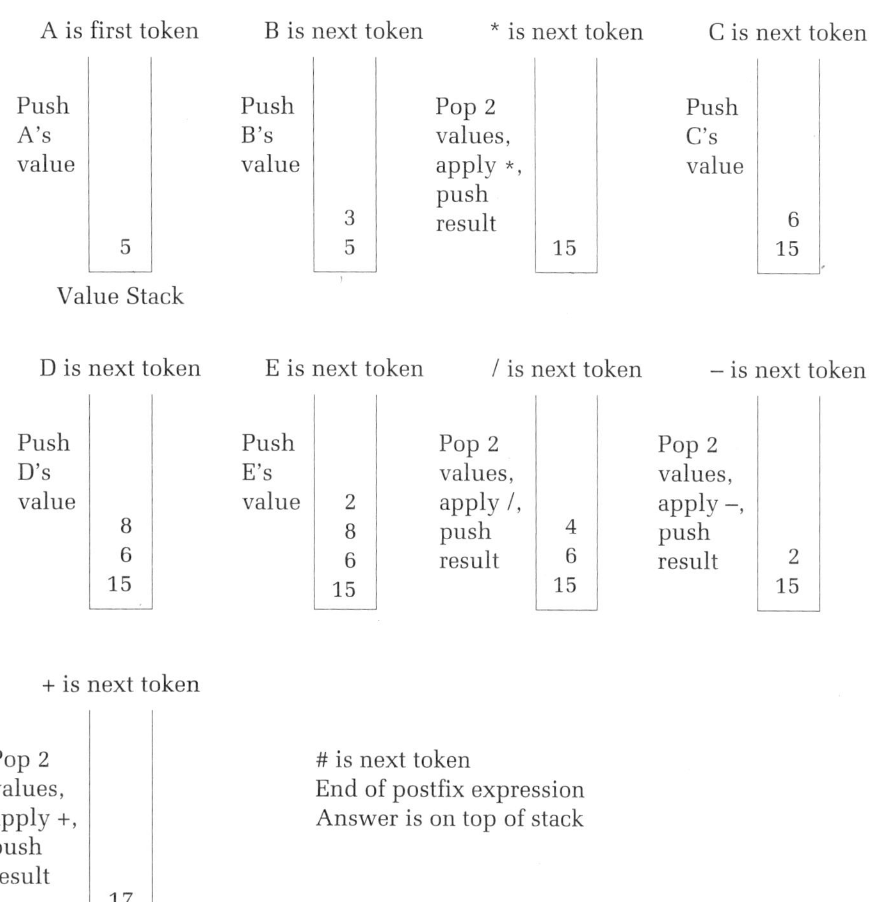

Assuming functions ValueOf, which will return the value associated with a particular symbol; Eval, which will return the result of applying an operator to two values; and NextToken, which will return the next token to be read from the postfix expression, the Pascal function to evaluate a postfix expression is given by

```
TYPE
  PostfixString = { Assume a suitable implementation of the string ADT, }
                  { augmented by a NextToken operation.  NextToken (S)  }
                  { is a function which returns successive characters   }
                  { from a string S.  That is, the first time it is     }
                  { called it returns the first character in S, then    }
                  { the second character in S, and so forth.            }
  StackData = real;
  Stack = { Assume a suitable ADT implementation }

  { Also we assume the existence of a function ValueOf which associates }
  { a character with its real value--similar to the fashion in which    }
  { each variable in a program is associated with a value.  Since our   }
```

```
  { tokens are only single characters, an easy way of implementing       }
  { ValueOf would be to use an array of reals indexed by the subrange    }
  { 'A' .. 'Z'.  In effect, this would create a mini, 26-location        }
  { "memory."  Finally, we assume the existence of an Eval function      }
  { which receives two real operands and the operator to apply to them.  }
  { Eval returns the result of applying that operator to the operands.   }

FUNCTION Evaluate (Postfix : PostfixString) : real;

  {  Given:   Postfix representation of algebraic expression             }
  {           in Postfix.                                                }
  {  Task:    Evaluate the expression, using the value of each           }
  {           token.                                                     }
  {  Return:  The real result of that evaluation.                        }

  VAR
    Ch : char;
    V, V1, V2 : real;
    ValueStack : Stack;

  BEGIN
    Create (ValueStack);
    Ch := NextToken (Postfix);
    { Read character tokens from Postfix string until                    }
    { delimiter is encountered.                                          }
    WHILE Ch <> '#' {  the ending delimiter  } DO
      BEGIN
        IF ('A' <= Ch) AND (Ch <= 'Z') THEN {Operand}
          Push (ValueStack, ValueOf (Ch))
        ELSE
          BEGIN
            Pop (ValueStack, V2);
            Pop (ValueStack, V1);
            V := Eval(V1, V2, Ch);
            Push (ValueStack, V)
          END;
        Ch := NextToken (Postfix)
      END;
      {  What's left on stack is the answer we want  }
      Evaluate := OnTop (ValueStack)
  END; {  of FUNCTION Evaluate  }
```

Exercises 5.2

1. What are the infix, postfix, and prefix forms of the expression

   A + B * (C − D)/(P − R)?

2. Trace the contents of the stack as the postfix form of the expression in Exercise 1 is evaluated. Assume the following assignment of values: A = 6, B = 4, C = 3, D = 1, P = 12, and R = 11.

3. Consider the expression with the infix notation

   P+(Q−F)/Y

   Using the algorithm discussed in this section to transform this into a postfix expression, trace the state of both the operator stack and postfix string as each character of the infix expression is processed. Conduct your trace following the style of Table 5.1.

4. Using the postfix expression you have obtained in Exercise 3, trace the stack of real values that would develop as the postfix expression is evaluated. You should indicate the numeric values on the stack as each character in the postfix expression is processed. Assume the values F = 4, P = 10, Q = 18, and Y = 2.

5. Parse the infix expression

   P * (Q/Y) + A − B + D * Y#

   using the following definitions of InfixPriority and StackPriority:

Priority	*	/	+	−	(	)	#
Infix	2	2	4	4	5	0	0
Stack	1	1	3	3	0	undefined	0

   Trace this parsing operation following the style of Table 5.1.

6. Using the postfix string you have obtained in Exercise 5, trace the stack of real numeric values that would develop as the postfix expression is evaluated. You should indicate the values on the stack as each character in the postfix expression is processed. Assume the values A = 4, B = 3, D = 2, P = 1, Q = 4, and Y = 2.

7. Write an implementation of the Append operation suitable for use with postfix strings in this section's Convert procedure.

8. Write implementations of the NextToken, Value, and Eval operations suitable for this section's Evaluate function.

9. Explain how the relationship between the stack priorities and infix priorities of (,), *, /, +, −, and # controls the parsing of the infix expression. Then explain how you would extend the definition of the stack and infix priority functions of this section to include an exponentiation operator ^. The exponentiation operator should be right associative; that is, in an expression such as A^B^C, the exponentiations should occur in right-to-left order.

10. How would the functions InfixPriority and StackPriority be extended to include the Boolean operators <, >, <=, >=, =, < >, **AND**, **OR**, and **NOT**? Justify your choices of priority values for these Boolean operators.

■ ■ ■ ■

■ 5.3 The Queue Abstract Data Type: Its Use and Implementations

OBJECTIVES

- to understand the definition of the queue ADT
- to understand what is meant by a computer simulation
- to be able to use the queue ADT in a simulation program
- to examine three implementations of the queue ADT: array, circular array, and linked list

The stack ADT that we have studied in the first two sections of this chapter is a last-in, first-out list. The next type of restricted list that we will examine, the queue, is a first-in, first-out list. All additions to a queue occur at one end, which we will designate as the rear of the queue. Items that enter the queue at the rear must move up to the front of the queue before they can be removed.

The operations on a queue thus parallel the dynamics of a waiting line. The linear order underlying a queue is determined by the length of time an item has been in the queue. This concept is depicted in Figure 5.6. The analogy of a waiting line makes a queue the obvious ADT to use in many applications concerned with scheduling. Before we explore such applications, however, we must formally define a queue as an ADT.

> **Queue.** A queue is merely a restricted form of a list. In particular, the restrictions upon a queue are that all additions to the queue occur at one end, the rear, and all removals from the queue occur at the other end, the front. The effect of these restrictions is to insure that the earlier an item enters a queue, the earlier it will leave the queue. That is, items are processed on a first-in, first-out basis.

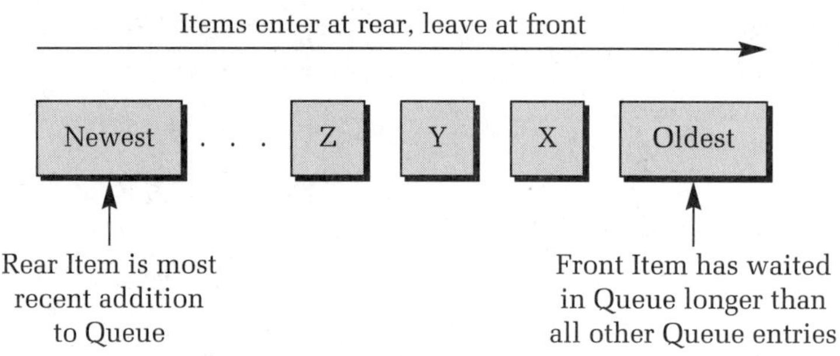

FIGURE 5.6
Abstract data type queue as computer embodiment of waiting line

The five basic operations on a queue are specified by the following pre- and postconditions.

Create operation	
Preconditions:	*Q* is an arbitrary queue in unknown state.
Postconditions:	*Q* is initialized to the empty queue.
Empty operation	
Preconditions:	*Q* is a previously created queue.
Postconditions:	*Empty* returns **true** if *Q* is empty, **false** otherwise.
Full operation	
Preconditions:	*Q* is a previously created queue.
Postconditions:	*Full* returns **true** if *Q* is full, **false** otherwise.
Enqueue operation	
Preconditions:	*Q* is a previously created queue. *Item* is a value to be added to the rear of the queue.
Postconditions:	*Q* is returned with *Item* added to the rear of the queue. If *Q* is full, it is left unchanged.
Dequeue operation	
Preconditions:	*Q* is a previously created queue.
Postconditions:	*Q* has its front value removed. *Item* contains the value that was at the front of *Q*. If *Q* is empty, contents of *Item* are unreliable.

EXAMPLE 5.5

To help conceptualize queue operations, consider the following sequence of actions on a queue of integers.

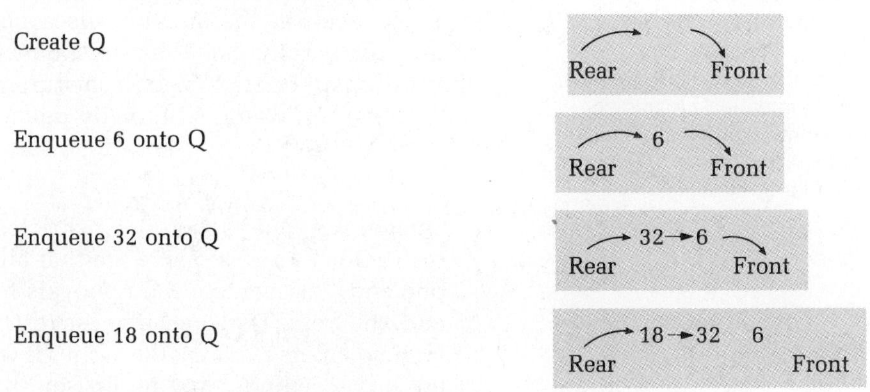

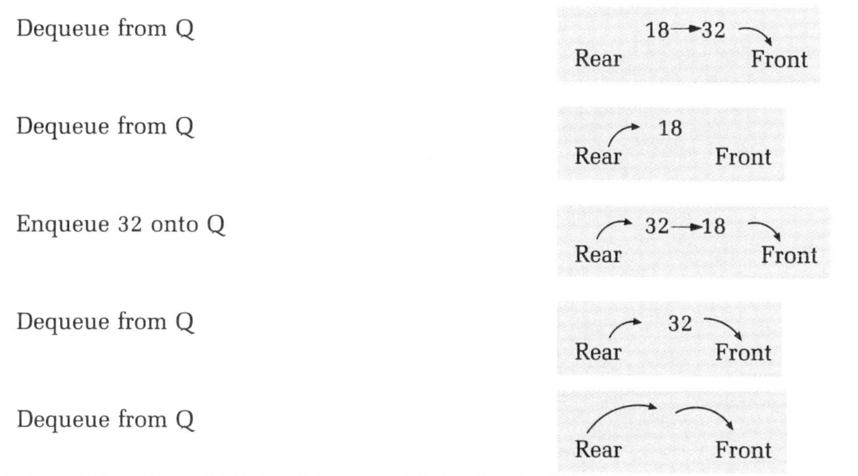

Application of a Queue in Computer Simulation

Before discussing implementations of a queue, we will examine how this ADT can be used in an application known as computer *simulation.* To introduce the notion of a simulation, consider the following question.

> *The star car washing team at Octopus Car Wash requires precisely four minutes to wash a car. On the average, a car arrives at Octopus every four minutes. In a typical 10-hour day at Octopus, how long does a car have to wait between its arrival and beginning its wash?*

It's tempting to answer this question by reasoning that the combination of four minutes to wash a car and four minutes between arrivals implies that no car should wait at all. However, such reasoning would not reflect the reality that cars arrive sporadically. Such sporadic arrival patterns are what can cause dreadful waiting lines.

That cars arrive, on the average, every four minutes really means that, in any given minute, there is a 25 percent chance that a car will arrive. We wish to reflect the notion of "chance" in a program that models the operation of Octopus Car Wash during a typical day. A computer simulation is a program that models a real-life event. To incorporate chance into simulations, a special function known as a *random number generator* is used.

A random number generator is a function that returns an unpredictable numerical value each time it is called. For our purposes, the value returned from a random number generator will be a real value greater than or equal to zero but less than 1. We will approach a random number generator as a "black box" function. That is, we will not worry about the internal logic of how such numbers are generated. Many versions of Pascal supply a random number generator; if yours doesn't, you might use the one given in Appendix 9. Our only concern in using a random number generator is that if we call on the **FUNCTION** Random in a loop such as the following

```
FOR K := 1 TO 100 DO
  BEGIN
    X := Random  {  A parameterless function  }
  END;
```

then we should see 100 values that obey statistical properties of randomness. Essentially these properties require that no pattern of values tends to recur and that values are evenly spread over the interval from 0.0 to 1.0.

How will a random number generator be used to reflect the "reality" of cars arriving at Octopus Car Wash? We will view each iteration through a loop as one minute in the daily operation of Octopus. On each iteration, we will call on Random to generate a random number. If it is less than or equal to 0.25 (corresponding to the 25 percent chance of an arrival), our program will interpret that as a car arriving during that minute. If the random number is greater than 0.25, the program decides that no car arrived during that minute.

When a car does arrive, it will be added to the waiting queue of cars. So that we may accumulate some statistical results, the car will be time-stamped with the time that it entered the queue. This time stamp will allow us to determine how long a car has been in the queue before it finally reaches the front. Conceptually, the queue at the core of this simulation is depicted in Figure 5.7.

FIGURE 5.7
Cars waiting at Octopus Car Wash, time-stamped with the minute of their arrival

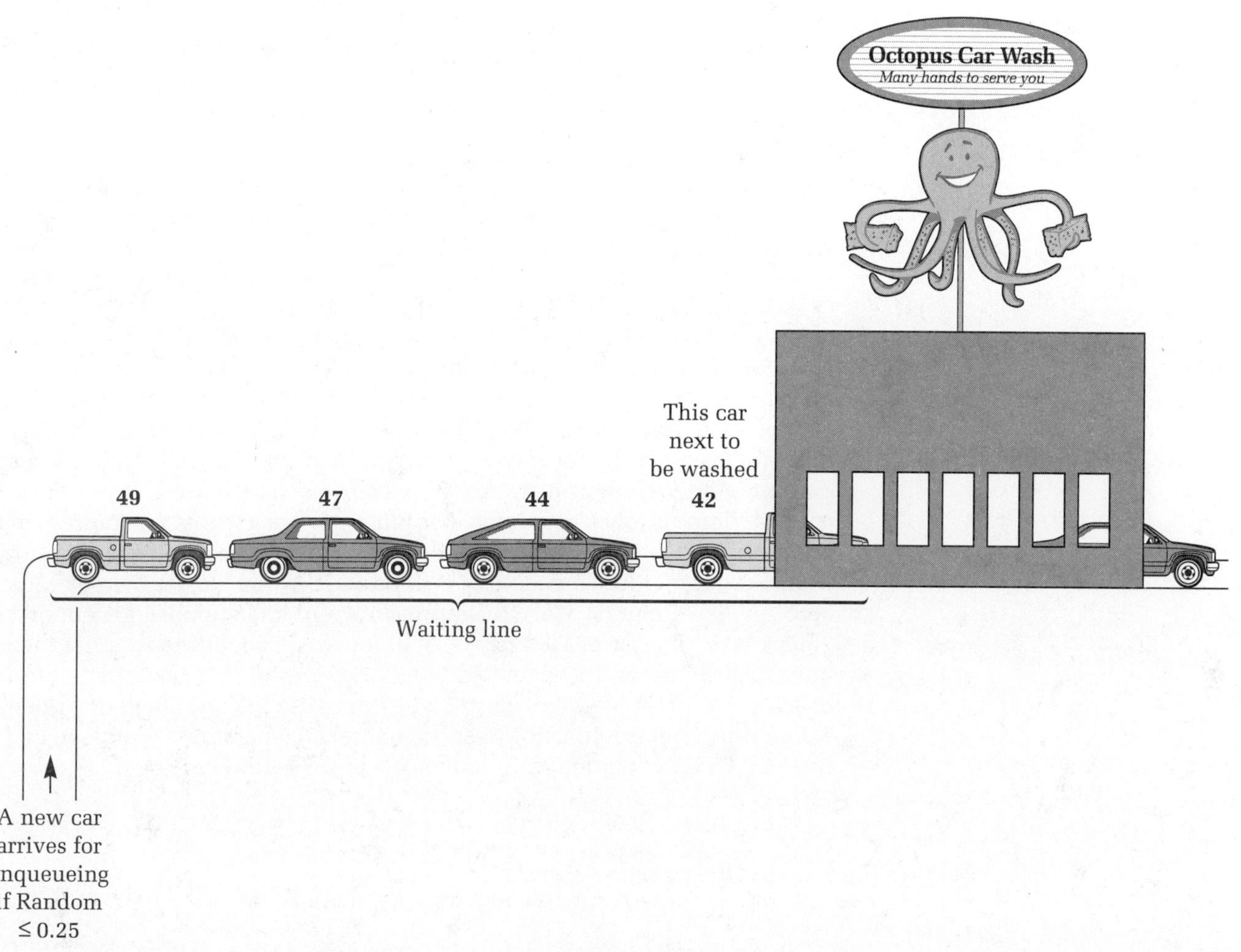

Pseudocode for the Octopus Car Wash simulation is

1. Initialize statistical counters
2. Create the queue of time-stamped cars
3. **FOR** each Minute in the day's operation
   3.1 Call on the random number generator to determine if a new car arrived
   3.2 **IF** a new car arrived **THEN**
      3.2.1 Time-stamp and enqueue in onto the queue of cars
   3.3 **IF** no car is currently being washed **AND** the queue of waiting cars is not empty **THEN**
      3.3.1 Dequeue a car from the queue for washing
      3.3.2 Use the time stamp for the car just dequeued to determine how long it waited
      3.3.3 Add that wait time to the accumulating total wait time
      3.3.4 Record that we have just begun to wash a car
   3.4 **IF** a car is being washed **THEN**
      3.4.1 Reduce by one minute the time left before we are done washing it

To refine this pseudocode into a Pascal main program, we must establish a formal Pascal interface for the queue ADT.

Pascal Interface for the Queue Abstract Data Type

```
TYPE
  QueueData = { The type of each data item in the queue };

PROCEDURE Create (var Q : Queue);

  {  Given:   An arbitrary queue variable Q in unknown state          }
  {  Task:    Initialize Q to the empty queue                         }
  {  Return:  Q initialized to the empty queue.                       }

FUNCTION Empty (Q : Queue) : boolean;

  {  Given:   A previously created queue                              }
  {  Task:    Determine if Q is empty                                 }
  {  Return:  True if Q is empty, false otherwise.                    }

FUNCTION Full (Q : Queue) : boolean;

  {  Given:   A previously created queue                              }
  {  Task:    Determine if Q is full                                  }
  {  Return:  True if Q is full, false otherwise.                     }

PROCEDURE Enqueue (VAR Q : Queue;
                   Item : QueueData);

  {  Given:   A previously created queue Q                            }
  {           An item to be added to the rear of the queue            }
  {  Task:    Add the item to the queue                               }
  {  Return:  Q with Item added to the rear of the queue.  If         }
  {           the queue is full, it is left unchanged.                }

PROCEDURE Dequeue (VAR Q : Queue;
                   VAR Item : QueueData);

  {  Given:   A previously created queue Q                            }
  {  Task:    Remove the item at the front of the queue               }
```

```
{  Return:  Q with its front value removed.                          }
{           Item  contains the value that was at the front of        }
{           queue.  If Q is empty, contents of Item are unreliable.  }
```

■ EXAMPLE 5.6

Use the preceding Pascal interface to write a main program for the Octopus Car Wash simulation. Assume the existence of a Random function.

```
PROGRAM Octopus (input, output);

  { A program to simulate the operation of the Octopus Car Wash over      }
  { 10 hours (600 minutes) of operation.  The variables TimeForWash       }
  { and ProbOfArrival represent the time it takes to run one car through  }
  { Octopus's star car wash team and the probability that a car          }
  { arrives for a wash in any given minute.  This program assumes the     }
  { existence of a Queue data type and a random number generator invoked  }
  { by a call to the parameterless function Random.                       }

TYPE
  QueueData = integer;
  Queue = { Assume appropriate implementation };

VAR
  TimeForWash,                 { Time to wash one car }
  Minute,                      { Loop counter }
  TimeEnteredQueue,            { Used for time-stamping car in queue }
  CarsWashed,                  { Total cars washed }
  TotalQueueMin,               { Total minutes spent waiting }
  TimeLeftOnCar : integer;     { Time left for washing current car }
  ProbOfArrival : real;
  CarQueue : Queue;
  .
  .    { Queue operations and random number generator, if needed }
  .

BEGIN
  write ('Enter time to wash one car ');
  readln (TimeForWash);
  write ('Enter probability of arrival in any minute ');
  readln (ProbOfArrival);
  Create (CarQueue);
  CarsWashed := 0;
  TotalQueueMin := 0;
  TimeLeftOnCar := 0;
  FOR Minute := 1 TO 600 DO  { Iterate through minutes of day }
    BEGIN
      IF Random < ProbOfArrival THEN  { Have new arrival in this minute }
        Enqueue (CarQueue, Minute);
      IF (TimeLeftOnCar = 0) AND NOT Empty (CarQueue) THEN
        BEGIN
          Dequeue (CarQueue, TimeEnteredQueue);
          TotalQueueMin := TotalQueueMin + (Minute - TimeEnteredQueue);
          CarsWashed := CarsWashed + 1;
          TimeLeftOnCar := TimeForWash
        END;
      IF TimeLeftOnCar <> 0 THEN
        TimeLeftOnCar := TimeLeftOnCar - 1
    END;
  writeln (CarsWashed : 4, ' cars were washed');
  writeln ('Average wait in queue ', TotalQueueMin/CarsWashed : 8 : 2)
END.
```

A sample run would appear as follows:

```
Enter time to wash one car 4
Enter probability of arrival in any minute 0.25
 150 cars were washed
Average wait in queue     15.53
```

The sample run of the program in Example 5.6 provides an indication of how the sporadic arrival of cars can cause a backlog of work at Octopus Car Wash. One of the great values of simulation programs is that they allow cost-free experimentation with various scenarios to see if a situation might improve or worsen. For instance, the program we have written for Octopus could be used to explore how adding help to the car wash team (and correspondingly reducing the amount of time it takes to wash a car) could affect the build-up of cars waiting for service. You will get a chance to explore further the use of queues for computer simulations in the Exercises and Problems.

Another noteworthy point about Example 5.6 is that it works with a queue even though we have no idea of how the queue of cars is actually implemented. Of course, this should not be surprising; this is the value of designing programs and data structures from an ADT perspective. However, given the high-level logic in our example, we should now turn our attention to ways in which the scheduling queue might be implemented.

A NOTE OF INTEREST

Computer Simulations: Blessing or Curse?

The computer's ability to condense a large span of time (such as 600 minutes in Example 5.6) into the very short time frame required for a run of a simulation program is the blessing and the curse of computer simulations. It makes the computer a very valuable experimental tool. In addition to providing a much faster means of experimentation, simulation programs allow researchers and decision-makers to set up initial conditions that would be far too risky if allowed in real life.

For example, consider the area of environmental studies. Here researchers can use simulation programs to create scenarios that would be far too time-consuming and dangerous if they were carried out in the environment. Researchers could use simulation software to see what might happen if pollution of a river were allowed to continue in an uncontrolled manner. If the results of the simulation indicate that all fish in the river would be gone within ten years, nothing has really been lost. Moreover, some valuable information has been gained; decision-makers in the environmental arena would know that some sort of pollution controls are necessary. Further experimentation with the simulation could be done to determine exactly what type and degree of controls should be imposed.

What can go wrong with decisions based on the result of computer simulation? Clearly, if the model upon which the program is based is not an accurate reflection of the situation being simulated, results could be produced that would disastrously mislead decision-makers. Additionally, we saw in Example 5.6, building the complex mathematical models used in simulation programs is a very sensitive process. Even models that seem to be relatively comprehensive can produce surprisingly inaccurate output. Hence, the real issue in using simulation results to support the decision-making process is the accuracy of the model on which the program is based. The authors of such a program must combine expertise in programming techniques with high levels of sophisticated knowledge in the relevant discipline(s). This is a situation in which computer science must truly become interdisciplinary.

The importance of simulation as an area of application within computer science is reflected in two issues of the *Communications of the ACM* that have been dedicated to this topic. The November 1985 issue (Vol. 28, No. 11) reported on simulation models in such diverse areas as molecular genetics, aviation, and seismology. The October 1990 issue (Vol. 33, No. 10) explored simulation in the context of parallel events, on-line scheduling, and semiconductor manufacturing.

Array Implementation of a Queue

From the definition of a queue, it is evident that two pointers will suffice to keep track of the data in a queue: one pointer to the front of the queue and one to the rear. This premise underlies all of the queue implementations which we will discuss in this section.

Let us consider computer jobs being scheduled in a batch processing environment, a good example of a queue in use. Suppose further that all job names are strings and that jobs are scheduled strictly in the order in which they arrive. Then an array and two pointers can be used to implement the scheduling queue. We will encapsulate the array and pointers into a single record type.

```
TYPE
  QueueData = String;
  QueueArray = ARRAY [1..MaxQueueSize] OF QueueData;
  Queue = RECORD
            List : QueueArray;
            Front, Rear : integer
          END;
VAR
  JobQueue : Queue;
```

Here MaxQueueSize would be set by a **CONST** declaration to the maximum number of entries that the field List may contain. We shall see that this is different from the actual number of entries that the queue may contain at a given time in processing.

If the Front and Rear pointers are initially set to 1 and 0 respectively, the state of the queue before any insertions or deletions appears as shown in Figure 5.8.

FIGURE 5.8
Empty queue

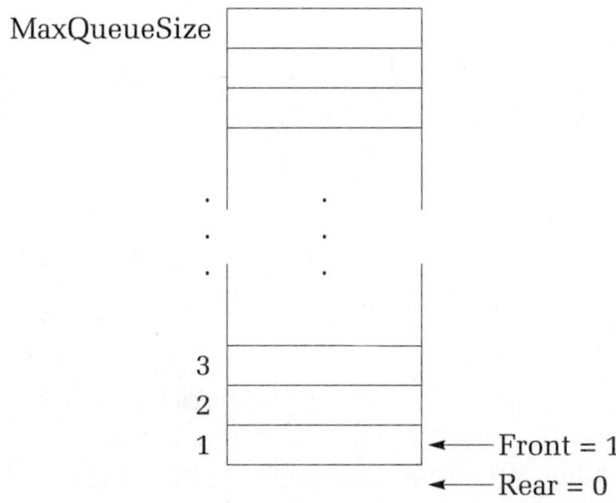

Recalling that insertions may be made only at the rear of the queue, suppose that job NEWTON now arrives to be processed. The queue then changes to the state pictured in Figure 5.9.

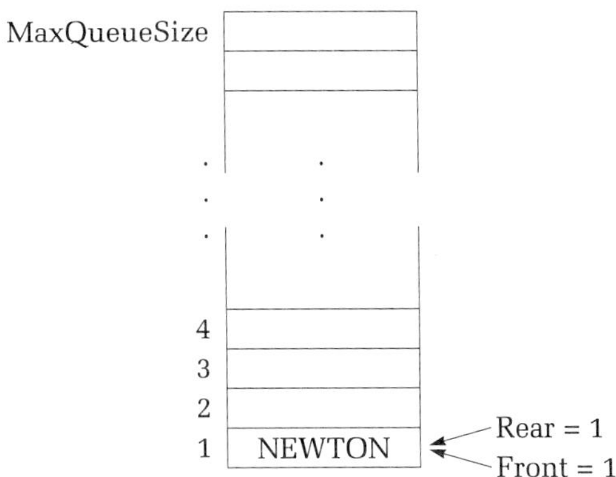

FIGURE 5.9
NEWTON added to the rear of the queue

If job NEWTON is followed by PAYROLL, the queue's status must change to that of Figure 5.10, which shows that the addition of any Item to the queue requires two steps:

```
Q.Rear := Q.Rear + 1;
Q.List[Q.Rear] := Item;
```

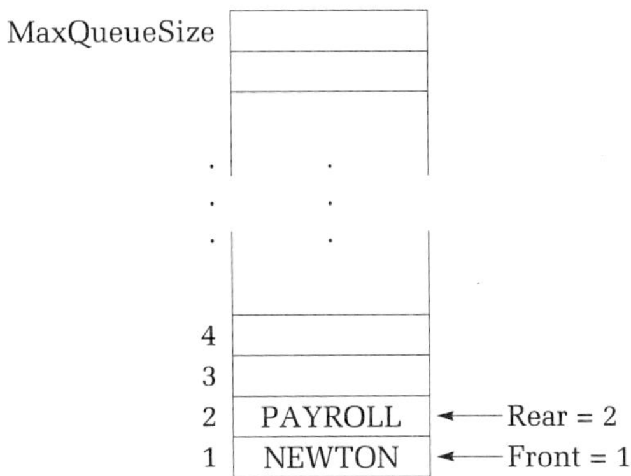

FIGURE 5.10
PAYROLL added after NEWTON

If the system is now ready to process NEWTON, the front entry must be removed from the queue to an appropriate location designated by Item in Figure 5.11.

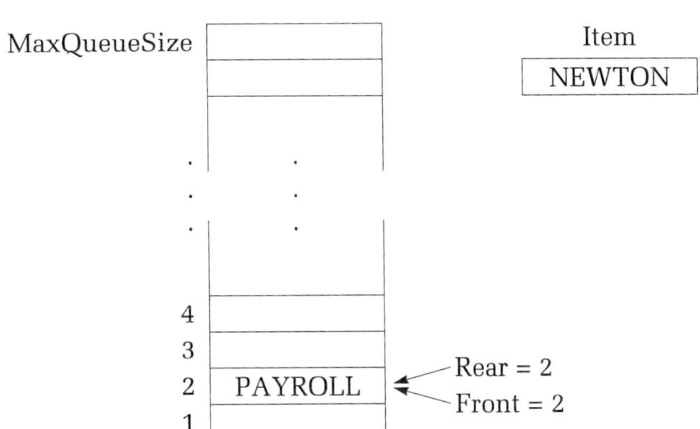

FIGURE 5.11
NEWTON removed from the queue

Here the instructions

```
Item := Q.List[Q.Front];
Q.Front := Q.Front + 1;
```

achieve the desired effect.

It should be clear that the conditions in Table 5.2 signal the associated boundary conditions for an array implementation of a queue.

TABLE 5.2
Boundary condition checks for array implementation of queue

Condition	Special Situation
Rear < Front	Empty queue
Front = Rear	One-entry queue
Rear = MaxQueueSize	No more entries may be added to queue

The conditions allow us to develop our brief two-line sequences for adding to and removing from a queue into full-fledged procedures. These in turn assume the existence of the Boolean-valued functions Empty and Full to check whether or not the Enqueue and Dequeue operations are possible. In the Exercises, you will be asked to write the Create, Empty, and Full operations.

EXAMPLE 5.7

Write the Enqueue and Dequeue operations for an array implementation of the queue ADT.

```
PROCEDURE Enqueue (VAR Q : Queue;
                   Item : QueueData);

  {  Given:   A previously created queue Q                          }
  {           An item to be added to the rear of the queue          }
  {  Task:    Add the item to the queue                             }
  {  Return:  Q with Item added to the rear of the queue.  If       }
  {           the queue is full, it is left unchanged.              }

  BEGIN
    WITH Q DO
      IF NOT Full (Q) THEN
        BEGIN
          Rear := Rear + 1;
          List[Rear] := Item
        END
  END; {  of PROCEDURE Enqueue  }
```

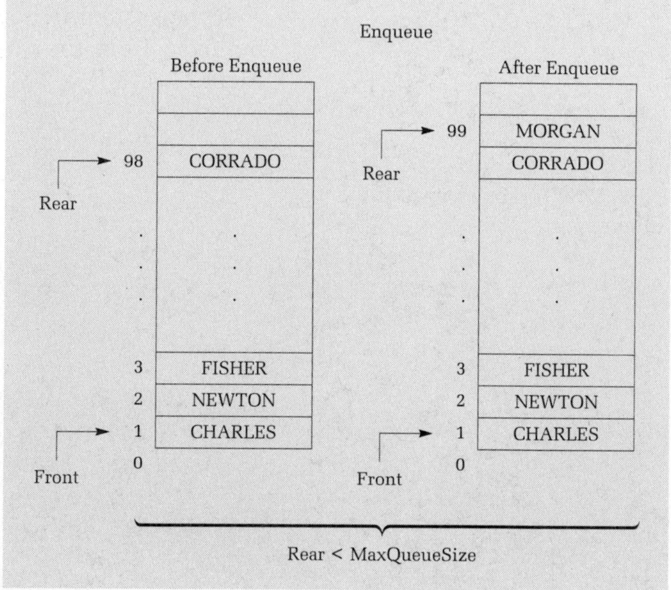

```
PROCEDURE Dequeue (VAR Q : Queue;
                   VAR Item : QueueData);

  {  Given:   A previously created queue Q                            }
  {  Task:    Remove the item at the front of the queue               }
  {  Return:  Q with its front value removed.                         }
  {           Item contains the value that was at the front of        }
  {           queue.  If Q is empty, contents of Item are unreliable. }

  BEGIN
    WITH Q DO
      IF NOT Empty (Q) THEN
        BEGIN
          Item := List[Front];
          Front := Front + 1
        END
  END; { of PROCEDURE Dequeue }
```


As it now stands, our implementation of a queue as a scheduling structure for jobs in a batch environment functions effectively until Rear matches MaxQueueSize. Then a call to Enqueue fails even though only a small percentage of slots in the array may actually contain data items currently in the queue structure. In fact, given the queue pictured in Figure 5.12, we should be able to use slots 1–997 again.

This is not necessarily undesirable. For example, it may be that the mode of operation in a given batch environment is to process 1,000 jobs, then print a statistical report on these 1,000 jobs, and finally clear the queue to start

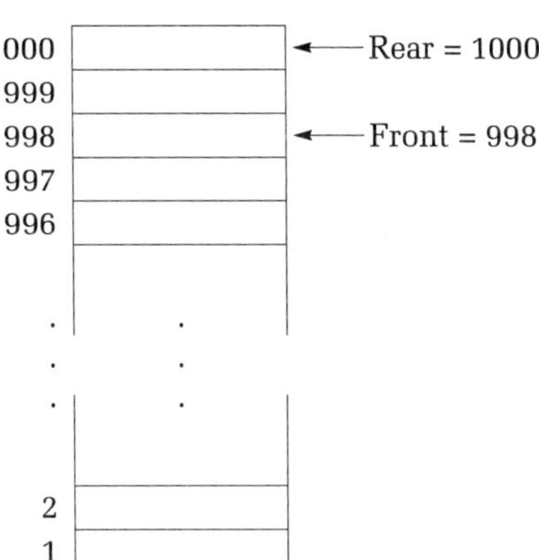

FIGURE 5.12
A full queue

another group of 1,000 jobs. In this case, the queue in Figure 5.12 is the ideal structure because data about jobs are not lost even after they have left the queue.

However, if the goal of a computer installation were to provide continuous scheduling of batch jobs, without interruption after 1,000 jobs, then the queue of Figure 5.12 would not be effective. One strategy that could be employed to correct this situation is to move the active queue down the array upon reaching the condition Rear = MaxQueueSize, as illustrated in Figure 5.13.

FIGURE 5.13
Active queue moved down

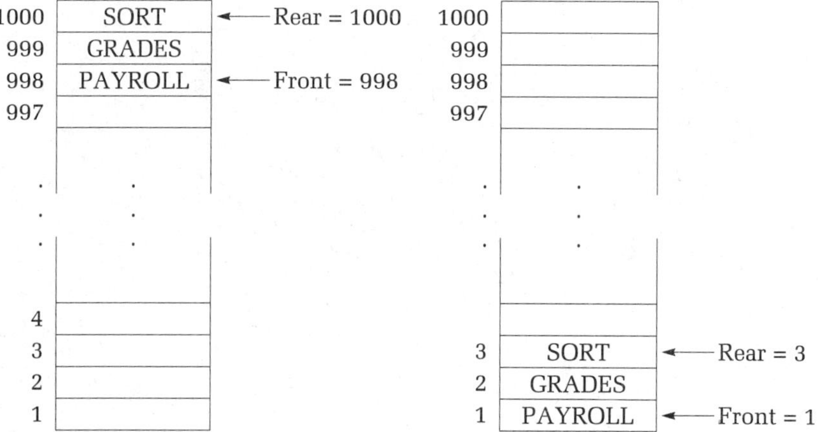

If the queue contains a large number of items, however, this strategy would not be satisfactory because it would require moving all of the individual data items. We will discuss two other strategies that allow the queue to operate in a continuous and efficient fashion: a circular implementation and a linked list implementation.

Circular Implementation of a Queue

This technique essentially allows the queue to wrap around upon reaching the end of the array. This transformation is illustrated by the addition of the Item, UPDATE, to the queue in Figure 5.14.

To handle the pointer arithmetic necessary for this implementation of a queue, we must make the Front and Rear pointers behave in a fashion analogous to an odometer in a car that has exceeded its mileage capacity. A convenient way of doing this is to use Pascal's **MOD** operator. For instance, if we replace

```
Front := Front + 1
```

in Example 5.7 with

```
Front := Front MOD MaxQueueSize + 1
```

and

```
Rear := Rear + 1
```

with

```
Rear := Rear MOD MaxQueueSize + 1
```

we will achieve the wraparound effect depicted in Figure 5.14.

FIGURE 5.14
Queue wraps around when UPDATE is added

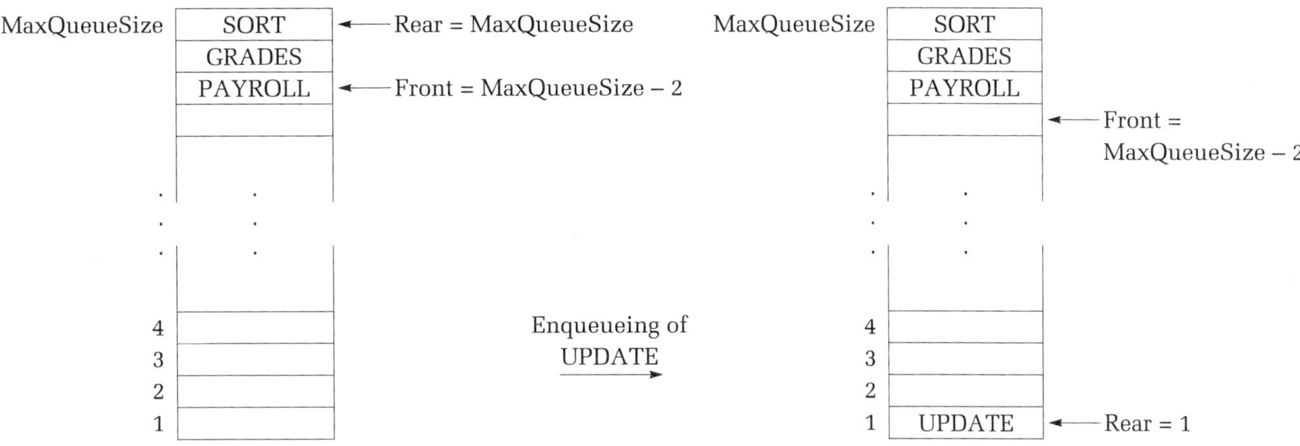

Unfortunately, it is clear from Figure 5.14 that Rear < Front will no longer suffice as a condition to signal an empty queue. To derive this condition, consider what remains after we remove an item from a queue that has only a single item in it. There are two possible situations, as illustrated in Figure 5.15.

FIGURE 5.15
Removing from one-entry queue

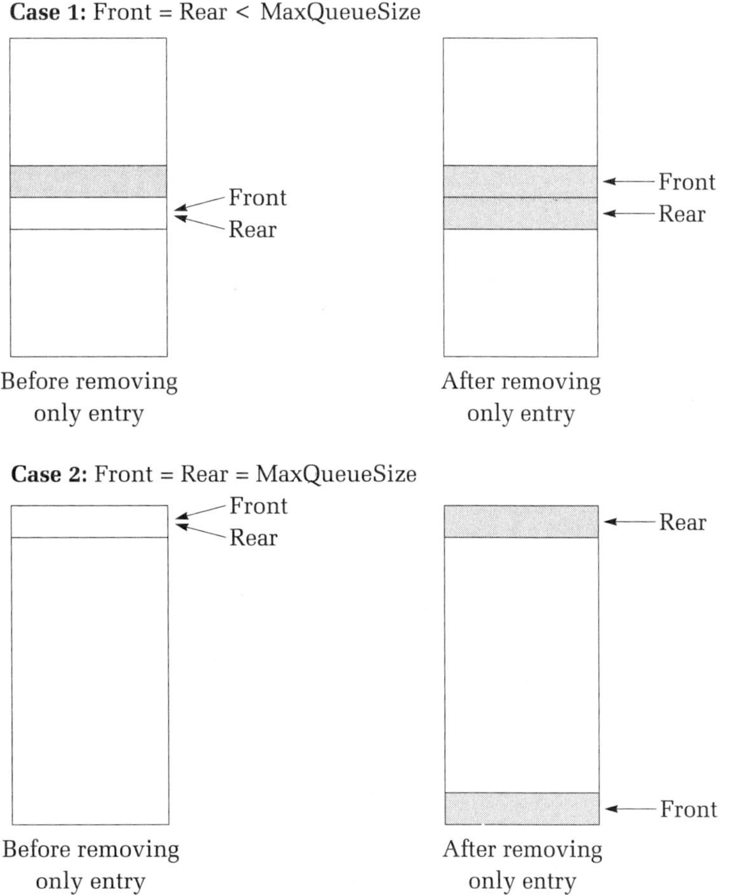

An inspection of both cases reveals that after the lone entry has been removed, the relationship

(Rear **MOD** MaxQueueSize) + 1 = Front

holds between the pointers. There is a problem, however, with immediately adopting this as a check for an empty queue. This same relationship between pointers also exists when the queue is full.

This apparent contradiction can be avoided easily if we add a counter to our encapsulation of the queue to keep track of the number of items currently in the queue. Then, as Table 5.3 indicates, tests for Empty and Full conditions need merely check this counter.

TABLE 5.3
Boundary condition checks for circular queue with encapsulated counter

Condition	Special Situation
Counter is 1	One-entry queue
Counter is 0	Empty queue
Counter is MaxQueueSize	Full queue

The actual implementation of queue operations using a circular array strategy is left for you to do in the Exercises.

Linked List Implementation of a Queue

The linked list method allows a queue to be completely dynamic with size restrictions imposed only by the pool of available nodes. Essentially, the queue is represented as a linked list with an additional rear pointer to the last node in the list so that the list need not be traversed to find this node. To reduce the necessity of handling special cases, we follow the strategy described in Section 4.4 of having a dummy header, which carries no actual data, as the first node in the list. Hence the linked list implementation of the queue containing PAYROLL, GRADES, and SORT would appear as in Figure 5.16.

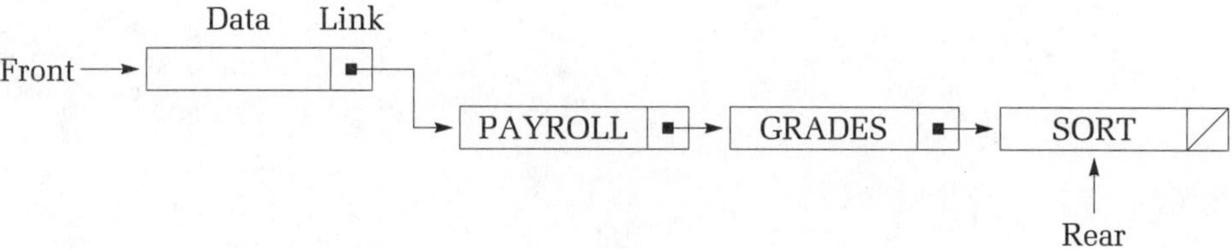

FIGURE 5.16
Queue with three data nodes and dummy header

We will follow the convention that the front pointer for the queue points at the dummy header. Hence we access the first actual item in the queue through the dummy header. Table 5.4 summarizes the conditional checks that signal an empty, one-entry, or full queue.

TABLE 5.4
Conditional checks for special situations in linked list implementation (using a dummy header)

Condition	Special Situation
Rear = Front	Empty queue
Rear = Front ↑ .Link	One-entry queue
Handled by GetNode or **new** procedures of Chapter 18	Full queue

Appropriate procedures for handling additions to and removals from the queue follow. Notice that from a calling module's perspective, it would make little difference whether these low-level procedures used an array or a linked list to implement the queue. For each implementation, we have bundled all the information involved with the queue into a single record of type Queue. Hence the calling protocol for these modules is the same regardless of the implementation being used. Remember that is the essence of data abstraction: the details of how a data structure is actually implemented are hidden as deeply as possible in the overall program structure.

EXAMPLE 5.8

Code the Enqueue and Dequeue operations for a linked list implementation of a queue. Assume that a dummy header is used.

```
{  Global declarations  }

TYPE
  QueueData = { Type of data item in queue };
  QueuePointer = ^QueueNode;
  QueueNode = RECORD
                Data : QueueData;
                Link : QueuePointer
              END;
  Queue = RECORD
            Front, Rear : QueuePointer
          END;

PROCEDURE Enqueue (VAR Q : Queue;
                   Item : QueueData);

  {  Given:    A previously created queue Q                            }
  {            An item to be added to the rear of the queue            }
  {  Task:     Add the item to the queue                               }
  {  Return:   Q with Item added to the rear of the queue.  If         }
  {            the queue is full, it is left unchanged.                }

  VAR
    P : QueuePointer;
```

```
    BEGIN
      new(P);
      P^.Data := Item;
      P^.Link := NIL;
      Q.Rear^.Link := P;
      Q.Rear := P
    END; {  of PROCEDURE Enqueue  }
```

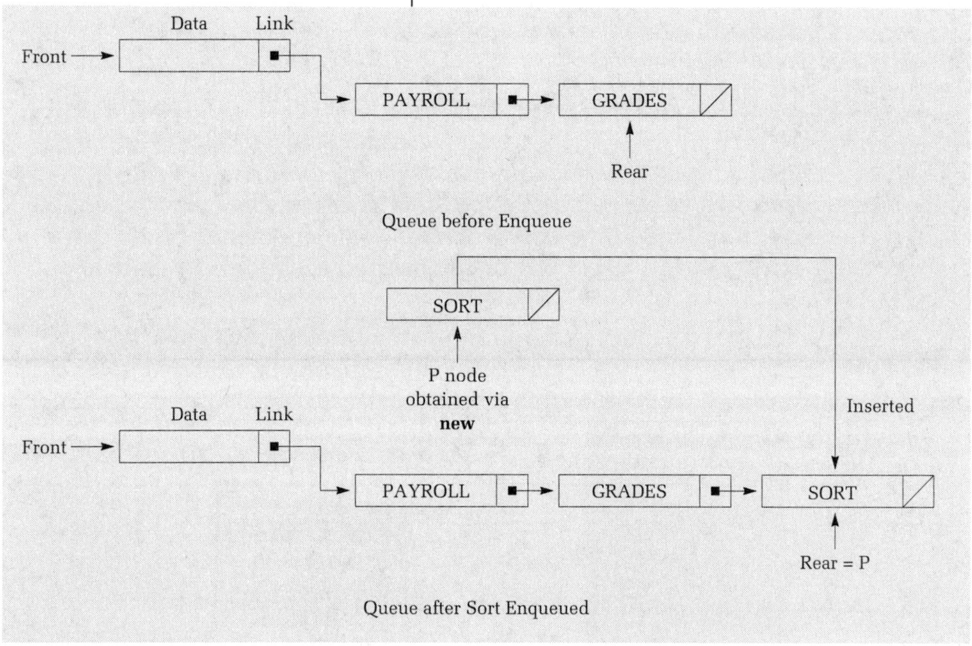

```
PROCEDURE Dequeue (VAR Q : Queue;
                   VAR Item : QueueData);

  {  Given:   A previously created queue Q                             }
  {  Task:    Remove the item at the front of the queue                }
  {  Return:  Q with its front value removed.                          }
  {           Item contains the value that was at the front of         }
  {           queue.  If Q is empty, contents of Item are unreliable.  }

  VAR
    P : QueuePointer;

  BEGIN
    IF NOT Empty (Q) THEN
      BEGIN
        P := Q.Front^.Link;
        Item := P^.Data;
        Q.Front^.Link := P^.Link;
```

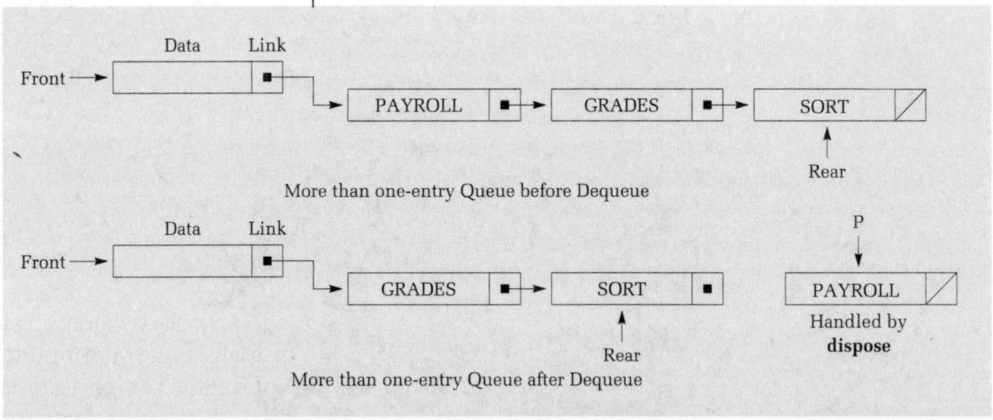

```
      IF Q.Rear = P THEN {  Removed from one-entry queue  }
        Q.Rear := Q.Front;
      dispose(P)
    END
END; {  of PROCEDURE Dequeue  }
```

Data Link
Front
SORT
Rear
One-entry Queue before Dequeue

Data Link
Front
Rear
One-entry Queue after Dequeue

Priority Queues

So far we have used a batch scheduling application as an example of how a queue might be used in an operating system. Typically, such batch scheduling might also give higher priorities to certain types of jobs. For instance, at a university computer center, students in introductory computer science courses may receive the highest priority for their jobs to encourage a quick turnaround. Students in upper-division courses may have the next highest priority, whereas jobs related to faculty research, which require a great deal of computation, get the lowest possible priority. These jobs could be classified as types A, B, and C respectively. Any A job is serviced before any B or C job, regardless of the time it enters the service queue. Similarly, any B job is serviced before any C job. A data structure capable of representing such a queue requires just one *front pointer* but three *rear pointers,* one for each of the A, B, and C priorities.

A queue with eight jobs waiting to be serviced might appear as shown in Figure 5.17, which tells us that STATS, PRINT, and BANK are the A jobs awaiting service; COPY and CHECK, the B jobs; and UPDATE, AVERAGE, and TEST, the C jobs. If a new A job, PROB1, were to arrive for service, it would be inserted at the end of the A queue, between BANK and COPY. Because jobs can be serviced only by leaving the front of the queue, PROB1 would be processed before any of the B or C jobs.

FIGURE 5.17
Priority queue with eight jobs at three priority levels

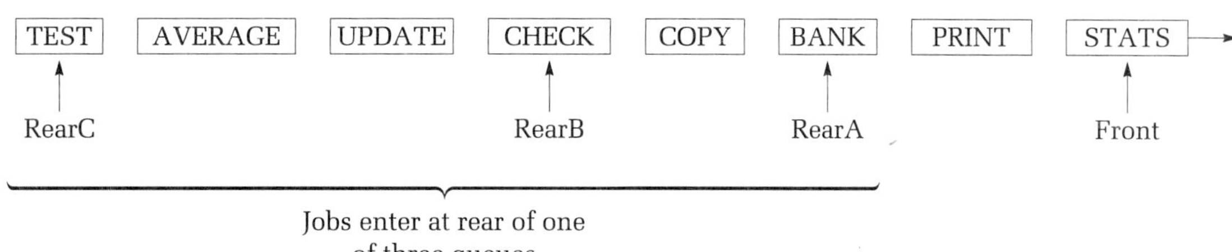

Because insertions in such a *priority queue* need not occur at the absolute rear of the queue, it is clear that an array implementation may require moving a substantial amount of data when an item is inserted at the rear of one of the higher priority queues. To avoid this, you can use a linked list to great advantage when implementing a priority queue. Whenever an item arrives to be inserted into a given priority level, the rear pointer for that priority gives us an immediately accessible pointer to the node after which the item is to be inserted. This avoids a costly sequential search for the insertion point. If a dummy leader is included at the beginning of the list, the empty conditions for any given priority are as shown in Table 5.5.

TABLE 5.5
Empty conditions for a priority queue

Condition	Priority
Front = Rear1	For priority 1, the highest priority
Rear1 = Rear2	For priority 2
Rear(n − 1) = Rear$n$	For priority n

The specifics of writing a formal ADT definition of a priority queue and providing an implementation for it are included as exercises at the end of this section. In Chapter 7, we will see that priority queues may also be implemented using the special type of tree structure known as a heap (not to be confused with the heap maintained in Pascal as described in Chapter 4). Unlike the implementation we have just discussed, the heap will conveniently allow an unrestricted number of different priorities.

A NOTE OF INTEREST

Operating Systems and Scheduling Resource Use in a Time-Sharing Environment

One of the primary problems facing designers of operating systems is the allocation and scheduling of resources that must be shared by a number of users. For instance, consider a simple time-sharing system which allows multiple users, each on a video terminal, and also has one shared printer. Suppose that the currently running process, called process A, makes a request to use the printer. Then, before this process completes its task on the printer, its allotted time (often called a time burst) expires, and it is replaced by process B as the currently running process. If process B requests the printer while it is running, we have a clear problem. If process B is granted the printer, its output will be interspersed with that from Process A, which did not complete its printing before its time burst expired. Obviously, we cannot let process B continue to run.

The solution developed by operating systems designers to honor both of these requests is to use multiple queues—one containing those processes that have cleared access to all resources they require to run, and one for processes that have requested a resource currently owned by another process. The former of these queues is often called the *ready queue;* the latter is termed the *blocked queue.* Hence the solution to the scenario described in the first paragraph involves two steps.

1. Move process A from its currently running state to the ready queue when its time burst expires (because it has all the necessary resources to start running again).
2. Move process B to the blocked queue when it requests the printer already owned by process A. Here it would remain until process A is done with the printer, at which time the front entry in the blocked queue for the printer (B in this case) would be moved to the ready queue.

In practice, the addition and removal of processes to and from these queues is controlled by special flags called *semaphores.* For a thorough exposition on operating system queues and semaphores, see H. M. Deitel's *Introduction to Operating Systems,* second edition (Reading, Mass.: Addison-Wesley, 1990) and Andrew Tanenbaum's *Operating Systems: Design and Implementation* (Englewood Cliffs, N.J.: Prentice-Hall, 1987).

Exercises 5.3

1. Suppose that you are given a queue that is known to contain only positive integers. Use only the fundamental queue operations to write a procedure

```
PROCEDURE Replace (VAR Queue : QueueType; Old, New : integer)
```

   which replaces all occurrences of the positive integer Old in the Queue with the positive integer New. Other than doing this, the queue is to remain unchanged. Avoid passing through the queue more than once.

2. Suppose that you are given a queue of real numbers. Using only the fundamental queue operations, write a function that returns the average value of an entry in the queue.

3. Augment the simulation program of Example 5.6 by
   a. Counting the number of minutes during the day when the Octopus Car Wash team is idle; that is, there are no cars in the queue waiting to be washed.
   b. Counting how many cars are left waiting in the queue at the end of the day.

   Make no assumptions about how the CarQueue might be implemented.

4. Consider a circular array implementation of a queue in which the array is declared to have an index range 1..5. Trace the status of the array and the front and rear pointers after each of the following successive operations.

   Enqueue *SMITH*
   Enqueue *JONES*
   Enqueue *GREER*
   Dequeue
   Enqueue *CARSON*
   Dequeue
   Enqueue *BAKER*
   Enqueue *CHARLES*
   Enqueue *BENSON*
   Dequeue
   Enqueue *MILLER*

5. Implement the Create, Empty, and Full operations for a (noncircular) array implementation of a queue. Be sure that your answers are consistent with the implementation of Enqueue and Dequeue in Example 5.7.

6. Provide declarations for a circular array implementation of a queue. Then use these declarations to implement each of the five basic queue operations.

7. Implement the Create, Empty, and Full operations for a linked list (with dummy header) implementation of a queue. Be sure that your answers are consistent with the implementations of Enqueue and Dequeue in Example 5.8.

8. Implement all five basic queue operations using a linked list representation that does not include a dummy header.

9. Suppose that we adopt the following conventions for the front and rear pointers associated with a queue. Front is to point at the next item to be removed from the queue. Rear is to point at the first available location, that is, the next location to be filled. Following these conventions, implement all five queue operations for a noncircular array representation of the ADT.

10. Repeat Exercise 9 for a circular array representation.

11. In a queue used to schedule batch jobs on a computer system, it is often convenient to allow users to remove a job from the queue after submitting it. (They may, for example, realize that they accidentally submitted a job with an infinite loop.) Develop a procedure header for this removal operation. Be sure

that you document it appropriately. Then implement it for a circular array representation of a queue.

12. Repeat Exercise 11 for a linked list (with dummy header) representation of a queue.
13. Provide a formal ADT definition for the priority queue. Then implement the ADT under the assumption that possible priority values are drawn from a set that could be used to index an array. See if you can make your implementation of each operation O(1) in its efficiency.
14. Discuss ways in which the Octopus Car Wash simulation of Example 5.6 does not reflect the way in which a car wash really operates. Then discuss ways in which the pseudocode logic behind this example should be modified to overcome these shortcomings.

■ ■ ■ ■

FOCUS ON PROGRAM DESIGN

The application of the parsing algorithm described in Section 5.2 is not limited to compilers. Many of the programs typically used by scientists, engineers, and mathematicians can be greatly enhanced by allowing the user to interactively enter an algebraic expression as opposed to embedding the expression inside the program. Consider, for instance, the situation described in the following memorandum from the head of the physics department at the University of Hard Knocks.

MEMORANDUM
University of Hard Knocks

TO: Director of Computer Center
FROM: Head of Physics Department
DATE: November 22, 1996
RE: Making integration program more versatile

In physics we find frequent application to take the integral of a function $f(x)$ over the interval from a to b on the real number line. As you are aware, this essentially means that we wish to find the area under the graph of the function between endpoints a and b, as indicated in the following diagram:

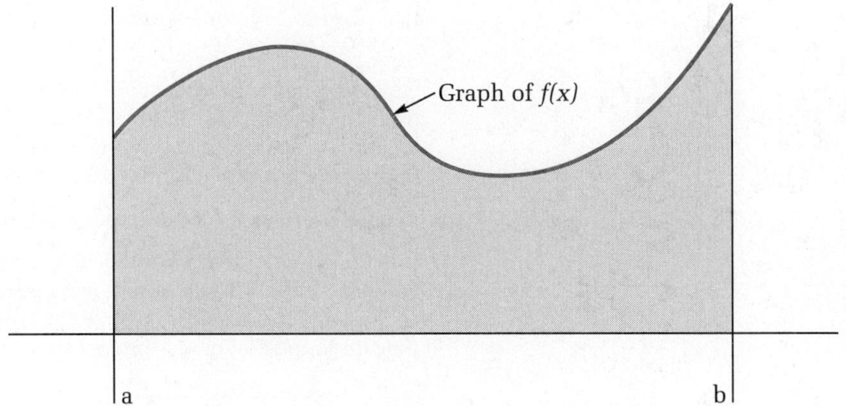

We presently have a program which obtains a good approximation of this area by adding up the areas of a large number of small rectangles, each with base along the interval from *a* to *b* and top passing through the graph of *f*(*x*). This concept is highlighted in the next diagram.

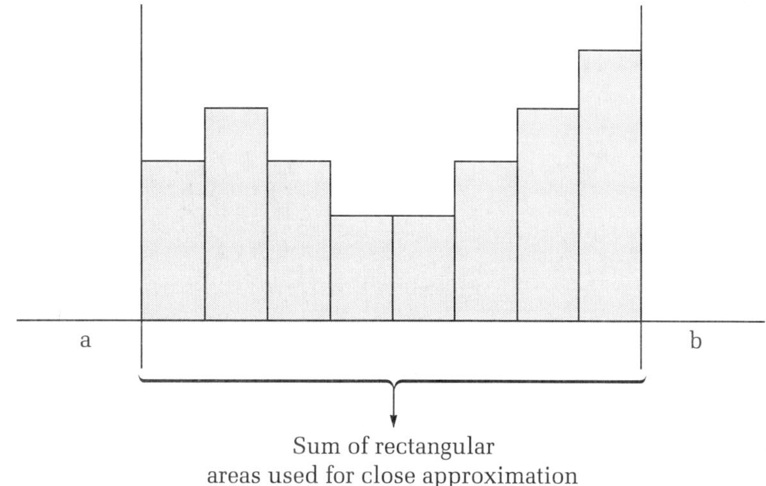

Sum of rectangular areas used for close approximation

The user of our program can interactively enter the endpoints *a* and *b* and the number of rectangles. The result is a very good approximation when enough rectangles are used.

Our problem is not with the accuracy of the approximation but with the fact that, to change the function *f*(*x*), the user must edit the definition of the function in the source program and then recompile. Can you help us by writing a program which will allow the user to enter the function *f*(*x*) interactively? The functions we integrate in this fashion can be defined in terms of the standard arithmetic operations addition, subtraction, multiplication, division, and exponentiation. Thanks in advance for your prompt assistance.

The physics department head has presented us with a substantial task in the preceding memorandum. Consider some of the subordinate problems with which we will be faced in writing this program.

- The evaluation of integrals; that is, areas under graphs of functions. Obtaining numerical answers to mathematical problems of this variety will serve to introduce us to a subject known as *numerical analysis.*
- The interactive parsing and evaluation of a function will give us an opportunity to adapt the algorithms introduced earlier.
- For the type of functions described in the memorandum, the problem of finding the next token in the expression can become complicated. Consider, for instance, a function defined by the expression

  ```
  3.14*X^3 + X^2
  ```

  where ^ is used to denote exponentiation. Here, from a stream of incoming characters, we must be prepared to select a token which may be a real number, the variable X, or an arithmetic operator. The problem of recognizing tokens in an incoming stream of characters is called *lexical analysis.*

To keep our situation relatively simple, we will assume that all tokens must be separated by a space and no other operations such as trigonometric functions may be used in defining the function *f*.

Modular Structure Chart for the Integral Evaluation System

With these comments in mind, we turn our attention toward designing a solution to the integration problem. Recall that the first step in this design process is to develop a modular structure chart reflecting the way in which we will partition the problem into subproblems. (See Figure 5.18). Since both conversion from infix to postfix and the evaluation of a postfix expression require fundamental stack operations, we have located our stack processing modules at the deepest level of the structure chart. Here they will be accessible by both the parsing and evaluation algorithms.

Interestingly, our system will also make use of a queue. Because the tokens in the postfix expression are now more complicated objects than single characters, we need a data structure to append tokens to as they are processed by the infix-to-postfix algorithm. A queue emerges as a very nice ADT for this purpose. Hence the structure chart also indicates the presence of fundamental queue operations at a level accessible by both the parsing and evaluation algorithms.

Data Structures for the Integral Evaluation System

We will need a queue to store the postfix expression that is built as the infix expression goes through our conversion algorithm. The data in this queue are more complex than characters, however. This is because the tokens needed from the infix string being entered by the user are not necessarily individual characters. Rather, such tokens will fall into one of the three following categories:

1. A real number. If the token is a real number, the lexical analysis phase of our algorithm must convert it from the appropriate stream of digits and decimal point as typed by the user.
2. The variable X. The infix expression defines the function in terms of this general variable. When the function is evaluated, a particular value is then substituted for X.
3. An operator. We broadly include +, −, *, /, ^, (,), and the special delimiter # in this category.

The problem with a token that may be either a real number or a character is that we essentially need a data type that can assume one of several identities, depending upon the current token. This is exactly the purpose for which Pascal's variant record type is defined. Hence, the following declarations provide a suitable data type for all three of the categories we have described:

```
TYPE
  TokenType = (RealValue, VarX, Operator);
              {  Number, variable, or operator/parenthesis  }

  TokenRec = RECORD
               CASE Token : TokenType OF
                 RealValue : (Value : real);
                 VarX : (XChar : char);
                 Operator : (OpChar : char)
               END;
```

FIGURE 5.18
Modular structure chart for integration problem

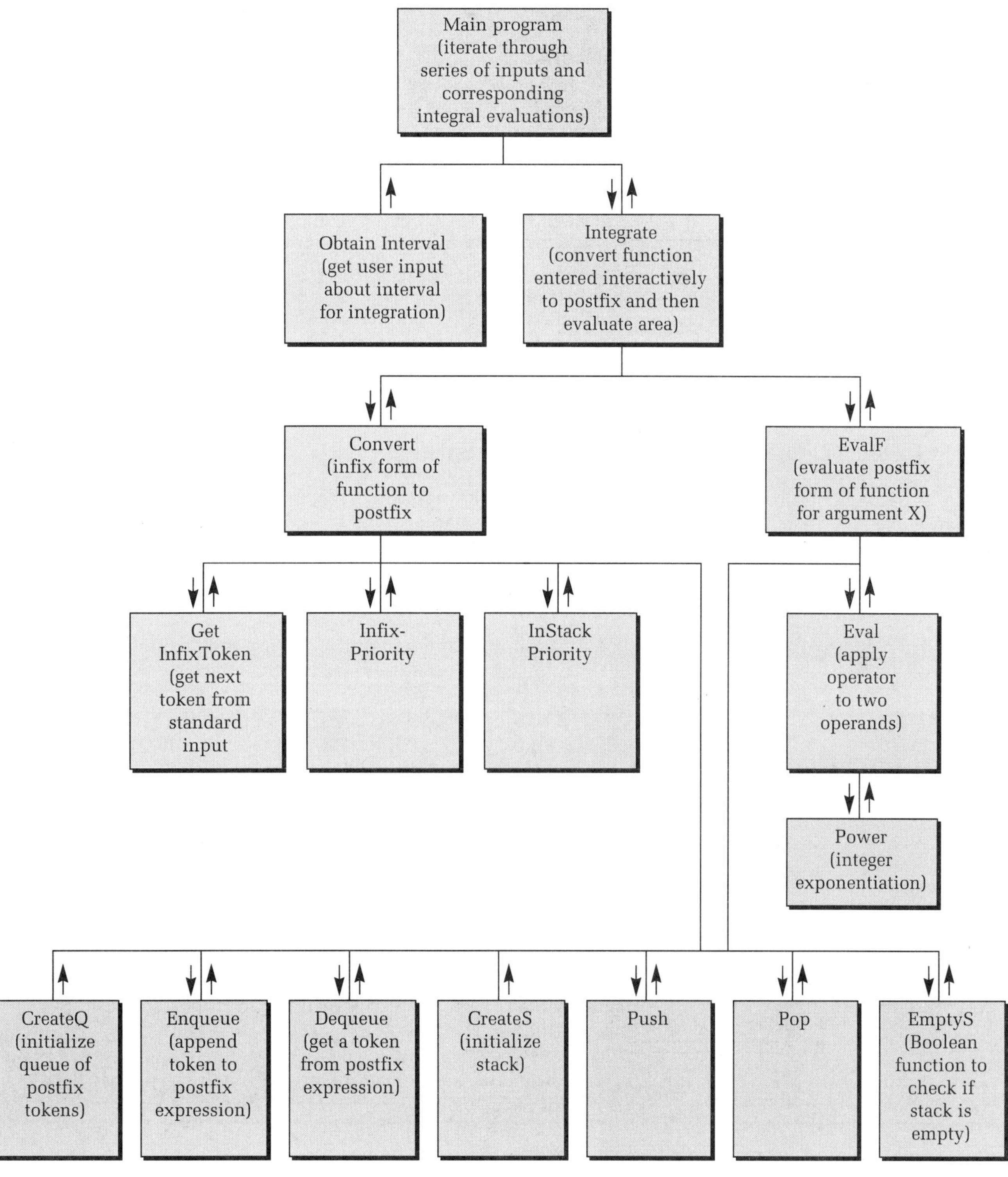

Given these declarations, an appropriate data structure for the postfix expression is a queue whose elements are of type TokenRec.

The final data structure needed by our program is a stack. Actually, two conceptual stacks are needed: one for operator symbols during the parsing phase and one for values during the evaluation phase. However, by making TokenRec the base data type of items in the stack, we can use just one stack structure for both of the conceptual stacks that are needed.

The module specifications for the integral evaluation problem posed by the head of the physics department follow.

1. Main Program Module
   Logic: Repeatedly call on modules to obtain input specifications and then evaluate integral.
2. ObtainInterval Module
   Data received: None
   Information returned: Interval endpoints a and b
   NumberOfRectangles to use in approximating area
   Logic: Issue appropriate prompts and read user input.
   Terminate when $a >= b$.
3. Integrate Module
   Data received: Endpoints a and b
   NumberOfRectangles for which area is to be accumulated
   Information returned: Approximation to area under graph of function entered interactively by user
   Logic: Compute Width of each rectangle as
   $(b - a)$/Number of Rectangles.
   Call on module Convert to convert Infix expression read from standard input to Postfix notation.
   Initialize Area to zero.
   Repeatedly evaluate f at the midpoint of the base of the current rectangle, multiply this by the width of the base, add resulting product to Area accumulation.
4. Convert Module
   Data received: Nothing
   Information returned: Postfix queue of TokenRec records, delimited by '#', corresponding to what user enters from standard input
   Logic: Follow algorithm described in Section 5.2 of text.
5. GetInfixToken Module {*Note:* This module responsible for lexical analysis.}
   Data received: Infix expression being read from standard input
   Information returned: FromInfix, a TokenRec containing the next token read from standard input
   Logic: {*Note:* We assume all tokens separated by one space.}
   Initialize Value field of FromInfix to zero.
   {In case token is a real number.}
   REPEAT
   Let c be next character read from standard input

CASE *c* **OF**

1. *c* is a space: We are done.
2. *c* is a 'X': Set FromInfix to *c*.
3. *c* is '+', '−', '*', '/', '^', '(', ')', '#':
   Set FromInfix to *c*.
4. *c* is decimal point: Set a Multiplier to 0.1 for future accumulation.
5. *c* is a digit:
   IF left of decimal **THEN** Set Value to
   10 * Value plus numeric form of *c*.
   ELSE Set Value to Value +
   Multiplier times numeric form of *c*.
   Divide Multiplier by 10 for next iteration.

UNTIL *c* is a space

6. <u>InfixPriority Module</u>
   Data received: *t,* a TokenRec record
   Information returned: Infix priority rank of *t*.
   Logic: See Section 5.2 of text.
7. <u>InStackPriority Module</u>
   Data received: *t,* a TokenRec record
   Information returned: InStack priority rank of *t*
   Logic: See Section 5.2 of text.
8. <u>EvalF Module</u>
   Data received: Postfix queue representation of function *f*
   x, the real number at which *f* is to be evaluated
   Information returned: The real number *f*(*x*)
   Logic: See evaluation algorithm in Section 5.2 of text.
9. <u>Eval Module</u>
   Data received: v1, v2: the values of two operands
   Op: character containing operator +, −, *, /, ^
   Information returned: Numeric result of applying Op to v1 and v2.
   Logic: Select the appropriate Pascal operation based on Op.
10. <u>Power Module</u>
    Data received: *b,* a base, and *p,* an integer exponent
    Information returned: b^p
    Logic: Use loop to perform appropriate number of multiplications.

In addition to these specific modules, we will need a package of procedures for stack and queue operations. To avoid name clashes between the Create, Empty, and Full operations for these ADTs, we shall use CreateS, EmptyS, and FullS for stack operations and CreateQ, EmptyQ, and FullQ for the corresponding queue operations.

The complete Pascal program for the integral evaluation system follows, with reference to the module specifications. Also included are graphic documentation and sample runs to give you a more detailed grasp of how the program functions in its interaction with a user.

```
PROGRAM TakeIntegral (input, output);

  {  Program to compute area under curve of function entered        }
  {  interactively.  A stack is used to convert function expression to  }
  {  postfix notation (which is stored in a queue) and then to          }
```

```
{  evaluate.  Valid function expressions can contain the variable X,  }
{  numeric constants, operators +, -, *, /, ^ (for                    }
{  exponentiation) and appropriate parentheses.                       }

CONST
  EndToken = '#'; {  End token corresponding to algorithm             }
                  {  described in text                                }

VAR
  A, B : real;
  NumberOfRectangles : integer;
  Area : real;

{ ******************************************************************** }

  PROCEDURE ObtainInterval (VAR A, B : real;
                            VAR NumberOfRectangles : integer);

    {  Given:   Nothing.                                               }
    {  Task:    Issue prompts, obtain user input regarding interval    }
    {           of integration.                                        }
    {  Return:  Interval endpoints A  and B.  NumberOfRectangles,      }
    {           the number of rectangular areas to accumulate in       }
    {           approximating the area.                                }

    VAR                                                                  2
      K : integer;

    BEGIN
      write ('Enter left and right endpoints (left >= right to quit)--> ');
      readln (A, B);
      IF A < B THEN
        BEGIN
          write ('Enter number of rectangles for computing area--> ');
          readln (NumberOfRectangles)
        END
    END; { of PROCEDURE ObtainInterval }

{ ******************************************************************** }

  PROCEDURE Integrate (A, B : real;
                       NumberOfRectangles : integer;
                       VAR Area : real);

    {  Given:   Parameters for interval of integration:  interval      }
    {           endpoints A and B, NumberOfRectangles to accumulate    }
    {           in approximating area.                                 }
    {  Task:    Approximate area under interactively entered function  }
    {           between A and B.                                       }
    {  Return:  Approximated area.                                     }

    TYPE
      TokenType = (RealValue, VarX, Operator);
                  { Number, X, or operator/paren }
      TokenRec = RECORD
                   CASE Token : TokenType OF
                     RealValue :
                       (Value : real);                                   3
                     VarX :
                       (XChar : char);
                     Operator :
                       (OpChar : char)
                 END;
```

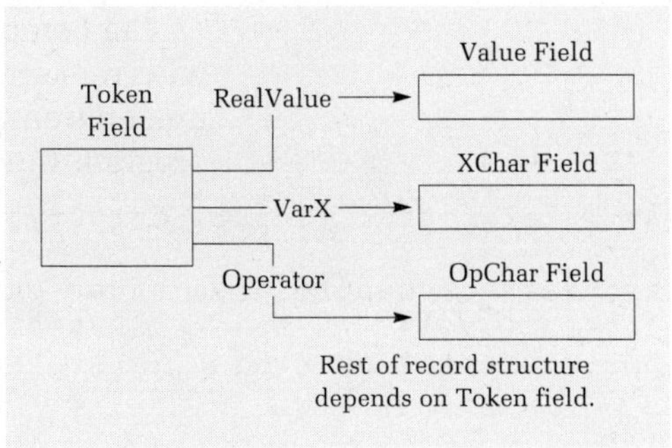

Token Field

RealValue → Value Field

VarX → XChar Field

Operator → OpChar Field

Rest of record structure depends on Token field.

```
    StackData = TokenRec;
    Stack = { A hidden implementation of the stack ADT }
    QueueData = TokenRec;
    Queue = { A hidden implementation of the queue ADT }
    PfString = Queue;    { To store postfix form of infix expression }

  VAR
    TokenStack : Stack;
    Postfix : PfString;
    Count : integer;
    Width, X : real;

{ ********************************************************************** }

     { Stack and queue operations here.  To avoid name clashes          }
     { stack operations are CreateS, EmptyS, and FullS.  Queue          }
     { operations referenced by CreateQ, EmptyQ, and FullQ.             }

{ ********************************************************************** }

  PROCEDURE Convert (VAR Postfix : PfString);

    {  Given:   Infix expression being entered from standard input    }
    {  Task:    Apply parsing algorithm of Section 5.2                }
    {           to infix expression.                                  }
    {  Return:  Postfix, a queue of tokens representing the           }
    {           function in postfix notation.                         }

    VAR
      BottomStack, FromStack, FromInfix : TokenRec;

    PROCEDURE GetInfixToken (VAR FromInfix : TokenRec);

      {  Given:   Nothing.                                          }
      {  Task:    Get the next token from standard input.           }
      {  Return:  This next token in FromInfix.                     }

    CONST Space = ' ';

    VAR
      C : char;
      Multiplier : real;
      LeftOfDecimal : boolean;

    BEGIN
      FromInfix.Value := 0;
      LeftOfDecimal := true;
      REPEAT
        IF NOT eoln THEN
          read (C)
        ELSE
          C := EndToken;
        CASE C OF
          '.':              {  Encountered decimal point  }
            BEGIN
              LeftOfDecimal := false;
              Multiplier := 1.0E-1
            END;
          '+', '-', '*', '/', '^', '(', ')',
          EndToken :      { Operator }
```

4

5

3.14
↑
We are currently here. Must prepare to accumulate digits to right of decimal.

```
        BEGIN
          FromInfix.Token := Operator;
          FromInfix.OpChar := C
        END;
      '0', '1', '2', '3', '4', '5', '6', '7', '8', '9' :
        BEGIN
          FromInfix.Token := RealValue;
          IF LeftOfDecimal THEN
            FromInfix.Value := FromInfix.Value * 10.0 + (ord(C) -
                                 ord('0'))
          ELSE
            BEGIN
              FromInfix.Value := FromInfix.Value +
                                  (ord(C) - ord('0')) * Multiplier;
              Multiplier := Multiplier / 10.0
            END
        END;
      'X' :                                      {  Variable X  }
        BEGIN
          FromInfix.Token := VarX;
          FromInfix.XChar := C
        END;
      Space :       {  Blank signals end of current token.     }
        BEGIN       {  So we do nothing.                        }
        END
    END {  CASE  }
  UNTIL eoln OR (C = Space) OR (C = EndToken);
  IF C = EndToken THEN
    readln
END; {  of PROCEDURE GetInfixToken  }
```

23.14
For digits to left of decimal, must multiply accumulated value by 10 and add digit.

23.14
For digits to right of decimal, add digit scaled to appropriate decimal value by Multiplier.
{ Digit }

```
{ ************************************************************************ }

    FUNCTION InfixPriority(T : TokenRec) : integer;

      {  Given:   T, a token read from the infix form of the          }
      {           function being integrated.                           }
      {  Task:    Determine infix priority value of T.                 }
      {  Return:  The infix priority value.                            }

      BEGIN
        CASE T.OpChar OF
          '^' :
            InfixPriority := 3;
          '*', '/' :
            InfixPriority := 2;
          '+', '-' :
            InfixPriority := 1;
          '(' :
            InfixPriority := 4;
          ')', EndToken :
            InfixPriority := 0
        END
      END;

{ ************************************************************************ }

    FUNCTION InStackPriority(T : TokenRec) : integer;

      {  Given:   A token T on the operator stack.                     }
      {  Task:    Determine in-stack priority of T.                    }
      {  Return:  The in-stack priority.                               }
```

6

```
      BEGIN
        CASE T.OpChar OF
          '^' :
            InStackPriority := 3;
          '*', '/' :                                                      7
            InStackPriority := 2;
          '+', '-' :
            InStackPriority := 1;
          '(', EndToken :
            InStackPriority := 0
        END
      END; {  of FUNCTION InStackPriority  }

{ ************************************************************************ }

    BEGIN {  Convert  }
      CreateS (TokenStack);
      {  CreateS must push EndToken to correspond with algorithm in Section 5.2 }
      BottomStack.Token := Operator;
      BottomStack.OpChar := EndToken;
      CreateQ (PostFix);
      writeln ('Enter function with spaces between tokens, then <RETURN>');
      REPEAT
        GetInfixToken(FromInfix);
        IF (FromInfix.Token = RealValue) OR (FromInfix.Token = VarX) THEN
          {  We have an operand -- variable or number.  }
          Enqueue (Postfix, FromInfix)
        ELSE IF FromInfix.OpChar = ')' THEN
          BEGIN
            Pop(TokenStack, FromStack);
            WHILE FromStack.OpChar <> '(' DO
              BEGIN
                Enqueue (Postfix, FromStack);
                Pop(TokenStack, FromStack)
              END
          END
        ELSE IF FromInfix.OpChar = EndToken THEN
          WHILE NOT EmptyS (TokenStack) DO
            BEGIN
              Pop(TokenStack, FromStack);
              Enqueue (Postfix, FromStack)
            END
        ELSE
          { We have one of arithmetic operators +, -, *, /, ^  or ) }
          BEGIN
            Pop(TokenStack, FromStack);
            WHILE InStackPriority(FromStack) >=
                  InfixPriority(FromInfix) DO
              BEGIN
                Enqueue (Postfix, FromStack);
                Pop(TokenStack, FromStack)
              END;
            Push(TokenStack, FromStack);
            Push(TokenStack, FromInfix)
          END
      UNTIL (FromInfix.Token = Operator) AND
            (FromInfix.OpChar = EndToken)
    END; {  of PROCEDURE Convert  }

{ ************************************************************************ }

  FUNCTION EvalF(Postfix : PfString;
                 X : real) : real;
```

```
    {  Given:   Postfix, containing the postfix form of the        }
    {           function to be integrated, and X, a point          }   8
    {           at which the function is to be evaluated.          }
    {  Task:    Evaluate the function at X.                        }
    {  Return:  Result of the evaluation.                          }

    VAR
      T, T1, T2, T3 : TokenRec;

{   *****************************************************************   }

    FUNCTION Eval(V1, V2 : real;
                  Op : char) : real;

      {  Given:   Two real operands, V1 and V2, and an             }   9
      {           arithmetic operator Op.                          }
      {  Task:    Apply operator to the two operands.              }
      {  Return:  Result of the application.                       }

{   *****************************************************************   }

      FUNCTION Power(B : real;
                     P : integer) : real;

        {  Given:   B, a real representing a base, and P, an       }
        {           integer exponent.                              }
        {  Task:    Evaluate B raised to the power P.              }
        {  Return:  Result of the evaluation.                      }

        VAR
          Prod : real;
          K : integer;

        BEGIN                                                          10
          Prod := 1;
          K := 1;
          WHILE K <= P DO
            BEGIN
              Prod := Prod * B;
              K := K + 1
            END;
          Power := Prod
        END; {  of FUNCTION Power  }

{ ********************************************************************** }

      BEGIN {  Eval  }
        CASE Op OF
          '+' :
            Eval := V1 + V2;
          '-' :
            Eval := V1 - V2;
          '*' :
            Eval := V1 * V2;
          '/' :
            Eval := V1 / V2;
          '^' :
            Eval := Power(V1, round(V2))
        END {  CASE  }
      END; {  of FUNCTION Eval  }

{ ********************************************************************** }
```

```
    BEGIN { EvalF }
      CreateS (TokenStack); {  Will push EndToken  }
      Dequeue (Postfix, T1);
      { Put token back into queue for next call to EvalF            }
      Enqueue (Postfix, T1);
      {  We're done when encounter operator that is                 }
      {  EndToken.  Just testing for EndToken not enough            }
      {  because coincidentally we could get match for              }
      {  EndToken when not an operator.                             }
      WHILE (T1.Token <> Operator) OR (T1.OpChar <> EndToken) DO
        BEGIN
          IF T1.Token <> Operator THEN
            IF T1.Token = RealValue THEN
              Push(TokenStack, T1)
            ELSE
              BEGIN
                T1.Token := RealValue;
                T1.Value := X;
                Push(TokenStack, T1)
              END
          ELSE
            BEGIN
              Pop(TokenStack, T2);
              Pop(TokenStack, T3);
              T.Token := RealValue;
              T.Value := Eval(T3.Value, T2.Value, T1.OpChar);
              Push(TokenStack, T)
            END;
          Dequeue (Postfix, T1);
          { Put token back into queue for next call to EvalF }
          Enqueue (postfix, T1)
        END;
      Pop(TokenStack, T);
      EvalF := T.Value
    END; {  of FUNCTION EvalF  }

{ ************************************************************************** }


  BEGIN {  Integrate  }
    Width := (B - A) / NumberOfRectangles;
    Count := 0;
    X := A;
    Area := 0;
    Convert(Postfix);
    WHILE Count < NumberOfRectangles DO
      BEGIN
        Area := Area + EvalF(Postfix, X + Width / 2.0) * Width;
        X := X + Width;
        Count := Count + 1
      END
  END; {  of PROCEDURE Integrate  }
```

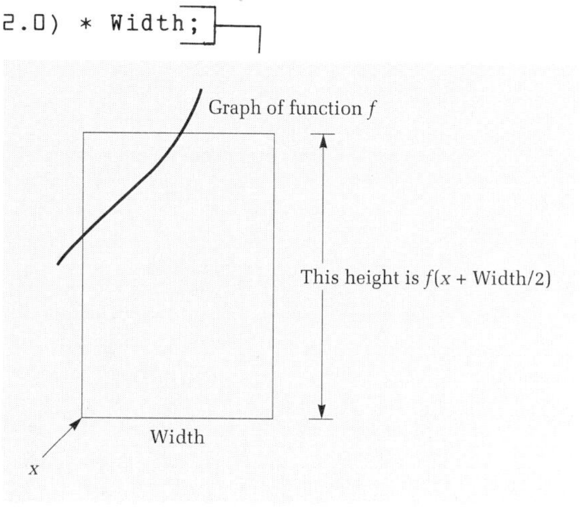

Graph of function f

This height is $f(x + \text{Width}/2)$

Width

x

```
{ ************************************************************************* }

  BEGIN { Main program }
    ObtainInterval(A, B, NumberOfRectangles);
    WHILE A < B DO
      BEGIN
        Integrate(A, B, NumberOfRectangles, Area);
        writeln ('Approximation to area is ', Area: 10 : 3);
        writeln;
        ObtainInterval(A, B, NumberOfRectangles)
      END
  END.
```

```
Sample runs

Enter left and right endpoints (left >= right to quit)--> 0 3
Enter number of rectangles for computing area--> 10
Enter function with spaces between tokens, then <RETURN>
3
Approximation to area is      9.000

Enter left and right endpoints (left >= right to quit)--> 0 3
Enter number of rectangles for computing area--> 10
Enter function with spaces between tokens, then <RETURN>
X ^ 2
Approximation to area is      8.978

Enter left and right endpoints (left >= right to quit)--> 0 3
Enter number of rectangles for computing area--> 100
Enter function with spaces between tokens, then <RETURN>
X ^ 2
Approximation to area is      9.000

Enter left and right endpoints (left >= right to quit)--> 0 1
Enter number of rectangles for computing area--> 100
Enter function with spaces between tokens, then <RETURN>
( X + 2 ) ^ 3 / ( X + 1 )
Approximation to area is     10.526

Enter left and right endpoints (left >= right to quit)--> 0 0
```

RUNNING AND DEBUGGING TIPS

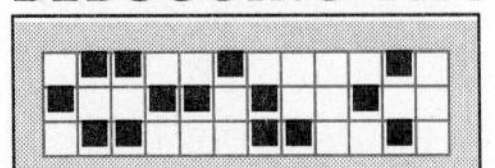

1. In applications in which the size to which a stack or queue may grow is hard to predict, use a linked list to implement the ADT. That way, you can take advantage of Pascal's dynamic memory management to avoid having to worry about a full data structure.
2. Many scientific and mathematical application programs can be enhanced by allowing users to enter function definitions at run-time. This chapter's Focus on Program Design section provides an example of how such run-time definitions of a function can be done.
3. When debugging simulations, use a random number sequence that remains the same over different runs of the program. Without such a sequence, your program will behave differently on separate runs even though you provide it with identical inputs. This is because you are getting a different pattern of random numbers. Appendix 9 indicates how you can ensure a fixed sequence of random numbers from one run of the program to the next.

Summary

Key Terms

blocked queue
first-in, first-out (FIFO)
front pointer
infix
infix priority
last-in, first-out (LIFO)
lexical analysis
numerical analysis
parsing
pop
postfix
prefix
priority queue
push
queue
random number generator
ready queue
rear pointer
semaphores
simulation
stack
stack priority
tokens
top

Key Concepts

- Conceptually, a stack is simpler than a queue since all additions and deletions are limited to one end of the structure, the top. For this reason, a stack is also known as a last-in, first-out (LIFO) list. Like a queue, a stack may be implemented using either an array or a linked list.
- The simplicity of the stack as an abstract structure belies the importance of its application. Stacks play a crucial role in the parsing done by language compilers.
- Parsing, as we have studied it in this chapter, involves the conversion of an expression from infix to postfix notation. In infix notation, an algebraic operator is located between its two operands. In postfix notation, the operator follows its two operands.
- Expressions in postfix notation do not require parentheses to override the standard hierarchy of algebraic operations.
- Stacks process procedure calls when a program executes.
- A queue is a first-in, first-out (FIFO) data structure used in processing of data such as job scheduling in a large university computer environment. There are two basic pointers, Front and Rear, associated with this structure. New data items are added to the rear of the queue, and the data item that is about to be processed is removed from the front of the queue.
- The relative advantages and disadvantages of three implementations of queues—array, circular array, and linked list—are summarized in the following table.

Implementation	Advantages	Disadvantages
Array	A record of queue entries entries remains even after they have been removed.	Static allocation of storage limits overall queue size. Array locations cannot be reused once entries are removed from queue.
Circular Array	Array locations can be reused once entries are removed from the queue.	Static allocation of storage limits overall queue size.
Linked List	With Pascal pointer variables, the queue can grow dynamically to take full advantage of all space available in Pascal's heap.	Could be less space-efficient than array implementations since each node in queue must include a pointer field as well as data fields.

- Primary applications of queues are in the areas of operating systems and computer simulation of events.

■ Programming Problems and Projects

1. Write a program that will parse infix expressions into prefix form.
2. Write a program to call for input of a decimal number and convert it to its binary equivalent using the method described in the following flowchart.

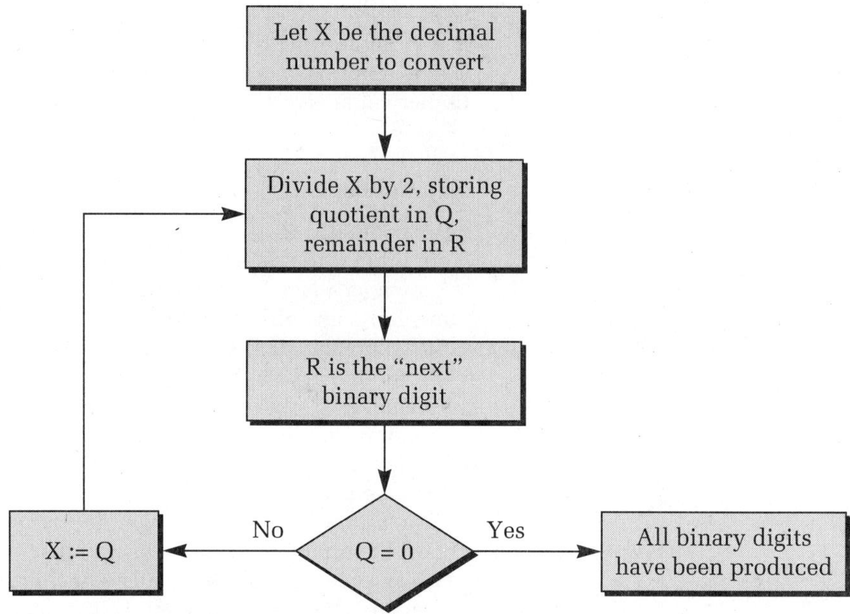

Note that this method produces the binary digits for the given number in reverse order. Use a stack to get them printed in the correct order.

3. In the Programming Problem 2 for Chapter 4, you developed a passenger list processing system for the various flights of Wing-and-a-Prayer Airlines. Wing-and-a-Prayer management would now like you to extend this system so that it processes logical combinations of flight numbers. For example, the command

```
LIST 1 OR 2
```

should list all passengers whose name appears on the flight 1 list or the flight 2 list. Your program should also accept the logical operators **AND** and **NOT** and allow parenthesized logical expressions obeying the standard logical hierarchy

NOT
AND
OR

4. A tax form may be thought of as a sequence of items, each of which is either a number or defined by an arbitrary mathematical formula involving other items in the sequence. To assist them in their tax-planning strategy, top management at the Fly-by-Night credit card company desire a program that would allow them to interactively enter numbers or formulas associated with given lines of a tax form. Once all such lines have been defined, users of the program may redefine the number or formula associated with a particular line, and all other lines dependent on that one should be appropriately updated.

Note that, since formulas may be entered interactively, your program will have to use a stack to evaluate them. You will in effect have written a small-scale spreadsheet program.

5. Write a program that will accept commands of the following form:

- **INPUT** ⟨variable name⟩
- ⟨variable name⟩ = infix expression involving variables names and arithmetic operators +, −, *, /
- **PRINT** ⟨variable name⟩
- **GO**

These commands are to be stored in an array of strings until the **GO** command is entered. Once the **GO** command is entered, your program should execute the previously stored commands. "Execute" here means

- For an **INPUT** command: Send a question mark to the terminal and allow the user to enter a real number; this real number is then stored in the variable name.
- For an assignment statement: Parse the expression into postfix form and then evaluate it, storing the results in the variable name on the left of the equality sign.
- For a **PRINT** instruction: Write to the terminal the numerical contents of the specified variable name.

To make things relatively easy you may assume a syntax that

- Allows variable names consisting of one uppercase alphabetical character.
- Allows only one variable name following the commands for **INPUT** or **PRINT**.
- Allows one blank space after the commands for **INPUT** and **PRINT** and no blank spaces anywhere else.

For an additional challenge, enable your program to handle successfully the exponentiation operator ^ within assignment statement expressions. The following example should illustrate the need for care in handling this exponentiation operator:

$3^{2^3} = 3^8$, not 9^3

6. This problem is an extension of Problem 5 for a "compiler" for a primitive programming language. Write a program that will accept commands of the following form:

- **INPUT** ⟨variable name⟩
- **PRINT** ⟨variable name⟩
- ⟨variable name⟩ = infix arithmetic expression involving variable names and arithmetic operators +, −, *, /, ^
- **GOTO** ⟨line⟩ { **ALWAYS**, or
IF infix logical expression involving variable names and operators +, −, *, /, ^, & (for **AND**), ! (for **OR**), ~ (for **NOT**), <, >, = }
- **STOP**
- **RUN**

These commands are to be stored in an array of strings until the **RUN** command is entered. Upon encountering the **RUN** command, your program should execute the previously stored commands. "Execute" here means:

- For an **INPUT** command: Send a question mark to the terminal and allow the user to enter a real number, which is stored in the variable name.
- For a **PRINT** command: Write to the terminal the numerical contents of the specified variable name.
- For an assignment command: Parse the expression into postfix form and then evaluate it. Store the result in the variable name on the left of the equality sign.
- For a **GOTO** command: Branch to the line number specified when the **ALWAYS** condition follows the line number or when the infix expression that follows the **IF** evaluates to true. Here "line number" refers to the relative position of the line in the sequence of lines that were entered prior to the Run command. The first line number in this sequence is "00".
- For a **STOP** command: Halt execution.

To make things relatively easy, you may assume a syntax that

- Specifies that one and only one blank space follows **INPUT**, **PRINT**, **GOTO**, and line number. No other blanks appear anywhere.
- Allows only one variable name to follow **INPUT** or **PRINT**.
- Only allows variable names consisting of one uppercase alphabetical character.
- Only allows line numbers consisting of two digits: 00 through 99.

The usual hierarchy for operators is assumed.

7. Modify **PROGRAM** TakeIntegral (Focus on Program Design section) so that it also integrates expressions involving the functions **sin, cos, tan, exp,** and **ln.** Test your modified program by having it evaluate the following integrals:
   a. **sin** (X * 2) + **cos** X / 2 between 0 and 1
   b. 3 * (X + 4) ^ 2 + **tan** (X / 2) between 0 and 1
   c. 3 * (X + 4) ^ 2 + **tan** X / 2 between 0 and 1
   d. **exp ln** X ^ 3 between 1 and 3
   e. **exp ln** (X ^ 3) between 1 and 3
8. If you have access to a graphics library in your version of Pascal, write a program that allows a user to interactively define a function and then displays a graph of the function between two specified endpoints.
9. Develop a program to simulate the processing of batch jobs by a computer system. The scheduling of these jobs should be handled via a queue (or priority queue for more of a challenge). Examples of commands that your program should be able to process are

Command	Purpose
Add	To add an entry to queue.
Delete	To take an item out of the queue.
Status	To report on items currently in queue.

10. A bank has asked you to develop a program to simulate the arrival of customers in a waiting line at the bank. Factors to consider are the average time it takes to service one customer, the average number of customers that arrive in a given time period, and the number of service windows maintained by the bank. These factors should be provided as input to your program. Statistics such as the length of time the average customer has to spend in the waiting line could be very helpful in the bank's future planning.

11. Here is a problem typically encountered in text formatting applications.

    Given a file of text, that text delimited by special bracketing symbols [and] is to be considered a footnote. Footnotes, when encountered, are not to be printed as normal text but are instead stored in a footnote queue. Then, when the special symbol # is encountered, all footnotes currently in the queue are printed and the queue should be returned to an empty state.

    What you learn in solving this problem will allow you to make good use of string storage techniques discussed in earlier chapters.

12. In order to improve their services, the Fly-by-Night credit card company (Problem 3, Chapter 4) has decided to give incentives to their customers for prompt payment. Customers who pay their bills two weeks before the due date receive top priority and a 5 percent discount. Customers who pay their bills within one week of the due date receive next priority and a 1 percent discount. Third priority is given to customers who pay their bills on or within two days after the due date. The customers who pay their bills thereafter are assigned the lowest priority. Write a program to set up a priority queue to access customer records accordingly.

13. The Bay Area Brawlers professional football team (Problem 4, Chapter 4) has been so successful in recent weeks that the team management is considering the addition of several new ticket windows at the team's stadium. However, before investing a sizable amount of money in such an improvement, they would like to simulate the operation of ticket sales with a variety of ticket window configurations. Develop a computer program that allows input of such data as number of ticket windows, average number of fans arriving each hour as game time approaches, and average length of time to process a ticket sale. Output from your program should include statistics such as the average waiting-line length each hour as game time approaches and the amount of time the average fan had to wait in line before having his or her ticket request processed. Use queues to represent each of the waiting lines.

14. Consider the design for an implementation of the radix sort algorithm and its associated bin (sublist) structure that was discussed in Chapter 4's Focus on Program Design section. Note that queues could provide an alternative implementation for the bin structure needed by radix sort. What queue implementation would provide the most space-efficient bin structure for radix sort? Why? Develop a complete radix sort program that uses queues to implement the bins needed by the algorithm and then accesses these bins *only* through the defined ADT operations for a queue.

Is this implementation of radix sort more or less time efficient than that described in Chapter 4's Focus on Program Design section? Justify your answer in a written memorandum.

15. As Director of Computer Operations for Wing-And-A-Prayer Airlines, you receive the following memorandum. Design and write a simulation program according to the specifications in the memorandum.

> MEMORANDUM
> Wing-and-a-Prayer Airlines
>
> TO: Director of Computer Operations
> FROM: President, Wing-and-a-Prayer Airlines
> DATE: September 30, 1996
> RE: Wasted Fuel and Time
>
> Wing-and-a-Prayer Airlines is becoming increasingly concerned about the amount of fuel being wasted as its planes wait to land at and take off from world-famous O'Hair Airport. Could you please help us write a program to simulate the operation of one day's activity at O'Hair and report on the times spent waiting to land and take off for each Wing-and-a-Prayer flight? Input data to the program should include
>
> - Average number of Wing-and-a-Prayer arrivals each hour
> - Average number of other airline arrivals each hour
> - Average number of Wing-and-a-Prayer departures each hour
> - Average number of other airline departures each hour
> - Number of available runways
> - Average time runway in use for an arrival
> - Average time runway in use for a departure
>
> By appropriately adjusting these parameters, we hope to do some valuable "what-if" analyses regarding the time spent waiting for a runway by our arrivals and departures.

16. If an arithmetic expression is written in prefix notation, then there is no need to use parentheses to specify the order of operators. For this reason, some compilers translate infix expressions (such as 2 + 8) to prefix notation (+ 2 8) first and then evaluate the prefix string.

Write a program that will read prefix expressions and then compute and display the value of the indicated arithmetic expression. Assume that the operands are single-digit positive integers separated by blanks. The operators can be +, −, *, and /, also separated by blanks and having their usual meanings of add, subtract, multiply, and divide.

17. Implement the following robustness enhancements for **PROGRAM** TakeIntegral in this chapter's Focus on Program Design section.
    a. Make the GetInfixToken module more robust by allowing the user to separate individual tokens with an arbitrary number of zero or more spaces.
    b. Make the GetInfixToken module more robust by guarding against input of an invalid arithmetic operator.

c. Make the GetInfixToken module more robust by guarding against an invalid character in a stream of characters intended to be a real number. When such an invalid character is detected, allow the user to recover from the point of error rather than forcing the user to retype the entire line.

18. This chapter's Note of Interest on "Computer Simulations: Blessing or Curse?" cites two issues of the *Communications of the ACM* that have been dedicated to the topic of simulation. Using these two issues as a starting point, research and prepare a written report on computer simulation. Your report could discuss any or all of the following:
   a. Examples of disciplines and industries in which simulation has been used to great advantage.
   b. Limitations and inaccuracies that arise in modeling a system by computer simulation. Techniques that can be used to measure and monitor such inaccuracies.
   c. The reliance of many simulation programs on the effective generation of random numbers.
   d. The potential danger in relying on the results of simulation programs without examining the validity of their underlying models.

19. This chapter's Focus on Program Design section demonstrated how a computer program can be used to solve a mathematical problem in interactive fashion. In particular, the type of problem solved by this program is the evaluation of integrals. Explore other types of mathematical problems that can be solved interactively by software systems available at your school. (The *Mathematica* program from Wolfram Research is one example of such a system available at many universities.)

    Prepare a report on the results of your explorations. In keeping with the theme of this chapter's Focus on Program Design section, be sure that your report includes a discussion of the types of mathematical expressions that can be parsed and evaluated by such systems.

It's déjà vu all over again.
Lawrence Peter (Yogi) Berra

Research is the process of going up alleys to see if they are blind.
Marston Bates

More about Recursion

Recall that Pascal allows a procedure or function to call itself. In computer science this form of self-reference is called *recursion*.

In many introductory programming courses and textbooks the first examples of problems solved using recursion are often better suited to nonrecursive solutions that use iterative control structures such as **WHILE, REPEAT,** and **FOR** loops. As a result, recursion appears to be an alternative way of doing something that could be done by other iterative control strategies. There are, however, many complex problems for which recursion presents the most natural and elegant solution. We are now ready to embark on the detailed study of such problems.

In this chapter, we will first review the essentials of recursive procedures. Now that we are familiar with stack operations, we will also be able to explain more completely how recursion is implemented. The "invisible" data structure underlying *recursive procedures* is the stack used by the system to process the call-and-return pattern of procedures in a program (Section 5.1). By examining the role of this system stack more closely, you will build confidence in your ability to express algorithms recursively. In time, you will use this technique without hesitation in your problem-solving.

Then we will begin to use recursion to explore problems for which nonrecursive solutions would be exceedingly difficult to fathom. We hope that you will be amazed at the ease with which recursion handles such problems. We will demonstrate that recursion is a natural and elegant way to solve many complex problems. We will also begin to explore the price paid for this elegance: the compactness of a recursive solution to a complex problem is not necessarily an accurate statement of its time or space efficiency.

Finally, we will use recursion to develop a problem-solving methodology known as *trial-and-error,* or non-deterministic, *backtracking.* In theory this technique can solve a large variety of problems. Unfortunately, in practice, the technique is so computationally expensive that it can only be used to solve small instances of such problems in a reasonable amount of time.

■ 6.1 A Closer Look at Controlling Simple Iteration with Recursion

OBJECTIVES

- to review the essentials of controlling simple iteration by recursion.
- to be able to identify and distinguish tail-recursive algorithms.
- to understand what is meant by the stack frame associated with a procedure or function call
- to understand the role of the system stack in processing calls made to a recursive procedure, particularly a procedure that is not tail-recursive
- to be able to trace the contents of the system stack during execution of recursive procedures with only one embedded recursive call

Recall that any recursive algorithm must have a well-defined stopping state, or *termination condition.* Without careful logical control by means of such conditions, recursive procedures can fall prey to looping in endless circles. To illustrate this, let us suppose that we have access to an output device known as a pen plotter. Such a device is equipped with a pen held by a mechanical hand that is under control of the computer.

Typical procedures to manipulate the pen could include

Procedure	Action
Line(n)	Draw a line of length n in the current direction.
RightTurn(d)	Alter current direction by rotating d degrees in clockwise direction.

Such procedures are not unlike those found in the Logo programming language or the "turtle" graphics tool kits that accompany many popular Pascal compilers. If you have access to such a compiler, you may wish to explore developing some recursive graphic figures.

If we assume that the pen is initially set to draw a line toward the north—the top of the plotting page—then the sequence of instructions

```
Line(10);
RightTurn(90);
Line(10);
RightTurn(90);
Line(10);
RightTurn(90);
Line(10);
```

will clearly draw a square with sides of length 10.

Let us now try to predict what will happen when the following recursive procedure Draw is invoked by the initial call Draw(1).

```
PROCEDURE Draw(Side : integer);

  BEGIN
    Line(Side);
    RightTurn(90);
    Draw(Side + 3) {  Recursive call  }
  END;
```

The initial call Draw(1) will result in a line of length 1 in a northerly direction. We then rotate the pen toward the east and, via a recursive call, generate a line of length 4. This is followed by a rotation to the south and a new invocation for a line of length 7. The emerging pattern should now be clear; the resulting right-angled spiral is shown in Figure 6.1.

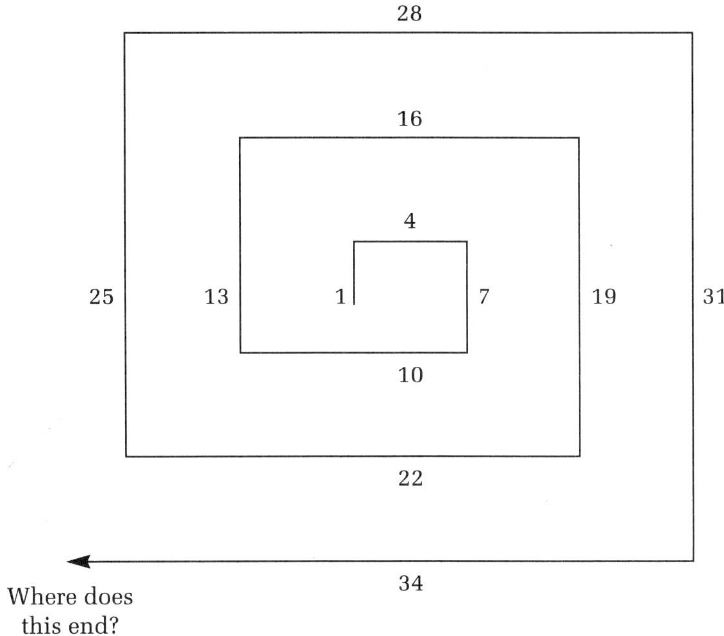

FIGURE 6.1
Runaway recursive spiral

Unfortunately, our spiral-producing procedure has tumbled into a vicious circle loop of self-reference. There presently is no way to turn off the *recursive calls* made to Draw. Consider what happens, however, if we provide ourselves with a *recursive termination condition* (or recursive out) as in the following new version of Draw.

```
PROCEDURE Draw(Side : integer);

  BEGIN
    IF Side <= 34 THEN {  Recursive termination condition  }
      BEGIN
        Line(Side);
        RightTurn(90);
        Draw(Side + 3)
      END
  END;
```

Now after drawing the line of length 34 in Figure 6.1, our procedure Draw invokes itself once more, passing 37 for the parameter Side. Since the recursive termination condition is now false, no line of length 37 will be drawn. More importantly, no further recursive invocation of Draw will be made. Hence, we return immediately from the call to Draw with Side being 37. Moreover, that return triggers returns (in reverse order) from all the previous invocations of Draw, eventually ending up at the instruction following our initial call; that is, Draw(1).

The important point to stress here is that, to appropriately use recursion, we must use a recursive termination condition to avoid an infinite series of recursive calls. If we were to view each recursive call as a descent one level deeper into an algorithm's logic, we in effect must use a recursive termination condition to allow a corresponding ascent back to the level of the first call to the procedure. This concept is highlighted in Figure 6.2.

FIGURE 6.2
Unwinding from descent through recursive calls

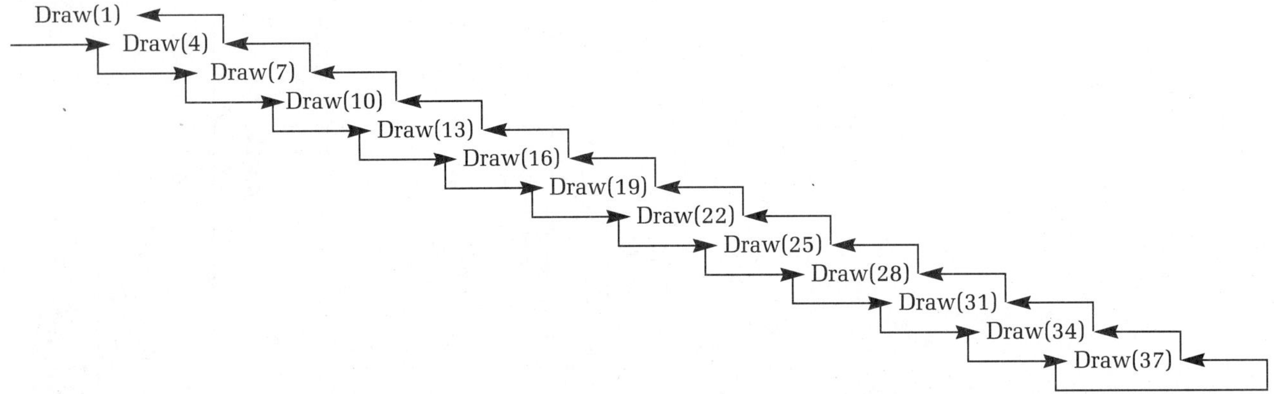

Linked Lists as Recursive Data Structures

In Section 4.1 we defined the linked list ADT. We can now reformulate that definition from a recursive perspective. The key to such a perspective is the realization that the pointer leading from each linked list node references another linked list. More formally:

> **Linked List.** A linked list is a pointer that is either *Null* (the recursive termination condition signaling an empty list) or references a node designated as the head node. The head node contains a data field and a pointer that satisfies the criteria for being a linked list.

Though an English composition teacher may find fault with our defining a linked list in terms of itself, our new definition is nonetheless completely free of ambiguity. For instance, to verify that the list in Figure 6.3 is a linked list, we note that:

1. The head node in the three-item structure contains a pointer to an embedded two-item structure, which we must verify as a linked list.
2. The head node in the two-item structure contains a pointer to an embedded one-item structure.
3. The head node in the one-node structure contains a Null pointer.
4. By the recursive termination condition, a Null pointer meets the criteria for being a linked list.
5. Hence the one-node structure in step 3 contains a pointer to a linked list and meets the criteria for being a linked list.
6. Similarly, we climb up the recursive ladder to verify that the two-node and, consequently, the three-node structures in steps 1 and 2 meet the criteria for being linked lists.

Not only does our recursive definition unambiguously specify the linked list ADT, but it also provides a natural way to implement linked list operations by recursive procedures. Consider the following example.

FIGURE 6.3
Recursive view of a linked list

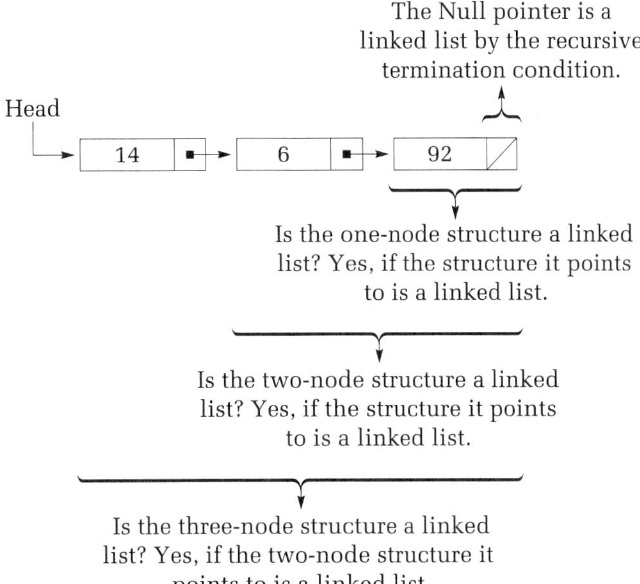

EXAMPLE 6.1

A linked list is implemented by Pascal pointer variables in the following declarations.

```
TYPE
  Pointer = ^LinkedListNode;
  LinkedListNode = RECORD
                     Data : LinkedListData;
                     Link : Pointer
                   END;
```

Develop a recursive implementation of the LinkedTraversal operation.

The implementation literally flows from our recursive definition of the linked list structure. That is, if the list we are traversing is empty there is nothing to do; otherwise we must process the data in the head node and recursively traverse the linked list referenced by the Link field in the head node. This logic is embodied in the following Pascal procedure.

```
PROCEDURE LinkedTraverse (Head : Pointer;
                          PROCEDURE ProcessNode (VAR Item : LinkedListData));

  {  Given:   Linked list referenced by Head pointer          }
  {  Task:    Traverse the list in the linear order           }
  {           determined by the links, applying the           }
  {           procedure ProcessNode to each record            }
  {           in the list                                     }
  {  Return:  The list referenced by Head with each node      }
  {           affected by ProcessNode                         }

  BEGIN
    IF Head <> NIL THEN    { the only condition under which action is taken }
      BEGIN
        ProcessNode (Head^.Data);
        LinkedTraverse (Head^.Link)
      END
  END;  { of PROCEDURE LinkedTraverse }
```

■

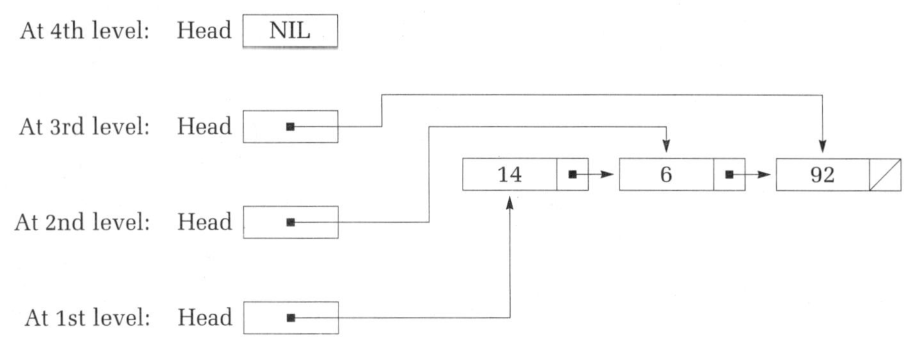

FIGURE 6.4
Trace of recursive LinkedTraverse on linked list of Figure 6.3

A trace of the recursive **PROCEDURE** LinkedTraverse for the list of Figure 6.3 is given in Figure 6.4. This trace shows that the procedure is initially called with a Head pointer to the node containing 14. The data are processed, and the first recursive call then passes in a Head pointer to the node containing 6. The data item 6 is processed, and a Head pointer to the node containing 92 is recursively passed to the procedure. The node containing 92 is processed, and a **NIL** head pointer is recursively passed to the procedure. Since the recursive termination condition (Head = **NIL**) is now met, we unwind from the series of recursive calls. As we return to each prior recursive level, there is nothing left to do since the recursive call is the last operation at that level.

A recursive procedure is called *tail-recursive* if only one recursive call appears in the procedure and that recursive call is the last operation performed at that procedural level. (That is, nothing else must be done after returning from a deeper recursive level.) The LinkedTraverse procedure of Example 6.1 is clearly tail-recursive. Typically, such a tail-recursive procedure can be easily recast in the form of a nonrecursive procedure using a **WHILE** or **REPEAT** control structure. We have already seen how to do this for LinkedTraverse in Chapter 4.

How Is Recursion Implemented?

As we begin to examine recursive algorithms that are not tail-recursive, we will also need to understand in detail *how* a computer language implements recursion. Here again we encounter the abstraction-implementation duality we have emphasized throughout the book. Recursion is a powerful conceptual tool. But unless you understand details of how recursion is implemented, your use of it will be limited to an intuitive approach that often employs a trial-and-error strategy to reach a solution.

In Section 5.1, we indicated that the stack is an essential data structure in a compiler's implementation of procedure calls. The role of a system stack being manipulated by the procedure calls in your program becomes even more crucial as we use recursion. To illustrate this, let us consider a problem more computationally oriented than our previous graphics and linked list examples. N factorial, denoted N!, is defined by

$$N! = N \times (N - 1) \times (N - 2) \times \ldots \times 2 \times 1$$

That is, N! is the product of the first N integers. We note that the alternate way of defining N! is by means of using (N − 1)!

$$N! = \begin{cases} 1 \text{ if } N = 1 \text{ or } N = 0 \\ N * (N - 1)! \text{ otherwise} \end{cases}$$

A NOTE OF INTEREST

Language Definition

In the *Pascal User Manual and Report* (Berlin: Springer-Verlag, 1974), Kathleen Jensen and Niklaus Wirth made famous a diagrammatic way of representing Pascal syntax. By way of example, a syntax diagram which defines a Pascal statement is presented here. One interesting feature to note about this diagram is that the term *statement* is used eight times in defining statement. (Where are the recursive termination conditions in this diagram?)

Jensen and Wirth's diagrams are recursive in nature, and they point out the fact that the syntax of most computer languages can be recursively defined. This is of tremendous importance in the writing of compilers, most of which rely heavily upon stacks and recursion to parse source programs.

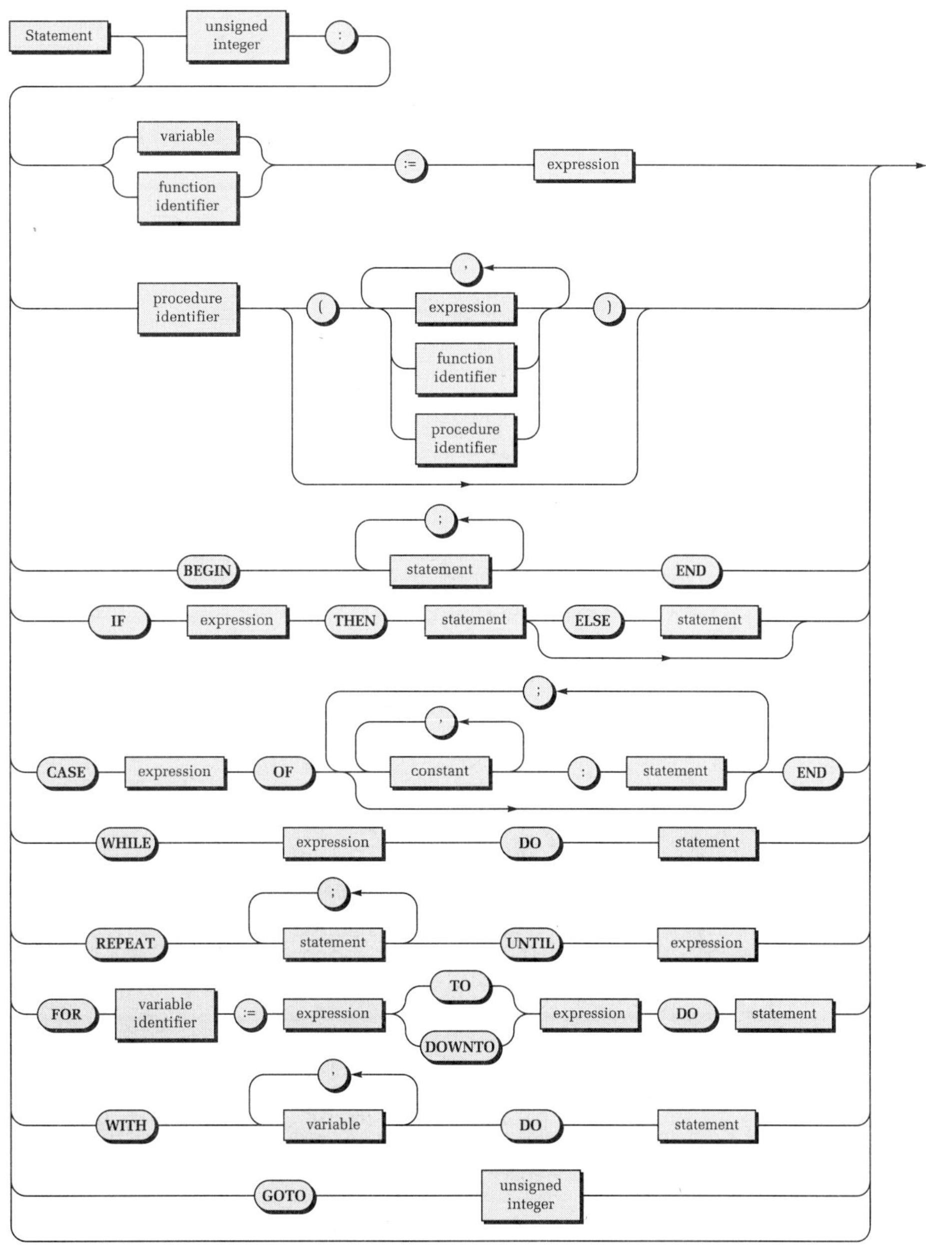

(*continued*)

A NOTE OF INTEREST

Language Definition (*continued*)

A broader question than the definition and parsing of programming languages is the ability of the computer to process natural languages such as English. Researchers in the field of artificial intelligence are attempting to use more general recursive techniques to define the syntax of natural languages and, consequently, program the computer to cope with this more complex type of language. To date, their work has met with success in only-highly restricted domains of natural language such as that used to express word problems in algebra. Despite these present limitations, research in language definition and the consequent processing of that language by computer should be one of the most intensely explored fields within computer science in the future.

Notice that this alternative definition is a *recursive definition* because it uses the notion of factorial to define factorial. Despite this circularity, we have a perfectly valid definition because of the recursive termination condition in the special definition of 1!.

To see how recursion works for factorial computation, think of the preceding definition as a series of clues which eventually will allow us to unravel the mystery of how to compute N!. That is, to compute N!, the recursive definition really tells us to

1. Remember what N is.
2. Go compute (N − 1)!.
3. Once we've computed (N − 1)!, multiply that by N to get our final answer.

Of course, when we use the definition to determine how to compute (N − 1)!, we find out that we must, in turn, compute (N − 2)!. Computing (N − 2)! will involve finding (N − 3)!. This downward spiral will eventually end with 1!, allowing us to begin the actual series of multiplications that will bring us to the appropriate answer. Figure 6.5 illustrates the logic of the recursive method for computing N factorial. In particular, if N were 4, the sequence of recursive invocations of the definition and resulting computations would be as shown in Figure 6.6.

The program in Example 6.2 calls a recursively defined Factorial function. The associated run indicates the behavior of the program for an input of 4.

EXAMPLE 6.2

```
PROGRAM RecursiveDemo (input, output);

  {  Illustrate how recursion may be used to compute factorial  }

  VAR
    M : integer;

  FUNCTION Factorial (N : integer) : integer;

    {  Given:    Nonnegative integer N.                          }
    {  Task:     Use recursion to compute N factorial.           }
    {  Return:   Computed factorial value.                       }
```

FIGURE 6.5
Recursive computation of N!

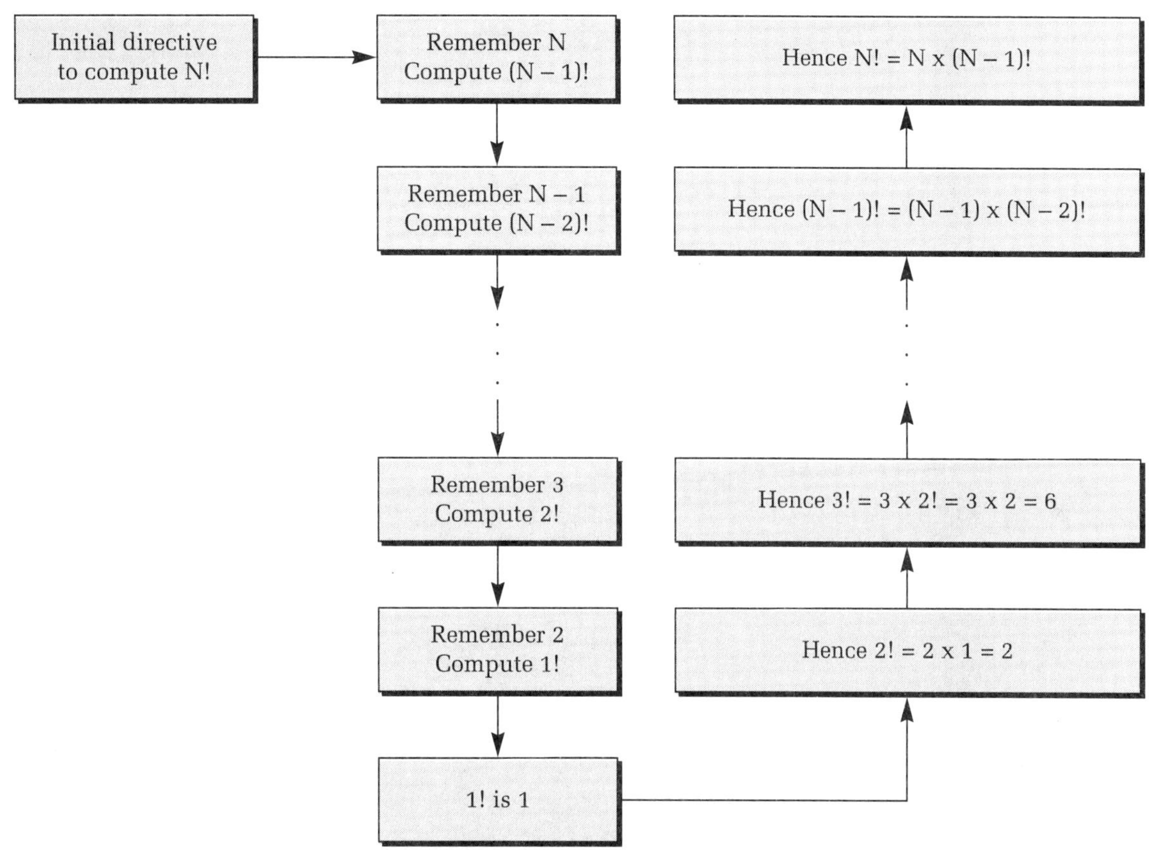

FIGURE 6.6
Recursive computation of 4!

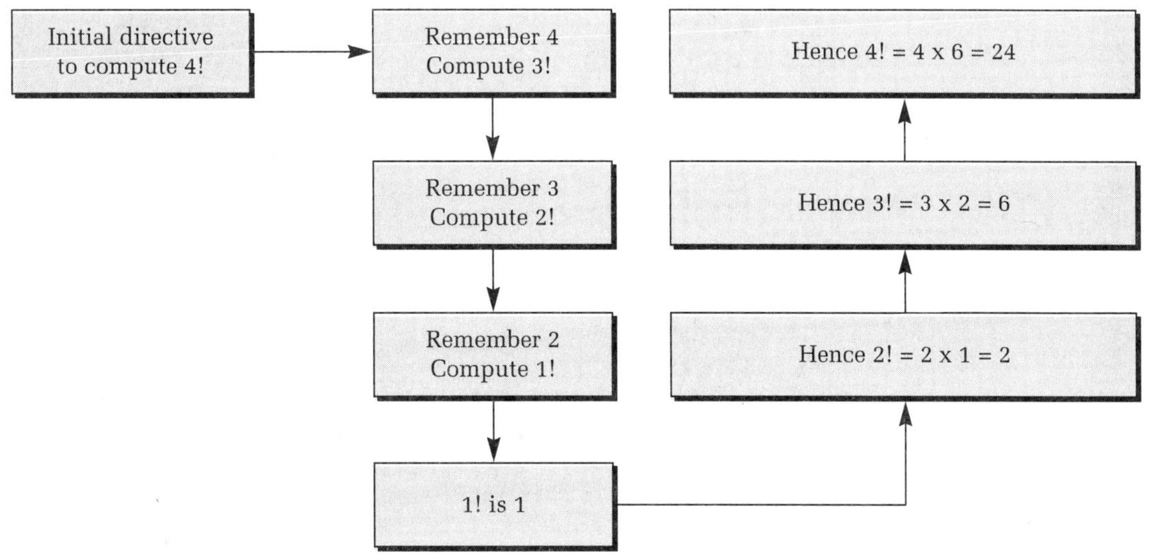

```
    BEGIN
      writeln ('ENTERING FACTORIAL WITH N = ', N);
      IF (N = 1) OR (N = 0) THEN
        Factorial := 1
      ELSE
        Factorial := N * {  Return Point 2  } Factorial (N - 1);
      writeln ('LEAVING FACTORIAL WITH N = ', N)
    END; {  of FUNCTION Factorial  }

BEGIN {  Main program  }
  write ('ENTER NUMBER FOR FACTORIAL COMPUTATION-->');
  readln (M);
  writeln (Factorial(M)) {  Return Point 1  }
END.
```

A sample run for the preceding code follows.

```
ENTER NUMBER FOR FACTORIAL COMPUTATION-->4
ENTERING FACTORIAL WITH N = 4
ENTERING FACTORIAL WITH N = 3
ENTERING FACTORIAL WITH N = 2
ENTERING FACTORIAL WITH N = 1
LEAVING FACTORIAL WITH N = 1
LEAVING FACTORIAL WITH N = 2
LEAVING FACTORIAL WITH N = 3
LEAVING FACTORIAL WITH N = 4
     24
```

The **writeln** statements upon entry to and exit from **FUNCTION** Factorial in Example 6.2 are not necessary but have been included to demonstrate the precise call and return sequence triggered by the initial call of Factorial(4) in the main program. It is crucial to note that the output from **writeln** statements implies that we must in some sense have multiple copies of the variable N, one copy for each descent to a recursively deeper level. As we shall see, a stack keeps track of these multiple copies of N in the appropriate fashion.

It is also important to emphasize that **FUNCTION** Factorial would not be tail-recursive even if the **writeln** statements were removed. This is because the recursive call to Factorial is not the last operation performed by the algorithm. After a return from the call to Factorial (N − 1), we must multiply by N. It is this multiplication that is the final operation performed. The fact that we multiply by N after returning from a recursive call indicates that, for algorithms that are not tail-recursive, we must have some means of preserving the values of parameters and local variables at each level of the recursive execution of the algorithm.

The comments { Return Point 1 } and { Return Point 2 } in Example 6.2 will allow us to trace the role played by a stack as this program is run. We have already alluded to the existence of a general system stack onto which return addresses are pushed each time a function or procedure call is made. Let us now explain it more fully. Each time a procedure or function call is made, an item called a *stack frame* will be pushed onto the system stack. The data in this stack frame consist of the return address and a copy of each local variable and parameter for the procedure or function. Figure 6.7 illustrates how stack frames are pushed and popped from the system stack when Factorial(4) is invoked. Return addresses have been indicated by referring to the appropriate comments in the Pascal code.

FIGURE 6.7
Sequence of pushes and pops in computing 4!

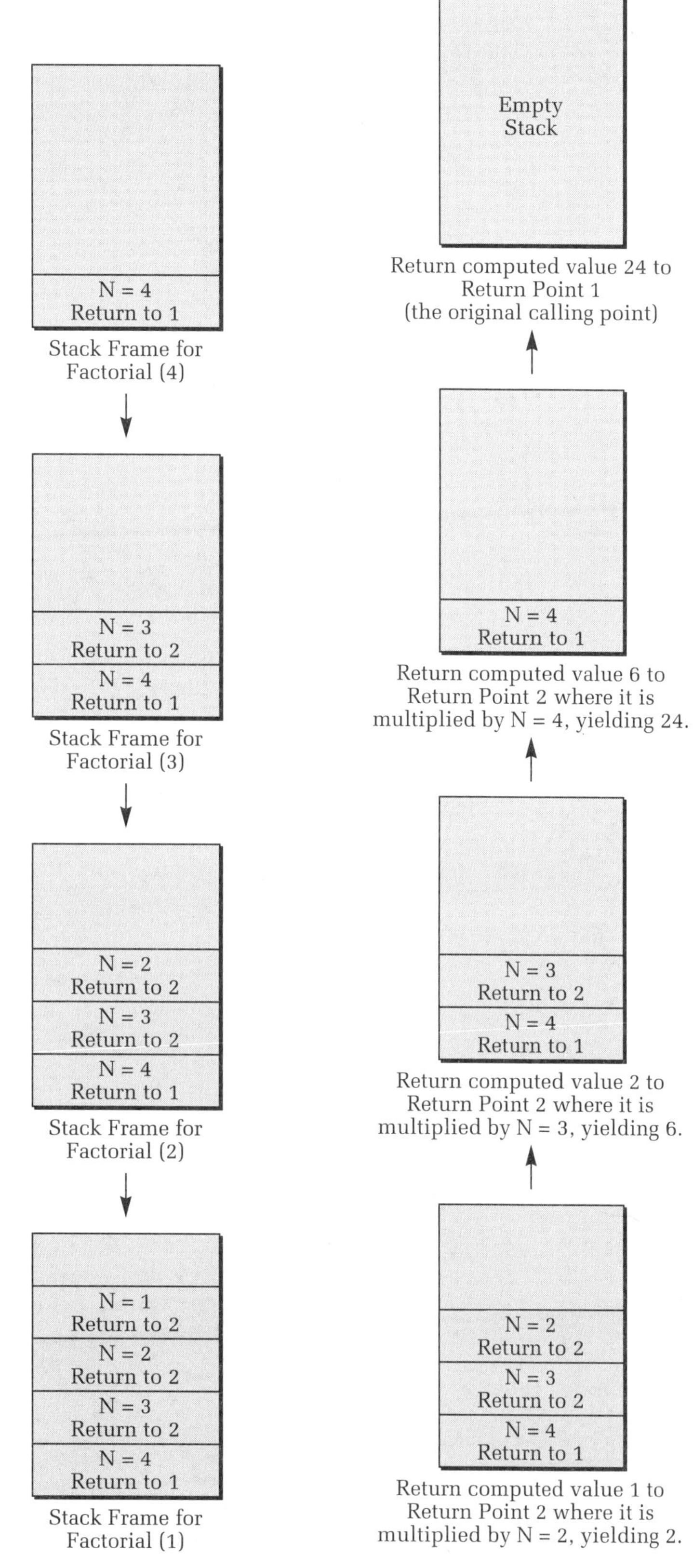

Although **FUNCTION** Factorial of Example 6.2 provides an illustration of an algorithm that is not tail-recursive, you could still validly argue that the computation of N! could be achieved more easily by a nonrecursive, iterative loop structure. In order to sense the real power and elegance of recursion, we must begin to explore algorithms that more subtly manipulate the stack frames hidden below the surface of recursive processing. These stack frames provide us with a "free" stack data structure; that is, a structure that we need not declare formally and that we control completely by the recursive calling pattern of our algorithm.

Exercises 6.1

1. Stand between two parallel mirrors and see how recursion works for you.
2. Consider the following function to compute N!

```
FUNCTION Factorial (N : integer) : integer;

  VAR J : integer;

  BEGIN
    Factorial := 1;
    FOR J := 2 TO N DO
      Factorial := Factorial * J
  END; {  of FUNCTION  Factorial  }
```

   Is this recursive or nonrecursive? Will it work? Explain why or why not.

3. Each of the following procedures offers a slight variation on the LinkedTraverse procedure developed in Example 6.1. For each procedure, indicate what output would be produced if the procedure were called initially with the linked list of Figure 6.3 and the ProcessNode procedure merely printed the data field of each node. If the procedure would crash with a run-time error for the data of Figure 6.3 or any other test case, explain why.

a.

```
PROCEDURE LinkedTraverse (Head : Pointer;
                          PROCEDURE ProcessNode (VAR Item : LinkedListData));

  BEGIN
    IF Head <> NIL THEN
      BEGIN
        LinkedTraverse (Head^.Link);
        ProcessNode (Head^.Data)
      END
  END;  {  of PROCEDURE LinkedTraverse  }
```

b.

```
PROCEDURE LinkedTraverse (Head : Pointer;
                          PROCEDURE ProcessNode (VAR Item : LinkedListData));

  BEGIN
    ProcessNode (Head^.Data);
    IF Head^.Link <> NIL THEN
      LinkedTraverse (Head^.Link)
  END;  {  of PROCEDURE LinkedTraverse  }
```

c.

```
PROCEDURE LinkedTraverse (Head : Pointer;
                          PROCEDURE ProcessNode (VAR Item : LinkedListData));
```

```
BEGIN
  IF Head^.Link <> NIL THEN
    BEGIN
      ProcessNode (Head^.Data);
      LinkedTraverse (Head^.Link)
    END
END;  {  of PROCEDURE LinkedTraverse  }
```

4. Which of the procedures in Exercise 3 are tail-recursive?

5. The following programs are intended to read a string character-by-character, put each character on the system stack, and then print out the string of characters in reverse order. Which one(s) actually achieve the intent? Which one(s) don't? Why not? What will be the output of each program for input of 'MADAM'?

a.
```
PROGRAM Palindrome (input, output);

    {  Print out a string in reverse order to check if palindrome  }

    PROCEDURE Reverse;

      {  Keep recursively stacking characters until end of string.  }
      {  Then print it out in reverse by unstacking.                }

      VAR
         c : char;  {  Here c is local to Reverse.  }

      BEGIN
        read (c);
          IF NOT eoln THEN
            Reverse;
          write(c)
      END;  {  Reverse  }

      BEGIN
        Reverse
      END.
```

b.
```
PROGRAM Palindrome (input, output);

    {  Print out a string in reverse order to check if palindrome  }

    VAR
      c : char; { Here c is global }

    PROCEDURE Reverse;

     {  Keep recursively stacking characters until end of string.  }
     {  Then print it out in reverse by unstacking.  }

      BEGIN
        read (c);
        IF NOT eoln THEN
          Reverse;
        write (c)
      END;  {  Reverse  }

    BEGIN
      Reverse
    END.
```

6. Given the declarations for the linked list structure in Example 6.1, write a recursive procedure to search the list for a particular item and return a pointer to the item in the list if it is found. If the item is not found in the list, a **NIL** pointer should be returned.

7. Suppose that NumberArray is declared as follows:

```
TYPE NumberArray = ARRAY [1..100] OF integer;
```

Study the following function and determine what it computes. (*Hint:* Try to trace it for several small instances of the array and N values.)

```
FUNCTION Compute (A : NumberArray; N : integer) : integer;

  BEGIN
    IF N = 1 THEN
      Compute := A[N]
    ELSE IF A[N] < Compute (A, N - 1) THEN
      Compute := A[N]
    ELSE
      Compute := Compute (A, N - 1)
  END;  { of Compute }
```

8. Write a recursive function of two integer arguments *M* and *N*, both greater than or equal to zero. The function should return M^N.

9. Write a recursive function of two integer arguments *M* and *N*, $M > 1$ and $N > 0$. The function should return the integer log of *N* to the base *M*. This is defined to be the least integer *L* such that $M^{L+1} > N$. (*Hint:* Though your function only receives two arguments, embed within it an auxiliary function of three arguments—*M*, *N*, and *L*. Call on the auxiliary function initially with $L = 0$; the auxiliary function is then called recursively.)

10. Given the declaration of NumberArray in Exercise 7, write a **FUNCTION** Product that receives two arguments, one of type NumberArray and another argument N that indicates the logical size of the NumberArray. Remember that the logical size of an array is the number of indices that store well-defined data items. **FUNCTION** Product should return the product of the entries in the array from indices 1 through N.

11. Insert tracer output instructions at strategic points and use them to debug the following version of a function, which attempts to recursively compute factorials. After you've debugged the function, write a statement in which you explain the behavior of the function as originally coded and also why the function did not work in this original form.

```
FUNCTION Factorial (N : integer);

  {  Given:    Integer N greater than or equal to zero.  }
  {  Task:     Compute N factorial                       }
  {  Return:   The computed value.                       }

  BEGIN
    IF (N=0) OR (N=1) THEN
      Factorial := 1
    ELSE
      BEGIN
        N := N - 1;
        Factorial := N * Factorial(N)
      END
  END;  {  of FUNCTION Factorial  }
```

■ ■

6.2 Weaving More Complex Recursive Patterns

OBJECTIVES

- to recognize problems particularly suited to recursive solutions
- to be able to state the solutions to such problems as a simpler instance of the same problem
- to be able to trace the performance of a recursive algorithm using a run-time trace diagram
- to use an algorithm's run-time trace diagram to estimate the time and space efficiency of the algorithm
- to see how recursive algorithms that potentially involve more than one recursive call at each level may lead to an exponential time efficiency
- to develop an intuitive approach for developing recursive solutions to problems

The recursive algorithms we have examined so far share the property that, at each level of recursive execution of the algorithm, at most one recursive call will be made. The pattern of operations on the system stack for such algorithms is that a series of stack frames is pushed, a recursive termination condition is reached, and then all stack frames are successively popped until we return to the execution level of the main program. More complex recursive algorithms involve multiple recursive calls at each level of execution. Correspondingly, the pattern of operations on the system stack will not be a series of uninterrupted pushes followed by a series of uninterrupted pops. Instead, the system stack will initially grow a bit, then shrink, then grow again, then shrink, and so forth.

Towers of Hanoi Problem

We introduce this more complex type of recursion via the "Towers of Hanoi" problem. This problem, although impractical, is excellent for illustrating the technique involved. As you may recall, in the Towers of Hanoi problem monks were given the painstaking task of moving a collection of N stone disks from one pillar, designated as pillar A, to another, designated as pillar C. Moreover, the relative ordering of the disks on pillar A had to be maintained as they were moved to pillar C. That is, as illustrated in Figure 6.8, the disks, all of different sizes, were to be stacked from largest to smallest, beginning from the bottom. Additionally, the monks were to observe the following rules in moving disks:

- Only one disk could be moved at a time.
- No larger disk could ever be placed on top of a smaller disk on any pillar.
- A third pillar B could be used as an intermediate to store one or more disks while they were being moved from their original source A to their destination C.

Consider the following recursive solution to this problem:

1. If N = 1, merely move the disk from A to C.
2. If N = 2, move the first disk from A to B. Then move the second disk from A to C. Then move the first disk from B to C.

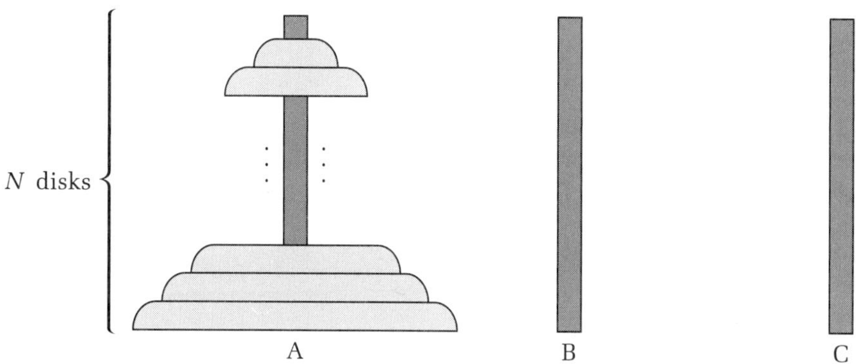

FIGURE 6.8
Towers of Hanoi problem

3. If N = 3, call upon the technique already established in step 2 to move the first two disks from A to B using C as intermediate. Then move the third disk from A to C. Then use the technique in step 2 to move the first two disks from B to C using A as an intermediate.

.

.

.

N. For general N, use the technique in the previous step to move N - 1 disks from A to B using C as an intermediate. Then move one disk from A to C. Then use the technique in the previous step to move N - 1 disks from B to C using A as an intermediate.

Notice that this technique for solving the Towers of Hanoi describes itself in terms of a simpler version of itself. That is, it describes how to solve the problem for N disks in terms of a solution for N - 1 disks. In general, any problem you hope to solve recursively must be approached in this fashion. This strategy is important enough to state as a principle.

> **Principle of Recursive Problem Solving.** When trying to solve a problem by recursion, always ask yourself "What could I do if I had a solution to a simpler version of the same problem?"

If you can see how to use the solution to a smaller version of the problem in solving the original problem, you have hurdled your toughest obstacle. All that remains is to determine the recursive termination conditions. This can be done by answering the question "Under what circumstances is this problem so simple that a solution is trivial?" Your answer to this question will define parameter values that trigger an immediate return from the recursive algorithm.

EXAMPLE 6.3

Implement a Pascal solution to the Towers of Hanoi problem. Our earlier discussion has indicated that the problem for N disks can be defined in terms of N - 1 if we switch the roles played by certain pillars. This switching can be achieved by altering the order in which parameters are passed when recursive calls are made. When a value of 1 is passed in for N, we have reached the recursive termination condition. The comments { Return Point 1 } and { Return Point 2 } in the following Pascal code will be used in a later trace of **PROCEDURE** Hanoi.

```
PROCEDURE HANOI (N : integer;
                 Source, Destination, Intermediate : char);

  {  Given:   N, the number of disks to be transferred, and    }
  {           character representations of Source,             }
  {           Destination, and Intermediate pillars.           }
  {  Task:    Apply recursive logic to specify a sequence      }
  {           of moves which will successfully transfer        }
  {           the N disks from Source to Destination.          }
  {  Return:  Nothing.                                         }
```

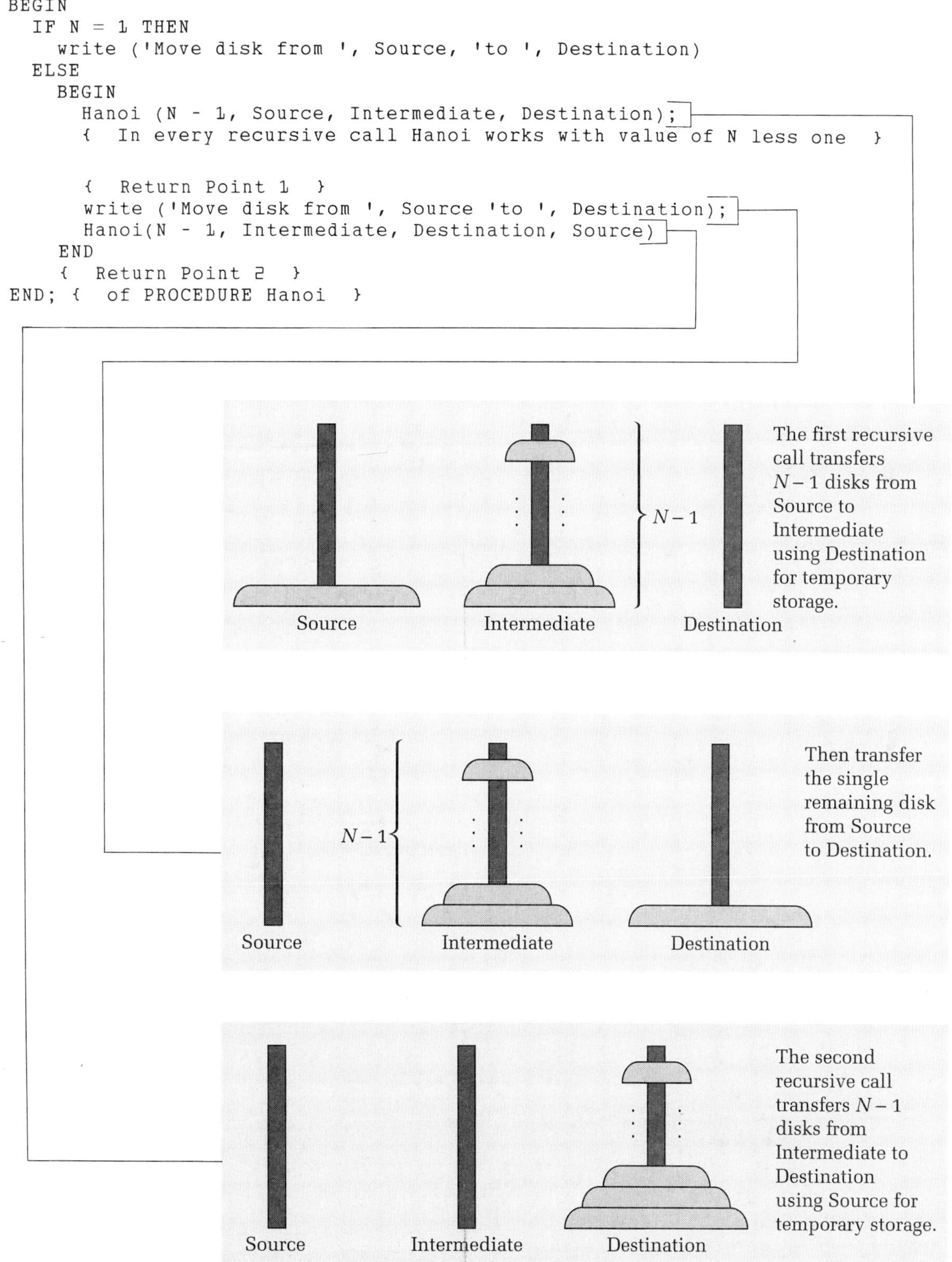
BEGIN
IF N = 1 THEN
write ('Move disk from ', Source, 'to ', Destination)
ELSE
BEGIN
Hanoi (N - 1, Source, Intermediate, Destination);
{ In every recursive call Hanoi works with value of N less one }
{ Return Point 1 }
write ('Move disk from ', Source 'to ', Destination);
Hanoi(N - 1, Intermediate, Destination, Source)
END
{ Return Point 2 }
END; { of PROCEDURE Hanoi }
N – 1
Source
Intermediate
Destination
The first recursive call transfers N – 1 disks from Source to Intermediate using Destination for temporary storage.
N – 1
Source
Intermediate
Destination
Then transfer the single remaining disk from Source to Destination.
Source
Intermediate
Destination
The second recursive call transfers N – 1 disks from Intermediate to Destination using Source for temporary storage.

Unlike previously studied recursive algorithms in which only one recursive call was made each time the procedure was invoked, **PROCEDURE** Hanoi will re-invoke itself twice each time it is called with N > 1. The result is a more complicated algorithm that could not be implemented easily by using mere iterative control structures. Implicitly, through its recursive calls, **PROCEDURE** Hanoi is weaving an intricate pattern of push and pop operations on the system stack.

EXAMPLE 6.4

To illustrate, we trace through the actions affecting the system stack when a call of the form

```
Hanoi(3, 'A', 'C', 'B')
```

is initiated. The values in the return address portion of the stack are the documentary { Return Point } labels in our Hanoi procedure.

1. We enter Hanoi with the following stack frame. N is not 1, so the condition in the **IF** statement is **false.**

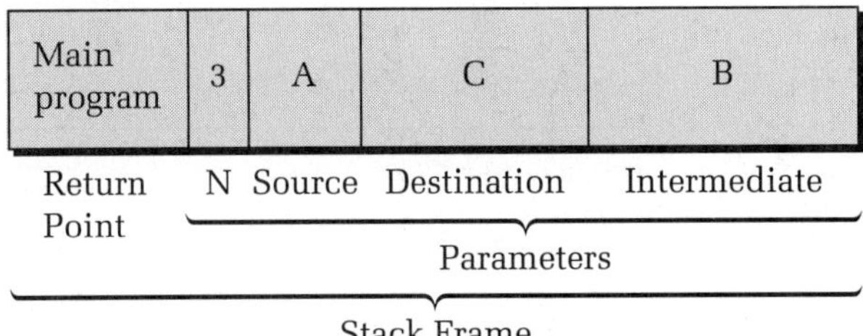

2. We encounter Hanoi(N − 1, Source, Intermediate, Destination) with A, B, C as first, second, and third arguments. Because this represents a (recursive) procedure call, some stacking must be done.

Return Point	N	Source	Destination	Intermediate
1	2	A	B	C
Main program	3	A	C	B

Parameters

Stack Frames

3. We reenter Hanoi. Notice that as we enter this time, the procedure's view of the parameters is N = 2, Source = A, Destination = B, and Intermediate = C. Because N is not 1, the condition in the **IF** statement is **false.**

4. We encounter Hanoi (N − 1, Source, Intermediate, Destination). Because this is a recursive call, stacking occurs.

Return Point	N	Source	Destination	Intermediate
1	1	A	C	B
1	2	A	B	C
Main program	3	A	C	B

Parameters: N, Source, Destination, Intermediate

Stack Frames

5. We reenter Hanoi with N = 1, Source = A, Destination = C, and Intermediate = B. Because N = 1, the condition in the **IF** statement is **true.**

6. Hence

```
Move disk from A to C
```

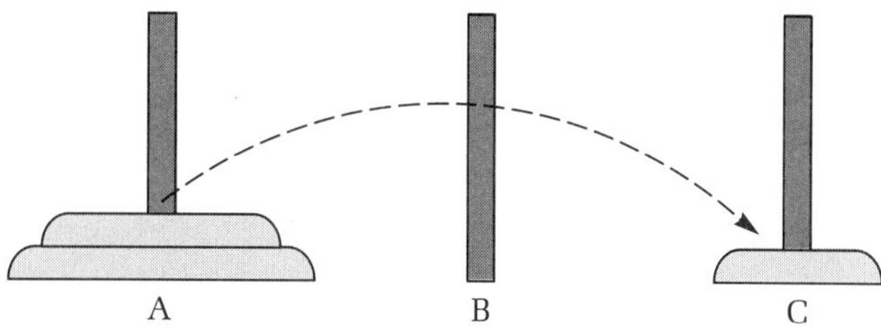

is printed and a return triggers a popping of a return address (1) and four parameters, leaving the system stack as follows:

Return Point	N	Source	Destination	Intermediate
1	2	A	B	C
Main program	3	A	C	B

Parameters: N, Source, Destination, Intermediate

Stack Frames

7. Because the return address popped was 1

```
Move disk from A to B
```

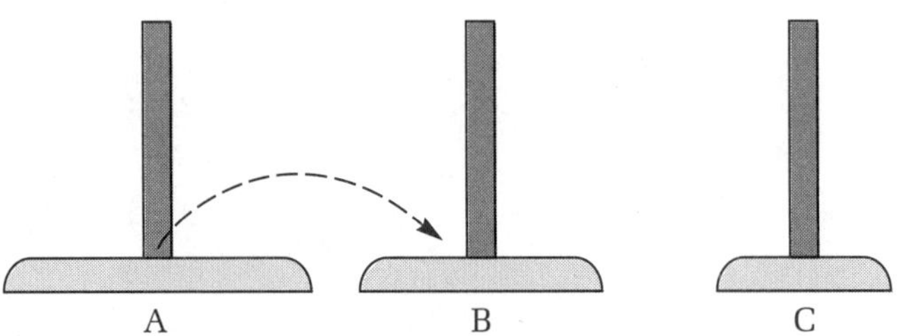

is printed and

```
Hanoi (N - 1, Intermediate, Destination, Source)
```

is encountered with N = 2, Source = A, Destination = B, and Intermediate = C.

8. The call pushes a return address and four parameters onto the system stack.

Return Point	N	Source	Destination	Intermediate
2	1	C	B	A
1	2	A	B	C
Main program	3	A	C	B

Parameters

Stack Frames

9. We reenter Hanoi, this time with N = 1, Source = C, Destination = B, and Intermediate = A.

10. Because N = 1, the **IF** statement generates the output

```
Move disk from C to B
```

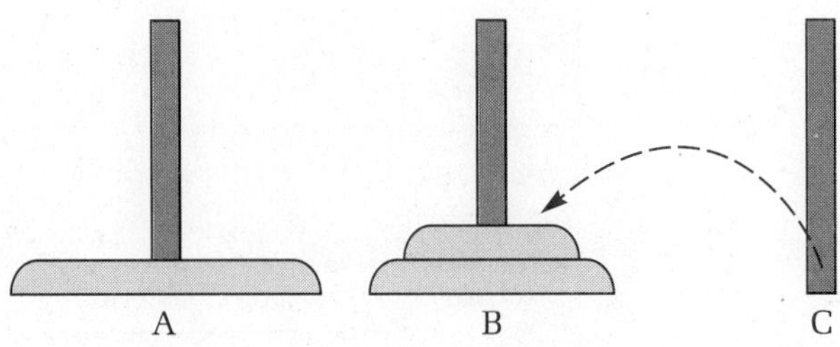

and a return.

11. The return pops a frame from the system stack and we return to the statement labeled by 2 with N = 2, Source = A, Destination = B, and Intermediate = C.

12. But statement 2 triggers a return itself, so a stack frame is popped again and we return to the statement labeled 1 with N = 3, Source = A, Destination = C, Intermediate = B.

13. Statement 1 triggers the output

    ```
    Move disk from A to C
    ```

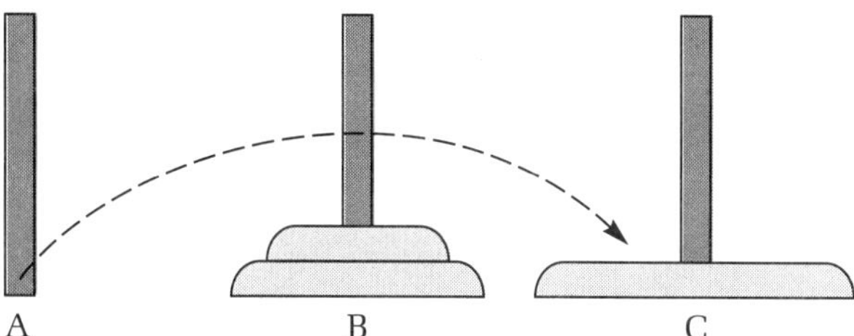

and we are immediately at another call

```
Hanoi (N - 1, Intermediate, Destination, Source)
```

Hence the status of the system stack is changed to

Return Point	N	Source	Destination	Intermediate
2	2	B	C	A
Main program	3	A	C	B

Parameters: N, Source, Destination, Intermediate

Stack Frames

14. We reenter Hanoi with N = 2, Source = B, Destination = C, and Intermediate = A. Because N is not 1, another call is executed and more values are stacked.

Return Point	N	Source	Destination	Intermediate
1	1	B	A	C
2	2	B	C	A
Main program	3	A	C	B

Parameters: N, Source, Destination, Intermediate

Stack Frames

15. We reenter Hanoi, with N = 1, Source = B, Destination = A, and Intermediate = C. Because N = 1, we print

```
Move disk from B to A
```

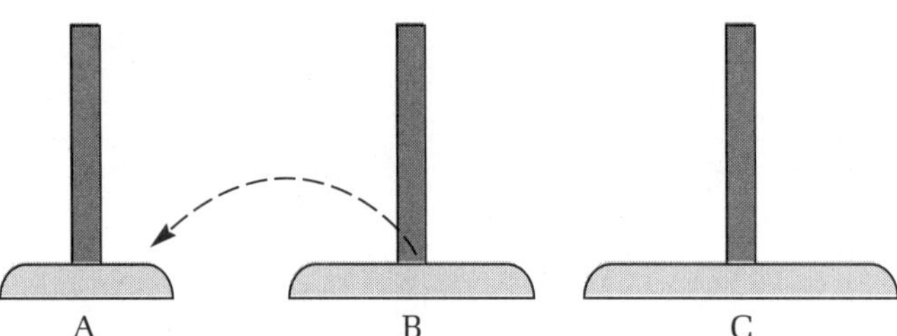

and return.

16. The return prompts the popping of the system stack. The return address popped is the statement labeled 1. Statement 1 causes output

```
Move disk from B to C
```

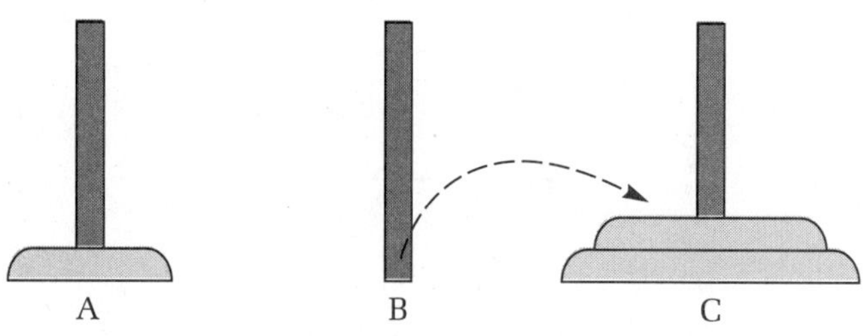

with the stack frames left at

Return Point	N	Source	Destination	Intermediate
2	2	B	C	A
Main program	3	A	C	B

Parameters (N, Source, Destination, Intermediate)

Stack Frames

17. The output from statement 1 is followed by a recursive call

```
Hanoi (N - 1, Intermediate, Destination, Source)
```

Hence another frame is pushed onto the stack.

Return Point	N	Source	Destination	Intermediate
2	1	A	C	B
2	2	B	C	A
Main program	3	A	C	B

Parameters: N, Source, Destination, Intermediate

Stack Frames

18. We reenter Hanoi (for the last time), with N = 1, Source = A, Destination = C, and Intermediate = B. Because N = 1, we output

```
Move disk from A to C
```

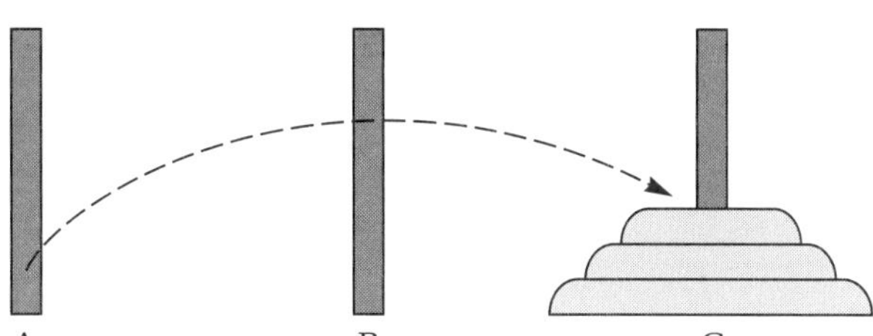

and return.

19. But now the return pops return address 2 from the stack, so return to statement 2 with the system stack given by

Return Point	N	Source	Destination	Intermediate
2	2	B	C	A
Main program	3	A	C	B

Parameters: N, Source, Destination, Intermediate

Stack Frames

20. Statement 2 is another return, so pop the stack again. The return address popped is 2, the same return point. But this time the return will transfer control back to the original calling location—and we are done!

Long-winded as this example is, it is essential that you understand it. Recursive procedures are crucial to many of the algorithms used in computer science, and you can acquire the necessary familiarity with recursion only by convincing yourself that it really works. If you have some doubt or are not sure you understand, we recommend that you trace through the Hanoi procedure with N = 4 (be prepared to go through a lot of paper).

Efficiency Analysis of the Recursive Towers of Hanoi Algorithm An analysis of the time and space efficiency of a recursive algorithm is dependent upon two factors. The first of these is the depth, that is, number of levels, to which recursive calls are made before reaching the recursive termination condition. Clearly, the greater the depth, the greater the number of stack frames that must be allocated and the less space efficient the algorithm becomes. It is also clear that recursive calls to a greater depth will consume more computer time and hence make the algorithm less time efficient. The second factor affecting efficiency analyses (particularly time efficiency) of recursive algorithms is the amount of resource (time or space) consumed at any given recursive level.

Figure 6.9 portrays this leveled view of a recursive algorithm as a hierarchy of the recursive calls that are (potentially) made as the algorithm exe-

FIGURE 6.9
Generalized hierarchy of calls by recursive algorithm

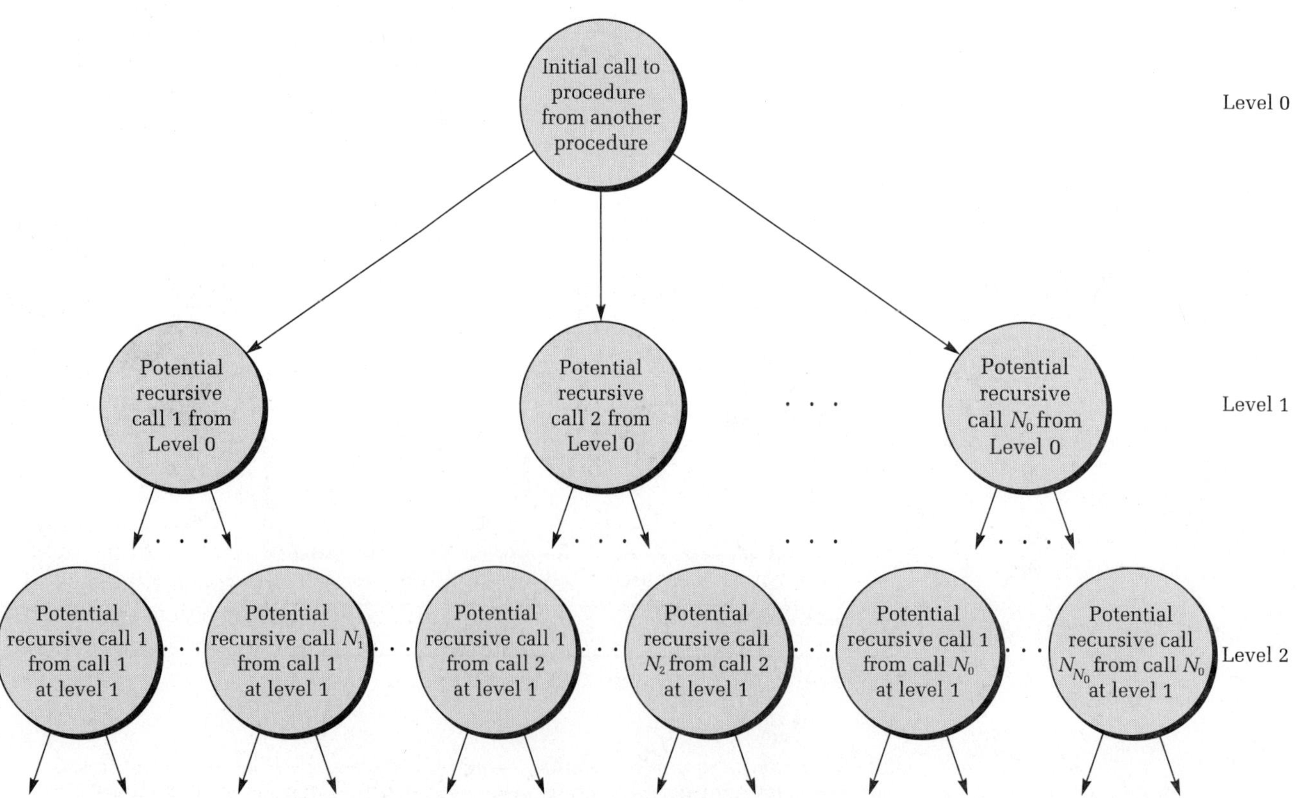

cutes. Such a hierarchy can be used as a diagrammatic model of the run-time behavior of a recursive algorithm. Consequently, we will call the hierarchy associated with the execution of a particular recursive program a *run-time trace diagram* for that algorithm. Figure 6.10 presents a run-time trace diagram for the Towers of Hanoi algorithm with N = 4 disks.

FIGURE 6.10
Run-time trace of procedure Hanoi with N originally 4 (Numbers next to circles indicate order of recursive calls)

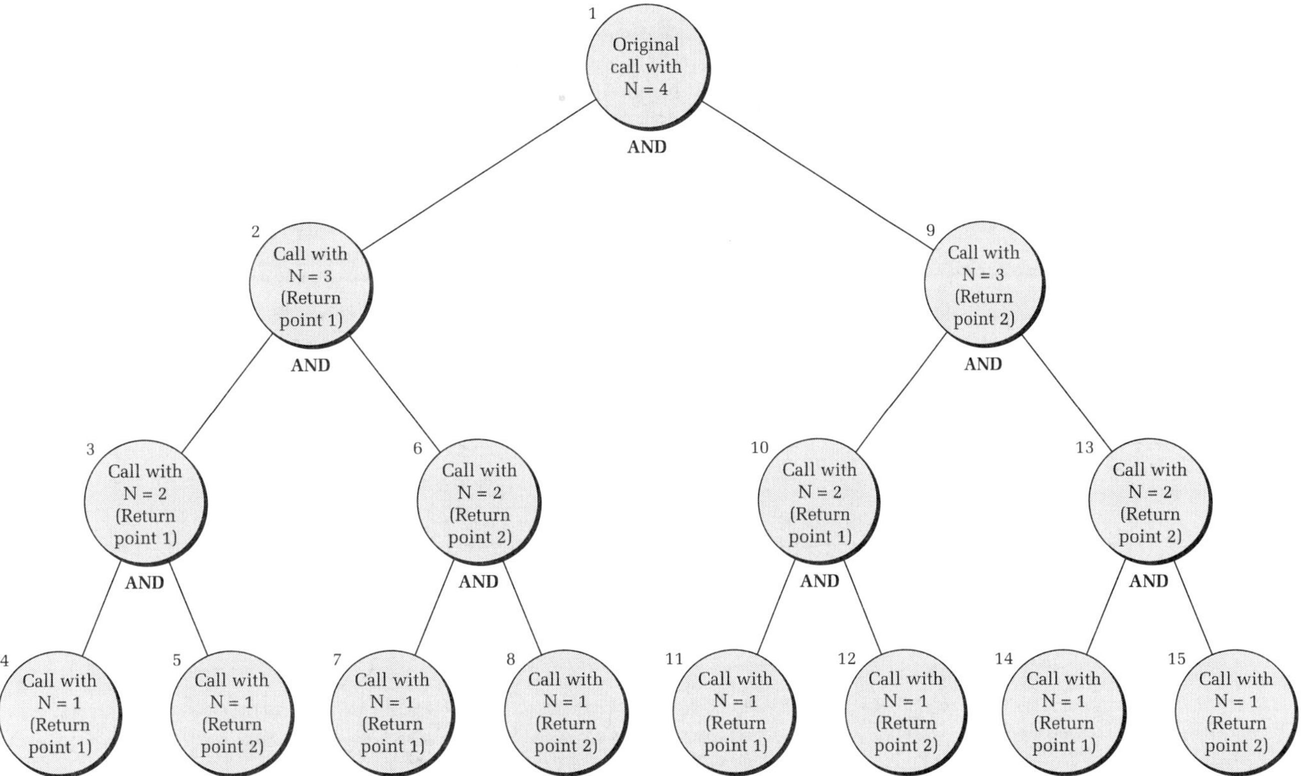

A run-time trace diagram can often be used in analyzing the time and space efficiency of an algorithm. We will provide two general principles for carrying out such analyses and then illustrate them in the context of the Towers of Hanoi algorithm.

Space Efficiency of a Recursive Algorithm. Because a stack frame must be allocated at each level of recursive execution, the space efficiency of a recursive algorithm will be proportional to the deepest level at which a recursive call is made for a particular set of values; that is, the deepest level in its run-time trace diagram.

Time Efficiency of a Recursive Algorithm. Because processing time is associated with each recursive call, the time efficiency of a recursive algorithm will be proportional to the sum, over all levels, of the times spent processing at each level.

EXAMPLE 6.5

Use the run-time trace diagram of **PROCEDURE** Hanoi to analyze the time and space efficiency of the algorithm.

A graphic representation of this diagram for four disks is given in Figure 6.10. Note that the two calls descending from each call are linked by **AND.** This is to emphasize that, when N is not 1, both potential recursive calls in the **PROCEDURE** Hanoi will be made. The fact that both potential calls are made has a rather dramatic effect on the time efficiency of the algorithm. In particular, calling Hanoi initially with N = 4 results in a total of 15 calls in the run-time trace. The numbers outside the circles in Figure 6.10 indicate the order in which these 15 calls are made. Increasing N to 5 in this figure would add an additional level with 16 calls to the run-time trace. In general, adding one disk adds only one level to the run-time trace diagram but doubles (plus 1) the number of calls in the diagram. This implies that the space efficiency of Hanoi relative to the system stack is O(N), but, since every call in the run-time trace diagram will be made, the time efficiency is $O(2^N)$.

■ ■

The analysis carried out in the preceding example demonstrates that the Hanoi algorithm falls into the class of exponential algorithms as defined in Section 1.3. This is the first exponential algorithm we have encountered. Recall from our discussion of algorithm efficiency in Section 1.3 that such algorithms are impractical to run for even moderate values of N. We shall at this point complete the Hanoi legend by noting that, if the monks of Hanoi use the recursive algorithm that we have described here, the exponential efficiency of the algorithm insures that the world will exist for many more centuries.

Recursive Implementation of the Binary Search Algorithm

Do not let our solution to the Towers of Hanoi problem mislead you into thinking that every recursive algorithm having more than one recursive call will be exponential in its efficiency. Consider, for example, a recursive formulation of the binary search algorithm. Recall the interface to this algorithm that we developed in Section 1.5.

```
PROCEDURE  BinarySearch (Target : KeyType;
                         N : integer;
                         SearchList : DataArray;
                         VAR InfoWanted : DataRec;
                         VAR Found : boolean);

  {  Given:   List of sorted records in SearchList, Target    }
  {           storing key value being sought, and N storing   }
  {           number of records in the list.                  }
  {  Task:    Apply binary search algorithm.                  }
  {  Return:  DataRec associated with Target in InfoWanted.   }
  {           If not found, return false in boolean           }
  {           variable Found.                                 }
```

The principle of recursive problem-solving (stated in our discussion of the Hanoi problem) directs us to solve the binary search problem in terms of a simpler version of itself. Toward this end, we employ a perspective often used in recursive algorithms that act upon an array: we view the algorithm as occurring between a certain subrange of array indices. For the binary search, that subrange is specified by Low. .High where Low is initially 1 and High is initially N. The "simpler version" of the binary search needed for a recursive statement of the algorithm is then a version that works on a smaller subrange of array indices. This subrange ultimately may become so small that it triggers the recursive termination condition for an unsuccessful search.

An intuitive recursive statement of the binary search logic then becomes:

```
IF (recursive termination for unsuccessful search) THEN
  Found := false (and recursion terminated)
ELSE
  BEGIN
    Compute Mid index between Low and High
    IF (Target is found at Mid index) THEN
      Search is successful (and recursion terminated)
    ELSE IF (Target is less than data at Mid index) THEN
      Recursively call with same Low and Mid - 1 as High
    ELSE
      Recursively call with Mid + 1 as Low and same High
```

According to this logic, the recursive calls result in a continual narrowing of the range to be searched until either the Target is found or a recursive termination condition for an unsuccessful search is reached.

To determine what this unsuccessful recursive termination condition is, consider Figure 6.11. It portrays successive recursive calls on an array in which the Target does not exist. The shaded regions of these array snapshots indicate the index subrange in which Target = 152 could possibly be found on successive recursive calls. Note that, on the fourth recursive call, no

FIGURE 6.11
Unsuccessful search for array with 15 key values

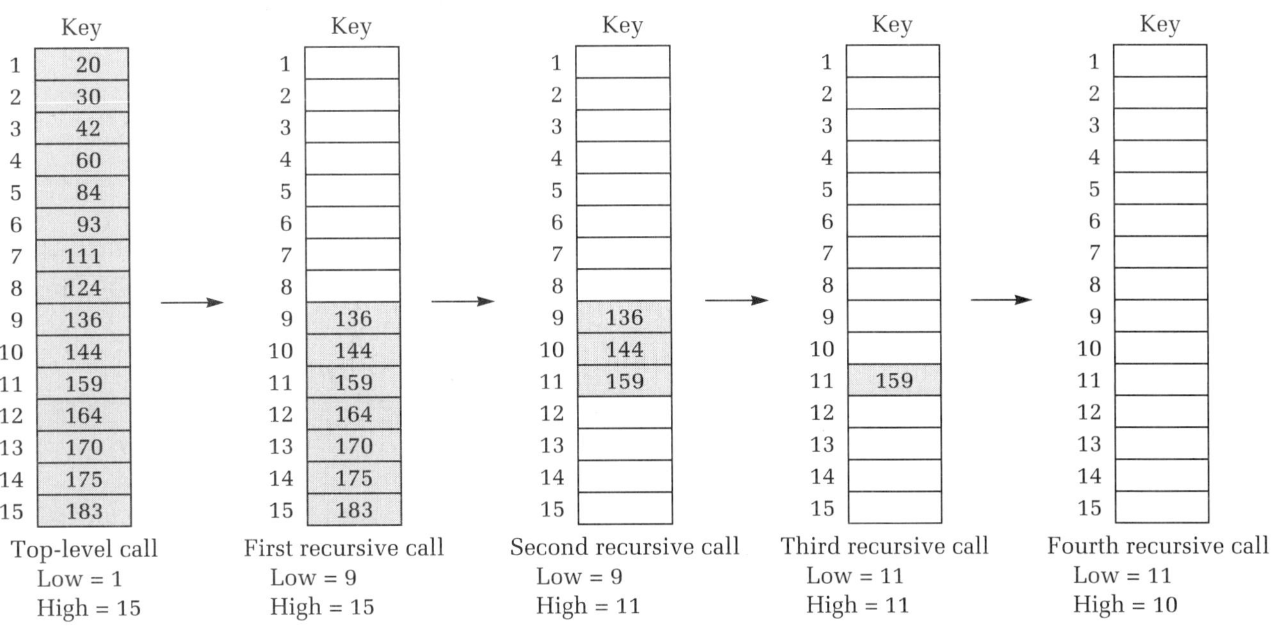

portion of the array is shaded; the condition High < Low exists. This condition is therefore the recursive termination check for an unsuccessful search. The following example presents the code for the recursive binary search in its entirety.

EXAMPLE 6.6

Developing a recursive version of the binary search requires that we use a local auxiliary procedure to work with the index subrange Low. .High. Using this auxiliary procedure will allow us to preserve the interface to **PROCEDURE** BinarySearch. This interface should not require its user to pass in an initial Low value of 1. Instead the user need only pass in the N: the number of records in SearchList. From there, the front-end portion of **PROCEDURE** BinarySearch need only call on its auxiliary local procedure, passing in 1 for Low and N for High.

```
PROCEDURE  BinarySearch (Target : KeyType;
                         N : integer;
                         SearchList : DataArray;
                         VAR InfoWanted : DataRec;
                         VAR Found : boolean);

  {  Given:   List of sorted records in SearchList, Target    }
  {           storing key value being sought, and N storing   }
  {           number of records in the list.                  }
  {  Task:    Apply binary search algorithm.                  }
  {  Return:  DataRec associated with Target in InfoWanted.   }
  {           If not found, return false in boolean           }
  {           variable Found.                                 }

  PROCEDURE BinarySearchAux (Low, High : integer);

    {  Given:   Low and High--array indices in SearchList between     }
    {           which Target may still be found.                      }
    {  Task:    Check if Target is in the middle index between Low    }
    {           and High or if Low and High meet the recursive        }
    {           termination condition for an unsuccessful search.     }
    {  Return:  If Target is in the middle index, then the DataRec    }
    {           associated with Target is returned in InfoWanted and }
    {           Found is set to true.  If recursive termination       }
    {           condition for an unsuccessful search is met, then     }
    {           Found is false.  Otherwise recur to next level with   }
    {           smaller index range.                                  }

    VAR
      Mid : integer;

    BEGIN
      IF High < Low THEN    { Recursive termination when not found }
        Found := false
      ELSE
        BEGIN
          Mid := (Low + High) DIV 2;
          IF SearchList[Mid].Key = Target THEN { Recursive termination when found }
            BEGIN
              InfoWanted := SearchList[Mid];
              Found := true
            END
```

```
      ELSE IF Target < SearchList[Mid].Key THEN { Work with lower subrange }
        BinarySearchAux (Low, Mid - 1)
      ELSE                                { Work with higher subrange }
        BinarySearchAux (Mid + 1, High)
    END
  END;   { of PROCEDURE BinarySearchAux }

BEGIN
  BinarySearchAux (1, N)
END; {  of PROCEDURE BinarySearch  }
```

Efficiency Analysis of the Recursive Binary Search As we did for the Towers of Hanoi problem, we will use a run-time trace diagram of potential recursive calls to analyze the efficiency of the recursive implementation of the binary search algorithm. This diagram appears in Figure 6.12. For the specific case of an array with 15 data items, the run-time trace stops at level 3, as indicated in Figure 6.13. The **OR**s that appear in these two figures are

FIGURE 6.12
Run-time trace diagram of potential calls for recursive binary search algorithm

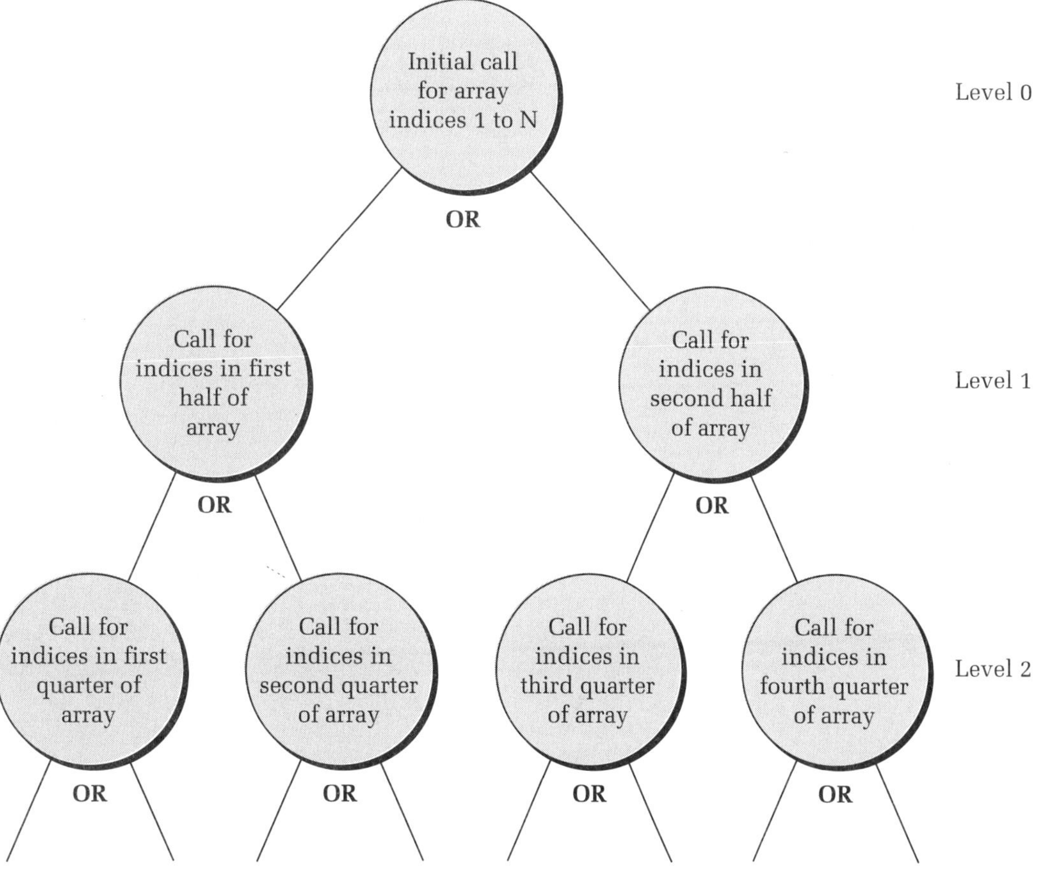

FIGURE 6.13
Trace of Figure 6.12 for specific case of array with 15 data items

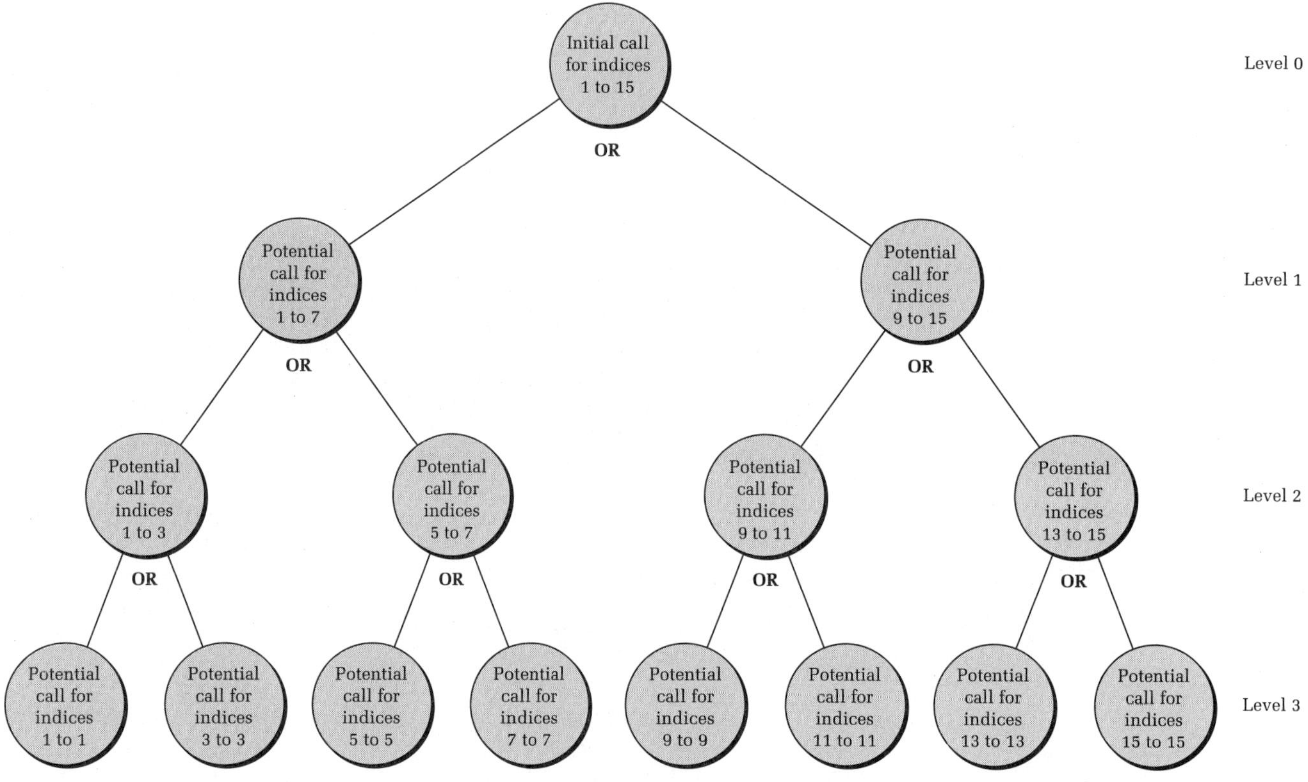

indicative of the fact that, at any given level, we will make, at most, one recursive call or the other, but not both. This is important and, as we have seen, different from the **AND** pattern of recursive calls in the Hanoi problem. It implies that the work done at any given level is simply the work done at one node along that level.

In the binary search, the work done at any node is O(1) since we are merely comparing the Target item to the data at the Mid position. Hence the time efficiency of the recursive version of this algorithm will merely be proportional to the number of levels in the run-time trace for an array with N items. In Figures 6.12 and 6.13, we can see that doubling the number of items in the array will merely add one level to the run-time trace diagram. That is, the number of levels in the diagram is $\log_2 N + 1$ (truncated). With the O(1) work done at each level, we can thus conclude that the time efficiency of a recursive binary search is $O(\log_2 N)$. Similarly, since a stack frame will be allocated for each recursive level, the additional space requirements of the algorithm (beyond the array itself) are $O(\log_2 N)$. Note that our earlier nonrecursive implementation of the binary search algorithm did not carry with it this additional cost in space efficiency.

Recursive Computation of "N Choose K"

The preceding discussion of the binary search algorithm has honed our ability to use the run-time trace diagram to measure the efficiency of a recursive algorithm. It did not, however, represent a solution to a problem that would be difficult to conceptualize without recursion. We close this section with an example in the latter category.

The phrase "N choose K" is often used in the combinatorics branch of mathematics to refer to the number of ways that we could choose K objects from among N different objects. For instance, "52 choose 13" represents the number of ways that you could be dealt a bridge hand (that is, 13 cards out of 52). We now seek a recursive function to compute N choose K for arbitrary N and K, $K \leq N$.

Our principle of recursive problem solving asks us to consider how we could use a solution to a simpler version of the same problem. For N choose K, a simpler version of the same problem could mean a solution for a smaller value of N or K. Let us designate our N objects as object #1, object #2, . . . , object #(N - 1), object #N. Figure 6.14 indicates that we can partition

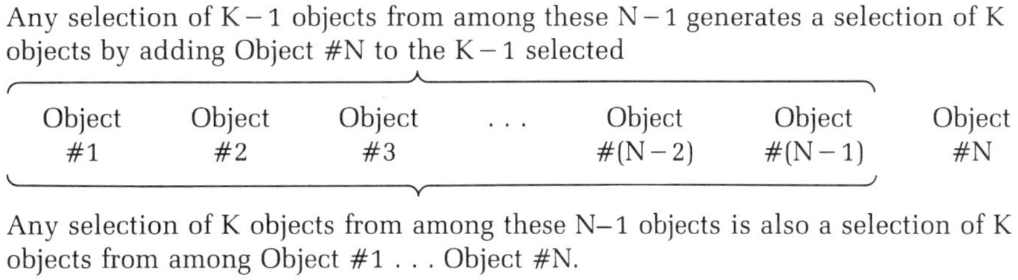

FIGURE 6.14
Formulating Choose (N, K) in terms of Choose (N − 1, K) and Choose (N − 1, K − 1)

Any selection of K − 1 objects from among these N − 1 generates a selection of K objects by adding Object #N to the K − 1 selected

Object #1	Object #2	Object #3	. . .	Object #(N − 2)	Object #(N − 1)	Object #N

Any selection of K objects from among these N−1 objects is also a selection of K objects from among Object #1 . . . Object #N.

selections of K objects from these N as those groups of K objects that come strictly from objects 1, 2, . . . , N - 1 and those groups of K objects that include object #N in addition to K - 1 chosen among objects 1, 2, . . . , N - 1. In other words,

Choose (N,K) = Choose (N − 1, K) + Choose (N − 1, K − 1)

- Choose (N − 1, K): Ways of selecting K objects from among the first N − 1
- Choose (N − 1, K − 1): Ways of selecting K − 1 objects from among the first N − 1 and then including object #N

The preceding equation appears to be the recursive key we need to write our function. We need only develop recursive termination conditions to complete the puzzle. Note from the preceding equation that one of the terms being summed, Choose (N − 1, K), will recursively reduce N until it eventually equals K. But, in such a case, we are merely asking for the number of combinations of N objects selected N at a time—and there is trivially only one such combination. Hence, our first recursive termination condition is when N = K, for which we immediately return the value 1.

To develop the second recursive termination condition, we examine the second term, Choose (N − 1, K − 1), in the sum. Since both N and K will be reduced by this recursion, K will eventually reach 0. But the number of ways of choosing 0 objects from among N is again trivially 1. Consequently, the second recursive termination condition is when K = 0; this condition flags the immediate return of the value of 1.

EXAMPLE 6.7

Implement a recursive N choose K function based on the preceding discussion.

```
FUNCTION Choose (N, K : integer) : integer;

  {  Given:    N, the number of objects we are selecting from         }
  {            K, the number of objects being selected                }
  {  Task:     Compute N choose K; that is, the number of ways of     }
  {            selecting K objects from N                             }
  {  Return:   The computed value of N choose K                       }

  BEGIN
    IF K = 0 THEN              { recursive termination condition  }
      Choose := 1
    ELSE IF N = K THEN         { recursive termination condition  }
      Choose := 1
    ELSE
      Choose := Choose (N - 1, K) + Choose (N - 1, K - 1)
  END;  {  of FUNCTION Choose  }
```

EXAMPLE 6.8

Trace the Choose (N, K) function by developing the run-time trace diagram for Choose (4, 2).

This diagram is provided in Figure 6.15. The numbers next to the circles indicate the order in which calls are made.

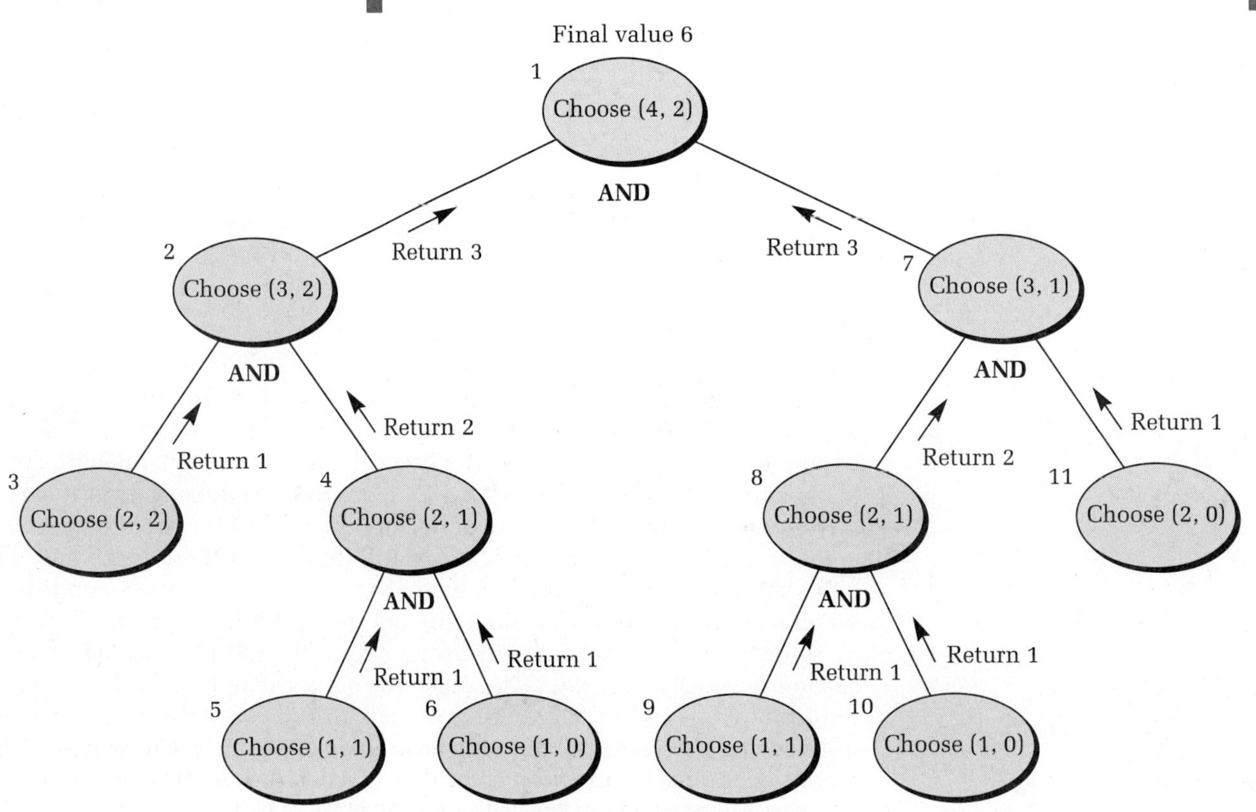

FIGURE 6.15
Run-time trace diagram for Choose (4, 2)

Exercises 6.2

1. Trace the stack frames that are pushed and popped from the system stack as the Towers of Hanoi algorithm executes for N = 4 disks.

2. Is the recursive binary search algorithm presented in this section tail-recursive? Provide a written rationale for your response.

3. Construct run-time trace diagrams in the style of Example 6.8 for a variety of values of N and K in the **FUNCTION** Choose (N, K). Judging from the run-time trace diagrams you construct, make conjectures about the time and space efficiency of this algorithm. Support these conjectures in a written statement.

4. Consider the following version of the **PROCEDURE** BinarySearchAux from Example 6.6 to which a tracer **writeln** statement has been added. What output would be produced from this tracer **writeln** if we were to call on **PROCEDURE** BinarySearch from Example 6.6 with a SearchList of 16 integers containing the key values

   12 34 67 89 113 125 169 180 191 201 225 237 256 270 299 304

   and a Target of 191?

```
PROCEDURE BinarySearchAux (Low, High : integer);

  {  Given:   Low and High--array indices in SearchList between    }
  {           which Target may still be found.                     }
  {  Task:    Check if Target is in the middle index between Low   }
  {           and High (or if Low and High meet the recursive      }
  {           termination condition)                               }
  {  Return:  If Target is in the middle index, then DataRec       }
  {           associated with Target is in InfoWanted and Found    }
  {           is true.  If recursive termination condition is met  }
  {           then Found is false.  Otherwise recur to next level  }
  {           with smaller index range.                            }

  VAR
    Mid : integer;

  BEGIN
    writeln (Low, High);  { <-- Note the output added here        }
    IF High < Low THEN    { Recursive termination when not found }
      Found := false
    ELSE
      BEGIN
        Mid := (Low + High) DIV 2;
        IF SearchList[Mid].Key = Target THEN { Recursive termination when found }
          BEGIN
            InfoWanted := SearchList[Mid];
            Found := true
          END
        ELSE IF Target < SearchList[Mid].Key THEN  { Work with lower subrange }
          BinarySearchAux (Low, Mid - 1)
        ELSE                                       { Work with higher subrange }
          BinarySearchAux (Mid + 1, High)
      END
  END;   { of PROCEDURE BinarySearchAux }
```

5. Repeat Exercise 4 but this time with a Target value of 6.

6. We have chosen not to include SearchList as a formal value parameter to the **PROCEDURE** BinarySearchAux in Example 6.6. Analyze what would be the cost in space and time efficiency if SearchList were to be included as a value parameter to this procedure.

7. Consider the following recursive function and associated top-level call. Comments of the form { Return Point N } label possible return points from recursive calls. What would a stack frame for this function contain? Show by a series of stack "snapshots" how the stack would be manipulated for the calls indicated. Finally, provide the output that would be produced by these calls.

```
PROGRAM Mystery (input, output);

  FUNCTION Weird (M, N: integer) : integer;

    BEGIN
      writeln (M, N);
      IF M = 0 THEN
        Weird := N + 1
      ELSE IF N = 0 THEN
        Weird := Weird(M - 1, 1)
                   {  Return Point 2  }
      ELSE
        Weird := Weird(M - 1,             Weird(M, N - 1))
                   {  Return Point 4  } {  Return Point 3  }
    END; { Weird }

  BEGIN
    writeln (Weird(1, 3))
                       {  Return Point 1  }
  END.
```

8. **PROCEDURE** Hanoi developed in this section specified the sequence of disk moves that would have to be performed to complete the Towers of Hanoi problem for N disks. Now write a recursive function that computes the exact number of disk moves needed to solve the Towers of Hanoi problem for N disks. (*Hint:* Express the number of individual moves necessary to transfer N disks in terms of the number of moves necessary to transfer N − 1 disks.)

9. Write a recursive procedure to determine the minimum entry in an array of N integers.

10. Write a recursive implementation of the insertion sort algorithm.

11. Suppose we have an amount of money M that is divisible evenly by 10 cents. Write a recursive function that computes the number of ways that M can be broken down into half dollars, quarters, and dimes.

12. In essay form, discuss some of the trade-offs in terms of time and space efficiency that are made when recursion is used.

13. Both a modular structure chart and a run-time trace diagram reflect a hierarchical pattern of how procedures are called in a program. In a carefully written statement, explain the differences between these two diagrammatic techniques.

■ ■ ■ ■

■ 6.3 Recursion, Trial-and-Error Backtracking, and Generalized Nested Loops

OBJECTIVES

- to use recursion in implementing a search strategy called trial-and-error backtracking
- to realize that trial-and-error backtracking requires that loops be nested to arbitrarily deep levels
- to be able to construct a run-time trace diagram for a program that uses trial-and-error backtracking to search for solutions
- to understand what a permutation is
- to be able to use trial-and-error backtracking to develop a program that produces permutations of a size not determined until run-time
- to see how trial-and-error backtracking, as studied in the context of the permutation problem, represents a strategy that can be generalized to solve a wide variety of problems

In the previous section, we have seen examples of recursive algorithms in which the number of recursive calls at each recursive level is (potentially) more than one. In this section we shall consider what happens when the number of recursive calls made on any given level is under the control of an iterative control structure such as a **FOR, WHILE,** or **REPEAT** loop.

As an example of the class of problems we will study in this section, consider the notion of a permutation.

Permutation. A permutation of the integers 1, 2, . . . , *N* is an ordered arrangement of these integers in which each integer appears exactly once.

For instance, two possible permutations of the integers 1, 2, 3, 4 are

```
3 2 1 4
2 4 3 1
```

The Permutation Problem

We now pose the following problem: For input of *N,* devise a program that outputs all permutations of the integers 1, 2, . . . , *N.*

■ EXAMPLE 6.9

The following program solves this problem, but only for the special case where N = 4.

```
PROGRAM LimitedPermutations (input, output);

  { Produce all permutations of 1, 2, 3, 4 }

  VAR K1, K2, K3, K4 : integer;

  BEGIN
    FOR K1 := 1 TO 4 DO
      FOR K2 := 1 TO 4 DO
        IF K2 <> K1 THEN
          FOR K3 := 1 TO 4 DO
            IF (K3 <> K2) AND (K3 <> K1) THEN
              FOR K4 := 1 TO 4 DO
                IF (K4 <> K3) AND (K4 <> K2) AND (K4 <> K1) THEN
                  writeln (K1:2, K2:2, K3:2, K4:2)
  END.
```

The strategy of this program is to use a **FOR** loop to control a variable which runs through the four possibilities for each of the four permutation positions. Hence four loops emerge, nested within each other. When an inner loop generates a number that matches one at a previously generated position, the **IF** statement is used to reject that number.

The program in Example 6.9 constitutes a simple and straightforward approach to the permutation problem. But it falls far short of solving the general problem as originally posed because it works only for the number 4, not for a general N to be input when the program runs. Note that the requirement that N be entered at run-time is what causes the major complication. Certainly, the strategy of using nested loops would allow us to write one program that works for $N = 2$, another that works for $N = 3$, another for $N = 4$, and so on. However, in addition to having a ridiculous number of nested **FOR** loops for reasonably large N, the decision as to which permutations to generate would instead be made at the time the appropriate program is compiled and not when it runs. Computer scientists typically call this a *binding time problem.* Here we would prefer to bind a value to N when our program runs instead of when it compiles. Clearly, the later the binding time, the more versatile the program. To do this, we need some means of simulating arbitrarily deep nested loops when the program runs.

To see how we can use recursion to achieve such a simulation, consider the diagram of permutation possibilities in Figure 6.16. This diagram bears a resemblance to what we called a run-time trace of recursive calls in the preceding section. Interpret the diagram by viewing any given path from the node labeled Start down to the base level of the diagram as a potential candidate for a permutation of 1, 2, . . . , N. As we progress from one level to the next along a path, we encounter the next digit in this potential permutation.

FIGURE 6.16
Candidates for permutations

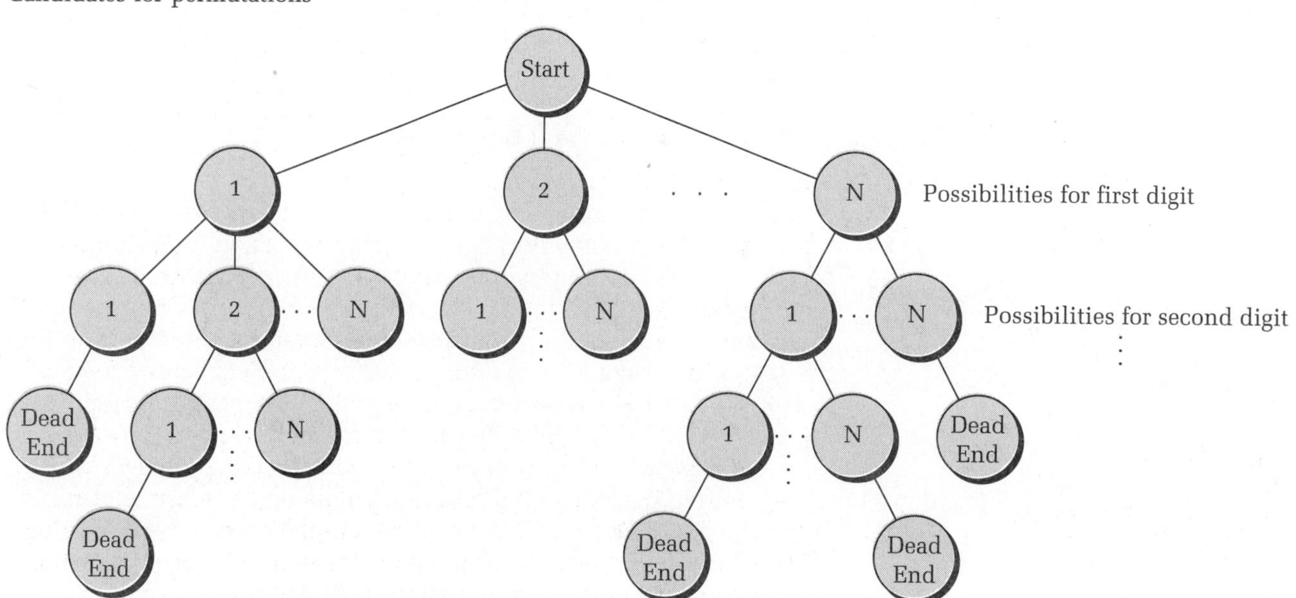

Conceptually we must use recursion to generate all the paths that appear in the figure. As soon as we generate a path with two equal numbers on it, we abandon that dead-end path and backtrack one level to continue the path along a potentially more fruitful route. If we ever complete one entire permutation along a path, we will output it, backtrack a level, and continue looking for more permutations that share the beginning of this path. At a given point in our search for a permutation, we need only store the current path. For this, a simple global array will do. Thus, the array CurrentPermutation of Figure 6.17 will store in its Jth subscript the number in the Jth position of the permutation currently being generated. The limiting factor on the size of permutations generated by our program will be the dimension of this array.

FIGURE 6.17
Current exploration of permutations beginning with 2 1 4

CurrentPermutation | | | | | | MaxPermutation

1	2	3	4	5	. . .	Size
2	1	4	Undefined	Undefined	. . .	Undefined

A complete program to solve our permutation problem follows. The heart of the program is the recursive procedure Try. Try receives three parameters.

Parameter	Explanation
N	The number of numbers to be permuted in the current run.
Level	The level in the tree of Figure 6.16; that is, the position in CurrentPermutation at which Try is to attempt placement of a new value.
Possibility	The new value to be placed at this Level.

Try initially calls on a procedure AddToCurrentPath to actually place Possibility at the appropriate Level. Once this placement is made, there are three states in which the CurrentPermutation array could be.

1. The placement of the value Possibility at the designated Level could have completed a successful permutation. In this case, call on a procedure to print out the permutation and then remove Possibility from CurrentPermutation at the given Level so that we may continue seeking additional permutations.
2. The placement of the value Possibility at the designated Level did not complete a permutation but does represent a valid beginning of length Level for a potential permutation. For instance, this case would occur if *N*, Level, and Possibility were 6, 4, and 5 respectively and we called Try with CurrentPermutation as pictured in Figure 6.17. The CurrentPermutation array would be extended to contain 2 1 4 5. Here what we must do is to test the possible candidates for a value at the next position; that is, at depth (Level + 1). This is done by an iterative series of recursive calls to Try, passing a variety of values for Possibility at (Level + 1). This iterative series of recursive calls is what achieves the desired simulation of nested looping. After all of these deeper-level possibilities (that is, those below the beginning of the current permutation in Figure 6.16) have been ex-

plored, we return and can remove Possibility from CurrentPermutation at position Level since (recursively) all permutations with this beginning arrangement will have been generated.

3. The placement of the value Possibility at Level destroys the viability of the current path by adding a number that appeared earlier in the permutation. For instance, calling on Try with N = 6, Level = 4, and Possibility = 1 would cause an invalid path for the state of CurrentPermutation given in Figure 6.17. In this case we do nothing but retract from the placement of this invalid Possibility before attempting to place other possible values.

You should carefully study how these three potential cases are handled in our recursive procedure Try in the program VersatilePermutations. The modular structure chart presented in Figure 6.18 indicates how Try invokes

FIGURE 6.18
Modular structure chart for **PROGRAM** VersatilePermutations

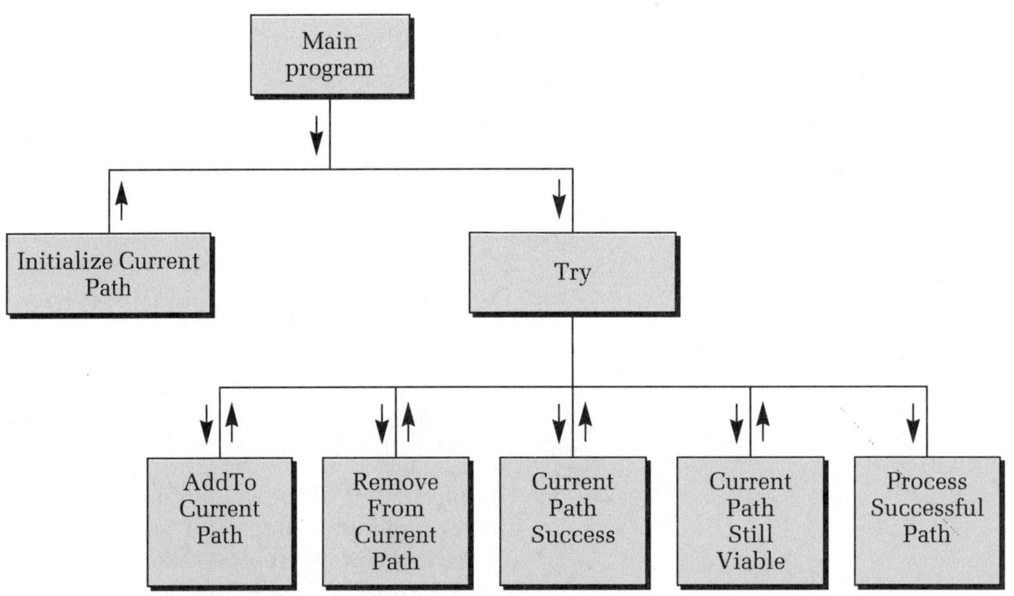

other procedures and functions. In the Focus on Program Design section, we adapt the technique illustrated here to a broader class of problems.

```
PROGRAM VersatilePermutations (input, output);

  {  Use recursion to find all permutations of 1,2, ..., N.  }

  CONST
    MaxPermutationSize = 100;
    Undefined = MaxInt;

  VAR
    N, K : integer;
    CurrentPermutation : ARRAY [1..MaxPermutationSize] OF integer;
```

```
PROCEDURE InitializeCurrentPath;

  {  Given:   CurrentPermutation array in unreliable        }
  {           state.                                        }
  {  Task:    Initialize all indices in                     }
              CurrentPermutation array to Undefined flag.   }
  {  Return:  Initialized array.                            }

  VAR
    K : integer;

  BEGIN
    FOR K := 1 TO MaxPermutationSize DO
      CurrentPermutation[K] := Undefined
  END; {  of PROCEDURE InitializeCurrentPath  }

PROCEDURE Try (N, Level, Possibility : integer);

  {  Given:   N, the number of numbers we are trying to       }
  {           permute.  Level, the current depth of the       }
  {           solution path as portrayed in Figure 6.16.      }
  {           Possibility, the number we wish to              }
  {           place at that level.                            }
  {  Task:    After locating Possibility at specified         }
  {           Level, check if we have a permutation.  If      }
  {           so, print it.  If not, check whether or not     }
  {           a permutation is still possible for this        }
  {           placement of Possibility.  If so, attempt       }
  {           placement at deeper Level by recursive call.    }
  {  Return:  Relative to this Level, CurrentPermutation      }
  {           array is returned unaltered.  However, if       }
  {           permutation was found, contents of this         }
  {           array are printed.                              }

  VAR
    K : integer;

  PROCEDURE AddToCurrentPath (Level, Possibility : integer);

    {  Given:   Level, the current depth of the solution       }
    {           path.  Possibility, the number to place at     }
    {           that Level.                                    }
    {  Task:    Assign Possibility to this Level.              }
    {  Return:  Suitably altered CurrentPermutation array.     }

    BEGIN
      CurrentPermutation[Level] := Possibility
    END; { of PROCEDURE  AddToCurrentPath }

  PROCEDURE RemoveFromCurrentPath (Level : integer);

    {  Given:   The deepest Level to which solution path       }
    {           has grown.                                     }
    {  Task:    Remove the value at that Level.                }
    {  Return:  Suitably altered CurrentPermutation array.     }

    BEGIN
      CurrentPermutation[Level] := Undefined
    END; { of PROCEDURE RemoveFromCurrentPath }

  FUNCTION CurrentPathSuccess (N, Level : integer) : boolean;
```

```
  {  Given:   CurrentPermutation array.  Level, the depth     }
  {           to which solution path has grown.  N, the       }
  {           number of numbers we are trying to permute.     }
  {  Task:    Check if contents of CurrentPermutation array   }
  {           through index Level constitute a complete       }
  {           permutation of the first N numbers.             }
  {  Return:  True if permutation, false otherwise.           }

  VAR
    Success : boolean;
    K : integer;

  BEGIN
    Success := true;
    IF N > Level THEN  {  Level must be N for successful permutation  }
      Success := false
    ELSE  {  Are all entries different from that at index Level?  }
      BEGIN
        K := 1;
        WHILE (K <= (Level - 1)) AND Success DO
          BEGIN
            Success := (CurrentPermutation[K] <> CurrentPermutation[Level]);
            K := K + 1
          END
      END;
    CurrentPathSuccess := Success
  END; {  of FUNCTION CurrentPathSuccess  }

FUNCTION CurrentPathStillViable (Level : integer) : boolean;

  {  Given:   CurrentPermutation array.  Level, the           }
  {           depth to which solution path has grown.         }
  {           N, the number of numbers we are trying to       }
  {           permute.                                        }
  {  Task:    Check if contents of CurrentPermutation         }
  {           array through index Level constitute a          }
  {           viable beginning for permutation of the         }
  {           first N numbers.                                }
  {  Return:  True if viable, false otherwise.                }

  VAR
    Viable : boolean;
    K : integer;

  BEGIN
    Viable := true;
    K := 1;
    WHILE (K <= (Level - 1)) AND Viable DO
      BEGIN
        Viable := (CurrentPermutation[K] <> CurrentPermutation[Level]);
        K := K + 1
      END;
    CurrentPathStillViable := Viable
  END; {  of FUNCTION CurrentPathStillViable  }

PROCEDURE ProcessSuccessfulPath (N : integer);

  {  Given:   CurrentPermutation array and N, the number      }
  {           we are trying to permute.                       }
  {  Task:    Write out first N indices of                    }
  {           CurrentPermutation.                             }
  {  Return:  Nothing.                                        }
```

```
    VAR
      K : integer;

    BEGIN
      FOR K := 1 TO N DO
        write (CurrentPermutation[K]:3);
      writeln
    END; {  of PROCEDURE ProcessSuccessfulPath  }

  BEGIN {  Try  }
    AddToCurrentPath (Level, Possibility);
    IF CurrentPathSuccess (N, Level) THEN
      ProcessSuccessfulPath (N)
    ELSE IF CurrentPathStillViable (Level) THEN
      FOR K := 1 TO N DO
        Try (N, Level + 1, K);
    RemoveFromCurrentPath (Level)
  END; {  of PROCEDURE Try  }

BEGIN {  Main program  }
  InitializeCurrentPath;
  write ('Permutation of integers from 1 to ? ');
  readln (N);
  FOR K := 1 TO N DO
    Try (N, 1, K)
END.
```

You may have noticed that certain efficiency considerations have not been taken into account in writing the previous program. For example, the initialization of the CurrentPermutation array actually is unnecessary in this particular implementation. Also, the call to RemoveFromCurrentPath could have been eliminated since the Undefined flag that this procedure assigns is quickly replaced without ever being explicitly used. Finally, additional global data could be used to keep track of information that would eliminate the necessity of using loops in the CurrentPathSuccess and CurrentPathStillViable procedures. You will be asked to rewrite the program taking these economies into account in the Exercises.

Our purpose in this section has not been to present the most compact version of a permutations program, but rather to illustrate how recursion can be used to simulate *generalized nested loops* whose nesting depth can be established at run-time. Such generalized nested loops can then be used in situations where trial-and-error backtracking is an appropriate strategy in searching for a problem's solution. In this context, we have intended the permutations program to be illustrative of a general problem-solving approach rather than a solution to a particular problem.

Consider what we must abstract from the permutations program to view it as a general template for trial-and-error backtracking instead of a mere permutation printer. Figure 6.16 presents the problem of finding permutations as a problem in finding certain types of paths through a maze. We probe deeper and deeper along a given path (that is, add new numbers to the current permutation) until we reach a predefined goal or reach a dead end. As we take a new step along the current path, we must analyze the state in which it has placed us.

1. Have we reached a goal state?
2. Have we reached a state that, though not itself a goal, is still a viable start toward that goal?
3. Have we reached a dead end?

For each of the three cases we take appropriate action such as

1. Processing a goal state; for example, printing it out, tallying a counter, or setting a flag signaling that we are done.
2. Probing further along a viable path by recursively taking another step.
3. No action in the case of a dead end.

After taking the appropriate action, we then retract from the step that led us to the current state, possibly returning to a higher recursive level where we may find ourselves in the midst of a similar three-state analysis. The essence of this trial-and-error backtracking logic is illustrated in Figure 6.19. Upon reaching a dead end for path A, you must retrace steps 9 → 8 → 7 → 6 → 5 before you can try new path B. The retracing of states that have been visited previously is conveniently done by unwinding from recursive calls.

FIGURE 6.19
Backtracking problem illustrated by maze solution

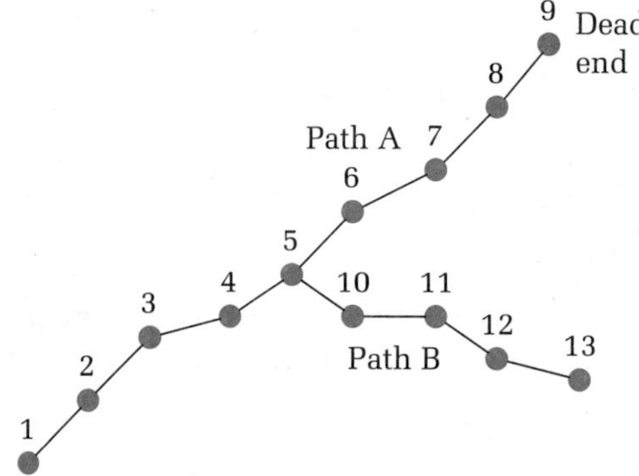

In this chapter's Focus on Program Design section and the Programming Problems, you will see how this type of logic can be used to solve a wide variety of problems.

Exercises 6.3

1. Consider the VersatilePermutations program discussed in Section 6.3. Suppose that $N = 3$ in a particular run of this program and that we printed out the contents of the CurrentPermutation array each time the Try procedure was invoked in this run. How many times would the array be printed? What would be the overall output?
2. Suppose you used the permutations procedure of this section to compute all permutations of 1, 2, 3, and 4. What would the complete run-time trace diagram of recursive procedure calls look like for such a run? Can you generalize from this diagram of procedure calls the efficiency of the permutations procedure? State your answer in big-O terms with respect to both stack size and number of stack operations. Provide justification for your answer in a written statement.
3. Rewrite **PROGRAM** VersatilePermutations in a fashion that takes into account the efficiency considerations discussed in Section 6.3. These considerations are discussed in the paragraph that follows the program.
4. What is the output from the following program?

```
PROGRAM X(output);

  PROCEDURE Y(A, B, C: integer);
    VAR K : integer;
```

```
    BEGIN
      IF B <= C THEN
        BEGIN
          writeln(A);
          FOR K := B TO C DO
            Y(K, B + 1, C)
        END
    END;

  BEGIN
    Y(16,1,4)
  END.
```

5. What is the output from the following program?

```
PROGRAM Easy(output);

  PROCEDURE Tough(B, C, D: integer);
    VAR K : integer;
    BEGIN
      IF B <= C THEN
        BEGIN
          writeln(D);
          FOR K := B TO C DO
            Tough(B + 1, C, K)
        END
    END;

  BEGIN
    Tough(1,4,12)
  END.
```

6. A car's odometer may be viewed as a physical implementation of a nested loop. Each loop cycles through the digits 0..9, with the one's digit cycling the fastest, then the ten's digit, and so forth. Write a procedure to simulate an *N*-digit odometer (*N* determined at run-time) by creating a generalized nested loop structure that will run through, in sequence, all possible settings for the odometer.

FOCUS ON PROGRAM DESIGN

We have emphasized throughout this text that computer scientists must work at varying levels of abstraction. With this in mind, consider the program of the last section not merely as a permutation printer but rather as illustrative of a more abstract problem-solving technique. In fact, a careful examination of the **PROCEDURE** Try in **PROGRAM** Versatile Permutations will show that it is nearly independent of the particular problem of searching for permutations. That is, the algorithm behind Try could be used in any analogous search for a solution in which there were *N* additional possibilities at the current level. We shall now indicate the power of this abstract approach to trial-and-error backtracking by sketching a solution to another problem that could be solved with the same methodology. You will then complete the solution in the Programming Problems.

The Eight Queens Problem

Consider what has come to be known as the Eight Queens Problem. This problem has long intrigued chess fanatics. It requires determining the various ways in which eight queens could be configured on a chessboard so that none of them could capture any other queen. (The rules of chess allow a queen to move an arbitrary number of squares in a horizontal, vertical, or diagonal fashion.) Figure 6.20 illustrates one such configuration.

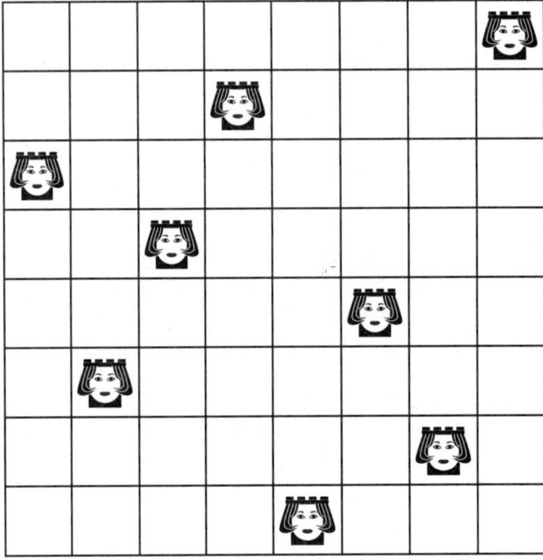

FIGURE 6.20
One successful eight queens configuration

Applying backtracking logic to this problem we could attempt to find a path to a configuration by successively trying to place a queen in each column of a chessboard until we reach a dead end: a column in which the placement of queens in prior columns makes it impossible to place the queen being moved. This situation is pictured in Figure 6.21. Here, the sixth queen cannot be placed due to the placement of the first five queens.

When we reach such a dead end, we must backtrack one column (to column 5 in Figure 6.21), and attempt to find a new placement for the queen

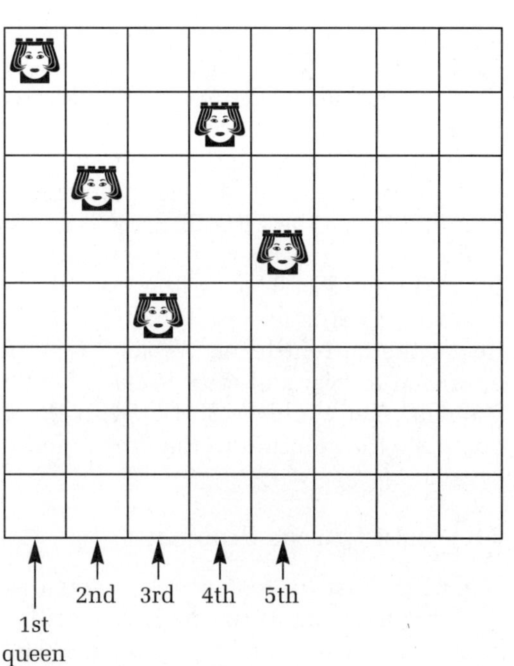

FIGURE 6.21
Dead end in queen placement

A NOTE OF INTEREST

Recursion, LISP, and the Practicality of Artificial Intelligence

Artificial intelligence, the science of implementing on computers the problem-solving methods used by human beings, is one of the most rapidly expanding fields within computer science. Research in this field includes enabling computers to play games of strategy, to understand natural languages, to prove theorems in logic and mathematics, and to mimic the reasoning of human experts in fields such as medical diagnosis. Only recently has artificial intelligence become a commercially viable area of application, capable of solving some real-life problems apart from the idealized setting of a pure research environment. More and more, we are seeing artificial intelligence systems which perform such practical functions as aiding business executives in their decision-making processes and providing a "near-English" user-interface language for data-base management software.

What has sparked the sudden emergence of artificial intelligence? Why wasn't it possible to produce commercially feasible programs in this field until recently? One of the primary answers to these questions is tied to the language in which most artificial intelligence programming is done. This language is called *LISP* (for LISt Processor). Interestingly, the control structures of LISP are based almost entirely on recursion. What a Pascal programmer would view as normal iterative control structures (for example, **WHILE, REPEAT,** and **FOR** loops) appear in various versions of LISP only as infrequently used, nonstandard extensions to the language.

One of the reasons that a recursively based language such as LISP is so ideally suited to this field is that most problem-solving methods in artificial intelligence involve searching for a particular goal state; that is, searching for a path leading to a complete problem solution. This is similar to the approach we have taken in the permutation problem and the Eight Queens Problem in this chapter.

The complexity of problems studied in artificial intelligence leads to run-time trace diagrams of enormous size. Interestingly, LISP has been available as a recursive language ideally suited to such problems for a long time. It is one of the oldest high-level programming languages, having been first developed by John McCarthy in the late 1950s.

Researchers who work in artificial intelligence have realized since LISP's introduction that its ability to recursively process general data structures was, on a theoretical basis, exactly what they needed. The problem through the years has been that, because of the very high overhead associated with recursion (and some other features built into LISP), computer hardware has not been fast enough to run LISP programs in practical applications. Thus, researchers were restricted not by LISP itself but rather by the ability of computer hardware to execute LISP programs in reasonable times. One of the major reasons for the recent emergence of artificial intelligence has been the increase in speed of computing hardware and the decrease in cost of this same hardware. This has made it possible for users to have dedicated computer resources capable of meeting the demands of LISP's recursive style. As hardware continues to improve, so will applications in LISP and artificial intelligence become increasingly sophisticated.

If you are curious about LISP and the important role that it plays at some of the frontiers of research in programming languages, consult the September 1991 issue of the *Communications of the ACM* (vol. 34, no. 9). This entire issue was devoted to LISP and described its ability to adapt to many computing environments.

in that column. If placement in the previous column is impossible, we must backtrack yet another column to attempt the new placement. This backtracking through previous columns continues until we finally are able to reposition a queen. At that point, we can begin a new path by again attempting to position queens on a column-by-column basis until another dead end is reached or until a fully successful configuration is developed.

The key to a program that finds all possible configurations for the eight queens is a procedure that attempts to place a queen in a given square and, if successful, recursively calls itself to attempt the placement of another queen in the next column. Such a procedure in skeletal pseudocode form follows:

```
PROCEDURE TryQueen (K, J)

{    Place a queen in row K, column J. Analyze        }
{    state reached by this placement. If appropriate,  }
{    recurse to place queen in next column.           }
```

1. Actually put queen at position K, J
2. **IF** this results in successful configuration **THEN**
   Tally this configuration
   ELSE IF no queen in immediate danger **THEN**
   FOR L := 1 to 8 **DO**
   TryQueen(L, J + 1)
3. Retract from position K, J

END { of **PROCEDURE** TryQueen }

The similarities between this sketch of a solution to the Eight Queens Problem and our complete solution to the permutation problem should convince you that, from an abstract perspective, both problems are really the same. We have intentionally left the Eight Queens Problem unfinished. Still to be resolved are such issues as:

- The initial call(s) to TryQueen.
- How to represent the chessboard.
- How to check whether placing a queen at position K, J puts it in immediate danger. That is, how to determine whether there is currently another queen sharing the same row, column, or diagonal.

The resolution of these issues is left for your enjoyment in the Programming Problems at the end of the chapter. Additional problems given there further illustrate the far-reaching applicability of the trial-and-error backtracking method.

RUNNING AND DEBUGGING TIPS

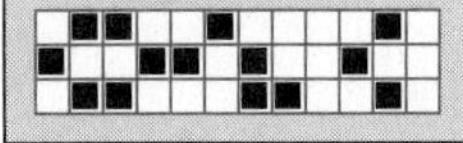

1. Recursion is an elegant and powerful tool. It combines iterative control with a built-in data structure, the system stack. To properly control that iteration, be sure that you provide an appropriate recursive termination condition for your algorithms.

2. Be sure that, when you invoke a procedure recursively, you are in some sense passing in a smaller, simpler version of the problem being solved. Otherwise, your algorithm will infinitely recur.

3. The use of tracer output can be valuable in debugging recursive algorithms. However, you must be careful not to insert so many tracer **write** statements that you become lost in the copious output they produce. Remember that recursive algorithms are often exponential in efficiency and, consequently, may be exponential in the amount of output produced by tracers also. You must be careful to insert tracer **write** statements judiciously. Where appropriate, use a Boolean constant that can be toggled to **true** or **false** to control whether or not the tracer output is produced.

■ Summary

Key Terms

binding time problem
generalized nested loops
LISP
recursive call
recursive definition
recursive procedure
recursive termination condition
run-time trace diagram
stack frame
tail-recursion
termination condition
trial-and-error backtracking

Key Concepts

- Stacks process procedure calls when a program executes. Understanding the role of the stack in this application is essential to effectively using the programming technique known as recursion.

- A recursive procedure or function invokes itself with a simpler version of the same problem it was originally given. Ultimately there must be a recursive termination condition to break a series of recursive procedure calls.
- In tail-recursion, no further processing occurs at any level of recursion after a return from a recursive call is made.
- A procedure's stack frame contains memory locations for all parameters and local variables and the machine address of the point to return to after the procedure completes execution at the current level.
- A run-time trace diagram can often be used to help analyze the efficiency of a recursive algorithm. If the diagram indicates that multiple recursive calls are made at each level, there is a good chance that the algorithm is in the class of exponential algorithms.
- Recursion can be used to solve a complex class of search problems by using a trial-and-error backtracking strategy. However, often such solutions can consume a tremendous amount of resources, particularly in terms of run-time efficiency.
- Do not be misled into thinking that recursion is necessarily the most efficient programming technique because the code that expresses it is often compact and lacking in any explicit loop control statements such as **WHILE** or **REPEAT.** The very nature of a recursive call generates iteration without any need for **WHILE** or **REPEAT.** The iteration control mechanism in recursion is the recursive termination condition which triggers a series of returns before another recursive call is made. Hence, from a time-efficiency perspective, a recursive algorithm's measure of effectiveness is closely tied to the number of times it must iterate its recursive call-and-return pattern. Moreover, with recursion, we pay a price in memory efficiency that is not present in other iterative control structures. This price is system stack space.
- The value of recursion lies in the way in which it enables us to express algorithms compactly and elegantly for a certain class of problems. Since we use recursion frequently throughout the rest of this text, you will learn to acquire a feel for the type of problems particularly suitable to this powerful technique. In the next chapter, we will see that recursion is an indispensable strategy for manipulating a data structure known as a tree. In later chapters, recursion will be explored as a means of sorting and searching.

Programming Problems and Projects

1. Write a program to call for input of a decimal number and convert it to its binary equivalent using the method described in the following flowchart.

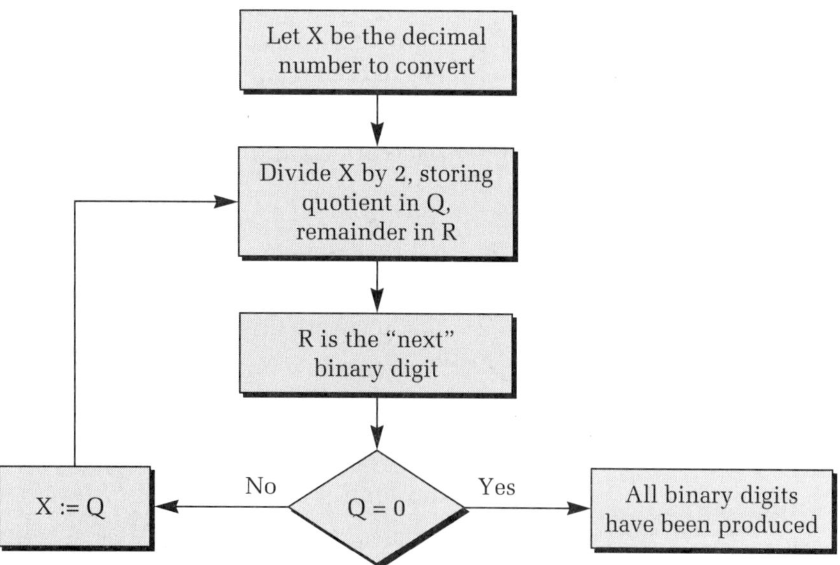

Note that this method produces the binary digits for the given number in reverse order. One strategy for printing out the digits in the correct order would be to store them in an array as they are produced and then print out the array. However, this strategy would have the drawbacks of allocating unnecessary storage for an array and then limiting the size of the binary number to the size of the array. Your program is not to employ this strategy. Rather call for input of the decimal number in your main program and then immediately transfer control to a procedure that in turn is called recursively, stacking the binary digits as they are produced. Once division by 2 yields 0, the succession of returns can be used to print out the digits one by one as they are popped from this stack.

2. The Nth Fibonacci number is defined by

   1 if N is 1.
   1 if N is 2.
   The sum of the previous two Fibonacci numbers otherwise.

   Write a recursive function to compute the Nth Fibonacci number. Then, using a run-time trace diagram, analyze the efficiency of your function.

3. Euclid devised a clever algorithm for computing the greatest common divisor of two integers. According to Euclid's algorithm,

$$\text{GCD(M,N)} = \begin{cases} \text{GCD(N,M) if N} > \text{M} \\ \text{M if N} = 0 \\ \text{GCD(N,M MOD N) if N} > 0 \end{cases}$$

   Write a recursive procedure to compute greatest common divisors via Euclid's method.

4. Suppose that you have N thousand dollars and can use it to buy a combination of Orange computers (which cost $1,000 each), HAL computers (which cost $2,000 each), or MAX computers (which cost $4,000 each). How many different combinations of Orange, HAL, MAX computers could be bought with your N thousand dollars?

   Write a program that receives N as input and responds with the number of possible combinations. *Hint:* If N were 100, then the number of combinations is

   The number of combinations totaling $100,000 and involving Orange and HAL computers only

   PLUS

   The number of combinations totaling $96,000 and involving potentially all three brands

   Think about this hint for a while and extend it to a recursive function that answers this question.

5. Ackermann's function is defined recursively for two nonnegative integers m and n as follows:

$$\text{Ackermann}\ (m,n) = \begin{cases} n + 1 \text{ if } m = 0 \\ \text{Ackermann}\ (m - 1, 1) \text{ if } n = 0 \\ \text{Ackermann}\ (m - 1, \text{Ackermann}\ (m,n - 1)) \text{ otherwise} \end{cases}$$

Write a recursive version of this function. Develop a run-time trace diagram for the function when $m = 2$ and $n = 3$. Attempt to deduce the big-O efficiency of the recursive version with respect to stack size and stack operations. Justify your answer in a written statement.

6. If you have access to an appropriate graphics device, write the procedures Line and RightTurn described in Section 6.1. Then experiment by writing recursive procedures that call on these procedures (and others you may develop) to produce a variety of interesting figures.

7. Write a procedure that receives a set of N integers and then prints all subsets of this set.

8. Write a program that completes the solution of the Eight Queens Problem as sketched in the Focus on Program Design section.

9. A K-permutation of the first N positive integers, $K \leq N$, is a permutation of a K-element subset of $\{ 1, 2, \ldots, N \}$. Write a procedure to generate all possible K-permutations of the first N positive integers.

10. A continued fraction is a number of the form that follows (where each a_i is an integer):

$$a_1 + \cfrac{1}{a_2 + \cfrac{1}{a_3 + \cfrac{1}{a_4 + \cfrac{\ddots}{\quad \cfrac{1}{a_n}}}}}$$

Though a continued fraction is composed of integers a_i, it has a real value. For example, consider the following continued fraction and its indicated real value.

$$1 + \cfrac{1}{2 + \cfrac{1}{6 + \cfrac{1}{5}}} = 1 + \cfrac{1}{2 + \cfrac{1}{\frac{31}{5}}} = 1 + \cfrac{1}{2 + \cfrac{5}{31}} = 1 + \cfrac{1}{\frac{67}{31}} = \frac{98}{67} = 1.46$$

Provide a **TYPE** definition of your implementation of a continued fraction. Then, write a recursive function that receives a continued fraction and returns its associated real value.

11. There are five other teams in the same league as the Bay Area Brawlers (Problem 4, Chapter 4 and Problem 13, Chapter 5). Over a given five-week period, the Brawlers must play each of the other teams exactly once. Using recursion, write a program to determine the ways in which such a five-week schedule could be accomplished. For an added challenge, introduce more realistic scheduling considerations into this problem. For instance, have your program determine the ways in which a fifteen-game schedule could be constructed such that each of the six teams in the league plays each of the other teams exactly three times, but never consecutively.

12. Write a procedure that uses a random number generator to produce mazes. One way of viewing a maze is as a two-dimensional array of records.

```
RECORD
  NorthBlocked,
  EastBlocked,
  SouthBlocked,
  WestBlocked : boolean
END
```

At each square in the array, the Boolean fields are set to indicate whether or not we can proceed in the indicated direction. After your maze-generating procedure is working, develop a procedure that uses trial-and-error backtracking to solve the maze.

13. A transportation network such as the following can be represented as a two-dimensional integer array with rows and columns indexed by the cities in the network. The number stored at position (K, J) of such an array represents the distance of the link between two cities. Zero indicates that two cities are not directly linked.

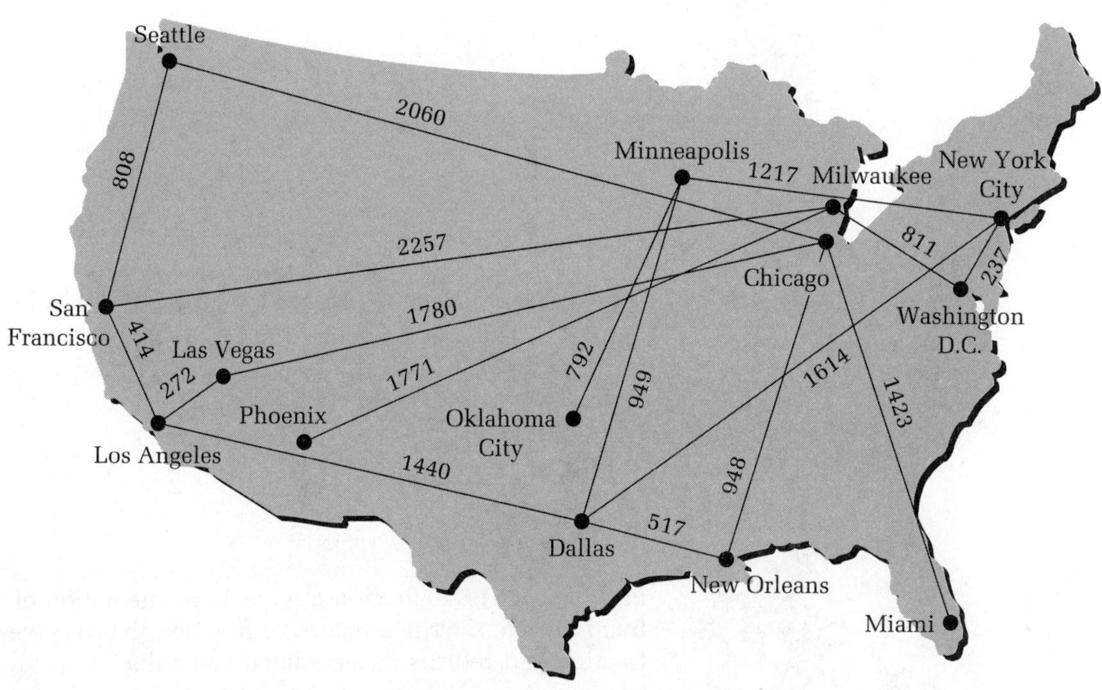

Write a program which, for input of two cities, outputs all possible paths connecting the two cities. Then modify the program so that it outputs only the shortest path linking the two cities. Use a trial-and-error backtracking strategy to do this. We will discuss a more efficient algorithm for solving this problem in the next chapter.

14. Another classic chess problem that can be solved by trial-and-error backtracking is known as the Knight's Tour. Given a chessboard with a knight initially placed at coordinates x_0, y_0, the problem is to specify a series of moves for the knight that will result in each board location being visited exactly once. From a given square on the chessboard, a knight may move to any of the eight numbered squares in the following diagram:

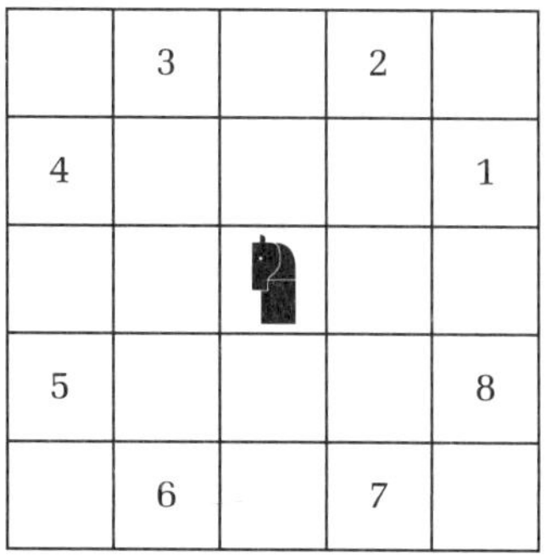

	3		2	
4				1
5				8
	6		7	

Write a program to find a valid Knight's Tour.

15. A famous theorem in mathematics states that four colors are enough to color any map in a fashion which allows each region on the map to be a different color from any of its adjacent neighbors. Write a program that initially allows input of a map. One way of doing this is to input each region followed by a list of its adjacent neighbors. This information can then be stored in a two-dimensional Boolean array with rows and columns indexed by region names. Store **true** at row K, column J if region K and region J are neighbors; otherwise store **false.** Once your program has appropriately stored the information associated with the input map, it should use trial-and-error backtracking to find a pattern for coloring the map with four colors. Note that the Four-Color Theorem from mathematics guarantees that such a pattern can be found.

16. Write a program to find a solution to the following stable marriage problem (or indicate that no solution exists for the input data). According to this problem, we have n men and n women, each of whom has stated distinct preferences for their possible partners. The data regarding these preferences is the input for this problem. It can be stored in two two-dimensional arrays: one in which each woman has rated each of the men as 1st choice, 2nd choice, . . . , nth choice and another in which each man has similarly rated each of the women. Given this input, a solution to the stable marriage problem is to find n couples (marriages) such that

1. Each man is part of exactly one couple (marriage).
2. Each woman is part of exactly one couple (marriage).
3. There does not exist a man and a woman who are not married to each other but who would prefer each other to their current spouses.

If a pair as specified in requirement 3 does exist, then the assignment of n couples is said to be unstable and should be avoided. Note that the stable marriage problem is representative of many real-life problems in which assignments have to be made according to preferences.

17. Write a program to analyze football team scores by computing the point spread for any team A playing any team B. Your program should compute the point spreads for

Level I Analysis: Team A played B in past
Level II Analysis: Average point spreads for situations such as

A played C—point spread 3 *C played B—point spread 7*

Total point spread 10

Level III Analysis: Average point spread for situations such as

A played C—point spread 3 *C played D—point spread −14 (C lost)* *D played B—point spread 7*

Total point spread −4

Level IV Analysis: Average point spreads for situations such as

A played C—point spread 3 *C played D—point spread −14* *D played E—point spread 21* *E played B—point spread 4*

Total point spread 14

All level II point spreads are then averaged for a final level II point spread figure. Point spreads are similarly averaged for levels III and IV. Items that potentially need to be stacked (via recursion) in this program include

- Accumulated point spread at current position.
- Number of scores reflected in the accumulated point spread at current position.
- Current position; that is, team A playing team B.
- Path to the current position; that is, teams played to get to the current position.

18. Many business phone numbers contain embedded words that correspond to the digits of the phone number and, at the same time, remind customers of the business's product name. For instance, because of the pattern of digits and letters on a phone (pictured below), the phone number for Caswell Catering and Convention Service, 227–9355, may also be interpreted as CASWELL.

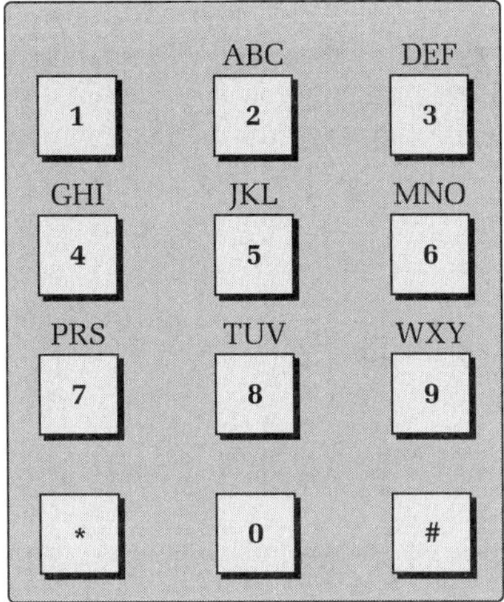

Because businesses often want to know which letter combinations are embedded in their phone number, the phone company would like you to write a procedure based upon the following:

```
TYPE
  PhoneNumber = ARRAY [1..10] OF integer; { used to store phone numbers of up to 10 digits }
  PhoneLetters = ARRAY [2..9] OF ARRAY [1..3] OF char; { used to store the three letters }
                                                      { associated with each dialing    }
                                                      { digit 2..9                      }
PROCEDURE PrintWords (NumDigits : integer;
                      Number    : PhoneNumber);

      { Given:   A phone number of up to 10 digits between 2 and 9 in Number and the actual      }
      {          number of digits in the phone number in NumDigits.                                }
      { Task:    Print out all letter combinations corresponding to this phone number.  Hence     }
      {          if Number were 56 and NumDigits were 2, your output should be the strings         }
      {          JM, JN, JO, KM, KN, KO, LM, LN, and LO.  }
      { Assume:  You may assume the existence of a global array Letters of type PhoneLetters       }
      {          that has been initialized to contain 'ABC' in index 2, 'DEF' in index 3, ...,    }
      {          'WXY' in index 9, corresponding to the matchup of three letters per phone          }
      {          digit.                                                                              }
      { Hint:    Remember the generalized nested looping that can be achieved at run-time by        }
      {          recursion.  Also, though it may not be the only way to do it, consider nesting     }
      {          another subordinate procedure within PrintWords, with that being the procedure      }
      {          that is called recursively. Then incorporate your procedure into a main program    }
      {          appropriate for testing it.                                                         }
```

19. Write a solution to the Towers of Hanoi problem in which you use a nonrecursive iterative control structure and a stack. In effect, your stack will simulate the role played by the system stack in the recursive version of the algorithm.

In a written statement, compare the time and space efficiency of your nonrecursive solution to the recursive solution presented in this chapter. Is your solution faster than the exponential recursive solution? If so, explain why it is. Otherwise, explain why it is still exponential in its run-time.

20. If you have had a course in discrete mathematics, then you may be familiar with recurrence relations and methods for explicitly solving them. Use your knowledge of recurrence relations to analyze the time and space efficiencies of the Towers of Hanoi and recursive binary search algorithms. Your analysis should be presented as a precise mathematical argument, citing any results that you use but do not prove.

Except during the nine months before he draws his first breath, no man manages his affairs as well as a tree does.

George Bernard Shaw
1856–1950

Binary Trees, General Trees, and Graphs

Human beings organize much of the world around them into *hierarchies*. For instance, an industrial or governmental body functions effectively only by defining a collection of supervisor-subordinate relationships among its participants. We have emphasized throughout the text that computer scientists design a software system by breaking it down into modules and defining hierarchical boss-worker relationships among those modules. In Chapter 6, we used hierarchical run-time trace diagrams to analyze the efficiency of recursive algorithms. To continue this discussion, we now introduce the idea of trees.

The familial parent-child relationship allows a natural breakdown of a family's history into a genealogical tree. In computer science, a *tree* is a data structure that represents such hierarchical relationships between data items.

To introduce some of the terminology of tree structures, consider the record of a student at a typical university. In addition to the usual statistical background information such as social security number, name, and address, a typical student record contains listings for a number of courses, exams and final grades in each course, overall grade point average, and other data relating to the student's performance at the college. Figure 7.1 is a tree structure representing such a student record. As in genealogical trees, at the highest *level* (0) of a tree is its *root* (also called the *root node*). Here STUDENT is the root node. The nodes NAME, ADDRESS, SSN, COURSE, and GPA, which are directly connected to the root node, are the *child nodes* of the *parent node* STUDENT. The child nodes of a given parent constitute a set of *siblings*. Thus NAME, ADDRESS, SSN, COURSE, and GPA are siblings. In the hierarchy represented by a tree, the child nodes of a parent are one level

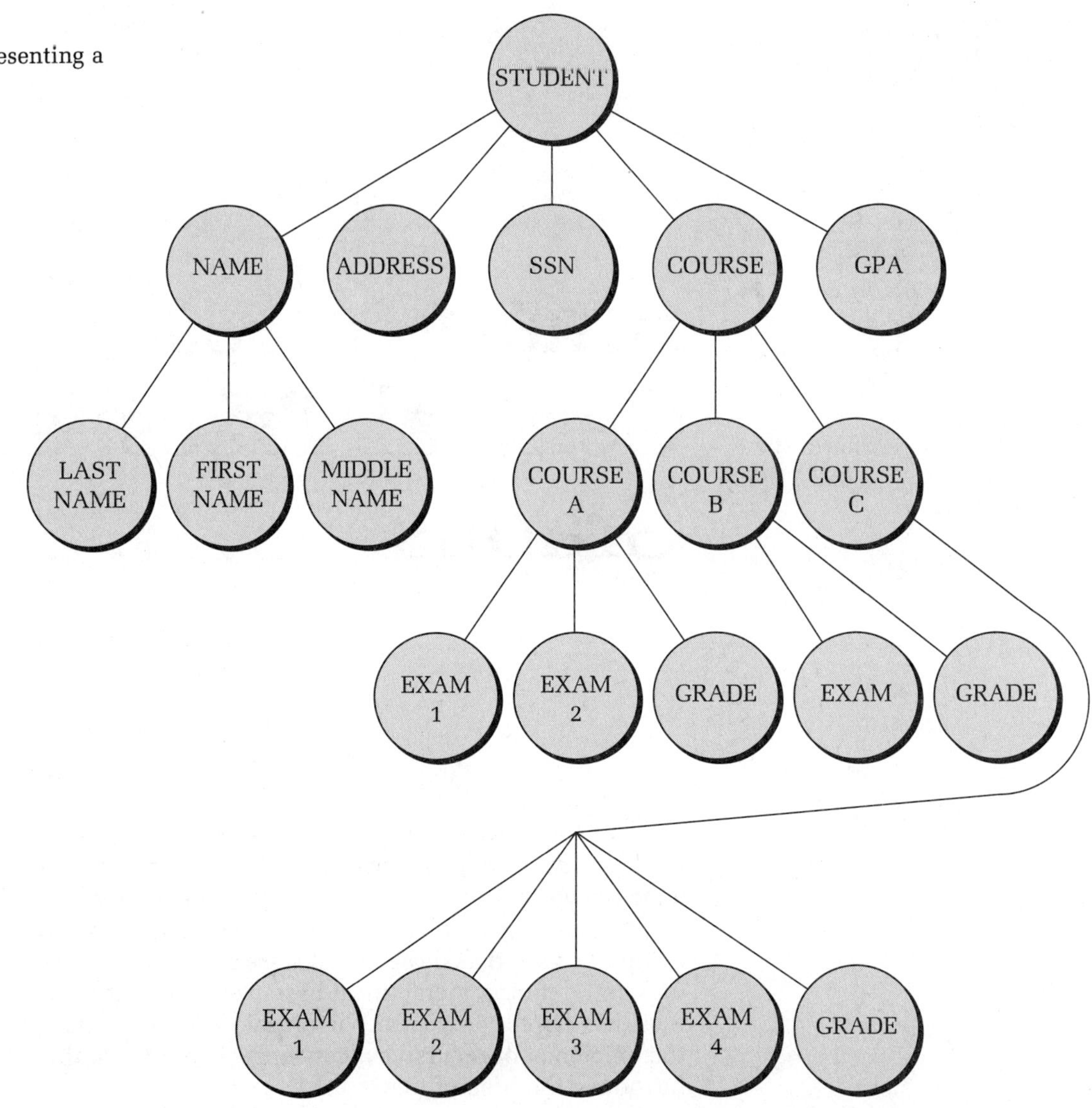

FIGURE 7.1
Tree structure representing a student record

lower than the parent node. Thus NAME, ADDRESS, SSN, COURSE, and GPA are at level 1 in Figure 7.1.

A link between a parent and its child is called a *branch* in a tree structure. Each node in a tree except the root must descend from a parent node via a branch. Thus LASTNAME, FIRSTNAME, and MIDDLENAME descend from the parent node NAME. The root of the tree is the *ancestor* of all the nodes in the tree. Each node may be the parent of any number of nodes in the tree.

A node with no children is called a *leaf node.* In Figure 7.1, GPA is a leaf node. LASTNAME, FIRSTNAME, MIDDLENAME, EXAM1, and EXAM2 also are leaf nodes.

A *subtree* is a subset of a tree that is itself a tree; the tree in Figure 7.2 is a subtree of the tree in Figure 7.1. This subtree has the root node NAME. Similarly, the tree in Figure 7.3 is another subtree of the tree in Figure 7.1. Notice that the tree in Figure 7.3 is a subtree of the tree in Figure 7.1 and the tree in Figure 7.4.

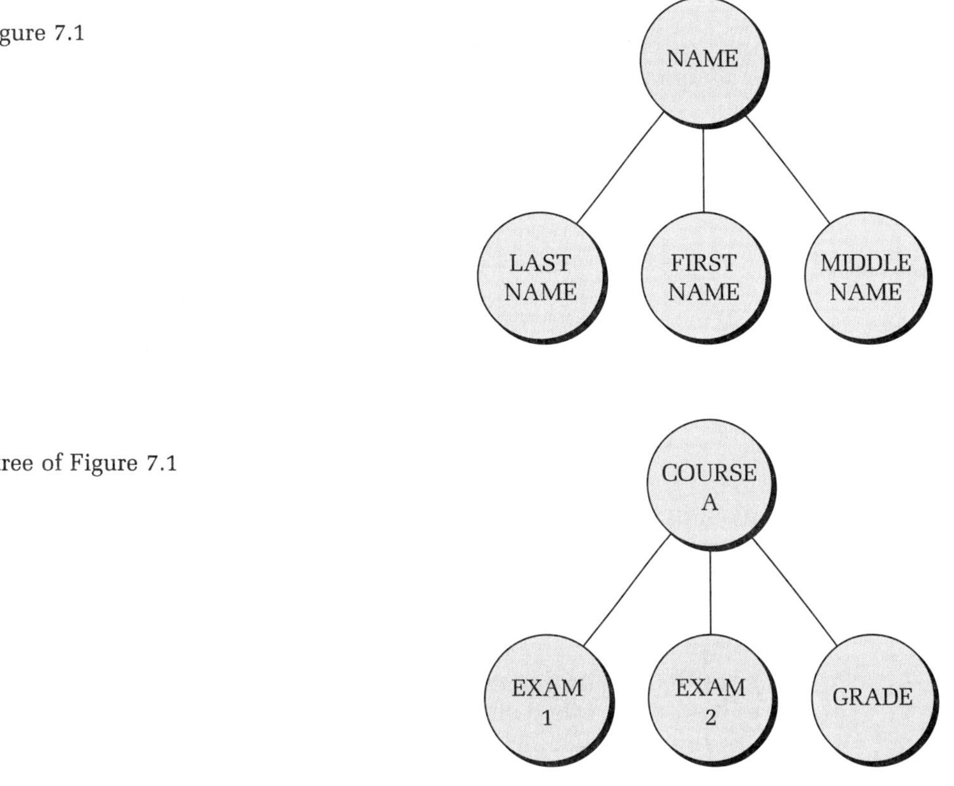

FIGURE 7.2
Subtree of Figure 7.1

FIGURE 7.3
Another subtree of Figure 7.1

FIGURE 7.4
Another subtree of Figure 7.1

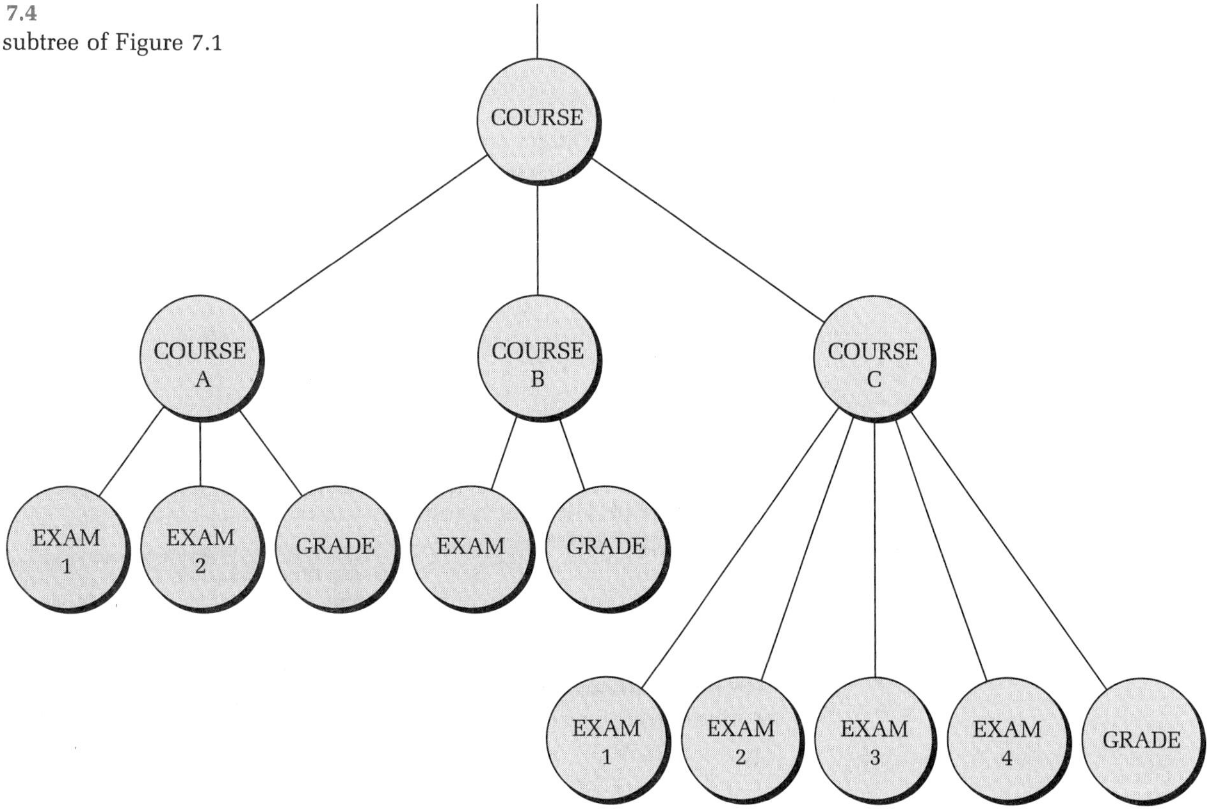

7.1 General Trees and Binary Trees as Abstract Data Types

OBJECTIVES

- to define partially the general tree ADT
- to define completely the binary tree ADT
- to understand conceptually the effect of each of the binary tree operations
- to become familiar with some examples of binary trees such as heaps, arithmetic expression trees, and binary search trees

It is evident from the preceding discussion that a tree has the following interesting property: Any given node within a tree is itself the root node of a completely analogous tree structure. That is, a tree is composed of a collection of substructures, each of which also meets the criteria for being a tree. This sounds dangerously circular, and, to formally describe a tree in this fashion, we must be sure to give ourselves an escape from the recursion. This is done via the following definition of a tree as an abstract data type:

> **Tree.** A *general tree* is a set of nodes that is either empty (the recursive termination condition), or has a designated node called the root from which (hierarchically) descend zero or more subtrees. Each subtree itself satisfies the definition of a tree.

We will defer completing the definition of a general tree to Section 7.5. There we will more formally discuss the operations associated with this ADT.

Two points about this partial definition should be emphasized. First, the recursive fashion in which a tree is defined should provide a strong hint that most tree-processing algorithms will also be recursive. Second, most operations on the tree data structure are closely linked to the hierarchical relationship among nodes for that particular tree. This hierarchical relationship may vary greatly from tree to tree. To consider some examples of such relationships which are found quite often in computer science applications, let us restrict our attention for the moment to an abstract data type called a *binary tree.*

> **Binary Tree.** A binary tree is a tree in which each node has exactly two subtrees. These two subtrees are designated as the left and right subtrees respectively. Note that either or both of these subtrees could be empty.

We specify the following operations on a binary tree in terms of pre- and postconditions.

Create operation
- Preconditions: *BT* is a binary tree, potentially not initialized.
- Postconditions: *BT* is initialized to the empty binary tree.

Empty operation
- Preconditions: *BT* is a previously created binary tree.
- Postconditions: *Empty* returns **true** if the tree is empty, **false** otherwise.

Full operation
- Preconditions: *BT* is a previously created binary tree.
- Postconditions: *Full* returns **true** if the tree is full, **false** otherwise.

AddNode operation

Preconditions: *BT* is a previously created binary tree based upon a particular hierarchical property. *Item* is a value to be inserted in *BT*.

Postconditions: If the tree *BT* is full, *Item* is not inserted and *BT* is left unaltered. Otherwise *Item* is added to *BT* in a way which maintains *BT*'s hierarchical property.

PreorderTraversal operation

Preconditions: *BT* is a previously created binary tree, and *ProcessNode* is an algorithmic process that can be applied to each node in the tree *BT*.

Postconditions: Each node of *BT* is visited in the following order: root of *BT* first, then recursively all nodes in left subtree, then recursively all nodes in right subtree. As each node is visited, *ProcessNode* is applied to it.

InorderTraversal operation

Preconditions: *BT* is a previously created binary tree, and *ProcessNode* is an algorithmic process that can be applied to each node in the tree *BT*.

Postconditions: Each node of *BT* is visited in the following order: first visit recursively all nodes in left subtree of *BT*, then visit the root of *BT*, then recursively all nodes in right subtree. As each node is visited, *ProcessNode* is applied to it.

PostorderTraversal operation

Preconditions: *BT* is a previously created binary tree, and *ProcessNode* is an algorithmic process that can be applied to each node in the tree *BT*.

Postconditions: Each node of *BT* is visited in the following order: first visit recursively all nodes in left subtree of *BT*, then visit recursively all nodes in right subtree, then visit the root of *BT*. As each node is visited, *ProcessNode* is applied to it.

Several remarks are in order concerning this definition. First, the three traversal procedures require some clarification. With a linked list, there is only one obvious traversal because there was only one node that could be reached from any given node. However, with a binary tree, at any node, there are some choices to be made.

- Should we apply ProcessNode to the data field of the root before proceeding to the left and right subtrees?
- Should we apply ProcessNode to the nodes in the left subtree and right subtree before processing the data in the root?
- Should we apply ProcessNode to all the nodes in one of the subtrees, then to the root, and finally to all the nodes in the other subtree?

The answers to these questions determine the type of traversal. Figure 7.5 demonstrates the different orders in which nodes are visited under the three traversals.

FIGURE 7.5
Differences between preorder, inorder, and postorder traversals

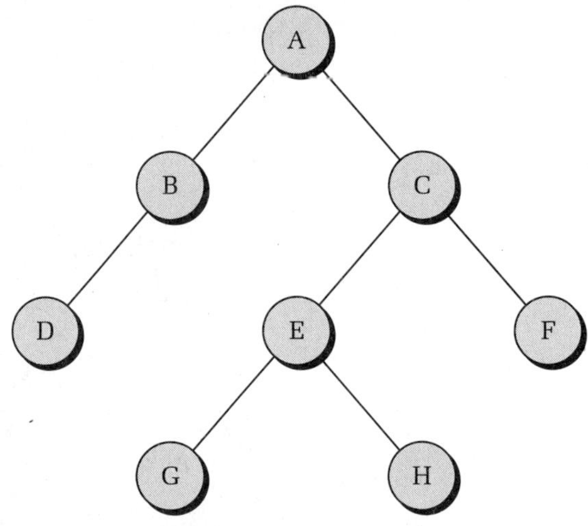

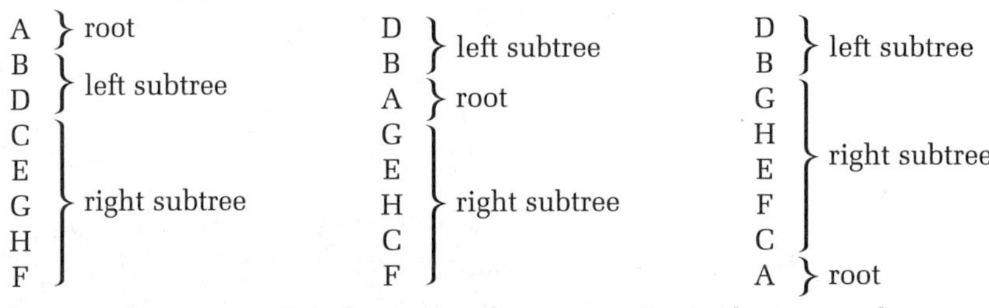

Second, the AddNode operation specified in our ADT definition for a binary tree provides a generic tree-building operation. That is, repeated applications of the AddNode operation on an initially empty binary tree are typically the way that a binary tree is constructed. However, it is virtually impossible to define or implement the AddNode operation in a way that is general enough for all applications that will use a binary tree. Each instance of a binary tree is highly dependent on the hierarchical relationship between nodes that defines that particular binary tree. Therefore, we have linked our specification of the AddNode operation to the hierarchical relationship underlying a particular binary tree.

The following three examples provide illustrations of hierarchical relationships that can be used in defining binary trees. We will often use trees based on these hierarchical properties as examples in the remainder of the chapter. However, these three properties should by no means be considered exhaustive—virtually every application that uses a binary tree will have its own definitional property. The point to be emphasized now is that the AddNode operation must, in its implementation, always be tailored to the property that defines a tree.

■ EXAMPLE 7.1

The tree of Figure 7.6 is a binary tree. Each node of this tree has two subtrees (null or non-null) designated as the left subtree and the right subtree. The particular hierarchical relationship underlying this tree is that the data in any given node of the tree are greater than or equal to the data in its left *and*

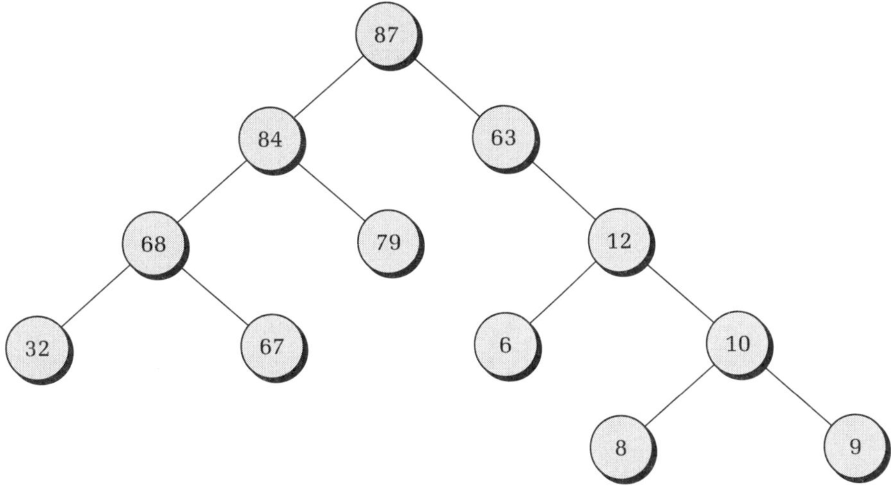

FIGURE 7.6
Binary tree with the heap property

right subtrees. A tree with this property is said to be a *heap* and to have the *heap property*. (This notion is not to be confused with the heap maintained by Pascal for allocating space to pointer variables as described in Chapter 4.) We will discuss heaps in more detail in the next section. Also, they will prove particularly important in our discussion of more powerful sorting methods in Chapter 8. The Programming Problems at the end of this chapter also indicate how a heap may be used to implement the priority queue abstract data structure introduced in Chapter 5. The heap property is one example of a hierarchical relationship that can underlie a tree and hence must be preserved when various operations are performed upon the tree.

■ ■

■ EXAMPLE 7.2

A second example of a hierarchical relationship underlying a binary tree structure is shown in Figure 7.7.

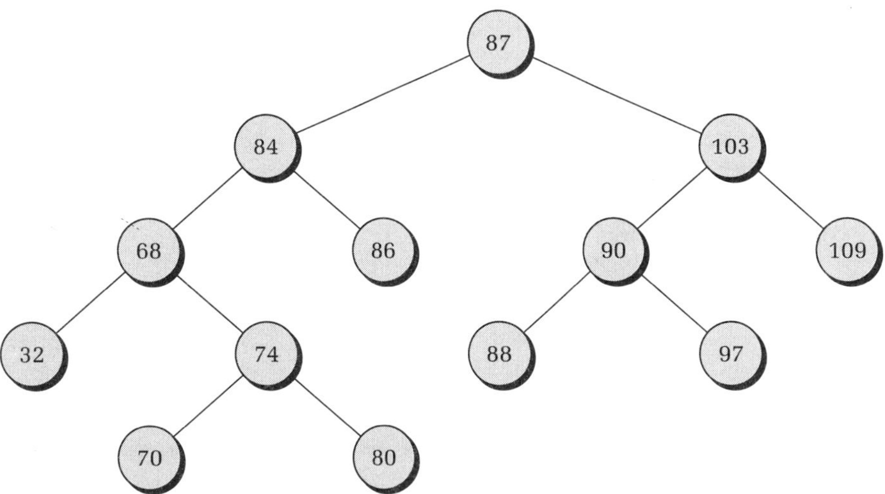

FIGURE 7.7
Binary search tree with the ordering property

This binary tree exhibits the property known as the *ordering property;* the data in each node of the tree is greater than all of the data in that node's left subtree and less than or equal to all the data in the right subtree. A binary tree with the ordering property is often called a *binary search tree.* We shall see the importance of trees possessing this property when we explore binary trees as a means of implementing a keyed list in Section 7.3.

EXAMPLE 7.3

As a final example of a hierarchical relationship that can determine the arrangement of data in a binary tree, consider Figure 7.8, in which we have a binary tree representation of the infix algebraic expression

(A − B) + C * (E/F)

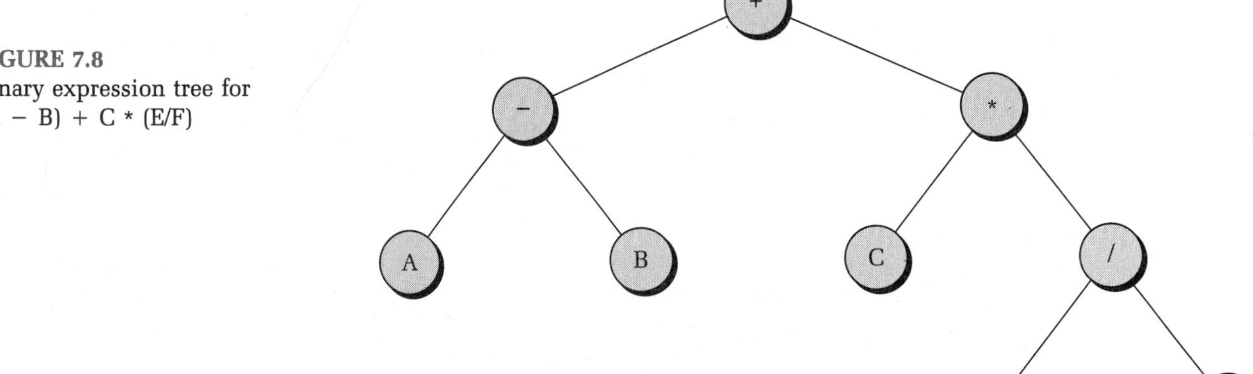

FIGURE 7.8
Binary expression tree for (A − B) + C * (E/F)

Take a moment to make particular note of Figure 7.8. Since we will be referring back to it frequently throughout this chapter, you may want to clip the page or mark it with a bookmark.

The hierarchical relationship of parent to children in this tree is that of algebraic operator to its two operands. Note that an operand may itself be an expression (that is, a subtree) which must be evaluated before the operator in the parent node can be applied. Note also that, if the order of evaluation in the expression changes as in

(A − B) + C * E/F

then the corresponding binary expression tree must also change as reflected in Figure 7.9.

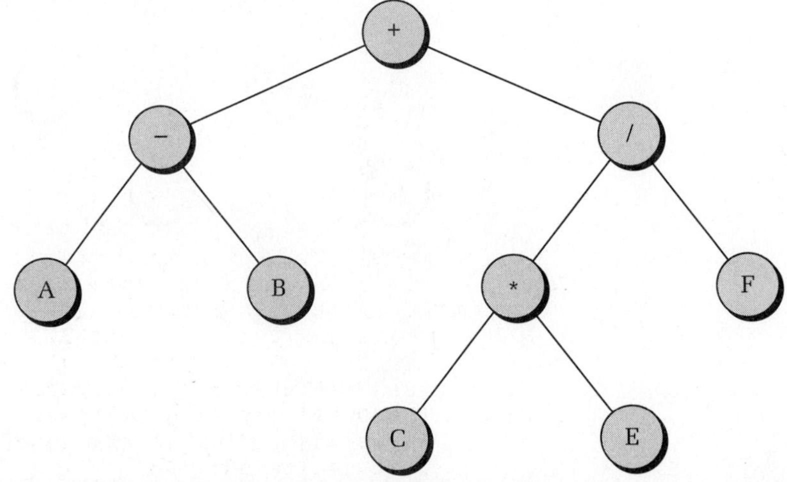

FIGURE 7.9
Binary expression tree for (A − B) + C * E/F

Contemporary compilers make use of tree structures in obtaining forms of an arithmetic expression for efficient evaluation. As we've seen, there are basically three forms for an arithmetic expression such as that corresponding to Figure 7.8: infix, prefix, and postfix.

Expression	Form
(A − B) + C * (E/F)	infix
+ − AB*C/EF	prefix
AB − CEF/* +	postfix

All three of these forms are immediately available to us if we know exactly how the corresponding tree should be traversed. The *inorder traversal* of the binary tree for an arithmetic expression gives us the expression in unparenthesized infix form. The *preorder traversal* of the same tree leads us to the prefix form of the expression, whereas the *postorder traversal* of the tree yields the postfix form of the expression. We shall study procedures for these three traversals in Section 7.2, when we discuss a method of implementing a binary tree.

We close this section with a Pascal interface for the binary tree ADT. In the sections that follow, we will analyze two implementations that adhere to this interface.

Pascal Interface for the Binary Tree ADT

```
TYPE
  TreeDataNode =  { This specifies the data in a given tree node. };
  BinaryTree   =  { This is the binary tree data type.            };

PROCEDURE Create (VAR BT : BinaryTree);

  {  Given:   BT a binary tree, potentially not initialized.      }
  {  Task:    Initialize BT to an empty binary tree.              }
  {  Return:  Initialized tree.                                   }

FUNCTION Empty (BT : BinaryTree) : boolean;

  {  Given:   BT, a binary tree.                                  }
  {  Task:    Check if the tree BT is empty.                      }
  {  Return:  True if the tree is empty, false otherwise.         }

FUNCTION Full (BT : BinaryTree) : boolean;

  {  Given:   BT, a binary tree.                                  }
  {  Task:    Check if the tree BT is full.                       }
  {  Return:  True if the tree is full, false otherwise.          }

PROCEDURE AddNode (VAR BT : BinaryTree;
                       Item : TreeDataNode);

  {  Given:   BT, a binary tree based upon a particular           }
  {           hierarchical property.  Item, a value               }
  {           to be inserted in tree BT.                          }
  {  Task:    Insert Item in tree BT maintaining the              }
  {           tree's hierarchical property.                       }
  {  Return:  Appropriately altered tree.  If the tree            }
  {           BT is full, Item is not inserted and BT is          }
  {           left unaltered.                                     }
```

```
PROCEDURE PreorderTrav (BT : BinaryTree;
                        PROCEDURE ProcessNode (VAR Item : TreeDataNode));

  { Given:    Binary tree BT.                                    }
  { Task:     Perform preorder traversal--root of BT first,      }
  {           then left subtree, then right subtree--            }
  {           applying ProcessNode to each Item in tree.         }
  { Return:   BT with each node affected by ProcessNode.         }

PROCEDURE InorderTrav (BT : BinaryTree;
                       PROCEDURE ProcessNode (VAR Item : TreeDataNode));

  { Given:    Binary tree BT.                                    }
  { Task:     Perform inorder traversal--left subtree            }
  {           first, then root of BT, then right subtree--       }
  {           applying ProcessNode to each Item in tree.         }
  { Return:   BT with each node affected by ProcessNode.         }

PROCEDURE PostorderTrav (BT : BinaryTree;
                         PROCEDURE ProcessNode (VAR Item : TreeDataNode));

  { Given:    Binary tree BT.                                    }
  { Task:     Perform postorder traversal--left subtree          }
  {           first, then right subtree, then root of BT--       }
  {           applying ProcessNode to each Item in tree.         }
  { Return:   BT with each node affected by ProcessNode.         }
```

Exercises 7.1

1. Draw a binary tree for the following expression:

   A * B − (C + D) * (P/Q)

2. Represent the following StudentRec as a binary tree:

```
Name = RECORD
         FirstName : ARRAY [1..10] OF char;
         LastName : ARRAY [1..10] OF char
       END;

Year = RECORD
         FirstSem : ARRAY [1..2] OF char;
         SecondSem : ARRAY [1..2] OF char
       END;

StudentRec = RECORD
               StudentName : Name;
               YearOfStudy : Year
             END;
```

3. What, in an abstract sense, does a tree structure represent?

4. Indicate which of the following are binary search trees with the ordering property. Carefully explain what is wrong with those that are not.

   a.

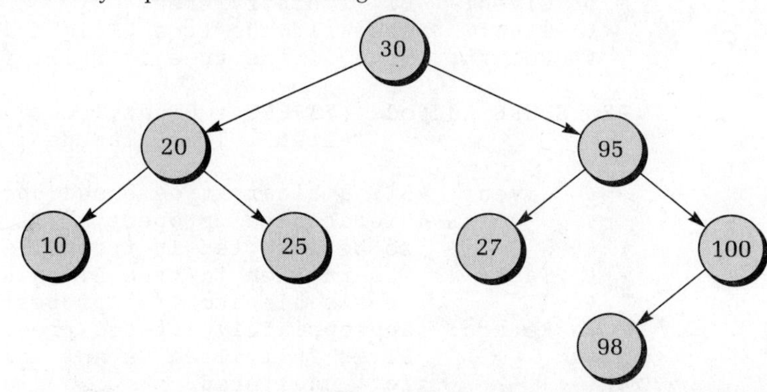

b.

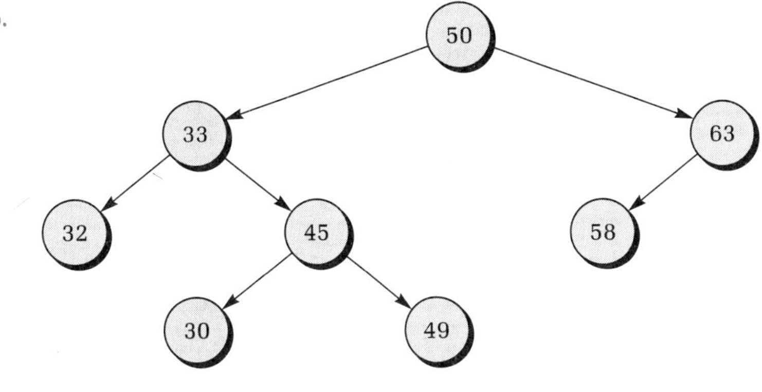

c.

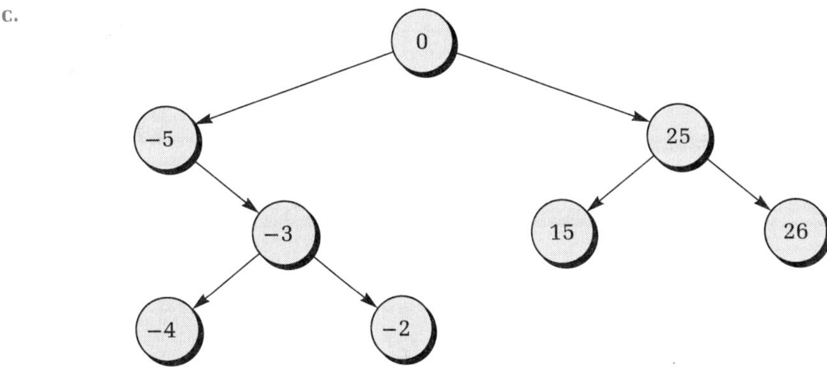

d.

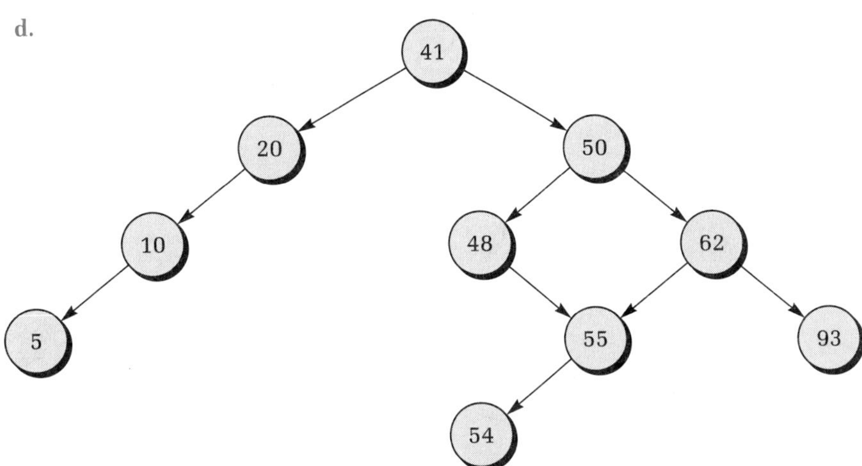

5. Indicate which of the following are binary trees with the heap property. Carefully explain what is wrong with those that are not.

a.

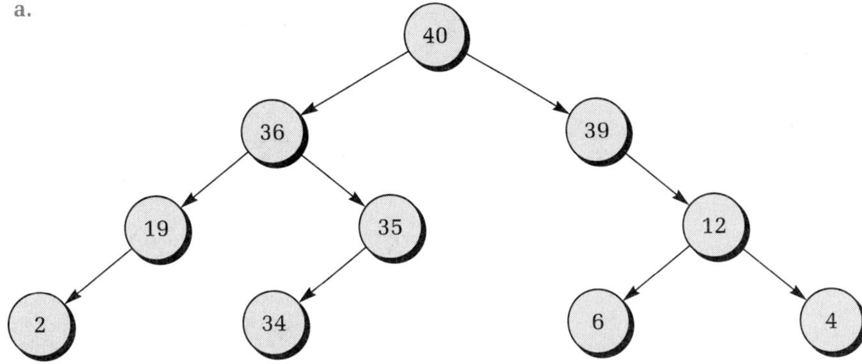

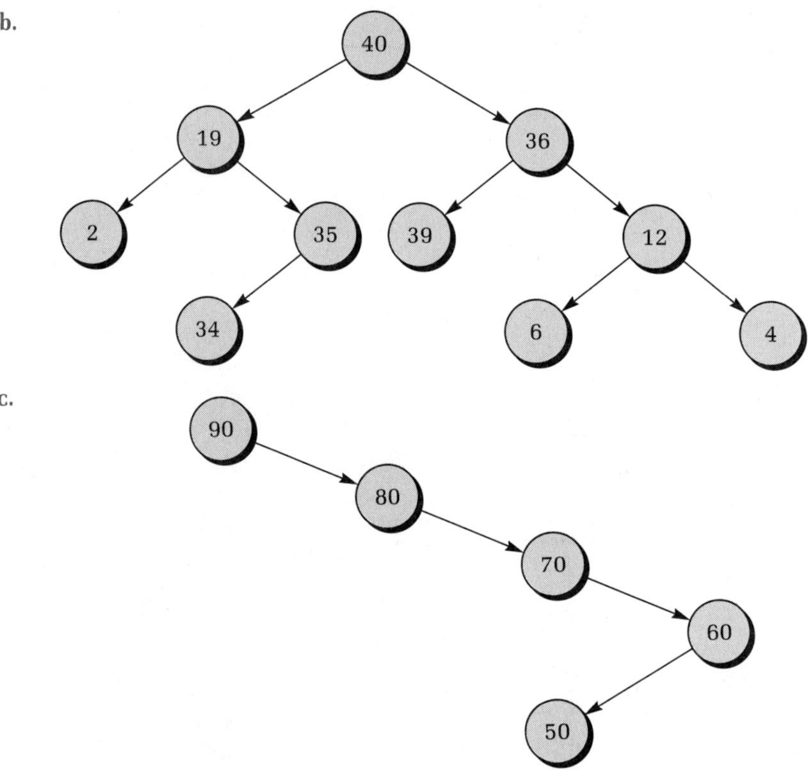

6. Given the following binary tree, indicate the order in which nodes would be processed for each of the preorder, postorder, and inorder traversals.

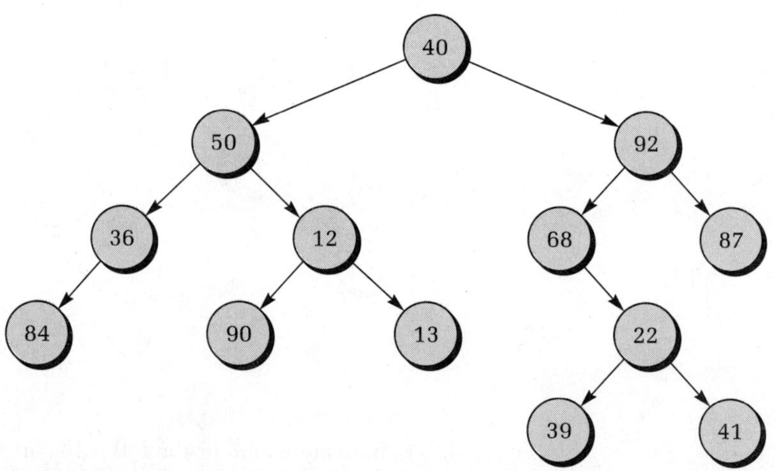

7. Construct some binary search trees with the ordering property. Then do some inorder traversals of these trees. What do you observe about the order in which nodes are processed? Be as specific as possible in stating your answer.

8. Given the following postorder and inorder traversals of a binary tree, draw the tree

   Postorder: ABCDEFIKJGH
   Inorder: CBAEDFHIGKJ

   Attempt to deduce your answer in a systematic (and recursive) fashion, not by trial-and-error methods. After you have solved this problem, write a statement in which you describe the method you used to solve it and explain how this method could be applied to similar problems.

9. Draw binary expression trees corresponding to the algebraic expression whose:
   a. infix representation is P/(Q + R) * X − Y.
   b. postfix representation is XYZPQR* +/− *.
   c. prefix representation is + * −MNP/RS.
10. In a written statement, explain how the arrangement of data in a binary expression tree reflects the order of operations in the corresponding expression.

■ ■ ■ ■

7.2 Linked Implementation of a Binary Tree

OBJECTIVES

- to become familiar with the linked implementation of the binary tree ADT
- to be able to implement the AddNode operation for a binary search tree with the ordering property
- to see how the shape of a binary search tree is dependent on the order in which data arrive for insertion into the tree
- to develop algorithms for the three traversal operations on the linked implementation of a binary tree

Consistent with the way in which we have studied other data structures, we now have a very good idea of *what* a tree is without any consideration of *how* we will implement it. This latter issue must now be explored.

There are two common methods for implementing binary trees. One method, known as *linked implementation,* uses pointers. The other, which does not require the overhead of maintaining pointers, is called a *linear implementation.* In this section and the next, we will focus on the linked implementation. We will see how this implementation is particularly well-suited for binary search trees and binary expression trees.

Because each node in a binary tree may have two child nodes, a node in a linked implementation has two pointer fields, one for each child, and one or more data fields. When a node has no children, the corresponding pointer fields are **NIL.** Figure 7.10 is a linked representation of the binary expression tree of Figure 7.8. The LeftChild and RightChild fields are pointers to (that is, memory addresses of) the left child and the right child of a node.

For the moment, let us give a detailed description of the linked representation of the binary tree of Figure 7.8, using an array of records. This is similar to the way in which we first discussed linked lists in Chapter 4. By doing this, we will actually be able to trace the values of the pointers. Once the concept is thoroughly understood, we will then return to using Pascal pointer variables for the actual implementation of binary trees. For example,

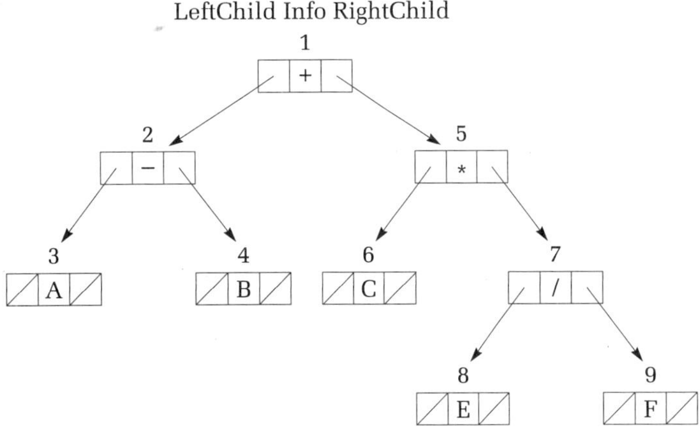

FIGURE 7.10
Linked representation of the binary expression tree of Figure 7.8

we can implement the tree of Figure 7.10 as shown in Table 7.1, using the strategy of building the left subtree for each node before considering the right subtree. The numbers on top of the cells in Figure 7.10 represent the addresses given in the LeftChild and RightChild fields.

TABLE 7.1
Implementation of Figure 7.10 using array of records

Node	Info	LeftChild	RightChild
1	+	2	5
2	–	3	4
3	A	NIL	NIL
4	B	NIL	NIL
5	*	6	7
6	C	NIL	NIL
7	/	8	9
8	E	NIL	NIL
9	F	NIL	NIL

In the linked representation, insertions and deletions involve no data movement except the rearrangement of pointers. Suppose we wish to modify the tree in Figure 7.8 to that in Figure 7.11. (This change might be needed due to some recent modification in the expression represented by Figure 7.8.) The insertion of the nodes containing – and P into the tree structure can be achieved easily by simply adding the nodes – and P in the next available spaces in the array and adjusting the corresponding pointers.

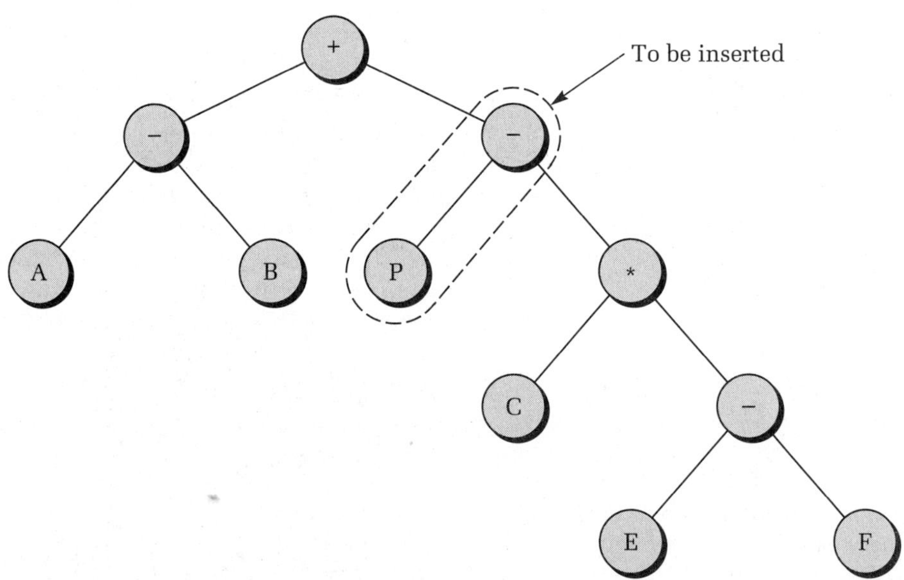

FIGURE 7.11
Desired modification of Figure 7.8

For the implementation of the tree shown in Figure 7.10, the effect of this insertion is given by Table 7.2. The adjusted pointers and data fields have

TABLE 7.2
Modification of Table 7.1 by insertions into the tree of Figure 7.8

Row	Info	LeftChild	RightChild
1	+	2	(10)
2	–	3	4
3	A	NIL	NIL
4	B	NIL	NIL
5	*	6	7
6	C	NIL	NIL
7	/	8	9
8	E	NIL	NIL
9	F	NIL	NIL
10	–	(11)	(5)
11	P	(NIL)	(NIL)

been circled. Notice that the change in row 1 of RightChild and the additional rows 10 and 11 are all that is necessary. No data were moved.

Similarly, if we wish to shorten the tree in Figure 7.8 by deleting the nodes * and C, then all we must do is rearrange the pointers to obtain the altered tree, as shown in Figure 7.12. The effect of this deletion is given in Table 7.3. As before, the adjusted pointers and data fields have been circled.

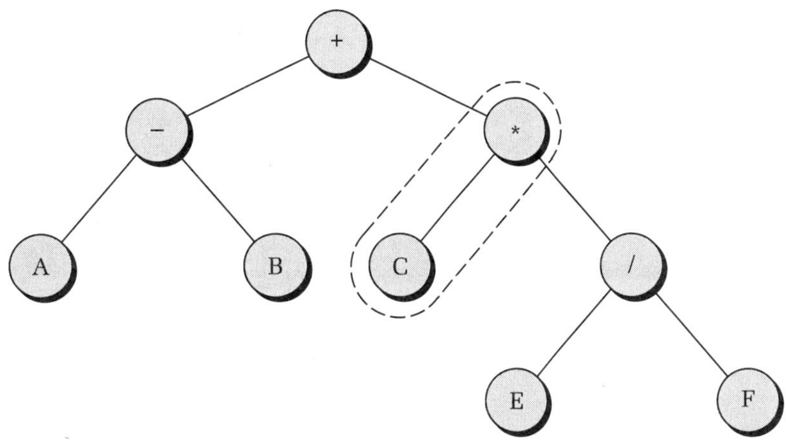

FIGURE 7.12 Another modification of Figure 7.8

TABLE 7.3 Modification of tree of Figure 7.8

Row	Info	LeftChild	RightChild	Modified tree
1	+	2	7	
2	−	3	4	
3	A	NIL	NIL	
4	B	NIL	NIL	
5	*			unused space after
6	C			deletion of '*' and 'C'
7	/	8	9	
8	E	NIL	NIL	
9	F	NIL	NIL	

A more formal statement of the algorithm underlying such insertions and deletions is dependent upon the hierarchical property that forms the basis for the tree structure. We will soon examine in detail insertion and deletion algorithms for binary search trees.

Now that we have explained the linked representation of a binary tree by using arrays to contain pointer values that can be explicitly traced, we will use the following general record description with Pascal pointer variables to implement this structure in the remainder of this and the next sections.

```
TYPE
  TreeDataNode = { whatever is being stored in individual node };
  BinaryTree = ^RootNode;
  RootNode = RECORD
               LeftChild : BinaryTree;
               Info : TreeDataNode;
               RightChild : BinaryTree
             END;
```

EXAMPLE 7.4

Using the linked representation of a binary tree, implement the AddNode operation for a binary search tree with the ordering property.

```
PROCEDURE AddNode (VAR BT : BinaryTree;
                       Item : TreeDataNode);

  {  Given:   BT, a binary search tree with ordering                }
  {           property, implemented by Pascal pointer variables.   }
  {           Item, a value to be inserted in tree BT.              }
  {  Task:    Insert Item in tree BT, maintaining                   }
  {           the tree's ordering property.                         }
  {  Return:  Appropriately altered tree.                           }

  BEGIN
    IF BT = NIL THEN  { Add a new node  at leaf level }
      BEGIN
        new (BT);
        BT^.Info := Item;
        BT^.LeftChild := NIL;
        BT^.RightChild := NIL
      END
    ELSE IF Item < BT^.Info THEN { Move down the tree }
      AddNode (BT^.LeftChild, Item)
    ELSE
      AddNode (BT^.RightChild, Item)
  END; {  of PROCEDURE AddNode  }
```

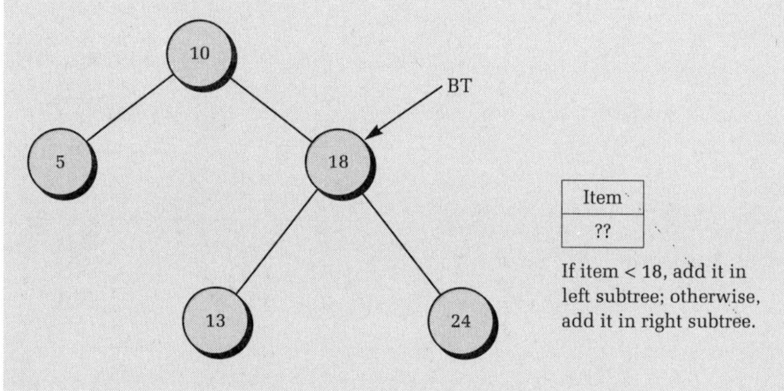

The algorithm of Example 7.4 implies that insertion of new nodes will always occur at the leaf nodes of a tree. As with insertion into a linked list, no data are moved; only pointers are manipulated. However, unlike the steps required by a linked list, we do not have to traverse the list sequentially to determine where the new node belongs. Instead, using the *insertion rule*—if less than, go left; otherwise, go right—we need merely traverse one branch of the tree to determine the position for a new node.

For example, if the AddNode procedure of Example 7.4 is successively fed numerical items in the following order:

16 8 −5 20 30 101 0 10 18

the binary search tree that results can be traced by the sequence in Figure 7.13. Note that the shape of the binary search tree is dependent on the order in which data items are given to AddNode. This dependency of the shape of the tree on the order in which data arrive for insertion complicates any attempt to analyze the efficiency of the AddNode procedure in Example 7.4. We will provide a more detailed analysis of binary search trees with the ordering property in Section 7.3.

FIGURE 7.13
Growth of search tree when data arrive in order
16 8 −5 20 30 101 0 10 18

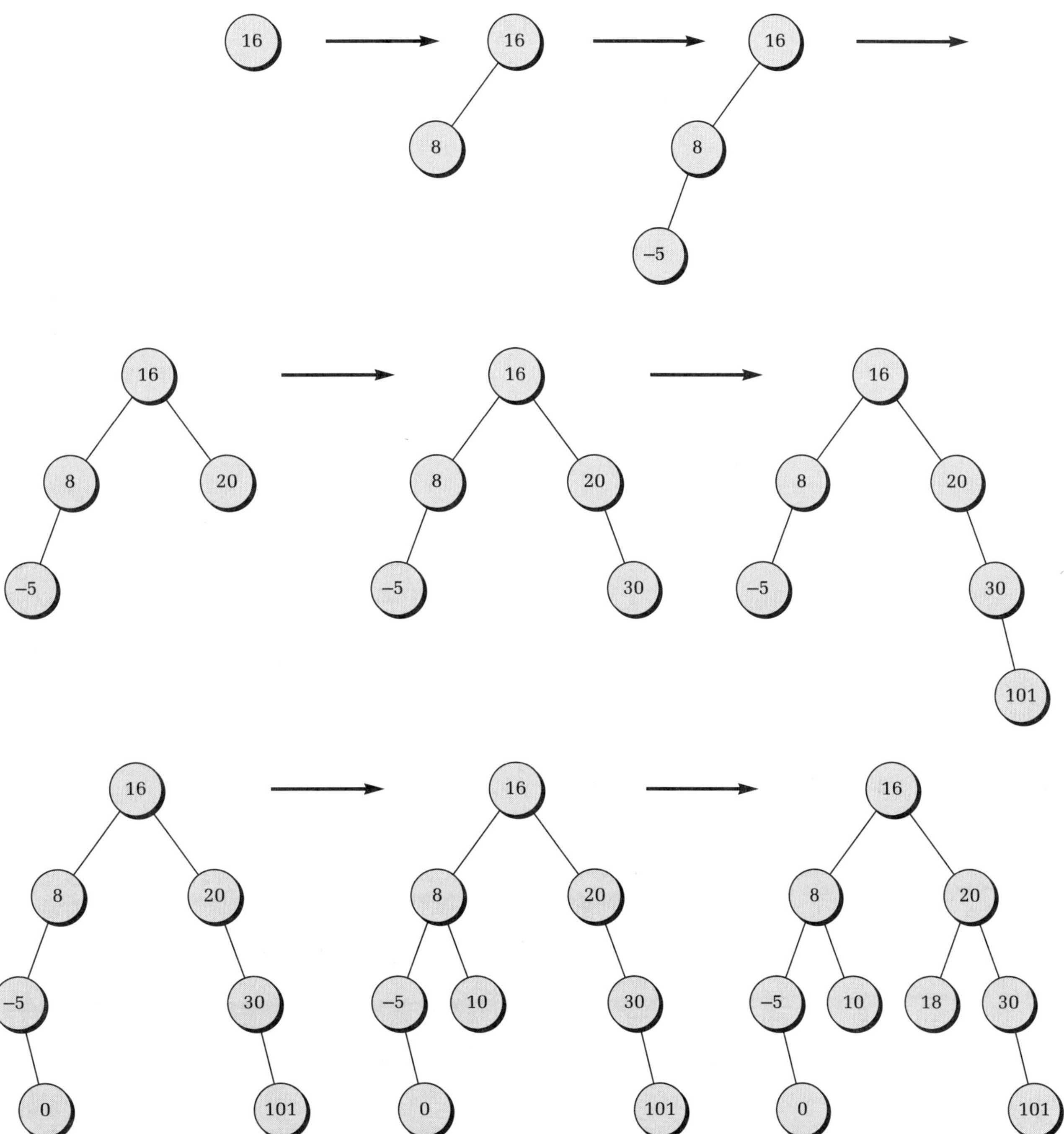

Implementing Traversal Operations on a Binary Tree

In Section 7.1 we described conceptually three different traversal operations on a binary tree: preorder, inorder, and postorder. In Example 7.3, we established correspondences between these three traversals and the prefix, infix, and postfix forms of the algebraic formula represented by a binary expression tree. However, it is important to reiterate that the three traversals apply broadly to all binary trees, regardless of the hierarchical relationship underlying their structure.

Recall from Section 7.1 the threefold dilemma facing us at each node we visit in a traversal of a binary tree.

1. Do we process the data contained in the node at which we are currently located?
2. Do we remember the location of the current node (so that we can return to process it) and visit (and process) all nodes in its left subtree?
3. Do we remember the location of the current node (so that we can return to process it) and visit (and process) all nodes in its right subtree?

Each of the three choices represents a valid choice. The route chosen out of the three-way dilemma dictates the order in which the nodes are visited and processed.

Preorder Traversal of a Binary Tree

In a preorder traversal, the three options are combined in the following order:

1. First, process the root node.
2. Then, recursively visit all nodes in the left subtree.
3. Finally, recursively visit all nodes in the right subtree.

These three ordered steps are recursive. Once the root of the tree is processed, we go to the root of the left subtree, and then to the root of the left subtree of the left subtree, and so on until we can go no farther. Following these three steps, the preorder traversal of the tree of Figure 7.8 would process nodes in the order

$$+ \; - AB * C/EF$$

which is the prefix form of the expression

$$(A - B) + C * (E/F)$$

Hence we conclude that if to process a node means to print it, then a preorder traversal of a binary expression tree will output the prefix form of the expression.

The preorder traversal of an existing binary tree implemented via the linked representation can be accomplished recursively using the following procedure:

```
PROCEDURE PreorderTrav (BT : BinaryTree;
                        PROCEDURE ProcessNode (VAR Item : TreeDataNode));

  { Given:   Binary tree BT implemented by Pascal pointer variables. }
  { Task:    Perform preorder traversal--root of BT first,            }
  {          then left subtree, then right subtree--applying          }
  {          ProcessNode to each Item in the tree.                    }
  { Return:  BT with each node affected by ProcessNode                }
```

```
BEGIN
  IF BT <> NIL THEN
    BEGIN
      ProcessNode (BT^.Info);
      PreorderTrav (BT^.LeftChild, ProcessNode);
      PreorderTrav (BT^.RightChild, ProcessNode)
    END
END; {  of PROCEDURE PreorderTrav  }
```

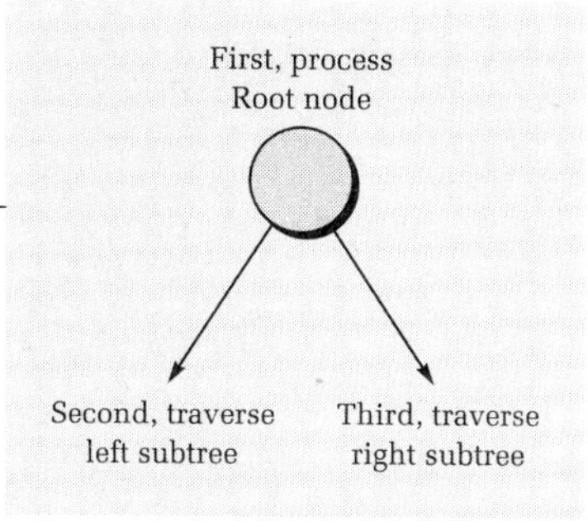

Inorder Traversal of a Binary Tree

The inorder traversal of a binary tree proceeds is outlined in the following three ordered steps:

1. First, recursively visit all nodes in the left subtree.
2. Then, process the root node.
3. Finally, recursively visit all nodes in the right subtree.

By carefully following these steps for the tree of Figure 7.8 and assuming "process" means "print," we obtain the readily recognizable infix expression

A − B + C * E/F

Unless we add parentheses, this infix expression is not equivalent to the order of operations reflected in the tree of Figure 7.8. The fact that prefix and postfix notations do not require parentheses to avoid such ambiguities makes them distinctly superior to infix notation for evaluation purposes.

An implementation of the recursive algorithm for an inorder traversal is given in the following procedure for a linked representation of a binary tree:

```
PROCEDURE InorderTrav (BT : BinaryTree;
                       PROCEDURE ProcessNode (VAR Item : TreeDataNode));

  {  Given:   Binary tree BT implemented by Pascal pointer variables. }
  {  Task:    Perform inorder traversal--left subtree first, then     }
  {           root of BT, then  right subtree--applying               }
  {           ProcessNode to each Item in the tree.                   }
  {  Return:  BT with each node affected by ProcessNode               }

  BEGIN
    IF BT <> NIL THEN
      BEGIN
        InorderTrav (BT^.LeftChild, ProcessNode);
        ProcessNode (BT^.Info);
        InorderTrav (BT^.RightChild, ProcessNode)
      END
  END; {  of PROCEDURE InorderTrav  }            }
```

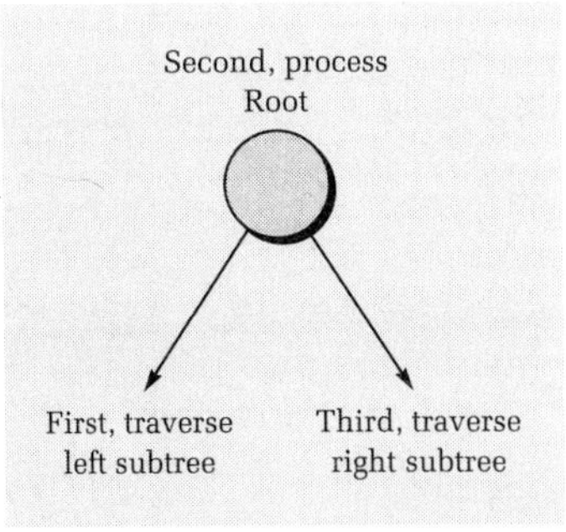

Postorder Traversal of a Binary Tree

The third standard traversal of a binary tree, the postorder traversal, entails an arrangement of options which postpones processing the root node until last.

1. First, recursively visit all nodes in the left subtree of the root node.
2. Then, recursively visit all nodes in the right subtree of the root node.
3. Finally, process the root node.

Applying these three steps to the binary expression tree of Figure 7.8 yields the postfix form of the underlying expression:

A B − C E * F / +

The actual implementation of the postorder traversal operation is completely analogous to the inorder and preorder operations. Consequently, we will leave it as an exercise.

Although we have illustrated the three traversal algorithms using binary expression trees, we emphasize that the traversals apply in general to *any* binary tree. Indeed, as we shall see in the next section, the inorder traversal when used in combination with a tree exhibiting the hierarchical ordering property of a binary search tree will neatly allow us to implement a keyed list using a binary tree.

Exercises 7.2

1. You are writing a program that uses a binary tree. To make it easy to trace the structure, you use an array of records instead of pointer variables. Consider the following binary tree:

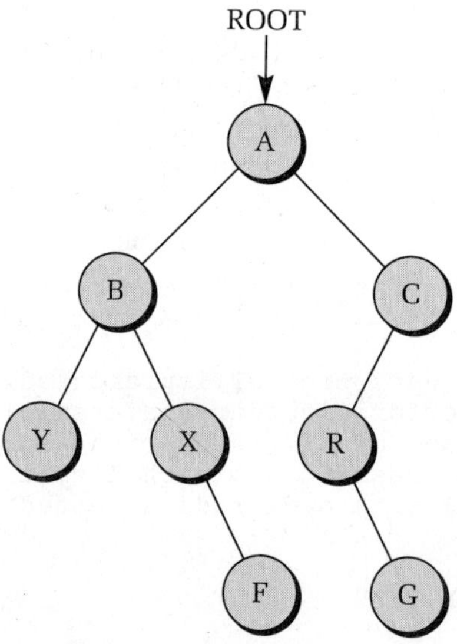

a. Indicate the contents of Root and Avail pointers and LeftChild and RightChild fields in the array Tree that follows:

Tree

Location	Info	LeftChild	RightChild
1	C		
2	R		
3	G		
4	F		
5	X		
6	Y		
7	B		
8	A		
9			

Root

Avail

b. Show the contents of Root and Avail and LeftChild and RightChild fields after a node containing J has been inserted as the left child of X and R has been deleted with G becoming the left child of C.

2. Using a preorder traversal of the tree you derived in Exercise 1 from Section 7.1, obtain the prefix form of the expression in that exercise.

3. Sketch the binary search tree that would result when the AddNode procedure of Example 7.4 is used for data that arrive in the following orders:

a. 100 90 80 70 60 50 40 32 20 10

b. 60 80 30 90 70 100 40 20 50 10

c. 60 50 70 40 80 30 90 20 100 10

Provide a brief written statement in which you describe how the shape of the binary search tree is related to the order in which data arrive for insertion into the tree.

4. Consider the following search trees with the ordering property. For each, specify an order of arrival of data items which would result in that particular tree if the AddNode procedure of Example 7.4 is used.

a.

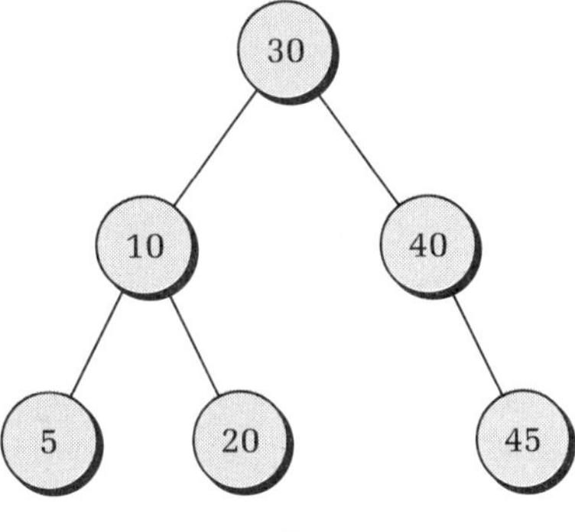

b.

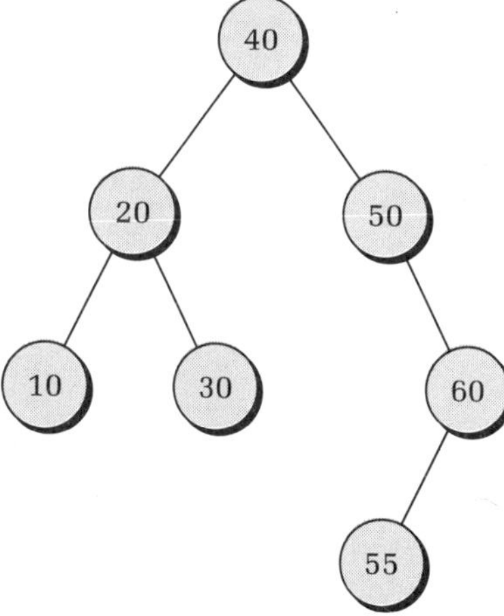

c.

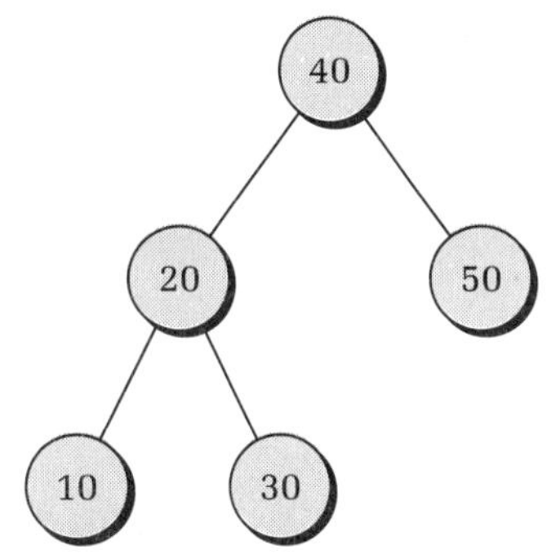

5. What is the output produced by the following procedure for the pictured tree?

```
PROCEDURE TreeWalk (BT : BinaryTree);

  BEGIN
    IF BT = NIL THEN
      writeln ('OOPS')
    ELSE
      BEGIN
        TreeWalk (BT^.RightChild);
        TreeWalk (BT^.LeftChild);
        writeln (BT^.Info)
      END
  END;
```

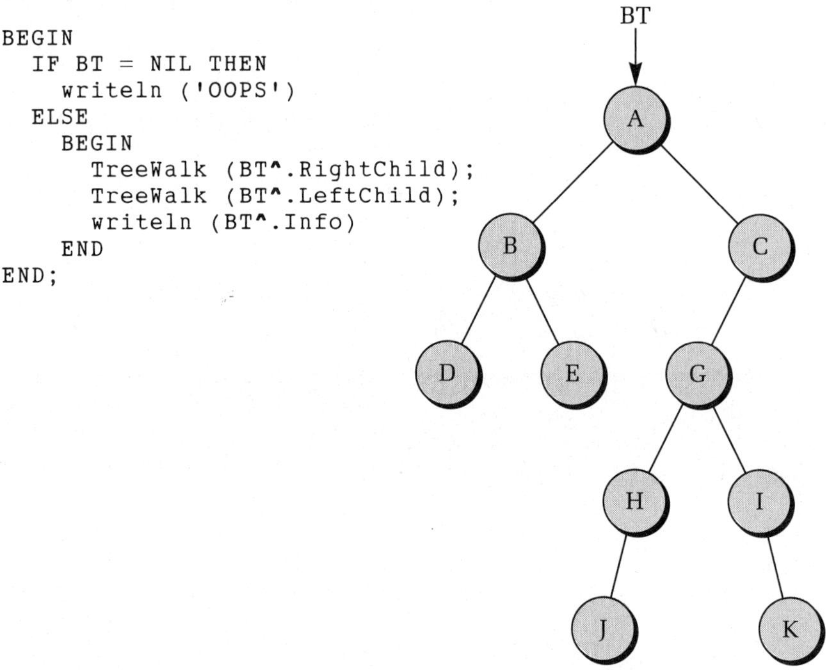

6. How does the output from Exercise 5 change if the statement

   `writeln (BT^.Info)`

   is moved ahead of the recursive calls to TreeWalk?

7. How does the output from Exercise 5 change if the statement

   `writeln (BT^.Info)`

   is located between the recursive calls to TreeWalk?

8. Repeat Exercises 5, 6, and 7 for the following tree:

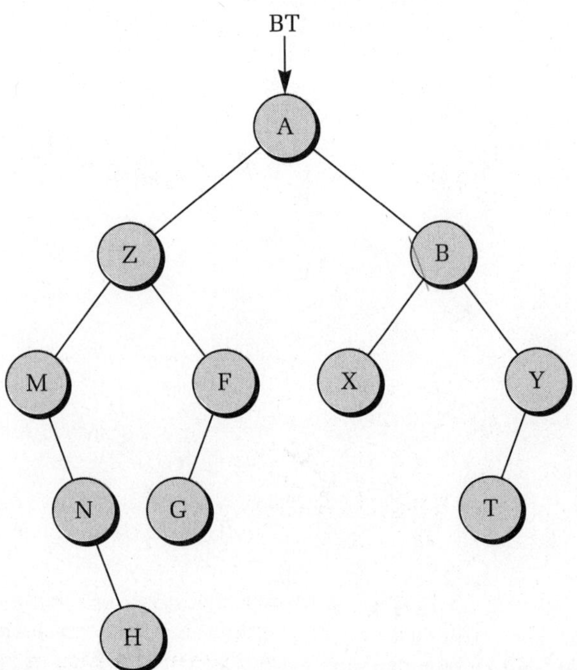

9. A *ternary tree* is a tree in which each node may have at most three children. A pointer/record structure for a linked implementation of such a tree could thus be given by the following declarations:

```
TYPE
  TreePointer = ^TreeNode;
  TreeNode = RECORD
               LeftChild : TreePointer;
               MiddleChild : TreePointer;
               RightChild : TreePointer;
               Data : char
             END;
```

What would be the output produced by the following TreeWalk procedure

```
PROCEDURE TreeWalk (Root : TreePointer);
  BEGIN
    IF Root = NIL THEN
      writeln ('NIL')
    ELSE
      BEGIN
        writeln (Root^.Data);
        TreeWalk (Root^.RightChild);
        TreeWalk (Root^.MiddleChild);
        TreeWalk (Root^.LeftChild)
      END
  END; {  of PROCEDURE TreeWalk  }
```

if it were initially called with the root pointer to the tree in the following diagram?

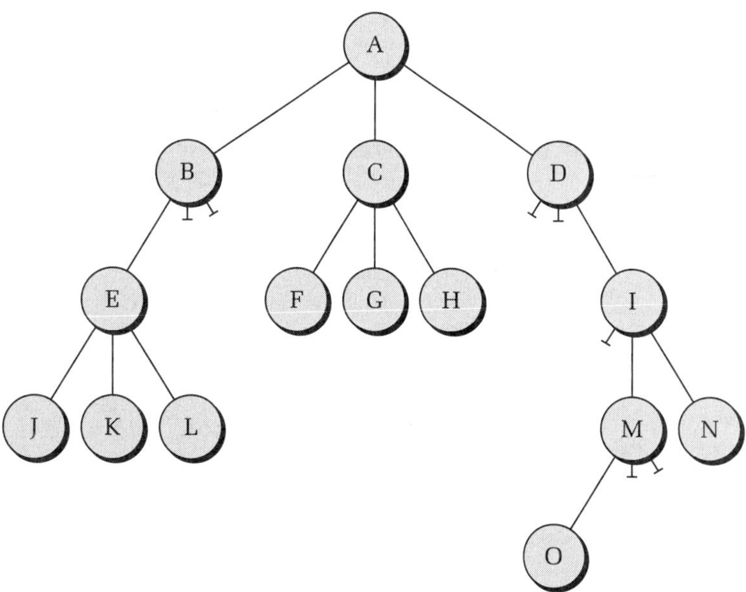

10. Write implementations of the Create, Empty, and Full operations for a binary search tree with the ordering property using the linked representation method.

11. Write an implementation of the postorder traversal operation for a linked representation of a binary tree.

12. Write a procedure that reads an algebraic expression in prefix notation and builds the binary tree corresponding to the expression (see Example 7.3). Assume that all tokens in the expression are individual characters.

13. Write a procedure that reads an algebraic expression in postfix notation and builds the binary tree corresponding to the expression (see Example 7.3). Assume that all tokens in the expression are individual characters.

14. Implement one of the traversal algorithms in a nonrecursive fashion by using a stack to keep track of pointers to nodes that must be visited when you finish processing the current subtree. Your stack will approximate the role played by the system stack in the recursive version of the algorithm.

15. Suppose that you have a binary tree representation of an algebraic expression consisting of the operators +, −, *, / and operands that are uppercase letters. Suppose also that you have a function Value which, given an operand, will return the numeric value associated with that operand. Write a recursive function to evaluate the expression tree.

16. Write a procedure to solve the following puzzle. Assume that TreeNodeData is **char** data. Your procedure receives two strings of the same length. The first represents the order in which the nodes of a tree would be visited by a preorder traversal. The second represents the order in which nodes from the same tree would be visited by an inorder traversal. Your procedure is to construct the tree from these two traversals.

17. Write a Boolean-valued function that receives two binary trees composed of the same type of data. The function should return **true** if the two trees are identical: that is, if they have precisely the same shape and have the same values in each node. Otherwise, it should return **false.**

18. How could the inorder traversal of a binary tree be used to logically sort data? Provide your answer in the form of a precise written statement.

■ ■ ■ ■

■ 7.3 Binary Search Tree Implementation of a Keyed List

OBJECTIVES

- to realize how a binary search tree with the ordering property may be used to provide an effective implementation of the keyed list ADT introduced in Chapter 2
- to develop an algorithm for deleting a node from a binary search tree
- to analyze the efficiency of this new implementation of the keyed list ADT
- in particular, to compare the efficiency of this new keyed list implementation with the efficiencies of other implementations we have previously studied

The implementations we have considered for the keyed list have been found lacking in certain respects. The physically ordered array implementation of Chapter 1 allowed for the fast inspection of records via the binary search algorithm but necessitated excessive data movement when records were added to or deleted from the list. The linked list implementation suggested in Chapter 4 handled adds and deletes nicely but presented us with an undesirable $O(n)$ search efficiency due to the lack of random access.

In this section, we shall see that by implementing a keyed list using a binary tree with the ordering property, we can achieve efficiency in both searching and adding or deleting while at the same time keeping the list in order. Moreover, we do not have to pay too great a price in other trade-offs to achieve this best of both worlds. Indeed, binary trees with the ordering property are called binary search trees precisely because of their frequent application in efficiently implementing keyed lists.

A binary search tree is organized via the hierarchical ordering property discussed in Example 7.2 in Section 7.1. Recall that this ordering property stipulates the following:

> *For any given data item X in the tree, every node in the left subtree of X contains only items that are less than X with respect to a particular type of ordering. Every node in the right subtree of X contains only items that are greater than or equal to X with respect to the same ordering.*

For instance, the tree of Figure 7.14 illustrates this property with respect to alphabetical ordering.

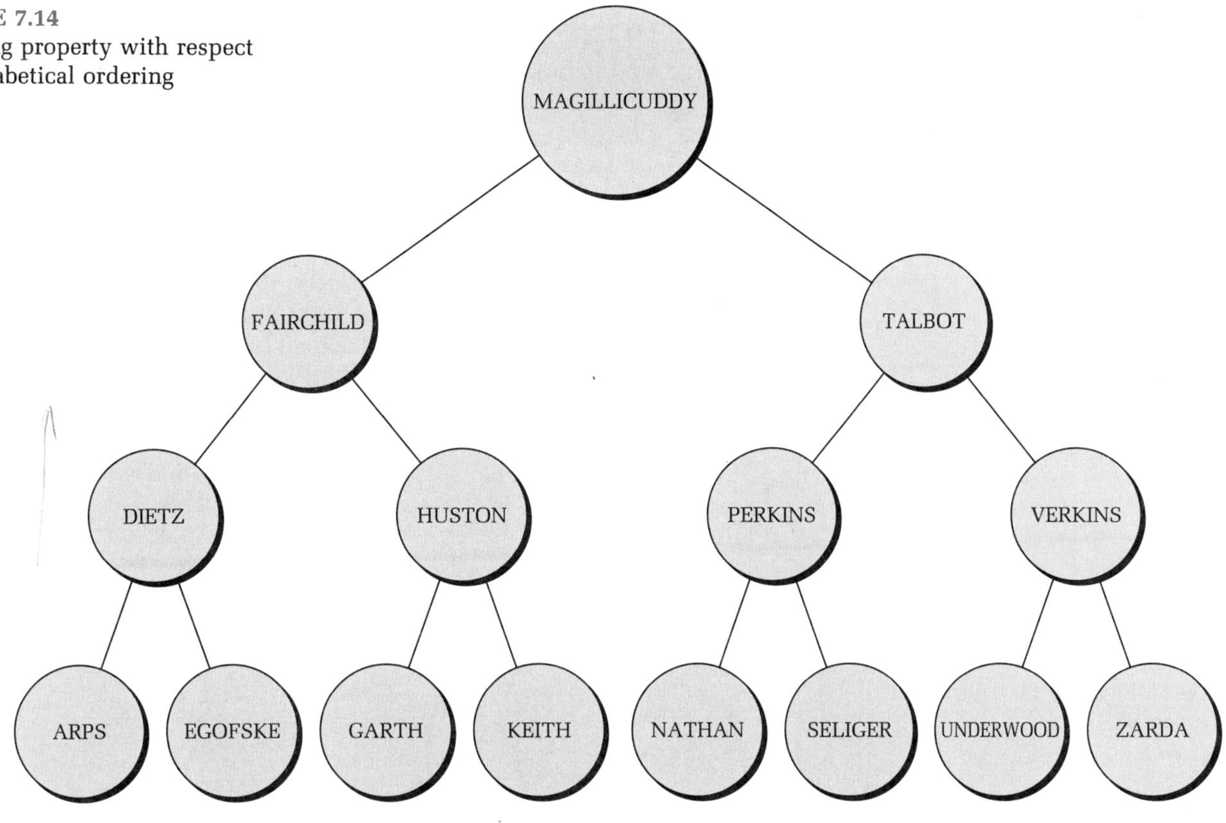

FIGURE 7.14
Ordering property with respect to alphabetical ordering

You can quickly verify that an inorder traversal of this tree (in which the processing of each node consists merely of printing its contents) leads to the following alphabetized list:

ARPS
DIETZ
EGOFSKE
FAIRCHILD
GARTH
HUSTON
KEITH
MAGILLICUDDY
NATHAN
PERKINS
SELIGER
TALBOT
UNDERWOOD
VERKINS
ZARDA

This allows us to reach the following important conclusion. That is, an inorder traversal of a binary search tree will visit nodes in ascending order. Hence such a tree may be viewed as an ordered list. The first list element is the first item visited by the inorder traversal. More generally, the *n*th element visited by the inorder traversal corresponds precisely to the *n*th element in the list. Given this view of a binary search tree as an implementation of a keyed list, let us now consider the operations of adding, deleting, and finding (retrieving) nodes in the list.

Adding Nodes to the Binary Search Tree Implementation of a List

Insertion of a new string into such a tree is a fairly easy process that may well require significantly fewer comparisons than insertion into a linked list. The specifics of the AddNode operation have already been developed in Example 7.4. Consider, for example, the steps necessary to insert the string 'SEFTON' into the tree of Figure 7.14 in such a fashion as to maintain the ordering property. We must

1. Compare SEFTON to MAGILLICUDDY. Because SEFTON is greater than MAGILLICUDDY, follow the right child pointer to TALBOT.
2. Compare SEFTON to TALBOT. Because SEFTON is less than TALBOT, follow the left child pointer to PERKINS.
3. SEFTON is greater than PERKINS. Hence follow the right child pointer to SELIGER.
4. SELIGER is a leaf node, so SEFTON may be added as one of its children. The left child is chosen because SEFTON is less than SELIGER.

The resulting tree for the sample insertion is given in Figure 7.15.

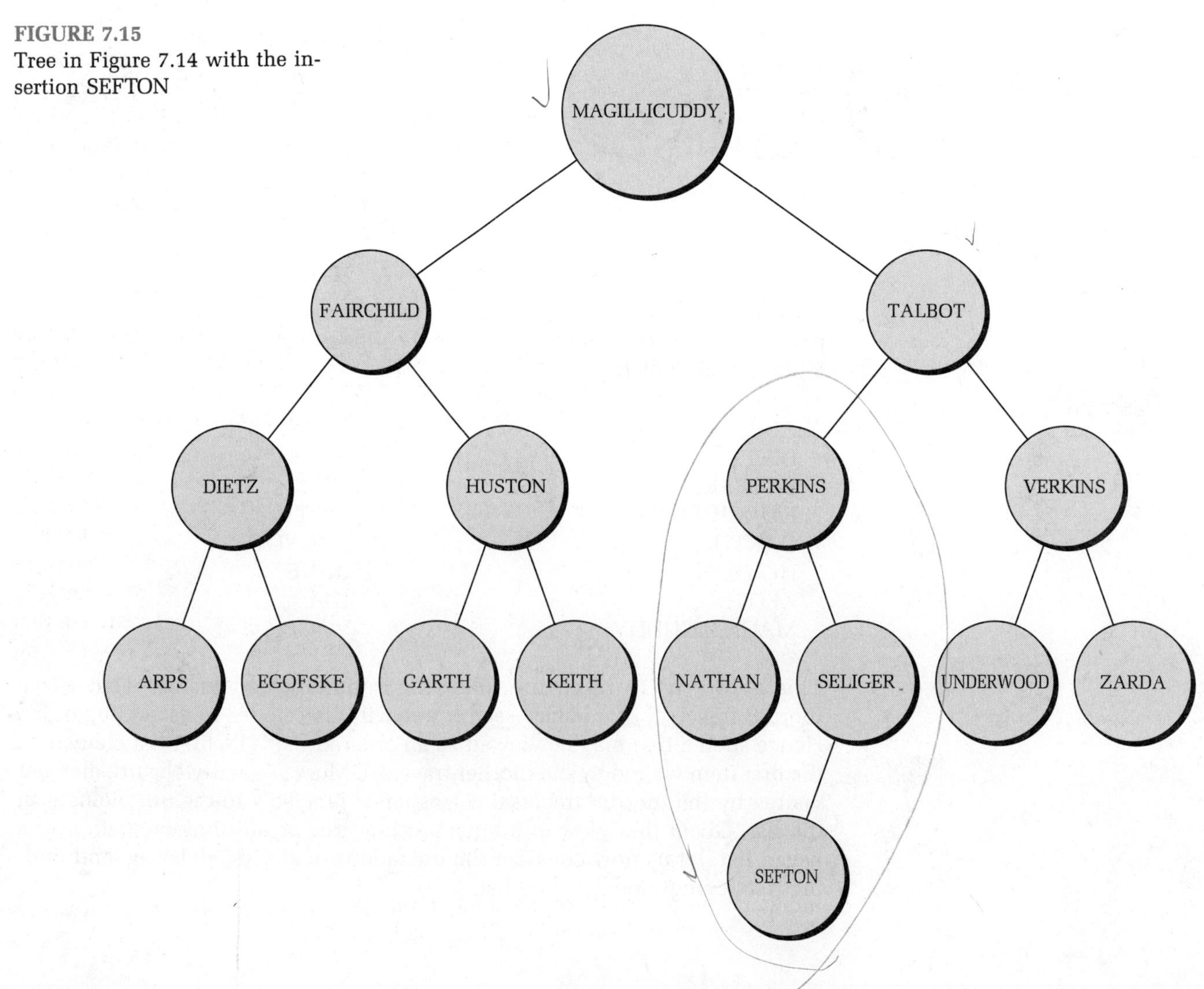

FIGURE 7.15
Tree in Figure 7.14 with the insertion SEFTON

Provided that the tree maintains a full shape, the number of nodes on a given branch will be at most

$$\log_2 n + 1$$

where n is the total number of nodes in the tree. By *full* we mean that all nodes with fewer than two children must occur at level m or $m - 1$ where m is the deepest level in the tree. In other words, all nodes above level $m - 1$ must have exactly two children. Hence, adding ROBERTS to the tree of Figure 7.15 by the insertion rule would destroy its fullness.

Given this definition of full, the ($\log_2 n + 1$) figure for the maximum number of nodes on a branch emerges immediately upon inspection or, more formally, using a proof by mathematical induction. Our purpose here, however, is not to give the details of such a proof but rather to emphasize that a binary search tree presents an alternative to a linked list structure for the type of processing involved in maintaining ordered lists. Moreover, it is a particularly attractive alternative when the tree is full, because substantially fewer comparisons are needed to locate where in the structure an insertion is to be made. For instance, if n is 1,024, the linked list may require as many as 1,024 comparisons to make an insertion. Because $\log_2 1024$ is 10, the full binary search tree method will require at most 11 comparisons. This difference becomes even more dramatic as n gets larger. For an ordered list with 1,000,000 entries, a linked list may require that many comparisons, but the full binary search tree requires a mere 21 comparisons.

What happens when the tree is not full? We will comment on that situation at the end of this section, when we discuss the overall efficiency considerations for this implementation of a list. Before that, however, consider the operations of finding and deleting data in a binary search tree.

Searching for Data in a Binary Search Tree Implementation of a List

The insertion rule also dictates the search path followed through a binary search tree when we are attempting to find a given data item. Interestingly, if we trace the nodes visited on such a search path for a full tree, we will probe exactly the same items that we would in conducting a binary search on a physically ordered array containing the same data. For instance, if we are searching for SMITH in the tree of Figure 7.14, we will have to probe MAGILLICUDDY, TALBOT, and PERKINS. These are precisely the items that would be probed if the binary search algorithm were applied to the physically ordered list associated with Figure 7.14. Our analysis of such a tree has allowed us to conclude that, as long as the binary search tree remains full, search efficiency for this method of implementing a keyed list matches that of the physically ordered array implementation. That is, the search efficiency is $O(\log_2 n)$.

Deleting Data in a Binary Search Tree Implementation of a List

The deletion algorithm for a binary search tree is conceptually more complex than that for a linked list. Suppose, for instance, that we wish to remove TALBOT from the list represented by the tree of Figure 7.14. Two questions arise.

1. Can such a deletion be achieved merely by manipulating pointers?
2. If so, what does the resulting tree look like?

To answer these questions, begin by recalling that all that is necessary to represent a keyed list with a binary search tree is that, for each node in the tree

1. The left subtree must contain only items less than it.
2. The right subtree must contain only items greater than or equal to it.

With the preservation of this ordering property as the primary goal in processing a deletion, one acceptable way of restructuring the tree of Figure 7.14 after deleting TALBOT appears in Figure 7.16; essentially, SELIGER moves up to replace TALBOT in the tree. The choice of SELIGER to replace TALBOT is made because SELIGER represents the greatest data item in the left subtree of the node containing TALBOT. As long as we choose this greatest item in the left subtree to replace the item being deleted, we guarantee preservation of the crucial ordering property that enables the tree to represent the list accurately.

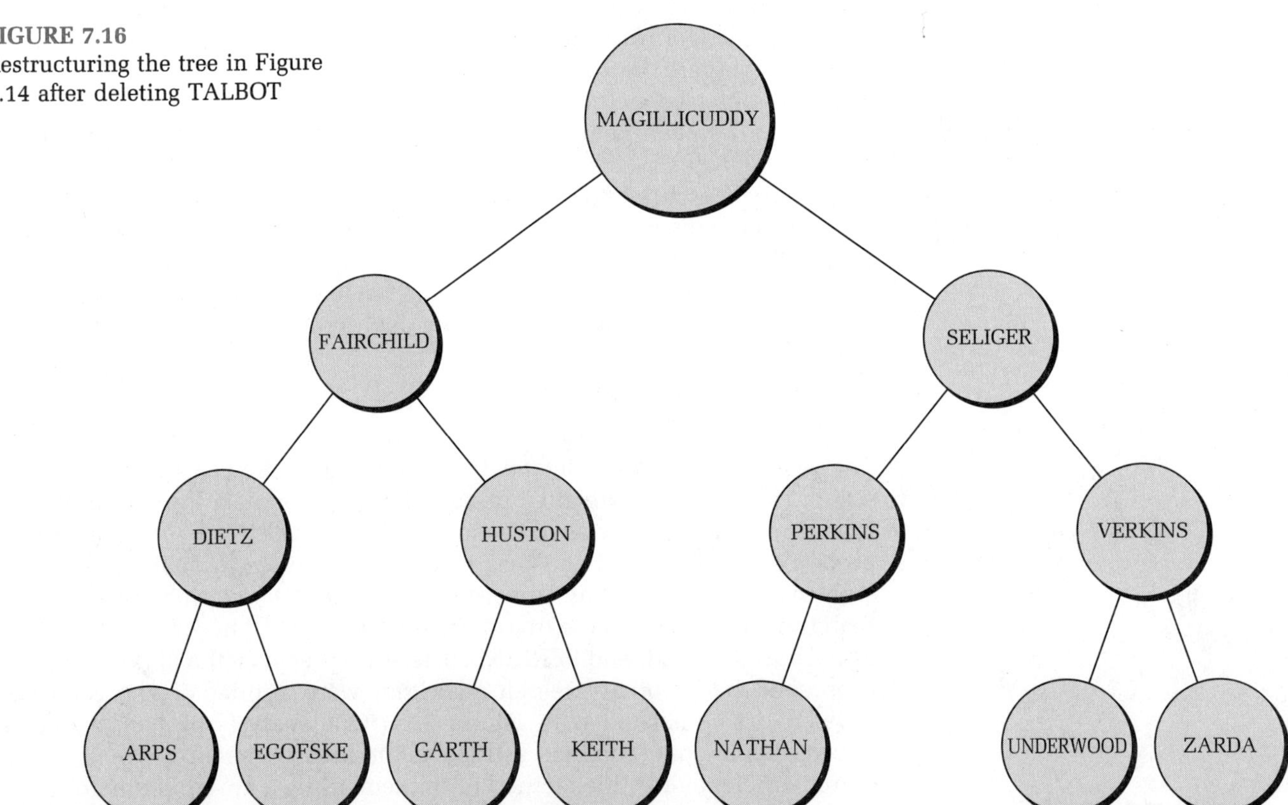

FIGURE 7.16
Restructuring the tree in Figure 7.14 after deleting TALBOT

Given this general motivation for choosing a node to replace the one being deleted, let us now outline a case-by-case analysis of the deletion algorithm. Throughout this analysis, we assume that we have a pointer P to the item that we wish to delete. The pointer P may be one of the following:

1. The root pointer for the entire tree.
2. The left child pointer of the parent of the node to be deleted.
3. The right child pointer of the parent of the node to be deleted.

Figure 7.17 highlights these three possibilities; the algorithm applies whether 1, 2, or 3 holds.

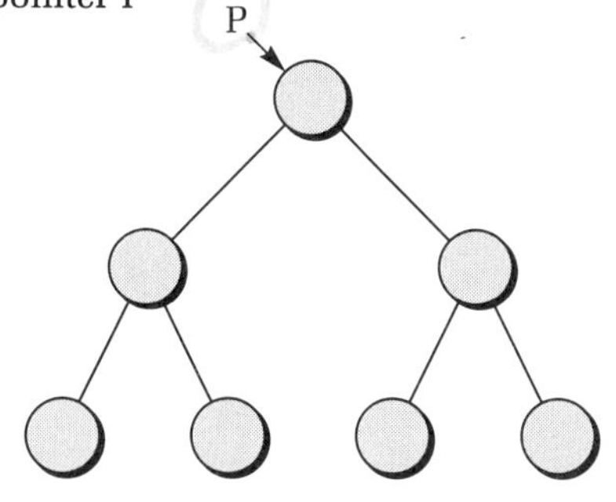

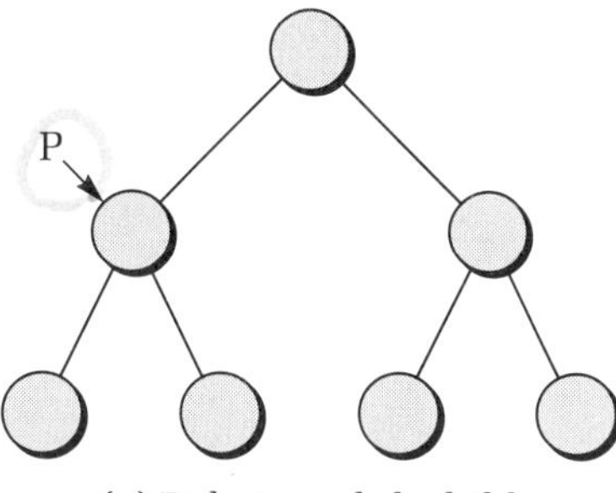

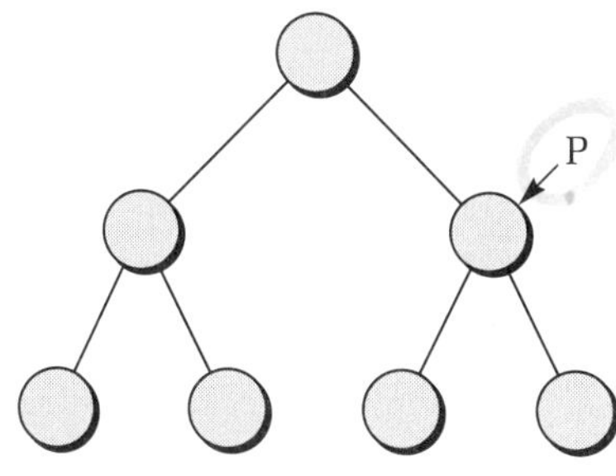

FIGURE 7.17
Three possibilities for the pointer P

(1) Deleting the root (2) Deleting a left child (3) Deleting a right child

We now examine three cases of node deletion on a binary search tree.

1. The node to be deleted has no children.
2. The node to be deleted has a right child but no left child.
3. The node to be deleted has a left child.

Case 1. The node pointed to by P, that is, the node to be deleted, has no children. This is the easiest of all the cases. It can be compactly handled

```
X := P;
P := NIL;
dispose (X);
```

Case 2. The node pointed to by P, that is, the node to be deleted, has a right child but no left child. This case poses no more problems than Case 1 and is described in Figure 7.18. The node to be deleted is merely replaced by its right child. The necessary Pascal coding is

```
X := P;
P := X^.RightChild;
dispose (X);
```

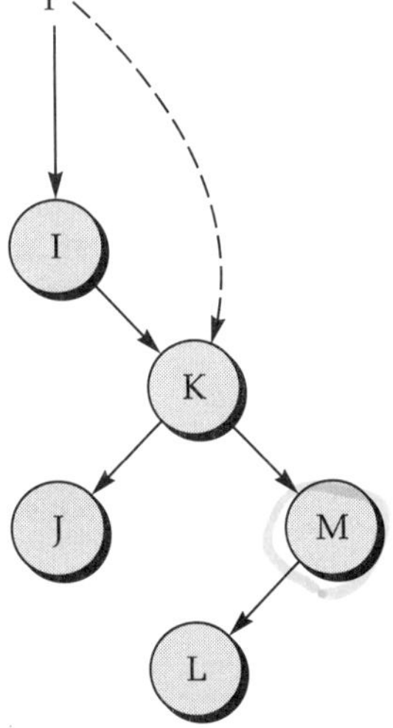

FIGURE 7.18
In Case 2 the node pointed to by P has a right but no left child

Case 3. The node pointed to by P, that is, the node to be deleted, has a left child. In Figure 7.19, node M is to be deleted, and it has left child K. In this case, because we have a non-null left subtree of the node to be deleted, our previous discussion indicates that we must find the greatest node in that left subtree. If the node pointed to by P^.LeftChild (node K in the figure) has no right child, then the greatest node in the left subtree of P is P^.LeftChild itself. Figure 7.19 pictorially describes this situation; the dotted lines indicate new pointer values.

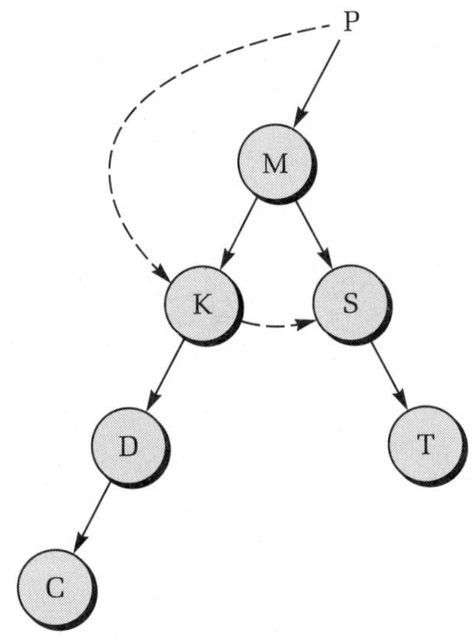

FIGURE 7.19
Case 3 with P^.LeftChild (node K) having no right children

The partial coding to achieve this pointer manipulation is given by:

```
X := P;
P := X^.LeftChild;
P^.RightChild := X^.RightChild;
dispose (X);
```

If the node pointed to by P^.LeftChild does have a right child, then to find the greatest node in the left subtree of P we must follow the right branch leading from P^.LeftChild as deeply as possible into the tree. In Figure 7.20, node R is the one chosen to replace the deleted node. This figure gives the

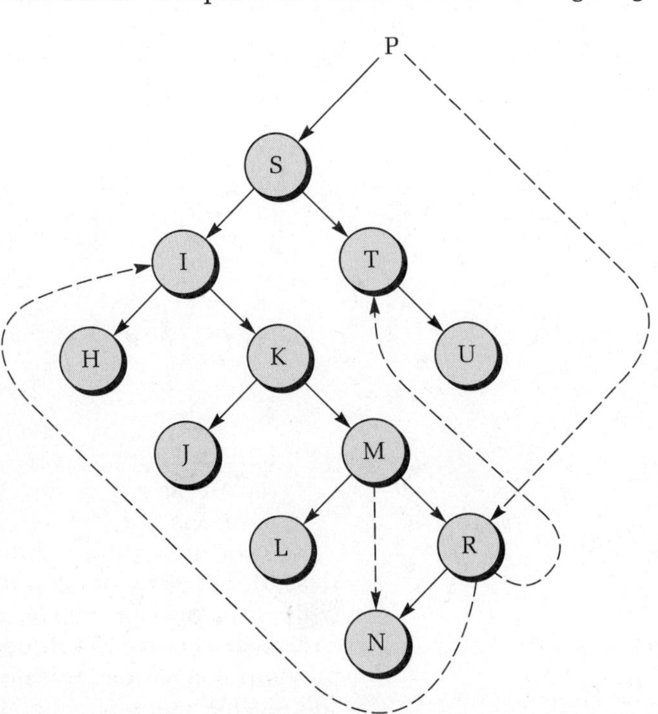

FIGURE 7.20
Case 3 with P^.LeftChild having a right child

schematic representation, with the pointer changes necessary to complete the deletion. The coding necessary for this slightly more complicated version of Case 3 is

```
X := P;
Q := X^.LeftChild^.RightChild;
QParent := X^.LeftChild;

{ Q will eventually point to node which will replace P. }
{ QParent will point to Q's parent.                      }
{ The following loop forces Q as deep as possible        }
{ along the right branch from P^.LeftChild.              }

WHILE Q^.RightChild <>NIL DO
  BEGIN
    Q := Q^.RightChild;
    QParent := QParent^.RightChild
  END;

{ Having found node Q to replace P, adjust pointers      }
{ to appropriately link it into the tree.                }

Q^.RightChild := X^.RightChild;
P := Q;
QParent^.RightChild := Q^.LeftChild;
Q^.LeftChild := X^.LeftChild;
dispose (X);
```

Efficiency Considerations for Binary Search Tree Implementation of a Keyed List

It is important to note that, in all three cases, the deletion of a node from the tree involved only pointer manipulation and no actual data movement. Hence, in a list maintained with a binary search tree, we are able to process both insertions and deletions by the same pure pointer manipulation that makes linked lists so desirable. Moreover, the binary search tree approach apparently allows us to locate data for retrieval, insertion, or deletion much faster than a linked list representation would. However, there are aspects of the binary tree method that tarnish its performance in comparison to a linked list. In particular:

- The binary search tree implementation requires more memory in two respects. First, each node has two pointers instead of the one required in a singly linked list. This proliferation of pointers is particularly wasteful because many of the pointers may be **NIL**. Second, we presently can traverse the tree in order only by using recursive techniques. Even in a language that allows recursion, a substantial amount of overhead is needed to maintain the stack used by recursive calls.
- The $O(\log_2 n)$ efficiency of the binary search tree method is only an optimal, not a guaranteed, efficiency. It is contingent upon the tree's remaining nearly full. The tree's remaining full is in turn contingent upon the order in which the data are added and deleted. In the worst possible case, data entering the tree structure in the wrong order can cause the tree to degenerate into a glorified linked list with a corresponding $O(n)$ efficiency. (The Exercises at the end of this section have you explore this relationship between the order in which data arrive for insertion and the resulting search efficiency of the binary search tree.)

Both of these drawbacks can be overcome. We can avoid the overhead associated with recursion if we use a technique (known as *threading*) that puts to good use the pointers that are otherwise wasted as **NIL.**

Moreover, by using a technique known as *height balancing,* the binary search tree may be maintained in a fashion which approaches fullness at all times, regardless of the order in which data arrive for entry. This nearly full form is enough to completely guarantee the $O(\log_2 n)$ search efficiency. Originally devised by G. M. Adelson-Velskii and Y. M. Landis, the height-balancing algorithm is sufficiently complex to be beyond the scope of this book. In-depth treatments of it and the threading technique cited above are given in *Data Structures in Pascal* by Ellis Horowitz and Sartaj Sahni (New York, N.Y.: Computer Science Press, 1990) and in *Introduction to Data Structures and Algorithm Analysis with Pascal* by Thomas L. Naps and George J. Pothering (St. Paul, Minn.: West Publishing, 1992).

Overall, the binary search tree implementation of a keyed list would seem to be the best of the three implementations we have studied for situations in which additions, deletions, and searches must all be processed efficiently. Even when steps are not taken to correct the two disadvantages we have cited, it offers the addition/deletion advantages of a linked list with a search efficiency that is bounded between $O(\log_2 n)$ and $O(n)$.

Exercises 7.3

1. Which of the following binary search trees are full?

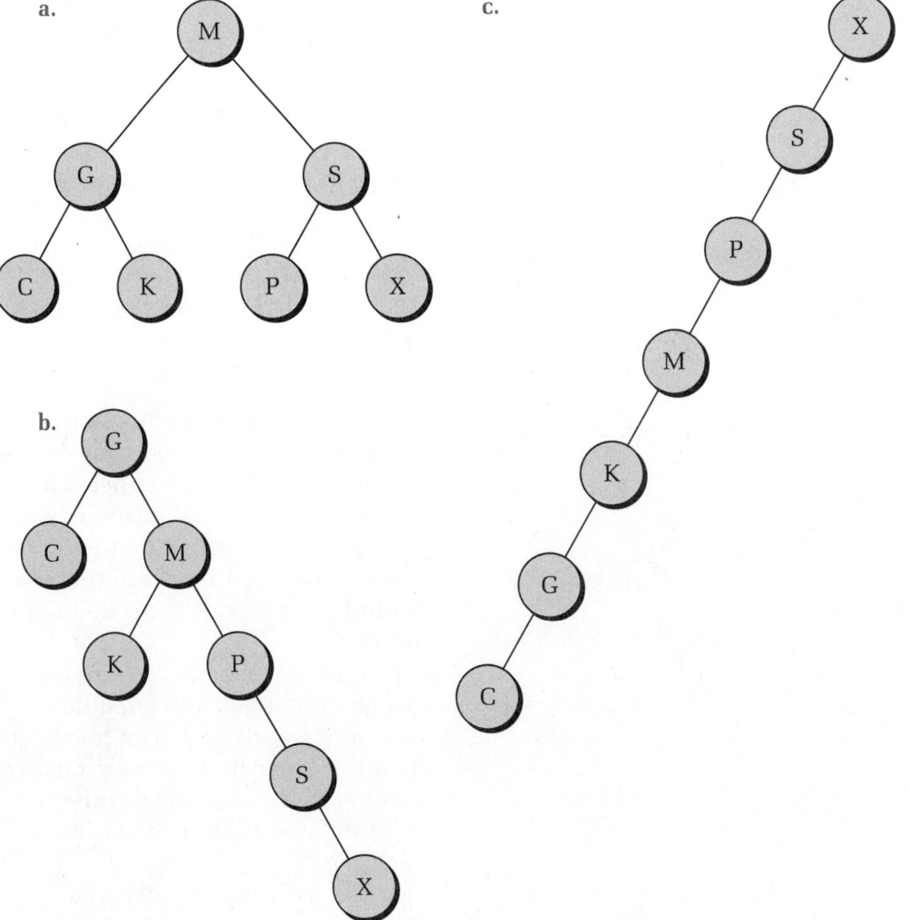

2. The key values 1 through 10 are to be inserted in a binary search tree. Specify orders of arrival for these values to create trees that correspond with each of the following shapes.

   a.

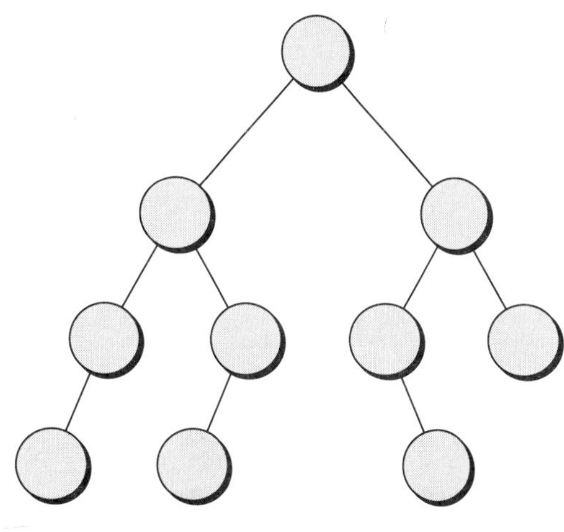

b.

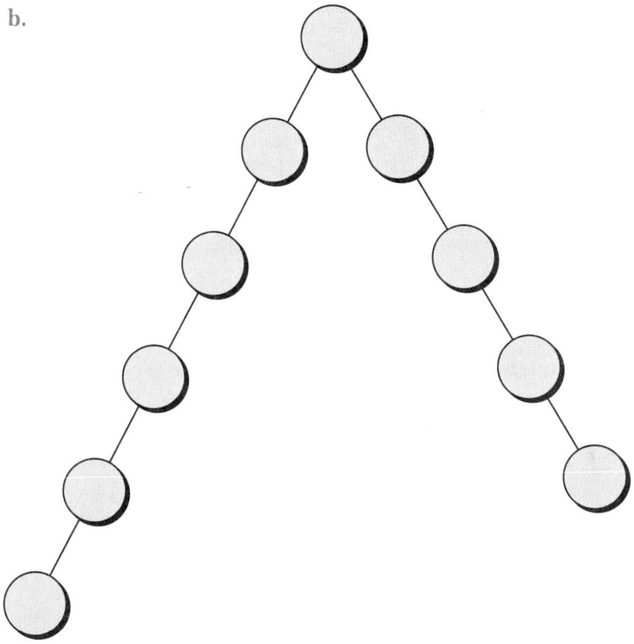

c.

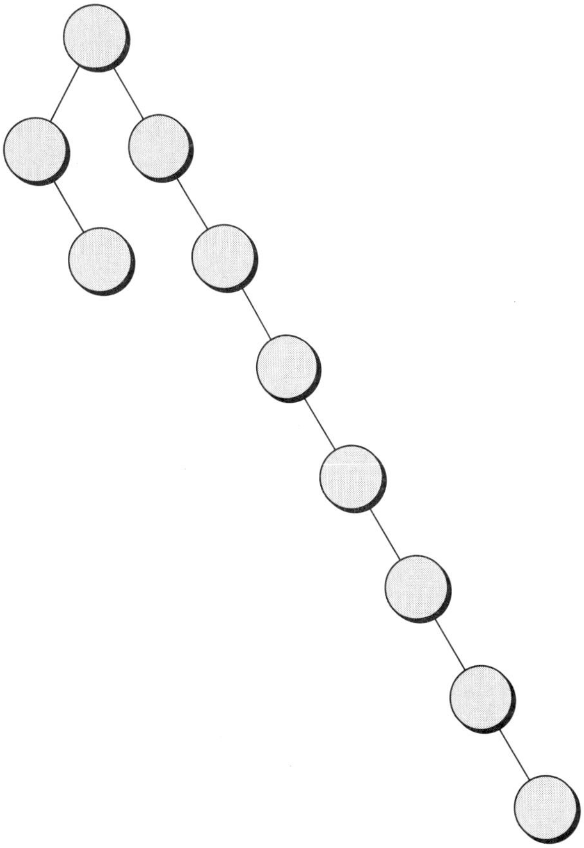

3. In an essay, discuss the relative merits of maintaining a keyed list by a binary search tree, a singly linked list, and a doubly linked list.

4. In an essay, discuss how the order in which data are entered into a binary search tree affects the fullness of the tree. Be sure to identify the best and worst possible cases. Analyze the efficiency of tree operations to add, delete, and find data for each of these cases.

5. The node containing 46 is to be deleted from each of the following binary search trees. Assuming the deletion algorithm described in this section is used, draw the tree after the deletion of 46.

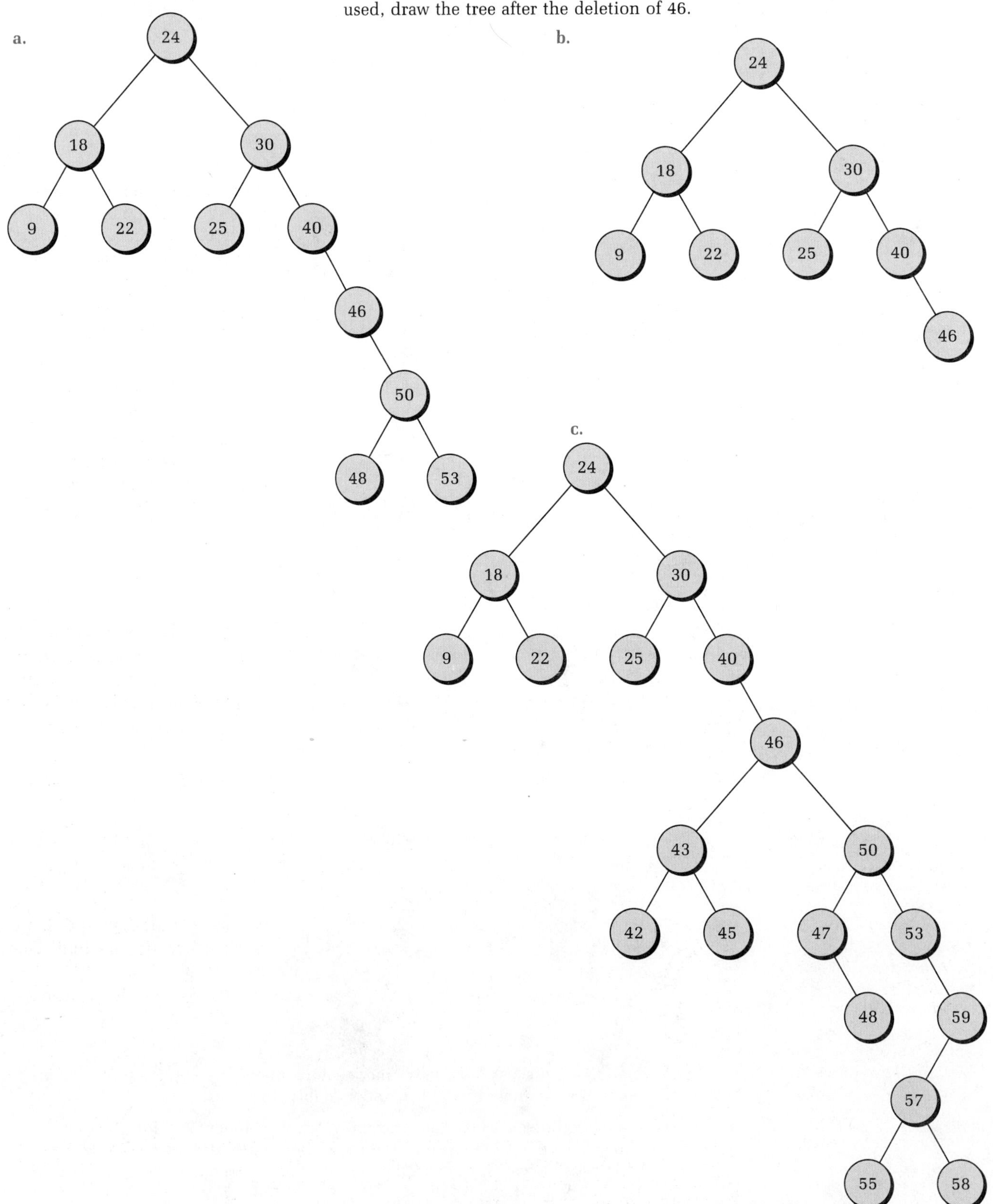

6. In Example 7.4 we provided an implementation of the AddNode operation for a binary search tree. What does the procedure in that example do when we try to insert a key value that already exists in the tree? Modify the procedure so that, when we try to insert such a key value, the tree is left unaltered.
7. The implementation of the AddNode operation for a binary search tree in Example 7.4 is recursive. Write a nonrecursive implementation of this operation.
8. Develop recursive and nonrecursive implementations of the algorithm to search for a particular data item in a binary search tree.
9. Develop a complete implementation of the algorithm to delete an item from a binary search tree. This will essentially require that you combine into one module the three cases discussed in this section. For an added challenge, try writing the procedure so that it handles deletion by using the "mirror image" of these three cases.
10. Look back to the definition of the keyed list ADT in Chapter 2. Provide a complete implementation of the keyed list operations using a binary search tree as the underlying data structure.
11. Suppose you are given a list of data in increasing order of keys. Develop a Pascal algorithm that will load this list into an optimal binary search tree.
12. A binary search tree could itself be considered an ADT that is derived from the more generic binary tree ADT defined in Section 7.1. Write a complete definition and a Pascal interface for the binary search tree as an ADT. Be sure that the set of operations you describe will allow your binary search tree ADT to be used as an implementation strategy for the keyed list ADT.

■ ■ ■ ■

7.4 Linear Implementation of the Binary Tree Abstract Data Type

OBJECTIVES

- to become familiar with the linear implementation of the binary tree ADT
- to recognize the advantages and disadvantages of the linear implementation versus the linked implementation
- to see why the linear implementation is particularly well-suited to representing a binary tree with the heap property
- to analyze the efficiency of the AddNode operation for a linear implementation of a binary tree with the heap property

The linear implementation of a binary tree uses a one-dimensional array of size $(2^{(d+1)}-1)$ where d is the depth of the tree, that is, the maximum level of any node in the tree. In the tree of Figure 7.8, the root + is at the level 0, the nodes − and * are at level 1, and so on. The deepest level in this tree is the level of E and F, level 3. Therefore, $d = 3$ and this tree will require an array of size $2^{(3+1)}-1 = 15$.

Once the size of the array has been determined, the following method is used to represent the tree:

1. Store the root in the first location of the array.
2. If a node is in location n of the array, store its left child at location $2n$, and its right child at location $(2n + 1)$.

With the aid of this scheme, the tree of Figure 7.8 is stored in the array BTData of size 15 shown in Figure 7.21. Locations BTData[8] through BTData[13] are not used.

An encapsulated definition of the binary tree ADT for this linear representation is given by:

```
CONST
  MaxTreeNodes = { Appropriate size for array, determined by maximum level }
                 { of any node in the tree.                                 }
  Null = { An appropriate value to signal that an array }
         { location does not  currently contain a node  }
```

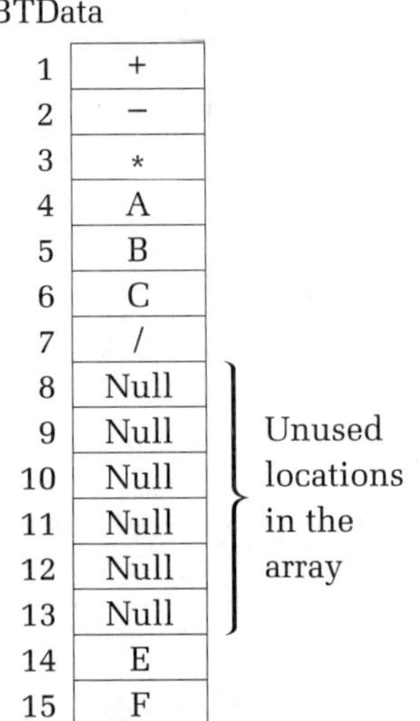

FIGURE 7.21
Tree of Figure 7.8 stored in a linear representation using an array

```
          { in the tree.  Since this value is used       }
          { as a flag, it should be chosen to be         }
          { a value that would never actually be         }
          { stored in the tree.                          }
TYPE
  TreeDataNode = { Data type of each individual node };
  BTArray = ARRAY [1..MaxTreeNodes] OF TreeDataNode;
  BinaryTree = RECORD
                 BTData : BTArray;
                 NumberNodes : integer { Number of nodes currently in tree }
               END;
```

The Create operation simply sets the NumberNodes field to zero and initializes all array locations to the Null value. The Null values are necessary to detect whether or not a given tree node has children. A tree node at location n has a left subtree if and only if location $2n$ contains a non-Null value. A similar consideration applies to the right subtree of the tree node at location n.

Efficiency Considerations for the Linear Representation

The main advantages of this method lie in its simplicity and the fact that, given a child node, its parent node can be determined immediately. If a child node is at location n in the array, then its parent node is at location n **DIV** 2.

In spite of its simplicity and ease of implementation, the linear representation method has all the costs that come with physically ordering items. Insertion or deletion of a node in a fashion that maintains the hierarchical relationships within the tree may cause considerable data movement up and down the array and hence use an excessive amount of processing time. Also, depending on the application, there may be wasted memory locations (such as locations 8 through 13 in Figure 7.21) due to partially filled trees.

Using the Linear Implementation for a Heap

One type of binary tree for which the linear implementation of a binary tree proves to be ideal is the heap, as defined in Example 7.1. The data in a heap can be embedded in an array without ever wasting any locations. To prove this claim, we will show that, given a heap with N-1 nodes embedded in an array with no gaps, we can add an Nth node and maintain the dense packing of data in the array.

To illustrate the algorithm for doing this, consider the heap with eight nodes pictured in Figure 7.22. The numbers outside the circular nodes in this figure indicate the array indices where data would be stored in the linear representation of a binary tree.

FIGURE 7.22
A heap with eight nodes

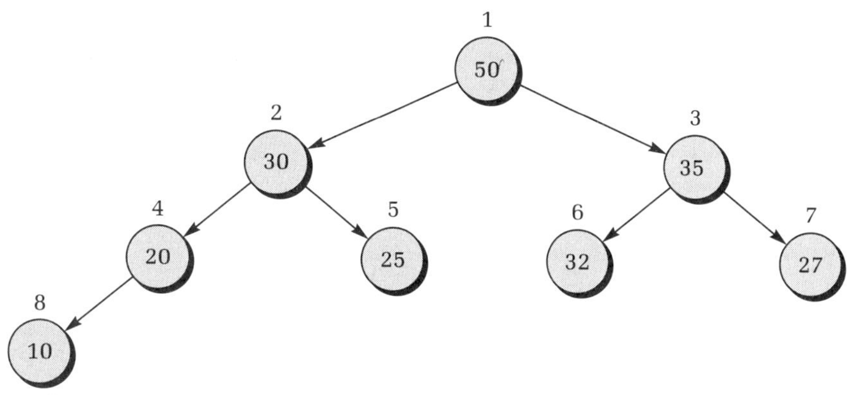

Now suppose we want to add 40 to the heap of Figure 7.22. We will begin by comparing 40 to the data in the least index which does not yet have two children: 20 at index 4 in Figure 7.22. Figure 7.23 shows a series of data interchanges that "walk 40 up" a path until the tree is transformed into a heap. The algorithm to achieve this "walking up" is given in the following example.

FIGURE 7.23
Transforming heap to accommodate insertion of 40 (Numbers outside circles indicate array index positions)

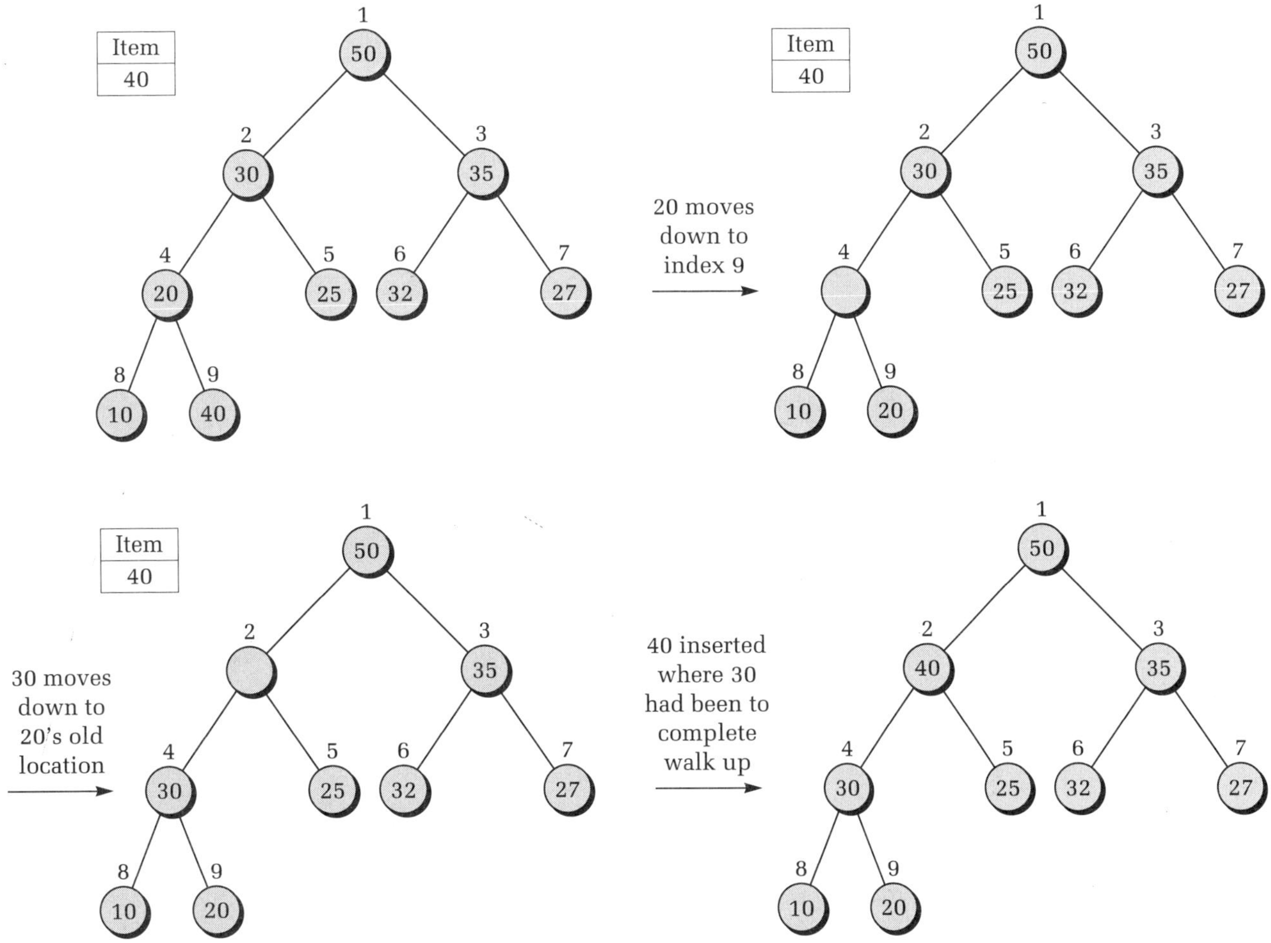

EXAMPLE 7.5

Implement the AddNode operation for a linear representation of a binary tree with the heap property.

```
TYPE
  TreeDataNode =  { any data type which has < relationship between
                    its values };
  BTArray = ARRAY [1..MaxTreeNodes] of TreeDataNode;
  BinaryTree = RECORD
                 BTData : BTArray;
                 NumberNodes : integer
               END;

PROCEDURE AddNode(VAR BT : BinaryTree;
                  Item : TreeDataNode);

  {  Given:   BT, a linear representation of binary tree with the    }
  {           heap property.  Item, a value to be inserted in        }
  {           tree BT.                                               }
  {  Task:    Insert Item in tree BT, maintaining                    }
  {           the tree's heap property.                              }
  {  Return:  Appropriately altered tree.  If there is no room       }
  {           for insertion, BT is not altered.                      }

  VAR
    K, L : integer;

  BEGIN
    IF BT.NumberNodes <> MaxTreeNodes THEN  { BT is not full }
      BEGIN
        BT.NumberNodes := BT.NumberNodes + 1;
        { Now walk the new item up the tree, starting at position L }
        L := BT.NumberNodes;
        K := L DIV 2;  { K references L's parent }
        WHILE (K >= 1) AND (BT.BTData[K] < Item) DO
          BEGIN
            BT.BTData[L] := BT.BTData[K];
            L := K;      { L moves up the tree }
            K := L DIV 2  { And so does K }
          END;
        BT.BTData[L] := Item  { L marks the spot for Item }
      END
  END;  { of PROCEDURE AddNode }
```

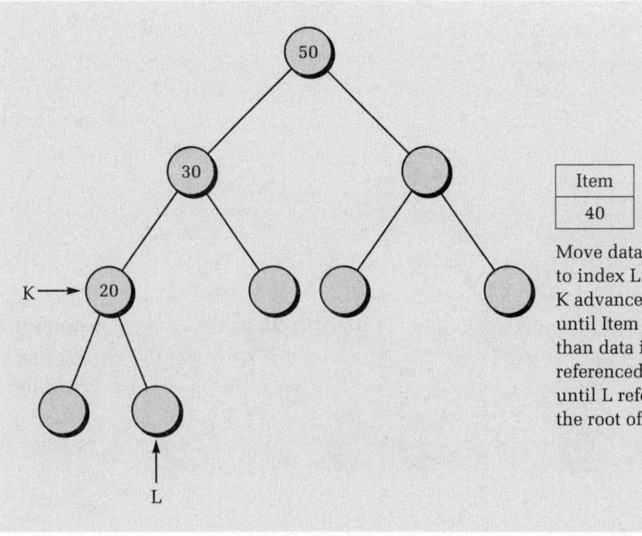

Move data at index K to index L. Then L and K advance up the tree until Item is less than data in node referenced by K or until L references the root of tree.

A NOTE OF INTEREST

Computer Security and Tree-Structured File Systems

One of the prime concerns in developing operating systems for multiuser computers is to insure that a user cannot, in an unauthorized fashion, access system files or the files of other users. A convenient data structure to implement such a file directory system is a tree such as that pictured here.

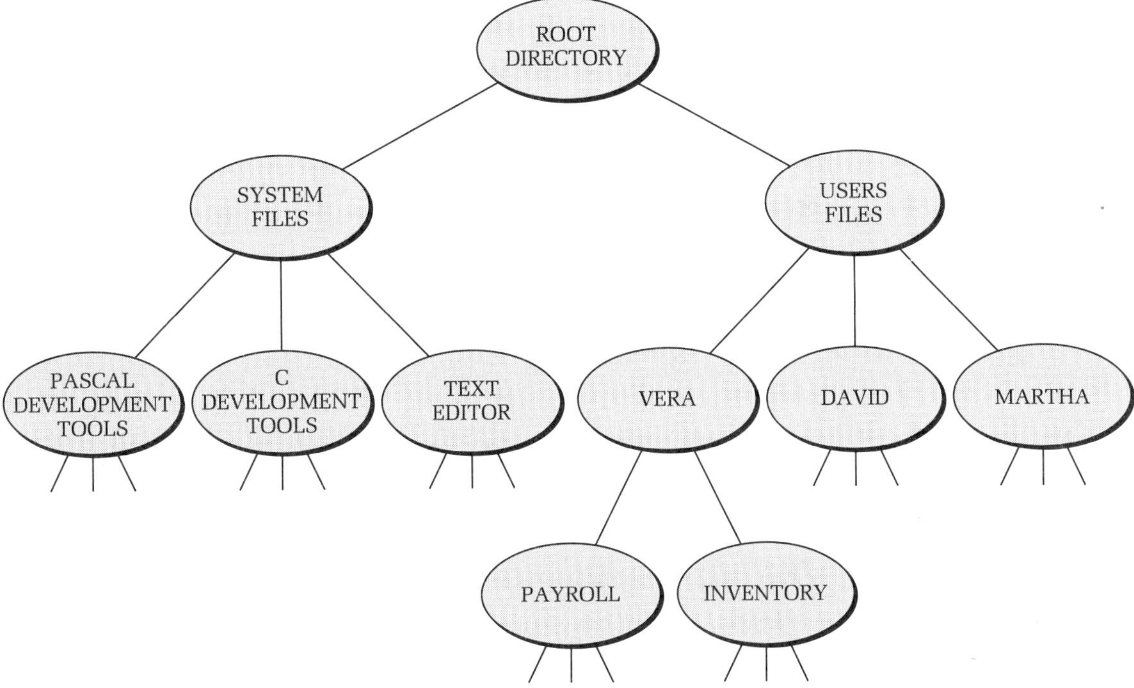

Each interior node of the tree can be viewed as a directory containing various system information about those files or subdirectories that are its descendants. Leaf nodes in the tree are the actual files. Hence, in the diagram, files can be broken down into system files and user files. System files consist of the PASCAL DEVELOPMENT TOOLS, the C DEVELOPMENT TOOLS, and the TEXT EDITOR. User directories are called VERA, DAVID, and MARTHA. One of the very convenient features of such a system is that it allows the user to extend this tree structure as deeply as desired. For instance, in the given tree directory structure, we see that user VERA has created subdirectories for files related to PAYROLL and INVENTORY. DAVID and MARTHA could have similarly partitioned subdirectories to organize their work.

In addition to offering users the convenience of being able to appropriately group their files into subdirectories, such a file system offers a very natural solution to the problem of file security. Since each individual user is, in effect, the root of a miniature subordinate file system within the overall system, a user is given, by default, free access to every node in his or her subtree. That is, the user is viewed as the owner of every node in the subtree. To jump outside of this subtree of naturally owned files and directories requires that special permissions be given the user by other users or by the operating system itself. Hence the tree structure offers convenience as well as a means of carefully monitoring the integrity of the file system.

AT&T's UNIX operating system, developed at Bell Laboratories in the early 1970s, was one of the first to use such a tree-structured directory system. The widespread popularity of UNIX today and the adoption of this scheme by a significant number of other operating systems is evidence of the attractive way in which it combines user convenience with system security. However, this is not to say that such systems are completely free of security problems. Once the security of such a system is slightly compromised, the tree structure lends itself to a cascade of far-reaching security breaks. Brian Reid's article "Reflections on Some Recent Widespread Computer Break-ins" in the February 1987 issue of *Communications of the ACM* (Vol. 30, No. 2) provides an interesting account of how such security problems surfaced at Stanford University and spread to an entire network of computers. An entertaining narrative of another security incident is presented by Clifford Stoll in *The Cuckoo's Egg* (Doubleday, New York, 1989).

Efficiency Analysis of AddNode for Linear Representation of Heap

Clearly the time efficiency of adding an item to the heap is directly proportional to the length of the path that the item must "walk up" as its appropriate position is determined. Because the linear representation of a heap leaves no unused gaps between values stored in the array, doubling the number of items in the heap will add only one level to the resulting binary tree. Thus, a heap with n nodes will have $\log_2 n$ levels using the linear representation. In other words, the length of the path that a new item will follow, and hence the efficiency of the AddNode operation, is $O(\log_2 n)$.

In the Exercises at the end of this section, you will explore an algorithm to delete a node from a heap. That exploration will show how a heap could be used to implement the priority queue ADT defined in Chapter 5.

EXAMPLE 7.6

In this example, we illustrate how the postorder traversal algorithm may be implemented for a linear array implementation of a binary tree. The algorithm is slightly more difficult for this representation since the tree is the encapsulation of an array and a count of the number of nodes. Unlike the linked implementation, there is not an explicit root pointer for the tree; instead, the root of the entire tree is understood to be at index 1. The following **PROCEDURE** PostorderTrav compensates for this by acting as a mere "front-end" for a local auxillary procedure which is where the actual recursion takes place. Our front-end **PROCEDURE** PostorderTrav simply passes a root pointer value of 1 to the auxillary procedure to start the recursion. We must also assume that a flagging Null value occupies array locations that are not currently storing data in the tree. This allows the auxiliary procedure to detect when the equivalent of a **NIL** pointer is passed.

```
PROCEDURE PostorderTrav (BT : BinaryTree;
                         PROCEDURE ProcessNode (VAR Item : TreeDataNode));

  {  Given:   Binary tree BT implemented by linear array representation. }
  {  Task:    Perform postorder traversal--left subtree                  }
  {           first, then right subtree, then root of BT--               }
  {           applying ProcessNode to each Item in the tree.             }
  {  Return:  BT with each node affected by ProcessNode                  }

  PROCEDURE PostorderTravAux (NodeLocation : integer);

    {  This procedure is the behind-the-scenes recursive helper        }
    {  of PostorderTrav.  The interface to PostorderTravAux is not     }
    {  seen by users of the ADT.  Assumption:  Array locations         }
    {  not presently storing data in the tree have been flagged        }
    {  with an appropriate Null value.                                 }
```

```
BEGIN
    IF NodeLocation <= MaxTreeNodes THEN
      IF BT.BTData[NodeLocation] <> Null THEN
        BEGIN
          PostorderTravAux (2 * NodeLocation);      { Left subtree  }
          PostorderTravAux (2 * NodeLocation + 1);  { Right subtree }
          ProcessNode (BT.BTData[NodeLocation])
        END
END;  { of PROCEDURE PostorderTravAux }
```



```
BEGIN
  IF BT.NumberNodes <> 0 THEN
    PostorderTravAux (1 { The location of the root of BT } )
END; {  of PROCEDURE PostorderTrav  }
```

Exercises 7.4

1. Suppose that items arrive for insertion into a heap in the following order:

   10 20 30 40 50 60 70 80 90 100

   Using the algorithm of Example 7.5, trace the contents of the BTData array after each item is added to the heap.

2. Write implementations of the Create, Empty, and Full operations for a binary tree with the heap property using the linear array implementation. Be sure that your Create operation is consistent with the postorder traversal algorithm of Example 7.6.

3. Write implementations of the preorder and inorder traversal operations for a linear array implementation of a binary tree.

4. The linear array implementation of a binary tree discussed in this section assumes the existence of a Null value to signal array locations that do not contain tree data. In some applications it may be impossible or highly inconvenient to determine such a Null value because you are, in effect, disallowing the Null value from ever occurring in the tree itself. Devise a strategy whereby you could still employ the linear array implementation with its mapping of $n \rightarrow 2n$ for left child and $n \rightarrow 2n + 1$ for right child but *not* have to assume the existence of a flagging Null value.

   Describe your strategy and, in a written statement, discuss why it works. Then implement the Create operation and one of the traversal operations using your strategy.

5. Implement the following operation for a linear representation of a binary tree with the heap property.

```
PROCEDURE Remove (VAR BT : Binary Tree;
                  VAR Item : TreeDataNode);
```

```
{ Given:    BT, a binary tree with the heap property      }
{ Task:     Remove the value at the root of BT, then      }
{           reshape the tree into a heap.                 }
{ Return:   The old root of BT in Item. BT with the       }
{           old root removed, reshaped to retain the      }
{           heap property.                                }
```

(*Hint:* When the root is removed, temporarily replace it by the tree node in the last active index of the array. Then develop an algorithm to walk this new root down a branch of the tree until the tree becomes a heap again.)

In a written statement, indicate how the AddNode procedure of Example 7.5 and the Remove procedure that you have written for this exercise could be used to implement a priority queue (Chapter 5) using a heap.

6. In a written statement discuss the relative advantages and disadvantages of the linear array implementation of a binary tree versus the linked implementation described in Section 7.2.

■ ■ ■ ■

7.5 General Trees

OBJECTIVES

- to understand how a general tree may be implemented using a linked representation of a binary tree
- given the implementation of a general tree by a binary tree, to examine which traversal operations for the underlying binary tree make sense when it is interpreted as a general tree

We began this chapter with a discussion of the many ways in which hierarchical structures are used to organize information around us. We then quickly imposed a birth control dictate of at most two children which focused all of our attention on the seemingly restricted case of the binary tree. What about all of those applications requiring a hierarchical relationship where a parent may have an unrestricted number of children? You may have become suspicious that we are avoiding such considerations because they are too difficult.

Fortunately, we have a much more educationally sound reason. That is, we may use a binary tree to implement a general tree. The nice implication of this rather surprising statement is that we will not have to spend a significant amount of time discussing general trees because we have unknowingly studied them in our thorough analysis of binary trees. Moreover, the formal operations on a general tree may be viewed as operations derived from those associated with a binary tree.

The real key to using a restricted type of tree such as a binary tree to implement a more general type of tree is to adjust our perspective. For example, consider the general genealogical tree of Figure 7.24.

FIGURE 7.24
Genealogical tree

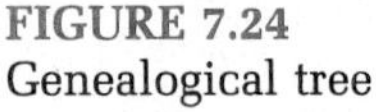

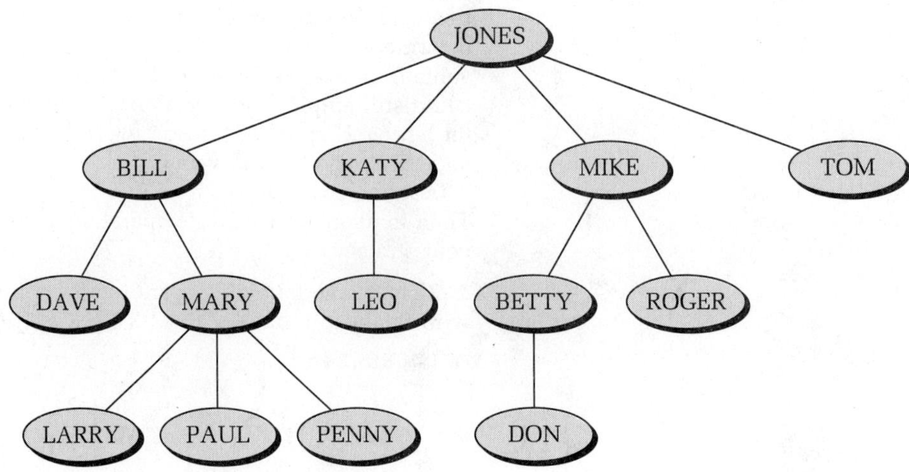

Here BILL is the first child of the JONES family, with KATY, MIKE, and TOM as BILL's siblings. Similarly, LARRY is the first child of MARY, with PAUL and PENNY as siblings. Now, in a linked representation of binary tree, we have two pointer fields associated with each node. We have called these pointer fields LeftChild and RightChild because it suited our perspective at the time. However, we shall now switch that perspective in the following way. One of the pointer fields is to be viewed as pointer to the leftmost child of a node in a general tree. The second pointer identifies the next sibling to the right of the node under consideration in the general tree. Since the children of a node taken in this context form an ordered set of nodes, we can regard the leftmost child of a node as FirstChild and the sibling to the right of this node as Sibling. We will henceforth adopt this terminology for the two link fields involved with the binary tree representation of a general tree. Figure 7.25 gives the binary representation of the general genealogical tree shown in Figure 7.24.

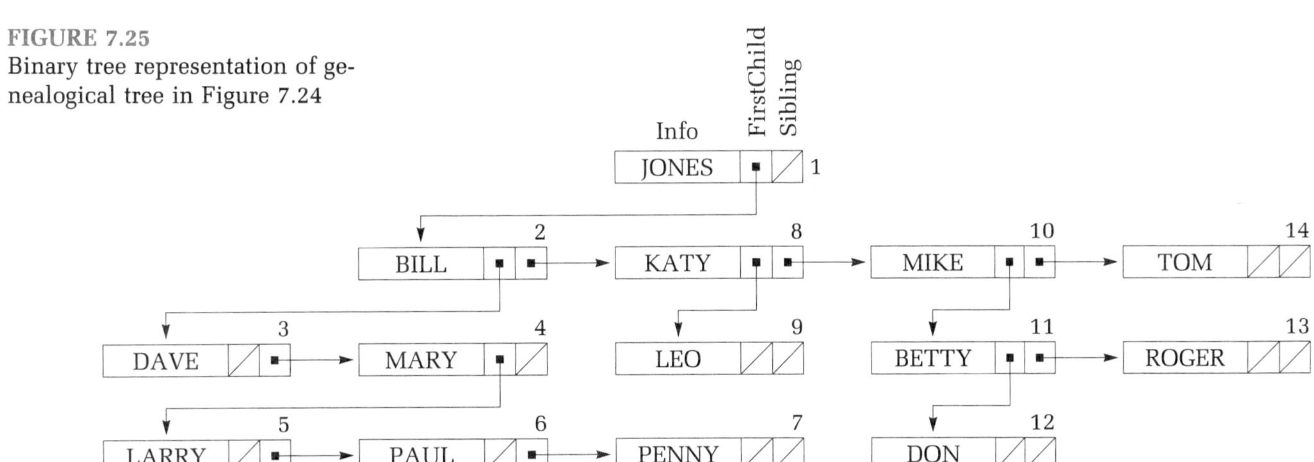

FIGURE 7.25
Binary tree representation of genealogical tree in Figure 7.24

TABLE 7.4
Tree in Figure 7.24 stored in array of records for data and pointers

Location	Data	FirstChild	Sibling
1	JONES	2	0
2	BILL	3	8
3	DAVE	0	4
4	MARY	5	0
5	LARRY	0	6
6	PAUL	0	7
7	PENNY	0	0
8	KATY	9	10
9	LEO	0	0
10	MIKE	11	14
11	BETTY	12	13
12	DON	0	0
13	ROGER	0	0
14	TOM	0	0

Although we will typically use Pascal pointer variables for such a binary tree implementation of a general tree, it is worth noting that an array of records with integer pointer fields can still be used just as it was for a linked list in Chapter 4. Indeed, because this array perspective allows us to specify some actual values for pointers, we have portrayed the tree of Figure 7.24 as an array of records in Table 7.4. You should carefully check all FirstChild and Sibling values to convince yourself that the scheme used to fill this array was to store a node before any of its children, and then recursively store the leftmost child.

The analogous representation in terms of Pascal pointer variables (and the representation we shall henceforth use) requires the following type declarations:

```
GenTree = ^GenTreeNode;
GenTreeNode = RECORD
                Info : TreeDataNode
                FirstChild : GenTree;
                Sibling : GenTree
              END;
```

Traversals of a General Tree Implemented via a Binary Tree

Since this implementation scheme for a general tree is nothing more than a special interpretation of a binary tree, all of the traversals defined for a binary tree clearly exist for the general tree. A more relevant question than the mere existence of a traversal, however, is the significance of the order in which the nodes of a general tree are visited when its corresponding binary tree is traversed. Of particular interest in this regard are the preorder and postorder traversals.

You should verify that the preorder traversal algorithm for a binary tree applied to Figure 7.24 visits nodes in the following order:

JONES
    BILL
        DAVE
        MARY
            LARRY
            PAUL
            PENNY
    KATY
        LEO
    MIKE
        BETTY
            DON
        ROGER
    TOM

The indentation here has been added to highlight the fact that the preorder traversal will recursively process a parent node, and then process the child nodes from left to right.

Relative to the general tree pictured in Figure 7.24, we see that the effect of the preorder traversal is to fix on a node at one level of the tree and then run through all of that node's children before progressing to the next node at the same level (the sibling). There is a hint here of a generalized nested loop situation which, as you will see, has some interesting applications in the Programming Problems.

The other traversal of interest in a binary tree representation of a general tree is the postorder traversal. In this regard, it should first be verified that the postorder traversal applied to Figure 7.24 (and its binary tree implementation in Figure 7.25) yields the following listing:

PENNY
PAUL
LARRY
MARY
DAVE
LEO
DON
ROGER
BETTY
TOM
MIKE
KATY
BILL
JONES

In general, the postorder traversal works its way up from the leaf nodes of a tree, insuring that no given node is processed until all nodes in the subtree below it have been processed.

Exercises 7.5

1. How would you implement a preorder traversal to print nodes in a fashion that has children indented under their parents?
2. Consider the following abstract graphical representation of a general tree.

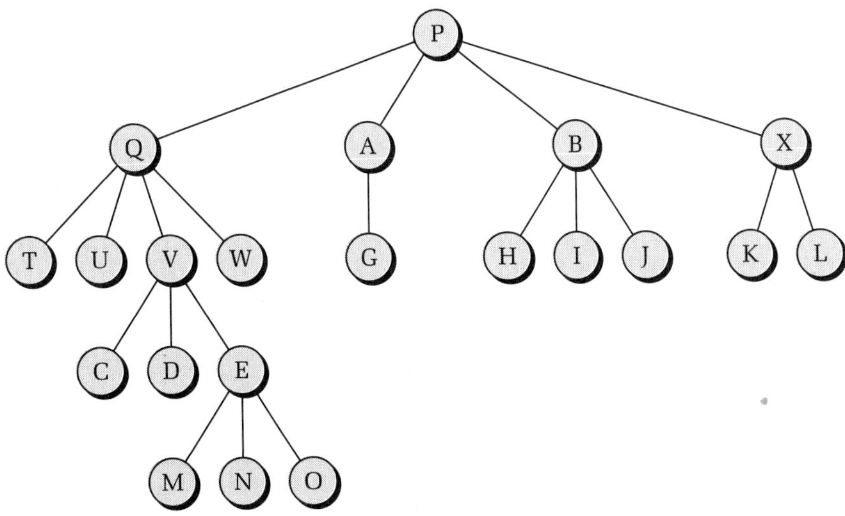

   Provide a specific Pascal record description for a node in this tree as you would represent it. (Do not make any assumption about maximum possible number of children.) Then draw a specific picture of how this tree would actually be stored using the record description you have chosen.
3. Given the tree from Exercise 2, in what order would nodes be visited by a preorder traversal? A postorder traversal?

4. For this exercise you are to assume a linked binary tree representation of a general tree. Write a procedure that meets the following specification.

```
PROCEDURE AddChild (VAR GT : GenTree;
                        ST : GenTree;
                        K : integer;

  { Given:   GT, a nonempty general tree.                    }
  {          ST, another nonempty general tree.              }
  {          K>= 1.                                          }
  { Task:    Insert ST as the Kth subtree descending from    }
  {          the root node of GT.                            }
  { Return:  GT with ST inserted as the Kth subtree of its   }
  {          root. If the root node of GT already has        }
  {          K or more subtrees, ST becomes the Kth          }
  {          subtree, and the former Kth subtree becomes     }
  {          the (K+1)st subtree. If the root node of GT     }
  {          has fewer than K subtrees, then ST is           }
  {          inserted as the last subtree of the root node.  }
```

5. Use the procedure you developed for Exercise 4 in another procedure to generate the following tree. Verify that you have generated the correct tree with a traversal procedure that outputs the tree in appropriate fashion.

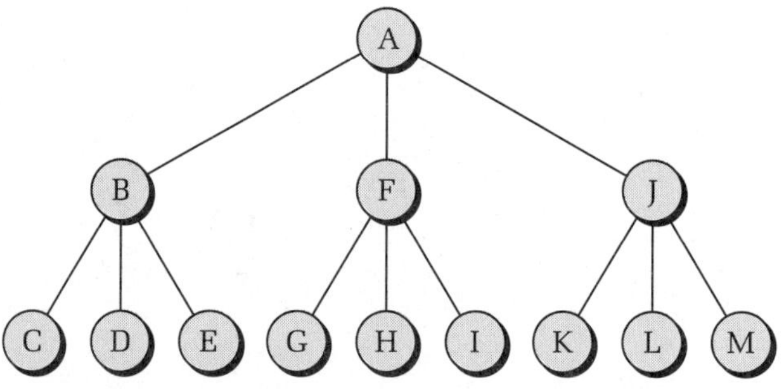

6. Is a binary tree a special case of a general tree? Provide a written rationale to justify your answer.

7.6 Graphs and Networks: Bidirectional Trees

OBJECTIVES

- to understand the definition and operations for the graph ADT
- to understand the definition and operations for the network ADT
- to understand how a two-dimensional table may be used to implement the graph and network ADTs
- to realize why the two-dimensional table representation of a graph or network often results in a sparse matrix

Objectives continued.

The key defining characteristic of a tree is the hierarchical relationship between parent and child nodes. In a tree, this hierarchical relationship is a one-way relationship. That is, within the tree there is pointer information that allows us to descend from parent to child. However, there is generally no pointer information within the tree which allows us to ascend from a child node to its parent. In many information storage applications such a one-way relationship is not sufficient.

Consider, for instance, the relationship between students and courses at a university. Each student is enrolled in several courses and could thus be viewed as a parent node with children consisting of the courses he or she is taking. Conversely, each course enrolls many students and could thus be viewed as a parent node with children consisting of the students enrolled in that particular course. The data structure that emerges from this type of bidirectional relationship is pictured in Figure 7.26.

Objectives continued.

- to understand traversal algorithms for graphs and networks
- to understand Dijkstra's algorithm for finding the shortest path between two nodes in a network

FIGURE 7.26
Bidirectional relationship between students and courses

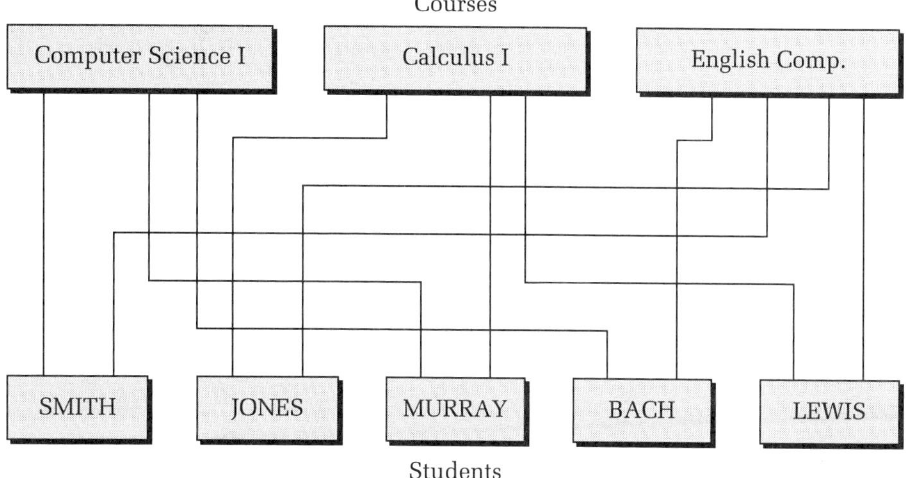

In terms of an abstract data-type, the representation of such a bidirectional relationship between nodes is called a *graph*.

> **Graph.** A graph consists of two sets. One set is a fixed set of objects called *nodes*. The other is a set of *edges,* the contents of which vary depending on the operations that have been performed upon the graph. A node is a data element of the graph, and an edge is a direct connection between two nodes. A node may also be called a *vertex* of the graph. If an edge exists between two nodes, we say that the second node is adjacent to the first node.

The operations associated with the graph ADT are specified in terms of the following pre- and postconditions:

Create operation	
Preconditions:	*G* is an arbitrary graph variable.
Postconditions:	Graph *G* initialized to a state with no edges. That is, no nodes are connected to any other nodes, including themselves.
AddEdge operation	
Preconditions:	*G* is an arbitrary graph that has been initialized by Create and, potentially, affected by other operations. *Node1, Node2* are two nodes in graph *G*.
Postconditions:	*G* is returned with an edge from *Node1* to *Node2*. If an edge already existed from *Node1* to *Node2*, *G* is not affected.
RemoveEdge operation	
Preconditions:	*G* is an arbitrary graph that has been initialized by Create and, potentially, affected by other operations. *Node1, Node2* are two nodes in graph *G*.

Postconditions:	If there is an edge from *Node1* to *Node2*, it is removed. Otherwise *G* is not affected.
Edge operation	
Preconditions:	*G* is an arbitrary graph that has been initialized by Create and, potentially, affected by other operations. *Node1, Node2* are two nodes in graph *G*.
Postconditions:	*Edge* returns **true** if there is an edge from *Node1* to *Node2*, **false** otherwise.
Traversal operation	
Preconditions:	*G* is an arbitrary graph that has been initialized by Create and, potentially, affected by other operations. *Start* is a node at which the traversal is to start. *ProcessNode* is an algorithmic process that can be applied to each Graph node.
Postconditions:	*G* is returned with each node that can be reached from *Start* affected by *ProcessNode*. A given node can be reached from *Start* if the given node is the *Start* node or if there is a sequence of edges $E_0, E_1, \ldots, E_n$ such that E_0 begins at the *Start* node, the node at which E_{i-1} ends is the node at which E_i begins, and E_n is the given node. In effect, the sequence of edges determines a path from *Start* to the given node. The path is composed of edges between adjacent nodes. *ProcessNode* is not applied to any node more than once.

Notice that, as it relates to Figure 7.26, the formal definition of a graph does not rule out the possibility of an edge connecting two courses or connecting two students. It is merely the nature of this course-student relationship that makes the existence of such a course-to-course edge or student-to-student

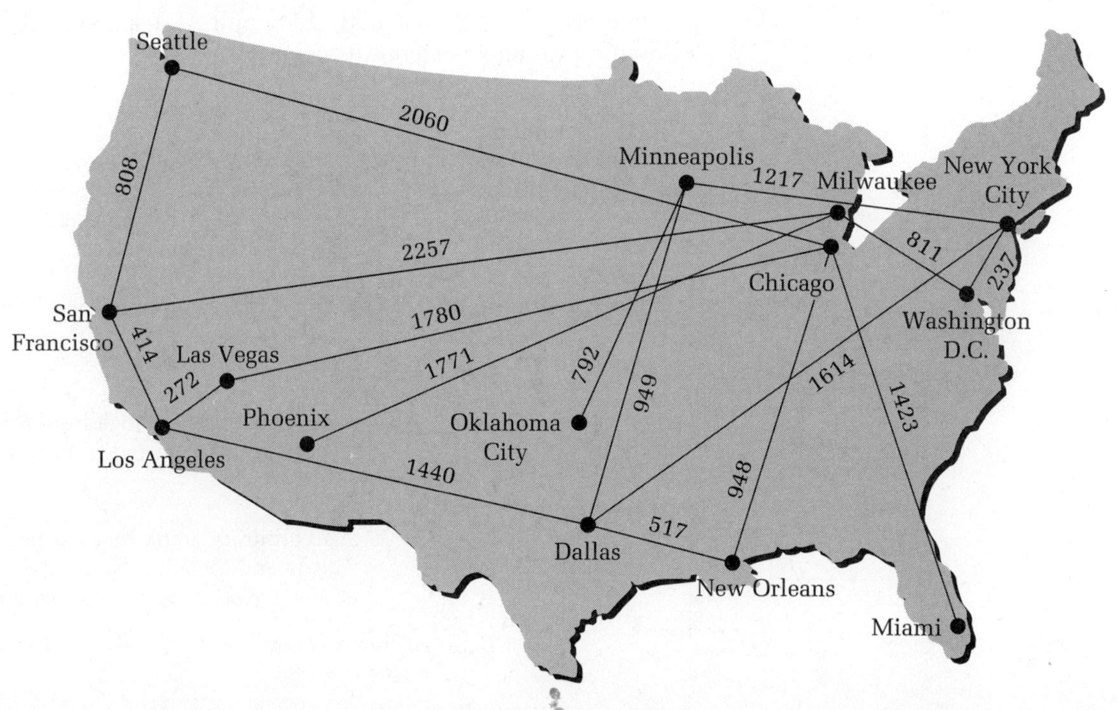

FIGURE 7.27
Transportation network as graph in which edges represent flights between cities

edge impractical. In other applications, such as the transportation network pictured in Figure 7.27, it may be entirely feasible for any node in the graph to have an edge connecting it to any other node.

To illustrate how a graph grows from an initial state with no edges, suppose that we start with a set of nodes labeled A, B, C, D. Figure 7.28 traces the effect of a sequence of AddEdge and RemoveEdge operations on a graph with these nodes.

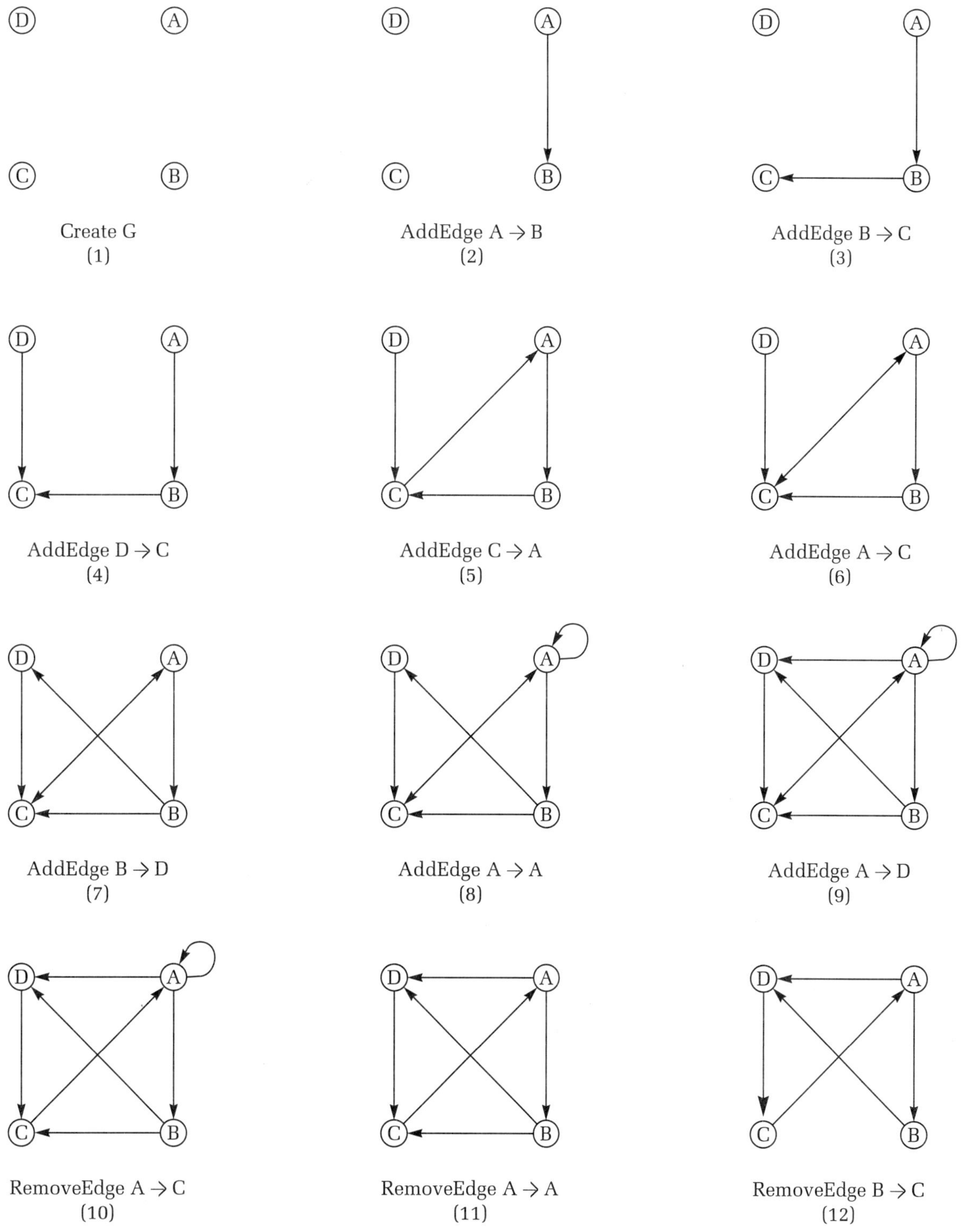

FIGURE 7.28
Graph affected by sequence of AddEdge and RemoveEdge operations

Create G
(1)

AddEdge A → B
(2)

AddEdge B → C
(3)

AddEdge D → C
(4)

AddEdge C → A
(5)

AddEdge A → C
(6)

AddEdge B → D
(7)

AddEdge A → A
(8)

AddEdge A → D
(9)

RemoveEdge A → C
(10)

RemoveEdge A → A
(11)

RemoveEdge B → C
(12)

Note from this figure that the concept of an edge carries with it the notion of a direction. That is, it is possible to have an edge from Node1 to Node2 in a graph G without there being a corresponding connection in the opposite direction. Figure 7.28 (8) also illustrates that it is possible to have an edge from a node to itself.

By convention, when we draw a graph without arrows on the edges, it is implicit that all edges run in both directions. Thus, in Figure 7.27, the line connecting San Francisco and Los Angeles implicitly represents two edges—the one from San Francisco to Los Angeles and the one from Los Angeles to San Francisco.

We will sometimes use the terminology *directional graph,* or *digraph,* to emphasize that a particular graph has some edges that exist only in one direction. Figure 7.29 illustrates a digraph. In a digraph, we use arrows on edges to specify the direction of an edge between nodes.

Before providing a Pascal interface for the graph ADT, we should clarify a point of ambiguity in the definition of the traversal operation. In particular, this operation does not establish a unique order of visiting nodes that can be reached from the Start node. The following examples illustrate two potential orders in which nodes can be visited starting at A in the graph of Figure 7.29.

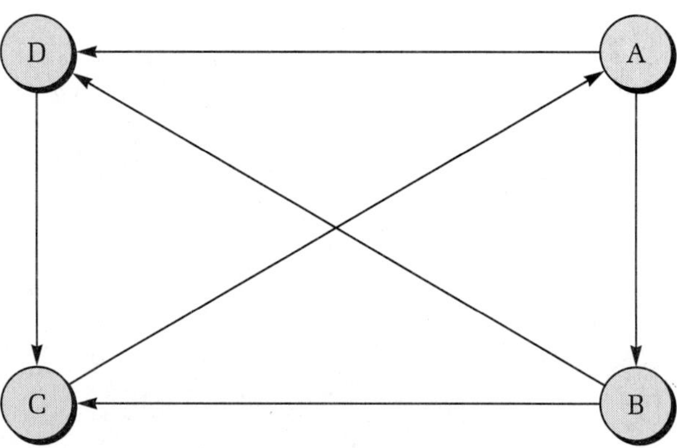

FIGURE 7.29
A four-node digraph

■ EXAMPLE 7.7

Consider a traversal from Start node A in the digraph of Figure 7.29 guided by the following strategy: a given path starting at A should be explored as deeply as possible before another path is probed. If we assume that B is the first node adjacent to A, then the traversal will proceed from A to B. If we then assume that C is the first node adjacent to B, the traversal will continue from B to C. From C, it is not possible to visit any nodes that have not already been visited. Hence, we will backtrack to B and, from there, continue the traversal to D since D is adjacent to B. Hence the overall order in which nodes would be visited by a traversal under the strategy and assumptions of this example is

A, B, C, D

The strategy exemplified here is often called a *depth-first traversal* since a given path is probed as deeply as possible before we backtrack and explore another path.

■ ■

EXAMPLE 7.8

Indicate the order in which nodes would be visited in a traversal starting at node A in the digraph of Figure 7.29 following a strategy that does not probe one path as deeply as possible but rather "fans out" to all nodes adjacent to a given node. Hence we would proceed from A to B and then to D, since both B and D are adjacent to A. Since all nodes adjacent to A have been exhausted, we would fan out from B, the first node we visited from A. This takes us to C by the edge B → C, completing the traversal in the overall order

A, B, D, C

The fan-out strategy exemplified here is often termed a *breadth-first traversal.*

Examples 7.7 and 7.8 just begin to scratch the surface of the variety of graph traversal strategies that exist. We shall soon examine the implementation of these traversal strategies more closely. At this time the point to emphasize is that the graph traversal operation is open to a variety of implementation techniques.

Pascal Interface for the Graph ADT

Before we can develop graph algorithms in detail, we must provide a Pascal interface for this ADT. This is done in the following procedure and function headers. The interface makes the assumption that the data in graph nodes are drawn from an appropriate subrange of an ordinal data type such as **integer**, **char**, or an enumerated type. Our reasons for making this assumption will become apparent when we discuss ways of implementing graphs.

```
CONST
  FirstNode = {The first value in the subrange for the GraphNode type};
  LastNode  = {The last value in the subrange for the GraphNode type};

TYPE
  GraphNode = FirstNode .. LastNode;
  Graph = { An appropriate implementation of the graph ADT };

PROCEDURE Create (VAR G : Graph);
  { Given:   G -- an arbitrary graph variable.                   }
  { Task:    Initialize G.                                       }
  { Return:  Graph G initialized to a state with no edges.       }
  {          That is, no nodes are connected to any other        }
  {          nodes, including themselves.                        }

PROCEDURE AddEdge (VAR G : Graph;
                   Node1, Node2 : GraphNode);

  { Given:   G -- an arbitrary graph that has been initialized   }
  {          by Create and, potentially, affected by other       }
  {          operations.                                         }
  {          Node1, Node2 -- two nodes in graph G.               }
  { Task:    Add an edge from Node1 to Node2 in G.               }
  { Return:  G with an edge from Node1 to Node2.  If an edge     }
  {          already existed from Node1 to Node2, G is not       }
  {          affected.                                           }

PROCEDURE RemoveEdge (VAR G : Graph;
                      Node1, Node2 : GraphNode);
```

```
  { Given:   G -- an arbitrary graph that has been initialized    }
  {          by Create and, potentially, affected by other         }
  {          operations.                                           }
  {          Node1, Node2 -- two nodes in graph G.                 }
  { Task:    Remove the edge from Node1 to Node2 in G.             }
  { Return:  If there is an edge from Node1 to Node2, it           }
  {          is removed.  Otherwise G is not affected.             }

FUNCTION Edge (G : Graph;
               Node1, Node2 : GraphNode) : boolean;

  { Given:   G -- an arbitrary graph that has been initialized    }
  {          by Create and, potentially, affected by other         }
  {          operations.                                           }
  {          Node1, Node2 -- two nodes in graph G.                 }
  { Task:    Determine if there is an edge from Node1 to Node2.    }
  { Return:  True if there is an edge from Node1 to Node2,         }
  {          false otherwise.                                      }

PROCEDURE GraphTraversal (VAR G : Graph;
                          VAR Start : GraphNode;
                          PROCEDURE ProcessNode (VAR Item : GraphNode));

  { Given:   G -- an arbitrary graph that has been initialized    }
  {          by Create and, potentially, affected by other         }
  {          operations.                                           }
  {          Start -- a node at which the traversal is to start.   }
  {          ProcessNode -- this procedure determines the          }
  {          process applied to each Graph node.                   }
  { Task:    Apply ProcessNode to each node that can be reached    }
  {          from Start in graph G.                                }
  { Return:  G with each node that can be reached from Start       }
  {          affected by ProcessNode.  ProcessNode is not          }
  {          applied to any node more than once.                   }
```

The Network ADT

Graphs such as that in Figure 7.27 are somewhat special in that the edges have weights associated with them, here representing distances between nodes (cities). Such a graph is an example of the *network* abstract data type.

Network. A network is a graph in which each edge has a positive numerical *weight*. The operations associated with the network ADT are the same as those for the graph ADT with the exceptions that the AddEdge operation must now specify the weight of the Edge being added and we must add an operation which, given two nodes, returns the weight of the edge that may exist between them.

These two new operations are specified by the following pre- and postconditions.

AddEdge operation

Preconditions: N is an arbitrary network that has been initialized by Create and, potentially, affected by other operations. *Node1, Node2* are two nodes in network N. *Wt* is a positive number representing the weight of an edge to be added from *Node1* to *Node2*.

Postconditions: N has an edge of weight *Wt* from *Node1* to *Node2*. If an edge already existed from *Node1* to *Node2*, the weight of that edge is now *Wt*.

EdgeWeight operation

Preconditions: N is an arbitrary network that has been initialized by Create and, potentially, affected by other operations. *Node1, Node2* are two nodes in network N.

Postconditions: *EdgeWeight* returns zero if there is no edge from *Node1* to *Node2* and the numerical value of the edge if it exists.

Graphs and networks provide excellent examples of how a theoretical area of mathematics has found very relevant application in computer science. It is beyond the scope of this text to provide a comprehensive treatment of graphs and networks. Rather, our purpose in the rest of this section is to provide you with an overview of a data structure which you will no doubt encounter again as you continue your study of computer science. More in-depth treatments of graphs and networks can be found in numerous advanced texts on data structures such as *Data Structures in Pascal* by Ellis Horowitz and Sartaj Sahni (New York, N.Y.: Computer Science Press, 1990) and *Introduction to Data Structures and Algorithm Analysis with Pascal* by Thomas L. Naps and George J. Pothering (St. Paul, Minn.: West Publishing, 1992).

Implementation of Graphs and Networks

A graph may be conveniently implemented using a two-dimensional table of Boolean values. For instance, the information in Figure 7.26 is contained in the following two-dimensional table (Table 7.5). In this table, the value **true** indicates the presence of an edge between two nodes and the value **false** indicates the absence of such an edge.

TABLE 7.5
Two-dimensional table implementation of graph from Figure 7.26

Course	SMITH	JONES	MURRAY	BACH	LEWIS
Computer Science	**true**	**false**	**true**	**true**	**false**
Calculus I	**false**	**true**	**true**	**false**	**true**
English Comp.	**true**	**true**	**false**	**true**	**true**

In the case of a network, the two-dimensional table implementation still applies. Now, however, the data stored in the table is of a type compatible with edge weights. Such a two-dimensional table implementation of the transportation network from Figure 7.27 is given in Table 7.6. Note that the data are mirrored across the diagonal of the table because all edges are bidirectional.

TABLE 7.6
Two-dimensional table implementation of network from Figure 7.27

	NY	Wash	Miami	Milw	Chi	NOrl	Mpls	OklC	Dals	LVeg	Phex	Stl	SFran	LA
NY		237					1217		1614					
Wash	237			811										
Miami					1423									
Milw		811									1771		2257	
Chi			1423			948				1780		2060		
NOrl					948				517					
Mpls	1217							792	949					
Oklc							792							
Dals	1614					517	949							1440
LVeg					1780									272
Phex				1771										
Stl					2060									808
SFran				2257								808		414
LA									1440	272			414	

Table 7.6 illustrates a quality typically found in two-dimensional table implementations of large graphs and networks: the sparseness of nontrivial data. Hence, the methods we have discussed for implementing sparse tables actually provide alternative implementation strategies for graphs and networks. In fact, the pilot/flight data-base problem of Wing-and-a-Prayer Airlines, with which we introduced the sparse matrix ADT in Chapter 2, may now be viewed as a graph problem. This problem presented us with a bidirectional tree in which each pilot could have multiple flights as child nodes and, conversely, each flight could have multiple pilots as child nodes.

In the discussion of the two graph/network algorithms that follow, we do not tie ourselves to a particular implementation strategy for representing the underlying data structure. Rather, we discuss the algorithms in terms of the operations associated with the abstract data type involved and leave implementation considerations for the Exercises and Programming Problems at the end of the chapter.

Examples of Graph Algorithms: Depth-First and Breadth-First Traversals

In many practical applications of graphs, there is frequently a need to systematically visit all the nodes on a graph from a designated starting node. One such application occurs in a political campaign when the organizers of the campaign are interested in having their candidate visit all important political centers. The presence or absence of direct transportation routes (that is, edges) between such centers will determine the possible ways in which all the centers could be visited. At the moment, our only concern is the development of an algorithm which insures that all possible nodes are visited. Such an algorithm will provide an implementation for the graph traversal operation. Later in the chapter we investigate how to determine the shortest possible distances from one node to all others.

Depth-First Traversal. This technique was illustrated in Example 7.7. The main logic of the depth-first algorithm is analogous to the preorder traversal of a tree. It is accomplished recursively as follows:

1. Designate the starting node as the search node and mark it as visited.
2. Find a node adjacent to the search node (that is, connected by an edge from the search node) which has not yet been visited. Designate this as the new search node (but remember the previous one) and mark it as visited.
3. Repeat step 2 using the new search node. If no nodes satisfying step 2 can be found, return to the previous search node and continue from there.
4. When a return to the previous search node in step 3 is impossible, the search from the originally chosen search node is complete.

This algorithm is called a depth-first traversal because the search continues progressively deeper into the graph in a recursive manner.

To illustrate this procedure more clearly, consider Figure 7.30; its table implementation is shown in Table 7.7.

FIGURE 7.30
Graph to illustrate depth-first search

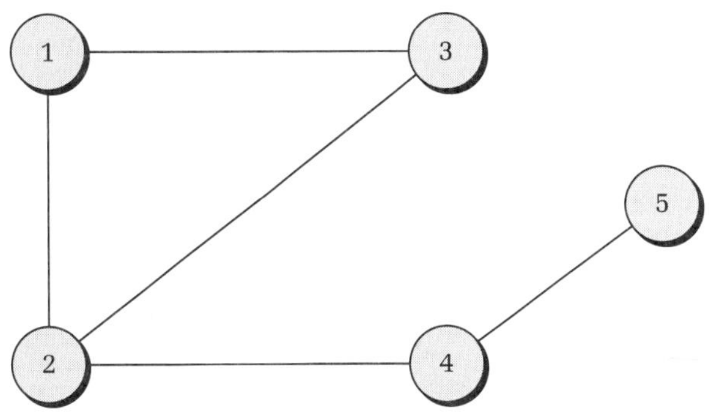

TABLE 7.7
Table implementation of Figure 7.30

	1	2	3	4	5
1	**false**	**true**	**true**	**false**	**false**
2	**true**	**false**	**true**	**true**	**false**
3	**true**	**true**	**false**	**false**	**false**
4	**false**	**true**	**false**	**false**	**true**
5	**false**	**false**	**false**	**true**	**false**

Suppose we have a procedure called SearchFrom which is invoked to begin a depth-first traversal from a given node on the graph. The steps followed by the algorithm are

1. We begin by marking node 1 visited and invoke SearchFrom(1).
2. Both nodes 2 and 3 are adjacent to node 1 according to the matrix implementation of the graph, but node 2 is encountered first on a left-to-right scan of the row for 1; so the search goes to node 2. We invoke SearchFrom(2), and node 2 is marked as visited.
3. Since node 3 is the first unvisited node adjacent to node 2, the search now goes to node 3, SearchFrom(3) is invoked, and node 3, is marked as visited.

4. Since there is no unvisited node adjacent to node 3, we say that this node has exhausted the search; the search goes back to its predecessor, that is, to node 2.
5. From node 2, we visit node 4.
6. From node 4, we proceed to node 5. All nodes have now been visited, and the depth-first traversal is complete.

Use Table 7.7 to verify these steps.

We note that the order in which nodes are visited in a depth-first traversal is not unique. This is because the order is dependent upon the manner in which "adjacent" nodes are chosen. That is, given two unvisited nodes adjacent to another node, which one should be chosen to invoke the SearchFrom procedure? In practice, this will usually be determined by the ordering of the data type used to implement the nodes in the graph.

EXAMPLE 7.9

Implement the depth-first traversal algorithm under the assumption that the GraphNode data type is a subrange of an ordinal type.

As with our implementation of the postorder traversal operation for a binary tree in Example 7.6, we use an auxiliary procedure as the real recursive workhorse. The **PROCEDURE** GraphTraversal itself is merely a front-end which appropriately sets the stage for the auxiliary **PROCEDURE** SearchFrom.

```
{  Global declarations  }

TYPE
  GraphNode = FirstNode .. LastNode;
  Graph = {  Appropriate implementation of the graph ADT  }

PROCEDURE GraphTraversal (VAR G : Graph;
                          VAR Start : GraphNode;
                          PROCEDURE ProcessNode (VAR Item : GraphNode));

  { Given:   G -- an arbitrary graph that has been initialized         }
  {          by Create and, potentially, affected by other             }
  {          operations.                                               }
  {          Start -- a node at which the traversal is to start.       }
  {          ProcessNode -- this procedure determines the              }
  {          process applied to each Graph node.                       }
  { Task:    Apply ProcessNode to each node that can be reached        }
  {          from Start in graph G.  Use a depth-first traversal to    }
  {          determine these nodes.                                    }
  { Return:  G with each node that can be reached from Start           }
  {          affected by ProcessNode.  ProcessNode is not              }
  {          applied to any node more than once.                       }

  VAR
    K : GraphNode;
    Visited : ARRAY [GraphNode] OF boolean;

  PROCEDURE SearchFrom (K : GraphNode);

    { Given:   K -- a single node in G.                                }
    { Task:    Conduct depth-first traversal from node K until all     }
    {          possibilities have been exhausted.                      }
    { Return:  Each node reachable from K affected by ProcessNode      }
```

```
  VAR
    J : GraphNode;

  BEGIN
    Visited[K] := true;
    ProcessNode (K);
    FOR J := FirstNode TO LastNode DO
      IF NOT Visited[J] AND Edge (G, K, J) THEN
        SearchFrom(J)  {  Recursively progress deeper into graph }
  END; {  of PROCEDURE SearchFrom  }

BEGIN {  DepthFirstTraversal  }
  FOR K := FirstNode TO LastNode DO
    Visited[K] := false;  {  Initially no nodes visited  }
  {  Begin traversal from Start node.  }
  SearchFrom (Start)
END; {  of PROCEDURE DepthFirstSearch  }
```

We can now see the reason for the restriction placed upon the type GraphNode in our Pascal interface for the graph ADT. It must be a type capable of indexing an array and an iterative loop structure. Both of these properties are assumed in the code of Example 7.9.

Breadth-First Traversal. An alternate graph traversal to the depth-first strategy is the breadth-first traversal. Instead of proceeding as deeply as possible along one path from the current node in the graph, the breadth-first traversal examines all nodes adjacent to the current node before proceeding more deeply along any given path. Hence, for the graph of Figure 7.31 implemented by Table 7.8, a breadth-first traversal starting at node 1 would visit nodes in the order 1, 2, 3, 4, 5 (as opposed to the order 1, 2, 4, 5, 3 that a depth-first traversal would dictate).

FIGURE 7.31
Graph to illustrate breadth-first traversal

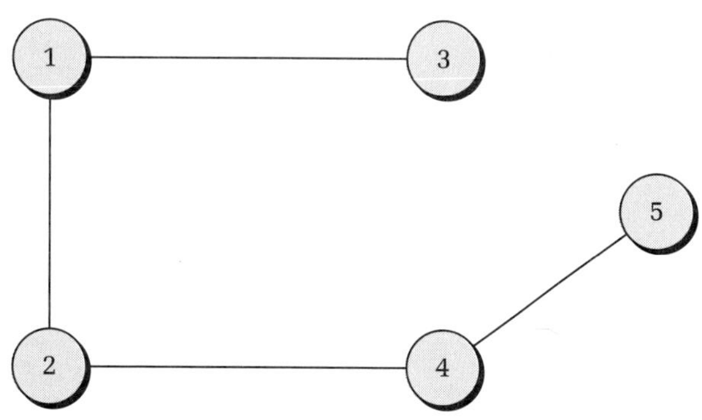

TABLE 7.8
Table implementation of Figure 7.31

	1	2	3	4	5
1	false	true	true	false	false
2	true	false	false	true	false
3	true	false	false	false	false
4	false	true	false	false	true
5	false	false	false	true	false

A breadth-first traversal of a graph involves the following steps:

1. Begin with the Start node, and mark it as visited.
2. Proceed to the next node having an edge connection to the node in step 1. Mark it as visited.
3. Come back to the node in step 1, descend along an edge toward an unvisited node, and mark the new node as visited.
4. Repeat step 3 until all nodes adjacent to the node in step 1 have been marked as visited.
5. Repeat steps 1 – 4 starting from the node visited in 2, then starting from the nodes visited in step 3 in the order visited. Keep this up as long as possible before starting a new scan.

You will be asked to explore this strategy in the Programming Problems at the end of the chapter.

Example of a Network Algorithm: Finding Shortest Paths

If the graph under consideration is a network in which edge weights represent distances, then an appropriate question is: From a given node called the Source, what is the shortest distance to all other nodes in the network?

For instance, the network of Figure 7.32 could be thought of as showing airline routes between cities. An airline would be interested in finding the most economical route between any two given cities in the network. The numbers listed on the edges would, in this case, represent distances between cities. Thus, the airline wishes to find the shortest path that can be flown from node 3 in order to reach nodes 1, 2, 4, and 5.

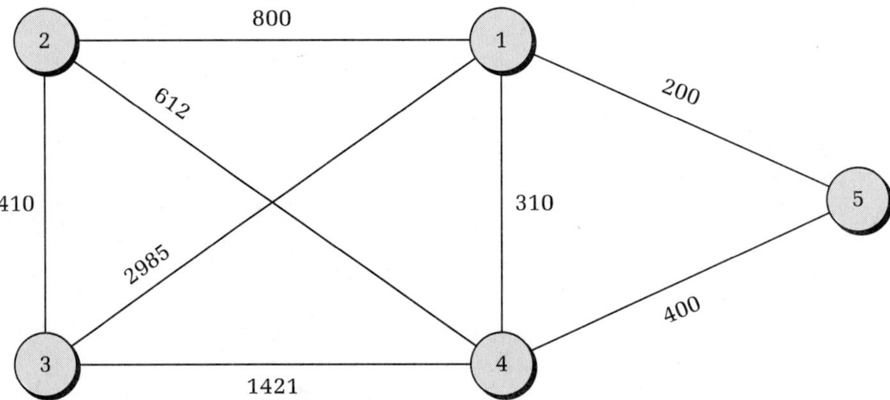

FIGURE 7.32
Network with edge weights representing distances

Suppose we want to find the shortest path from node 1 to node 3. From Figure 7.32, we note that this path would be 1→2→3, yielding a total weight of 800 + 410 = 1,210. An algorithm to find such a path was discovered by E. W. Dijkstra. For convenience in discussing Dijkstra's algorithm, often called the shortest path algorithm, let us assume that the nodes in the network under consideration are numbered 1, 2, . . ., NumberOfNodes. That is, the type GraphNode is the subrange of the integers given by 1 . . NumberOfNodes.

Given such a collection of nodes, Dijkstra's algorithm requires three arrays in addition to a suitable implementation of the network M. These three arrays are identified as follows:

```
VAR
  Distance, Path : ARRAY [GraphNode] OF integer;
  Included : ARRAY [GraphNode] OF boolean;
```

Identifying one node as the Source, the algorithm proceeds to find the shortest distance from Source to all other nodes in the network. At the conclusion of the algorithm, the shortest distance from Source to node J is stored in Distance[J] while Path[J] contains the immediate predecessor of node J on the path determining this shortest distance. While the algorithm is in progress, Distance[J] and Path[J] are being continually updated until Included[J] is switched from **false** to **true.** Once this switch occurs, it is known definitely that Distance[J] contains the shortest distance from Source to J. The algorithm progresses until all nodes have been so included. Hence it actually gives us the shortest distance from Source to every other node in the network.

Given the Source node in the network M, the algorithm may be divided into two phases: an initialization phase followed by an iteration phase in which nodes are included one by one in the set of nodes for which the shortest distance from Source is known definitely.

During the initialization phase, we must

1. Initialize Included[Source] to **true** and Included [J] to **false** for all other J.
2. Initialize the Distance array via the rule

$$\text{Distance[J]} = \begin{cases} 0 \text{ if J} = \text{Source} \\ \text{EdgeWeight(M,Source,J) if EdgeWeight(M,Source,J)} <> 0 \\ \text{Infinity if J is not connected to Source by a} \\ \quad \text{direct edge (that is, if} \\ \quad \text{EdgeWeight(M,Source,J)} = 0) \end{cases}$$

3. Initialize the Path array via the rule

$$\text{Path[J]} = \begin{cases} \text{Source if EdgeWeight (M,Source,J)} <> 0 \\ \text{Undefined otherwise} \end{cases}$$

Given this initialization, the iteration phase may be expressed in a generalized pseudocode form as follows:

REPEAT

1. Find the node J which has the minimal Distance among those nodes not yet Included;
2. Mark J as now Included;
3. **FOR** each R not yet Included
   - 3.1 **IF** there is an edge from J to R **THEN**
     - 3.1.1 **IF** Distance[J] + EdgeWeight (M,J,R) < Distance[R] **THEN**
       - 3.1.1.1 Distance[R] := Distance[J] + EdgeWeight (M,J,R)
       - 3.1.1.2 Path[R] := J

UNTIL all nodes are Included

The crucial part of the algorithm occurs within the innermost **IF** of the **FOR** loop. Figure 7.33 provides a pictorial representation of the logic involved here. The nodes included with the circle represent those nodes already Included prior to a given iteration of the **REPEAT** loop. The node J in Figure 7.33 represents the node found in the first step of the **REPEAT** loop; R represents another arbitrary node which has not yet been Included. The lines emanating from Source represent the paths corresponding to the current entries in the Distance array. For nodes within the circle—that is, those already Included—these paths are guaranteed to be the shortest-distance paths. If J is the node having the minimal entry in Distance among those not yet Included, we will add J to the circle of Included nodes and then check to see if J's connections to other nodes in the network which are not yet Included may result in a newly found shorter path to such nodes.

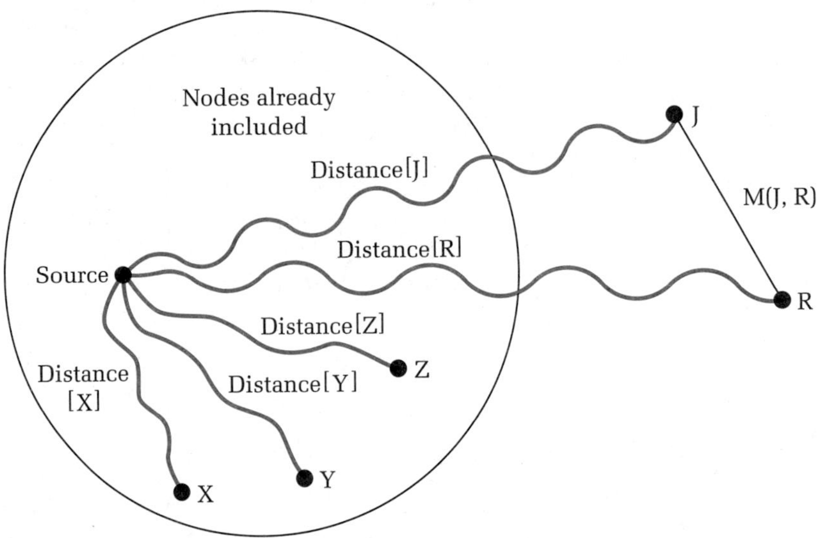

FIGURE 7.33
REPEAT loop logic in shortest-path (Dijkstra's) algorithm

Referring to Figure 7.33 again, the sum of two sides of a triangle

Distance [J] + EdgeWeight(M,J,R)

may in fact be shorter than the third side,

Distance[R]

This geometric contradiction is possible because these are not true straight-sided triangles, but "triangles" whose sides may be very complicated paths through a network.

It is also apparent from Figure 7.33 why Dijkstra's algorithm works. As the node J in this figure is found to have the minimal Distance entry from among all those nodes not yet Included, we may now Include it among the nodes whose minimal distance from the Source node is absolutely known. Why? Consider any other path P to J containing nodes which are not yet Included at the time J is Included. Let X be the first such non-Included node on the path P. Then clearly, as the first non-Included node on the Path P, X must be adjacent to an Included node. However as Figure 7.34 indicates, the criterion that dictated the choice of J as an Included node insures that

Distance[J] ≤ The total edge weight through node X on the path P
≤ Total edge weight of Path P

This inequality demonstrates that, once J is Included, there exists no other path P to J through a non-Included node that can yield a shorter overall distance. Hence we have verified our claim that Including a node guarantees our having found a path of shortest possible distance to that node.

FIGURE 7.34
Guaranteeing the minimality of Distance to J once it is Included

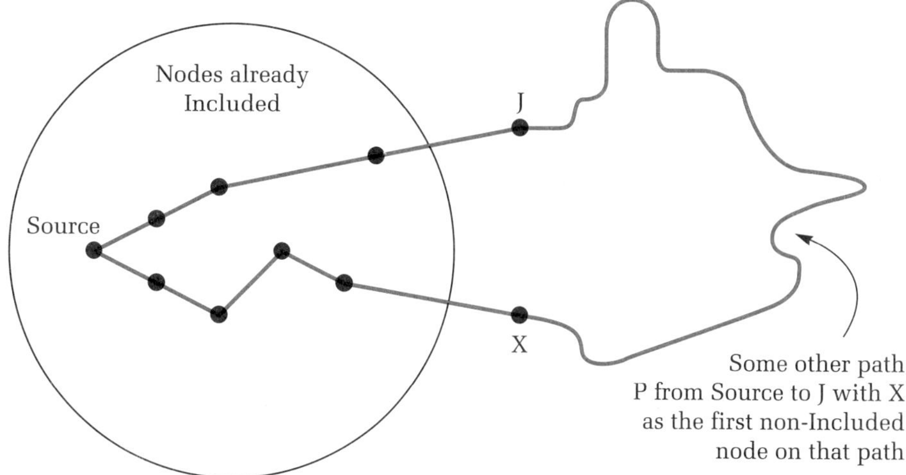

Criterion for Including J ensures
Distance [J] ≤ Distance[X] ≤ Length of path P

A NOTE OF INTEREST

Computer Networks: More Than an Abstract Data Type

Beginning with ARPANET (Advanced Research Projects Agency Network) in 1969, a relatively large number of computer networks have been developed, linking computers at various sites. These networks offer users the ability to trade information between computers across electronic communications lines. Typically, this information takes the form of electronic mail and text files. Electronic mail allows users working on related projects at distant sites to keep in touch at costs that are much cheaper than long-distance phone calls and at speeds of transmission that are *much* faster than postal service.

Using electronic mail is as easy as typing your message into the computer and then specifying the electronic mail address of the recipient. Usually these electronic mail addresses are a combination of the recipient name and computer installation. For example, one of the authors has the address NAPST@LAWRENCE.EDU on the InterNet network. Anyone using a computer with access to InterNet could send electronic data to Naps by routing the message to this address.

Among the best-known networks are ARPANET and MILNET, largely for the military and defense-oriented research; CSNET for computer science research; company networks such as DEC's Easynet and Xerox's Internet; and cooperative networks among users with common interests such as BITNET and InterNet (largely academic) and USENET (users of the UNIX operating system).

Although such networks are a godsend for users, the problems connected with their development have been monumental. One such problem concerns the routing of information from node to node along the network as data travel from originator to destination. Complicating this issue is the fact that individual networks often interconnect at so-called gateway nodes, making it possible for users on one network to relay information to someone on a completely different network. The information follows some interesting paths. For instance, to send a message from Wisconsin to New Jersey, one of the authors observed that the eventual path chosen by the routing software included computers at the University of Utah and the University of Texas. Clearly, the software does not employ Dijkstra's shortest path algorithm! (See Section 7.6.)

An excellent survey of existing computer networks appeared in *Scientific American* 265, No. 3 (September 1991). The entire issue is dedicated to articles on communications, computers, and networks. You should consult it for more information on this subject.

■ EXAMPLE 7.10

To be sure you understand Dijkstra's algorithm before you attempt to implement it, trace it through on the network of Figure 7.32 with Source = 1. Initially, we would have

```
Distance[2] =  800  Path[2] = 1
Distance[3] = 2985  Path[3] = 1
Distance[4] =  310  Path[4] = 1
Distance[5] =  200  Path[5] = 1
```

in accordance with steps 2 and 3 of the initialization phase. According to the iteration phase of the algorithm, we would then, in order

1. Include node 5; no change in Distance and Path needed.

```
Distance[2] =  800  Path[2] = 1
Distance[3] = 2985  Path[3] = 1
Distance[4] =  310  Path[4] = 1
Distance[5] =  200  Path[5] = 1
```

2. Include node 4; update Distance and Path to

```
Distance[2] =  800  Path[2] = 1
Distance[3] = 1731  Path[3] = 4
Distance[4] =  310  Path[4] = 1
Distance[5] =  200  Path[5] = 1
```

(Note that it is shorter to go from node 1 to node 4 to node 3 than to follow the edge directly connecting node 1 to node 3.)

3. Include node 2; update Distance and Path to

```
Distance[2] =  800  Path[2] = 1
Distance[3] = 1210  Path[3] = 2
Distance[4] =  310  Path[4] = 1
Distance[5] =  200  Path[5] = 1
```

(Now we find that traveling from node 1 to node 2 to node 3 is even better than the path determined in step 2.)

4. Finally node 3 is Included with (obviously) no changes made in Distance or Path.

■ ■

Exercises 7.6

1. Indicate the order that nodes would be visited if a depth-first traversal of the network in Figure 7.27 were initiated from SEATTLE. Use the adjacency relationships from Table 7.6.
2. Repeat Exercise 1 but initiate the traversal from MIAMI.
3. Repeat Exercise 1 for a breadth-first traversal.
4. Repeat Exercise 2 for a breadth-first traversal.
5. Trace the contents of the Distance, Path, and Included arrays as Dijkstra's shortest path algorithm is applied to the transportation network of Figure 7.27. Use PHOENIX as the Source node.

6. Repeat Exercise 5 with MILWAUKEE as the Source node.
7. Using a two-dimensional table, write procedures to implement each of the basic operations for the graph abstract data type. Then provide a big-O time efficiency analysis of each of the operations. How is this analysis affected by a particular sparse matrix technique that may be underlying the two-dimensional table? Be as specific as possible in stating your answer.
8. Using a two-dimensional table, write procedures to implement each of the basic operations for the network abstract data type.
9. In a written statement, discuss the implications of eliminating the requirement that **TYPE** GraphNode be a subrange of an ordinal type in the Pascal interface for the graph ADT. Your statement should identify problems that this would cause and outline strategies for solving such problems.

■ ■ ■ ■

FOCUS ON PROGRAM DESIGN

Throughout this text we have emphasized the importance of big-O algorithm analysis as a means of predicting beforehand the practicality of an algorithm in a given application. In this regard, big-O notation and analysis serves a vital purpose—the estimation of the time and space requirements of an algorithm in order of magnitude terms. However, when designing software systems in the very competitive and demanding real world, we often require a more detailed measurement of an algorithm's performance than that which can be achieved simply with a big-O analysis. One reason for this is the variety of complications that cannot be conveniently plugged into a big-O formula. Included among these complications are

- The variety of hardware on which an algorithm must ultimately be executed. There will be vast differences in both the time and space limitations of such hardware. Moreover, the details of such limitations are often buried deep in system reference manuals and can be exceedingly hard to find.
- Discrepancies that frequently arise between a user's projection of his or her computer needs and the unforeseen demands that materialize once the software system is put into use. A good systems analyst can hold those discrepancies to a minimum but not totally eliminate them.
- The elements of chance and probability that are inherent in many algorithms.

An example of this final point is the order of arrivals for insertion into a binary search tree. We can guarantee that search efficiency in a binary search tree will be between $O(n)$ and $O(\log_2 n)$. We can specify best and worst cases. But what happens in between? When do we cross over from response times that are acceptable to those that are not? Real-life data are rarely best case or worst case. Hence the "in-between" question is often of vital importance. Yet it is also the one that a pure big-O analysis leaves relatively unanswered.

In this section, we present a program that can serve as a start toward further exploration of the questions just posed. The program reads a list of unordered integers from a file, creates a binary search tree containing those integers, and then prints the binary search tree using indentation to reflect the level at which various nodes occur in the tree. In its present form, the program will allow you to test hypotheses about the relationship of the order of arrivals for insertion into a binary search tree and the resulting shape of the tree. In the first Programming Problem, you will extend the exploratory capabilities of the program, making it a substantive experimental tool.

A modular structure chart for the program is given in Figure 7.35.

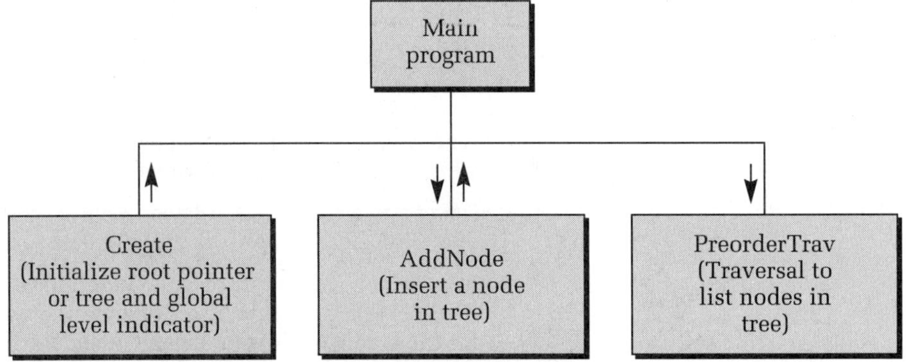

FIGURE 7.35
Modular structure chart for **PROGRAM** BinarySearchTree

The program essentially brings together tree processing modules that we have already discussed on an individual basis; therefore, we do not provide the module specifications here. Pseudocode for the main program is

1. Create root for tree
2. **WHILE NOT eof DO**
   2.1. get a number
   2.2. add a node
3. Print the tree

One twist is needed in the preorder traversal algorithm. To achieve indentation reflecting the depth of a node in the tree, we must keep track of our current level as we recursively call and then return from **PROCEDURE** PreorderTrav. The ideal solution would be to declare a local counter in the procedure that would retain its value from one invocation of the procedure to the next. Unfortunately, this is impossible with local variables in Pascal.

We are left with two alternatives: tag the level counter along as an additional **VAR** parameter for the PreorderTrav procedure or use a global level counter. The former alternative will alter the procedural interface to the PostorderTrav operation and hence violate the ADT implementation rule (formulated in Chapter 2). Hence we choose the latter alternative—use of a global variable—as the lesser of two evils. You should be aware that the need to preserve the value of a variable between invocations of a procedure is one instance in which the use of a global variable in a procedure can be justified, provided that you carefully document its use.

The complete program and a sample run follow. You will have the chance to explore the program more thoroughly in the Problems.

```
PROGRAM BinarySearchTree (input, output);

  {  This program illustrates working with a binary tree.     }
  {  Input is an unordered list of integers.  Output is a     }
  {  character-based representation of the binary search      }
  {  tree that is constructed from the read integers.         }
  {                                                           }
  {  Global variables:                                        }
  {  Number--integer read from the data file                  }
  {  BT--pointer to indicate the tree root                    }
  {  Level--global variable used to control indentation in    }
  {  printing the tree                                        }

  CONST
    Space = ' ';
```

```
TYPE
  TreeDataNode = integer;
  BinaryTree = ^RootNode;
  RootNode = RECORD
               LeftChild : BinaryTree;
               Info : TreeDataNode;
               RightChild : BinaryTree
             END;

VAR
  BT : BinaryTree;
  Number : TreeDataNode;
  Level : integer;

PROCEDURE Create (VAR BT : BinaryTree);

  {  Given:  BT, a binary tree, potentially not initialized.      }
  {  Task:   Initialize BT to an empty tree.                      }
  {  Return: Initialized tree.                                    }

  BEGIN
    BT := NIL;
    Level := 0  { In addition to initializing the root pointer to }
                { NIL, we initialize the Level counter used to    }
                { control indentation in printing.                }
  END; {  of PROCEDURE Create  }

PROCEDURE AddNode (VAR BT : BinaryTree;
                   Item : TreeDataNode);

  {  Given:   BT, a binary search tree with                       }
  {           ordering property, implemented by Pascal pointer    }
  {           variables.  Item, a value to be inserted            }
  {           in tree BT.                                         }
  {  Task:    Insert Item in tree BT, maintaining                 }
  {           the tree's ordering property.                       }
  {  Return:  Appropriately altered tree.                         }

  BEGIN
    IF BT = NIL THEN  {  Add a new node  }
      BEGIN
        new (BT);
        BT^.Info := Item;
        BT^.LeftChild := NIL;
        BT^.RightChild := NIL
      END
    ELSE IF Item < BT^.Info THEN { Move down the list }
      AddNode (BT^.LeftChild, Item)
    ELSE
      AddNode (BT^.RightChild, Item)
END; {  of PROCEDURE AddNode  }

PROCEDURE PreorderTrav (BT : BinaryTree;
                        PROCEDURE ProcessNode (VAR Item : TreeDataNode));

  {  Given:   Binary tree BT implemented by Pascal pointer          }
  {           variables.                                            }
  {  Task:    Perform preorder traversal--root of BT first,         }
  {           then left subtree, then right subtree--applying       }
  {           ProcessNode to each Item in the tree.                 }
  {  Return:  BT with each node affected by ProcessNode             }
```

```
  BEGIN
    IF BT <> NIL THEN
      BEGIN
        ProcessNode (BT^.Info);
        Level := Level + 1;    { We're recursing, so increase Level   }
        PreorderTrav (BT^.LeftChild, ProcessNode);
        PreorderTrav (BT^.RightChild, ProcessNode);
        Level := Level - 1    { Done recursing, so decrease Level    }
      END
    ELSE
      writeln (Space : Level * 4, ' NIL') { NIL to highlight end of }
                                          { branch                  }
 END; {  of PROCEDURE PreorderTrav  }

PROCEDURE PrintNode (VAR Item : TreeDataNode);

  { Given:   Item, a value in the binary search tree             }
  { Task:    Print Item, appropriately indented to reflect its    }
  {          position in the tree                                 }
  { Return:  Nothing                                              }

  BEGIN
    IF Level = 0 THEN
      writeln (Item : 4)
    ELSE
      writeln (Space : Level * 4, Item : 4)
  END;  { of PROCEDURE PrintNode }

  BEGIN  {  Main program  }
    Create (BT);
    WHILE NOT eof DO
      BEGIN
        readln (Number);
        AddNode (BT, Number)
      END;
    PreorderTrav (BT, PrintNode)
  END.  {  of main program  }
```

A sample run with the input file

results in the following output. Graphic lines have been added to highlight how the indentation reflects the tree structure.

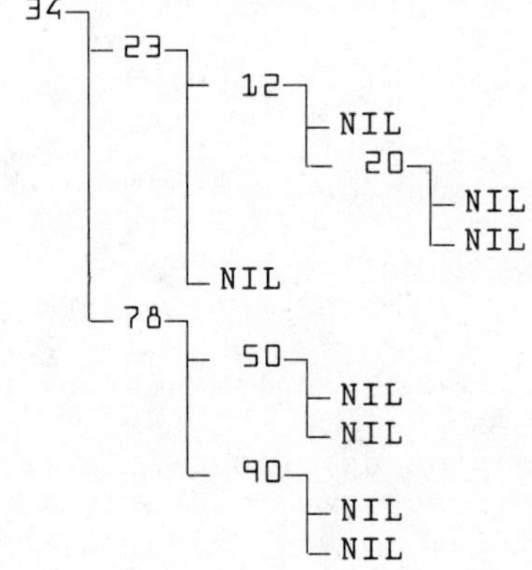

RUNNING AND DEBUGGING TIPS

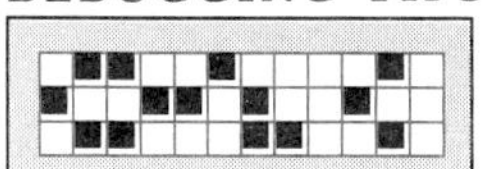

1. Trees are inherently recursive data structures, so learn to think recursively when devising algorithms that process trees.
2. When using the linear array representation of a binary tree, remember that all array locations must be initialized to a flagging Null value if the implementations of other operations are to work correctly.
3. The use of a preorder traversal to print a tree with indentation to reflect the depth of a node is a handy tracing tool to use when debugging a tree program that has gone awry. Keep such a procedure in your library, so it is readily available when the need arises. For more information, see this chapter's Focus on Program Design section.
4. When using a binary search tree to implement a keyed list, some experimentation may be necessary to determine the efficiency of this technique for the particular data of your application.

■ Summary

Key Terms

ancestor
binary search tree
binary tree
binary tree
  implementation of
  general tree
binary
  implementation of
  a keyed list
branch
breadth-first traversal
child node
depth-first traversal
digraph
directional graph
edge
general tree
graph
heap
heap property
height balancing
hierarchy
inorder traversal
insertion rule
leaf node
level
linear representation
linked representation
network
ordering property
parent node
postorder traversal
preorder traversal
root
root node
siblings
subtree
ternary tree
threading
tree
tree traversal
vertex
weight

Key Concepts

- Trees are a data structure used to reflect a hierarchical relationship among data items. Indicative of this hierarchy is the parent-child terminology used to express the relationship between items on successive levels of the tree. Trees are by nature recursive structures, with each node of a tree being itself the root of a smaller, embedded subtree.
- Binary trees are trees in which each parent may have at most two child nodes. Although this seems like a major restriction, binary trees find a wide range of applications. Three such applications are the representation of algebraic expressions, keyed lists, and priority queues.
- Two ways of implementing a binary tree are the linear representation and the linked representation. The former method uses an array and requires no pointers but is prone to wasting a large number of array locations. The latter uses pointers and consequently is able to take advantage of Pascal's dynamic memory allocation.
- There are three standard ways of traversing a binary tree: that is, three ways of visiting all nodes exactly once. These are the preorder, postorder, and inorder traversals.
- In a preorder traversal, the current root node is processed, followed recursively by the nodes in its left subtree and then its right subtree.

- In a postorder traversal, all nodes in the left subtree of the current root are recursively processed. Then all nodes in the right subtree are processed, and the root itself is processed last.
- In an inorder traversal, the nodes in the left subtree are processed first, followed by the root node, and finally the nodes in the right subtree of the root. The inorder traversal is critical in the binary tree implementation of a keyed list since the order in which it visits nodes corresponds precisely to the ordering of items as 1st, 2nd, 3rd, . . . , within the list represented by the tree.
- The binary search tree implementation of a keyed list is the third such list implementation we have studied. The other two were the array implementation (Chapter 2) and the linked list implementation (Chapter 4). The following table summarizes the relative advantages and disadvantages of the three methods.

Method	Search	Additions/ Deletions	Other Comments
Physically Ordered Array	$O(\log_2 n)$ with binary search	Excessive data movement	Data must be physically ordered
Linked List	Requires sequential search, hence $O(n)$	Only pointer manipulation required	
Binary Search Tree	Bounded between $O(\log_2 n)$ and $O(n)$ though advanced methods can guarantee the former	Only pointer manipulation required	May necessitate the overhead associated with recursive traversals

- The binary tree may be used to implement the general tree structure. The preorder and postorder traversals emerge as the most important for this particular application.
- Graphs and networks are abstract data structures that are more complex than trees because they reflect bidirectional rather than hierarchical relationships. Depth-first and breadth-first traversals and finding the shortest path are examples of algorithms that manipulate graphs and networks.

■ Programming Problems and Projects

1. Extend and experiment with the program from this chapter's Focus on Program Design section in the following ways.
   a. Use the program as it presently appears to acquire a feel for the relationship between the order of input data and the shape of the binary search tree that results.
   b. Instead of reading data from a file, randomly generate the data being inserted in the tree. Use a random number generator available in your version of Pascal or, if none is available, the random number generator that appears in Appendix 9.
   c. After a tree has been generated, add the capability to selectively delete nodes from the tree. Reprint the tree after deleting a node as verification that is has retained the critical ordering property.
   d. Use the random generation capability from part b to build some very large trees. Instead of printing out these trees after they have been generated, compute the length of the average path that must be followed to find a node in the tree.

Do the results of your experiment indicate that, for random data, binary search trees yield a search efficiency that is $O(\log_2 n)$ or $O(n)$? Justify your conclusion with a written statement that is backed up by empirical data provided from your experimental runs.

e. Extend part d by computing the maximal path length in each randomly generated tree. What percentage of randomly generated trees have a maximal path length that is $O(n)$?

f. Depending upon the availability of graphics procedures in your version of Pascal, change the present character-based tree printout into a more appealing graphical representation.

2. Use a binary tree to implement the keyed list in the registrar's system from Example 2.1.

3. Modify the airline reservation system you developed for Wing-and-a-Prayer Airlines in Problem 2, Chapter 4 so that the alphabetized lists are maintained with binary trees instead of linked lists.

4. Write a program that sorts the records of the Fly-by-Night credit card company file (Problem 3, Chapter 4) in alphabetical order by the last name and then the first name of the customer. Use a binary tree and its inorder traversal to accomplish the sort.

5. Recall the roster maintenance system that you wrote for the Bay Area Brawlers in Programming Problem 4 from Chapter 4. The system has been so successful that the league office would like to expand the system to include all the players in the league. Again the goal is to maintain the list of players in alphabetical order, allowing for frequent insertions and deletions as players are cut, picked up, and traded among teams. In addition to storing each player's height, weight, age, and university affiliation, the record for each player should be expanded to include team affiliation, years in league, and annual salary. Because the data base for the entire league is many times larger than that for just one team, maintain this list as a binary search tree to increase efficiency.

6. Write a program that reads an expression in its prefix form and builds the binary tree corresponding to that expression. Then write procedures to print the infix and postfix forms of the expression using inorder and postorder traversals of this tree. Then see if you can extend the program to evaluate the expression represented by the tree.

7. Given a file containing some arbitrary text, determine how many times each word appears in the file. Your program should print out in alphabetical order the words that appear in the file, with their frequency counts. For an added challenge, do not assume any maximum word length; this will enable you to combine trees with the string handling methods you have already learned.

8. Here is a problem you will encounter if you write statistical analysis software. Given an arbitrarily long list of unordered numbers with an arbitrary number of different values appearing in it, determine and print out the marginal distribution for this list of numbers. That is, count how many times each different value appears in the list and then print out each value along with its count (frequency). The final

output should be arranged from smallest to largest value. This problem can be solved in elegant fashion using trees.

An example of such output as produced by the COSAP (Conversationally Oriented Statistical Analysis Package) of Lawrence University follows:

```
Command?  Marginals Judge
                    Pine County Criminal Cases

                M A R G I N A L   F R E Q U E N C I E S
Variable Judge        JUDGE BEFORE WHOM CASE BROUGHT (2)
Value label           Value        Absolute          Relative
                                   Frequency         Frequency

ALLEN                  1             677               80.8%
JONES                  2              88               10.5%
KELLY                  3              26                3.1%
MURDOCK                5              47                5.6%

       838 Valid  0 Missing  838 Total Observations
```

Here the data file contained 838 occurrences of the values 1, 2, 3, and 5. Each value was a code number assigned to a particular judge.

9. Many compilers offer the services of a cross-referencing program to aid in debugging. Such a program will list in alphabetical order all the identifiers that appear in a program and the various lines of the program that reference them. Write such a cross-referencer for your favorite language using a binary tree to maintain the list of identifiers that are encountered.

10. A relatively easy game to implement with a binary tree is to have the computer try to guess an animal about which the user is thinking by asking the user a series of questions that can be answered by yes or no. A node in the binary tree to play this game could be viewed as

    Yes/No pointers leading to

    1. *Another question.*
    2. *The name of the animal.*
    3. ***NIL***.

    If **NIL**, have your program surrender and then ask the user for a new question that uniquely defines the animal being thought of. Then add this new question and animal to the growing binary tree data base.

11. For this problem, you are to write a program which will differentiate expressions in the variable X. The input to this program will be a series of strings, each representing an infix expression to be differentiated. Each such expression is to be viewed as a stream of tokens. Valid tokens are integers, the variable X, the binary operators (+, −, *, /, ^), and parentheses. To make scanning for tokens easy, you may assume that each token is followed by exactly one space, with the exception of the final token, which is followed by **eoln.**

    First your program will have to scan the infix expression, building up an appropriate binary tree representation of it. For this you should be able to borrow significantly on the work you did in parsing expressions in Chapter 5. The major difference here is that the end result of this parse is to be a binary tree instead of a postfix string.

Once the binary expression tree is built, traverse it, building up another binary expression tree which represents the derivative of the original expression. The following differentiation rules should be used in this process:

Suppose C is a constant, and S and T are expressions in X

Diff(C) = 0
Diff(X) = 1
Diff(S + T) = Diff(S) + Diff(T)
Diff(S − T) = Diff(S) − Diff(T)
Diff(S * T) = S * Diff(T) + T * Diff(S)
Diff(S / T) = ((T * Diff(S)) − (S * Diff(T))) / (T ^ 2)
Diff(S ^ C) = (C * S ^ (C − 1)) * Diff(S) { the infamous chain rule }

Finally, once the binary expression tree for the derivative has been built, print the expression. Print it in completely parenthesized infix notation to avoid ambiguity.

Note that there are three distinct phases to this problem.

- Parsing of the original infix expression into a binary tree representation.
- Building a binary tree representation of the derivative.
- Printing out the derivative in completely parenthesized infix notation.

For an added challenge on this problem, simplify the derivative before printing it out. Simplify the expression for the derivative according to the following rules:

S + 0 = S
0 + S = S
S − 0 = S
S * 0 = 0
0 * S = 0
S * 1 = S
1 * S = S
0 / S = 0
S ^ 0 = 1
S ^ 1 = S
S − S = 0
0 / S = 0
S / S = 1
S / 0 = 'DIVISION BY ZERO'
0 / 0 = 'UNDEFINED'

12. Wing-and-a-Prayer Airlines (Problem 3) is expanding their recordkeeping data base. This data base may now be pictured hierarchically as

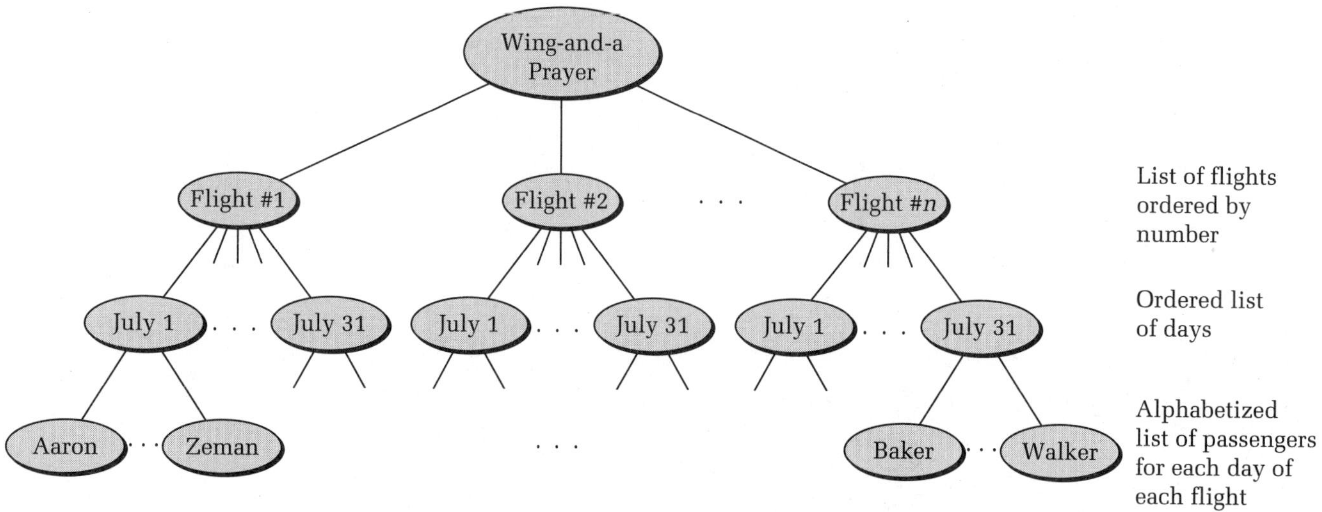

Write a program to maintain this data base. Your program should process requests to add, delete, or list the following:

- Specified flight number.
- Specified day of the month (for a given flight number)
- Specified passenger or all passengers (for a given flight number and day of the month).

13. Many statistical analysis packages support a "cross-tabulation" command designed to explore the relationship between statistical variables. A cross-tabulation between two variables produces a two-dimensional table containing a frequency count for each possible ordered pair of values of the two variables. However, these statistical packages typically allow this type of analysis to proceed even further than merely exploring two variables. For instance, in a legal-system data base, we might be interested in cross-tabulating a defendant's age with the judge before whom the defendant stood trial. We may then wish to cross-tabulate this result with the sex of the defendant. Sex in this case is called the control variable. We would output one such cross-tabulation table for each possible value of sex.

Note that this type of output is not limited to just one control variable. There may be an arbitrary number of control variables and tables to cycle through. Moreover, the variables have an arbitrary number of observations and are all in arbitrary order. Yet for each variable the list of possible values is always printed out in smallest to largest order.

The general tree structure that emerges for handling cross-tabulation is

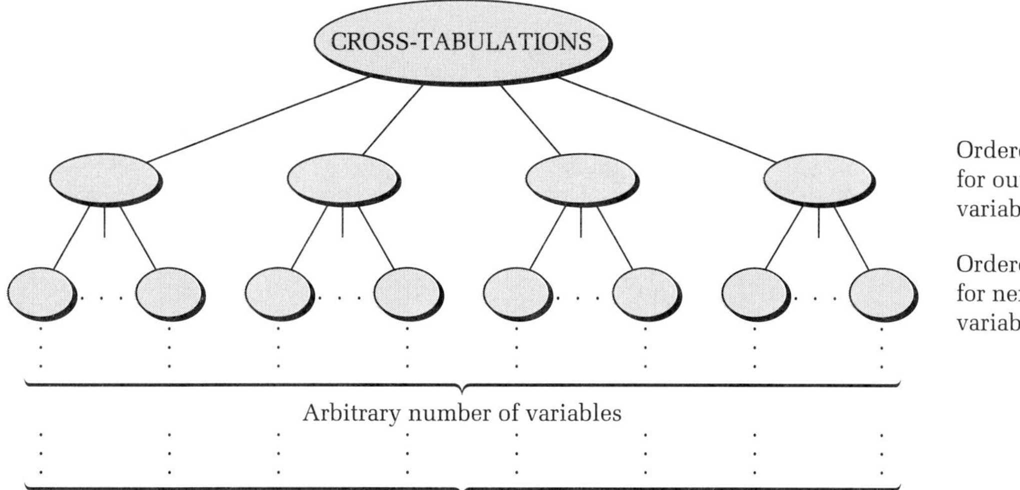

Write a program to handle the task of producing statistical cross-tabulations.

14. Write a program to print out the nodes of a tree level by level; that is, all level 0 nodes, followed by all level 1 nodes, followed by all level 2 nodes, and so on. *Hint:* This program will afford an excellent opportunity to practice using a queue in addition to a tree.

15. Operating systems often use general trees as the data structure on which their file directory system is based. Leaf nodes in such a system represent actual files or empty directories. Interior nodes represent nonempty directories. For instance, consider the following situation:

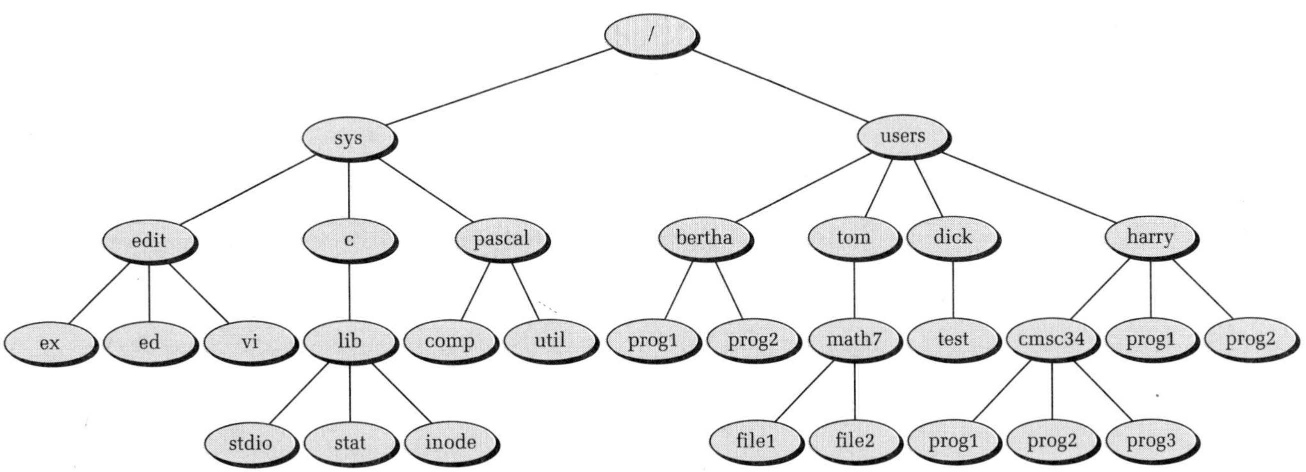

A directory entry is specified by its pathname. A pathname consists of tree node names separated by slashes. Such a pathname is absolute if it starts at the root; that is, if it starts with a slash (/). It is relative to the current directory if it does not start with a slash.

In this assignment, you are to write a command processor that will allow a user to manipulate files within such a directory structure. The commands accepted by your processor will be in the form of numbers associated with particular operations and pathnames, as shown in the following table:

Number	Operation	Pathname
1	Change directory	Absolute pathname, relative pathname, or ". ." for parent
2	Make a new directory	Absolute or relative pathname
3	Make a new file	Absolute or relative pathname
4	Remove a file	Absolute or relative pathname
5	Remove a directory, but only if it is empty	Absolute or relative pathname
6	Remove a directory and, recursively, everything below it	Absolute or relative pathname
7	Print directory entries in alphabetical order	Absolute or relative pathname
8	Recursively print directory entries in alphabetical order	Absolute or relative pathname
9	Print current directory name	
10	Quit processing commands	

Since even intelligent tree-walking users can easily get lost, your command processor should be prepared to trap errors of the following variety:

- Specifying a nonexistent pathname.
- Specifying a pathname that is a file when it should be a directory.
- Specifying a pathname that is a directory when it should be a file.

Upon detecting such an error, have your command processor print an appropriate error message and then return to accept the next user command.

16. Trees have significant applications in the area of artificial intelligence and game playing. Consider, for instance, the game of FIFTEEN. In this game, two players take turns selecting digits between 1 and 9 with the goal of selecting a combination of digits that add up to 15. Once a digit is chosen, it may not be chosen again by either player.

Rather than immediately considering a tree for the game of FIFTEEN, let us first consider a tree for the simpler game of SEVEN with digits chosen in the range 1 to 6. A tree that partially represents the states that may be reached in this game follows:

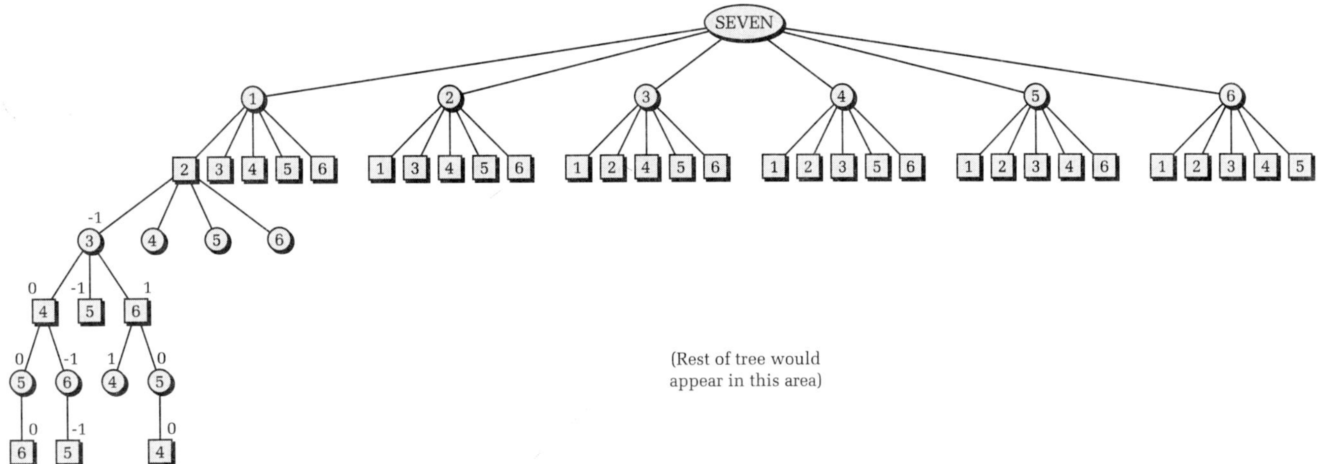

In this tree, circular nodes represent the states that may be reached by the player who moves first (the computer), and square nodes represent the states that may be reached by the player who moves second (a human opponent). The $+1$, 0, or -1 attached to each node represent weighting factors designed to help the computer choose the most advantageous move at any given stage of the game. The rules used to compute these weighting factors are

- If the node is a leaf node, its weight is determined by some static weighting function. In this case, the static weighting function used was to assign $+1$ to a leaf node representing a computer win, 0 to a leaf node representing a draw, and -1 to a leaf node representing a human win.
- If the node is a node in which the computer will move next (that is, a state occupied by the human opponent), then the weighting factor of the node is the maximum of the weighting factors of its children.
- If the node is a node in which the human opponent will move next, then the weighting factor of the node is the minimum of the weighting factors of its children.

In its turn, the computer should always choose to move to the node having the maximum possible weighting factor. The rationale behind this technique, called the minimax technique, is that the computer will move in such a way as to always maximize its chances of winning. The human opponent, if playing intelligently, will always move to a node having a minimum weighting factor. Thus in the partial game shown, the computer would choose 4 if the human had been naive enough to select the 6 node with the weighting factor of $+1$.

Write a program to build a weighted game tree for the game of FIFTEEN and then have the computer play against a human opponent. Note that this game is really the game of tic-tac-toe if one considers the following matrix.

4	9	2
3	5	7
8	1	6

All winning tic-tac-toe paths add up to 15

Give some consideration as to the time and efficiency of your algorithm. Many games simply cannot be completely represented via a general tree because of space limitations. Consequently, a partial game tree is built in which the leaf nodes may not actually be the final moves made in the game. In such situations, the static weighting function applied to the leaf nodes in the game tree requires a bit more insight to develop.

17. Consider a priority queue (see Chapter 5, Section 5.3) in which each item is assigned a different priority. Discuss how a binary tree with the heap property could be used to maintain such a priority queue. Write procedures for a heap implementation of the basic priority queue operations:

    Create(PriorityQueue)
    Empty(PriorityQueue)
    Full(PriorityQueue)
    Add(Item, PriorityQueue)
    Remove(Item, PriorityQueue)

    Categorize the run-time efficiency of the Add and Remove operations in big-O terms. Would a linear implementation or a linked implementation of the binary tree be most advantageous for this application? Explain why.

    Finally, use your priority queue implementation to solve a problem such as Programming Problem 12 in Chapter 5 or to simulate the servicing of priority-rated jobs on a time-sharing computing system.

18. Implement Dijkstra's shortest path algorithm using a suitable sparse table representation scheme to store the network data. Test your program with the transportation network pictured in Figure 7.27. Note that this same problem appeared in Chapter 6 as Problem 13. There you used a different algorithm for solving it. In a written statement, compare the efficiencies of the two algorithms.

19. A breadth-first traversal of a graph was discussed in Section 7.6. Implement this algorithm as a Pascal procedure. *Hint:* Use a queue.

20. You are given a binary tree of integers implemented by a linked representation. Such a tree is said to be *weight-balanced* if the sum of all the entries in the left subtree of the root equals the sum of all the entries in the right subtree of the root. Write a Boolean-valued function that receives a root pointer to such a tree and returns **true** if the tree is weight-balanced and **false** otherwise. Then write a complete program to test your function. Finally, adjust your procedure so that it returns **true** only when *every* subtree of the original tree is weight-balanced.

21. Explore some additional graph and network algorithms in one of the advanced texts cited earlier in this chapter (Horowitz and Sahni, *Data Structures in Pascal* (New York, N.Y.: Computer Science Press, 1990) or Naps and Pothering, *Introduction to Data Structures and Algorithm Analysis with Pascal* (St. Paul, Minn.: West Publishing, 1992)). Then prepare a written or oral report in which you explain the logic behind one of the algorithms you explore.

Never mistake motion for action.

Ernest Hemingway
1889–1961

More Powerful Sorting Methods

In Chapter 1 we analyzed three simple sorting algorithms: bubble sort, insertion sort, and selection sort. We also discussed a technique, called a pointer sort, which can be combined with any of these three algorithms to minimize data movement when large records are being sorted by a particular key field. The essence of the pointer sort is to maintain an array of pointers that dictates the logical order of the records in an array of records. When the sorting algorithm dictates a swap, only the pointers must be interchanged, not the actual records.

With all three of our sorting algorithms, however, we ran into a barrier. This barrier was a run-time efficiency of $O(n^2)$ comparisons. Since the pointer sort technique reduces data movement but not the number of comparisons, this barrier exists whether or not we incorporate the pointer sort idea into the sorting algorithm. Our goal in this chapter is to study sorting algorithms that break the $O(n^2)$ comparisons barrier. These new algorithms will make use of what we have learned since Chapter 1. In particular, both recursion and a conceptual understanding of trees are essential prerequisites to analyzing these more powerful methods.

Here we make one small simplification to the general setup for sort algorithms. Instead of sorting potentially large records with one key field, we limit ourselves to arrays consisting solely of the keys being sorted. That is, we will not worry about the other data associated with a key. This simplification will allow us to focus more directly on our primary concern in this chapter: reducing the number of comparisons made by a sorting algorithm. If you then want to generalize any of the algorithms to sorting records, the changes require only trivial syntactical considerations in Pascal.

General setup for the sort algorithms of this chapter is

```
CONST
  MaxIndex = {  Appropriate size for array to be sorted  };

TYPE
  SortType = {  Any data type with a well-defined ordering  };
  SortArray = ARRAY [1..MaxIndex] OF SortType;
```

```
PROCEDURE Sort (VAR Key : SortArray;
                N : integer);

  {  Given:    Array Key containing entries in indices        }
  {            1 through N.                                   }
  {  Task:     Apply appropriate sorting algorithm to these   }
  {            entries.                                       }
  {  Return:   Array Key with first N entries arranged in     }
  {            ascending order.                               }
```

Although our algorithms for this chapter are presented in the context of sorting arrays in ascending order, they apply more generally to any list whose elements can be directly accessed (for example, random access files) and they can be easily modified to sort in descending order. Moreover, one of the methods we discuss (merge sort) actually does not require direct access into the list. Hence it could be applied to lists that are just sequentially accessible such as sequential files and linked lists.

8.1 The Shell Sort Algorithm

OBJECTIVES

- to understand the logic behind the shell sort algorithm
- to see the relationship between shell sort and insertion sort
- to develop a Pascal procedure to perform shell sort
- to analyze the efficiency of the shell sort algorithm

The *shell sort,* named after its inventor D. L. Shell, incorporates the logic of the insertion sort to a certain extent. However, instead of sorting the entire array at once, it first divides the array into smaller, noncontiguous segments which are then separately sorted using the insertion sort. The advantage of doing this is twofold. First, where a comparison dictates a swap of two data items in a segment, this swap within a noncontiguous segment of the array moves an item a greater distance within the overall array than the swap of adjacent array entries in the usual insertion sort. This means that one swap is more likely to place an element closer to its final location in the array when using shell sort than when using the simple insertion sort. For instance, a large-valued entry which appears near the front of the array will more quickly move to the tail end of the array because each swap moves it a greater distance in the array. The second advantage of dividing the array into segments is tied to the first. That is, because early passes tend to move elements closer to their final destination than early passes would in a straight insertion sort, the array becomes partially sorted quite fast. The fact that the array is likely to become partially sorted relatively early then allows the embedded insertion sort logic to make more frequent use of its check for an early exit from its inner loop. (Recall that this check is what makes the insertion sort particularly efficient for arrays that are partially sorted.) An example will help clarify this shell sort rationale.

EXAMPLE 8.1

Suppose we have an array Key containing the following integers:

80 93 60 12 42 30 68 85 10

We first divide this into three segments of three elements each.

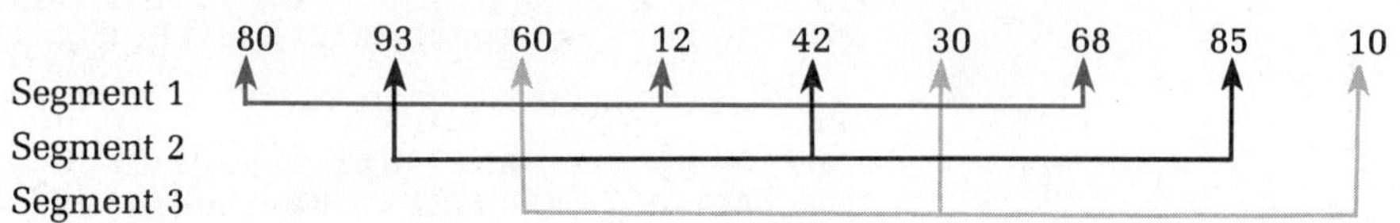

80	12	68→	Segment 1
93	42	85→	Segment 2
60	30	10→	Segment 3

and sort each of the segments.

12	68	80
42	85	93
10	30	60

The original array, partially sorted, now appears as

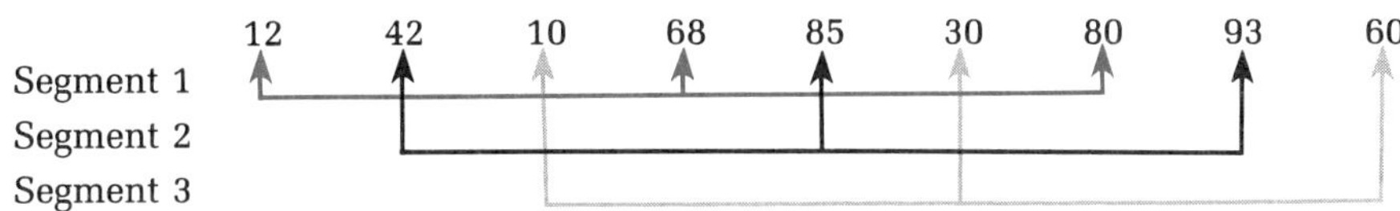

We divide this partially sorted array as

12	10	85	80	60	→	Segment 1
42	68	30	93		→	Segment 2

These segments are then sorted and the array Key takes the form

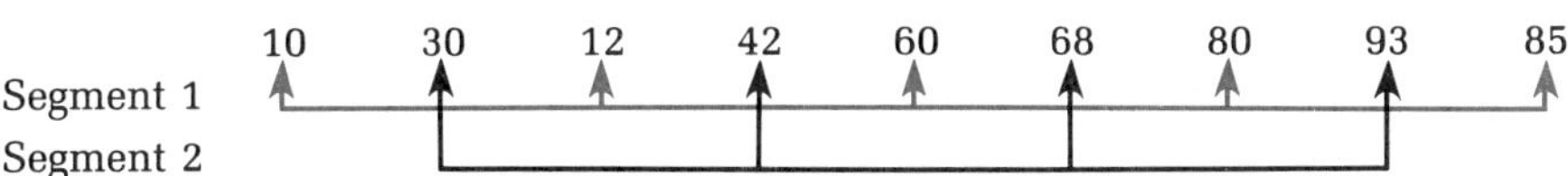

Finally, this array is sorted as one segment; 12 and 30, and 93 and 85 are swapped to give us the sorted array

10 12 30 42 60 68 80 85 93

■ ■

The key to the shell sort algorithm is that the whole array is first fragmented into K segments for some number K, where K is preferably a prime number. These K segments are given by

```
Key[1], Key[K + 1], Key[2 * K + 1], ...
Key[2], Key[K + 2], Key[2 * K + 2], ...
   .
   .
   .
Key[K], Key[2 * K], Key[3 * K], ...
```

Because each segment is sorted, the whole array is partially sorted after the first pass. For the next pass, the value of K is reduced, which increases the size of each segment, hence reducing the number of segments. Preferably, the next value of K is also chosen so that it is prime relative to its previous value, or *relatively prime.* (Two integers are said to be relatively prime to each other if they have no common factor greater than 1.) The process is repeated until K = 1, at which point the array is sorted. The insertion sort is applied to each segment, so each successive segment is partially sorted. Consequently, the later applications of the insertion sort become very efficient, dramatically increasing the overall efficiency of the shell sort.

To emphasize the fashion in which the shell sort algorithm relies on the logic of insertion sort, we present a SegmentedInsertionSort procedure which arranges each of K segments in an N-element array into ascending order. Compare this procedure with the procedure for insertion sort that was given in Chapter 1. You willl see that SegmentedInsertionSort moves an item from position J to position J + K. When K = 1, this is precisely the original insertion sort algorithm.

```
PROCEDURE SegmentedInsertionSort (VAR Key : SortArray;
                                  N, K : integer);

  {  Given:   N-element array Key, viewed as being divided     }
  {           into K segments.                                 }
  {  Task:    Arrange each segment into ascending order using  }
  {           insertion sort logic.                            }
  {  Return:  Array Key with K sorted segments.                }

  VAR L, J : integer;
      ItemToInsert : SortType;
      StillLooking : boolean;

  BEGIN
    { On the Lth pass, insert item L into its correct position among }
    { the previous entries in its segment.                           }
    FOR L := K + 1 TO N DO
      BEGIN
        { Walk backwards through segment, looking for slot to insert Key[L] }
        ItemToInsert := Key[L];
        J := L - K;     { J counts down through current segment }
        StillLooking := true;
        WHILE (J >= 1) AND StillLooking DO
          {.ItemToInsert is compared to Key[J] }
          IF ItemToInsert < Key[J] THEN
            BEGIN
              Key[J + K] := Key[J];
              J := J - K
            END
          ELSE
            StillLooking := false;
        { Upon leaving loop, J + K is the index where ItemToInsert belongs }
        Key[J + K] := ItemToInsert
      END  { FOR }
  END;  { of PROCEDURE SegmentedInsertionSort }
```

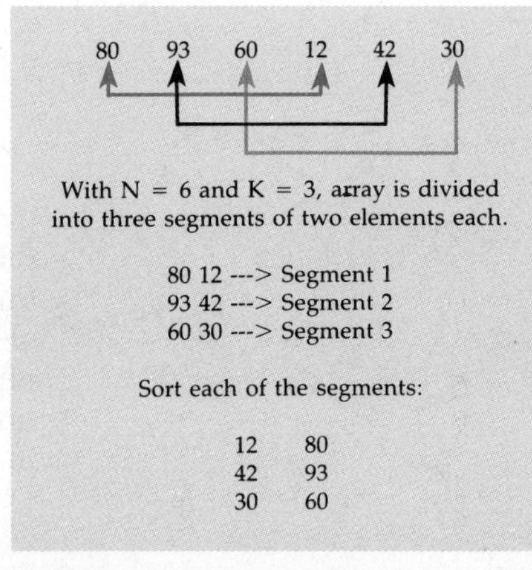

Given the SegmentedInsertionSort procedure, we now merely call on this with values of K that become successively smaller. Eventually, SegmentedInsertionSort must be called with K = 1 to guarantee that the array, viewed as one segment, is completely sorted.

The procedure ShellSort that follows illustrates these successive calls to SegmentedInsertionSort for values of K which are repeatedly halved.

```
PROCEDURE ShellSort (VAR Key : SortArray;
                     N : integer);

  {  Given:   Array Key with entries in indices 1 through N.  }
  {  Task:    Apply shell sort algorithm.                     }
  {  Return:  Array Key with first N entries arranged in      }
  {           ascending order.                                }

  VAR
    K : integer;

  PROCEDURE SegmentedInsertionSort (VAR Key : SortArray;
                                    N, K : integer);

  {  This procedure would be local to ShellSort.  }

  BEGIN {  PROCEDURE ShellSort  }
    K := N DIV 2;  {  K represents current number of segments.  }
    WHILE K > 0 DO
      BEGIN
        SegmentedInsertionSort (Key, N, K);
        K := K DIV 2   {  Reduce number of segments  }
      END
  END;  {  of PROCEDURE ShellSort  }
```

Efficiency of the Shell Sort

The shell sort is also called the *diminishing increment sort* because the value of k (the number of segments) continually decreases. The method is more efficient if the successive values of k are kept relatively prime to each other, thereby helping to ensure that a pair of values previously compared to each other are not compared again. D. E. Knuth has mathematically estimated that, with relatively prime values of k, the shell sort will execute in an average time proportional to $O(n(\log_2 n)^2)$. (See Donald E. Knuth, *Searching and Sorting.* Vol. 3 of *The Art of Computer Programming.* (Menlo Park, Calif.: Addison-Wesley, 1973).) However, the sort will work for any values of k, as long as the last value of k is 1. For instance, note that in the version of ShellSort we have given, the successive values of k will not often be relatively prime. When the values of k are not relatively prime, then the efficiency of the shell sort is of the order $O(n^r)$, where $1 < r < 2$. The particular value of r makes the sort less efficient than $O(n(\log_2 n)^2)$ for large values of n, but better than the $O(n^2)$ methods of Chapter 1.

The shell sort is most efficient on arrays that are nearly sorted. In fact, the first chosen value of k is large to insure that the whole array is fragmented into small individual arrays, for which the insertion sort is highly effective. Each subsequent sort causes the entire array to be more nearly sorted, so that the efficiency of the insertion sort as applied to larger partially sorted arrays is increased. Trace through a few examples to convince yourself that the partially ordered status of the array for one value of k is not affected by subsequent partial sorts for a different value of k.

It is not known with what value of k the shell sort should start, but Knuth suggests a sequence of values such as 1, 3, 7, 15, . . . , for reverse values of

k; that is, the $(j + 1)$th value is two times the jth value plus 1. Knuth suggests other possible values of k, but generally the initial guess at the first value of k is all that you need. The initial guess will depend on the size of the array, and, to some extent, on the type of data being sorted.

Exercises 8.1

1. Consider the ShellSort procedure given in this section. Suppose that we were to trace the contents of the array being sorted after each call to the procedure SegmentedInsertionSort. What would we see as output if we called ShellSort with the following key array?

   60 12 90 30 64 8 6

2. Repeat Exercise 1 for a six-element array that initially contains

   1 8 2 7 3 6

3. Why is the shell sort called by that name?
4. Why is the shell sort most efficient when the original data are in almost sorted order?
5. What advantage do the relatively prime values of the increments have over other values in a shell sort? Formulate your answer in a precise written statement that explains why relatively prime values are better.
6. What property must the sequence of diminishing increments in the shell sort have to insure that the method will work?
7. Provide examples of best-case and worst-case data sets for the shell sort algorithm presented in this section. Justify your data sets by explaining why they generate best-case and worst-case performance.
8. In Chapter 1, PointerSort used an index of pointers to sort data logically without rearranging it. Identify the sort algorithm that was behind the Pascal PointerSort procedure. Adapt the pointer sort procedure to the shell sort algorithm.
9. The version of shell sort presented in this section uses the following sequence of diminishing increments

   N **DIV** 2, N **DIV** 4, . . ., 8, 4, 2, 1

   Rewrite the shell sort so that the following sequence of diminishing increments is used.

   K, . . ., 121, 40, 13, 4, 1

   Here K represents the largest member of this sequence which is <= N where N is the logical size of the array being sorted.

■ ■ ■ ■

■ 8.2 The Quick Sort Algorithm

OBJECTIVES

- to understand the logic behind the quick sort algorithm
- to understand the role played by the partitioning subalgorithm in quick sort

Objectives continued.

Even though the shell sort provides a significant advantage in run-time over its $O(n^2)$ predecessors, its average efficiency of $O(n(\log_2 n)^2)$ may still not be good enough for large arrays. The next group of methods, including the *quick sort,* have an average execution time of $O(n\log_2 n)$ which is the best that can be achieved. Compared to $O(n (\log_2 n)^2)$ or $O(n^r)$ for $1 < r < 2$, an $O(n\log_2 n)$ sort is often a good choice as the main vehicle for large sorting jobs.

The essence of the quick sort algorithm, originally devised in 1961 by C.A.R. Hoare, is to rely on a subordinate algorithm to partition the array. The process of partitioning involves moving a data item, called the *pivot,* in the correct direction just enough for it to reach its final place in the array. The

- to develop a Pascal procedure to perform quick sort
- to analyze the efficiency of the quick sort algorithm; in particular, to see the relationship between the efficiency of the quick sort algorithm and the way in which the subordinate partitioning subalgorithm splits the array.

partitioning process, therefore, reduces unnecessary interchanges and potentially moves the pivot a great distance in the array without forcing it to be swapped into intermediate locations. Once the pivot item is chosen, moves are made so that data items to the left of the pivot are less than (or equal to) it, whereas those to the right are greater (or equal). The pivot item is thus in its correct position. The quick sort algorithm then recursively applies the partitioning process to the two parts of the array on either side of the pivot until the entire array is sorted.

In the next example, we illustrate the mechanics of this partitioning logic by applying it to an array of numbers.

EXAMPLE 8.2

Suppose the array Key contains integers initially arranged as

15 20 5 8 95 12 80 17 9 55

Table 8.1 shows a partitioning pass applied to this array.

TABLE 8.1
Each call to QuickSort partitions an array segment

Line Number	Key[1]	Key[2]	Key[3]	Key[4]	Key[5]	Key[6]	Key[7]	Key[8]	Key[9]	Key[10]
1	15*	20	5	8	95	12	80	17	9	55
2	9	20	5	8	95	12	80	17	( )	55
3	9	( )	5	8	95	12	80	17	20	55
4	9	12	5	8	95	( )	80	17	20	55
5	9	12	5	8	( )	95	80	17	20	55
6	9	12	5	8	15	95	80	17	20	55

The following steps are involved:

1. Remove the first data item, 15, as the pivot, mark its position, and scan the array from right to left, comparing data item values with 15. When you find the first smaller value, remove it from its current position and put in position Key[1]. (This is shown in line 2.)
2. Scan line 2 from left to right beginning with position Key[2], comparing data item values with 15. When you find the first value greater than 15, extract it and store it in the position marked by parentheses in line 2. (This is shown in line 3.)
3. Begin the right to left scan of line 3 with position Key[8] looking for a value smaller than 15. When you find it, extract it and store it in the position marked by the parentheses in line 3. (This is shown in line 4.)
4. Begin scanning line 4 from left to right at position Key[3]. Find a value greater than 15, remove it, mark its position, and store it inside the parentheses in line 4. (This is shown in line 5.)
5. Now, when you attempt to scan line 5 from right to left beginning at position Key[5], you are immediately at a parenthesized position determined by the previous left-to-right scan. This is the location to

put the pivot data item, 15. (This is shown in line 6.) At this stage, 15 is in its correct place relative to the final sorted array.

Notice that all values to the left of 15 are less than 15, and all values to the right of 15 are greater than 15. The method will still work if two values are the same. The process can now be applied recursively to the two segments of the array on the left and right of 15. Notice that these recursive calls eventually result in the entire array's being sorted. The result of any one call to **PROCEDURE** QuickSort is merely to partition a segment of the array so that the pivotal item is positioned with everything to its left being less than or equal to it and everything to its right being greater than or equal.

The procedure Partition that follows achieves one partitioning pass in the overall QuickSort algorithm as described in Example 8.2. The indices Lo and Hi represent the pointers that move from the left and right respectively until they meet at the appropriate location for the Pivot. The pivotal value is initially chosen to be Key[Lo]. We will later discuss the possible implications of choosing a different pivotal value. Note that it is crucial for Partition to return in PivotPoint the position where the pivotal value was finally inserted. This information will allow the QuickSort procedure that calls upon Partition to determine whether or not a recursive termination condition has been reached.

```
PROCEDURE Partition (VAR Key : SortArray;
                     Lo, Hi : integer;
                     VAR PivotPoint : integer);

  {  Given:   Key array, indices Lo and Hi.                    }
  {  Task:    Partition Key array between indices Lo and Hi.   }
  {           That is, using Key[Lo] as pivotal value, arrange }
  {           entries between Lo and Hi indices so that all    }
  {           values to left of Pivot are less than or equal   }
  {           to it and all values to right of Pivot are       }
  {           greater than or equal to it.                     }
  {  Return:  Partitioned array Key, and PivotPoint            }
  {           containing final location of Pivot.              }

  VAR Pivot : SortType;

  BEGIN
    Pivot := Key[Lo];
    {  Lo and Hi start to move toward each other.  }
    WHILE Lo < Hi DO
      BEGIN
        {  Begin right-to-left scan  }
        WHILE (Pivot < Key[Hi]) AND (Lo < Hi) DO
          Hi := Hi - 1;
        IF Hi <> Lo THEN
          {  Move entry indexed by Hi to left side of partition.  }
          BEGIN
            Key[Lo] := Key[Hi];
            Lo := Lo + 1
          END;
```

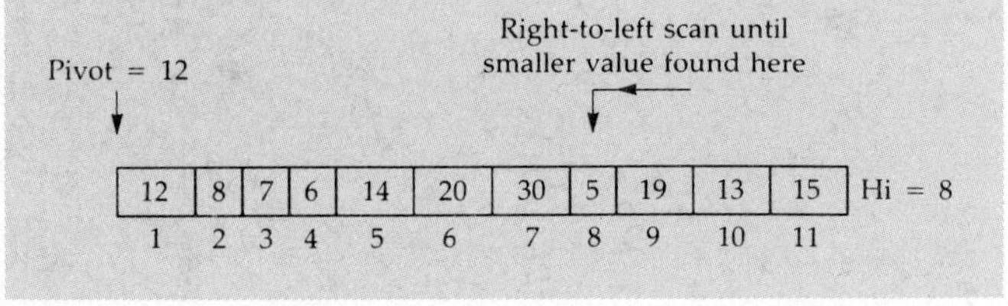

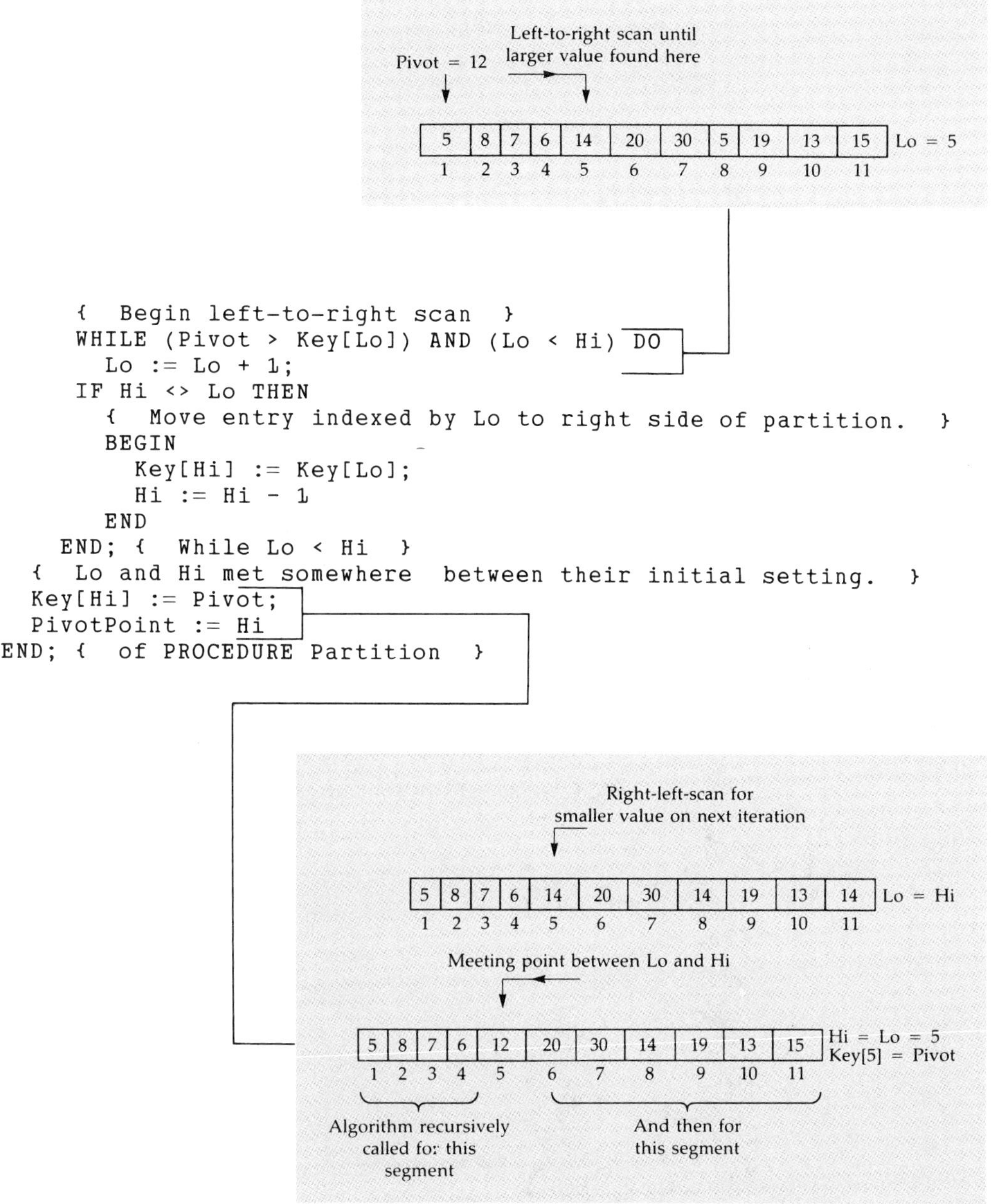


```
      {  Begin left-to-right scan  }
      WHILE (Pivot > Key[Lo]) AND (Lo < Hi) DO
        Lo := Lo + 1;
      IF Hi <> Lo THEN
        {  Move entry indexed by Lo to right side of partition.  }
        BEGIN
          Key[Hi] := Key[Lo];
          Hi := Hi - 1
        END
     END; {  While Lo < Hi  }
   {  Lo and Hi met somewhere  between their initial setting.  }
   Key[Hi] := Pivot;
   PivotPoint := Hi
 END; {  of PROCEDURE Partition  }
```

Given the previous Partition procedure, QuickSort itself must call on Partition and then use the returned value of PivotPoint to decide whether or not recursive calls are necessary to perform more refined partitioning of the segments to the left and right of PivotPoint. The recursive logic for this decision is given in the following **PROCEDURE** QuickSort. Partition would be incorporated as a subordinate local procedure within QuickSort.

```
PROCEDURE QuickSort (VAR Key : SortArray;
                     Lower, Upper : integer);

  {  Given:   Array Key with indices Lower and Upper.       }
  {           Assume Lower <= Upper.                        }
  {  Task:    Apply  quick sort logic to Key between Lower  }
  {           and Upper indices.                            }
```

```
{  Return:  Array Key with entries between Lower and Upper   }
{           indices arranged in ascending order.              }

VAR  PivotPoint : integer;

PROCEDURE Partition (VAR Key : SortArray;
                     Lo, Hi : integer;
                     VAR PivotPoint : integer);

  {  Previously discussed Partition procedure would appear   }
  {  here, subordinate to QuickSort                          }

BEGIN  {  PROCEDURE QuickSort  }
  Partition (Key, Lower, Upper, PivotPoint);
  {  Recursive calls partition left and right segments  }
  IF Lower < PivotPoint THEN
    QuickSort (Key, Lower, PivotPoint - 1);
  IF Upper > PivotPoint THEN
    QuickSort (Key, PivotPoint + 1, Upper)
END; {  of PROCEDURE QuickSort  }
```

For instance, after the first call to QuickSort for a partitioning pass on the data in Table 8.1, we would then recursively call on QuickSort with Lower = 1 and Upper = 4. This would trigger deeper-level recursive calls from which we would ultimately return, knowing that the segment of the array between indices 1 and 5 is now sorted. This return would be followed by a recursive call to QuickSort with Lower = 6 and Upper = 10.

The run-time trace diagam of recursive calls to QuickSort for the data of Table 8.1 is given in Figure 8.1. You should verify this call-return pattern by walking through the preceding procedure.

FIGURE 8.1
Run-time trace diagram of (recursive) calls to QuickSort for data in Table 8.1

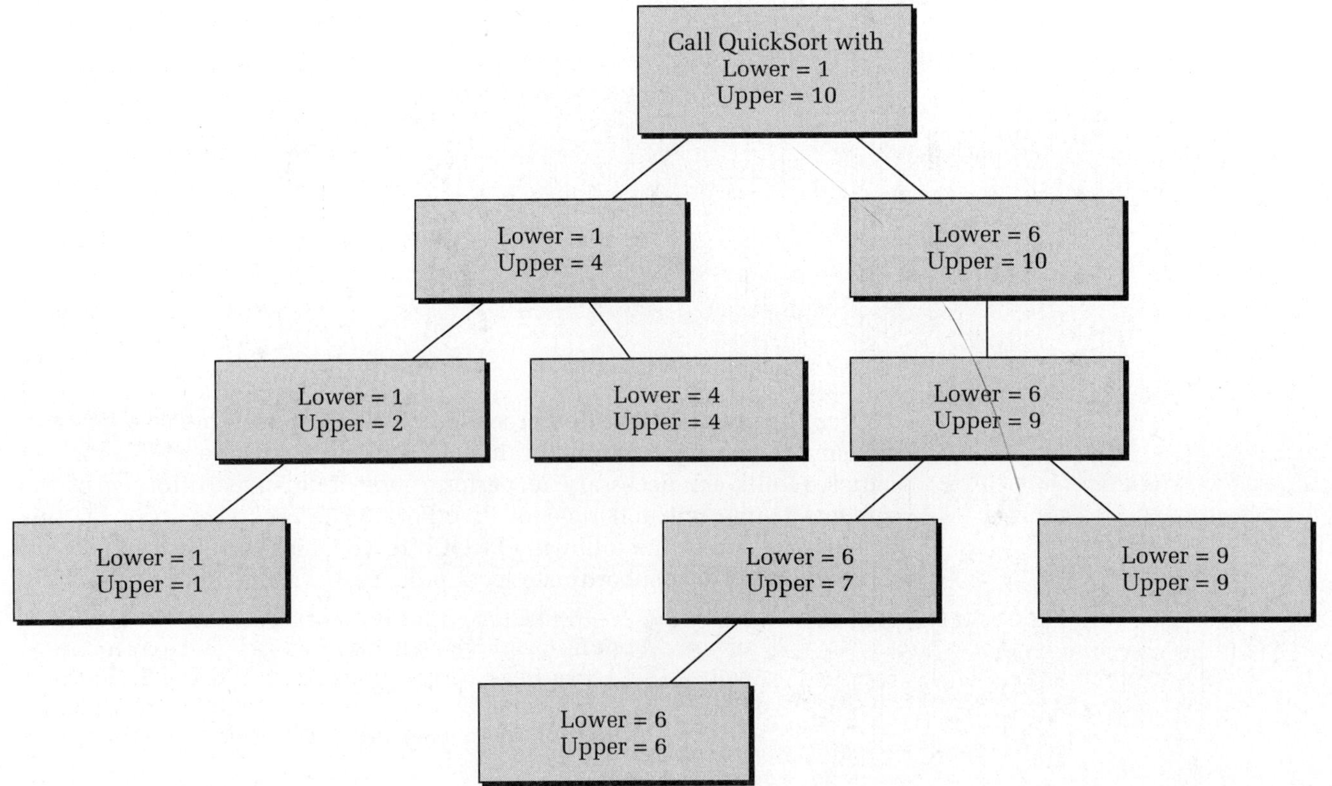

Efficiency of the Quick Sort

As mentioned earlier, the average run-time efficiency of the quick sort is $O(n\log_2 n)$, which is the best that has been achieved for a large array of size n. In the best case, it is quite easy to provide a rationale for this $O(n\log_2 n)$ figure. This best case occurs when each array segment recursively passed to QuickSort partitions at its midpoint; that is, the appropriate location for each pivotal value in the series of recursive calls is the midpoint of the segment being partitioned. In this case,

1 call to QuickSort (the first) is made with a segment of size n.
2 calls to QuickSort are made with segments of size n **DIV** *2.*
4 calls to QuickSort are made with segments of size n **DIV** *4.*
8 calls to QuickSort are made with segments of size n **DIV** *8.*
. .
. .
. .
n calls to QuickSort are made with segments of size 1.

Overall $\log_2 n$ levels

Since each call with a segment of size m requires $O(m)$ comparisons, it is clear that k calls with segments of size n **DIV** k will require $O(n)$ comparisons. Hence the total number of comparisons resulting from the preceding sequence of calls will be $O(n\log_2 n)$.

A NOTE OF INTEREST

Privacy Issues Kill Lotus Data Base

The August 1989 issue of *Communications of the ACM* (Vol. 32, No. 8) was dedicated to the role played by ethics in the education and career of a computer scientist. What are the social responsibilities that go along with state-of-the art capabilities to sort and search through gigabytes of information? A recent incident involving Lotus Development Corporation of Cambridge, Massachusetts illustrated the importance of a social conscience in computing.

In late 1990, Lotus had planned the release of a product called MarketPlace. Designed for use on a personal computer equipped with CD-ROM storage, the so-called "Household" version of MarketPlace supposedly contained information on 120 million Americans and 80 million households. This information included data on personal income, life-style, purchasing patterns, geographic location, and marital status. This data was compiled for Lotus by Equifax, the nation's largest credit reporting agency. Lotus foresaw a great demand for MarketPlace coming from a wide variety of large and small businesses. According to Michael W. Miller in the article "MarketPlace," which appeared in the November 13, 1990 issue of the *Wall Street Journal*:

> *"Advances in computers are making it easier to gather and piece together minutely detailed portraits of households, and marketers are gobbling these up to help choose targets for direct-mail and telephone campaigns."*

One of the early Lotus press releases for MarketPlace began with the headline "We Found You . . . And Quite Frankly, It Really Wasn't That Hard."

What Lotus had not properly anticipated was the storm of protest that would arise from consumer advocacy groups and individual consumers concerning MarketPlace's apparent insensitivity to privacy issues. Miller's *Wall Street Journal* article described these concerns:

> *"Privacy advocates' chief objection to MarketPlace was that it wouldn't be easy enough for consumers to delete their data, or correct any inaccuracies."*

Lotus demonstrated its sensitivity to the ethical issues that had been raised by MarketPlace. In January 1991, James Manzi, Lotus's chairman, announced that Lotus was canceling the MarketPlace project. Manzi stated, "What drove our decision was the volume and tenor of the concerns that were being raised by consumers all over the U.S." Though Lotus may have exercised poor judgment in the original conception of MarketPlace, their decision to pull the plug after a sizeable investment in the enterprise illustrates a high degree of social responsibility. Such ethical dilemmas are likely to play an increasing role in the careers of many computing professionals.

If segments partition away from the midpoint, the efficiency of quick sort begins to deteriorate. In the worst-case situation, when the array is already sorted, the efficiency of the quick sort may drop down to $O(n^2)$ due to the continuous right-to-left scan all the way to the last left boundary. In the Exercises at the end of the section, you will explore how the worst-case situation is affected by your choice of the pivotal element.

You may wonder how large a stack is needed to sort an array of size n. (Remember that this stack is implicitly created even whenever you use recursion.) Knuth has mathematically estimated that the size of the stack will generally not exceed $O(\log_2 n)$. However, in the worst case, it will be $O(n)$. (See D. E. Knuth's text, *Searching and Sorting,* cited toward the end of Section 8.1.)

Exercises 8.2

1. Consider the QuickSort procedure given in this section. Suppose that we were to insert the following tracer output immediately after the initial **BEGIN** for this procedure.

```
writeln (Lower, Upper);
FOR K := Lower TO Upper DO
  write(Key[K]);
writeln;
```

   What would we see as output from these tracers if we were to call on QuickSort with the key array initially containing the following seven entries?

   60 12 90 30 64 8 6

2. Repeat Exercise 1 for a six-element array that initially contains

   1 8 2 7 3 6

3. When is a bubble sort better than a quick sort? Explain your answer in a written statement.

4. Under what circumstances would you not use a quick sort? Explain your answer in a written statement.

5. How does the choice of the pivotal value affect the efficiency of the quick sort algorithm? Suppose that the middle value or the last value in a segment to be partitioned were chosen as the pivotal value. How would this alter the nature of best-case and worst-case data sets? Give examples to illustrate your answer.

6. Develop run-time trace diagrams of procedure calls to QuickSort for a variety of test data sets (analogous to what was done in Figure 8.1). Use these diagrams to analyze the efficiency of QuickSort. What types of data sets yield $O(n\log_2 n)$ efficiency? What types yield $O(n^2)$ efficiency?

7. In Chapter 1, PointerSort used an index of pointers to sort data logically without rearranging it. Adapt the pointer sort procedure to the quick sort algorithm.

8. Implement QuickSort in a nonrecursive fashion.

9. Implement a variation on the quick sort algorithm presented in this section, in which the pivot is chosen to be the median of the three values:

   Key[Lo], Key[(Lo + Hi) **DIV** 2], Key[Hi]

   In a carefully written statement, explain why this variation should be more efficient than the version that chooses the pivot to be Key[Lo].

8.3 The Heap Sort Algorithm

OBJECTIVES

- to understand the logic behind the heap sort algorithm
- to understand the relationship between heap sort and the linear representation of a binary tree in an array
- to develop a Pascal procedure to perform the heap sort
- to analyze the efficiency of the heap sort

The *heap sort* is a sorting algorithm that is roughly equivalent to the quick sort; its average efficiency is $O(n\log_2 n)$ for an array of size n. The method, originally described by R. W. Floyd, has two phases. In the first phase, the array containing the n data items is viewed as equivalent to a full binary tree. That is, the array to be sorted is viewed as the linear representation of a full binary tree containing n items (see Chapter 7). (If you want to read Floyd's description of this method, see his article, entitled "Algorithm 245: Tree Sort 3" found in *Communications of the ACM* 7 (1964):701.)

As an example, suppose we wish to sort the following array:

11	1	5	7	6	12	17	8	4	10	2

The tree now appears as shown in Figure 8.2.

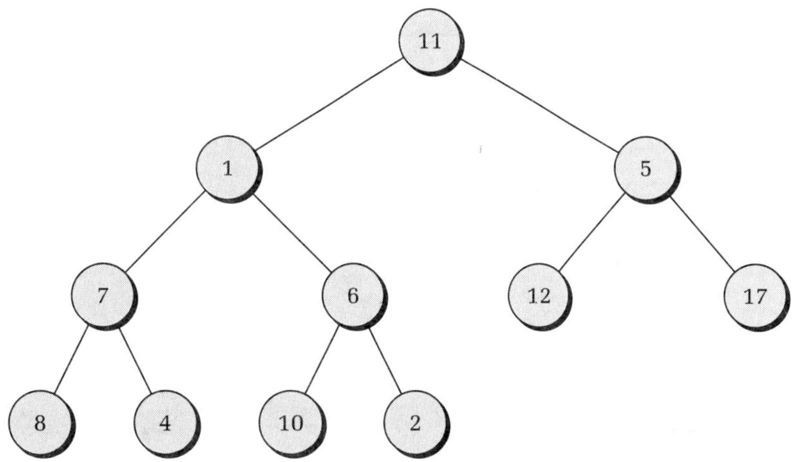

FIGURE 8.2
Full binary tree corresponding to array

The goal of phase 1 is to sort the data elements along each path from leaf node level to the root node. If we wish to sort in ascending order, then the numbers along any path from leaf node to root should be in increasing order. Eventually, after phase 1, the tree will be a heap as described in Chapter 7. That is, the data item at each node will be greater than or equal to both of its children. To achieve this, we take the following steps:

1. Process the node that is the parent of the rightmost node on the lowest level as follows: if its value is less than the value of its largest child, swap these values; otherwise do nothing.
2. Move left on the same level. Compare the value of the parent node with the values of the children. If the parent is smaller than the largest child, swap them.
3. When the left end of this level is reached, move up a level, and, beginning with the rightmost parent node, repeat step 2. Continue swapping the original parent with the larger of its children until it is larger than its children. In effect, the original parent is being walked down the tree in a fashion that insures all numbers will be in increasing order along the path.
4. Repeat step 3 until the root node has been processed.

Figure 8.3 shows these steps applied to Figure 8.2.

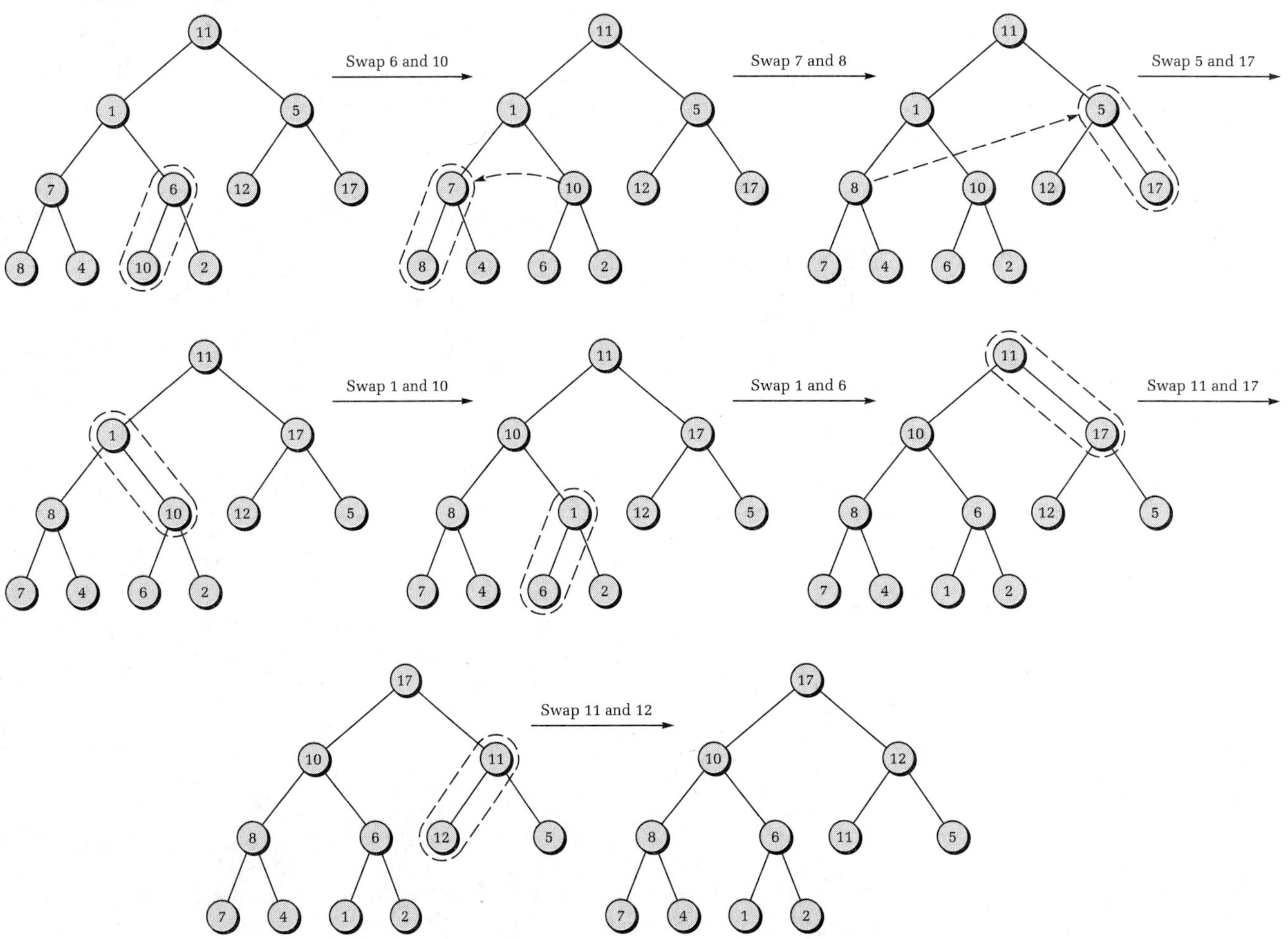

FIGURE 8.3
Phase 1 of heap sort applied to the binary tree in Figure 8.2

Phase 2 of the heap sort finds the node with the largest value in the tree and cuts it from the tree. This is then repeated to find the second largest value, which is also removed from the tree. The process continues until only two nodes are left in the tree; they are then exchanged if necessary. The precise steps for phase 2 are as follows:

1. Swap the root node with the bottom rightmost child, and sever this new bottom rightmost child from the tree. This is the largest value.
2. Continue swapping the new root value with the larger of its children until it is not exceeded by either child. In effect, this new root value is now being walked down a path in the tree to insure that all paths retain values arranged in ascending order from leaf node to root node. That is, the tree is being restored to a heap.
3. Repeat steps 1 and 2 until only one element is left.

Phase 2 of the heap sort begun in Figure 8.3 is shown in Figure 8.4 for the three highest values.

FIGURE 8.4
Phase 2 of heap sort for three values

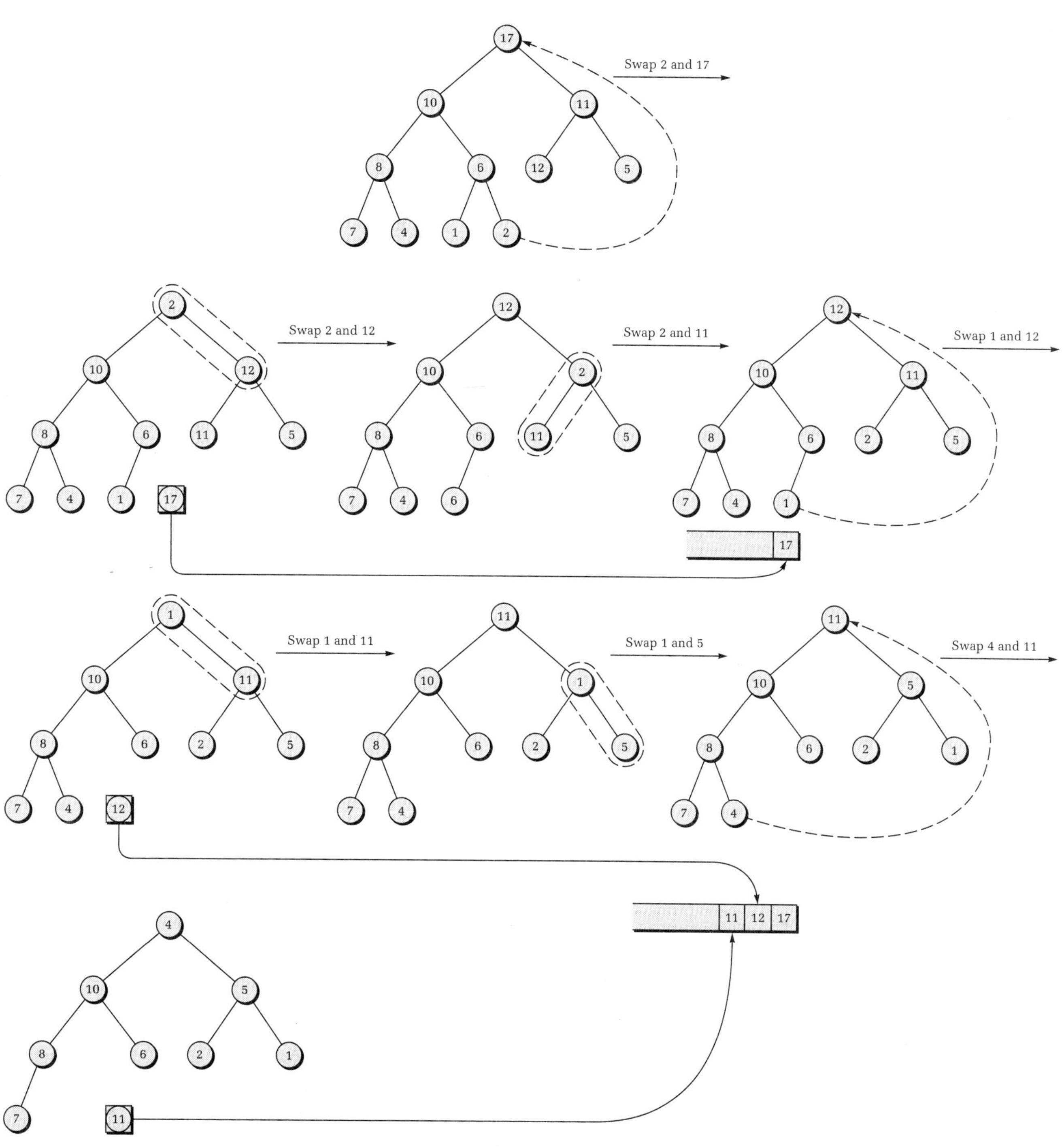

Both phase 1 and phase 2 use the same strategy of walking a parent down a path of the tree via a series of swaps with its children. The following procedure WalkDown isolates this crucial subordinate algorithm. In the linear representation of a tree assumed by WalkDown, the assignment statement K := 2 * L will make K reference the left child of the node indicated by L. That is, this statement will allow us to descend a level deeper into the tree.

```
PROCEDURE WalkDown (VAR Key : SortArray;
                    J, N : integer);

  {  Given:   Array Key to be viewed as full binary tree.  N,  }
  {           the number of entries in the array.  J, the      }
  {           index of a parent node within the tree.          }
  {  Task:    Repeatedly exchange this parent with child of    }
  {           greatest value until the original parent is      }
  {           greater than both of its children                }
  {  Return:  Tree array, as altered by this task.             }

  VAR
    L, K : integer;
    Ref : SortType;
    FoundSpot : boolean;

  BEGIN {  WalkDown  }
    FoundSpot := false;
    L := J;
    Ref := Key[L];
    {  Key [L] will move along the appropriate path in tree.  }
    K := 2 * L; { Initially K references left child of Key[L] }
    WHILE (K <= N) AND NOT FoundSpot DO
      BEGIN
        IF K < N THEN {  Have K reference largest child  }
            IF Key[K + 1] > Key[K] THEN
              K := K + 1;
        IF Key[K] > Ref THEN {  Child must move up  }
          BEGIN
            Key[L] := Key[K];
            L := K;
            K := 2 * L
          END
        ELSE  {  Appropriate spot has been found  }
          FoundSpot := true
      END;
    Key[L] := Ref
  END; {  of PROCEDURE WalkDown  }
```

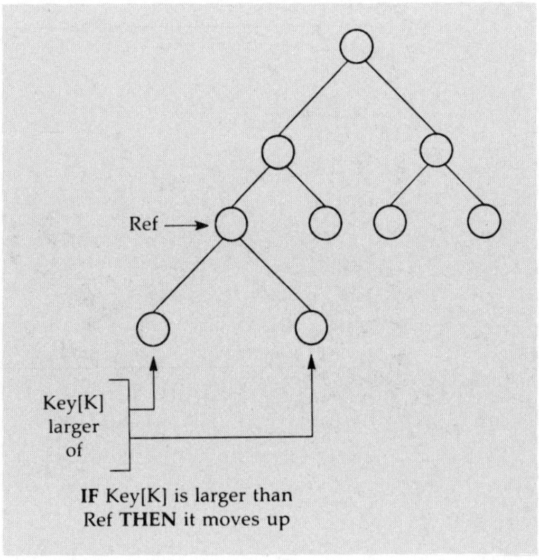

IF Key[K] is larger than Ref **THEN** it moves up

With the essential WalkDown logic isolated in a separate procedure, phases 1 and 2 of HeapSort may now be developed easily. The loop for phase 1 repeatedly calls on WalkDown to form the tree into a heap. Then a loop for phase 2 repeatedly swaps the root of the tree with the last child and calls on WalkDown to allow this new root to find an appropriate position in the heap.

```
PROCEDURE  HeapSort (VAR Key : SortArray;
                     N : integer);

  {  Given:   Array Key with entries in indices 1 through N.   }
  {  Task:    Apply heap sort logic to array.                   }
  {  Return:  Array Key with first N entries arranged in        }
  {           ascending order.                                  }

  VAR
    Y : integer;
    Temp : SortType;

  {  Here WalkDown would be located as a procedure local to HeapSort.  }

  PROCEDURE WalkDown (VAR Key : SortArray;
                      J, N : integer);

  BEGIN  {  PROCEDURE HeapSort  }

    {  First phase 1 arranges the tree into a heap.  }
    Y := N DIV 2;  {  Y starts at the last node to have child.  }
    WHILE  Y > 0 DO
      BEGIN
        WalkDown (Key, Y, N);
        Y := Y - 1
      END;

    {  Phase 1 done.  Now begin phase 2.  }
    {  In phase 2, Y is used to point at the current last array slot.  }
    Y := N;
    WHILE Y > 1 DO
      BEGIN
        {  Interchange root with bottom right leaf node.  }
        Temp := Key[1];
        Key[1] := Key[Y];
        Key[Y] := Temp;
        Y := Y - 1;
        WalkDown (Key, 1, Y)
      END  {  of WHILE  }
  END;  {  of PROCEDURE HeapSort  }
```

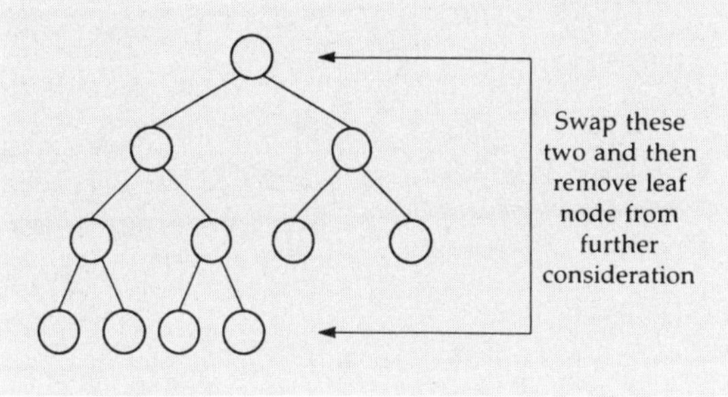

Efficiency of the Heap Sort

It is relatively easy to deduce that the heap sort requires $O(n\log_2 n)$ comparisons. To see this, note that the phase 1 loop in the preceding Pascal procedure will execute $n/2$ times. Inside this loop we call WalkDown, which in turn has a loop that will execute at most $\log_2 n$ times (because it merely follows a path down a full binary tree). Hence phase 1 requires at most

$$(n/2) * \log_2 n$$

iterations at its deepest level. Phase 2 may be similarly analyzed. The phase 2 loop iterates n times. Within each iteration, WalkDown is called, again resulting in at most $\log_2 n$ operations. Thus phase 2 requires at most $n * \log_2 n$ iterations at its deepest level. Overall, we get

$$1.5\ n * \log_2 n$$

as an upper bound for the number of iterations required by the combination of phases 1 and 2.

Thus, both quick sort and heap sort yield $O(n\log_2 n)$ efficiencies. In *Searching and Sorting,* referenced in Sections 8.1 and 8.2, Knuth has shown that, on the average, quick sort will be slightly faster since its big-O constant of proportionality will be smaller than that for heap sort. However, heap sort offers the advantage of guaranteeing an $O(n\log_2 n)$ efficiency regardless of the data being sorted. As we have already noted for quick sort, worst-case data can cause its performance to deteriorate to $O(n^2)$.

Exercises 8.3

1. Consider the HeapSort procedure given in this section. Note that WalkDown is called at two points in the procedure: once in phase 1 and again in phase 2. Suppose that we were to trace the contents of the array being sorted after each call to WalkDown. What would we see as output if we called HeapSort with an array that initially contained

   60 12 90 30 64 8 6

2. Repeat Exercise 1 for a six-element array that initially contains

   1 8 2 7 3 6

3. Why is the heap sort called by that name?
4. What is a heap?
5. Is a heap sort always better than a quick sort? When is it? When isn't it? Explain your answer in a written essay.
6. What is the worst-case and average-case efficiency of the heap sort?
7. Give examples of arrays that generate the best and worst performances respectively for the heap sort algorithm. Explain why these arrays generate the best and worst performance.
8. In Chapter 1, PointerSort used an index of pointers to sort data logically without rearranging it. Adapt the pointer sort procedure to the heap sort algorithm.

■ ■ ■ ■

■ 8.4 The Merge Sort Algorithm

OBJECTIVES

- to understand the logic behind the merge sort algorithm
- to understand merge sort's reliance on a subalgorithm that merges two sorted lists
- to develop a Pascal procedure to perform the merge sort
- to analyze the efficiency of the merge sort

The essential idea behind *merge sort* is to make repeated use of a procedure that merges two lists, each already in ascending order, into a third list, also arranged in ascending order. The merge procedure itself only requires sequential access to the lists. Its logic is similar to the method you would use if you were merging two sorted piles of index cards into a third pile. That is, start with the first card from each pile. Compare them to see which one comes first, transfer that one over to the third pile, and advance to the next card in that pile. Repeat the comparison, transfer, and advance operations until one of the piles runs out of cards. At that point, merely move what is left of the remaining pile over to the third merged pile.

This logic is reflected in the generalized Merge procedure that follows. For reasons that will become apparent when we incorporate it into a full sorting procedure, this version of Merge begins with the two sorted lists stored in one array. The first list runs from subscript Lower to Mid of array Source. The second runs from subscript Mid + 1 to Upper of the same array. The merged result of the two lists is stored in a second array Destination.

```
PROCEDURE Merge (Source : SortArray;
                 VAR Destination : SortArray;
                 Lower, Mid, Upper : integer);

  {  Given:   Array Source arranged in ascending order        }
  {           between indices Lower..Mid and Mid + 1..Upper   }
  {           respectively.                                   }
  {  Task:    Merge the two ordered segments of Source into   }
  {           one list arranged in ascending order.           }
  {  Return:  The complete ordered list in Destination.       }

  VAR  S1, S2, D : integer; { Pointers into two Source lists and Destination }

  BEGIN
    {  Initialize pointers  }
    S1 := Lower;
    S2 := Mid + 1;
    D := Lower;

    {  Repeat comparison of current item from each list.  }
    REPEAT
      IF Source[S1] < Source[S2] THEN
        BEGIN
          Destination[D] := Source[S1];
          S1 := S1 + 1
        END
      ELSE
        BEGIN
          Destination[D] := Source[S2];
          S2 := S2 + 1
        END;
      D := D + 1
    UNTIL (S1 > Mid) OR (S2 > Upper);

    {  Move what is left of remaining list.  }
    IF (S1 > Mid) THEN
      REPEAT
        Destination[D] := Source[S2];
        S2 := S2 + 1;
        D := D + 1
      UNTIL S2 > Upper
    ELSE
```

```
    REPEAT
      Destination[D] := Source[S1];
      S1 := S1 + 1;
      D := D + 1
    UNTIL S1 > Mid
END; {  of PROCEDURE Merge  }
```

Clearly Merge is an O(n) algorithm where n is the number of items in the two lists to be merged. A question remains: How can Merge be used to actually sort an entire array? To answer this we need another procedure called Order that will take the values in indices Lower through Upper of an array Source and arrange them in ascending order in subscripts Lower through Upper of another array called Destination. Notice that Order is itself almost a sorting procedure except that it produces a sorted list in a second array instead of actually transforming the array it originally receives. Our use of Order will be to obtain two sorted half-length sequences from our original array.

Then we will use the Merge procedure we have already developed to merge the two sorted half-length sequences back into the original array. Of course, this merely defers our original question of how to use Merge to sort because now we are faced with the question of how Order will be able to produce two sorted half-length sequences. Here is where recursion enters the picture. To produce a sorted half-length sequence, we use Order to produce two sorted quarter-length sequences and apply Merge to the results. Similarly, the quarter-length sequences are produced by calling on Order to produce sorted eighth-length sequences and apply Merge to the results. The recursive termination condition for this descent into shorter and shorter ordered sequences occurs when Order receives a sequence of length 1.

Given the crucial Order procedure, the MergeSort procedure itself is almost trivial. It need merely create a copy of the array to be sorted and then call on Order to sort the elements of the copy into the original. Note that, because Order continually calls on Merge and Merge cannot do its work within one array, the need to create a copy of the original array is unavoidable. Complete Pascal versions of MergeSort and Order follow:

```
PROCEDURE MergeSort (VAR Key : SortArray;
                     N : integer);

  {  Given:   Array Key with entries in indices 1 through N.   }
  {  Task:    Apply merge sort algorithm.                      }
  {  Return:  Key arranged in ascending order.                 }

  VAR
    CopyKey : SortArray;
    K : integer;

  PROCEDURE Merge (Source : SortArray;
                   VAR Destination : SortArray;
                   Lower, Mid, Upper : integer);

    {  Previously discussed Merge PROCEDURE would appear here.  }

  PROCEDURE Order (Source : SortArray;
                   VAR Destination : SortArray;
                   Lower, Upper : integer);

    {  Given:   Source and Destination, two arrays that are      }
    {           initially identical between indices              }
    {           Lower..Upper.                                    }
```

```
  {  Task:     Transfer Source in ascending order to        }
  {            Destination, between indices Lower..Upper.   }
  {  Return:   Destination arranged in order between Lower  }
  {            and Upper.                                   }

  VAR Mid : integer;

  BEGIN {  PROCEDURE Order  }
    IF Lower <> Upper THEN {  Recursively call to get smaller  }
                           {  pieces which are then ordered.   }
      BEGIN
        Mid := (Lower + Upper) DIV 2;
        Order (Destination, Source, Lower, Mid);
        Order (Destination, Source, Mid + 1, Upper);
        Merge (Source, Destination, Lower, Mid, Upper)
      END
  END; {  of PROCEDURE Order  }

BEGIN  {  PROCEDURE MergeSort  }
  {  Make copy for call to Order.  }
  FOR K := 1 TO N DO
    CopyKey[K] := Key[K];
  Order (CopyKey, Key, 1, N)
END; {  of PROCEDURE MergeSort  }
```

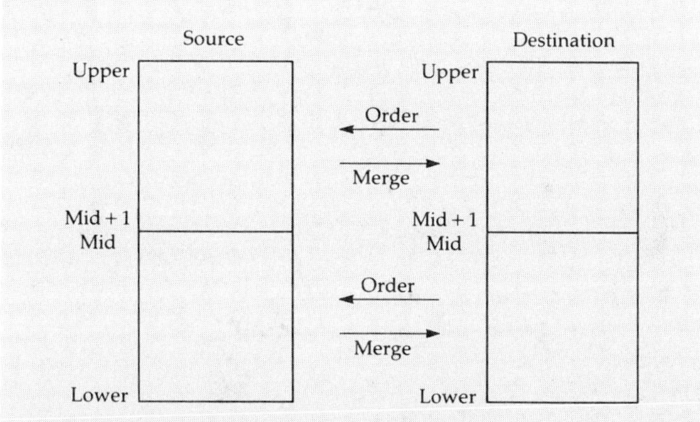

Recursively call Order to get two sorted segments in Source which are then merged into Destination. This requires that Destination originally be a copy of Source.

The run-time trace diagram of procedure calls in Figure 8.5 highlights the interaction between Order and Merge triggered by calling MergeSort with a sample array of size N = 11. The leaf nodes in this trace diagram represent the recursive termination condition reached when Lower = Upper.

Analysis of the Merge Sort

From a run-time trace of procedure calls such as that appearing in Figure 8.5, it is quite easy to deduce that merge sort requires $O(n\log_2 n)$ comparisons. The reasoning required for this deduction is as follows. All the merge operations across any given level of the trace diagram will require $O(n)$ comparisons. There are $O(\log_2 n)$ levels to the trace diagram. Hence, the

FIGURE 8.5
Run-time trace of procedure calls to Order and Merge

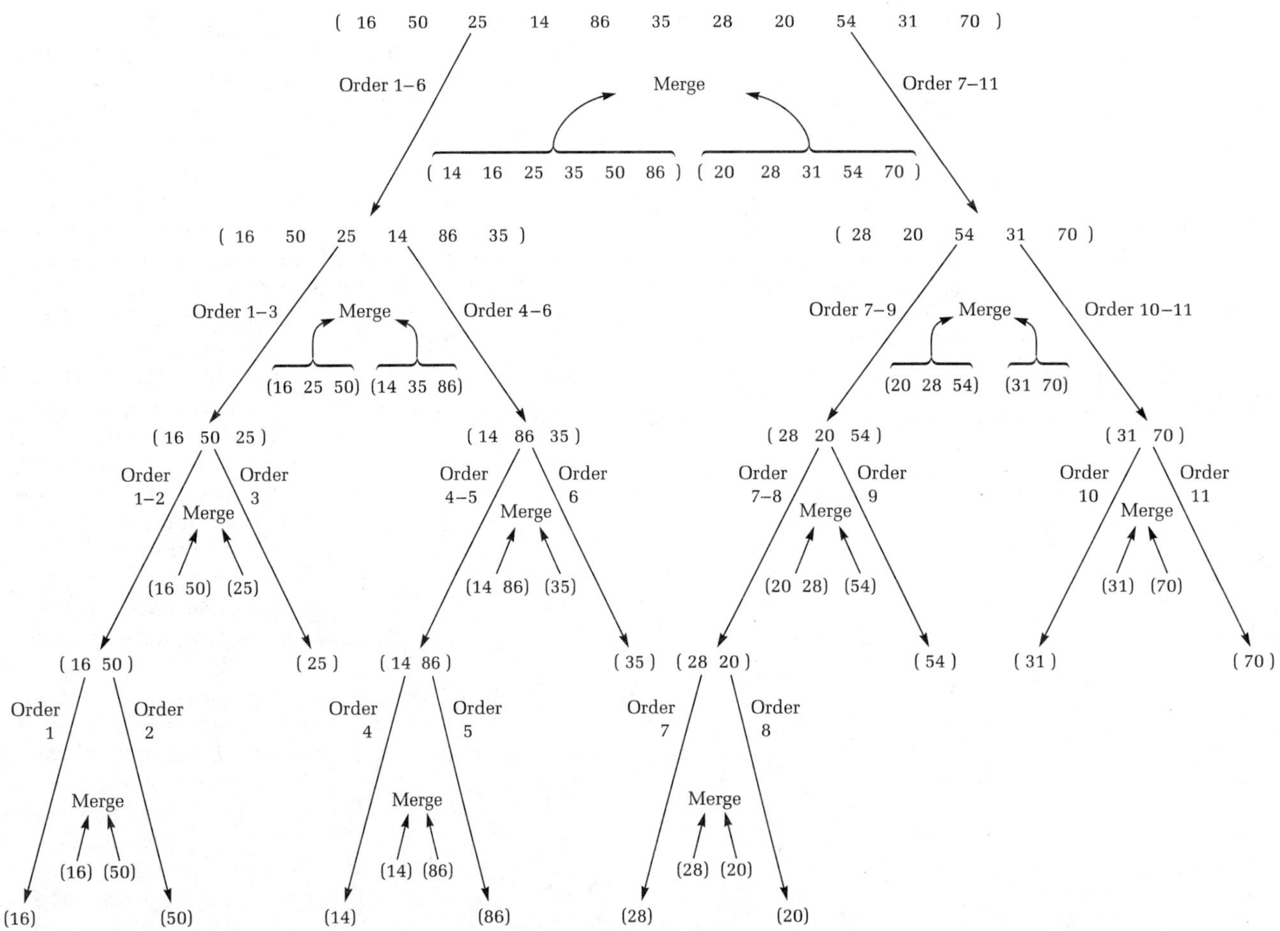

overall efficiency is the product $O(n\log_2 n)$. Notice that, like the heap sort, the merge sort can guarantee this efficiency regardless of the original data. That is, there is no worst case that can cause its efficiency to deteriorate (as there is for quick sort).

The price paid for using merge sort is in the memory space it requires. Of course, there is the stack space associated with recursion. More important, however, is the need for a duplicate copy of the array being sorted. In applications where the original array barely fits in memory, this space requirement will make merge sort totally impractical.

As steep as the memory price is, there is an added benefit to merge sort that makes it the only possible choice for certain applications: merge sort may be written in a way which necessitates only sequential access to the lists being manipulated. As we have presented it here, random access is required at only one point in the algorithm, namely, in the Merge procedure to access the second list beginning at subscript (Mid + 1) of Source. The need for this could have been eliminated by having Merge work with two separate source

A NOTE OF INTEREST

Public-Key Cryptography

The manner in which computers can sort through and in other ways manipulate information gives rise to concern over the security of electronic information. Cryptography is the science of encoding information to protect it from being viewed by unauthorized parties. Today, as an increasing amount of sensitive information is being transmitted in electronic and magnetic form, cryptography is becoming an increasingly important field. (For information on data transmission, see the Note of Interest entitled "Computer Networks: More Than an Abstract Data Type" in Chapter 7.)

A conventional encryption system works much like a mailbox with a combination lock. Anyone knowing the combination can open the box to leave a message or to read any of the messages in the box. In computerized information systems, the "combination" to the mailbox is a digital key; that is, a particular bit pattern which is applied to an electronic message to encode or decode it. In conventional systems, anyone knowing the digital key has access to the information in the electronic mailbox. Hence such systems are best suited to a small number of users and not to the networking of information among many computer installations that is possible with today's technology.

An interesting development in cryptography occurred in the early 1970s with the development of theory for public-key encryption systems. Such systems work on two different digital keys: one for writing information into the electronic mailbox and the other to read encoded information that has been left in the mailbox. As a user of such an encryption system, you could freely give out the write key to your mailbox (the public key), allowing anyone to send you an encoded letter. However, you would keep the read key (the decoding key) secret so that only you would be able to make sense out of your mail.

The best-known public-key encryption scheme is known as the RSA algorithm (after Rivest, Shamir, and Adleman, the mathematicians who developed it). This algorithm is based upon the difficulty of factoring large numbers that are the product of two prime numbers. For instance, the number $51 = 3 \times 17$ would satisfy this criterion except that it is not nearly large enough.

In the RSA system, the product of the two prime factors would be linked to your public key. However, this public key would include only the product, not the prime factors that comprise the product. Your private key would include each of the individual prime factors. Why should such numbers be large? The answer to this question lies in the present limitations of the area of mathematics known as number theory. It turns out that, given the product of two such prime factors without being told the factors themselves, number theory provides no known way of factoring the number into its prime factors in a reasonable amount of time, even using the most advanced supercomputers. From a security perspective, this means that your code could not be broken by outside agencies, even if they were using a computer to assist them.

The role of public-key cryptography in electronic data systems will no doubt become increasingly important in the future. For an excellent discussion of the method and some of the social concerns arising from it, you may want to read the article "Encryption: Technology, Privacy, and National Security," by Tom Athanasiou in *Technology Review* (August/September 1986): 57–66. A very readable description of the RSA and other encryption algorithms is presented in "Cloak and Dagger" by Rick Grehan in the June 1990 issue of *Byte* magazine (Vol. 15, No. 6: 311–324).

arrays. That is, we would merge ordered arrays Source1 and Source2 into Destination. This would be very costly with arrays since it would necessitate using three arrays to sort one array. However, it is less costly when the lists being manipulated are being implemented not by arrays but rather by dynamically allocated linked lists or sequential files. In both of these latter situations, the need to use sequential access would make the merge sort strategy the only appropriate sorting method. In the Exercises at the end of the section and the Programming Problems at the end of the chapter, you will be asked to adapt MergeSort to such sequential implementations of a list. In particular, when the list exists in a file instead of main memory, the sorting method employed is said to be an *external sort* (as opposed to the *internal sorts* we have studied in this chapter).

Exercises 8.4

1. Consider the MergeSort procedure given in this section. Note that this procedure contains a subordinate procedure called Order. Suppose that we were to insert the following tracer output immediately after the initial **BEGIN** for this procedure.

```
writeln (Lower,Upper);
FOR K := Lower to Upper DO {  K  declared as scratch variable.  }
    write (Source[K]);
writeln;
```

   What would we see as output from these tracers if we were to call on MergeSort with an array that initially contained

   60 12 90 30 64 8 6

2. Repeat Exercise 1 for a six-element array that initially contains

   1 8 2 7 3 6

3. Explain in what sense **PROCEDURE** MergeSort of this section would be more efficient if the Source parameter for the subordinate **PROCEDURE** Order were a **VAR** parameter instead of a value parameter.

4. Implement MergeSort in a nonrecursive fashion.

5. In Chapter 1, PointerSort used an index of pointers to sort data logically without rearranging it. Adapt the pointer sort procedure to the merge sort algorithm.

6. Identify and give an example of best-case and worst-case data sets for the merge sort algorithm. Explain why your data sets generate best- and worst-case performance.

7. A sorting method is said to be stable if two data items of matching value are guaranteed not to be rearranged with respect to each other as the algorithm progresses. For example, in the four-element array

   $60\ 42_1\ 80\ 42_2$

   a stable sorting method would guarantee a final ordering of

   $42_1\ 42_2\ 60\ 80$

   Classify each of the sorting algorithms studied in this chapter and in Chapter 1 as to their stability. (To see why stability may be important, consider Programming Problems 5 and 9 at the end of this chapter.)

8. You are to sort an array in a program in which the following considerations are to be taken into account. First, there is a large amount of data to be sorted. The amount of data to be sorted is so large that frequent $O(n^2)$ run-times will prove unsatisfactory. The amount of data will also make it impossible for your program to use a large amount of overhead data (for example, stack space) to make the sort efficient in its run-time. This is because the space required by the overhead data would potentially take up space needed by the array to be sorted. Second, you are told that the array to be sorted is often nearly in order to start with. For each of the seven sorting methods indicated, specify whether or not that method would be appropriate for this application and, in a brief statement, explain why your answer is correct.

   a. Bubble sort
   b. Insertion sort
   c. Selection sort
   d. Shell sort
   e. Quick sort

f. Heap sort
g. Merge sort

■ ■ ■ ■

FOCUS ON PROGRAM DESIGN

We have stressed repeatedly that analysis of algorithms combines formal mathematical techniques with experimental methodology. Certainly, nowhere is this better illustrated than in the analysis of sorting algorithms. For instance, among the four algorithms studied in this chapter, only two—heap sort and merge sort—can be placed with certainty in the $O(n\log_2 n)$ category by purely mathematical analysis. The other two—shell sort and quick sort—are apparently much more dependent on the original arrangement of the data being sorted.

In this section, we present components of a program whose structure facilitates experimentation with a sorting algorithm. In particular, our program will be useful in the exploration of the shell sort algorithm. However, the underlying structure of the program makes it easy to incorporate other sorting algorithms. All that must be altered is the procedure that implements the particular sorting algorithm being studied. This procedure must not only do the sorting, but also profile the algorithm in the sense described in Chapter 1. All the other modules in the program are geared toward construction of an environment in which you can experiment with the sorting algorithm. These modules remain the same regardless of which sorting algorithm is chosen.

Input to the program is the list of integers to be sorted. This input may be provided in one of three forms:

1. A randomly generated permutation of the integers from

   1, 2, 3, . . . Size–1, Size

   where Size is the logical size of the list being sorted. Recall that a permutation is an arrangement of the integers in which no repetitions occur.
2. A list of integers entered interactively, allowing input of particular data sets for which you want to profile the sorting algorithm.
3. A list of integers read one per line from a text file.

This final form of input, coupled with the program's ability to save a particular data set in the text file form which can later be read, allows you to fine-tune the sorting algorithm for data sets that proved particularly interesting from an efficiency perspective. That is, if you encounter a randomly generated or interactively input data set for which the efficiency of the sort algorithm seems to deteriorate, you can save that data set in a text file. Then you can adjust the sort algorithm to allow for the characteristics of that data set and rerun the program, loading the saved data set to see if your adjustments made a substantial improvement. This mode of experimental use of the program is illustrated in the following sample runs:

First run:

```
1 - Load a random array
2 - Interactively load an array
3 - Load array from previous round
```

```
    Enter 1, 2, or 3 -->1

    Enter the number of values -->10
    Do you want to see the array? (Y/N) -->y

 ARRAY[ 1] =  1
 ARRAY[ 2] =  3
 ARRAY[ 3] =  2
 ARRAY[ 4] =  4
 ARRAY[ 5] =  5
 ARRAY[ 6] =  8
 ARRAY[ 7] =  6
 ARRAY[ 8] =  9
 ARRAY[ 9] =  7
 ARRAY[10] = 10

Sort required 51 loop interation(s).
Sort required 4 swap(s) of data.
Sort required 78 comparison(s).

Do you want to see the array after sorting? (Y=N) -->y

      ARRAY[ 1] =  1
      ARRAY[ 2] =  2
      ARRAY[ 3] =  3
      ARRAY[ 4] =  4
      ARRAY[ 5] =  5
      ARRAY[ 6] =  6
      ARRAY[ 7] =  7
      ARRAY[ 8] =  8
      ARRAY[ 9] =  9
      ARRAY[10] = 10

Save this list for another run? (Y/N) -->y
Name for save file -->test.dat
Another Shell Sort? (Y/N) -->n
```

Then fine-tune the program to improve efficiency, and run again.

Second run:

```
          1 - Load a random array
          2 - Interactively load an array
          3 - Load array from previous round

          Enter 1, 2, or 3 -->3

          Enter the name of the file -->test.dat
          Do you want to see the array? (Y/N) -->y

      ARRAY[ 1] =  1
      ARRAY[ 2] =  3
      ARRAY[ 3] =  2
      ARRAY[ 4] =  4
      ARRAY[ 5] =  5
      ARRAY[ 6] =  8
      ARRAY[ 7] =  6
      ARRAY[ 8] =  9
      ARRAY[ 9] =  7
      ARRAY[10] = 10

Sort required 42 loop interation(s).
Sort required 4 swap(s) of data.
Sort required 61 comparisons(s).
```

```
Do you want to see the array after sorting? (Y/N) -->n

Save this list for another run? (Y/N) -->n
Another Shell Sort? (Y/N) -->n
```

Notice how the profiling output gives evidence of the improved efficiency of the second run.

The modular structure chart for our program is given in Figure 8.6. Modular specifications and a partial program listing follow. In the Programming Problems, you will be asked to complete the program and then use it in various forms of exploration with the shell sort. You will also be asked to incorporate the design of the program into a vehicle for exploring other sorting algorithms.

FIGURE 8.6
Modular structure chart for **PROGRAM** ShellExperimentation

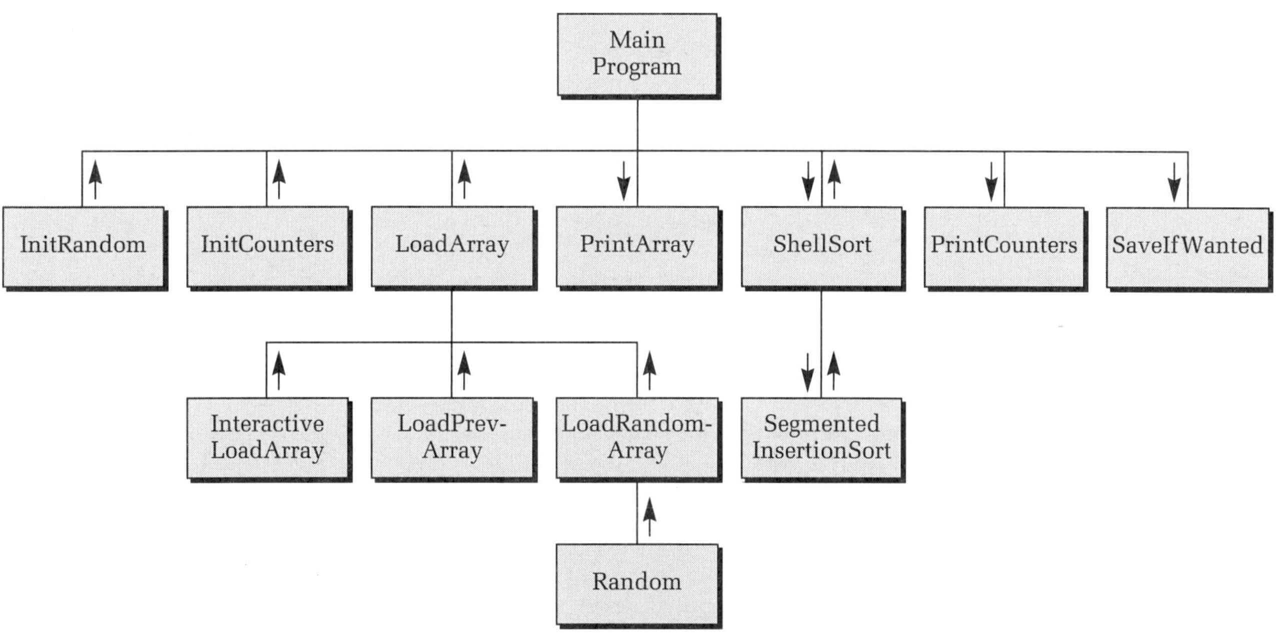

A first-level pseudocode development for the main program is

1. Initialize the random number generator (if necessary—see Appendix 9)
2. **REPEAT**
   - 2.1 Initialize the global profiling counters.
   - 2.2 Load the array by user-chosen method. Also return a duplicate copy of the array for potential saving in a file.
   - 2.3 Print the array if user wants to see it.
   - 2.4 Apply shell sort to the array.
   - 2.5 Output the global profiling counters.
   - 2.6 Print the sorted array if the user wants to see it.
   - 2.7 Save the copy of the original array if the user wants to.
   - 2.8 Inquire if the user wants to shell sort another array.

   UNTIL user indicates no more sorts.

Modular specifications corresponding to the modular structure chart of Figure 8.6 are as follows:

1. InitRandom Module
   Data received: None
   Information returned: None
   Logic: Initialize the random number generator as described in Appendix 9. May be unnecessary if your version of Pascal provides a random number generator.
2. InitCounters Module
   Data received: Profiling counters as global variables—for number of comparisons, number of swaps, and number of loop iterations.
   Information returned: Profiling counters set to zero.
   Logic: Obvious.
3. LoadArray Module
   Data received: None
   Information returned: The array to be sorted, a copy of that array for potential saving, number of values in array, integer indicating user choice for loading array: 1 for random permutation, 2 for interactive, 3 for file.
   Logic: Inquire about method for loading and then call on one of InteractiveLoadArray, LoadPrevArray, or LoadRandomArray.
4. InteractiveLoadArray Module
   Data received: None
   Information returned: Number of values in array, array to sort, and copy of that array for potential saving in file.
   Logic: Inquire as to number of values. Then iterate through interactive input of that many values.
5. LoadPrevArray Module
   Data received: None
   Information returned: Number of values in array, array to sort, and copy of that array for potential saving in file.
   Logic: Inquire as to name of file where array is stored. Then use **WHILE NOT eof** loop to read data from file into array.
6. RandomLoadArray Module
   Data received: None
   Information returned: Number of values in array, array to sort, and copy of that array for potential saving in file.
   Logic: Inquire as to size of array. Generate a random permutation of the values 1, 2, . . ., Size. There are several algorithms to do this. We leave it for you to discover one in the Programming Problems.
7. Random Module
   Data received: None
   Information returned: Randomly generated value.
   Logic: Use algorithm in Appendix 9 or random number generator provided with your version of Pascal.

8. PrintArray Module
Data received: Array and its logical Size.
Information returned: None
Logic: Iterate through output of each array value.

9. ShellSort and SegmentedInsertionSort Modules
Data received: Array of values and its logical Size.
Information returned: Array sorted in ascending order.
Logic: See Section 8.1.

10. PrintCounters Module
Data received: Global profiling counters.
Information returned: None.
Logic: Print profiling counters to report on efficiency of algorithm for data set just sorted.

11. SaveIfWanted Module
Data received: Copy of original array, logical Size of that array, integer indicating how user loaded array.
Information returned: None.
Logic: Inquire if user wants to save this list for further exploration. **IF** user wants to save and list not originally loaded from file **THEN** write array to file in form compatible with LoadPrevArray module.

A partial program listing follows:

```
PROGRAM ShellExperimentation(input, output, f);

  { This program allows the user to experiment with the ShellSort       }
  { algorithm on a variety of different arrays of data.  The sort       }
  { algorithm has been augmented to keep track of the number of         }
  { swaps, comparisons, and loop iterations necessary to sort the       }
  { current array. These can be used as a measure of comparison         }
  { among various initial data arrays or among different sorting        }
  { methods.  This method of measuring the amount of work required      }
  { to sort the array is used because standard Pascal has no built-in   }
  { method of timing program execution.                                 }
  {                                                                     }
  { The data file created by the program when an array is saved is      }
  { simply a text file with one element of the array per line of the    }
  { file.  Similarly, the program expects any file from which it is to  }
  { read an array to have this format.                                  }

  CONST { ShellExperimentation }
    MaxArraySize = 500;         { Maximum size of data array       }
    NameSize = 30;              { Maximum size of file name string  }

  TYPE { ShellExperimentation }
    SortType = integer;
    SortArray = ARRAY [1..MaxArraySize] OF SortType;
    NameString = PACKED ARRAY [1..NameSize] OF char;

  VAR { ShellExperimentation }
    Key, CopyOfKey: SortArray;  { Arrays to hold the data           }
    ArraySize: integer;         { Current size of array             }
    Query: char;                { User's response                   }
    f: text;                    { File variable                     }
    Seed: integer;              { Seed for random number generator  }
    ChoiceOfLoad: integer;      { User's choice for loading array   }
```

```
  { Global counters used to measure the amount of work required    }
  { to sort the data array.                                         }
  NumIterations: integer;   { Number of loop iterations             }
  NumSwaps: integer;        { Number of swaps of data               }
  NumComparisons: integer;  { Number of comparisons made            }

{ ******************************************************************** }
{              Random number modules appear here.                      }
{              See Appendix 9 or use function provided with            }
{                  your version of Pascal.                             }
.
.
.
{ ******************************************************************** }
{               Procedures to handle the data arrays                   }

PROCEDURE SaveIfWanted(ArraySize: integer;
                       VAR ArrayToSave: SortArray;
                       ChoiceOfLoad: integer);

  {  Given:   Array to save, Size of array, type of load performed.     }
  {  Task:    Write the array out to a file if the user indicates       }
  {           that he wants to save it for future runs.  The file       }
  {           handling may require modification on some systems.        }
  {  Return:  Nothing.                                                  }

.
.
.

PROCEDURE LoadArray(VAR Size: integer;
                    VAR Original, Copy: SortArray;
                    VAR ChoiceOfLoad: integer);

  {  Given:   Nothing.                                                  }
  {  Task:    Determine which method the user wants to use to           }
  {           load the array of data and call the appropriate           }
  {           procedure.                                                }
  {  Return:  Both arrays, the size of the arrays, and the              }
  {           user's selection of type of load to be performed.         }

  VAR { LoadArray }
    Valid: boolean;

  PROCEDURE InteractiveLoadArray(VAR Size: integer;
                                 VAR Orig, Copy: SortArray);

      {  Given:   Nothing.                                              }
      {  Task:    Prompt the user to input the data for the array,      }
      {           read it in, and make a copy of it.                    }
      {  Return:  Both arrays along with their size.                    }

      .
      .
      .

  PROCEDURE LoadPrevArray(VAR Size: integer;
                          VAR Orig, Copy: SortArray);

      {  Given:   Nothing.                                              }
      {  Task:    Open the file containing the previous array the       }
```

```
    {           user desires to use, read the data into the           }
    {           array, and make a copy of the array.  The file        }
    {           handling may require modification on some             }
    {           systems.                                              }
    {  Return:  Both arrays along with their size.                    }

    .
    .
    .

  PROCEDURE LoadRandomArray(VAR Size: integer;
                            VAR Orig, Copy: SortArray);

    {  Given:   Nothing.                                              }
    {  Task:    Fill the array with a randomly generated permutation of }
    {           the integers between 1..Size, and then make a copy of   }
    {           the array.                                            }
    {  Return:  Both arrays along with their size.                    }

    .
    .
    .

  BEGIN { LoadArray }
    REPEAT
      writeln;
      writeln;
      writeln;
      writeln('         1 - Load a random array');
      writeln('         2 - Interactively load an array');
      writeln('         3 - Load array from previous round');
      writeln;
      write('         Enter 1, 2, or 3 --> ');
      readln(ChoiceOfLoad);
      Valid := ((ChoiceOfLoad > 0) AND (ChoiceOfLoad < 4));
      IF Valid THEN
        CASE ChoiceOfLoad OF
          1:
            LoadRandomArray(Size, Original, Copy);
          2:
            InteractiveLoadArray(Size, Original, Copy);
          3:
            LoadPrevArray(Size, Original, Copy);
        END { CASE }
      ELSE
        writeln('\', ChoiceOfLoad: 1,
                '\ is not a valid response - try again')
    UNTIL Valid
  END; { of PROCEDURE LoadArray }

PROCEDURE PrintArray(VAR A: SortArray;
                     Low, High: integer);

  {  Given:   Array of data, low and high ends of the range of       }
  {           indices of the array to be printed.                    }
  {  Task:    Print the contents of the specified range of           }
  {           the array to the terminal.                             }
  {  Return:  Nothing.                                               }

  .
  .
  .
```

```
{************************************************************************ }
{               Procedures for the global counters                        }

PROCEDURE InitCounters;

  {  Given:   Nothing.                                                    }
  {  Task:    Initialize the global counters.                             }
  {  Return:  Nothing.                                                    }

  BEGIN { InitCounters }
    NumIterations := 0;
    NumSwaps := 0;
    NumComparisons := 0
  END; { InitCounters }

PROCEDURE PrintCounters;

  {  Given:   Nothing.                                                    }
  {  Task:    Print the statistics regarding the sort.                    }
  {  Return:  Nothing.                                                    }

  BEGIN { PrintCounters }
    writeln;
    writeln('Sort required ', NumIterations: 1, ' loop iteration(s).');
    writeln('Sort required ', NumSwaps: 1, ' swap(s) of data.');
    writeln('Sort required ', NumComparisons: 1, ' comparison(s).');
    writeln
  END; { PrintCounters }

{*********************************************************************** }
{                        Procedures for ShellSort                         }

PROCEDURE ShellSort(Size: integer;
                    VAR Key: SortArray);

  {  Given:   Array Key with entries in indices 1 through Size.           }
  {  Task:    Apply shell sort algorithm.                                 }
  {  Return:  Array Key with first "Size" entries arranged in             }
  {           ascending order.                                            }

  VAR { ShellSort }
    K: integer;

  PROCEDURE SegmentedInsertionSort(VAR Key: SortArray;
                                   N, K: integer);

      {  Given:   N-element array Key, viewed as being divided            }
      {           into K segments.                                        }
      {  Task:    Arrange each segment into ascending order using         }
      {           insertion sort logic.                                   }
      {  Return:  Array Key with K sorted segments.                       }

    VAR L, J : integer;
        ItemToInsert : SortType;
        StillLooking : boolean;

    BEGIN
      {  On the Lth pass, insert item L into its correct position among  }
      {  the previous entries in its segment.                            }
      FOR L : = K + 1 TO N DO
        BEGIN
          NumIterations := NumIterations + 1;         {  Update Efficiency Stats  }
```

```
        {  Walk backwards through segment, looking for slot to insert Key[L]  }
        ItemToInsert := Key[L];
        J := L - K;    {  J counts down through current segment  }
        StillLooking := true;
        NumComparisons := NumComparisons + 1;         {  Update Efficiency Stats}
        WHILE (J >= 1) AND StillLooking DO
          BEGIN
            NumIterations := NumIterations + 1;       {  Update Efficiency Stats}
            {  ItemToInsert is compared to Key[J] }
            NumComparisons := NumComparisons + 1;     {  Update Efficiency Stats}
            IF ItemToInsert < Key[J] THEN
              BEGIN
                Key[J + K] := Key[J];
                NumSwaps := NumSwaps + 1;             {  Update Efficiency Stats}
                J := J - K
              END
            ELSE
              StillLooking := false;
            NumComparisons := NumComparisons + 1      {  Update Efficiency Stats}
          END;  {  WHILE  }
        {  Upon leaving loop, J + K is the index where ItemToInsert belongs  }
        Key[J + K] := ItemToInsert
      END  {  FOR  }
  END;  {  of PROCEDURE SegmentedInsertionSort  }

  BEGIN { ShellSort }
    K := Size DIV 2;        { K represents current number of segments. }
    NumComparisons := NumComparisons + 1;                 { Update Efficiency Stats}
    WHILE K > 0 DO
      BEGIN
        NumIterations := NumIterations + 1;               { Update Efficiency Stats}
        SegmentedInsertionSort(Key, Size, K);
        K := K DIV 2; { Reduce number of segments }
        NumComparisons := NumComparisons + 1              { Update Efficiency Stats}
      END
  END; { of PROCEDURE ShellSort }

{******************************************************************* }
{                        The main program                            }

BEGIN { Main }
  InitRandom;
  REPEAT
    InitCounters;
    LoadArray(ArraySize, Key, CopyOfKey, ChoiceOfLoad);
    write('Do you want to see the array? (Y/N) --> ');
    readln(Query);
    IF (Query = 'Y') OR (Query = 'y') THEN
      PrintArray(Key, 1, ArraySize);
    ShellSort(ArraySize, Key);
    PrintCounters;
    write('Do you want to see the array after sorting? (Y/N) --> ');
    readln(Query);
    IF (Query = 'Y') OR (Query = 'y') THEN
      PrintArray(Key, 1, ArraySize);
    SaveIfWanted(ArraySize, CopyOfKey, ChoiceOfLoad);
    write('Another Shell Sort? (Y/N) --> ');
    readln(Query)
  UNTIL (Query = 'N') OR (Query = 'n')
END. { Main }
```

RUNNING AND DEBUGGING TIPS

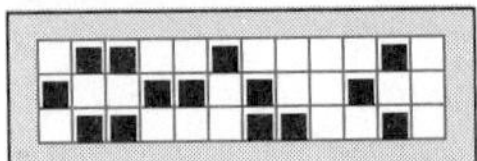

1. To describe and understand the more complex sort algorithms, it is helpful to present them via subordinate algorithms and stepwise refinement. To this end, we have found it convenient to initially focus on subalgorithms (SegmentedInsertionSort for ShellSort, Partition for QuickSort, WalkDown for HeapSort, and Merge for MergeSort). Our method is illustrative of the stepwise refinement approach to problem solving: break a complex problem down into smaller problems, solve these smaller problems, and then tie their solutions together to solve the original large problem.
2. Describing and understanding algorithms is a separate issue from their actual implementation in a specific programming language and on a real machine. One implication of this separation of algorithm description and algorithm implementation is the run-time cost associated with a procedure call. We must consider the hidden costs of making a procedure call and how deeply embedded the procedure call is in the iterative structure of the calling module.
3. Depending upon the machine you are using, calling a procedure instead of directly inserting the code necessary may mean that your program spends more run-time handling the hidden cost of procedure calls than it does in actually interchanging data items. If large data sets are being sorted and if run-time efficiency is of primary importance, then we should implement our algorithm without actually calling on a procedure.
4. Keep in mind the distinction between algorithm description and algorithm implementation when making decisions about whether or not to proceduralize a given sequence of instructions. What may be appropriately isolated as a trivial subalgorithm at the time when a designer is concerned with describing an algorithm may carry with it a steep price if implemented as a trivial procedure that is called upon many times when the resulting program is put into use.
5. In making the decision whether to use procedures or in-line code when implementing an algorithm, carefully weigh run-time considerations with respect to the clarity and readability of code. A useful rule of thumb is that only in exceptional circumstances should the code associated with a module exceed one printed page in length. This guideline allows in-line insertion of code for simple algorithmic units and assures that the overall software system does not become unwieldy.

■ Summary

Key Terms

diminishing increment sort
external sort
heap sort
internal sort
merge sort
partition
pivot
quick sort
relatively prime
shell sort

Key Concepts

- This chapter has added four sorting algorithms to those already presented in Chapter 1. This gives us a large variety of tools from which to choose when we need to perform a sorting job.
- The following comparison table summarizes the pros and cons of each sorting method we've covered.

Sorting Method	Chapter	Number of Comparisons in Terms of the Number of Data Items Being Sorted (*n*)	Space Requirement	Additional Comments
Binary tree	7	Between $O(n^2)$ and $O(n\log_2 n)$ depending on original data and whether tree height-balanced	Pointers for tree and possible stack space for recursive traversals	
Bubble	1	$O(n^2)$	No additional overhead	Loop check allows early exit as soon as array is ordered.
Heap	8	$O(n\log_2 n)$	No additional overhead	
Insertion	1	$O(n^2)$	No additional overhead	Loop check allows early exit as soon as item is correctly placed.
Merge	8	$O(n\log_2 n)$	Requires duplicate array and stack space for recursion	Since only requires sequential access, can be used for linked lists and sequential files.
Pointer	1	Depends on method with which it is combined	Required list of pointers to maintain logical order	Can be combined with any method to substantially reduce size of data items being interchanged.
Quick	8	$O(n\log_2 n)$ on the average but $O(n^2)$ for worst cases	Stack space for recursion	
Radix	1, 4	$O(n)$	Space for bins	Though $O(n)$, large constant of proportionality. Not generalizable to all types of data, for example, **real**.
Selection	1	$O(n^2)$	No additional overhead	
Shell	8	Between $O(n(\log_2 n)^2)$ and $O(n^{1.5})$ depending on increments used	No additional overhead	

Programming Problems and Projects

1. Complete the partial program presented in this chapter's Focus on Program Design section. Then use the completed program to explore empirically the shell sort algorithm. In particular, experiment with different sequences of diminishing increments.
   Write a report on your exploration. In your report you should compare various sequences of diminishing increments and rate them as to their performance on a variety of data sets.
2. Modify the shell sort so that it employs bubble sort logic on segments instead of insertion sort. Incorporate this change into the program presented in this chapter's Focus on Program Design section. Compare the observed efficiency of this new version of shell sort with the original on a variety of data sets. Which performs better? Explain your answer in a carefully written statement.
3. Modify the program presented in this chapter's Focus on Program Design section so that it becomes an experimental tool for quick sort, heap sort, or merge sort. Then use the modified program to conduct an experiment similar to that which you did for shell sort in Problem 1. For instance, for quick sort, you could experiment with the selection of a pivot element or try invoking insertion sort when the size of the array segment to be partitioned becomes sufficiently small. Whatever experimentation you choose to do, write a report on your exploration. In your report, draw conclusions about the efficiencies of various strategies. Support your conclusions with empirical data obtained from your exploratory runs.
4. Given a sequential file containing an unordered list of passengers and their flight numbers for Wing-and-a-Prayer Airlines (Problem 2, Chapter 4; Problems 3 and 12, Chapter 7), produce a listing arranged in flight-number order. Passengers on the same flight should be ordered by last name. The easy version of this program assumes that all information will fit in memory, allowing the use of an internal sort. For an added challenge, write the program using an external sort algorithm. (*Hint:* Adapt MergeSort along the lines discussed in the text.)
5. The Bay Area Brawlers professional football team (Problem 4, Chapter 4; Problem 5, Chapter 7) has stored the records of all the players who have played on the team during the history of the team. One player's record consists of

   Name
   Total points scored
   Number of touchdowns
   Number of field goals
   Number of safeties
   Number of extra points

   Write a program that lists players in order from the highest scorer in the team's history down to the lowest. Those players who have scored the same number of points should then be arranged in alphabetical order.
6. Take N randomly generated integers. Now apply a bubble sort, a shell sort, a quick sort, a heap sort, and a merge sort. Observe, compare, and plot their execution time for N = 100; N = 1,000; N = 10,000; N = 100,000, ...

7. Put some hypothetical data in an external file and apply a modified merge sort to them.

8. Write a Pascal program to complete the following steps.

   - Artificially create a file with a large number of randomly chosen names.
   - Read into an array all those names which begin with *A* through some letter, say *G*, chosen so that all the names will fit in the array.
   - Sort this array with one of the sorting algorithms from this chapter and store this sorted array into another file.
   - Now read into the array all those names from the file which begin with *H* through another appropriate letter.
   - Sort the array and append it to the end of the new file.

   Repeat this process until all names from the original file have been processed. The new file will be the sorted version of the original. Observe the execution time of your program. Analyze its efficiency in big-O terms.

9. Consider a list of records, each containing four fields.

   Name
   Month of birth
   Day of birth
   Year of birth

   Write a program to sort this list in oldest-to-youngest order. People with the same birth date should be arranged alphabetically. One strategy you could employ would be to concatenate strategically the four fields into one, and then sort just that one field. Another strategy would be to sort the list four times, each time by a different field. (Think carefully about which field to sort first.) Which of the strategies would require that you choose a stable sorting algorithm? (See Exercise 7 in Section 8.4.)

10. Modify MergeSort so that it will sort a linked list instead of an array.

I do not search, I find.
Pablo Picasso

More Powerful Search Methods

In earlier chapters, we've analyzed three methods of searching for items within a list: sequential search, binary search, and binary search tree. The sequential search, though easy to implement and applicable to short lists, is limited in many practical situations by its $O(n)$ search efficiency. The binary search offers a much faster $O(\log_2 n)$ search efficiency but also has limitations. Foremost among these limitations are the need to maintain the list in physically contiguous order and the need to maintain a count of the number of records in the list. Both of these limitations are particularly restrictive for volatile lists; that is, lists in which insertions and deletions are frequently made. In Chapter 7, a binary search tree emerged as offering the best of both worlds. Insertions and deletions can be done on a binary search tree by merely manipulating pointers instead of moving data, and an $O(\log_2 n)$ search efficiency can be achieved if the tree remains close to full. Unfortunately, to guarantee that the tree remains nearly full and hence insure the $O(\log_2 n)$ efficiency, a sophisticated technique known as height balancing (see Chapter 7) is required. The complications involved in implementing this technique frequently dictate that it not be used. Essentially, you must weigh the significant cost in development time to implement a height-balanced tree against the risk that the order in which data arrive for insertion may cause search efficiency to deteriorate from $O(\log_2 n)$ to $O(n)$. If data items arrive in a relatively random order, then taking that risk may well be the prudent choice.

The efficiency of all three of these techniques is dependent on the number of items in the list being searched. In this chapter, we shall study another alternative, called *hashing*. Its efficiency is measurable in terms of the amount of storage you are willing to waste. In this sense, hashing can achieve phenomenally fast search times regardless of how much data you have, provided that you can afford to keep a relatively large amount of unused list space available.

We shall also explore some of the special considerations that enter into searching for data stored in a disk file instead of main memory. These considerations lead to a variety of search schemes, all of which employ some variation of a data structure known as an *index*.

9.1 Density-Dependent Search Techniques

OBJECTIVES

- to understand what is meant by a key-to-address transformation, that is, a hashing function
- to develop techniques for constructing hashing functions
- to understand why, for most applications, hashing functions cannot transform all possible keys to a unique address
- to understand what the term *collision* means relative to hashing
- to develop methods for processing collisions: linear probing, quadratic probing, rehashing, linked (chained) probing, and bucket hashing
- to understand what the term *clustering* means relative to hashing

In an ideal data processing world, all identifying keys such as product codes, Social Security numbers, and so on, would start at 1 and follow in sequence thereafter. Then, in any given list, we would merely store the key and its associated data at the position that matched the key. The search efficiency for any key in such a list would be one access to the list, and all data processors could live happily ever after! Unfortunately, in the real world, users (not being concerned with the happiness of data processing personnel) desire keys that consist of more meaningful characters, such as names, addresses, region codes, and so on. For instance, it may be that in a given inventory-control application, product codes are numbered in sequence beginning with 10,000 instead of 1. A moment's reflection should indicate that this is still a highly desirable situation since, given a key, we need merely locate the key at position

KeyValue − 9999

in the list, and we still have a search efficiency of 1. What we have done here is to define what is known as a *key-to-address transformation,* or *hashing function.* The idea behind a hashing function is that it acts upon a given key in such a way as to return the relative position in the list where we expect to find the key.

Most hashing functions are not as straightforward as the preceding one and present some additional complications which we can quickly illustrate. Suppose we use the following hashing function:

Hash(KeyValue) = (KeyValue **MOD** 4) + 1

Then the set of keys 3, 5, 8, and 10 will be scattered as illustrated here.

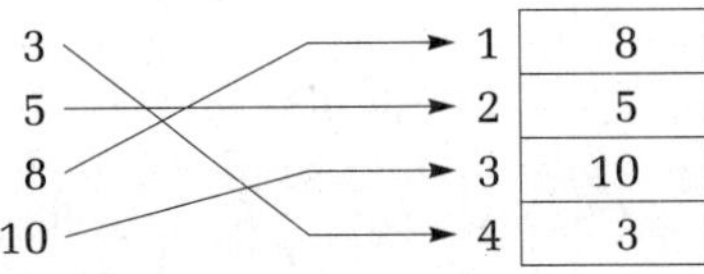

However, if we happen to have 3, 4, 8, and 10 as keys instead of 3, 5, 8, and 10, a problem arises: 4 and 8 hash to the same position. They are said to be *synonyms,* and the result is termed a *collision.* This situation, here a collision at position 1, is shown in the following illustration.

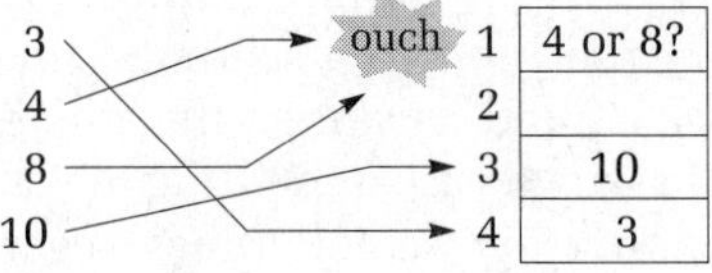

Clearly, one of the goals of the hashing functions we develop should be to reduce the number of collisions as much as possible.

The Construction of Hashing Functions

The business of developing hashing functions can be quite intriguing. The essential idea is to build a mathematical black box that will take a key value as input and issue as output the position in the list where that key value should be located. The position emitted should have a minimal probability of colliding with the position that would be produced for a different key. In addition, the black box we create must insure that a given key will always produce the same position as output. You should begin to note a similarity between some of the properties possessed by a good hashing function and a good random number generator such as that used in our simulation case study in Chapter 5. Indeed, list access via a hashing function is sometimes called *randomized storage,* and the first type of hashing function we discuss makes direct use of a random number generator.

Method 1: Use of a Random Number Generator. Many high-level languages provide a random number generator to produce random sequences of real values between 0 and 1. If one is not provided, you may easily write one using a method such as that described in Appendix 9. (For readable discussions of other methods of random number generation, see Chapter 7 of *Numerical Recipes* by William H. Press, Brian P. Flannery, Saul A. Teukolsky, and William T. Vetterling (Cambridge, England: Cambridge University Press, 1986).) Typically, all of these methods rely on having a global seed to start the process of generating random numbers. Computations done on this seed produce the random number. At the same time, the computations alter the value of the seed so that the next time the random number generator is called, a different random number will almost surely be produced.

In typical applications of random number generation, you need merely initialize the seed to some arbitrary value to start the random sequence. Once the seed is supplied, the random sequence is completely determined. If you have access to a system procedure that returns the current time, day, month, and year, this can be called to initialize the seed in a fashion that insures there is only a very small likelihood of generating the same random sequence twice.

How does all of this relate to hashing? For a hashing application, we must slightly alter the definition of our random number generator so that the seed is supplied as a value parameter. Then we supply the values of search keys as the seeds. The nature of the random number algorithm insures that

- Each time the same key is passed to the function, the same random value will be returned.
- It is unlikely that two different keys will yield the same random value.

The random number between 0 and 1 which is correspondingly produced can then be appropriately multiplied, truncated, and shifted to produce a hash value within the range of valid positions.

Method 2: Folding. In situations where the key to be positioned is not a pure integer, some preliminary work may be required to translate it into a usable form. Take, for instance, the case of a Social Security number such as

387–58–1505

Viewed as one integer, this would cause overflow on many machines. By a method known as *shift folding,* this Social Security number would be viewed as three separate numbers to be added

```
  387
   58
+1505
```

producing the result 1,950. This result could either be regarded as the hash position itself or, more likely, as a pure integer which now could be further acted upon by Method 1 or 4 to produce a final hash position in the desired range.

Another often-used folding technique is called *boundary folding.* The idea behind boundary folding is that, at the boundaries between the numbers making up the key under consideration, every other number is reversed before being added to the accumulated total. Applying this method to our Social Security number example, we would have

```
  387
   58 (this number reversed)
+1505
```

yielding a result of 1,977. Clearly, the two methods do not differ by much, and a choice between them must often be made on the basis of some experimentation to determine which will produce more scattered results for a given application.

Regardless of whether shift or boundary folding is used, one of the great advantages of the folding method is its ability to transform noninteger keys into an integer suitable for further hashing action. For keys such as names which contain alphabetic characters, the type of folding just illustrated may be done by translating characters into their ASCII (or other appropriate) codes.

Method 3: Digit or Character Extraction. In certain situations, a given key value may contain specific characters that are likely to bias any hash value arising from the key. The idea in *digit or character extraction* is to remove such digits or characters before using the result as a final hash value or passing it on to be further transformed by another method. For instance, a company may choose to identify the various products it manufactures by using a nine-character code which always contains either an A or B in the first position and either a 1 or 0 in the fourth position. The rest of the characters in the code tend to occur in less predictable fashion. Character extraction would remove the biased first and fourth characters, leaving a seven-character result to pass on to further processing.

Method 4: Division-Remainder Technique. All hashing presupposes a given range of positions that can be valid outputs of the hash function. In the remainder of this section, we assume the existence of a global constant RecordSpace which represents the upper limit of our hashing function. That is, the function should produce values between 1 and RecordSpace. It should than be evident that

Hash(KeyValue) = (KeyValue **MOD** RecordSpace) + 1

is a valid hashing function for integer KeyValue.

To begin examining criteria for choosing an appropriate RecordSpace, let us load the keys 41, 58, 12, 92, 50, and 91 into a list with RecordSpace 15. Figure 9.1 shows the results. In this array, zeros are used to denote empty positions.

FIGURE 9.1
Array with RecordSpace 15 loaded using a division remainder hashing function

Position	Key
1	0
2	91
3	92
4	0
5	0
6	80
7	0
8	0
9	0
10	0
11	0
12	41
13	12
14	58
15	0

However, if we keep RecordSpace the same and try to load the keys 10, 20, 30, 40, 50, 60, and 70, we have many collisions, as shown in Figure 9.2.

FIGURE 9.2
Array from Figure 9.1, loaded differently, with several collisions

Position	Key	
1	30	← 60 (collision)
2	0	
3	0	
4	0	
5	0	
6	20	← 50 (collision)
7	0	
8	0	
9	0	
10	0	
11	10	← 40 ← 70 (collision)
12	0	
13	0	
14	0	
15	0	

Hence a different set of keys can cause disastrous results even though the list seemingly has plenty of room available. On the other hand, if we choose RecordSpace to be 11, we have a list with considerably less room but no collisions. Figure 9.3 indicates the hashing positions when the same set of keys is acted upon by 11 instead of by 15.

FIGURE 9.3
Array with same keys as Figure 9.2, but with RecordSpace 11: no collision results

Position	Key
1	0
2	0
3	0
4	0
5	70
6	60
7	50
8	40
9	30
10	20
11	10

Although these examples of the *division-remainder technique* are far from conclusive, they suggest that choosing a prime number for RecordSpace may produce a more desirable hashing function. The Exercises at the end of this section have you explore this question more deeply. Apart from considerations of whether or not RecordSpace should be prime, it is clear that the nature of a particular application may dictate against the choice of certain RecordSpace values. For instance, in a situation where the rightmost digits of key values happen to follow certain recurring patterns, it would be unwise to choose a power of 10 for RecordSpace. (Why?)

Despite such considerations, usually a hashing function cannot rule out the possibility of collisions; it can only make them less likely. You should quickly be able to imagine a key value that will produce a collision for the hashing function used in determining the list of Figure 9.3. Notice that, as the list becomes more full, the probability that collisions will occur increases. Hence, when using hashing as a search strategy, one must be willing to waste some positions in the list; otherwise search efficiency will drastically deteriorate. How much space to waste is an interesting question that we will soon discuss. Further, since hashing functions generally cannot eliminate collisions, we must be prepared to handle them when they occur.

Collision Processing

The essential problem in collision processing is to develop an algorithm that will position a key in a list when the position dictated by the hashing function itself is already occupied. Ideally, this algorithm should minimize the possibility of future collisions; that is, the problem key should be located at a position that is not likely to be the hashed position of a future key.

However, the nature of hashing makes this latter criterion difficult to meet with any degree of certainty, since a good hashing function does not allow prediction of where future keys are likely to be placed. We will discuss five methods of collision processing: linear, quadratic, rehashing, linked, and buckets. In all of the methods, it will be necessary to detect when a given list position is not occupied. To signify this, we use a global constant Empty to distinguish unoccupied positions. As you read, give some thought to the question of how deletions could be processed from a list accessed via one of these hashing methods. In particular, will the Empty flag suffice to denote positions that have never been occupied *and* positions previously occupied but now vacant? This question is explored in the Exercises and Programming Problems.

Linear Collision Processing

The linear method of resolving collisions is the simplest to implement (and, unfortunately, the least efficient). *Linear collision processing* requires that, when a collision occurs, we proceed down the list in sequential order until a vacant position is found. The key causing the collision is then placed at this first vacant position. If we come to the physical end of our list in the attempt to place the problem key, we merely wrap around to the top of the list and continue looking for a vacant position. For instance, suppose we use a hashing function of

Hash(KeyValue) = (KeyValue **MOD** RecordSpace) + 1

with RecordSpace equal to 7, and attempt to insert the keys 18, 31, 67, 36, 19, and 34. The sequence of lists in Figure 9.4 shows the results of these insertions. When a collision occurs at the third insert, it is processed by the linear method; 67 is thus loaded into position 6.

FIGURE 9.4
Insertion with linear collision processing

First insert Hash(18) = 5		Second insert Hash(31) = 4		Third insert Hash(67) = 5		Fourth insert Hash(36) = 2		Fifth insert Hash(19) = 6		Sixth insert Hash(34) = 7	
1	0	1	0	1	0	1	0	1	0	1	34
2	0	2	0	2	0	2	36	2	36	2	36
3	0	3	0	3	0	3	0	3	0	3	0
4	0	4	31	4	31	4	31	4	31	4	31
5	18	5	18	5	18	5	18	5	18	5	18
6	0	6	0	6	67	6	67	6	67	6	67
7	0	7	0	7	0	7	0	7	19	7	19

EXAMPLE 9.1

Suppose that an array has been loaded with data using the linear collision processing strategy illustrated in Figure 9.4. Write a Pascal algorithm to seek a Target key in this array.

```
{ Global declarations }

CONST
  RecordSpace = { Appropriate size };
  Empty       = { Appropriate flagging value };

TYPE
  KeyType = { Appropriate data type for key field in record };
```

```
  DataRec = RECORD
              Key : KeyType;
              OtherData : {  Appropriate type  }
            END;
  DataArray = ARRAY [1..RecordSpace] OF DataRec;

PROCEDURE  LinearHash (Target : KeyType;
                       SearchList : DataArray;
                       VAR InfoWanted : DataRec;
                       VAR Found : boolean);

  {  Given:   List of records loaded by linear hashing method  }
  {           in SearchList.  Target, the value of a key       }
  {           field to be found in SearchList.                 }
  {  Task:    Use linear hashing algorithm to search           }
  {           SearchList for Target.                           }
  {  Return:  If record with key field matching Target is      }
  {           found, return Found as true and return           }
  {           associated information for that record in       }
  {           InfoWanted.  Otherwise return Found as false.    }

  VAR
    K, J : integer;
    Traversed : boolean;

  BEGIN
    Found := false;     {  Assume failure  }
    Traversed := false; {  Toggled to true if entire list is traversed  }
    K := Hash (Target); {  Call on hashing function  }
    J := K;             {  J is used to probe list  }
    WHILE (SearchList[J].Key <> Empty) AND NOT (Traversed OR Found) DO
      IF Target = SearchList[J].Key THEN
        BEGIN
          InfoWanted := SearchList[J];
          Found := true
        END
      ELSE
        BEGIN
          J := (J MOD RecordSpace) + 1;  {  MOD insures wraparound  }
          Traversed := (J = K)
        END
  END; {  OF PROCEDURE LinearHash  }
```

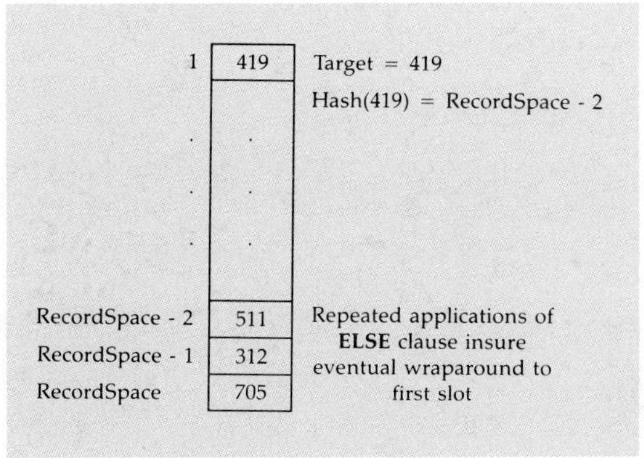

Several remarks are in order concerning the procedure in Example 9.1. First, note that the procedure as it stands would not handle list processing in which it was necessary to process deletions. In such a situation, an additional flagging value would be needed to indicate a list position that had once been occupied and is now vacant because of a deletion. Without this distinction, we would not know whether or not to exit the search loop upon encountering an empty slot. You will explore the problem of deletions from a list maintained by hashing in greater detail in the Exercises and Programming Problems. Second, note that the linear method is not without its flaws. In particular, it is prone to a problem known as *clustering*. Clustering occurs when a collision processing strategy relocates keys that have a collision at the same initial hashing position to the same region (known as a cluster) within the storage space. This usually leads to further collisions with other relocated values until everything is resolved. With linear collision processing, the clustering problem is compounded because, as one cluster expands, it can run into another cluster, immediately creating a larger cluster. This one large cluster ultimately causes collision resolutions to be drawn out longer than they would otherwise be. Hence, linear hashing is more likely to result in the clustering phenomenon pictured in Figure 9.5 than the other methods we discuss.

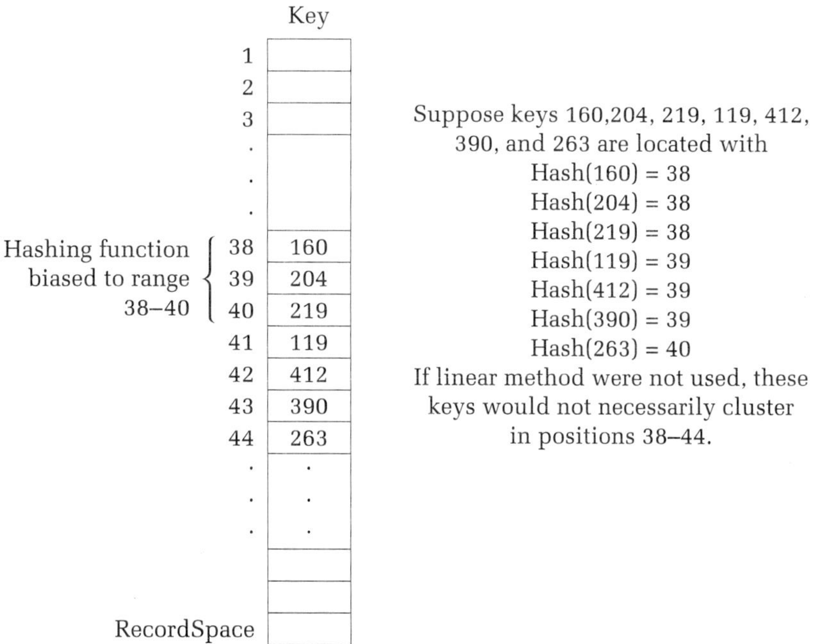

FIGURE 9.5
Clustering due to biased hashing function and linear processing

Efficiency Considerations for Linear Hashing. A final point to note about the linear hashing method is its search efficiency. Knuth has shown that the average number of list accesses for a successful search using the linear method is

$$(1/2) * (1 + 1/(1 - D))$$

where

D = (Number of currently active records)/RecordSpace

(See Donald E. Knuth, *Searching and Sorting*. Vol. 3 of *The Art of Computer Programming*. (Menlo Park, Calif.: Addison-Wesley, 1973).) An interesting fact about this search efficiency is that it is not solely dependent upon the number of records in the list but rather upon the density ratio of the number of records currently in the list divided by the total record space available. In other words, no matter how many records there are, a highly efficient result can be obtained if one is willing to waste enough vacant records. This is what is meant by a *density-dependent search technique*. In the case of searching for a key that cannot be found, Knuth's results indicate that the average search efficiency will be

$$(1/2) * (1 + 1/(1 - D)^2)$$

Table 9.1 illustrates the effectiveness of linear collision resolution by showing the computed efficiencies for a few strategic values of D.

TABLE 9.1
Average search efficiency for linear collision processing

D	Efficiency for Successful Search (number of accesses)	Efficiency for Unsuccessful Search (number of accesses)
0.10	1.06	1.18
0.50	1.50	2.50
0.75	2.50	8.50
0.90	5.50	50.50

Quadratic and Rehashing Methods of Collision Processing

Both the *quadratic* and *rehashing collision processing methods* attempt to correct the problem of clustering. They force the problem-causing key to immediately move a considerable distance from the initial collision. By the rehashing method, an entire sequence of hashing functions may be applied to a given key. If a collision results from the first hashing function, a second is applied, then a third, and so on, until the key can be successfully placed.

The quadratic method has the advantage of not requiring numerous hashing functions for its implementation. Suppose that a key value initially hashes to position K and a collision results. Then, on its first attempt to resolve the collision, the quadratic algorithm attempts to place the key at position

$$K + 1^2$$

Then, if a second attempt is necessary to resolve the collision, position

$$K + 2^2$$

is probed. In general, the Rth attempt to resolve the collision probes position

$$K + R^2$$

(with wraparound taken into account). Figure 9.6 highlights this scattering pattern. At this point you should verify that, if the hashing function

Hash(KeyValue) = (KeyValue **MOD** RecordSpace) + 1

is used with RecordSpace equal to 7, the keys 17, 73, 32, and 80 will be located in positions 4, 5, 6, and 1 respectively.

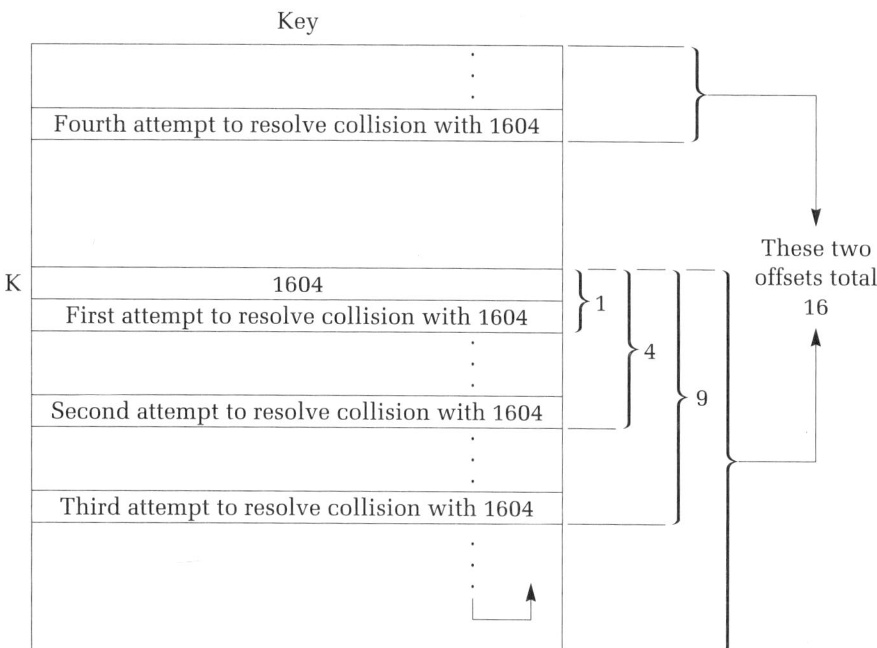

FIGURE 9.6
Quadratic collision processing

Efficiency Considerations for the Quadratic and Rehashing Methods. Knuth's results (see *Searching and Sorting,* cited earlier in this section) demonstrate the effectiveness of the rehashing and quadratic methods versus the linear method. For the quadratic method, average search efficiencies improve to

$$1 - \log_e(1 - D) - (D/2)$$

for the successful case and

$$1/(1 - D) - D - \log_e(1 - D)$$

for an unsuccessful search, where D is density ratio defined earlier in this section and *e* is the base for the natural logarithm function.

Rehashing with a completely random sequence of rehashing locations for each key improves slightly the efficiencies of the quadratic method to

$$-(1/D) * \log_e(1 - D)$$

for the successful case and

$$1/(1 - D)$$

for an unsuccessful search. Compare the numbers presented in Table 9.2 for quadratic collision processing and (ideal) random rehashing to those in Table 9.1 for linear collision processing.

TABLE 9.2
Average search efficiency for quadratic and rehashing collision processing

D	Efficiency for Successful Search (number of accesses)		Efficiency for Unsuccessful Search (number of accesses)	
	Quadratic	Rehashing	Quadratic	Rehashing
0.10	1.05	1.05	1.11	1.11
0.50	1.44	1.39	2.19	2.00
0.75	2.01	1.84	4.64	4.00
0.90	2.85	2.56	11.40	10.00

You may have surmised that the increased efficiency of the quadratic method entails at least some drawbacks. Firt, the computation of a position to be probed when a collision occurs is somewhat more obscure than it was with the linear method. We leave it for you to verify that the position for the Rth probe after an initial unsuccessful hash to position K is given by

$$(K + R^2 - 1)\ \textbf{MOD}\ \text{RecordSpace} + 1$$

A more significant problem, however, is that the quadratic method seemingly offers no guarantee that we will try every position in the list before concluding that a given key cannot be inserted. With the linear method, as the list became relatively dense when keys and insertions were attempted, the only way that the insertion could fail would be for every position in the list to be occupied. The linear nature of the search, although inefficient, insured that every position would be checked. However, with the quadratic method applied to the RecordSpace of Figure 9.7, you can confirm that an

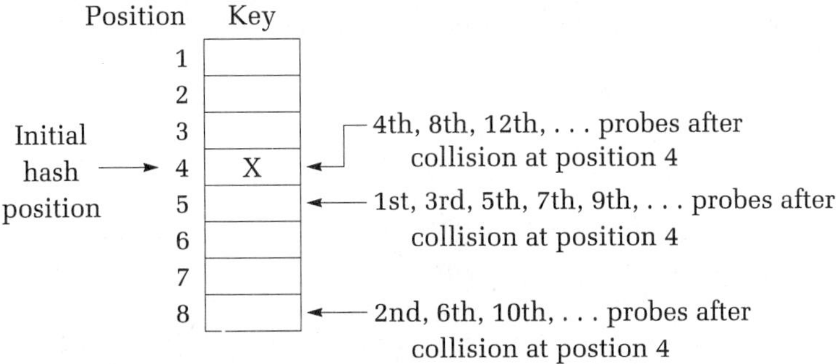

FIGURE 9.7
Quadratic probing after initial hash to 4

initial hash to position 4 will lead to future probing of positions 4, 5, and 8 only; it will never check positions 1, 2, 3, 6, or 7.

A satisfactory answer to the question of what portion of a list will be probed by the quadratic algorithm was fortunately provided by Radke for values of RecordSpace that are prime numbers which satisfy certain conditions. Radke's results and their application to the quadratic algorithm are explored in the Exercises at the end of the section. (If you wish to read Radke's results, see C. E. Radke, "The Use of Quadratic Residue Research." *Communications of the ACM* 13, No. 2, (February 1970): 103–105.)

Linked Method of Collision Processing

The logic of *linked collision processing* completely eliminates the possibility that one collision begets another. It requires a storage area divided into two regions: a *prime hash area* and an *overflow area.* Each record requires a Link field in addition to the Key and OtherData fields. The global constant RecordSpace is applicable to the prime hash area only. This storage concept is illustrated in Figure 9.8.

Initially, the hashing translates function keys into the prime hashing area. If a collision occurs, the key is inserted into a linked list with its initial node in the prime area and all following nodes in the overflow area (no dummy header is used). Figure 9.9 shows how this method would load the keys 22, 31, 67, 36, 29, and 60 for a RecordSpace equal to 7 and hashing function

Hash(KeyValue) = (KeyValue **MOD** RecordSpace) + 1

FIGURE 9.8
Storage allocation for linked collision processing

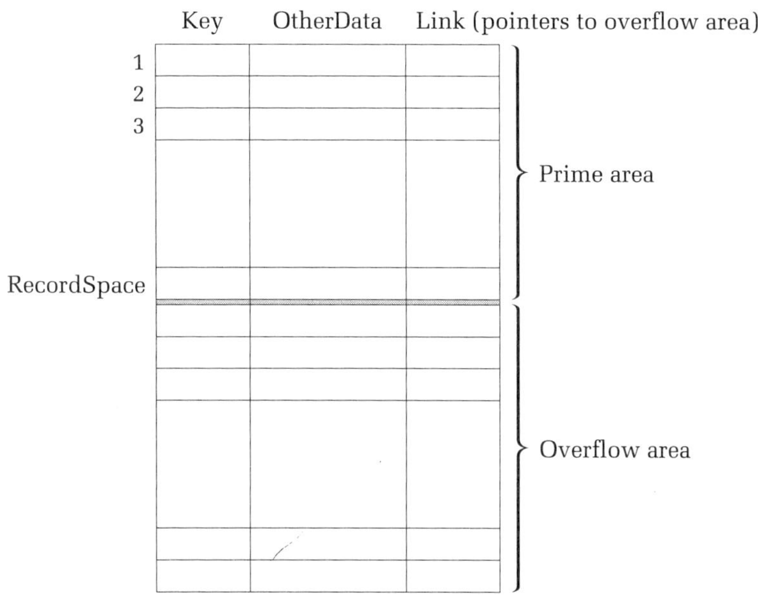

FIGURE 9.9
Loading keys with KeyValue **MOD** 7 + 1 and linked collision processing

	Key	Link
1	0	NULL
2	22	8
3	0	NULL
4	31	NULL
5	67	10
6	0	NULL
7	0	NULL
8	36	9
9	29	NULL
10	60	NULL
11	0	NULL
12	0	NULL
13	0	NULL
14	0	NULL
15	0	NULL
16	0	NULL
17	0	NULL

EXAMPLE 9.2

Suppose that an array has been loaded with data using the linked collision processing strategy illustrated in Figures 9.8 and 9.9. Write a Pascal procedure to find a Target key in this array.

We have made the Link fields integer pointers to other array locations instead of Pascal dynamic memory pointers to facilitate using the algorithm with a random access file. As written, the procedure assumes that all key locations in the prime area have had their corresponding Key and Link fields initialized to appropriate constant flags for Empty and Null respectively. The assumption is also made that no keys will be deleted.

```
{ Global declarations }

CONST
  RecordSpace = { Appropriate size for prime area };
  PrimePlusOverflow = { Actual array size };
```

```
    Empty = {  Appropriate flag for key field of empty record  };
    Null = {  Appropriate flag for end-of-list pointer  };

  TYPE
    KeyType = {  Appropriate type for key field in record  };
    DataRec = RECORD
                Key : KeyType;
                OtherData : {  Appropriate type  };
                Link : integer {  or Pascal pointer variable if desired  }
              END;
    DataArray = ARRAY [1..PrimePlusOverflow] OF DataRec;

  PROCEDURE  LinkedHash (Target : KeyType;
                         SearchList : DataArray;
                         VAR InfoWanted : DataRec;
                         VAR Found : boolean);

    {  Given:   List of records loaded by linked hashing method  }
    {           in SearchList.  Target, the value of a key       }
    {           field to be found in SearchList.                 }
    {  Task:    Use linked hashing algorithm to search           }
    {           SearchList for Target.                           }
    {  Return:  If record with key field matching Target is      }
    {           found, return Found as true and return           }
    {           associated information for that record in        }
    {           InfoWanted.  Otherwise return Found as false.    }

    VAR
      K : integer;

    BEGIN
      Found := false;      {  Assume failure  }
      K := Hash (Target); {  Call on hashing function, use K to probe list}
      REPEAT
        IF Target = SearchList[K].Key THEN
          BEGIN
            InfoWanted := SearchList[K];
            Found := true
          END
        ELSE
          K := SearchList[K].Link
      UNTIL Found OR (K = Null)
    END; {  of PROCEDURE LinkedHash  }
```

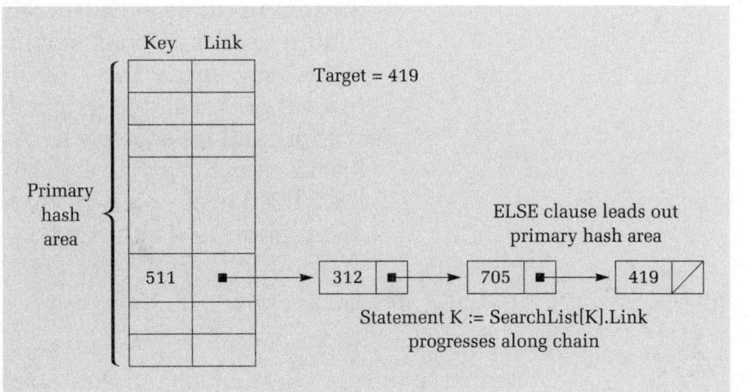

Efficiency Considerations for Linked Hashing. Knuth's efficiency results for the linked hashing method depend on a density factor (D) which is computed using the RecordSpace in the prime hashing area only. Hence, unlike the other hashing methods we have discussed, the linked method allows a density factor greater than 1. For example, if the RecordSpace for the primary hash area were 200 and the overflow area contained space for 300 additional records, then 400 active records would yield a density factor of 2. Given this variation, average search efficiencies for the successful and unsuccessful cases are 1 + D/2 and D respectively. Table 9.3 shows computations of this search efficiency for selected values of D, and should be compared to the corresponding results for the linear and quadratic methods, which were presented in Table 9.1 and Table 9.2, respectively.

TABLE 9.3
Average search efficiencies for the linked method

D	Efficiency for Successful Search (number of accesses)	Efficiency for Unsuccessful Search (number of accesses)
2	2	2
5	3.5	5
10	6	10
20	11	20

A NOTE OF INTEREST

Machine Translation

When the search algorithms discussed in this chapter were first discovered, they sparked a flurry of activity in an area known as machine translation. Programs in this area attempt to translate text from one natural language to another, for example, English to German. Early attempts at machine translation tended to view the process as essentially the searching of a large dictionary. Hence, to translate the English sentence

The sun is yellow.

the program would simply find each of the words in a disk-based version of an English-to-German dictionary and arrive at the German sentence

Die Sonne ist gelb.

However, machine translation activity was soon slowed by the complexities of syntax (grammar) and semantics (meanings) in natural language. The translation of some sentences by these early systems produced some rather humorous results. According to computer folklore cited in the article "Computers Gain as Language Translators Even Though Perfect Not They Always" by William M. Bulkeley (*Wall Street Journal,* February 6, 1985, p. 25), the following translations occurred in an early English-to-Russian system.

English Phrase	Russian Translation
The spirit is willing but the flesh is weak.	The vodka is good but the meat is rotten.
Out of sight, out of mind	Invisible maniac.

Results such as these caused a government panel to declare, in 1966, that computerized translation would never be practical. Today, as linguists have more successfully formalized rules of syntax and semantics, machine translation is making somewhat of a comeback. In restricted domains, such as the translation of language specific to technology and business, products are being developed as time-saving aids to human translators.

Two recent issues of the *Communications of the ACM*—Vol. 33, No. 5 (May, 1990) and Vol. 33, No. 8(August, 1990)—contain a variety of articles describing progress that has been made in processing natural languages. These articles provide an excellent starting point for you to explore this topic more thoroughly.

Bucket Hashing

In the bucket hashing strategy of collision processing, the hashing function transforms a given key to a physically contiguous region of locations within the list to be searched. This contiguous region is called a *bucket*. Thus, instead of hashing to the Kth location, a key would hash to the Kth bucket of locations. The number of locations contained in this bucket would depend upon the bucket size. (We assume that all buckets in a given list are the same size.) Figure 9.10 illustrates this concept for a list with seven buckets and a bucket size of 3.

FIGURE 9.10
Storage allocation for bucket hashing

		KEY
	1	
Bucket #1	2	
	3	
	4	
Bucket #2	5	
	6	
	7	
Bucket #3	8	
	9	
	10	
Bucket #4	11	
	12	
	13	
Bucket #5	14	
	15	
	16	
Bucket #6	17	
	18	
	19	
Bucket #7	20	
	21	

Having hashed to a bucket, the Target must then be compared in sequential order to all of the keys in that bucket. On the surface, it would seem that this strategy could do no better than duplicate the efficiency of the linked hash method discussed earlier. Indeed, because a sequential search is conducted in both cases after the initial hash is made, the average number of list accesses for a successful or unsuccessful search cannot be improved by using buckets. Moreover, provisions for linking to some sort of overflow area must still be made in case a series of collisions consumes all of the space in a given bucket.

What then could be a possible advantage of using buckets? If the list to be searched resides entirely in main memory, there is no advantage. However, if the list resides in a disk file, the bucket method will allow us to take advantage of some of the physical characteristics of the storage medium itself. To see this, we must realize that a one-surface disk is divided into concentric *tracks* and pie-shaped *sectors* as indicated in Figure 9.11.

There are two ways in which the bucket hashing strategy may take advantage of the organization of the data on the disk. First, when records in a contiguous random access file are stored on a disk, they are generally located in relative record number order along one track, then along an adjacent track,

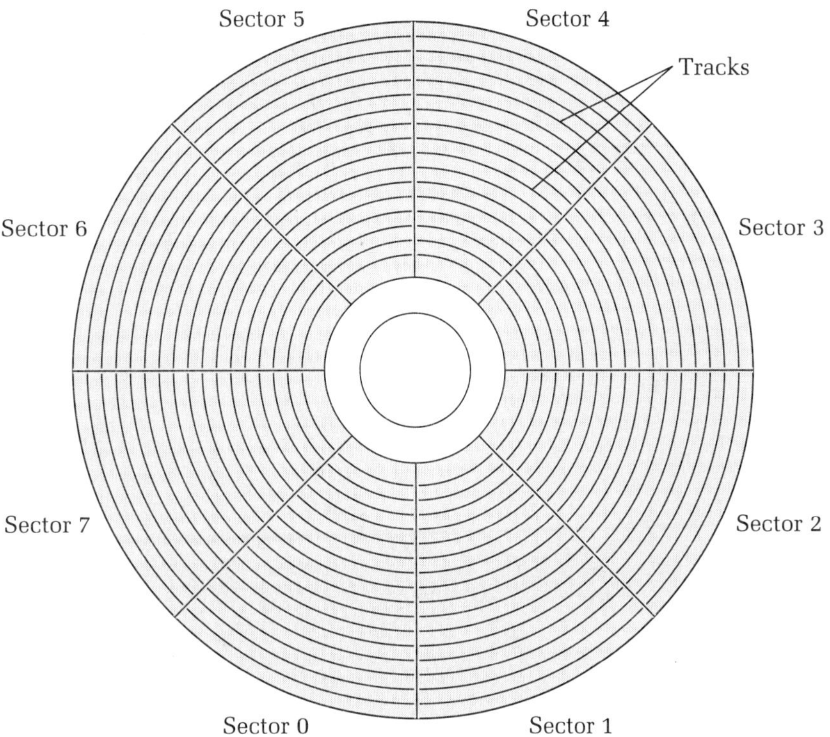

FIGURE 9.11
One-surface disk

and so on. The movement of the read-write head between tracks is generally the cause of the most significant delays in obtaining data from a disk. The farther the movement, the greater the delay. Hence, if our knowledge of the machine in question allows us to make a bucket coincide with a track on the disk, then hashing to the beginning of a bucket and proceeding from there using a sequential search within the bucket (that is, the track) will greatly reduce head movement. A linked hashing strategy, on the other hand, could cause considerable movement of the read-write head between tracks on the disk, thereby slowing program execution. This consideration is an excellent example of how one must examine more than just the number of list accesses when measuring the efficiency of a program involving disk files.

A second advantage in using the bucket hashing algorithm when disk files are being searched is related to the way in which records are transferred between the disk and main memory. Frequently, programming languages create the illusion that each record accessed requires a separate disk access. However, records are frequently blocked, that is, positioned in contiguous regions on a track of the disk, so that a fixed number of them are brought into main memory when a record in that block is requested. This means that, if the record requested happens to be part of the block presently in main memory, a program statement that requests a record may not even require a disk access but only a different viewing window applied to the block already in main memory. Since main memory manipulations are orders of magnitude faster than the rate of data transfer to and from a disk, this means that positioning our buckets to coincide with a disk block will necessitate only one disk access each time an entire bucket is sequentially searched. Here again, the more scattered nature of a purely linked hashing algorithm would not allow this disk-oriented efficiency consideration to be taken into account.

Exercises 9.1

1. Assume a hashing function has the following characteristics:

   Keys 459 and 333 hash to 1.
   Key 632 hashes to 2.
   Key 1090 hashes to 3.
   Keys 1982, 379, 238, and 3411 hash to 10.

   Assume that insertions into a hashed file are performed in the order 1982, 3411, 333, 632, 1090, 459, 379, and 238.

   a. Indicate the position of the keys if the linear method is used to resolve collisions.

Record No.	Key
1	
2	
3	
4	
5	
6	
7	
8	
9	
10	
11	

   b. Indicate the position of the keys if the quadratic method is used to resolve collisions.

Record No.	Key
1	
2	
3	
4	
5	
6	
7	
8	
9	
10	
11	

   c. Indicate the position of the keys and the contents of the link fields if the chaining (that is, linked) method is used to resolve collisions. Use zeros to represent **NIL** links and assume that the first record used in the overflow area is 12, then 13, then 14, and so on.

Record No.	Key	Link
1		
2		
3		
4		
5		
6		
7		
8		
9		
10		
11		

Prime Area

Record No.	Key	Link
12		
13		
14		
15		
16		
17		
18		
19		
20		
21		
22		

Overflow Area

2. Repeat Exercise 1 with the order of insertion of keys reversed.

3. We have covered binary search, linked lists, binary trees, and hashing as methods of implementing a keyed list ADT. Choose the method you would use to implement the data list involved for each of the following three real-world applications. In each case you should choose the most appropriate implementation technique. "Most appropriate" here means efficiently handling all of the required operations while not being too powerful; that is, not doing something that should be easy in an overly complicated way. Then provide a written rationale as to why yours would be the appropriate method.
   a. The list to be maintained is the card catalog of a library. Frequent additions to and deletions from this catalog are made by the library. Additionally, users are frequently searching for the data associated with a given book's key. However, the library rarely prints out an ordered list of all its holdings. Hence ordering the list is not to be considered a high priority.
   b. You are writing a program that maintains the lists of passengers on flights for an airline company. Passengers are frequently added to these lists. Moreover, quite often passengers cancel flight plans and must be removed from a list. You are also told that the airline frequently wants alphabetized listings of the passengers on a given flight and often needs to search out a particular passenger by name when inquiries are received from individuals.
   c. You are writing a program to access a large customer data base and build up counts for the numbers of customers from each of the 50 states (plus the District of Columbia). To do this you will use a list of records consisting of the two-character state abbreviation and an integer representing the count of customers from that state. For each customer you read in from the data base, you must find the customer's home state in your list and increase the corresponding count field. At the end, print out the counts in order alphabetized by the two-character state abbreviation.

4. Write procedures to insert a key into a list to be searched by
   a. Linear hashing.
   b. Quadratic hashing.
   c. Linked hashing.
   d. Bucket hashing.

5. Write procedures to search for a key via
   a. Quadratic hashing.
   b. Bucket hashing.

6. Devise strategies to delete keys from a list being maintained by each of the four hashing strategies in Exercise 4. Write Pascal versions for each of these algorithms. Given your deletion strategy, describe in detail the modifications (if any) that must be made in the various search and insertion procedures of Exercises 4 and 5.

7. In Section 9.1 we mentioned a result by Radke that answered the question of how many array slots would be probed by the quadratic hashing algorithm for certain values of RecordSpace. In particular, Radke showed that if RecordSpace is a prime number of the form $4m + 3$ for some integer m, then half of the array slots would be probed by the sequence of probes

   $K, K + 1^2, K + 2^2, K + 3^2, \ldots$

   where K is the original hash position. Radke also showed that the other half would be probed by the sequence

   $K - 1^2, K - 2^2, K - 3^2, \ldots$

Rewrite your insertion and search procedures for the quadratic method in Exercises 4 and 5 to take into account Radke's result.

8. a. Given the arrival of integer keys in the order 67, 19, 4, 58, 38, 55, 86 and RecordSpace = 9 with

Hash(KeyValue) = (KeyValue **MOD** RecordSpace) + 1

trace the insertion steps of linearly processing collisions.

Index	KeyValue
1	0
2	0
3	0
4	0
5	0
6	0
7	0
8	0
9	0

(0 indicates empty position)

b. Given the arrival of integer keys in the order 32, 62, 34, 77, 6, 46, 107 and RecordSpace = 15 with

Hash(KeyValue) = (KeyValue **MOD** RecordSpace) + 1

trace the insertion steps of quadratically processing collisions.

Index	KeyValue
1	0
2	0
3	0
4	0
5	0
6	0
7	0
8	0
9	0
10	0
11	0
12	0
13	0
14	0
15	0

(0 indicates empty position)

c. Given the arrival of integer keys in the order 5, 3, 16, 27, 14, 25, 4 and RecordSpace = 11 with initial hashing function

Hash_1(KeyValue) = (KeyValue **MOD** RecordSpace) + 1

trace the insertion steps of the rehashing collision processing method where the secondary hashing function is

Hash_2(KeyValue) = (5*KeyValue **MOD** RecordSpace) + 1

Assume that, if the secondary hashing function is not successful in locating a position for the key, then linear collision processing is used from the address indicated by the secondary hashing function.

Index	KeyValue
1	0
2	0
3	0
4	0
5	0
6	0
7	0
8	0
9	0
10	0
11	0

(0 indicates empty position)

Comment on the effectiveness of rehashing with this particular secondary hashing function. Can you think of a better one? Explain why yours is better.

9. In a written statement explain how hashing could be used to search for keys that were not unique. For instance, you might have several people identified by the same name.

■ ■ ■ ■

9.2 Two Abstract Data Types Revisited

OBJECTIVES

- to discuss how hashing could be used to implement the keyed list ADT
- to evaluate the efficiency of hashing as an implementation strategy for the keyed list ADT
- to discuss how hashing could be used to implement the sparse table ADT

We can analyze hashing from a pragmatic perspective by considering how it might be used to implement two ADTs introduced in Chapter 2: the keyed list and the sparse table. You will then be asked to carry out these implementations in the Exercises and Programming Problems at the end of the chapter.

The Keyed List ADT Implemented by Hashing

In this context, hashing emerges as yet another list maintenance strategy to be evaluated and compared to those strategies we have already discussed: array (or random access file) with binary search, linked list, and binary tree. Hence we must examine its performance with respect to the same Add, Retrieve, Delete, and TraverseInOrder operations that were introduced in Chapter 2 and then used to evaluate these other list implementation techniques. Assuming the existence of an appropriate hashing function to act on the key and a willingness to waste enough storage to allow for fast searching, hashing will clearly perform very well in all of these areas with the exception of ordering data. Here is where we have to pay a price for the scattered storage of records that are located via a hashing function.

Nonetheless, there are strategies that can be used to allow hashing and ordering of data to coexist. One such strategy would simply be to use a pointer sort algorithm (see Chapter 1) to logically sort the data when an ordered list is needed. This strategy has the drawback of not maintaining the list in order but actually performing a potentially costly sort algorithm each time an ordering is requested. Clearly, this strategy would not be wise if such an ordering were requested frequently and unpredictably.

In situations where requests for ordering would come frequently enough to make maintaining the list in order (as opposed to sorting) a necessity, we could follow a strategy that would combine the search speed of hashing with the ordered list advantages offered by a linked list implementation. This combination would have us use hashing to search for an individual record but would add link fields to each record so that a linked list for each desired ordering could be woven through the collection of hashed records. Implementing this combination of hashing and linked list would entail the following considerations with respect to the keyed list operations:

- Add. In effect, the hashing/collision processing algorithm would provide us with an available node to store data. Each linked list involved would then have to be traversed to link the node into each ordering in the appropriate logical location.
- Retrieve. There is no problem here because the hash algorithm should find the desired record quickly.
- Delete. This is similar to the retrieve operation. Use hashing to find the record to be deleted, then adjust the link field appropriately. A doubly linked list could prove to be particularly valuable here. (Why?)
- TraverseInOrder. There is no problem here because the linked lists constantly maintain the appropriate orderings.

The Sparse Table ADT Implemented by Hashing

We have already suggested two implementation strategies for sparse tables.

1. In Section 2.3 we described a strategy that would simply create a list of the rows and columns corresponding to nontrivial values in the table. Thus, determining the value of the data at a conceptual row/column location is simply a matter of searching this list.
2. In Chapter 4, we described a strategy that would form a linked list of the nontrivial columns in each row. Here, determining the value of the data at a conceptual row/column location is reduced to the problem of sequentially searching a relatively small linked list.

At the time we explored these two strategies, the first one appeared to be less attractive. Because the data in the list of row/column coordinates corresponding to nontrivial values are likely to be volatile, physically ordering the data for a binary search would not be practical. Yet, without a binary search, requests to inspect the value at any given location are met with the $O(n)$ response time of a sequential search. Hashing allows us to search for a row/column coordinate in the list of the first strategy in a very efficient fashion, probably faster than the sequential search along the linked list representing a given row required by the second strategy. Moreover, since the order of the data in the list is not important for this application, the scattered nature of hashed storage does not present any obstacle at all.

The considerations we have discussed with respect to these two ADTs make it evident that hashing is a very attractive list implementation technique. It will be extremely efficient in regard to the add, retrieve, and delete list operations if we are willing to pay the price of wasting enough storage to get a reasonably low density ratio. The only other drawback to hashing, in addition to this wasted storage, is the price that must be paid if various orderings of the data are frequently needed.

Exercises 9.2

1. Suppose that we combine hashing with a linked list in the fashion described in Section 9.2 so that all keyed list operations can be efficiently performed. Which of the variations on a linked list structure would be most effective in this context? Explain why in a carefully worded statement. (*Hint:* Think about the retrieve and delete operations.)

2. Give an example of an application where the hashing implementation of a two-dimensional table described in this section would be less efficient (overall) than the linked list implementation described in Chapter 4. Explain why in a carefully worded statement.

3. Provide implementations of all keyed list operations using the hashing strategy described in this section. Provide alternative implementations of the TraverseIn-Order operations: one should invoke a pointer sort and another should combine hashing with a linked list.

4. Provide implementations of all sparse table operations defined in Chapter 2 using the hashing strategy described in this section.

■ ■ ■ ■

9.3 Indexed Search Techniques (Optional)

OBJECTIVES

- to understand the differences between searching in main memory and in random access disk storage
- to understand how an index may be used to advantage when searching for data in a random access file
- to study how the indexed sequential search methodology is implemented
- to discuss the efficiency of the indexed sequential search strategy
- to understand how the B-tree data structure may be used to implement an index for a random access file
- to discuss the efficiency of B-trees
- to understand how the trie data structure may be used to implement the index for a random access file keyed by strings of variable length
- to discuss the efficiency of tries

All of the search strategies we have studied up to this point could be applied to lists implemented in main memory or on a random access disk. However, with the exception of bucket hashing, none of the methods we have studied actually take into account physical characteristics of disk storage in an attempt to enhance their efficiency. In practice, because retrieval of data from a disk file is orders of magnitude slower than retrieval from main memory, we often cannot afford to ignore these special characteristics of disk files if we want reasonable response time for our searching efforts. The indexing schemes that we are about to discuss in this section are primarily directed toward file-oriented applications and thus will take into account the operational properties of this storage medium. We encourage you to reread the discussion of bucket hashing at the end of Section 9.1 for a summary analysis of file storage considerations.

The idea behind the use of an index is analogous to the way in which we routinely use an address book to find a person whom we are seeking. That is, if we are looking for a person, we do not knock on the doors of numerous houses until we find the one where that person lives. Instead, we apply a search strategy to an address book. There we use the name of the person as a key to find a pointer—that is, an address—which swiftly leads us to where the person can be found. Only one actual "house access" must be made, although our search strategy may require numerous accesses into the address book index.

In a computer system, records (or more precisely blocks) could play the role of houses in the search scenario just described. Data records on disk are (when compared to main memory) terribly slow and awkward creatures to access. One of the reasons for this is that there is often so much data that must be moved from disk to main memory every time a record is accessed. Because of this, the conceptual picture for the general setup of an indexed search must be revised. The list of keys is no longer parallel to the actual data with which they are logically associated but rather is parallel to a list of pointers which will lead us to the actual data. The revised picture is presented in Figure 9.12.

The general strategy of an indexed search is to use the key to efficiently search the index, find the relative record position of the associated data, and from there make only one access into the actual data. Because the parallel lists of keys and relative record positions require much less storage than the data itself, frequently the entire index can be loaded and permanently held in main memory, necessitating only one disk access for each record being

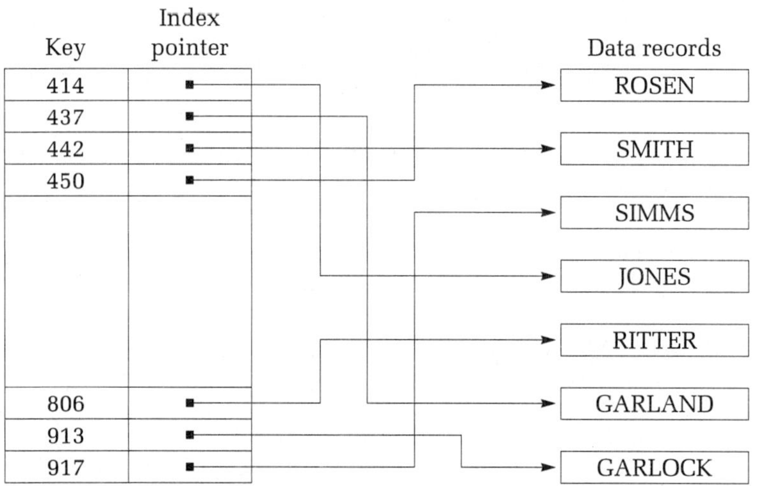

FIGURE 9.12
General setup for an indexed search

sought. For larger indices, it still remains true that large blocks of keys and associated pointers may be manipulated in main memory, thereby greatly enhancing search efficiency.

Indexed Sequential Search Technique

The *indexed sequential search* technique is also commonly recognized by the acronym *ISAM,* which stands for *Indexed Sequential Access Method.* Essentially it involves carefully weighing the disk-dependent factors of blocking and track size to build a partial index. The partial index, unlike some other index structures we will study, does not reduce to one the number of probes which must be made into the actual data.

To continue the analogy between searching for data and searching for a person, the indexed sequential strategy is somewhat like an address book that would lead us to the street on which a person lives but leave it to us to check each of the houses on that street. The ISAM method correspondingly leads us to an appropriate region (often a track or a cylinder containing multiple tracks within a disk pack) and then leaves it to us to search sequentially within that region.

As an example, let us suppose that we can conveniently fit the partial index, or directory, pictured in Figure 9.13 into main memory and that the organization of our disk file allows six records per track. This directory is formed by choosing the highest key value in each six-record track along with a pointer indicating where that track begins. Here our pointers are simply relative record numbers; in practice they could well be a more disk-dependent locator. The strategy to conduct an indexed sequential search is to

1. Search the main memory directory for a key which is greater than or equal to the Target.
2. Then follow the corresponding pointer out to the disk and there search sequentially until we find a match (success) or the key that the directory maintains as the high key within that particular region (failure).

For the data given in Figure 9.13, this technique would mean that the 36-record file would require no more than six main memory index accesses plus six disk accesses, all of which are located in the same track.

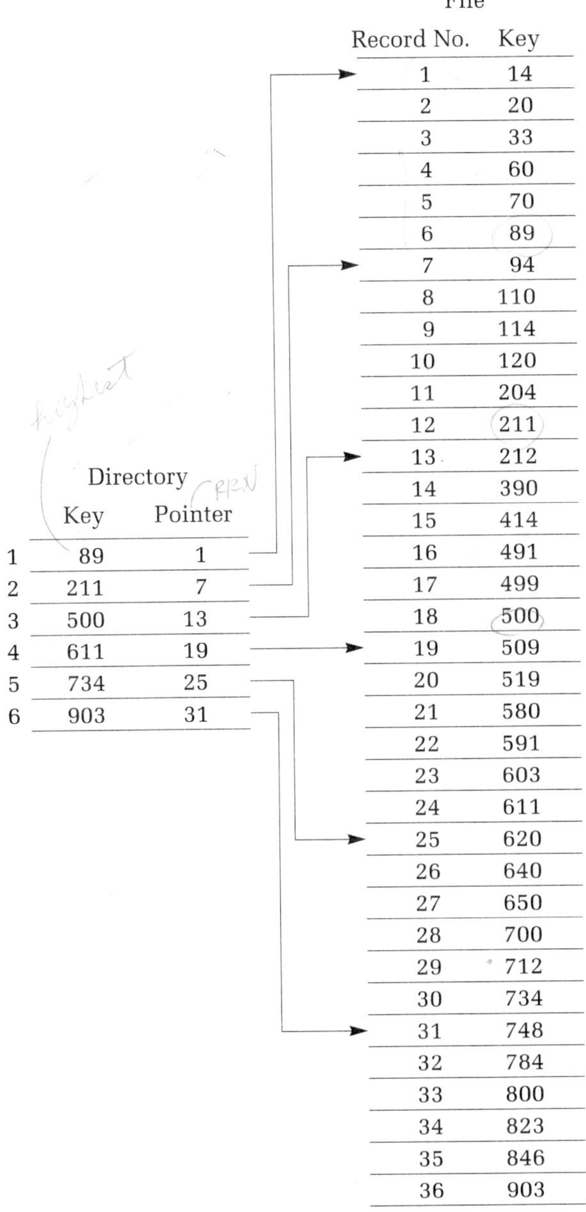

Directory

	Key	Pointer
1	89	1
2	211	7
3	500	13
4	611	19
5	734	25
6	903	31

File

Record No.	Key
1	14
2	20
3	33
4	60
5	70
6	89
7	94
8	110
9	114
10	120
11	204
12	211
13	212
14	390
15	414
16	491
17	499
18	500
19	509
20	519
21	580
22	591
23	603
24	611
25	620
26	640
27	650
28	700
29	712
30	734
31	748
32	784
33	800
34	823
35	846
36	903

FIGURE 9.13
One-level indexed sequential file

For larger files, it may be advantageous to have more than one level of these directory structures. Consider, for instance, the two-level directory structure for a file with 216 records given in Figure 9.14. Here we might suppose that storage restrictions allow the entire primary directory to be kept in main memory, the secondary directory to be brought in from a disk file in blocks of six key-pointer pairs each, and the actual data records to be stored six per track. The primary directory divides the file into regions of 36 records each. The key in the primary directory represents the highest-valued key in a given 36-record region, but the pointer leads us into the subdirectory instead of the actual file. So, we search the primary directory for a key greater than or equal to the target we are seeking. Once this is done, we follow the primary directory pointer into the secondary directory. Beginning at the

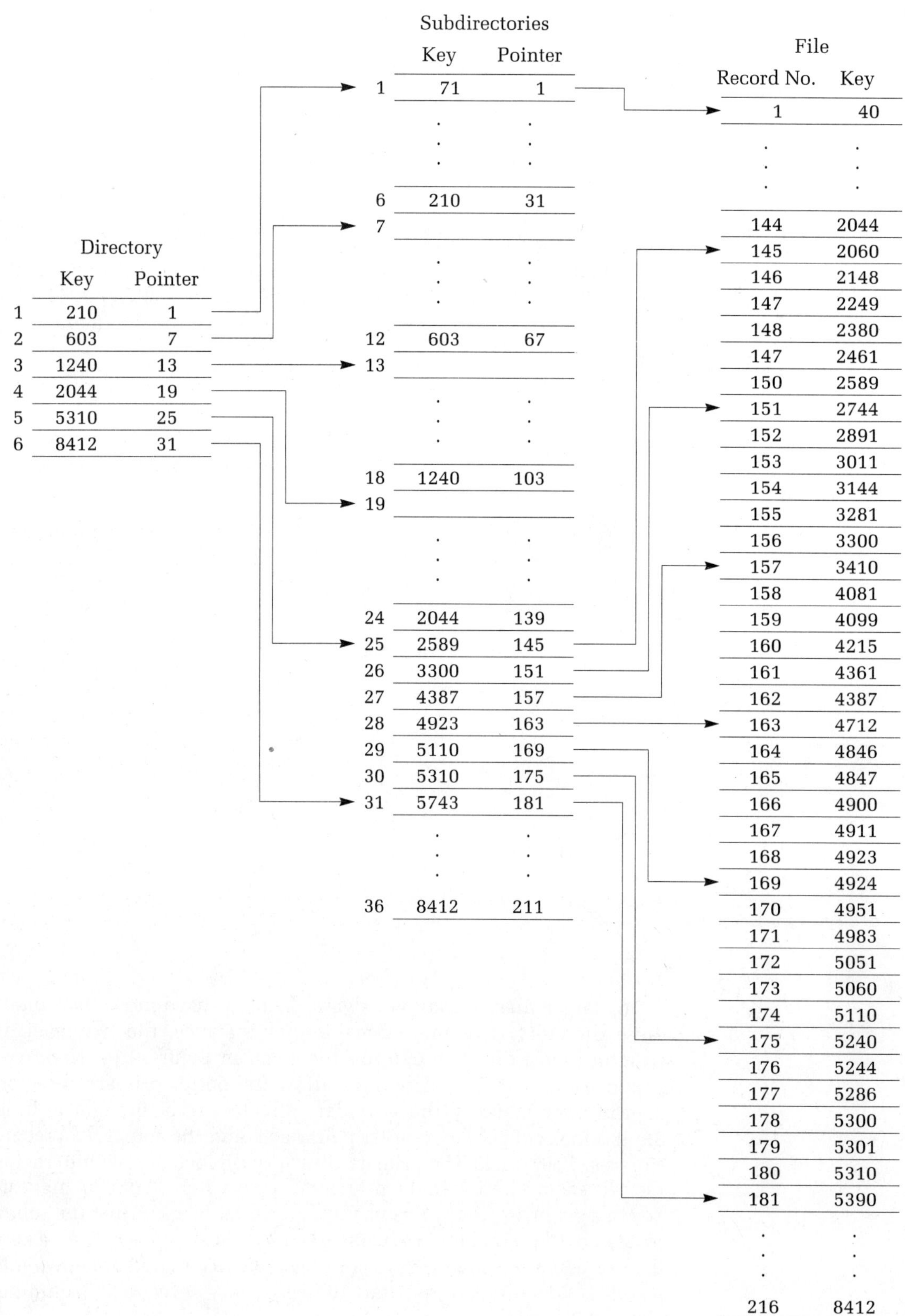

FIGURE 9.14
Two-level directory structure

position indicated by the primary directory's pointer, we again search for a key greater than or equal to the target. Notice that fetching one block of six key-pointer pairs from the subdirectory has necessitated one disk access in our hypothetical situation. In return for this single disk access, we are able to subdivide the 36-record region determined by the primary directory into six 6-record regions, each of which will lie entirely on one track by the time we get out to the actual disk file. Following the subdirectory's pointer to the file, we end up with a relatively short sequential search on the storage medium itself. In this example, the maximum number of disk accesses required to find any record would be seven, and six of those would be isolated on one track of the disk.

Efficiency Considerations for the Indexed Sequential Search. It should be clear from the preceding discussion that the search efficiency of the indexed sequential technique depends on a variety of factors. Included among them are

- To what degree the directory structures are able to subdivide the actual file.
- To what degree the directory structures are able to reside in main memory.
- The relationship of data records to physical characteristics of the disk such as blocking factors, track size, cylinder size, and so on.

It should also be clear that the indexed sequential method may not be ideal for a highly volatile file. This is because, as implicitly indicated in Figures 9.13 and 9.14, the actual data records must be physically stored in increasing (or decreasing) key order. The requirement for physical ordering is obviously not conducive to frequent insertions and deletions. In practice, the solution to this problem is that each file subregion which is ultimately the subject of a sequential search is equipped with a pointer to an overflow area. Insertions are located in this overflow area and linked to the main sequential search area. As the overflow area builds up, the search efficiency tends to deteriorate. In some applications, this deterioration can be so severe that data processing personnel have been known to refer to the ISAM technique as the Intrinsically Slow Access Method.

The way to avoid deterioration is to periodically reorganize the file into a new file with no overflow. However, such reorganization cannot be done dynamically. It requires going through the file in key sequential order and copying it into a new one. Along the way, the indices must be rebuilt, of course. These types of maintenance problems involved with the ISAM structure have led to the development of several more dynamic indexing schemes.

Binary Search Tree Indexing

The concept of a binary search tree has already been covered in Chapter 7. The only twist added when the binary tree plays the role of an index is that each node of the tree contains a key and a pointer to the record associated with that key in some larger data aggregate. The advantages of using a binary search tree as an index structure include:

- A search efficiency potentially proportional to $\log_2 n$.
- The ability to traverse the list indexed by the tree in key order.
- Dynamic insertion and deletion capabilities.

A NOTE OF INTEREST

Data Integrity, Concurrent Updates, and Deadlock

The problems of finding and allowing a user to access a particular record in a file are complicated somewhat in a system that allows several users to access that file simultaneously. To see why this is so, it is important to recall that when you actually manipulate a record or part of an index from a file, you really have a copy of that portion of the file in your main memory area. Now suppose that two users are not only accessing the same file simultaneously but also the same record in that file simultaneously. A scenario such as the following could emerge:

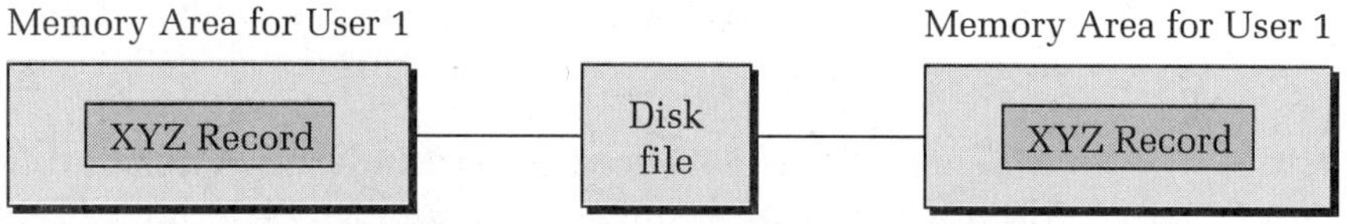

User 1 requests record associated with key XYZ.
User 2 requests record associated with key XYZ.
User 1 updates address field of that record.
User 2 updates inventory field of that record.
User 1 makes change in the file by writing that record to disk.
User 2 makes changes in the file by writing that record to disk.

What will be wrong with the new record that exists in the disk file? Clearly, the address change made by User 1 will have been destroyed when User 2's copy of the record is written back to the disk. We have what is known as a *data integrity* problem caused by the *concurrent updating* of the same record by two users. The situation can become much worse than merely losing an address change. Imagine the havoc created if one of the users deleted the record while the other was processing it or if the portion of the file being simultaneously updated by two users was not a data record but instead part of the file index.

The concurrent update problem must be avoided in any multiuser system if data integrity is to be insured. The solution used in many systems is that of a *record lock facility*. With such a facility, the user who has a file record in main memory for updating is considered the owner of that record to the exclusion of any other users accessing that record. That lock on the record exists until the user writes the (perhaps altered) record back to the disk file. Hence, in our scenario, User 2 would not have been able immediately to obtain the record for key XYZ. Instead, that user would sit idle in a wait state until the record became available.

Although the record-locking approach guarantees data integrity, it is not without its own set of problems. For instance, consider the following scenario:

User 1 requests and gets record for key XYZ.
User 2 requests and gets record for key ABC.
To process record XYZ, User 1 needs data associated with record ABC.
Because record is owned by User 2, User 1 must wait in idle state.
To process record ABC, User 2 needs data associated with record XYZ.
Because record is owned by User 1, User 2 must wait in idle state.

Though data integrity has been maintained, we now have two users in an infinite wait state known as a *deadlock* or, more glamorously, *fatal embrace*. The avoidance and/or detection of deadlock situations in a multiuser environment is a nontrivial problem. If you are interested in exploring it more deeply, see Harvey M. Deitel's *An Introduction to Operating Systems*. 2nd ed. (Reading, Mass.: Addison-Wesley, 1990).

These qualities make the binary search tree the ideal index structure for situations in which the entire tree can fit in main memory. However, if the data collection is so large that the tree index must itself be stored on disk, the efficiency of the structure is less than optimal. This is because each node of the index may lie in a disk block separate from the other nodes and hence require a separate disk access. Using an example of 50,000 keys, a search of a *binary tree index* could require 16 disk accesses. To solve this problem, we would like to cluster those nodes along a given search path into one, or at least relatively few, disk blocks. The *B-tree* index structure is a variation on the tree index which accomplishes this goal.

B-Tree Indexing

We begin this discussion of B-trees by reminding you that one index entry requires nothing more than a key and a pointer. Moreover, we have assumed that both the key and the pointer are integers, and we continue to operate under this assumption during our discussion of B-trees. We emphasize this point here because, in a B-tree, a given tree node will in fact contain many such key-pointer pairs. This is because a given B-tree node will in fact coincide with one disk block. The idea behind a B-tree is that we will somehow group key-pointer pairs which are related in the search algorithm into a few strategic B-tree nodes, that is, disk blocks. At this point, we make a formal definition; later, we'll clarify this definition via some examples.

B-Tree of Order *n*. A B-tree of order n is a structure with the following properties:

1. Every node in the B-tree has sufficient room to store $n - 1$ key-pointer pairs.
2. Additionally, every node has room for n pointers to other nodes in the B-tree (as distinguished from the pointers within key-pointer pairs, which point to the position of a key in the file).
3. Every node except the root must have at least $(n - 1)$ **DIV** 2 key-pointer pairs stored in it.
4. All terminal nodes are on the same level.
5. If a nonterminal node has m key-pointer pairs stored in it, then it must contain $m + 1$ nonnull pointers to other B-tree nodes.
6. For each B-tree node, we require that the key value in key-pointer pair KP_{i-1} be less than the key value in key-pointer pair KP_i, that all key pointer pairs in the node pointed to by P_{i-1} contain keys that are less than the key in KP_i, and that all key-pointer pairs in the node pointed to by P_i contain key values that are greater than the key in KP_i.

According to property 5 of the definition, we can think of a B-tree node as a list

$$P_0, KP_1, P_1, KP_2, P_2, KP_3, \ldots, P_{m-1}, KP_m, P_m$$

where P_i represents the ith pointer to another B-tree node and KP_i represents the ith key-pointer pair. Note that a B-tree node will always contain one more pointer to another B-tree node than it does key-pointer pairs. With this picture in mind, the sixth and final property of our definition makes sense. Figure 9.15 illustrates how this rather involved definition applies to a B-tree node with three key-pointer pairs.

As a further illustration of this definition, a complete B-tree of order 6 serving as an index structure for the 36-record file of Figure 9.13 appears in

FIGURE 9.15
Example of a B-tree node with three key-pointer pairs

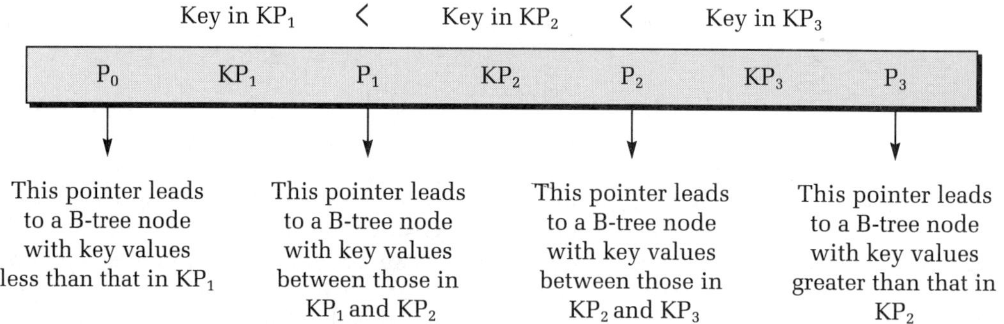

Figure 9.16. (In this figure, the slash between numbers denotes a key-pointer pair; ⊦ denotes a null pointer.) Carefully verify that all six defining properties are satisfied.

The choice of order 6 for Figure 9.16 was made only for the purposes of making the figure fit on a page of text. In practice, the order chosen would be the maximum number of B-tree pointers and key-pointer pairs that we could fit into one disk block. That is, the choice should be made to force a disk block to coincide with a B-tree node. It is also worth noting that B-trees of order 3 have special application as a data structure apart from indexing considerations. This application will be covered in the Programming Problems at the end of the chapter.

Efficiency Considerations for B-Tree Indexing. Let us now consider what is involved in searching a B-tree for a given key. Within the current node (starting at the root), we must search sequentially through the key values in the node until we come to a match, a key value that is greater than the one being sought, or the end of the key values in that particular node. If a match is not made within a particular B-tree node, we have a pointer to follow to an appropriate follow-up node. Again, you should verify this algorithm for several of the keys appearing at various levels of Figure 9.16. The sequential search on keys within a given node may at first seem unappealing. However, the important fact to remember here is that each B-tree node is a disk block which is loaded entirely into main memory. Hence, it may be possible to search sequentially on hundreds of keys within a node in the time it would take to load one new node from disk. Our main concern is to minimize disk accesses, and here we have achieved a worst-case search for our 36-entry file in three disk accesses.

What in general is the search efficiency for a B-tree index? It should be clear from the nature of the structure that the maximum number of disk accesses for any particular key will simply be the number of levels in the tree. So the efficiency question really amounts to knowing the maximum number of levels that the six defining criteria would allow for a B-tree containing n key-pointer pairs. That is, this number would be the worst-case search efficiency. To determine this number, we use the minimum number of nodes that must be present on any given level. Let L be the smallest integer greater than or equal to K/2 where K is the order of the B-tree in question.

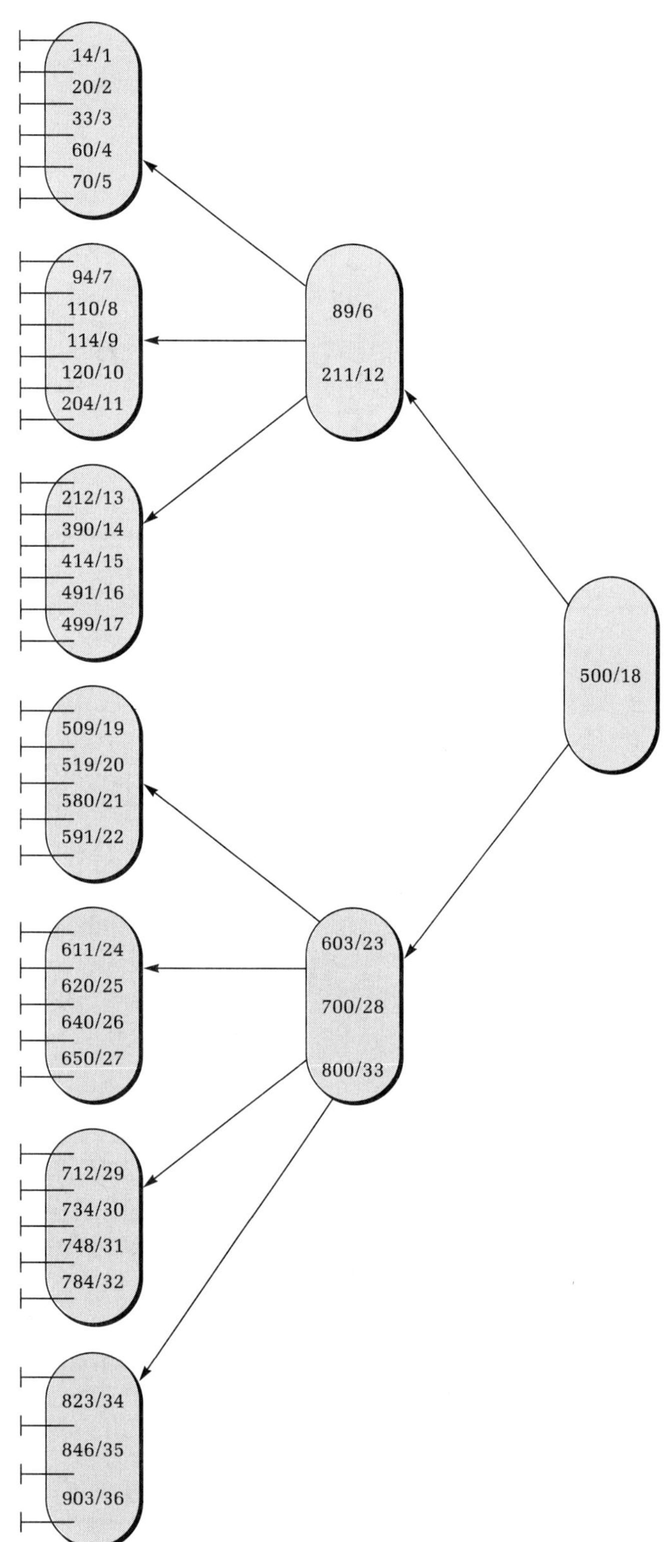

FIGURE 9.16
B-tree index of order 6 for file in Figure 9.13

Then

Level 0 contains at least 1 node.
Level 1 contains at least 2 nodes.
Level 2 contains at least 2L nodes.
Level 3 contains at least $2L^2$ nodes.

. .
. .
. .

Level m contains at least $2L^{m-1}$ nodes.

An argument based on Knuth's research (see *Searching and Sorting,* cited in Section 9.1) uses this progression to show that the maximum number of levels (and thus the worst-case search efficiency) for n key-pointer pairs is

$$\log_K((n + 1)/2)$$

Thus, a B-tree search has an $O(\log_K n)$ efficiency where n is the number of records and K is the order of the B-tree. Note that this can be considerably better than an $O(\log_2 n)$ search efficiency. As an example, the index for a file of 50,000 records which would require on the order of 16 disk accesses using a binary tree structure could be searched with 3 disk accesses using a B-tree of order 250. Note that, given typical block sizes for files, the choice of order 250 for this example is not at all unrealistic.

Unlike ISAM, the B-tree index can dynamically handle insertions and deletions without a resulting deterioration in search efficiency. We next discuss how B-tree insertions are handled; making deletions is left for an exercise. The essential idea behind a B-tree insertion is that we must first determine which bottom-level node should contain the key-pointer pair to be inserted. For instance, suppose that we want to insert the key 742 into the B-tree of Figure 9.16. By allowing this key to walk down the B-tree from the root to the bottom level, we could quickly determine that this key belongs in the node presently containing

712/29
734/30
748/31
784/32

Since, by the definition of a B-tree of order 6, this node is not presently full, no further disk accesses would be necessary to perform the insertion. We would merely need to determine the next available record space in the actual data file (37 in this case) and then add the key-pointer pair 742/37 to this terminal node, resulting in

712/29
734/30
742/37
748/31
784/32

A slightly more difficult situation arises when we find that the key-pointer pair we wish to add should be inserted into a bottom-level node that is already full. For instance, this would occur if we attempted to add the key 112 to the B-tree of Figure 9.16. We would load the actual data for this key into file position 38 (given the addition already made in the preceding paragraph) and then determine that the key-pointer pair 112/38 belongs in the bottom-level node

94/7
110/8
114/9
120/10
204/11

The stipulation that any B-tree node except the root have at least $(n - 1)$ **DIV** $2 = 2$ key-pointer pairs allows us to split this node, creating one new node with two key-pointer pairs and one with three key-pointer pairs. We also have to move one of the key-pointer pairs up to the parent of the present node. The resulting B-tree is given in Figure 9.17.

Although it does not happen in this particular example, note that it would be entirely possible that the moving of a key-pointer pair up to a parent node that is already full would necessitate a split of this parent node, using the same procedure. Indeed it is possible that key-pointer pairs could be passed all the way up to the root and cause a split of the root. This is in fact how a new level of the tree would be introduced. A split of the root would force the creation of a new root which would only have one key-pointer pair and two pointers to other B-tree nodes. However, at the root level this is still a sufficient number of pointers to retain the B-tree structure. Because the insertion algorithm for a B-tree requires checking whether a given node is full and potentially moving back up to a parent node, it is convenient to allow space within a node to store both of the following:

- A count of the number of key-pointer pairs in the node.
- A back pointer to the node's parent.

Trie Indexing

In all of the indexing applications we have discussed so far, the keys involved have been integers. In practice, however, we must be prepared to deal with keys of different types. Perhaps the worst case is that of keys that are variable length character strings. *Trie indexing* has developed as a means of retrieving keys in this worst case. (The term itself is derived from the four middle letters of "retrieve," though it is usually pronounced "try.")

Let us suppose that the strings in the following list represent a set of keys. Each string may be thought of as a last name followed by initials and a delimiting $.

ADAMS BT$
COOPER CC$
COOPER PJ$
COWANS DC$
MAGUIRE WH$
MCGUIRE AL$
MEMINGER DD$
SEFTON SD$
SPAN KD$
SPAN LA$
SPANNER DW$
ZARDA JM$
ZARDA PW$

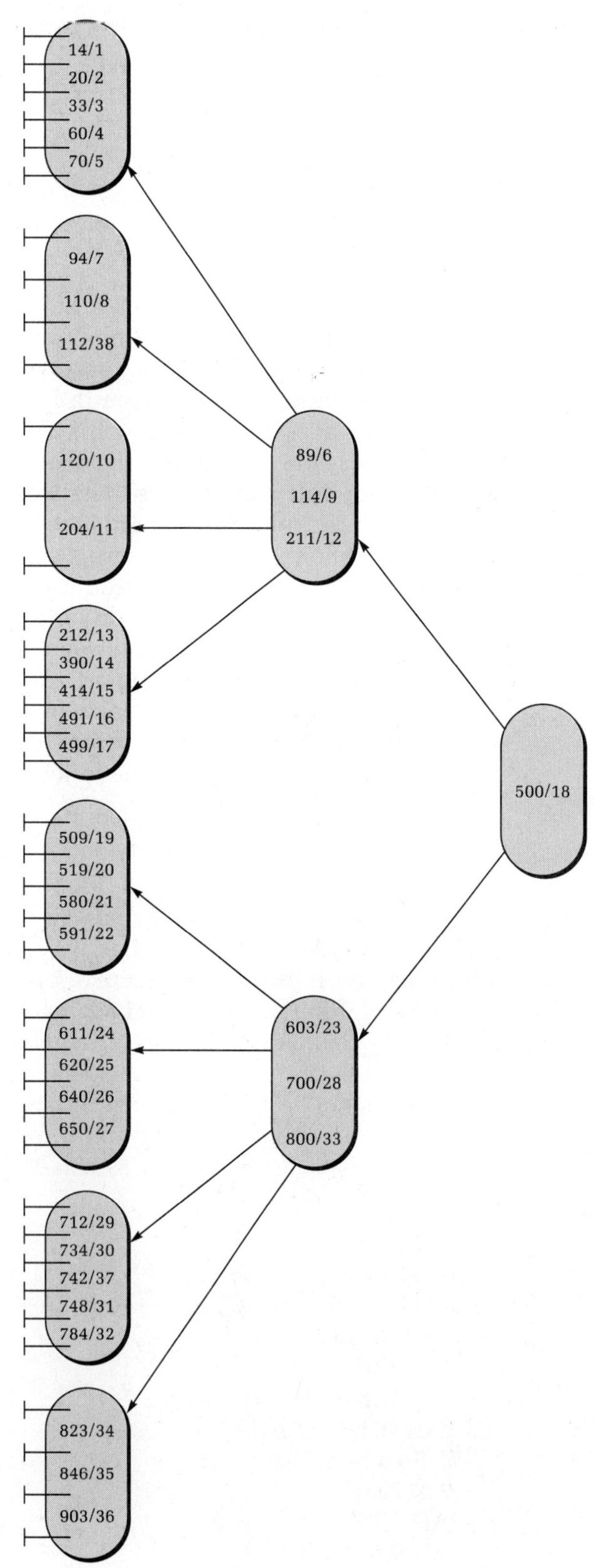

FIGURE 9.17
B-tree of Figure 9.16 after insertion of 112/38 and 742/37

An individual node in a trie structure for these keys follows:

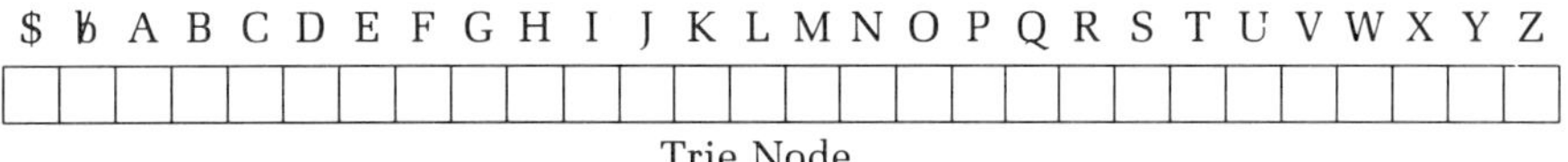

Trie Node

It is essentially a fixed length array of 28 pointers: one for each letter of the alphabet, one for a blank, and one for the delimiter. Each pointer within one of these nodes can lead to one of two entities—either another node within the trie or the actual data record for a given key. Hence it may be convenient to embed a Boolean flag in each pointer indicating the type of entity to which it is pointing. The trie structure for the preceding list of keys is given in Figure 9.18. In this figure, pointers to nodes labeled as data records lead us outside of the trie structure itself.

FIGURE 9.18
Trie index structure

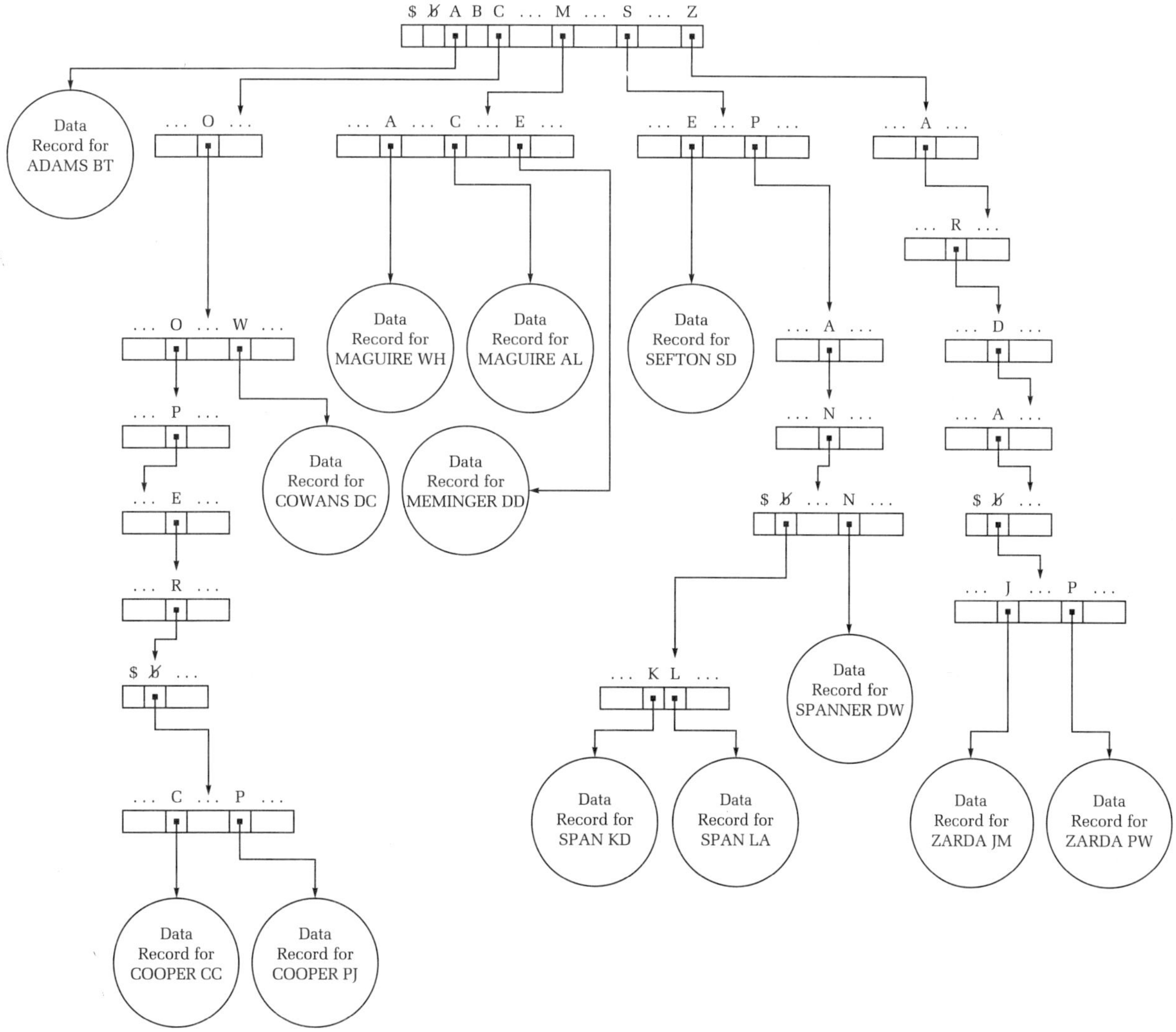

The logic behind a trie structure may best be seen by tracing through an example. This search algorithm involves examining the target key on a character-by-character basis. Let us begin by considering the easy case of finding the data record for ADAMS BT$. In this case, we look at A, the first character in the key, and follow the A pointer in the root node to its destination. From what we have previously said, we know that its destination will be either another node within the trie structure or an actual data record. If it were a node within the trie, it would be a node on the search path for all keys that begin with A. In this case, there is only one key in our list that begins with A, so the A pointer in the root node leads us directly to the actual data record for ADAMS BT$.

On the other hand, the search path to find the key COOPER CC$ in the trie is somewhat longer. We follow the C pointer from the root node down a level to a node shared by all keys starting with C. From there, the O pointer is followed to a trie node shared by all keys that start with CO. The process continues down level by level, following the O pointer to a trie node shared by all keys starting with COO, then the P pointer to a node for all keys starting with COOP, the E pointer to a node for all keys starting with COOPE, the R pointer to a node for all keys starting with COOPER, and the blank pointer to a node shared by all keys starting with COOPER followed by a blank. Notice that, as each character is read in, we must continue following these pointers from trie node to trie node (instead of from trie node to actual data record) until we finally reach a point where the next character to be read will uniquely define the key. At this point, the key in question need no longer share its pointer with other keys that match it on an initial substring. Hence the pointer may now lead to an actual data record. This is what happens in our example when we read in the next C to form the uniquely defined substring COOPER C.

Efficiency Considerations for Trie Indexing. The search efficiency for the trie index is quite easily determined. The worst case occurs when a key is not uniquely defined until its last character is read in. In this case, we may have as many disk accesses as there are characters in the key before we finally locate the actual data record. You may have observed, however, that there is another efficiency consideration to take into account when using the trie method. This is the amount of wasted storage in the trie nodes. In our example using a short list of keys, only a small percentage of the available pointers are ever used. In practice, however, a trie would only be used for an extremely large file, such as the list represented by a phone book with names as keys. In such a situation, a much larger number of character combinations occurs and the resulting trie structure is correspondingly much less sparse.

A final point to consider relative to trie indexes is their ability to dynamically handle insertions and deletions. Here, we discuss insertions; deletions are left as an exercise. Insertions may be broken down into two cases. For both we must begin by reading the key to be inserted, character by character, and following the appropriate search path in the trie until

- We come to a trie node which has a vacant pointer in the character position corresponding to the current character of the insertion key.

or

- We come to an actual data record for a key different from the one which is being inserted.

The first case is illustrated by trying to insert the key COLLINS RT$ into the trie of Figure 9.18. We would follow the search path pointers until we came to the trie node shared by all keys starting with CO. At this point, the L pointer is null. The insertion is completed by merely aiming the presently null L pointer to a data record for the key COLLINS RT$. The second case is illustrated by trying to insert the key COOPER PA$ into the trie of Figure 9.18. Here, following the search path of the trie would eventually lead us to the data record for the key COOPER PJ$. The dynamic solution is to get a new trie node, aim the P pointer presently leading to the data record for COOPER PJ$ to this new trie node, and use the A and J pointers in the new trie node to lead us to data records for COOPER PA$ and COOPER PJ$ respectively. Both the COLLINS RT$ and COOPER PA$ insertions are shown with the resulting trie in Figure 9.19.

FIGURE 9.19
Trie of Figure 9.18 after inserting COLLINS RT$ and COOPER PA$

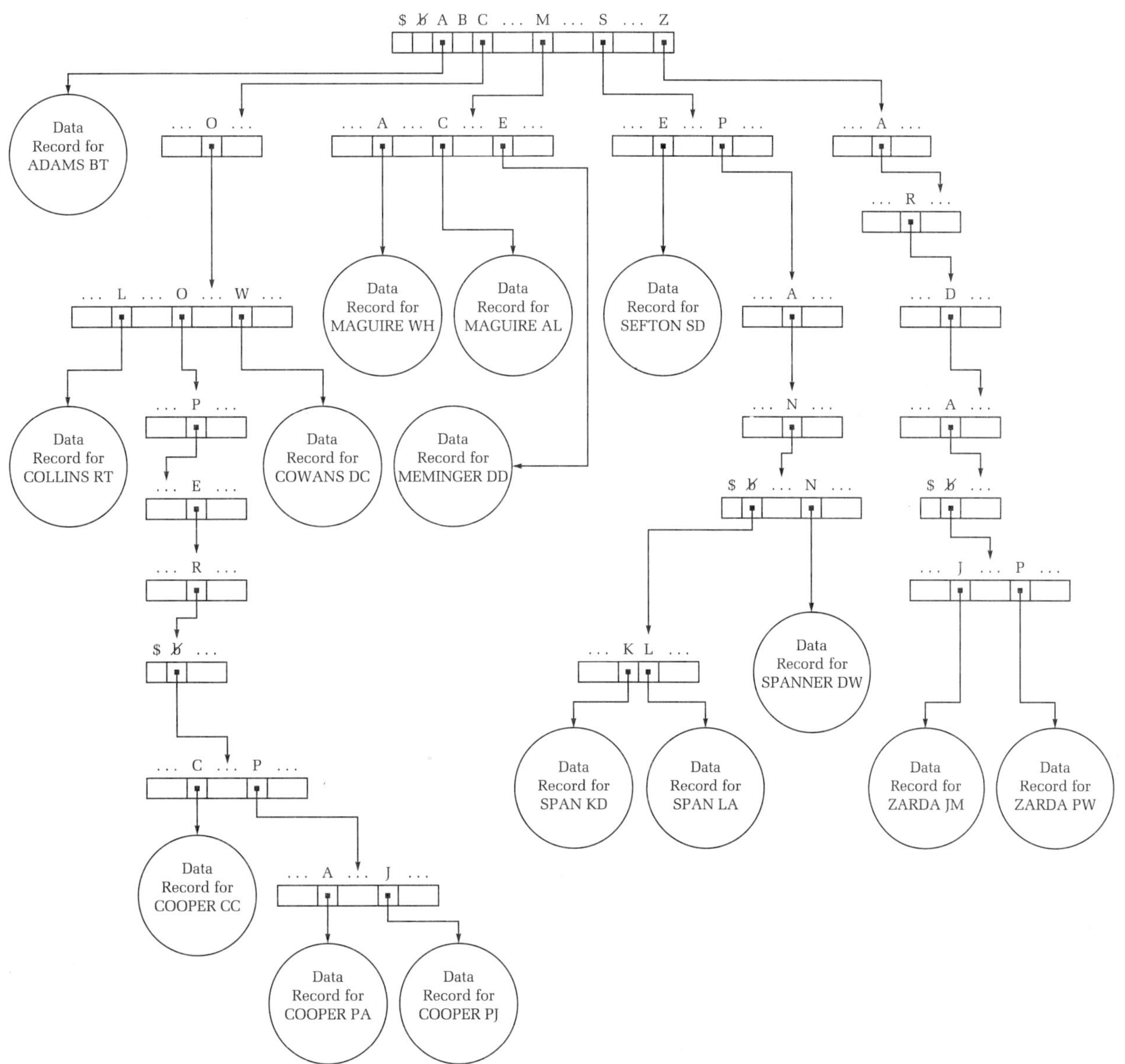

Exercises 9.3

1. a. Suppose that the records associated with keys 810, 430, 602, 946, 289, 106, and 732 are stored in positions 1, 2, 3, 4, 5, 6, and 7 respectively of a file. Draw a B-tree index of order 8 for this file.

   b. Suppose the key 538 then arrives for insertion in position 8. Redraw your B-tree of order 8 after this insertion.

2. Suppose that the following strings arrive for insertion into a trie index.

   CARTER
   HERNANDEZ
   HERMAN
   HERMANSKI
   HERSCHEL
   HALL
   CARSON
   CARSWELL
   CARSEN

   a. Draw the trie index.

   b. Draw the index after CARSWELL and HERMANSKI have been deleted.

3. Discuss the key deletion strategy for B-trees. Write a procedure that implements your strategy.

4. Discuss a key deletion strategy for trie indexes. Write a procedure to implement your strategy.

5. Carefully read your system reference material concerning the specifics of how disk file records are blocked. Then explain how this knowledge would influence your decisions in the construction of

   a. An ISAM index structure.

   b. A B-tree index structure.

   c. A trie index structure.

   d. A bucket hashing structure.

6. All of the search strategies we have discussed assume a key that is uniquely valued. That is, no two records have the same value for their key field. In practice this will not always be the case. We may have duplicate keys. For instance, a list of personnel records may contain two records for different people with the same name. In a carefully worded statement, discuss how each of the search strategies we have covered would have to be modified to perform a duplicate key search. What effect would these modifications have on the performance of the algorithm?

7. Develop a procedure to search a list via ISAM. Initially assume just one directory. Then alter the procedure so that it would work with one subdirectory.

8. Devise procedures to handle insertions into and deletions from a list maintained by the indexed sequential method. Do the strategies reflected by these procedures require any modifications in your answers to Exercise 7? If so, explain the nature of these modifications.

9. Write the algorithm to insert a key into a B-tree.

10. Write an algorithm to insert a key and its data record into a trie.

■ ■ ■ ■

FOCUS ON PROGRAM DESIGN

A theme of the Focus on Program Design section in the two previous chapters has been the development of programs that allow us to experiment with algorithms. Such programs are extremely useful for algorithms whose analysis defy purely mathematical techniques. Certainly the strategy of hashing, presented in Section 9.1, falls into this category of algorithms. The efficiency of hashing is dependent on a variety of factors: the randomness with which your hashing function scatters keys into the record space, the amount of space you are willing to sacrifice to empty storage locations, and the effectiveness of your collision-processing strategy in reducing clustering.

Because of hashing's dependency on these factors, an experimental tool for testing various hashing strategies can be very valuable in predicting how effective hashing will be for a particular application. In this section, we discuss the design of such an experimental program for situations in which we wish to study the effectiveness of hashing on keys that are strings.

As with the previous chapter's Focus on Program Design program, we want to choose between three forms of input for our experimentation:

1. A sequence of randomly generated string keys
2. A sequence of string keys that we enter interactively, so that we can enter specific data sets particularly relevant to our experimentation.
3. A sequence of string keys read one per line from a file

From last chapter's program, we will also borrow the facility to save a particularly interesting data set in a text file form that can later be read by the program. This will allow you to fine-tune the algorithm by altering the hashing function or selecting a different collision-processing method and then testing the new program with the same set of data. An example of such experimental runs with the program follows:

First Run: Hash Table with Record Space for 40, 30 Slots Filled with Random Strings.

```
How large is record space for hash table? 40
Choose method for loading hash table:

         1 - Load table with random strings
         2 - Interactively load the table
         3 - Load the table from a file

Enter 1, 2 or 3 --> 1

Enter number of values in table --> 30
Print the table? (Y/N) --> y
NONEMPTY SLOTS OF THE TABLE:

      ARRAY[ 2] = \TUFqY]Y-tlLcTIxGRnPHUjikDzoxy  {  Note random strings  }
      ARRAY[ ↑] = UVo{texGxxYSbwNMqI\-O7¨≠(??D4E
      1≠≠1?[ ↓] = Qrfh[O46×53S0=DCOTQO×AO4{paxhN
      ARRAY[ ι] = OTSK{onLIBZ^U'VfDwdKrmOhqbSjBx
      ARRAY[ 6] = MID\argowZc-Z[vMF[hZzBxkJiohiD
      ARRAY[ 7] = Pr]Rncs{CXOREpjkyYRtmmFRaXHbWv
      ARRAY[10] = 'kgPl^[lJrmTsSfbw\JBXrVOVDTose
      ARRAY[14] = O'S'[SL^sVJn'Pdw'aJ^votElbqLFZ
      ARRAY[15] = J[lsvd{LwcRvQyiF{SPPKLDyrIIpGl
      ARRAY[16] = LkYsfFhnyvdKPnPe'Niiup{xXHMxGj
      ARRAY[18] = pKiWMJzLLNfho-jYGcPxJzVsDRDiqE
      ARRAY[19] = YC's^ZPOXZEnHe{BnbI'Xp'uEvOgr\
      ARRAY[20] = bT{bZGcKmhwGfdFxH]IOPrIbHQJ]oS
      ARRAY[21] = NILYPSQnhr-H'u{CuDnErrunYr[kif
      ARRAY[22] = \]kmBdbnLhSQBN{ncqjtwe\II\WFPe
      ARRAY[23] = fByLV{fqOhOLSfotfZYZReHYTn{Wp\
      ARRAY[24] = ^NSsPsYp\{kSKOUw[ISOWOjnzHbIVU
```

```
        ARRAY[25] = eLWslIC'ZLPsUwHXgvhk\jzWpsHwlx
        ARRAY[26] = IxV'GzjKFeq[IXptTukEjhdbuQ-wSQ
        ARRAY[27] = HPyGpLkGZINJEh-pnVghemjPgZlJxx
        ARRAY[28] = XPDHfZTwyCzk\fGCMokZNEv]dCllXN
        ARRAY[29] = GvpO^bWgPubRY]\jEsI[OddGCRzM^]
        ARRAY[30] = EZzxgV'ih'nLJ-nCLsdnqISzHvyMJl
        ARRAY[31] = qwbs{HblUTCIwEzfox-nB^iHfRbPmu
        ARRAY[32] = KWQcS[WdJSyZl]FeJbpl\HMVjiTCzs
        ARRAY[35] = RUhjdEgb{x]d''NWPXx\OGjZaMcpOP
        ARRAY[36] = ysb[z-gCgghfDskqOiqKRiFOPZ'bM^
        ARRAY[37] = PngO'I\efYtwfJykbvnc-PWE'mqkiz
        ARRAY[38] = KB]Uiq]kLxmylwUdXUTLMmlSOkh-cq
        ARRAY[39] = iJtgsTbicsFueT]{uRqZdRKZGwdc\m

Average length for successful search    2.13
Average length for unsuccessful search    4.87

Save the input values for this table? (Y/N)--> y
Name for save file --> test.dat
Another table? (Y/N) --> n
```

Second Run: Now Adjust Hashing Function and/or Collision Processing, and Run Again.

```
How large is record space for hash table? 40
Choose method for loading hash table:

          1 - Load table with random strings
          2 - Interactively load the table
          3 - Load the table from a file

Enter 1, 2 or 3 --> 3

Enter the name of the file --> test.dat
Print the table? (Y/N) --> n
Average length for successful search 1.92
Average length for unsuccessful search 4.76

Save the input values for this table? (Y/N) --> n
Another table? (Y/N) --> n
```

Note the slight improvement in efficiency for the second run.

A modular structure chart for **PROGRAM** HashingExperimentation appears in Figure 9.20. Notice from the modular structure chart that a package of queue modules is used in the program. As a sequence of string keys is loaded into the hash table by the program, the keys are also placed on the queue. Then, after the hash table has been loaded, these keys are removed from the queue. As each key is removed from the queue, we search the hash table for it, accumulating a profiling counter as the search for the key is performed. The key is then returned to the tail of the queue. If the user chooses to save the sequence of string keys to a text file, we merely proceed through the queue, writing each key to the file as it is removed from the queue.

To accumulate the statistics for the average unsuccessful search, the program generates a fixed number of additional random keys—assuming that the probability of any such key matching one already in the table is virtually zero. The program is exercised by sending each of these randomly generated keys through the search algorithm. A profiling accumulator for unsuccessful searches is maintained as these keys are processed.

FIGURE 9.20
Modular structure chart for **PROGRAM** HashingExperimentation

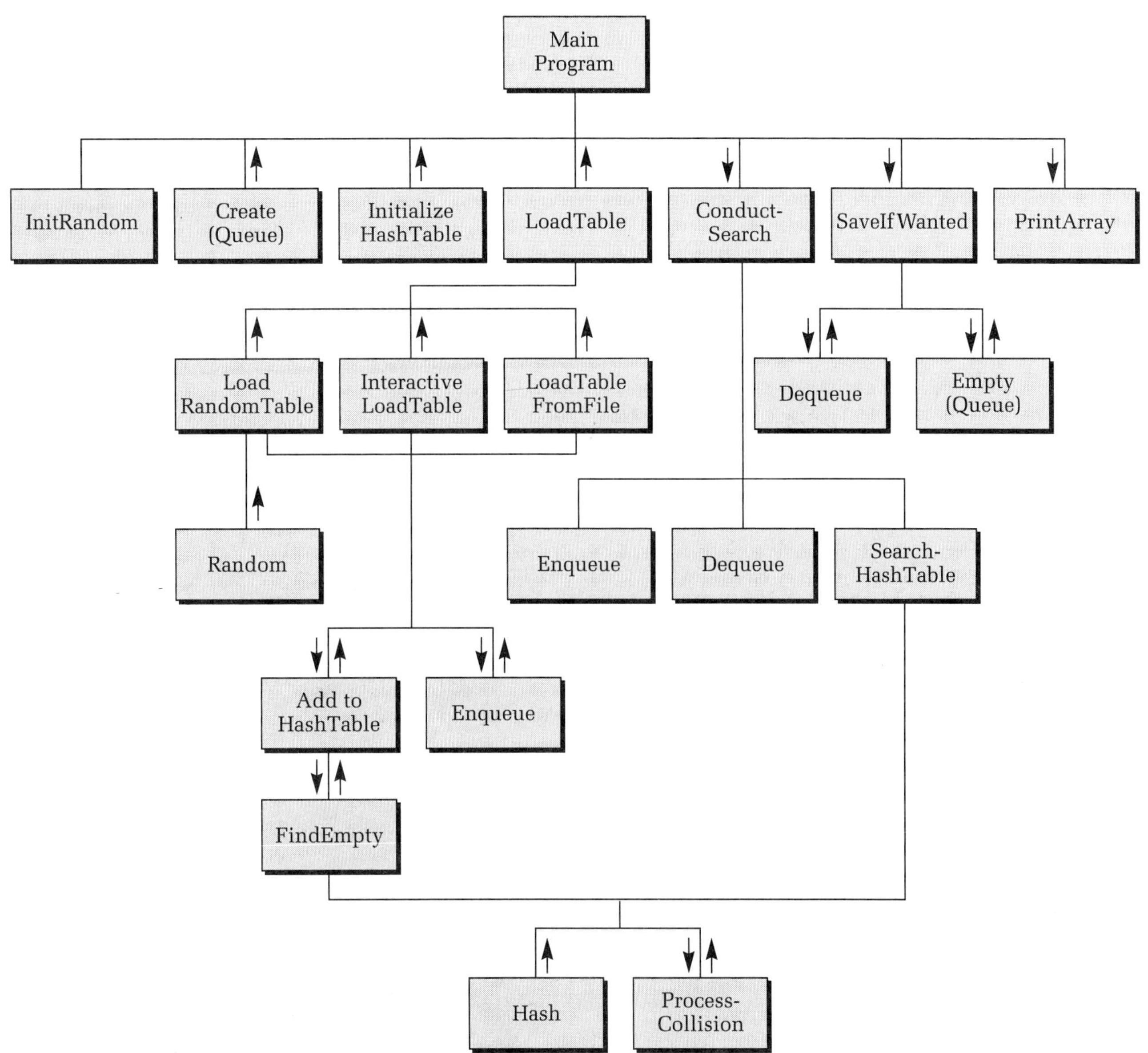

A first-level pseudocode development for the main program is given by:

1. Intialize the random number generator (See Appendix 9)
2. Create the queue used to store a copy of keys in order of generation
3. Initialize the value used to flag an empty slot
4. **REPEAT**
   4.1 Initialize hash table to all empty slots
   4.2 Load the table of a specified logical record space with number of keys specified by user, also returning a queue containing the sequence of keys generated

4.3 If tho user wants, print the hash table
4.4 Conduct searches: accumulate and print profiling counters for successful and unsuccessful searches
4.5 Save the sequence of keys from queue to a file if the user wants
4.6 Inquire if the user wants to load another table
UNTIL user indicates no more tables to load

Refinement of this pseudocode into Pascal yields the following main program:

```
PROGRAM HashingExperimentation(input, output, F);

  {  This program allows users to experiment with hashing on        }
  {  an array implementation of a list of strings.  A hashing       }
  {  function is provided, but users are encouraged to              }
  {  try their own hashing functions.  The current implementation   }
  {  makes use of the linear collision processing strategy, but     }
  {  is written in such a way that other strategies can be          }
  {  substituted easily.                                            }
  {                                                                 }
  {  The program is designed to create the list of strings          }
  {  in one of three ways:  allow a user to interactively           }
  {  specify the contents of the list, generate a random list,      }
  {  or read a previously-saved list in from a file.  The           }
  {  program will also save the contents of the list for later      }
  {  reuse if desired.                                              }
  {                                                                 }
  {  The data file created by the program when a table is saved is  }
  {  simply a text file with one element of the table per line of   }
  {  the file.  Similarly, the program expects any file from which  }
  {  it is to read a table to have this format.  Internally, the    }
  {  program uses a queue to store the incoming table elements      }
  {  in the order they arrive so that they can be saved to the      }
  {  file in that same order.                                       }

  CONST { HashingExperimentation }
    NameSize = 30;               { Maximum size of name string      }
    MaxHashTableSize = 2000;  { Maximum size of the hash table      }

  TYPE { HashingExperimentation }
    NameString = PACKED ARRAY [1..NameSize] OF char;
    InfoType = NameString;
    HashTable = ARRAY [1..MaxHashTableSize] OF NameString;
    Queue = { Appropriate implementation of this ADT }
    .
    .
    .

  VAR { HashingExperimentation }
    Table: HashTable;            { Hash table                         }
    Query: char;                 { User's response                    }
    F: text;                     { File variable                      }
    ChoiceOfLoad: integer;       { User's choice for loading table    }
    EmptySlot: NameString;       { String for empty hash table entry  }
    AveSearchLength: real;       { Statistics for search efficiency   }
    HashTableSize : integer;  { Logical size of hash table            }
    Copy : Queue;                { Copy of keys which are generated   }
  .
  .
  { You will fill procedures as part of programming problem          }
  .
  .
```

```
{**************************************************************}
{                The Main Program                              }

BEGIN { Main program }
  InitRandom;
  CreateQueue(Copy);
  InitString(EmptySlot);
  REPEAT
    InitializeHashTable(Table, EmptySlot);
    LoadTable(Table, ChoiceOfLoad, Copy);
    write('Print the table? (Y/N) --> ');
    readln(Query);
    IF (Query = 'Y') OR (Query = 'y') THEN
      PrintArray(Table, 1, HashTableSize);
    ConductSearch(Table);
    SaveIfWanted(Copy, ChoiceOfLoad);
    write('Another table? (Y/N) --> ');
    readln(Query)
  UNTIL (Query = 'N') OR (Query = 'n')
END. { of main program }
```

Specifications for individual modules in the program follow. You will implement these specifications in the Programming Problems, thereby providing yourself with a means of exploring the effectiveness of a variety of hashing functions and collision processing methods.

1. InitRandom Module
   Data received: None
   Information returned: None
   Logic: Initialize the random number generator as described in Appendix 9. This may be unnecessary if your version of Pascal provides a random number generator.
2. Create, Enqueue, Dequeue, Empty Modules
   Standard modules for performing operations on a queue.
3. InitializeHashTable Module
   Data received: Hash table in arbitrary state.
   Information returned: Hash table with all slots initialized to emtpy indicator.
   Logic: For each index in table, assign empty slot flag.
4. LoadTable Module
   Data received: Table, an empty hash table, and Copy, an empty queue.
   Information returned: An integer indicating the user's choice for loading the hash table: 1 for randomly generated strings, 2 for interactively loaded strings, 3 for strings read from file. Table is returned loaded with strings generated by chosen method. Copy contains sequence of strings generated by chosen method.
   Logic: Determine logical size of record space in table and choice for loading. Dispatch to LoadRandomTable, InteractiveLoadTable, or LoadTableFromFile respectively.

5 LoadRandomTable Module
   Data received: None
   Information returned: Hash table loaded with randomly generated strings and a queue Copy which contains each of the strings in the order of their generation.

Logic: 1. Inquire as to number of strings to generate.
2. For each string,
2.1 Fill it with randomly generated characters.
2.2 Call on AddToHashTable to load string into Table.
2.3 Call on Enqueue operation to add string to Copy queue.

6. Random Module
Data received: None
Information returned: Randomly generated value.
Logic: Use algorithm of Appendix 9 or random number generator provided with your version of Pascal.

7. InteractiveLoadTable Module
Data received: None
Information returned: Hash table loaded with strings entered interactively by user and a queue Copy which contains each of the strings in the order they were entered.
Logic: 1. Inquire as to number of strings that will be entered.
2. For each string,
2.1 Allow user to enter it interactively.
2.2 Call on AddToHashTable to load string into Table.
2.3 Call on Enqueue operation to add string to Copy queue.

8. LoadTableFromFile Module
Data received: None.
Information returned: Hash table loaded with strings read from file and a queue Copy which contains each of the strings in the order they were read.
Logic: 1. Inquire as to name of file to load.
2. **WHILE NOT eof**
2.1 Read string from file.
2.2 Call on AddToHashTable to load string into Table.
2.3 Call on Enqueue operation to add string to Copy queue.

9. AddtoHashTable Module
Data received: Hash table.
NewItem to be inserted in hash table.
Information returned: Table with NewItem added.
Logic: 1. Call on FindEmpty module to obtain index position for NewItem.
2. **IF** FindEmpty reports that Table is full or NewItem already in Table **THEN**
2.1 Print error message.
ELSE
2.2 Store NewItem at index position.

10. FindEmpty Module
Data received: Hash table.
Target value for which empty Index position in Table is needed.
Information returned: Boolean Found set to **true** if such an index position could be found. Boolean Exists set to **true** if Target already in Table.
Index: the position for Target when Found returned as **true**.

Logic: 1. Call on Hash function for initial placement of target.
2. **WHILE** (Target does not already exist in Table)
AND (Empty slot not found)
AND (All possible slots have not been checked)
2.1 Call on ProcessCollision module to obtain next index position.

11. Hash Module
Data received: A string key.
Information returned: Hashed index position for key.
Logic: Many possibilities exist; these are left for your experimentation in the Problems.

12. ProcessCollision Module
Data received: Previous index position visited.
Information returned: Next index position to check.
Logic: Determined by collision processing technique; left for your experimentation in the Problems.

13. ConductSearch Module
Data received: Hash table.
Copy queue containing string keys in order generated by LoadTable module.
Information returned: None.
Logic: Perform empirical testing on hashing method for this particular data.
1. For each queue in Copy queue.
1.1 Dequeue that key.
1.2 Call on SearchHashTable to find that key, accumulating a profiling count of number of probes into table that are required to find the key.
1.3 Enqueue that key back into Copy queue.
2. Report on average length for successful searches conducted in step 1.
3. For a fixed number of unsuccessful searches
3.1 Randomly generate a key not in Table.
3.2 Call on SearchHashTable to attempt to find that key, accumulating a profiling count of the number of probes into table that are required to determine that the key cannot be located.
4. Report profiling information for unsucessful searches.

14. SearchHashTable Module
Data received: Hash table.
Target to be found in Table.
Information returned: Index position of Target in Table if Found set to **true**.
Found set to **false** if Target not in Table.
Logic: 1. Call on Hash function for initial position of Target.
2. Increment profiling counter of number of table probes.
3. **WHILE** (EmptySlot not encountered)
AND (Target not found)
AND (All possible positions not checked)
3.1 Call on ProcessCollision to determine next index to check.
3.2 Increment profiling counter of number of table probes.

15. SaveIfWanted Module
    Data received: Copy queue containing keys in order originally generated.
    Information returned: None.
    Logic: Inquire if user wants to save this data set for further exploration.
    IF user wants to save and data set was not originally loaded from file **THEN**
    write Copy queue to file in form compatible with Load TableFrom File module.

16. PrintArray Module
    Data received: Hash table.
    Low and High: indices of table between which nonempty table positions are to be printed.
    Information returned: None.
    Logic: Iterate through Table from Low to High, printing nonempty slots.

RUNNING AND DEBUGGING TIPS

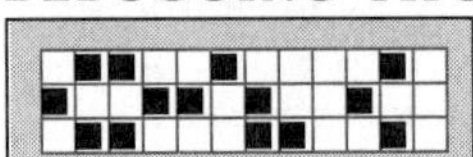

1. When using hashing as a search stratgey, provide yourself with a means of experimenting with your hashing function and collision-processing strategy. This will allow you to tailor your program to the particular kind of keys that are stored in the hash table.
2. Searching for data in a random access file involves different criteria than searching for data in main memory. Programs that search for data in random access files should minimize file accesses at the expense of main memory accesses. Indexed searches provide ways of doing this.
3. If a search program has to handle duplicate keys, that is, different records associated with the same key value, the search algorithm will have to be adjusted appropriately. Be sure you know and decide in advance whether this added complexity is necessary.

■ Summary

Key Terms

boundary folding
buckets
clustering
collision
density-dependent search techniques
digit/character extraction
division-remainder technique
folding
hashing
hashing function
index
key-to-address transformation
linear collision processing
linked collision processing
overflow area
prime hash area
quadratic collision processing
randomized storage
rehashing
rehashing collision processing
sectors
shift folding
synonyms
tracks

Key Terms (Optional)

binary tree index
B-tree
concurrent updating
data integrity
deadlock
fatal embrace
Indexed Sequential Access Method (ISAM)
indexed sequential search
record lock facility
trie indexing

Key Concepts

- The following table gives a concise synopsis of the search strategies that have been discussed in this and earlier chapters. Additional comments emphasize particular strengths or weaknesses of the strategy in terms of the keyed list operations we have considered throughout the text.

Method	Efficiency (n = Number of Records)	Other Components Regarding Keyed List Operations
Binary	$O(\log_2 n)$	Data must be maintained in physical order, hence making insertions and deletions inefficient.
Binary tree index	$O(\log_2 n)$ index probes, 1 file probe	Guaranteeing this efficiency requires height balancing.
B-tree index order K	Worst case requires $1 + \log_K((n + 1)/2)$ disk accesses for index	Choose K so that index node coincides with disk block.
Indexed sequential	O(size of index) index probes, O(n/(size of index)) file probes	Index and file require physical ordering to maintain efficiency.
Linear hashing	Average successful: $(1/2) * (1 + 1/(1 - D))$ Average unsuccessful: $(1/2) * (1 + 1/(1 - D)^2)$ where density $D = n/\text{RecordSpace}$	Data not maintained in any order.
Linked hashing	Average successful: $1 + D/2$ Average unsuccessful: D (where RecordSpace used in computation of D is that in primary hash area)	Data not maintained in any order.
Quadratic hashing	Average successful: $1 - \log_e(1 - D) - (D/2)$ Average unsuccessful: $1/(1 - D) - D - \log_e(1 - D)$	Data not maintained in any order.
Rehashing	Average successful: $-(1/D) * \log_e(1 - D)$ Average unsuccessful: $1/(1 - D)$	Data not maintained in any order.
Sequential	$O(n)$	
Trie index	O(number of characters in Target)	Specifically suited for character strings.

- In addition to hashing, other search strategies specifically oriented toward file structures include indexed sequential search, B-trees, and tries.
- As an implementation strategy for keyed lists, hashing fares very well in all of the operations except ordering. It thus represents a very viable addition to the list implementation strategies discussed in earlier chapters: array or random files with binary search, linked lists, and binary trees.

Programming Problems and Projects

1. Complete the program designed in this chapter's Focus on Program Design section. Then use the program as a means of conducting experiments on hashing. In your experiments, you should try a variety of hashing functions and collision-processing strategies. You might also try to adjust the generation of random strings so that, although

still random, the strings conform to rules for particular kinds of data. That is, if the data consist of names of the form

COOPER, J. C.

the random generation of characters could be modified based on the probabilities of certain letters being used and on the average length of last names.

Write up a report in which you analyze each of the hashing functions and collision-processing strategies you use. Back up your analysis with empirical profiling data obtained from the ConductSearches module of your program.

2. Implement the registrar's system described in Example 2.1 using hashing as a list maintenance technique. Be sure that you devise an appropriate strategy to output the ordered listings that the registrar must have.

3. Implement the Wing-and-a-Prayer flight/pilot data base (Section 2.3) using the implementation technique described in Section 9.2. For an added challenge, assume that the rows of the flight/pilot table are indexed by pilot name instead of pilot number. How could this complication be handled in a way which minimizes the memory needed to store the implementation of a sparse table?

4. A B-tree of order 3 is often called a 2-3 tree since each node has 2 or 3 children. Because of its low order, a 2-3 tree is not particularly applicable as a file index. However, if we store up to two actual data records in each node instead of up to two key-pointer pairs, then a 2-3 tree becomes an alternative to an ordered binary tree for implementing a list. Develop search, insertion, and deletion algorithms for such a 2-3 tree structure. Compare its performance characteristics with those of an ordered binary tree.

5. Implement the registrar's system of Problem 2 using a 2-3 tree representation of a list. (See Programming Problem 4.)

6. Wing-and-a-Prayer Airlines has the records of all its customers stored in the following form:

   - Last name.
   - First name.
   - Address.
   - Arbitrarily long list of flights on which reservations have been booked.

   Using a trie index, write a search-and-retrieval program that will allow input of a customer's last name (and, if necessary, the first name and address to resolve conflicts created by matching last names) and then output all flights on which that customer has booked reservations.

7. SuperScout Inc. is a nationwide scouting service for college football talent to which the Bay Area Brawlers professional team subscribes. As the pool of college talent increases in size, SuperScout has found that its old recordkeeping system has deteriorated considerably in its ability to quickly locate the scouting record associated with a given player in its file. Rewrite their scouting record system using a trie to

look up the record location of the data associated with a given player's name.

8. Using a large collection of randomly generated keys, write a series of programs that will test various hashing functions you develop. In particular, your programs should report statistics on the number of collisions generated by each hashing function. This information could be valuable in guiding future decisions about which hashing functions and techniques are most effective for your particular system.

9. Consider a student data record which consists of

   - Student identification number.
   - Student name.
   - State of residence.
   - Sex.

   Choose an index structure to process a file of such records. Then write a program to maintain such a file as a keyed list.

10. Suppose that data records for a phone book file consist of a key field containing both name and address, and a field containing the phone number for that key. Devise an appropriate index for such a file. Then write a program which calls for input of
    a. A complete key.
    b. If a complete key is not available, as much of the initial portion of a key as the inquirer is able to provide.

    In the case of situation **a**, your program should output the phone number corresponding to the unique key. In the case of situation **b**, have your program output all keys (and their phone numbers) that match the provided initial portion.

11. Consider the following problem faced in the development of a compiler. The source program contains many character-string symbols such as variable names, procedure names, and so on. Each of these character-string symbols has associated with it various attributes such as memory location, data type, and so on. However, it would be too time-consuming and awkward for a compiler to actually manipulate character strings. Instead, each string should be identified with an integer which is viewed as an equivalent to the string for the purpose of compiler manipulation. In addition to serving as a compact equivalent form of a string symbol within the source program, this integer can also serve as a direct pointer into a table of attributes for that symbol. Devise such a transformation that associates a string with an integer, and which in turn serves as a pointer into a table of attributes. Test the structure(s) you develop by using them in a program that scans a source program written in a language such as Pascal. You will in effect have written the symbol table modules for a compiler.

12. Write a spelling checker program. Such a program must scan a file of text, looking up each word it finds in a dictionary of correctly spelled words. When a word cannot be found in the dictionary, the spelling checker should convey this fact to its user, giving the user the opportunity to take one of the following steps:
    a. Skip the word.
    b. Change the spelling of the word in the text file.

c. Add the word to the dictionary so it will not be reported as incorrectly spelled in the future.

Since the dictionary for such a program will be searched frequently and is likely to become quite large, an efficient search algorithm is an absolute necessity. One possibility in this regard is to use a trie index with pointers into a large string workspace instead of the pointers to data records described in Section 9.3. Test your program with a text file and dictionary large enough to handle all of the possibilities your algorithm and data structure may encounter.

13. If you solved one of the problems from Chapter 2 that involved maintaining a keyed list, redo that problem using hashing combined with linked lists as an implementation technique. When finished, write a report in which you empirically compare the performance of your two implementations.

14. If you solved one of the problems from Chapter 2 that involved maintaining a sparse matrix, redo that problem using hashing of row and column indices as an implementation technique. When finished, write a report in which you empirically compare the performance of your two implementations.

Appendixes

Appendix 1 Reserved Words

The following words have predefined meanings in standard Pascal and cannot be changed. Each of these, except **GOTO** and **LABEL,** have been developed in the text. These statements are discussed in Appendix 7.

AND	**END**	**MOD**	**REPEAT**
ARRAY	**FILE**	**NIL**	**SET**
BEGIN	**FOR**	**NOT**	**THEN**
CASE	**FORWARD**	**OF**	**TO**
CONST	**FUNCTION**	**OR**	**TYPE**
DIV	**GOTO**	**PACKED**	**UNTIL**
DO	**IF**	**PROCEDURE**	**VAR**
DOWNTO	**IN**	**PROGRAM**	**WHILE**
ELSE	**LABEL**	**RECORD**	**WITH**

Appendix 2 Standard Identifiers

The standard identifiers for constants, types, files, functions, and procedures are set forth in this appendix. All have predefined meanings that could (but probably should not) be changed in a program. Summary descriptions are given for the functions and procedures.

Constants	*Types*	*Files*
false	**boolean**	**input**
maxint	**char**	**output**
true	**integer**	
	real	
	text	

Functions

Function	Parameter Type	Result Type	Value Returned
abs(*x*)	**integer**	**integer**	Absolute value of *x*
	real	**real**	
arctan(*x*)	**integer**	**real**	Arctangent of *x*
	real		(radians)
chr(*a*)	**integer**	**char**	Character with ordinal *a*
cos(*x*)	**integer**	**real**	Cosine of *x* (radians)
	real		
eof(F)	**file**	**boolean**	End-of-file test for F
eoln(F)	**file**	**boolean**	End-of-line test for F
exp(*x*)	**integer**	**real**	e^x
	real	**real**	
ln(*x*)	**integer** (positive)	**real**	Natural logarithm of *x*
	real (positive)		
odd(*a*)	**integer**	**boolean**	Tests for *a* an odd integer
ord(*x*)	nonreal scalar	**integer**	Ordinal number of *x*
pred(*x*)	nonreal scalar	same as *x*	Predecessor of *x*

Functions (continued)

Function	Parameter Type	Result Type	Value Returned
round(x)	**real**	**integer**	Rounds off x
sin(x)	**integer** **real**	**real**	Sine of x
sqr(x)	**integer** **real**	**integer** **real**	Square of x
sqrt(x)	**integer** **real**	**real**	Square root of x
succ(x)	nonreal scalar	same as x	Successor of x
trunc(x)	**real**	**integer**	Truncated value of x

Procedures

Procedure Call	Purpose of Procedure
dispose (Ptr)	Returns variable referenced by Ptr to available space list
get (F)	Advances the file pointer for the file F and assigns the new value to F^
new (Ptr)	Creates a variable of the type referenced by Ptr and stores a pointer to the new variable in Ptr
pack (U, J, P)	Copies unpacked array elements from U into the packed array P; copying starts with P[1] := U[J]
page (F)	Starts printing the next line of text F at the top of a new page
put (F)	Appends the current value of F to the file F
read (F, ⟨variable list⟩)	Reads values from file F into indicated variables; if F is not specified, **input** is assumed
readln (F, ⟨variable list⟩)	Executes the same as **read** and then advances the file pointer to the first position following the next end-of-line marker
reset (F)	Resets the pointer in file F to the beginning for the purpose of reading from F
rewrite (F)	Resets the pointer in file F to the beginning for the purpose of writing to F
unpack (P, U, J)	Copies packed array elements from P into the unpacked array U; copying starts with U[J] := P[1]
write (F, ⟨parameter list⟩)	Write values specified by parameter list to the text file F; if F is not specified, **output** is assumed
writeln (F, ⟨parameter list⟩)	Executes the same as **write** and then places an end-of-line marker in F

Appendix 3 Syntax Diagrams

Syntax diagrams in this appendix are listed in the following order:

```
Program
     Identifier
     File List
Declarations and Definitions
     Label Declaration
     Constant Definition
     Type Definition
          Type
               Enumerated Type
               Subrange Type
               Pointer Type
               Array Type
               Record Type
                    Field List
                         Fixed Part
                         Variant Part
                              Variant Description
               File Type
               Set Type
     Variable Declaration
     Procedure and Function Declarations
        Formal Parameter List
Body
     Compound Statement
          Statement
               Assignment Statement
                    Expression
                         Term
                              Factor
                                   Variable
                                   Set Value
                    Boolean Expression
               read or readln Statement
               write or writeln Statement
```

```
Procedure Statement
IF Statement
CASE Statement
     Case Label
WHILE Statement
REPEAT Statement
FOR Statement
WITH Statement
GOTO Statement
Empty Statement
```

Program

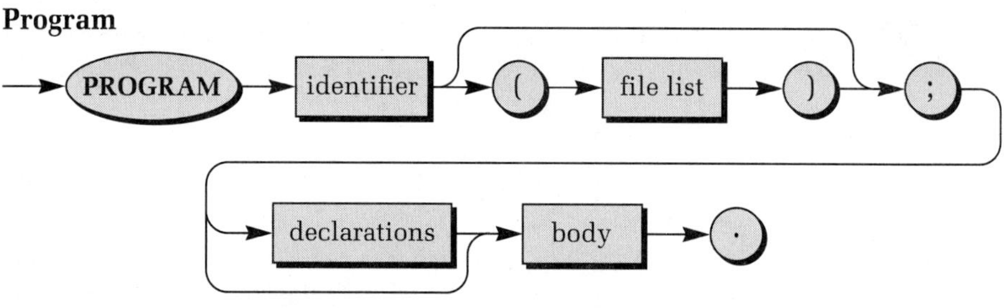

Identifier

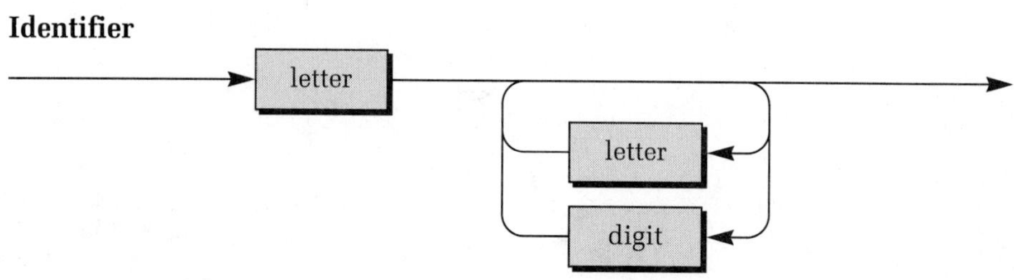

File List

identifier

,

Declarations and Definitions

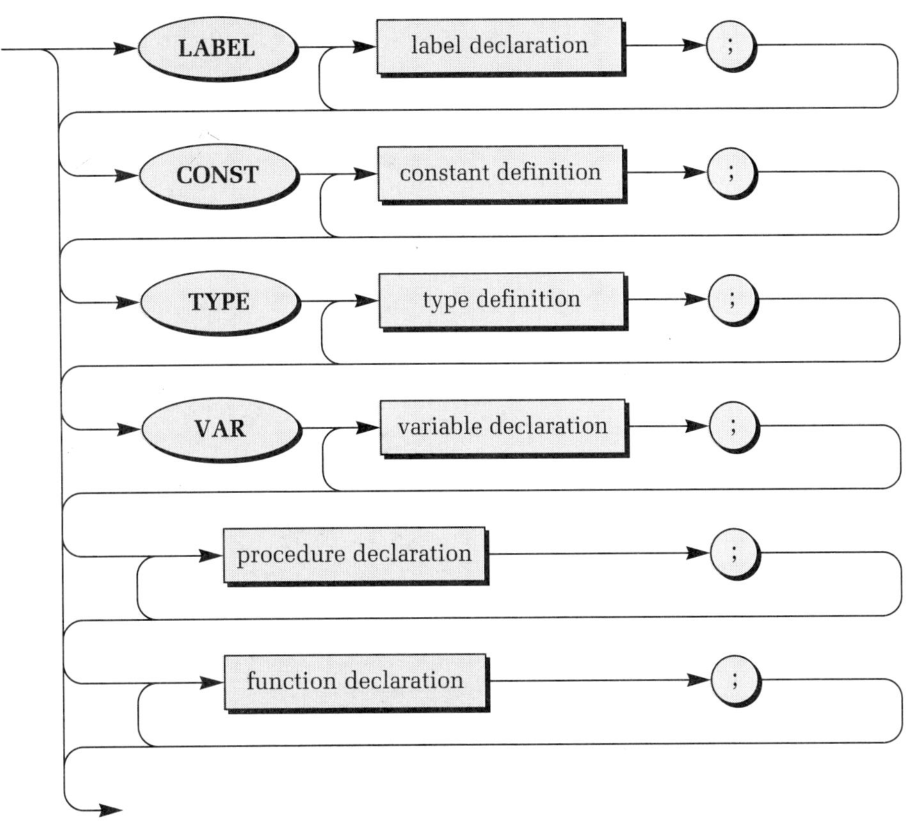

Label Declaration

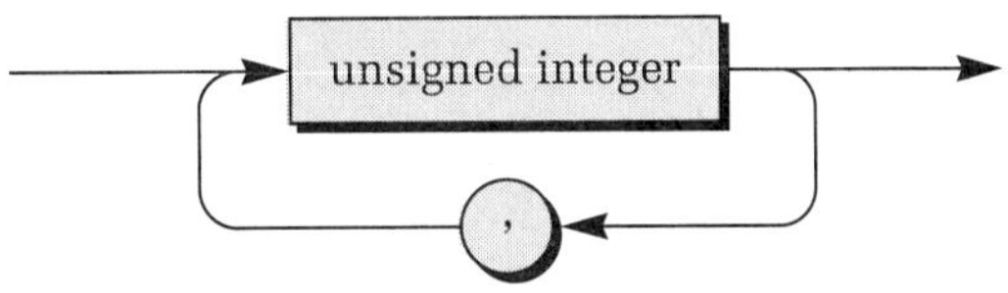

Constant Definition

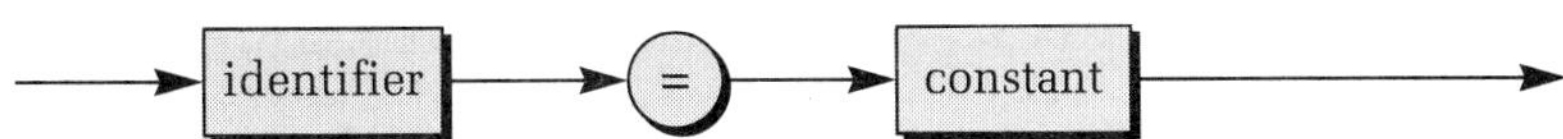

Type Definition

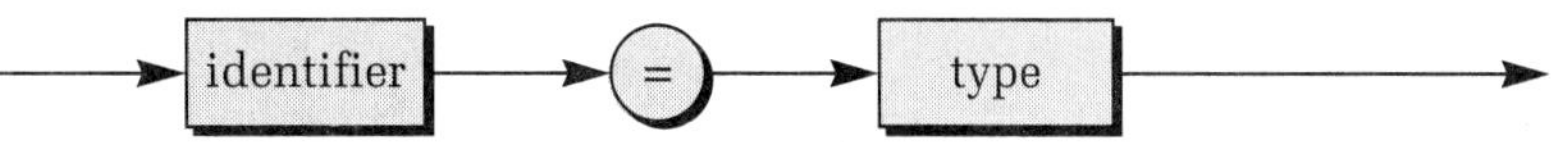

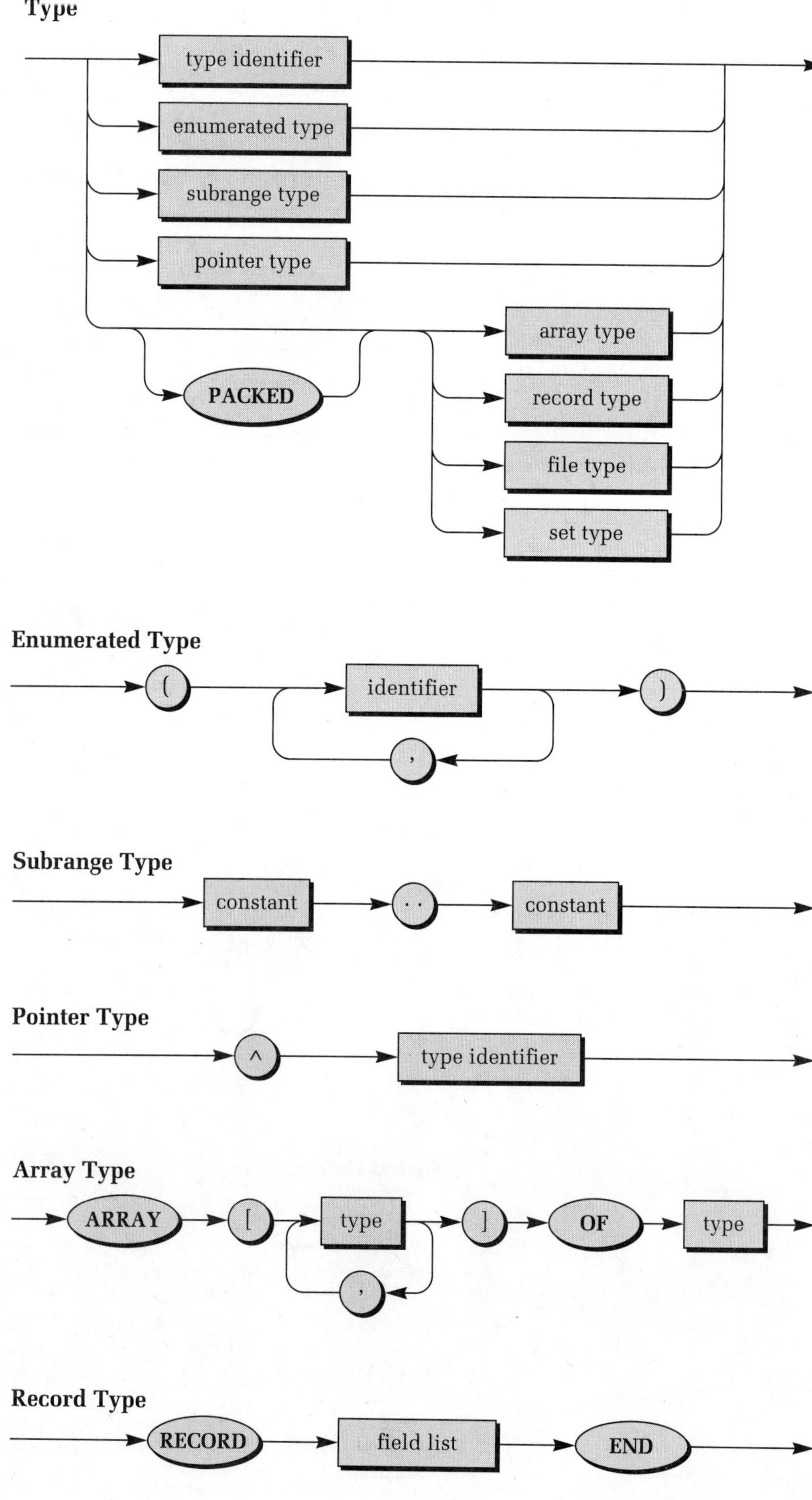
Type
type identifier
enumerated type
subrange type
pointer type
array type
PACKED
record type
file type
set type
Enumerated Type
(
identifier
)
,
Subrange Type
constant
..
constant
Pointer Type
^
type identifier
Array Type
ARRAY
[
type
]
OF
type
,
Record Type
RECORD
field list
END

Field List

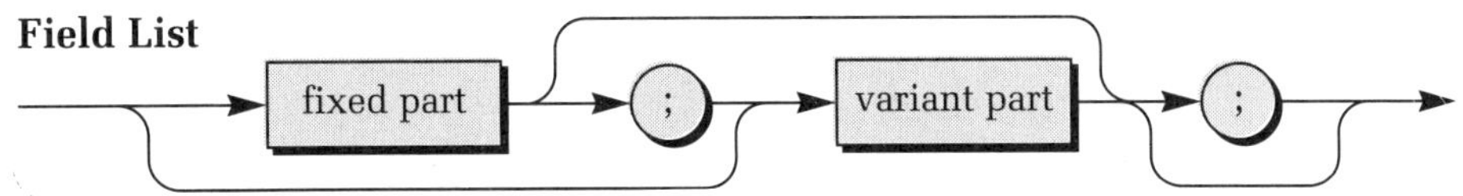

Fixed Part

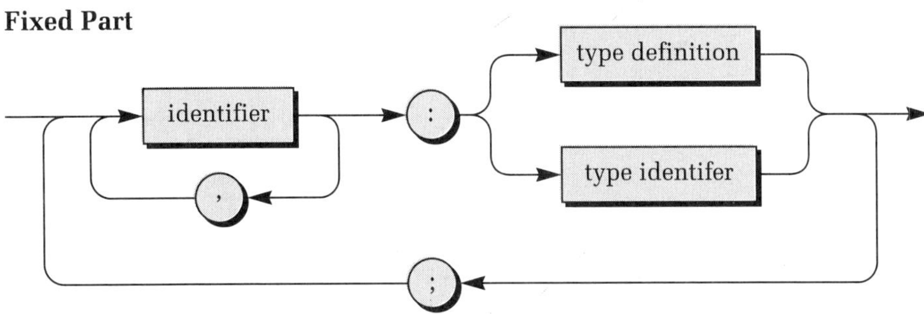

Variant Part

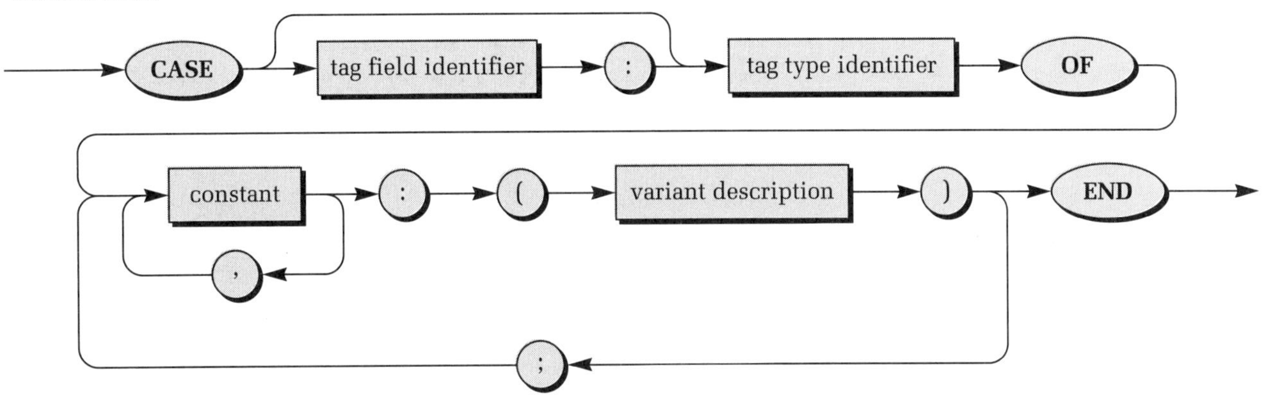

Variant Description

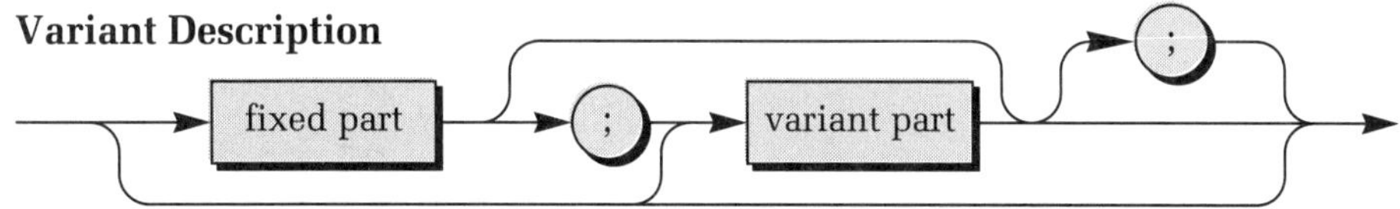

File Type

Set Type

Variable Declaration

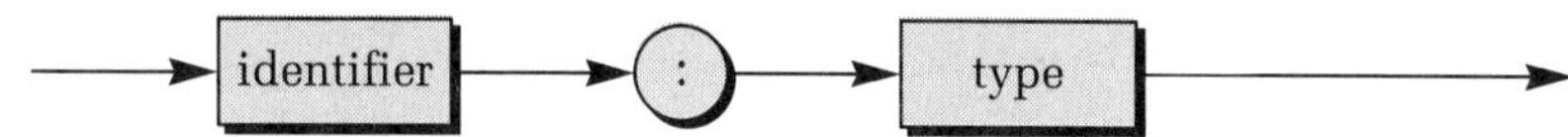

Procedure and Function Declarations

PROCEDURE identifier (formal parameter list) ;

FUNCTION identifier (formal parameter list)

: function type ;

declarations body ;

FORWARD

Formal Parameter List

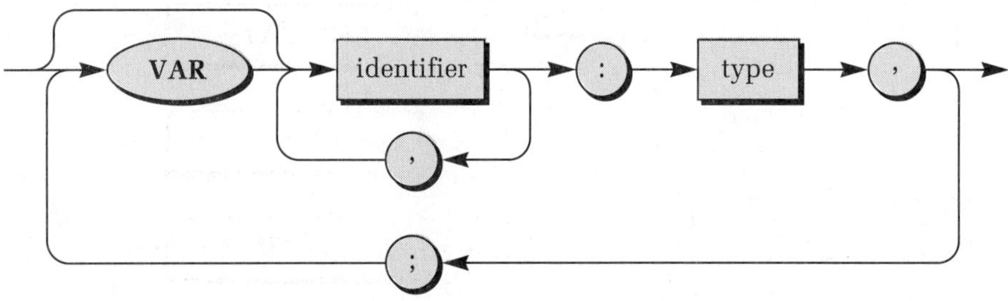

Body

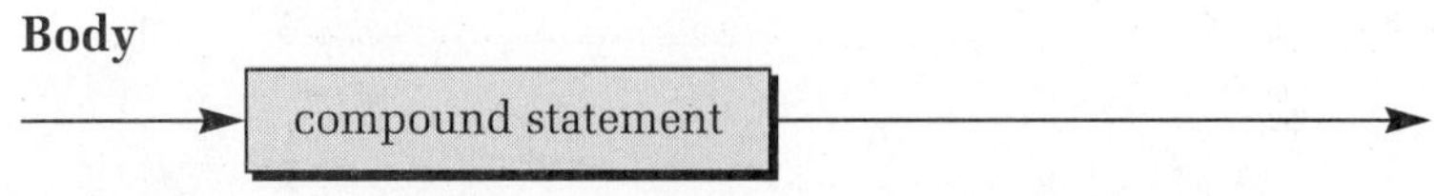

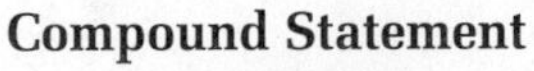

Compound Statement

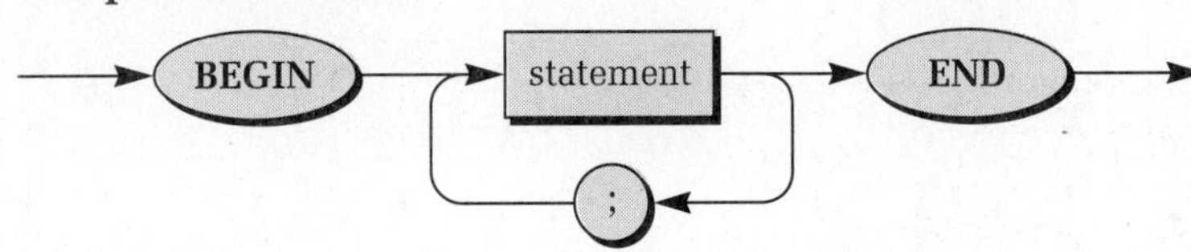

Statement

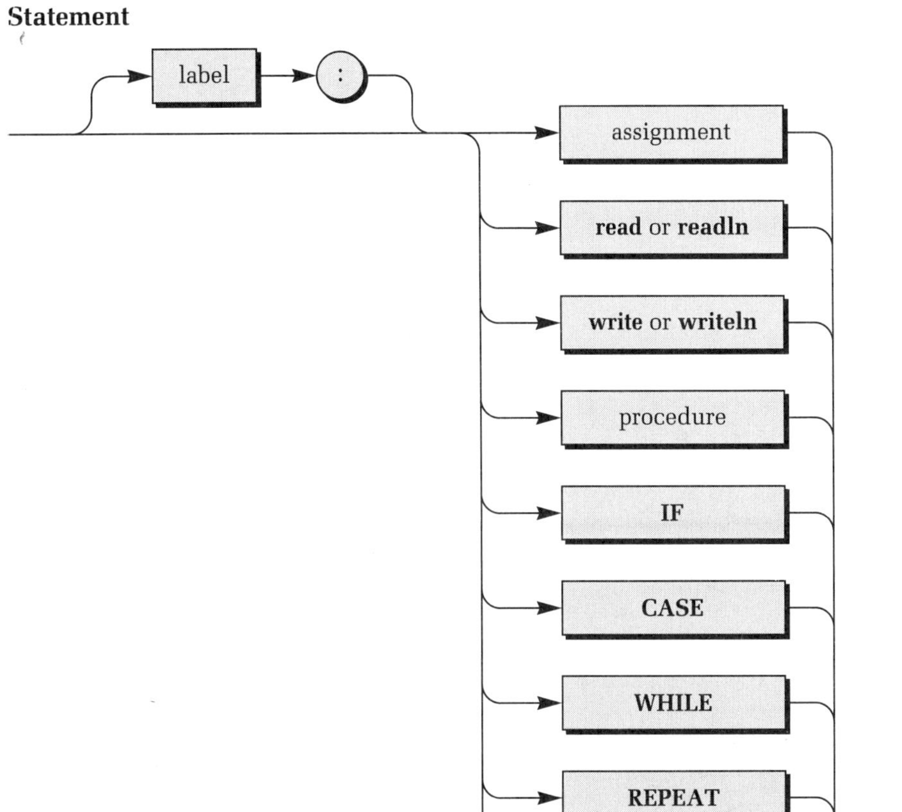

Assignment Statement

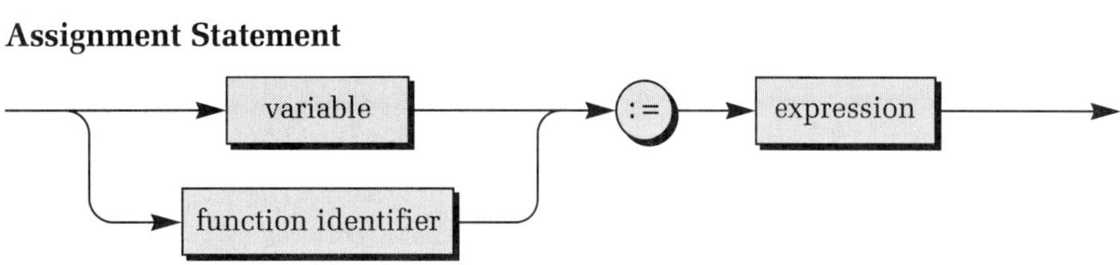

Expression

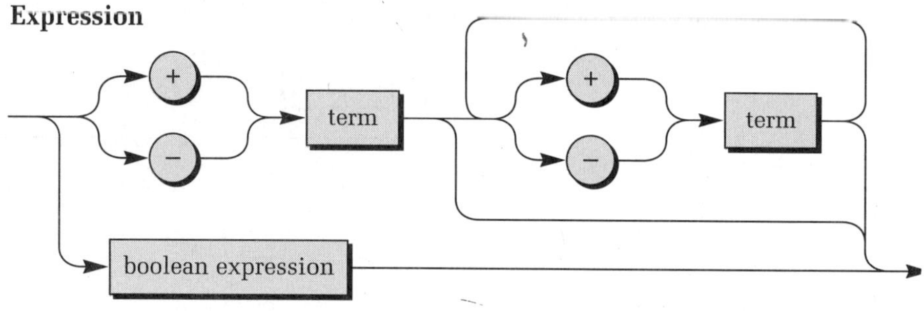

Term

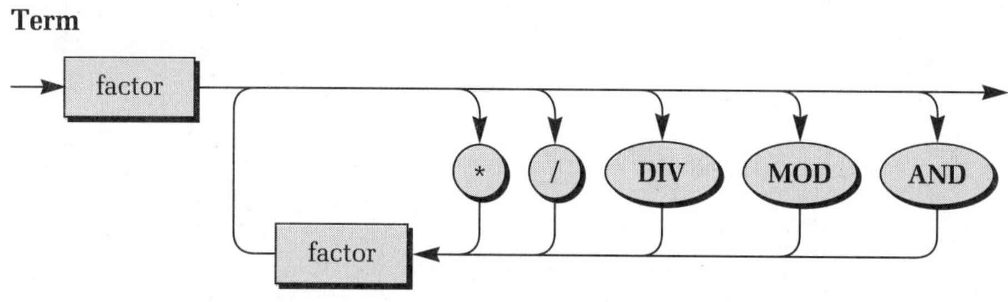

Factor

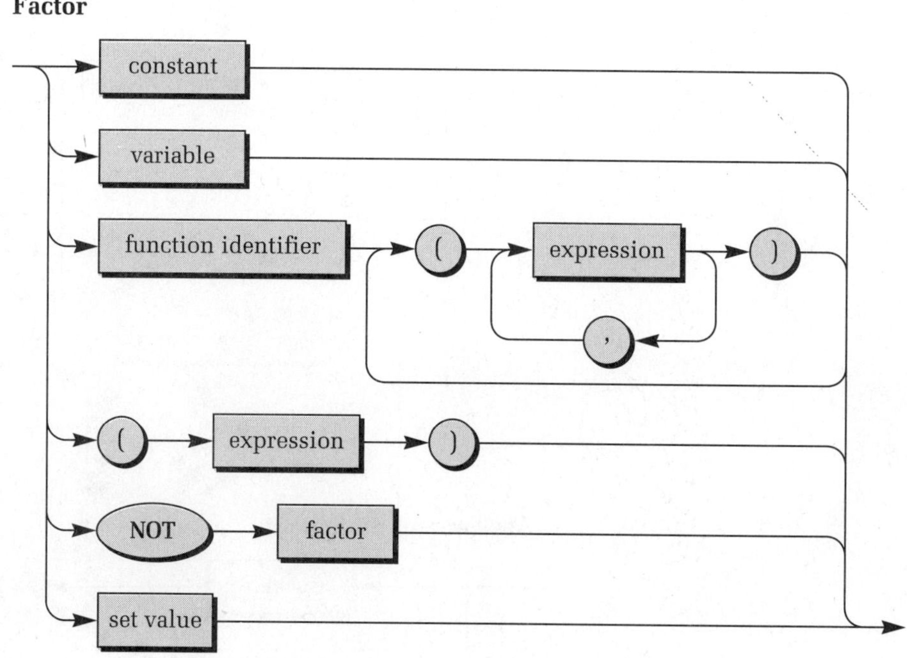

Variable

variable identifier
field identifier
[
expression
,
]
.
field identifier
^

Set Value

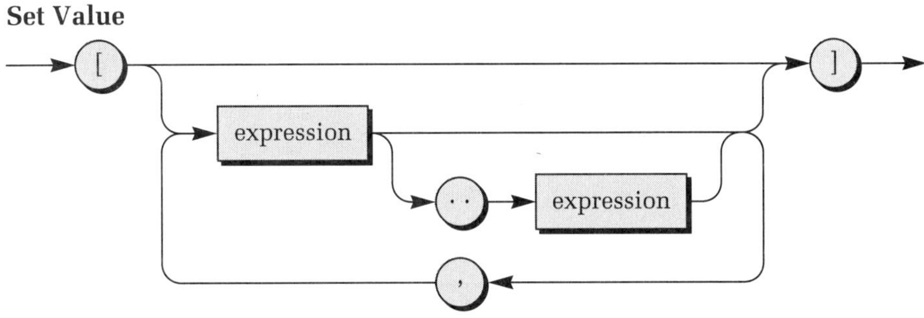

Boolean Expression

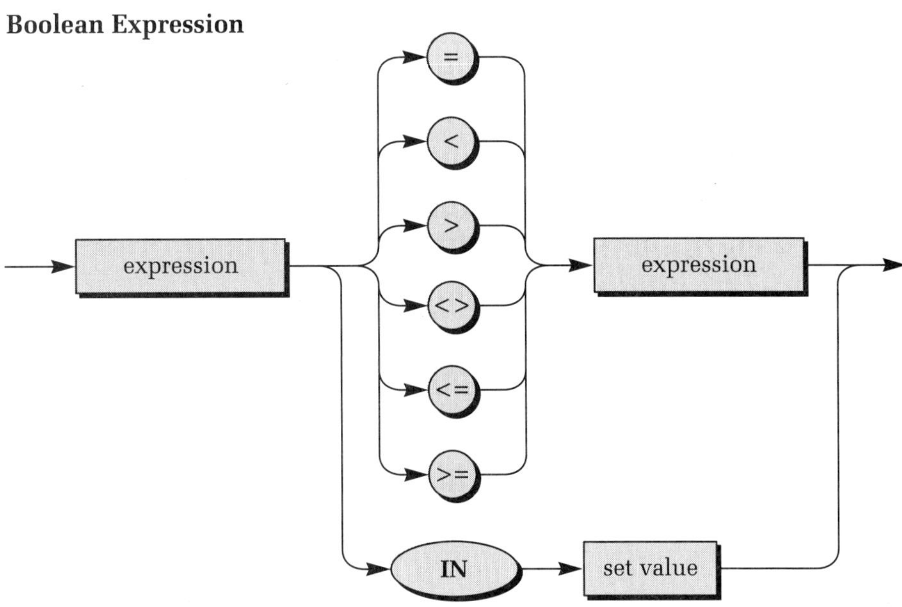

read or readln Statement

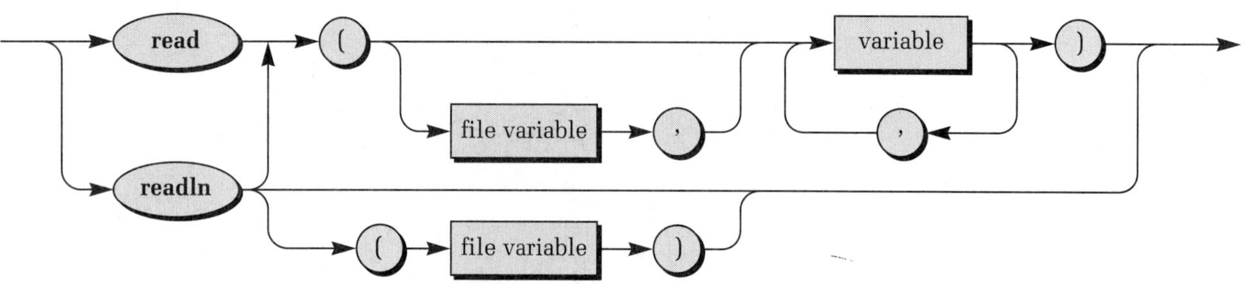

write or writeln Statement

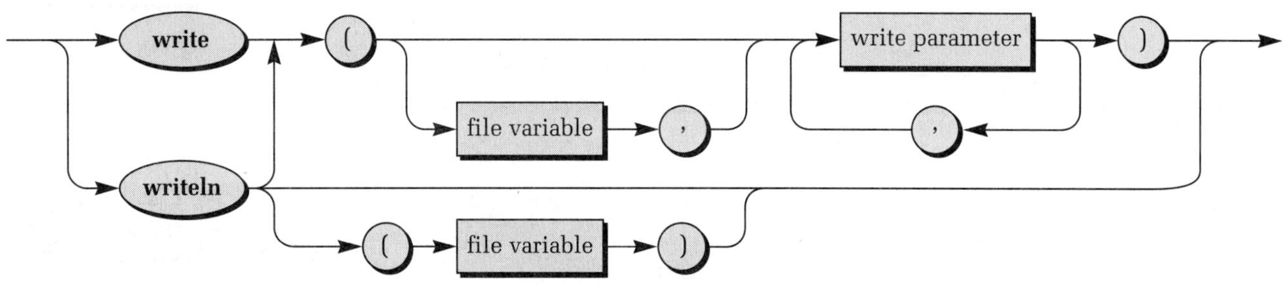

Procedure Statement

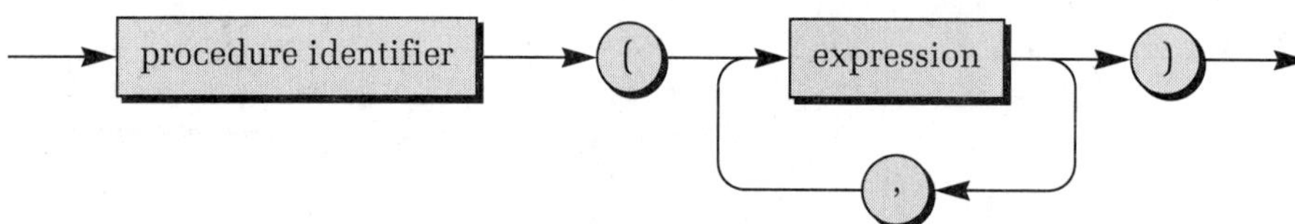

IF Statement

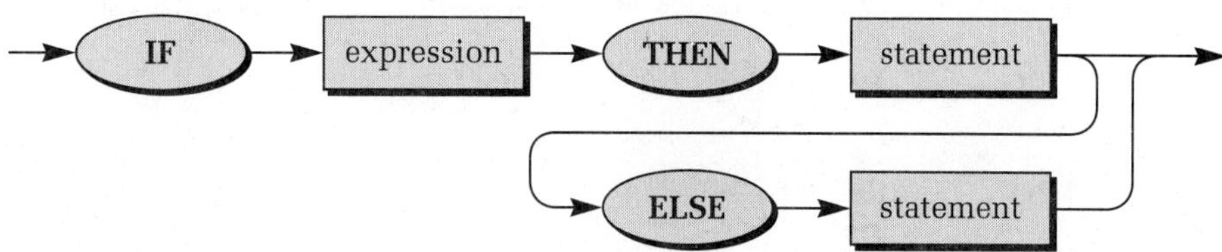

CASE Statement

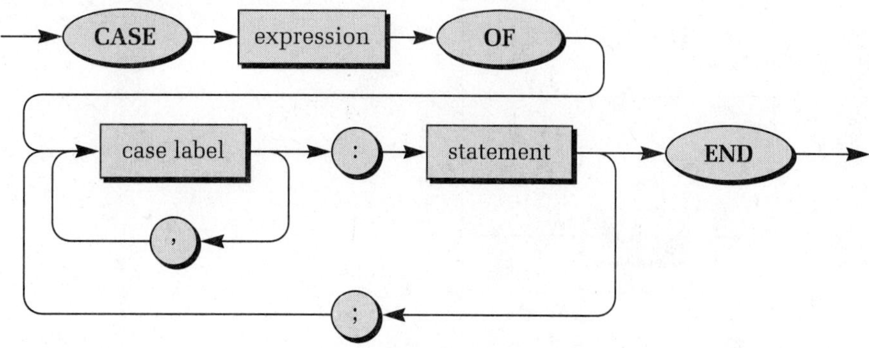

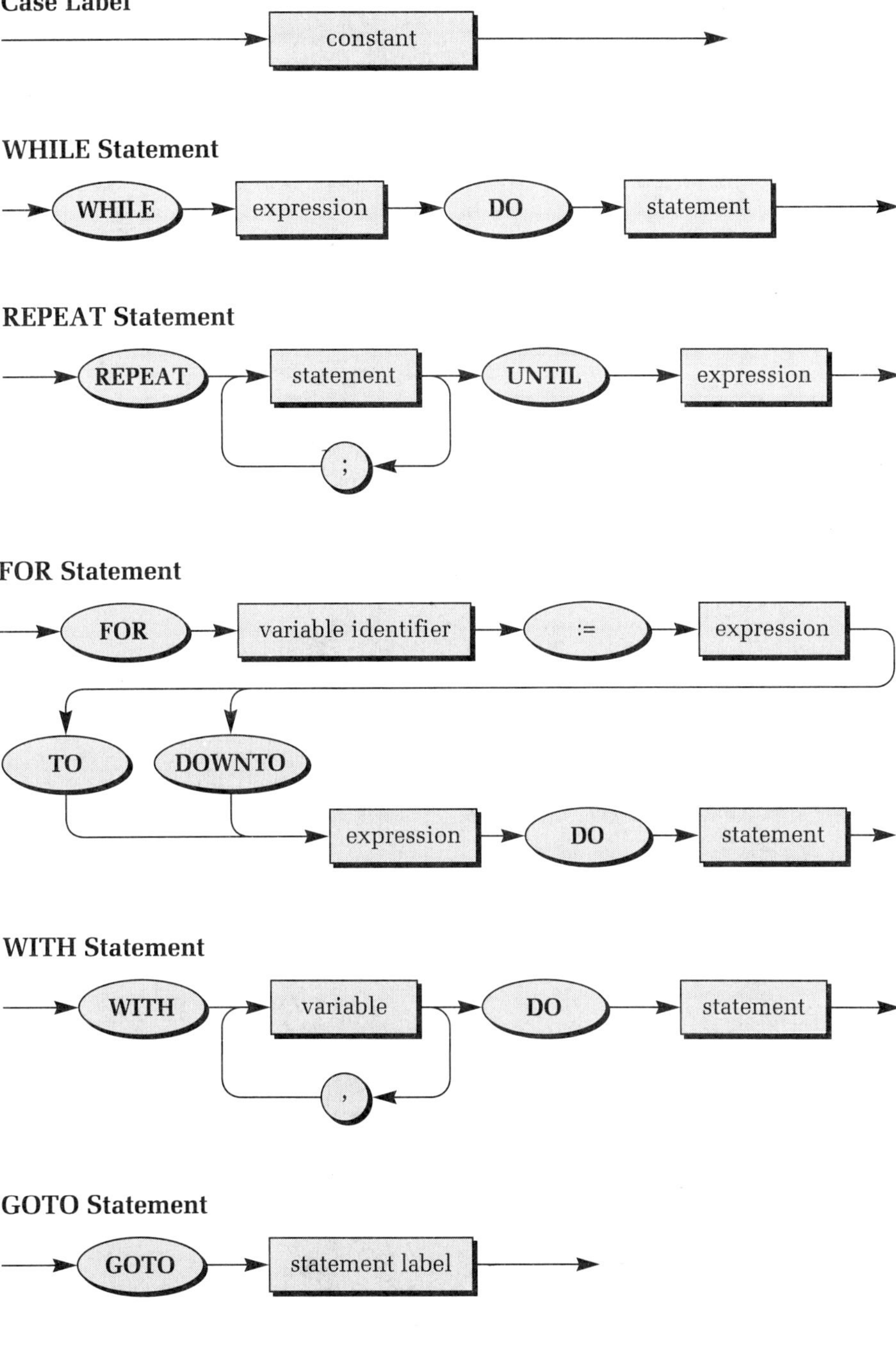
Case Label
constant
WHILE Statement
WHILE
expression
DO
statement
REPEAT Statement
REPEAT
statement
;
UNTIL
expression
FOR Statement
FOR
variable identifier
:=
expression
TO
DOWNTO
expression
DO
statement
WITH Statement
WITH
variable
,
DO
statement
GOTO Statement
GOTO
statement label
Empty Statement

Appendix 4 Character Sets

The two tables included here show the ordering of two common character sets. Note that only printable characters are shown for each set. Ordinals without character representations either do not have standard representation, or they are associated with unprintable control characters. In each list, the blank is denoted by "␢".

The American Standard Code for Information Interchange (ASCII)

Left Digit(s)	Right Digit									
	0	1	2	3	4	5	6	7	8	9
3			␢	!	"	#	$	%	&	'
4	(	)	*	+	,	-	.	/	0	1
5	2	3	4	5	6	7	8	9	:	;
6	<	=	>	?	@	A	B	C	D	E
7	F	G	H	I	J	K	L	M	N	O
8	P	Q	R	S	T	U	V	W	X	Y
9	Z	[	\	]	^	_	`	a	b	c
10	d	e	f	g	h	i	j	k	l	m
11	n	o	p	q	r	s	t	u	v	w
12	x	y	z	{	|	}	~			

*Codes less than 32 or greater than 126 are nonprintable.

The Extended Binary Coded Decimal Interchange Code (EBCDIC)

Left Digit(s)	Right Digit									
	0	**1**	**2**	**3**	**4**	**5**	**6**	**7**	**8**	**9**
6					b̸					
7					¢	.	<	(	+	|
8	&									
9	!	$	*	)	;	¬	-	/		
10							^	,	%	—
11	>	?								
12			:	#	@	'	=	"		a
13	b	c	d	e	f	g	h	i		
14						j	k	l	m	n
15	o	p	q	r						
16			s	t	u	v	w	x	y	z
17								\	{	}
18	[	]	-							
19				A	B	C	D	E	F	G
20	H	I								J
21	K	L	M	N	O	P	Q	R		
22							S	T	U	V
23	W	X	Y	Z						
24	0	1	2	3	4	5	6	7	8	9

*Codes not listed in this table are nonprintable.

Appendix 5 Compiler Error Messages

The following are typical error messages used by a compiler to identify compilation errors. Such errors will be identified by number with appropriate messages produced at the bottom of a compilation listing. Different compilers produce different error messages.

```
 1  ERROR IN SIMPLE TYPE.
 2  IDENTIFIER EXPECTED.
 3  'PROGRAM' EXPECTED.
 4  ')' EXPECTED.
 5  ' ' EXPECTED.
 6  UNEXPECTED SYMBOL.
 7  ERROR IN PARAMETER LIST.
 8  'OF' EXPECTED.
 9  '(' EXPECTED.
10  ERROR IN TYPE.
11  '[' EXPECTED.
12  ']' EXPECTED.
13  'END' EXPECTED.
14  ';' EXPECTED.
15  INTEGER CONSTANT EXPECTED.
16  '=' EXPECTED.
17  'BEGIN' EXPECTED.
18  ERROR IN DECLARATION PART.
19  ERROR IN FIELD-LIST.
20  ',' EXPECTED.
21  '..' EXPECTED.

40  VALUE PART ALLOWED ONLY IN MAIN PROGRAM.
41  TOO FEW VALUES SPECIFIED.
42  TOO MANY VALUES SPECIFIED.
43  VARIABLE INITIALIZED TWICE.
44  TYPE IS NEITHER ARRAY NOR RECORD.
45  REPETITION FACTOR MUST BE GREATER THAN ZERO.
```

50 ERROR IN CONSTANT.
51 ':=' EXPECTED.
52 'THEN' EXPECTED.
53 'UNTIL' EXPECTED.
54 'DO' EXPECTED.
55 'TO' OR 'DOWNTO' EXPECTED.
57 'FILE' EXPECTED.
58 ERROR IN FACTOR.
59 ERROR IN VARIABLE.
60 FILE TYPE IDENTIFIER EXPECTED.

101 IDENTIFIER DECLARED TWICE.
102 LOWBOUND EXCEEDS HIGHBOUND.
103 IDENTIFIER IS NOT OF APPROPRIATE CLASS.
104 IDENTIFIER NOT DECLARED.
105 SIGN NOT ALLOWED.
106 NUMBER EXPECTED.
107 INCOMPATIBLE SUBRANGE TYPES.
108 FILE NOT ALLOWED HERE.
109 TYPE MUST NOT BE REAL.
110 TAGFIELD TYPE MUST BE SCALAR OR SUBRANGE.
111 INCOMPATIBLE WITH TAGFIELD TYPE.
112 INDEX TYPE MUST NOT BE REAL.
113 INDEX TYPE MUST BE SCALAR OR SUBRANGE.
114 BASE TYPE MUST NOT BE REAL.
115 BASE TYPE MUST BE SCALAR OR SUBRANGE.
116 ERROR IN TYPE OF STANDARD PROCEDURE PARAMETER.
117 UNSATISFIED FORWARD REFERENCE.
119 FORWARD DECLARED; REPETITION OF PARAMETER LIST NOT ALLOWED.
120 FUNCTION RESULT TYPE MUST BE SCALAR, SUBRANGE, OR POINTER.
121 FILE VALUE PARAMETER NOT ALLOWED.
122 FORWARD DECLARED FUNCTION; REPETITION OF RESULT TYPE NOT ALLOWED.
123 MISSING RESULT TYPE IN FUNCTION DECLARATION.
124 FIXED-POINT FORMATTING ALLOWED FOR REALS ONLY.
125 ERROR IN TYPE OF STANDARD FUNCTION PARAMETER.
126 NUMBER OF PARAMETERS DOES NOT AGREE WITH DECLARATION.
127 INVALID PARAMETER SUBSTITUTION.
128 PARAMETER PROCEDURE/FUNCTION IS NOT COMPATIBLE WITH DECLARATION.
129 TYPE CONFLICT OF OPERANDS.
130 EXPRESSION IS NOT OF SET TYPE.
131 TESTS ON EQUALITY ALLOWED ONLY.
132 '<' AND '>' NOT ALLOWED FOR SET OPERANDS.
133 FILE COMPARISON NOT ALLOWED.
134 INVALID TYPE OF OPERAND(S).
135 TYPE OF OPERAND MUST BE BOOLEAN.
136 SET ELEMENT MUST BE SCALAR OR SUBRANGE.
137 SET ELEMENT TYPES NOT COMPATIBLE.
138 TYPE OF VARIABLE IS NOT ARRAY.
139 INDEX TYPE IS NOT COMPATIBLE WITH DECLARATION.
140 TYPE OF VARIABLE IS NOT RECORD.
141 TYPE OF VARIABLE MUST BE FILE OR POINTER.
142 INVALID PARAMETER SUBSTITUTION.
143 INVALID TYPE OF LOOP CONTROL VARIABLE.
144 INVALID TYPE OF EXPRESSION.
145 TYPE CONFLICT.
146 ASSIGNMENT OF FILES NOT ALLOWED.
147 LABEL TYPE INCOMPATIBLE WITH SELECTING EXPRESSION.
148 SUBRANGE BOUNDS MUST BE SCALAR.
149 INDEX TYPE MUST NOT BE INTEGER.
150 ASSIGNMENT TO THIS FUNCTION IS NOT ALLOWED.
151 ASSIGNMENT TO FORMAL FUNCTION IS NOT ALLOWED.

152 NO SUCH FIELD IN THIS RECORD.
155 CONTROL VARIABLE MUST NOT BE DECLARED ON AN INTERMEDIATE LEVEL.
156 MULTIDEFINED CASE LABEL.
157 RANGE OF CASE LABELS IS TOO LARGE.
158 MISSING CORRESPONDING VARIANT DECLARATION.
159 REAL OR STRING TAGFIELDS NOT ALLOWED.
160 PREVIOUS DECLARATION WAS NOT FORWARD.
161 MULTIPLE FORWARD DECLARATION.
164 SUBSTITUTION OF STANDARD PROCEDURE/FUNCTION NOT ALLOWED.
165 MULTIDEFINED LABEL.
166 MULTIDECLARED LABEL.
167 UNDECLARED LABEL.
168 UNDEFINED LABEL IN THE PREVIOUS BLOCK.
169 ERROR IN BASE SET.
170 VALUE PARAMETER EXPECTED.
172 UNDECLARED EXTERNAL FILE.
173 FORTRAN PROCEDURE OR FUNCTION EXPECTED.
174 PASCAL PROCEDURE OR FUNCTION EXPECTED.
175 MISSING FILE 'INPUT' IN PROGRAM HEADING.
176 MISSING FILE 'OUTPUT' IN PROGRAM HEADING.
177 ASSIGNMENT TO FUNCTION ALLOWED ONLY IN FUNCTION BODY.
178 MULTIDEFINED RECORD VARIANT.
179 X-OPTION OF ACTUAL PROCEDURE/FUNCTION DOES NOT MATCH FORMAL DECLARATION.
180 CONTROL VARIABLE MUST NOT BE FORMAL.
181 ARRAY SUBSCRIPT CALCULATION TOO COMPLICATED.
182 MAGNITUDE OF CASE LABEL IS TOO LARGE.
183 SUBRANGE OF TYPE REAL IS NOT ALLOWED.

198 ALTERNATE INPUT NOT FOUND.
199 ONLY ONE ALTERNATE INPUT MAY BE ACTIVE.

201 ERROR IN REAL CONSTANT DIGIT EXPECTED.
202 STRING CONSTANT MUST BE CONTAINED ON A SINGLE LINE.
203 INTEGER CONSTANT EXCEEDS RANGE.
204 8 OR 9 IN OCTAL NUMBER.
205 STRINGS OF LENGTH ZERO ARE NOT ALLOWED.
206 INTEGER PART OF REAL CONSTANT EXCEEDS RANGE.
207 REAL CONSTANT EXCEEDS RANGE.

250 TOO MANY NESTED SCOPES OF IDENTIFIERS.
251 TOO MANY NESTED PROCEDURES AND/OR FUNCTIONS.
255 TOO MANY ERRORS ON THIS SOURCE LINE.
256 TOO MANY EXTERNAL REFERENCES.
259 EXPRESSION TOO COMPLICATED.
260 TOO MANY EXIT LABELS.
261 TOO MANY LARGE VARIABLES.
262 NODE TO BE ALLOCATED IS TOO LARGE.
263 TOO MANY PROCEDURE/FUNCTION PARAMETERS.
264 TOO MANY PROCEDURES AND FUNCTIONS.

300 DIVISION BY ZERO.
302 INDEX EXPRESSION OUT OF BOUNDS.
303 VALUE TO BE ASSIGNED IS OUT OF BOUNDS.
304 ELEMENT EXPRESSION OUT OF RANGE.

350 ONLY THE LAST DIMENSION MAY BE PACKED.
351 ARRAY TYPE IDENTIFIER EXPECTED.
352 ARRAY VARIABLE EXPECTED.
353 POSITIVE INTEGER CONSTANT EXPECTED.

397 PACK AND UNPACK ARE NOT IMPLEMENTED FOR DYNAMIC ARRAYS.
398 IMPLEMENTATION RESTRICTION.

Appendix 6 Turbo Pascal Notes

This text is written using standard Pascal. The decision to use standard Pascal rather than some other version was made for three reasons.

1. Standard Pascal is still frequently used at many colleges and universities.
2. Although many different versions of Pascal are available, no single one is dominant.
3. Standard Pascal is the easiest version from which to adapt if some other version is being used.

Recently, however, Turbo Pascal has begun to grow rapidly in popularity. Turbo's popularity is a function of the increasing use of personal computers, good compiler programs, and Turbo's relatively low cost.

The third edition of this text has responded to the increasing use of Turbo Pascal by expanding this appendix on Turbo Pascal. Here, reference is made to parts of the text where specific differences occur between standard and Turbo Pascal. These differences are explained in some detail.

Using Turbo Pascal

Using a properly formatted disk containing Turbo Pascal, boot the system. When the prompt appears, enter 'TURBO' and press ⟨RETURN⟩. Next enter 'Y' or 'N' for error messages. At this stage, several options are available. Enter 'W' and you will be asked to enter a work file name. Enter 'Prac1' and press ⟨RETURN⟩. Then enter 'E' and you will be in the edit mode ready to write a program.

To see how the compiler works, input the following sample program. Enter this program exactly as written—complete with the error!

```
PROGRAM Practice;
  VAR
    A, B, Sum : integer;
  BEGIN
    A := 20
    B := 30;
    Sum := A + B;
    writeln ('Sum is', Sum:5)
  END.
```

Exit the edit mode by pressing Ctrl-K-D. Enter 'C' to compile the program. The error message

```
"Error 85: ';' expected. Press <Esc>"
```

appears. Press ⟨Esc⟩ and you will be returned to the program in the edit mode with the cursor under the 'B' of B := 30;. Move the cursor to where the missing semicolon belongs (after 20), enter the semicolon, and press Ctrl-K-D to exit. Compile again by entering 'C'. You now have an error-free program and can run it by entering 'R'.

You can save the program by entering 'S'. It will be saved as PRAC1.PAS. You can then exit by pressing 'Q'. Prac1 is now a permanent file. If you need to use it again, enter 'TURBO' and type in 'Prac1' when a work file name is requested.

Versions 5.0 and 6.0 have significantly different environments. After leaving the edit mode, menus are available for running and compiling. You run and/or compile a program by selecting the appropriate menu choice. A little practice with these menus should make you comfortable with their use.

The remainder of this appendix consists of specific page references in bold type, followed by appropriate comments. Turbo logos, (shown to the left), are used throughout the text to indicate a reference to this appendix.

Turbo Notes

Page 67: Turbo Pascal provides five predefined integer types. Each type denotes a specific subset of the whole numbers, as shown here:

Type	Range	Size
byte	0..255	8 bit
integer	−32768..32767	16 bit
longint	−2147483648..2147483647	32 bit
shortint	−128..127	8 bit
word	0..65535	16 bit

Page 70: Turbo's Random function may be used to return either a real or integer random number.

```
Syntax:
  Random [ ( Range: word) ]
```

If the optional word argument is used, then the result is a word random number within the range $0 <= x <$ Range. For a description of the word data type in Turbo, see the previous Turbo note. If the optional word argument is omitted, then a real random number in the range $0 <= x < 1$ is returned.

To initialize the random number generator, call Randomize, or assign a value to the global Turbo variable RandSeed.

Page 80: Turbo provides its own String data type with a library of operations. The caution here is that this makes String a reserved word in Turbo. Hence, if you work in Turbo, you will need to identify the String ADT in Chapter 16 by a different name.

Page 93: UNITs are the basis of modular programming with ADTs in Turbo Pascal. You use UNITs to create libraries and to divide large programs into logically related modules. The syntax for defining a UNIT file is as follows:

```
UNIT identifier;        { Heading }

INTERFACE               { Public symbols that define the interface for your ADT }
  USES . . . ;          { This clause specifies other UNITs used by this one }
  CONST . . . ;         { Constants }
  TYPE . . . ;          { Types }
  VAR . . . ;           { Variables }
```

```
    PROCEURE . . . ;        { Procedure headers for provided operations }
    FUNCTION . . . ;        { Function headers for provided operations }

  IMPLEMENTATION            { Private symbols that define your implementation of
                              the ADT. Users of your ADT cannot access symbols in
                              the IMPLEMENTATION section. }
    USES . . . ;
    CONST . . . ;           { Constants }
    TYPE . . . ;            { Types }
    VAR . . . ;             { Variables }
    PROCEDURE               { Procedure definitions to implement headers specified
  . . . ;                     in INTERFACE section }
    FUNCTION . . . ;        { Function definitions to implement headers specified in
                              INTERFACE section }

  BEGIN                     { Initialization necessary for implementation of ADT }
    Statement;              { Statements }
    . . .
    Statement
  END.
```

Page 110: Unfortunately, Turbo does not obey the syntax of standard Pascal when it comes to passing procedures as parameters to other procedures. Instead of directly including information about the number and type of a procedure's parameters in the formal parameter list of the procedure that is receiving another procedure as a parameter, Turbo requires that you define a type that includes this information. For instance, the following type declarations define a FUNCTION TYPE PrecedesRelation.

```
TYPE
  ElementType = integer;
  SortArray = ARRAY [1..IndexLimit] of ElementType;
  { The following type is for the function parameter }
  PrecedesRelation = FUNCTION (A, B : ElementType) : boolean;
                    {  Given:   Two values to compare              }
                    {  Return:  True if A precedes B in order      }
                    {           relationship on ElementType        }
```

Then, in the function that is to receive a function or procedure as a parameter, this type identifier must be used. The following example illustrates this usage.

```
PROCEDURE Sort ( VAR A : SortArray;
                 N : integer;
                 Precedes : PrecedesRelation);

  {  Given:   Array of values to be returned in order        }
  {           according to Precedes relation and N, the      }
  {           number of values in array.                     }
  {  Task:    Sort the array using a sort algorithm          }
  {  Return:  The array arranged in order by the Precedes    }
  {           relation passed in as parameter                }
```

Finally, note that Turbo requires that you enable the *far call model* when you are using parameters that are functions or procedures. See your Turbo reference manual as to how to set this switch in your version of the Turbo compiler.

Page 168: read and **write** must be used to access file records in Turbo. **get** and **put** are not supported in Turbo.

Page 168: Remember when using a **seek** statement in Turbo, such as

```
seek (Students, K)
```

that records in a file are numbered starting with zero. Hence, to access the fourteenth record in a file, K in the above example would be set to the value 13.

Page 175: In Turbo, an object is a data structure that contains data fields (like a record) and methods (unlike a record). These methods constitute ADT operations that are owned by the object.

The nature of this Appendix prevents any kind of detailed exposition on object-oriented programming. Briefly, the syntax would be as follows:

```
OBJECT
  <field declaration>;
  <field declaration>;
   .
   .
   .
  <method declaration>;
  <method declaration>
END;
```

For further information, you are encouraged to consult your Turbo reference manual. Note that only Turbo versions 5.5 or higher offer such object-oriented extensions.

Page 281: Refer to the previous Turbo note for page 70.

Appendix 7 GOTO Statement

In your work with computers, you may have heard of a **GOTO** statement. It is another statement in Pascal that allows a programmer to transfer control within a program. The **GOTO** statement has the effect of an immediate unconditional transfer to an indicated designation. You should not use **GOTO** statements in a Pascal program, but for the sake of completeness, you should be aware of their existence and how they work.

Early programming languages needed a branching statement; therefore, both FORTRAN and BASIC were designed using a **GOTO** statement for branching. Subsequent languages, particularly Pascal, included more sophisticated branching and looping statements. These statements led to an emphasis on structured programming, which is easier to design and read. If you are a beginning programmer and have not used the **GOTO** statement in another language, you should continue to develop your skills without including this statement. If you have already written programs in a language that uses **GOTO** statements, you should still attempt to write all Pascal programs without **GOTO** statements.

One instance in which **GOTO** statements might be appropriate is in making a quick exit from some part of the program. For example, if you are getting data from somewhere within a program and you have a check for valid data, your design could include a program segment such as

```
read data
IF (<bad data>) THEN
  BEGIN
    <write error message>;
    GOTO <end of program>
  END
ELSE
  <process data>
```

With the previous admonitions against using **GOTO** statements in mind, we will now briefly examine the form, syntax, and flow of control for these statements.

GOTO statements require the use of numerically labeled statements. Thus, your program could contain

```
LABEL
  <label 1>,
  <label 2>;
        .
        .
        .
GOTO 100;
        .
        .
        .
100: <program statement>;
        .
        .
        .
```

All labels must be declared in a label declaration section that precedes the constant definition section in a program. Each label can only be used for a single program statement. The form for the label declaration section is

> **LABEL**
> ⟨label 1⟩,
> ⟨label 2⟩,
> .
> .
> .
> ⟨label *n*⟩;

Correct form for a **GOTO** statement is

> **GOTO** ⟨numerical label⟩;

where numerical label is an integer from 1 to 9999 inclusive. Declared labels are then used with appropriate statements in a program. Proper syntax for labeling a statement is

> ⟨label⟩ : ⟨program statement⟩;

Consider the fragment

```
BEGIN
  read (Num);
  IF Num < 0 THEN
    GOTO 100
  ELSE
    Sum := Sum + Num;
        .
        .
        .
  100: writeln ('Data include a negative number,':40)
END.
```

In this instance, when a negative number is encountered as a data item, an appropriate message is printed and the program is terminated.

GOTO statements permit you to immediately transfer out of any control structure. As stated, we recommend you avoid the use of this statement whenever possible. However, if you must use it, use it only for an immediate exit from some point in the program; never use it to construct a loop in Pascal.

Appendix 8 Packing and Unpacking

The basic trade-off between working with arrays and packed arrays is that packed arrays require less memory but more time to access individual components. It is possible to facilitate working with packed and unpacked arrays (arrays that are not packed) by using assignment loops. For example, consider the following declarations.

```
TYPE
  String10 = PACKED ARRAY [1..10] OF char;
  Aray10 = ARRAY [1..10] OF char;
VAR
  PakName : String10;
  UnpakName : Aray10;
```

We now have reserved memory for

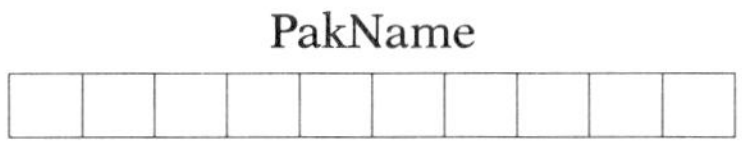

PakName

and

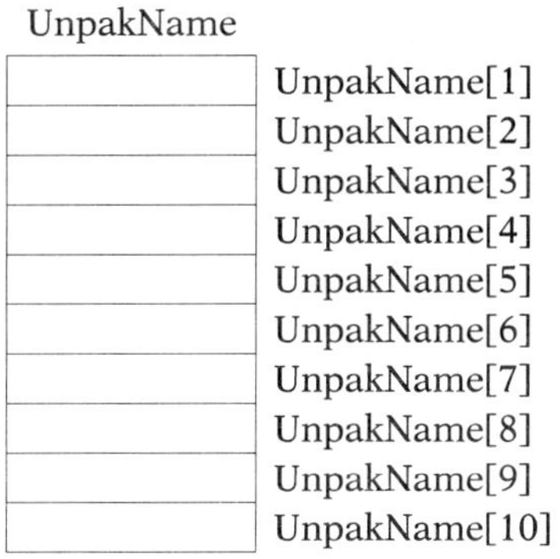

UnpakName

	UnpakName[1]
	UnpakName[2]
	UnpakName[3]
	UnpakName[4]
	UnpakName[5]
	UnpakName[6]
	UnpakName[7]
	UnpakName[8]
	UnpakName[9]
	UnpakName[10]

Now suppose that UnpakName contains the name 'John Smith'.

UnpakName
'J'
'o'
'h'
'n'
'S'
'm'
'i'
't'
'h'

and we wish to put the characters into a packed array for storage, sorting, or writing. This could be accomplished by

```
FOR J := 1 TO 10 DO
  PakName [J] := UnpakName[J];
```

and would produce the following:

PakName

'J'	'o'	'h'	'n'	' '	'S'	'm'	'i'	't'	'h'

This string can still be accessed as one packed array variable.

A **FOR** loop could also be used to transfer elements from a packed array to an unpacked array, but Pascal does provide standard procedures for both of these processes. An array can be packed by

```
pack (UnpackedArray, J, PackedArray);
```

This fills all of PackedArray with elements of UnpackedArray, starting with UnpackedArray [J]. An array can be unpacked by

```
unpack (PackedArray, UnpackedArray, K);
```

This copies all elements of PackedArray into UnpackedArray, putting the first element in UnpackedArray [K]. For these procedures, PackedArray and UnpackedArray do not have to be of the same length and K may be a constant or expression. Unfortunately, **pack** and **unpack** are difficult to use. Therefore, since **FOR** loops can accomplish the same results and are about as efficient, you would do well to use them if you wish to transfer between packed and unpacked arrays.

Appendix 9 Generating Random Numbers

The discussion of computer simulation in Chapter 5 cited the use of random numbers in determining the occurrence of a particular event. There are really two issues involved here:

- How to generate a sequence of random numbers
- How to use that sequence to simulate the occurrence (or nonoccurrence) of a particular event

For the discussion that follows, a sequence of random numbers is a sequence of real numbers $x_1, x_2, x_3, \ldots$ such that:

1. For each x_i, $0 \leq x_i < 1$.
2. The x_i are not biased toward any particular subinterval of the reals between 0 and 1. That is, members of the sequence should be evenly distributed between 0 and 1.
3. It should not be possible to predict the value of x_i from prior members of the sequence. That is, members of the sequence occur in an unpredictable fashion.

Random numbers generated by computer are often called pseudorandom. The origin of this term is due to the fact that sequences of such computer-generated numbers appear to be random even though there is a fixed mathematical formula underlying their generation. If you know the formula, you can in principle compute the sequence—hence, it is not truly unpredictable. However, if you merely observe the sequence without knowledge of the formula, the sequence appears to satisfy the three properties of randomness just cited.

Generating a Sequence of Random Numbers

Many Pascal compilers have a built-in random number generator. In case your compiler doesn't have such a function, we will describe a method for generating random numbers known as the *linear congruential algorithm*. The details of this method may be found in Knuth's "The Art of Computer Programming: Seminumerical Algorithms."

This algorithm is dependent on an integer value called the *seed.* The seed is acted on by two other integers, called the *multiplier* and the *adder,* using the following formula:

Multiplier × Seed + Adder

The result of this computation is then divided by another integer, called the *divisor.* The remainder of this division yields a new value for the seed, which is then divided by the divisor less 1 to yield a real value between 0 and 1. For appropriate choices of the divisor, multiplier, and adder, the sequence of real numbers produced by acting on a continually changing seed will give the appearance of a random sequence.

The preceding discussion is formalized in the following Pascal function and procedure:

```
{***************************************************************}
{       Procedures for random number generation                 }

FUNCTION Random : real;

  { Given:       A global variable Seed.  Must be global to insure that       }
  {              its value is retained between invocations of Random.         }
  { Task:        Seed is modified on each call to Random to insure a          }
  {              (probably) different random number on successive             }
  {              invocations of the function.  After Seed is modified,        }
  {              it is used to compute a real random value.                   }
  { Return:      A new value for global Seed and a real random value          }
  {              between 0 (inclusive) and 1.                                 }

  { The method of generating random numbers used here is known as the         }
  { linear congruential algorithm. The method is dependent on the word        }
  { size of your computer.  The choice of Divider below is appropriate        }
  { for a 32-bit machine.  In general, the Divider should be less than or     }
  { equal to 2 raised to the power ( B DIV 2 ) on a B-bit machine.  If        }
  { your machine does not flag integer overflow as a run-time error, then     }
  { Divider may be 2 raised to the power B.  The best choices for             }
  { Multiplier and Adder are relatively large, odd integers less than the     }
  { Divider.  By changing the Divider, Multiplier, and Adder constants in     }
  { this function, you can tailor the generation of random numbers to        }
  { your particular machine.                                                  }

  CONST { Random }
    Divider = 65536;          { 2^16 }
    Multiplier = 15625;
    Adder = 22221;

  BEGIN { Random }
    Seed := (Multiplier * Seed + Adder) MOD Divider; { Seed a global variable }
    Random := abs(Seed / (Divider - 1));
  END; { of function Random }

PROCEDURE InitRandom;

  { Given:       Global Seed for random number generation                     }
  { Task:        Initialize the Seed                                          }
  { Return:      Initialized Seed                                             }

  { The choice of Seed completely determines the random number sequence       }
  { that is generated.  The choice appearing here is one of many              }
  { appropriate Seed initializations for a 32-bit machine.  In general,       }
  { Seed should be an odd positive integer less than or equal to              }
```

```
  { 2 raised to the power ( B DIV 2 ) on a B-bit machine.  (This limit      }
  { becomes 2 raised to the B if your machine does not flag integer         }
  { overflow as a run-time error which halts your program.)  To generate    }
  { a different random number sequence, merely adjust the value of the     }
  { global variable Seed                                                    }

BEGIN { InitRandom }
  Seed := 44449;            { an odd prime }
END; { of PROCEDURE InitRandom }
```

Given this Pascal code, you merely call PROCEDURE InitRandom at the beginning of a program in which you wish to generate random numbers. Thereafter, each call to the FUNCTION Random will yield a random value between 0 and 1. Note that use of InitRandom and Random requires that you declare Seed as a global variable. This ensures that the value of Seed is retained from one invocation of Random to the next. Also, by choosing a different value for Seed in InitRandom, you can easily generate a different sequence of random numbers. Finally, the values for the Multiplier, Adder, and Divider used in the foregoing code are tailored to a Pascal compiler that uses 32 bits to store an integer. If your version of Pascal uses 16 bits, you should adjust the method as described in the documentation that accompanies InitRandom and Random.

Using Random Numbers to Simulate Events According to Probabilities

Here we describe three situations in which the generation of a random number may be used to simulate the occurrence of an event in a simulation. Our description is intended only to be brief and prescriptive in nature. An explanation of the theory underlying these and other applications of random number generation in simulation is given in *Modern Statistical, Systems, and GPSS Simulation* by Zaven Karian and Edward Dudewicz (New York, N.Y.: Computer Science Press, 1991).

Situation 1 An event occurs with a certain probability p. For example, in a given time unit of a simulation, there is a probability of 0.40 that a car will arrive in a queue waiting at a toll booth.

In this situation, generate a random number X. If X is less than p, declare that the event in question occurred; otherwise, declare that it did not occur. In the previous example, if X is less than 0.40, we process the event of a car's arrival; otherwise our simulation proceeds as if no car arrived.

Situation 2 The occurrence of an event is associated with a value, and that value is distributed uniformly over some interval $[a, b)$. Here the term *uniformly* means that the value associated with the event shows no bias to any portion of the interval $[a, b)$.

For instance, you must generate the time of day at which an event occurs, based on a 24-hour clock. The event is no more likely to occur at one time than another. Thus, you wish to generate a value in the interval [0, 24).

In this situation, generate a random number X, $0 \leq X < 1$. Then convert X to the desired value by the formula

$$a + (b - a)\,X$$

In our 24-hour clock example, if you generate a random value $X = 0.8125$, the formula above would convert it to 19.5, indicating a 7:30 P.M. time of occurrence.

A restricted case of this second situation occurs when the values to be generated are integers that are uniformly distributed over the range of integers given by Lo, Lo + 1, Lo + 2, . . . , Hi − 1, Hi. For instance, you are rolling a die and hence must generate an integer value uniformly distributed over the range 1, 2, 3, 4, 5, 6; that is, Lo = 1 and Hi = 6. In this situation, create the integer you want by generating a real number in the interval [Lo, Hi + 1) and then truncating this real to produce an integer. For instance, a random value $X = 0.24$ would yield a die's value of 2, according to the following evaluation:

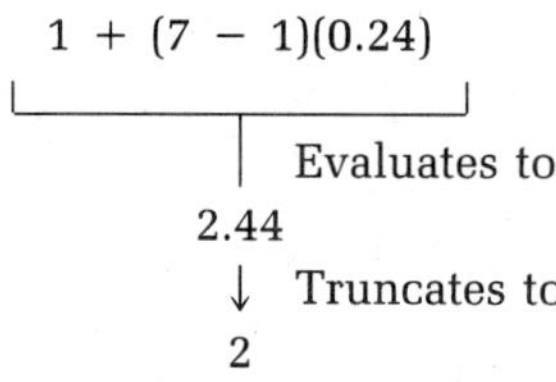

Situation 3 The occurrence of an event is associated with a value, and the value is *normally* distributed, with mean μ and standard deviation σ. We assume here a familiarity with the notion of a bell-shaped normal distribution and its associated mean and standard deviation. Such a distribution is used to model a variety of events in which values tend to aggregate around a middle value, known as the mean. For instance, test scores may be normally distributed around a mean of 70 with a standard deviation of 10, or temperature readings (in Fahrenheit) may be normally distributed around a mean of 60 with a standard deviation of 15. For a precise definition of the normal distribution, consult any introductory statistics text.

In such a situation, the normally distributed value may be approximated by generating 12 random numbers $X_1, X_2, X_3, \ldots, X_{12}$ and then using them in the following formula:

$$\mu + \sigma\left(\left(\sum_{i=1}^{12} X_i\right) - 6\right)$$

For instance, to generate a normally distributed temperature with mean 60 and standard deviation 15:

1. Generate 12 random values between 0 and 1 and form their sum. Suppose that this sum turns out to be 5.5.
2. Subtract 6 from the sum in step 1, obtaining -0.5.
3. Multiply the value in step 2 by the standard deviation 15, obtaining -7.5.
4. Add the result of step 3 to the mean 60, yielding a generated temperature of 52.5.

A justification of why this formula approximates a normally distributed variable is due to a famous theorem of statistics called the Central Limit Theorem. If you are interested in finding out more about this theorem, see Chapter 4 of the Karian and Dudewicz text cited earlier in this Appendix.

Appendix 10 Random Access File in Various Versions of Pascal

The original standard for Pascal developed by Kathleen Jensen and Niklaus Wirth (*Pascal User Manual and Report* (Berlin: Springer-Verlag, 1974)) made no provision for random (direct) access files. From the perspective of leaning structured programming concepts, this is not a serious omission. From the perspective of applying data structure concepts in the real world, however, it is a major omission. This is because most programs with a database orientation involve storing large amounts of data in files and then accessing the data by a search strategy that guarantees a quick response time. Without direct access, a tedious sequential search is the only method possible. Hence, what has emerged is that most implementors of Pascal compilers have developed their own procedures for directly accessing records that reside in a disk file. A general picture that applies in all of these various implementations follows:

A record from a random access file may be acted upon (for instance, updated) only when it has been retrieved as the currently available record in the main memory buffer associated with that file. (Actually, application programmers may think of the currently available record and the file's buffer as coinciding, though this is an oversimplification that can affect the efficiency of the search technique being considered. See Chapter 23 for a discussion of this point.) Hence the problem of programming in Pascal with random access files becomes one of being able to

1. Retrieve the Kth record from the file as the currently available record in main memory (where K is an arbitrary positive integer less than or equal to the number of records in the file).

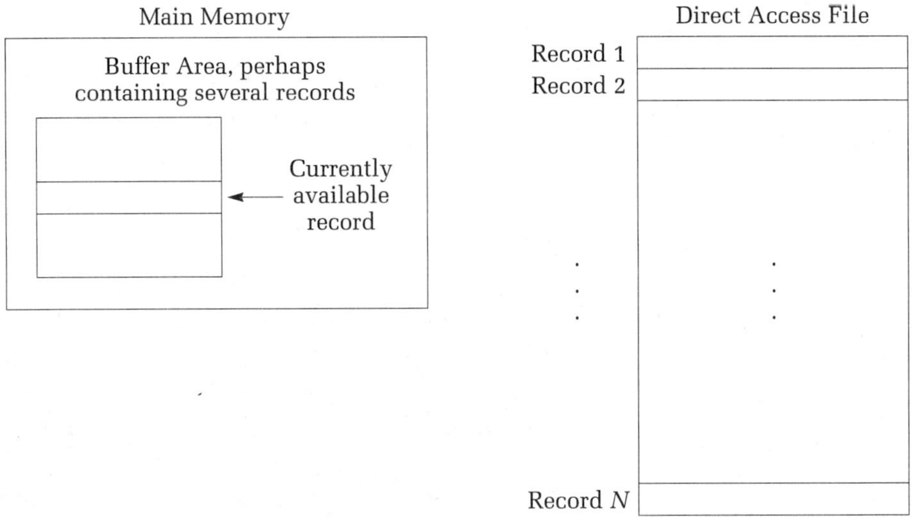

2. Update the currently available record in main memory.
3. Write the currently available record in memory to the Kth position in the file

Step 2 may typically be accomplished by using standard Pascal's up-arrow notation for a file variable. (See Chapter 12 for a discussion of this notation.) For example,

```
F1.IDNumber := 4918;
```

will assign the value 4918 to the IDNumber field of the record currently available in main memory. Note that this assignment is only made in memory; nothing is altered in the file until this record is written out to the appropriate file position.

Thus, only steps 1 and 3 require special nonstandard Pascal procedures. Once such procedures exist, search algorithms that apply to arrays may also be appropriately applied to random access files. Hence, a random access file may be conceptually thought of as a large array that resides on disk.

In the following examples, we assume that *F* is a Pascal file variable associated with records of an appropriate type (other than text). For each implementation of Pascal specified, we describe how to open, retrieve, and update records for random access file processing. If you do not see your system specified, the examples should nonetheless provide points of comparison to help you understand the local documentation describing similar facilities for your environment.

DEC's VAX-Pascal

- To open a file for random access:

```
open (F, access_method := direct, organization := relative);
```

- To fetch Kth record as currently available record:

```
find(F, K);
```

- To write currently available record to Kth position

```
locate(F, K)
put(F);
```

or

```
update(F); { if file already positioned at Kth record }
```

Macintosh and Lightspeed Pascal for the Apple Macintosh Family

- To open a file for random access:

```
open(F, filename);
```

- To fetch Kth record as currently available record:

```
seek(F, K);
```

- To write currently available record to Kth file position:

```
seek(F, K);
   .
   .
   .
put(F);
```

Oregon Software's (OMSI) Pascal-1 and Pascal-2

- To open a file for random access:

```
reset(F, filename specified with '=seek' switch);
```

- To retrieve Kth record as currently available record:

```
seek (F, K)
```

- To write currently available record to Kth file position:

```
seek (F, K)
   .
   . [ Appropriate updating ]
   .
put(F);
```

Turbo Pascal

- To open a file for random access:

```
assign(F, filename);
resest(F);
```

(Keep in mind that in Turbo Pascal, records are numbered beginning at 0.)

- To fetch Kth record into TempRec as the currently available record:

```
seek(F, K);
read(F, TempRec);
```

(In Turbo, the record is accessed in a declared record location, such as TempRec, instead of by accessing the buffer directly via F↑.)

- To write the currently available record in TempRec to Kth file position:

```
seek(F, K);
write (F, TempRec);
```

(For further information on Turbo Pascal, see Appendix 7.)

Glossary

abstract data type (ADT) A form of abstraction that arises from the use of defined types. An ADT consists of a class of objects, a defined set of properties of those objects, and a set of operations for processing the objects.

abstraction The description of data structures at a conceptual level, apart from their implementation using a particular technique and language.

abstract syntax tree *See* **parse tree.**

acceptance testing That testing phase in which the full system is released to the end users for their evaluation.

accumulator A variable used for the purpose of summing successive values of some other variable.

actual parameter A variable or expression contained in a procedure or function call and passed to that procedure or function. *See also* **formal parameter.**

Ada A newer, package-oriented programming language developed by the U.S. Defense Department.

address Once called address of a memory location, this is an integer value that the computer can use to reference a location. *See also* **value** and **pointer.**

ADT *See* **abstract data type.**

ADT implementation rule An implementation of an ADT must provide an interface that is entirely consistent with the operations specified in the ADT's definition.

ADT use rule An algorithm that uses an ADT should access variables of that abstract data type only through the operations provided in the ADT definition.

algorithm A finite sequence of effective statements that, when applied to the problem, will solve it.

analysis phase The first phase of the software system life cycle in which the systems analyst determines the user's needs and develops formal specifications describing the proposed system and its requirements.

ancestor A tree node which is hierarchically related to another tree node at a lower level in the tree.

application software Programs designed for a specific use.

argument A value or expression passed in a function or procedure call.

arithmetic/logic unit (ALU) The part of the central processing unit (CPU) that performs arithmetic operations and evaluates expressions.

array A structured variable designed to handle data of the same type.

array index The relative position of the components of an array.

array of records An array whose component type is a record.

artificial intelligence (AI) The field of computer science in which the goal is to program the computer to mimic intelligent human behavior.

ASCII collating sequence The American Standard Code for Information Interchange ordering for a character set.

assembler A computer program that automatically converts assembly language instructions to machine language.

assembly language A computer language that allows words and symbols to be used in an unsophisticated manner to accomplish simple tasks.

assertion Special comments used with selection and repetition that state what you expect to happen and when certain conditions will hold.

assignment statement A method of putting values into memory locations.

assignment, string The copying of one string variable to another.

automatic program synthesis Situation in which one computer program can be given the specifications for another computer program, generate the code to satisfy those specifications, and then prove the correctness of that code.

Backus-Naur grammar A standard form for defining the formal syntax of a language.

batch input Input for a program being run in batch mode. Also referred to as stream input.

batch processing A technique of executing the program by reading data from a file that has been created. User interaction with the computer is not required during execution. Also referred to as stream input.

BEGIN . . . END block The segment of code between **BEGIN** and **END** that, when a compound statement is executed within a program, is treated as a single statement.

best case The arrangement of data items prior to beginning a sort procedure that allows the sort procedure to finish in the least amount of time for that particular set of items. *See also* **worst case.**

big-O analysis A technique in which the time and space requirements of an algorithm are estimated in order of magnitude terms.

big-O notation Saying that an algorithm is $O(f(n))$ indicates that the function $f(n)$ may be useful in characterizing how efficiently the algorithm performs for large n. For such n, we are assured that the operations required by the algorithm will be bounded by a constant times $f(n)$.

bin sort *See* **radix sort.**

binary buddy system System used to coalesce blocks of memory in which all blocks have size 2^k for some integer k.

binary code A term often used as a synonym for machine language.

binary digit A digit, either 0 or 1, in the binary number system. Program instructions are stored in memory using a sequence of binary digits. Binary digits are called bits.

binary search The process of examining a middle value of a sorted array to see which half contains the value in question and halving until the value is located.

binary search tree A binary tree with the ordering property.

binary tree A tree such that each node can point to at most two children.

binary tree index A binary tree with the ordering property used as an index for the positions of keys in a random access file.

binary tree search A search algorithm driven by the hierarchical relationships of data items in a tree with the ordering property.

binding time The time at which a program variable is bound to a particular value. This can occur either at compile time or run time.

bit *See* **binary digit.**

black box testing The method of testing a module in which the tester is aware of only what the module is supposed to do, not the method of implementation or internal logic. *See also* **white box testing.**

block A contiguous area on a magnetic disk capable of storing a fixed amount of data.

block A program in Pascal can be thought of as a heading and a block. The block contains an optional declaration part and a compound statement. The block structure for a subprogram is a subblock. *See also* **subblock.**

blocked queue In an operating system, the queue of processes that have requested a resource currently owned by another process.

Boolean expression An expression whose value is either true or false. *See also* **compound Boolean expression** and **simple Boolean expression.**

bottom-up testing Independent testing of modules.

boundary conditions Values that separate two logical possibilities. These are important cases to check when testing a module.

boundary folding A variation on shift folding; in boundary folding, the digits in every other numeric section are reversed before the addition is performed.

boundary tag buddy system System for coalescing blocks of memory in which each block contains bookkeeping information at both its upper and lower boundaries.

branch In a tree, a link between a parent and its child node.

breadth-first traversal A visiting of all nodes in a graph; it proceeds from each node by first visiting all nodes adjacent to that node.

B-tree An efficient, flexible index structure often used in data-base management systems on random access files.

bubble sort Rearranges elements of an array until they are in either ascending or descending order. Consecutive elements are compared to move (bubble) the elements to the top or bottom accordingly during each pass. *See also* **heap sort, insertion sort, merge sort, quick sort, radix sort, selection sort,** and **shell sort.**

bucket In bucket hashing, an contiguous region of storage locations.

bucket hashing Method of handling collisions in which the hashing function sends the key to a bucket of locations rather than a single location. The key is then placed by performing a sequential search within the bucket.

buddy system Name applied to a variety of techniques which coalesce blocks of memory being returned from users.

buffer variable The actual vehicle through which values are passed to or from a file component.

built-in function *See* **standard function.**

bus A group of wires imprinted on a circuit board to facilitate communication between components of a computer.

byte A sequence of bits used to encode a character in memory. *See also* **word.**

call Any reference to a subprogram by an executable statement. Also referred to as invoke.

central processing unit (CPU) A major hardware component that consists of the arithmetic/logic unit (ALU) and the control unit.

character set The list of characters available for data and program statements. *See also* **collating sequence.**

child node A node that descends from another node in a tree.

children Nodes pointed to by an element in a tree.

circular linked list A linked list in which the last node of the list points to the first node in the list.

class object In object-oriented programming, the bundling of both the data fields and the operations for an ADT into the ADT's declaration.

cluster In a linked list implementation of a character string, the placement of more than one character per data node forms a cluster of data.

clustering Occurs when a hashing function is biased toward the placement of keys in a given region of the storage space.

coalescing The process by which two adjacent available blocks of memory are combined into one larger block.

code (writing) The process of writing executable statements that are part of a program to solve a problem.

coding phase The third phase of the software system life cycle. The code necessary to implement the system design specifications is produced in this phase.

cohesive subprogram A subprogram designed to accomplish a single task.

collating sequence The particular order sequence for a character set used by a machine. *See also* **ASCII** and **EBCDIC.**

collision Condition in which more than one key hashes to the same position with a given hashing function.

column major Implementation of a two-dimensional array as a one-dimensional array so that the columns are arranged in sequential order with all entries of the same column being adjacent.

comment A nonexecutable statement used to make a program more readable.

compaction The process of collecting all fragments of available memory and moving them to one end of memory to create one large block.

compatible (type) Variables that have the same base type. A value parameter and its argument must be of compatible type. *See also* **identical (type).**

compilation error An error detected when the program is being compiled. A complete list of compilation error messages is set forth in Appendix 5. *See also* **design error, run-time error,** and **syntax error.**

compiler A computer program that automatically converts instructions in a high-level language to machine language.

compiler symbol table A table kept by a compiler; it contains the identifiers used in the source program currently being compiled.

component of a file One element of the file data type.

component of a linked list *See* **node.**

component of an array One element of the array data type.

compound Boolean expression Refers to the complete expression when logical connectives and negation are used to generate Boolean values. *See also* **Boolean expression** and **simple Boolean expression.**

compound statement Uses the reserved words **BEGIN** and **END** to make several simple statements into a single compound statement.

computer graphics The use of computers to produce pictures.

concatenation, string The joining together of two character strings.

concurrent updating When two users each update the same record of a file at the same time.

conditional statement *See* **selection statement.**

constant The contents of a memory location whose contents cannot be changed.

constant definition section The section where program constants are defined for subsequent use.

control structure A structure that controls the flow of execution of program statements.

control unit The part of the central processing unit (CPU) that controls the operation of the rest of the computer.

counter A variable used to count the number of times some process is completed.

coupling The amount of interaction between a pair of modules.

cubic algorithm A polynomial algorithm in which the highest nonzero term is n^3.

data The particular characters that are used to represent information in a form suitable for storage, processing, and communication.

data about data Data that a program stores (for example, a pointer) in order to keep track of the data it is designed to be storing.

data abstraction The separation between the conceptual definition of a data structure and its eventual implementation.

data flow diagram A graphic tool used by a systems analyst to represent data flow and transformations in a conceptual process. Also referred to as a bubble diagram.

data integrity The problem of ensuring that no data are lost or corrupted due to concurrent updating.

data movement The physical transfer of data stored in computer memory from one location to another.

data type A formal description of the set of values that a variable can have.

data validation The process of examining data prior to use of the data in a program.

deadlock An infinite wait state in which two processes each own system resources the other needs and will not release these until they have obtained the remaining resources they need. Also referred to as fatal embrace.

debugging The process of eliminating errors or "bugs" from a program.

declaration section The section used to declare (name) all symbolic constants, data types, variables, and subprograms that are necessary to the program.

decrement To decrease the value of a variable.

deletion, string In text editing applications, removing a substring from the middle of string.

density The density is the number of storage locations used divided by the number of total storage locations available.

density-dependent search technique Search technique whose efficiency is determined solely by the density of the data.
depth-first traversal A visiting of all nodes in a graph; this traversal proceeds from each node by probing as deeply as possible along one path leading from that node.
design error An error such that a program runs, but unexpected results are produced. Also referred to as a logic error. *See also* **compilation error, run-time error,** and **syntax error.**
design phase Second phase of the software system life cycle. In this phase, a relatively detailed design plan is created from the formal specifications of the system as produced in the analysis phase.
difference The difference of set A and set B is A − B where A − B contains the elements that are in A but not in B. *See also* **intersection, subset,** and **union.**
digit/character extraction In creating a hashing function, the process of removing from a key those digits or characters that may bias the results of the hashing function.
digraph A graph in which some edges exist only in one direction.
diminishing increment sort A sort in which the number of segments on which the sort works on any one pass decreases with each successive pass. *See also* **shell sort.**
directional graph *See* **digraph.**
disk file A file that resides on a secondary storage medium (usually a magnetic disk) rather than in main memory.
division-remainder technique A technique used in creating hashing functions to ensure that the result will be a valid output. It uses the **MOD** function to scale the value into the proper range. *See also* **integer arithmetic operations.**
documentation The insertion of explanatory remarks into the program code to make maintenance of the program easier.
dominant term The highest power of n in a polynomial. For large n, the behavior of the entire polynomial will approach the behavior of the polynomial that contains only that term.
doubly-linked list A linked list in which each node has two pointers instead of one. One pointer points to the node preceding that node in the list and the other points to the node following that node in the list.
driver *See* **driver module.**
driver module A module used in testing another module. The driver module calls on the module being tested, sends it the values it needs, and then reports the values returned from that module.
dummy header A node preceding the first actual data node in a list and often containing information about the list.
dynamic memory manangement The allocation and reclamation of computer memory locations as necessary during program execution.
dynamic structure A data structure that may expand or contract during execution of a program.
dynamic variable Frequently designed as Ptr^ or Ptr↑, a dynamic variable is a variable accessed by a pointer variable.
EBCDIC collating sequence The Extended Binary Coded Decimal Interchange Code ordering for a character set.
echo checking A debugging technique in which values of variables and input data are displayed during program execution.
edge A direct connection between two nodes in graph.
effective statement A clear, unambiguous instruction that can be carried out.
efficiency ratio For a sparse table implementation method, the efficiency ratio is the number of storage locations used by that method divided by the number of storage locations used by standard row-major form.
element of an array *See* **component of an array.**
element of a set A value that has been assigned to a set.
embedded length implementation An implementation of the string ADT in which the length of the string is stored and maintained as part the record encapsulating the string.
empty set A set containing no elements. Also called a null set.
empty statement A semicolon used to indicate that no action is to be taken. Also referred to as a null statement.
encapsulation Grouping into a single record description all those data items necessary to implement an ADT.
encapsulation principle Whenever the implementation of an ADT involves several data items, these data items should be grouped into a record by which the ADT is identified to high-level logic.
end-of-file marker (eof) A special marker inserted by the machine to indicate the end of the data file. In this text it is represented by a black square (■).
end-of-line marker (eoln) A special marker inserted by the machine to indicate the end of a line in the data. In this text it is represented by a black column (▌).
entrance controlled loop *See* **pretest loop.**
enumerated data type A data type that is defined in the **TYPE** definition section by the programmer. Also referred to as user-defined data type.
equivalence classes A partitioning of all the logical possibilities that can be checked when testing a module. All test cases within a single equivalence class are identical from the standpoint of the logic of the module.
error *See* **compilation error, design error, run-time error,** and **syntax error.**
executable section Contains the statements that cause the computer to do something. Starts with the reserved word **BEGIN** and concludes with the reserved word **END.**
executable statement The basic unit of grammar in Pascal consisting of valid identifiers, standard identifiers, reserved words, numbers, and/or characters, together with appropriate punctuation.
execute To perform a program step-by-step.
exit controlled loop *See* **posttest loop.**

expert system Program able to reason as an expert in a limited domain world.

exponential algorithm An algorithm whose efficiency is dominated by a term of the form a^n.

exponential form *See* **floating point.**

extended IF statement Nested selection where additional **IF . . . THEN . . . ELSE** statements are used in the **ELSE** option. *See also* **nested IF statement.**

external file A file used to store data in secondary storage between runs of a program. *See also* **internal file.**

external sort A sort in which the list being sorted resides in a file rather than in memory.

factorial The product of the first N positive integers (denoted N!).

fatal embrace *See* **deadlock.**

Fibonacci buddy system System of coalescing blocks of memory in which all blocks of memory have a size corresponding to one of the numbers in the Fibonacci sequence.

field A component of a record.

field width The phrase used to describe the number of columns used for various output. *See also* **formatting.**

FIFO *See* **queue.**

file A data structure that consists of a sequence of components all of the same type.

file buffer An area in main memory associated with a file; the file buffer is capable of storing exactly one record from that file.

file window A term used in this book, though not designated by Pascal, to indicate an imaginary window through which values of a file component can be transferred.

finite state automata Algorithms driven by a table indexed by the possible states that can exist and the possible categories of input characters are called finite state algorithms. Machines that operate under such algorithms are called finite state automata.

finite state machine A method that conveniently employs enumerated types to perform a robustness check on strings of characters entered by a user.

first-in, first-out (FIFO) *See* **queue.**

fixed length method A method of storing strings in which a fixed amount of space is allocated for each string regardless of its actual length.

fixed repetition loop A loop used if the number of times a segment of code needs to be repeated is known in advance. **FOR . . . TO . . . DO** is a fixed repetition loop. Also referred to as an iterated loop.

fixed parts Fields in a record that exist for all records of a particular type. *See also* **variant part.**

fixed point A method of writing decimal numbers where the decimal is placed where it belongs in the number. *See also* **floating point.**

floating point A method for writing numbers in scientific notation to accommodate numbers that may have very large or very small values. Exactly one nonzero digit must appear on the left of the decimal. *See also* **fixed point.**

folding A method of constructing a hashing function in cases where the key is not an integer value whereby the nonnumeric characters are removed and the remaining digits are combined to produce an integer value.

FOR loop A fixed repetition loop causing a fragment of code to be executed a predetermined number of times. **FOR . . . TO . . . DO** and **FOR . . . DOWNTO . . . DO** are **FOR** loops.

formal parameter A variable, declared and used in a procedure or function declaration, that is replaced by an actual parameter when the procedure or function is called.

formal verification The use of the basic principles and axioms of logic to produce a proof of the correctness of an algorithm.

formatting Designating the desired field width when printing integers, reals, Boolean values, and character strings. *See also* **field width.**

forward reference A method of listing a subprogram heading without writing the subprogram. This allows a subprogram to be referenced by other subprograms before it appears as a complete subprogram in the list of subprograms.

fragmentation problem Problem faced by an operating system where after frequent allocation of memory to and reclamation of memory from users, the overall pattern of available memory is one of relatively small, disconnected fragments of available space.

front pointer The pointer to the front of a queue.

function *See* **standard function** and **user-defined function.**

functionally cohesive A functionally cohesive module achieves one particular predefined task without having unexpected side effects on the performance of other modules in the system.

general list A collection of data items, all of the same type, which are related to each other by their relative position in the list.

general tree A set of nodes that is either empty or has a designated node (called the root) from which descend zero or more subtrees.

generalized nested loops Nested loops whose nesting depth is determined at run-time using recursive logic.

global identifier An identifier that can be used by the main program and all subprograms in a program.

global variable *See* **global identifier.**

graph A set of data elements called nodes and the paths between those data elements called edges.

halting problem Problem concerned with determining whether or not a given program will terminate or loop indefinitely when provided with a given set of input data.

hardware The actual computing machine and its support devices.

hashing A density-dependent search technique in which the key for a given data item is transformed using a hashing function to produce the address in which that item is stored in memory.

hashing function A key-to-address transformation.

head pointer A pointer to the head or front of the list.

heap The portion of computer memory not required to store the program instructions, predeclared data storage locations, or various operating system requirements. The heap contains the memory used for dynamic memory requests.

heap A binary tree with the heap property.

heap property A binary tree has the heap property when the data at any given node are greater than or equal to the data in its left and right subtrees.

heap sort Sort in which the array is treated like the array implementation of a binary tree and the items are repeatedly manipulated to create a heap from which the root is removed and added to the sorted portion of the array. *See also* **bubble sort, insertion, merge sort, quick sort, radix sort, selection sort,** and **shell sort.**

height balancing A technique for ensuring that an ordered binary tree remains as full as possible in form.

heterogeneous A set of elements is heterogeneous if the elements are not all of the same type.

heuristics Rules of thumb which cut down on the number of possible choices to examine. They often lead to quick solutions but do not guarantee a solution the way an algorithm does.

hierarchy A relationship between nodes in which one is viewed as above or prior to another.

high-level language Any programming language that uses words and symbols to make it relatively easy to read and write a program. *See also* **assembly language** and **machine language.**

higher-dimensional array An array of more than two dimensions.

homogeneous A set of elements is homogeneous if the elements are all of the same type.

identical (type) Variables that are declared with the same type identifier. A variable parameter and its argument must be of identical type.

identifiers Words that must be created according to a well-defined set of rules but can have any meaning subject to these rules. *See also* **standard identifiers.**

implementation The process representing the abstract model of the system and its abstract data types in terms of declarations and instructions in a particular computer language.

index *See* **array index** or **loop index.**

indexed sequential access method (ISAM) The most common method of indexed sequential search.

indexed sequential search Use of a partial index based on disk-dependent factors to find the proper portion of the disk on which to sequentially search for the key.

index sort Sorting an array by ordering the indices of the components rather than exchanging the components.

index type The data type used for specifying the range for the index of an array. The index type can be any ordinal data type that specifies an initial and final value.

inductive assertion A method of formally proving the correctness of an algorithm by using an inductive proof.

infinite loop A loop in which the controlling condition is not changed in such a manner to allow the loop to terminate.

infix Algebraic notation in which the arithmetic operator appears between the two operands upon which it will be applied.

infix priority Function to hierarchically rank algebraic operators in order of precedence.

information hiding Characteristic of a package which allows it to be used by a calling program without that program requiring knowledge of how the package achieves the implementation.

inorder predecessor The node preceding a given node in an inorder tree traversal.

inorder successor The node following a given node in an inorder tree traversal.

inorder threads Pointers to the inorder predecessor and inorder successor of a node.

inorder traversal A binary tree traversal in which at any node, that node's left subtree is visited first, then that node is processed, and finally that node's right subtree is visited.

input Data obtained by a program during its execution. *See also* **batch input** and **interactive input.**

input assertion A precondition for a loop.

input device A device that provides information to the computer. Typical devices are keyboards, disk drives, card readers, and tape drives. *See also* **I/O device** and **output device.**

insertion rule For binary trees, rule whereby a new item is placed in the left subtree of an item greater than it or in the right subtree of an item less than it.

insertion sort Sorts an array of elements in either ascending or descending order. Starts with an empty array and inserts elements one at a time in their proper order. *See also* **bubble sort, heap sort, merge sort, quick sort, radix sort, selection sort,** and **shell sort.**

insertion, string In text editing applications, placing one string in the middle of another string.

instance In object-oriented programming, a specifically declared variable that belongs to a particular class of objects.

integer arithmetic operations Operations allowed on data of type **integer.** This includes the operations of addition, subtraction, multiplication, **MOD,** and **DIV** to produce integer answers.

interactive input A method of getting data into the program from the keyboard. User interaction is required during execution.

interface A formal statement of how communication occurs between subprograms, the main driver, and other subprograms.

interface for an ADT A collection of Pascal procedure and function headers for the operations which act on ADT objects.

internal file A file, also called a temporary or scratch file, that is used for processing only and not saved in secondary storage. *See also* **external file.**

internal sort A sort in which the list being sorted resides in memory.

intersection The intersection of set A and set B is A * B where A * B contains the elements that are in both A and B. *See also* **difference, subset,** and **union.**

invariant expression An assertion that is true before the loop and after each iteration of the loop.

invoke *See* **call.**

I/O device Any device that allows information to be transmitted to or from a computer. *See also* **input device** and **output device.**

iterated loop *See* **fixed repetition loop.**

iteration *See* **loops.**

key Field in a general list that is used to order or access elements of the list.

keyed list A collection of records, each of which is the same type. The records in the list are organized around a designated key field. This key field must take on a unique value for each record and have a well-defined ordering. The records are to be viewed as arranged in logical order by this key field.

keyed ordering Ordering imposed on the entries in a list by the value of a key field.

key-to-address transformation Transformation in which the key of the data item is transformed to provide the address at which the data are actually stored.

keywords Either reserved words or predefined identifiers.

last-in, first-out (LIFO) *See* **stack.**

leaf In a tree, a node that has no children.

length (of an array) The number of components of an array.

level All nodes in a tree with the same length path from the root node.

lexical analysis The task of recognizing valid language tokens in an incoming stream of characters.

LIFO *See* **stack.**

linear algorithm A polynomial algorithm in which the highest nonzero term is n.

linear collision processing Method of handling a collision in which the storage space is searched sequentially from the location of the collision for an available location where the new key can be placed.

linear ordering Any ordering of data in which there is an identifiable first element, second element, and so forth.

linear representation (of binary tree) An implementation of a binary tree in an array. For a given node stored at index position K, that node's left child is at position 2 * K, and the right child is at position 2 * K + 1.

linear search *See* **sequential search.**

link A pointer from one node to another.

linked collision processing Method of handling a collision in which the second key is stored in a linked list located in an overflow area.

linked list A collection of elements called nodes, each of which contains a data portion and a pointer to the node which follows that one in the linear ordering of the list.

linked representation An implementation of a binary tree in which pointer fields are used to reference the right and left child of a node in the tree (as opposed to the linear representation of a binary tree).

LISP (LISt Processor) A highly-recursive computer programming language used heavily in artificial intelligence (AI).

list traversal The process of sequentially visiting each node in a list.

local identifier An identifier that is restricted to use within a subblock of a program.

local variable *See* **local identifier.**

logarithmic algorithm An algorithm whose efficiency is dominated by a term of the form $\log_a n$.

logic error *See* **design error.**

logical operator Either logical connective **(AND, OR)** or negation **(NOT).**

logical order An ordering of data items according to some defined criterion such as alphabetic, increasing numeric, and so forth. That logical order of the data may or may not be the physical order of the data as stored in the computer.

logically sorted Data have been logically sorted when pointers to the data have been sorted, even though the data itself have not been touched. Hence, items that the sort places consecutively need not be physically adjacent.

$\log_2 n$ search algorithm A search algorithm whose efficiency is dominated by a term of the form $\log_2 n$.

loop goal expression *See* **invariant expression.**

loop index Variable used for control values in a **FOR** loop.

loop invariant An assertion that expresses a relationship between variables that remain constant throughout all iterations of the loop.

loops Program statements that cause a process to be repeated. *See also* **FOR loop, REPEAT . . . UNTIL loop,** and **WHILE . . . DO loop.**

loop variant An assertion whose truth changes between the first and final execution of the loop.

loop verification The process of guaranteeing that a loop performs its intended task.

low-level language *See* **assembly language.**

machine language This language is used directly by the computer in all its calculations and processing.

main block The part of a program consisting of both the declaration and executable sections.

main driver The main program when subprograms are used to accomplish specific tasks.

main memory Memory contained in the computer. *See also* **memory** and **secondary memory device.**

main unit A computer's main unit contains the central processing unit (CPU) and the main (primary) memory; it is hooked to an input device and an output device.

mainframe Large computers typically used by major companies and universities. *See also* **microcomputer** and **minicomputer.**

maintenance phase The fifth phase of the software system life cycle. In this phase, changes must be made in the original program either to fix errors discovered by the users of the program or to meet new user needs.

mapping function A function that transforms row-column array coordinates to the linear address of that array entry.

master file An existing external file.

maxint The largest integer constant available to a particular system.

memory The ordered sequence of storage cells that can be accessed by address. Instructions and variables of an executing program are temporarily held here. *See also* **main memory** and **secondary memory device.**

memory location A storage cell that can be accessed by address. *See also* **memory.**

merge The process of combining lists. Typically refers to files or arrays.

merge sort Sort in which the array is repeatedly split in half and then these pieces are merged together. *See also* **bubble sort, heap sort, insertion sort, quick sort, radix sort, selection sort,** and **shell sort.**

message In object-oriented programming, a signal to perform an operation on an object.

message-passing In object-oriented programming, one object's telling another object to perform an operation that is part of its encapsulation.

method of inductive assertions Method of formally verifying the correctness of an algorithm by identifying the input assertions, output assertions, and loop invariants of the algorithm and constructing a verification proof by mathematical induction.

microcomputer A personal computer with relatively limited memory, generally used by one person at a time. *See also* **mainframe** and **minicomputer.**

minicomputer A small version of a mainframe computer. It can be used by several people at once. *See also* **mainframe** and **microcomputer.**

mixed-mode Expressions containing data of both **integer** and **real** types; the value will be given as a real and not as an integer.

Modula-2 A newer, package-oriented programming language developed by Nicklaus Wirth (of Pascal fame).

modular development The process of developing an algorithm using modules. *See also* **module.**

modular specifications A description of the data received by, information returned from, and logic of a module within a system's design.

modular structure chart A graphic tool used by software designers to display the hierarchical relationships among the modules of the software system.

modular testing A method of testing in which each module is tested immediately after it has been completed rather than when the entire system has been completed.

modularity The property possessed by a program which is written using modules.

module An independent unit that is part of a larger development. Usually a procedure or function. *See also* **modular development.**

module specifications A description of data received, information returned, and logic used in the module.

multilinked list A linked list in which each node has two or more link fields.

natural language A language by which humans normally communicate (such as English), as opposed to a formal programming language (such as Pascal).

negation The use of the logical operator **NOT** to negate the Boolean value of an expression.

nested IF statement A selection statement used within another selection statement.

nested loop A loop as one of the statements in the body of another loop.

nested record A record as a field in another record.

nested selection Any combination of selection statements within selection statements. *See also* **selection statement.**

nested subprograms Functions or procedures within functions or procedures.

network A graph in which the edges have weight values associated with them.

node One data item in a linked list, tree, graph, or network.

null set *See* **empty set.**

null statement *See* **empty statement.**

numerical analysis A field concerned with obtaining numerical answers to mathematical problems which involve much computation.

object code *See* **object program.**

object-oriented programming A programming paradigm in which a data object is viewed as the owner of operations, as opposed to procedural programming in which an operation is passed data objects as actual parameters. Object-oriented programming emphasizes the ADT approach and allows the users of an ADT to extend the operations of an ADT library in a convenient and efficient fashion.

object program The machine code version of the source program.

opened for reading Positions a pointer at the beginning of a file for the purpose of reading from the file.

opened for writing Positions a pointer at the beginning of a file for the purpose of writing to the file.

opening a file Positions a pointer at the beginning of a file. *See also* **opened for reading** and **opened for writing.**

operating system A large program that allows the user to communicate with the hardware.

operations Actions to be performed on an abstract data type.

order of magnitude Power of ten. Two numbers have the same order of magnitude if their representations in scientific notation have identical exponents to designate the power of ten.

ordering A means of arranging the elements in a list.

ordering property In a binary tree, the data in each node of the tree are greater than or equal to all of the data in that node's left subtree and less than or equal to all of the data in its right subtree.

ordinal data type A data type ordered in some association with the integers; each integer is the ordinal of its associated character.
output Information that is produced by a program.
output assertion A postcondition for a loop.
output device A device that allows you to see the results of a program. Typically it is a monitor or printer. *See* **input device** and **I/O device.**
overflow In arithmetic operations, a value may be too large for the computer's memory location. A meaningless value may be assigned or an error message may result. *See also* **underflow.**
overflow area In linked collision processing, the area in which keys that cause collisions are placed.
packed array An array that has had data placed in consecutive bytes.
packed array implementation An implementation of the string ADT in which no data other than the characters composing the string are stored in the encapsulation of the string.
parallel arrays Arrays of the same length but with different component data types.
parallel processing The use of more than one processor to execute parts of a program concurrently. The effect is that these parts are completed in parallel rather than in sequence.
parameter *See* **argument.**
parameter list A list of parameters. An actual parameter list is contained in the procedure or function call. A formal parameter list is contained in the procedure or function heading.
parent In a tree, the node that is pointing to its children.
parse tree Tree representation of the syntactic structure of a source program produced by a compiler. Also referred to as abstract syntax tree.
parser A program that checks the syntax of an expression and represents that expression in a unique form.
parser generator A program that can take the input grammar for a language and produce the parser for that language.
parsing The procedure of checking the syntax of an expression and representing it in one unique form.
partition In quick sort, the process of moving the pivot to the location where it belongs in the sorted array and arranging the remaining data items to the left of the pivot if they are less than or equal to the pivot and to the right if they are greater than the pivot.
passed by reference When variable parameters are used in subprograms.
path A sequence of edges which connect two nodes in a graph or network.
peripheral memory *See* **secondary memory device** and **memory.**
permutation An ordered arrangement of the first n positive integers in which each integer appears exactly once.
physically ordered array implementation An implementation of the keyed list ADT in which the logical order of the items in the list matches their physical position in an array.
physically sorted Data are physically sorted when the sort routine has actually manipulated the data so that items that the sort places consecutively are also physically adjacent.
pivot Item used to direct the partitioning in quick sort.
pointer A memory location containing the location of another data item.
pointer sort A sort in which pointers to the data are manipulated rather than the data itself.
pointer variable A special data type used in Pascal to reference the location of other data. *See also* **address** and **dynamic variable.**
polymorphism That feature of object-oriented programming which allows one operation to have different meaning for different kinds of objects.
polynomial algorithm An algorithm whose efficiency can be expressed in terms of a polynomial.
pop A procedure that removes an item from the top of the stack.
postcondition An assertion written after a segment of code.
postfix Unambiguous algebraic notation in which the arithmetic operator appears after the two operands upon which it is to be applied.
postorder traversal A binary tree traversal in which at any node, that node's left subtree is visited first, then that node's right subtree is visited, and finally that node is processed.
posttest loop A loop where the control condition is tested after the loop is executed. **REPEAT . . . UNTIL** is a posttest loop. Also referred to as an exit controlled loop.
precondition An assertion written before a particular statement.
prefix Unambiguous algebraic notation in which the arithmetic operator appears before the two operands upon which it is to be applied.
preorder traversal A binary tree traversal in which at any node, that node is first processed, then that node's left subtree is visited, and finally that node's right subtree is visited.
pretest condition A condition that controls whether the body of the loop is executed before going through the loop.
pretest loop A loop where the control condition is tested before the loop is executed. **WHILE . . . DO** is a pretest loop. Also referred to as an entrance controlled loop.
primary memory *See* **main memory** and **memory.**
prime hash area In linked collision processing, the main storage area in which keys are placed if no collision occurs.
priority queue A queue in which the entries on the queue are ranked into groups according to priority. Such a queue requires a rear pointer for each different possible priority value.
procedural abstraction The process of considering only what a procedure is to do rather than details of the procedure.

procedure A subprogram designed to perform a specific task as part of a larger program. Procedures are not limited to returning a single value to the main program.

profile an algorithm A means of empirically measuring the execution of an algorithm by inserting counters to keep track of the number of times certain instructions are executed during a run of the program.

program A set of instructions that tells the machine (the hardware) what to do.

program heading The first statement of any Pascal program; it must contain the reserved word **PROGRAM.**

program proof An analysis of a program that attempts to verify the correctness of program results.

program protection A method of using selection statements to guard against unexpected results.

program walk-through The process of carefully following, using pencil and paper, steps the computer uses to solve the problem given in a program. Also referred to as a trace.

programmer-supplied identifier *See* **identifier.**

programming by personification In object-oriented programming, invoking an operation by sending a message to the object to perform an operation that is part of its encapsulation. The object is viewed as an actor who is told to perform a particular scene in a play.

programming language Formal language that computer scientists use to give instructions to the computer.

prompt A marker on the terminal screen that requests input data.

proportional Term applied to two algebraic functions whose quotient is a constant.

protection *See* **program protection.**

pseudocode A stylized half-English, half-code language written in English but suggesting Pascal code.

push A procedure that adds an item to the top of the stack.

quadratic algorithm A polynomial algorithm in which the highest nonzero term is n^2.

quadratic collision processing Method of handling a collision in which the storage space is searched in the k^2 place, for successive integer values of k starting at the location of the collision, until an available spot is found.

queue A dynamic data structure where elements are entered at one end and removed from the other end. Referred to as a FIFO (first-in, first-out) structure.

quick sort A relatively fast sorting technique that uses recursion. *See also* **bubble sort, heap sort, insertion sort, merge sort, radix sort, selection sort,** and **shell sort.**

radix sort Sorts integer data by repeatedly placing the items into bins and then collecting the bins, starting with the least significant digit for the first pass and finishing with the most significant digit. Also referred to as bin sort. *See also* **bubble sort, heap sort, insertion sort, merge sort, quick sort, selection sort,** and **shell sort.**

random access Ability to access any elements in a list without first accessing all preceding elements.

random access file A file whose components can be accessed using random access.

random number generator A function that returns a real number between 0 and 1 each time it is called. The numbers it returns are statistically random in that after repeated calls to the function, the sequence of numbers returned is evenly distributed over the interval yet each one is completely unpredictable.

randomized storage A name given to list access via a hashing function.

reading from a file Retrieving data from a file.

ready queue In an operating system, the queue of processes with cleared access to all the resources the processes require to run.

real arithmetic operations Operations allowed on data of type **real.** This includes addition, subtraction, multiplication, and division.

rear pointer The pointer to the rear of a queue.

record A data structure that is a collection of fields that may be treated as a whole or that will allow you to work with individual fields.

record lock facility Method used on many systems to maintain data integrity by allowing only one user at a time to have access to a record. Any other user wishing that same record must wait until the first user has released it.

recursion The process of a subprogram calling itself. A clearly defined stopping state must exist. Any recursive subprogram can be rewritten using iteration and a stack.

recursive call A statement in a procedure which invokes that same procedure.

recursive definition *See* **recursive definition.** (A definition that uses the term being defined to define itself.)

recursive out A condition that terminates a series of recursive calls and hence prevents an infinite series of such calls. Also referred to as recursive termination condition.

recursive procedure A procedure which contains a call to itself.

recursive step A well-defined step that leads to the stopping state in the recursive process.

recursive subprogram *See* **recursion.**

recursive termination condition A condition that signals the end of a series of recursive calls. Also referred to as recursive out.

rehashing Method of handling a collision in which a sequence of new hashing functions is applied to the key that caused the collision until an available location for that key is found.

rehashing collision processing Resolving a collision by invoking a sequence of hashing functions on a key.

relational operator An operator used for comparison of data items of the same type.

relative ordering Ordering imposed on the entries in a list by their relative positions in that list.

relatively prime Two numbers are relatively prime if and only if their only common factor is 1.

REPEAT . . . UNTIL loop A posttest loop examining a Boolean expression after causing a fragment to be executed. *See also* **FOR loops, loops,** and **WHILE . . . DO loop.**

repetition *See* **loops.**

reserved words Words with predefined meanings that cannot be changed. They are highlighted in text by capital boldface print; a list of Pascal reserved words is set forth in Appendix 1.

return type The data type for a function name.

robust The state in which a program is completely protected against all possible crashes from bad data and unexpected values.

root The first or top node in a tree.

row major Implementation of a two-dimensional array as a one-dimensional array so that the rows are arranged in sequential order with all entries of the same row adjacent.

run-time error Error detected when, after compilation is completed, an error message results instead of the correct output. *See also* **compilation error, design error,** and **syntax error.**

run-time trace diagram The leveled hierarchy of procedure calls associated with the execution of a particular recursive program. Such diagrams can help in analyzing the efficiency of recursive algorithms.

scope of identifier The largest block in which the identifier is available.

scratch file *See* **internal file.**

search algorithm An algorithm designed to find a particular data item in a large collection of such items.

secondary memory device An auxiliary device for memory, usually a disk or magnetic tape. *See also* **main memory** and **memory.**

sector A particular portion of a magnetic disk used at the machine language level in addressing information stored on the disk.

seed A global number used as the basis for generating random numbers in random number generating function.

selection sort A sorting algorithm that sorts the components of an array in either ascending or descending order. This process puts the smallest or largest element in the top position and repeats the process on the remaining array components. *See also* **bubble sort, heap sort, insertion sort, merge sort, quick sort, radix sort,** and **shell sort.**

selection statement A control statement that selects some particular logical path based on the value of an expression. Also referred to as a conditional statement.

self-documenting code Code that is written using descriptive identifiers.

semantics The semantics of an algorithmic statement is the action dictated by that statement.

semaphore In an operating system, special flags that regulate the addition and removal of processes to and from the blocked and ready queues.

sentinel value A special value that indicates the end of a set of data or of a process.

sequential access Requirement that elements of a list must be accessed according to the list's ordering so that before a particular element can be accessed, all preceding elements must be accessed first.

sequential access file A file whose components must be accessed using sequential access.

sequential algorithm *See* **straight-line algorithm.**

sequential search The process of searching a list by examining the first component and then examining successive components in the order in which they occur. Also referred to as a linear search.

set A structured data type that consists of a collection of distinct elements from an indicated base type (which must be ordinal).

shaker sort A variation on the bubble sort in which each pass through the data positions the (current) largest element in the (current) last array index *and* the (current) smallest element in the (current) first array index.

shell sort Sort that works by dividing the array into smaller, noncontiguous segments. These segments are separately sorted using the insertion sort algorithm. The number of these segments is repeatedly reduced on each successive pass until the entire array has been sorted. *See also* **bubble sort, heap sort, insertion sort, merge sort, quick sort, radix sort,** and **selection sort.**

shift folding A variation on folding in which each numeric part of the key is treated as a separate number, and these numbers are added to form an integer value. *See also* **boundary folding.**

siblings The child nodes of a given node.

side effect An unintentional change in a variable which is the result of some action taken in a program.

sieve of Eratosthenes A technique devised by the Greek mathematician Eratosthenes for finding all prime numbers greater than 2 and less than or equal to a given number.

simple Boolean expression An expression where two numbers or variable values are compared using a single relational operator. *See also* **Boolean expression** and **compound Boolean expression.**

simulation A computer model of a real-life situation.

simulation of system stack Technique used to eliminate recursion by making a program explicitly perform the duties of the system stack.

software Programs that make the machine (the hardware) do something, such as word processing, data-base management, or games.

software engineering The process of developing and maintaining large software systems.

software system A large program, typically composed of numerous modules that interact to solve one complex problem.

software system life cycle The process of development, maintenance, and demise of a software system. Phases include analysis, design, coding, testing/verification, maintenance, and obsolescence.

sort-merge The process of repeatedly subdividing a long list, sorting shorter lists, and then merging to obtain a single sorted list.

source program A program written by a programmer. *See also* **system program.**

sparse table A table in which a high percentage of data storage locations will be of one uniform value.
stack A data structure where access can be made from only one end. Referred to as a LIFO (last-in, first-out) structure.
stack frame The information placed on the system stack by the operating system when a procedure call is made.
stack priority Function to hierarchically rank algebraic operators in order of precedence.
standard function A built-in function available in most versions of Pascal.
standard identifiers Predefined words whose meanings can be changed if needed. Standard identifiers are highlighted in text by lowercase boldface print; a list of Pascal standard identifiers is set forth in Appendix 2.
standard simple types The predefined data types **integer, real, char,** and **boolean.**
state space The space of all possible states which can be generated in the solution to a given problem.
state-transition diagram A diagram used to model the logic of a finite state machine.
static variable A variable whose size (for example, array length) is fixed at compilation time. A certain memory area is reserved for each variable, and these locations are retained for the declared variables as long as the program or subprogram in which the variable is defined is active.
stepwise refinement The process of breaking a complex problem down into smaller problems, solving those smaller problems, and then tying those solutions together to solve the original large problem.
stopping state *See* **termination condition.**
straight-line algorithm Also called sequential algorithm, this algorithm consists of a sequence of simple tasks.
stream input *See* **batch input.**
string A list of characters that are related in linear fashion and that can be manipulated using string operations.
string ADT A sequence of characters viewed as a data object, along with the operations that may be performed on them.
string constant One or more characters used as a constant in a program.
string data type A data type that permits a sequence of characters. This is not available in standard Pascal, but can be simulated using a packed array of characters.
string operations Operations that manipulate character strings. *See* **assignment, string; concatenation, string; deletion, string; insertion, string.**
structure chart A graphic method of indicating the relationship between modules when designing the solution to a problem.
structured English A means of specifying the logic of a module using an English-like pseudocode description.
structured programming Programming that parallels a solution to a problem achieved by top-down design. *See also* **stepwise refinement** and **top-down design.**
stub module A module used to aid in testing another module. The stub module reports the values it was sent and sends back the values needed by the module being tested so it can continue execution.
stub programming A no-frills, simple version of a final program.
subblock A block structure for a subprogram. *See also* **block.**
subprogram A program within a program. Procedures and functions are subprograms.
subrange The defined subset of values of an existing ordinal data type.
subscript *See* **array index** and **loop index.**
subset Set A is a subset of set B if all the elements in A are also in B. *See also* **difference, intersection,** and **union.**
substring A portion of a string that is itself a string.
subtree A subset of a tree that is itself a tree.
symbol table A list of identifiers maintained by a compiler as it parses a source program.
synonyms Two keys that hash to the same position and therefore cause a collision.
syntax The formal rules governing construction of valid statements.
syntax diagramming A method to formally describe the legal syntax of language structures; syntax diagrams are set forth in Appendix 3.
syntax error An error in spelling, punctuation, or placement of certain key symbols in a program. *See also* **compilation error, design error,** and **run-time error.**
system program A special program used by the computer to activate the compiler, run the machine code version, and cause output to be generated. *See also* **source program.**
system software The programs that allow users to write and execute other programs, including operating systems such as DOS.
system testing Exercising the interfaces between modules instead of the logic of a particular module.
systems analyst The person responsible for analyzing the needs of the users and then formally specifying the system and its requirements to meet those needs.
tag field A field used in defining variant records. Values of the tag field determine the variant record structure.
tail recursion A type of recursion in which an initial return operation triggers a series of returns uninterrupted by further recursive calls.
temporary file *See* **internal file.**
termination condition *See* **recursive termination condition.**
test cases Collection of sets of test data that will exercise all the logical possibilities the module will encounter. Each test case has a corresponding expected result called the test oracle.
testing phase The fourth phase of the software system life cycle. In this phase, the program code is thoroughly tested in an effort to discover errors both in the design of the program and in the code itself.

test oracle The expected result for a particular test case when a module is being tested.

test program A short program written to provide an answer to a specific question.

text file A file of characters that is divided into lines.

thread A pointer contained in a tree node which leads to the predecessor or successor of the node relative to a specified traversal.

threaded tree A tree in which threading is used.

threading A technique of avoiding recursion in tree traversal algorithms whereby the pointers unused in tree formation are turned into pointers to the inorder predecessor and inorder successor of that node.

time/space trade-off The maxim that an attempt to make a program more efficient in terms of time will only come as a result of a corresponding decrease in efficiency in terms of space, and vice versa.

token A language symbol comprised of one or more characters in an incoming stream of characters. The basic unit in lexical analysis.

top The end of a stack at which entries are added and removed.

top-down design A design methodology for solving a problem whereby you first state the problem and then proceed to subdivide the main task into major subtasks. Each subtask is then subdivided into smaller subtasks. This process is repeated until each remaining subtask is easily solved. *See also* **stepwise refinement** and **structured programming.**

trace *See* **program walk-through.**

tracer output The values of the data received by and returned from a module through the use of **write** statements at the beginning and end of that module.

track A particular portion of a magnetic disk used at the machine language level in addressing information stored on the disk.

transaction file A file containing changes to be made in a master file.

transitions In a finite state machine, the possible actions taken upon encountering a particular character.

tree *See* **general tree.**

tree of recursive calls *See* **run-time trace diagram.**

tree traversal A means of processing every node in the tree.

trial-and-error backtracking Recursion in which more recursive calls may be made after the first return operation occurs.

trie index A type of indexing used when the keys are variable-length character strings. Although taken from the word *retrieve,* trie is pronounced "try."

Turing machine A hypothetical computing machine which consists of input and output units, and infinite memory in the form of a sequentially organized tape to store characters from a finite alphabet, a finite collection of states in which the machine could exist in at any given time, and a control unit capable of checking and potentially modifying the contents of any memory cell.

two-dimensional array An array in which each element is accessed by a reference to a pair of indices.

two-dimensional table A collection of data of the same type arranged as a rectangular grid whose rows and columns are each indexed by a separate contiguous range of an ordinal data type. Each entry in the grid can be specified by giving its row and column coordinates.

two-way merge The process of merging two sorted lists.

type *See* **data type.**

undecidable proposition A statement within an axiomatic system such that neither that statement nor its negation can be proven by reasoning within the system itself.

underflow If a value is too small to be represented by a computer, the value is automatically replaced by zero. *See also* **overflow.**

union The union of set A and set B is A + B where A + B contains any element that is in A or that is in B. *See also* **difference, intersection,** and **subset.**

universal set Any set that contains all possible values of the base type.

unordered array implementation An implementation of a keyed list in which data are stored in an array but not physically ordered to match the logical ordering of the list.

unpacked array An array in which data are not in consecutive bytes.

user-defined data type *See* **enumerated data type.**

user-defined function A subprogram (function) written by the programmer to perform a specific task. Functions return one value when called.

user-friendly A phrase used to describe an interactive program with clear, easy-to-follow messages for the user.

value Often called value of a memory location. Refers to the value of the contents of a memory location. *See also* **address.**

value parameter A formal parameter that is local to a subprogram. Values of these parameters are not returned to the calling program.

variable A memory location, referenced by an identifier, whose value can be changed during a program.

variable condition loop A repetition statement in which the loop control condition changes within the body of the loop.

variable declaration section The section of the declaration section where program variables are declared for subsequent use.

variable dictionary A listing of the meaning of variables used in a program.

variable parameter A formal parameter that is not local to a subprogram. Values of these parameters are returned to the calling program.

variant part The part of a record structure in which the number and type of fields can vary. *See also* **fixed part.**

vertex A data object (or node) in a graph.

volatile list A list that undergoes frequent insertions and deletions.

weight The numeric value associated with an edge in a network.

WHILE . . . DO loop A pretest loop examining a Boolean expression before causing a fragment to be executed.

white box testing The method of testing a module in which the tester is aware of the method of implementation and internal logic of that module. *See also* **black box testing.**

word A unit of memory consisting of one or more bytes. Words can be addressed.

workspace-index method A method of storing strings in which one large workspace is provided for storing all the strings and an index keeps track of the starting locations and lengths of each of the individual strings.

worst case The arrangement of data items prior to the beginning of the sort procedure which causes that procedure to take the longest amount of time for that particular set of items. *See also* **best case.**

writing to a file The process of entering data to a file.

Answers to Selected Exercises

CHAPTER 1

Section 1.2

1. Insertion sort provides for a possible early exit from its inner loop. This early exit can potentially reduce the number of comparisons necessary, especially for data that are "almost" in order.

3. Selection sort does not provide for an early exit from either the outer or the inner loop; however, it does guarantee that only n data exchanges will be made—fewer than either insertion or selection sort can guarantee (both require n^2 data exchanges on average).

5.

	K=1	K=2	K=3	K=4	K=5	K=6
43	12	12	12	12	12	12
40	40	18	18	18	18	18
18	18	40	24	24	24	24
24	24	24	40	39	39	39
39	39	39	39	40	40	40
60	60	60	60	60	60	43
12	43	43	43	43	43	60

7. This sort algorithm resembles a bubble sort, but is different in that small array entries "bubble up" instead of having large entries "bubble down" on each successive pass. That is, in the bubble sort we can guarantee that after the kth pass, the *largest* k array entries are in their rightful place; whereas, in this sort algorithm, we can guarantee that after the kth pass, the *smallest* k entries are in their rightful place.

Original	k=1	k=2	k=3	k=4	k=5	k=6
43	12	12	12	12	12	12
40	43	18	18	18	18	18
18	40	43	24	24	24	24
24	18	40	43	39	39	39
39	24	24	40	43	40	40
60	39	39	39	40	43	43
12	60	60	60	60	60	60

9. This sort algorithm resembles insertion sort in that it, too, positions the kth element in its rightful place among $k-1$ entries already in order. The difference between the two sorts lies in the section of the array each has sorted with each successive iteration. In insertion sort, the *first* $k+1$ entries are in order after the kth pass; in this sort, the *last* k entries are in order after the kth pass.

Original	k=1	k=2	k=3	k=4	k=5	k=6
43	43	43	43	43	43	12
40	40	40	40	40	12	18
18	18	18	18	12	18	24
24	24	24	12	18	24	39
39	39	12	24	24	39	40
60	12	39	39	39	40	43
12	60	60	60	60	60	60

11. The integers

20
30
40
50
10

or any such arithmetically or alphabetically ordered data cause the bubble sort to make comparisons, but no data are interchanged until the 10 is "bubbled up" to the top. For the insertion sort, the inner loop is shut off after a single comparison, until the final 10 is reached. Then the 10 is inserted at the top.

13.
```
PROCEDURE ModifiedInsertionSort (N:integer; VAR List:SortArray);
  { Same Given, Task, and Return as given in text for InsertionSort  }
  { New logic:  Move element only after all comparisons per loop are }
  {             finished                                              }

VAR  I,K,J: integer;
     Done: boolean;
     Remember: integer;

BEGIN
  FOR K := 2 TO N DO
    BEGIN
      J := K;
      Remember := J;            { remember the position being tested }
      Done := false;
      WHILE (J >=2) AND NOT Done DO
          IF List[Remember].Key < List[J-1].Key THEN
            J := J-1
          ELSE
            Done := true;
      IF J <> Remember THEN               { shuffle data from bottom up }
        BEGIN
          FOR K := Remember DOWNTO J+1 DO
            List[K] := List[K-1];
          List[J] := List[Remember]           { place in correct location }
        END
    END
END;
```

Section 1.3

1. a. Inner loop: $m-6$ repetitions. Outer loop: n repetitions. For each outer loop repetition, the inner loop is traversed $m-6$ times. Therefore, $(m-6) \times n$ overall repetitions are performed. This is $O(n^2)$.

   b. The inner loop will be executed $\log_2 n$ times and the outer loop will be executed n times. Thus the loops are $O(n \log_2 n)$.

   c. The inner **REPEAT** is executed $n/2$ times for each execution of the outer loop. The outer **REPEAT** is executed n times. Thus there are $n \times (n/2)$ repetitions. Thus the loops are $O(n^2)$.

3. The efficiency of the algorithm in question is constant—32 operations—for all input. Remembering that in big-O analysis, we are concerned primarily with the order of magnitude of the algorithm's efficiency, we write this algorithm's efficiency as O(1) * 32. And recalling that constants bear no importance except in comparing algorithms with the same big-O, we drop the constant 32 to arrive at the big-O that most accurately characterizes the algorithm—O(1).

5. a. The $n^3\log_2 n$ term dominates and this is $O(n^3\log_2 n)$.

   b. The 4^n exponential term will (eventually) dominate any polynomial terms. Thus this is $O(4^n)$.

   c. The 2^n exponential term will (eventually) dominate any polynomial terms. Thus this is $O(2^n)$.

7. For this small set of integers, the trace of the insertion sort is

20	20	20	20	10
30	30*	30	30	20
40	40	40*	40	30
50	50	50	50*	40
10	10	10	10	50

The inner loop of the insertion sort is "shut off" after one comparison for each value of K, until the "bottom" 10 is reached. At that point, four swaps are required to move it into the "top" position. For this almost ordered data, the insertion sort is $O(n)$.

9. Since n^2 dominates $n^2 + \log_2 n$, $O(n^2 + \log_2 n)$ is the same as $O(n^2)$. Hence, we have the following answers for a–d.

   a. You are both correct for any algorithm whose performance is dominated by a term such as n^k for $k \geq 2$ or a^n for any base $a > 1$.

   b. You are both wrong for any linear or logarithmic algorithm.

   c. No.

   d. No.

Section 1.4

1.

	K=1 J=1	K=1 J=2	K=1 J=3	K=1 J=4	K=1 J=5	K=1 J=6
1	2	2	2	2	2	2
2	1	3	3	3	3	3
3	3	1	4	4	4	4
4	4	4	1	5	5	5
5	5	5	5	1	6	6
6	6	6	6	6	1	7
7	7	7	7	7	7	1

K=2 J=1	K=2 J=2	K=2 J=3	K=2 J=4	K=2 J=5
3	3	3	3	3
2	2	2	2	2
4	4	5	5	5
5	5	4	6	6
6	6	6	4	7
7	7	7	7	4
1	1	1	1	1

K=3 J=1	K=3 J=2	K=3 J=3	K=3 J=4
3	3	3	3
2	5	5	5
5	2	2	2
6	6	6	7
7	7	7	6
4	4	4	4
1	1	1	1

K=4 J=1	K=4 J=2	K=4 J=3
3	3	3
5	5	5
2	2	7
7	7	2
6	6	6
4	4	4
1	1	1

K=5 J=1	K=5 J=2
3	3
5	7
7	5
2	2
6	6
4	4
1	1

K=6 J=1
7
3
5
2
6
4
1

3. Ten passes would be made through the outer **WHILE** loop of the radix sort algorithm because the length of the longest data item is ten characters. It is assumed that strings are padded with space beyond their last alphabetical character.

Pass 0:

List: CHOCOLATE VANILLA CARAMEL PEACH STRAWBERRY CHERRY

Pass 1:

Bins: Space: CHOCOLATE VANILLA CARAMEL PEACH CHERRY
Y: STRAWBERRY
List: CHOCOLATE VANILLA CARAMEL PEACH CHERRY STRAWBERRY

Pass 2:

Bins: Space: VANILLA CARAMEL PEACH CHERRY
E: CHOCOLATE
R: STRAWBERRY
List: VANILLA CARAMEL PEACH CHERRY CHOCOLATE STRAWBERRY

Pass 3:

Bins: Space: VANILLA CARAMEL PEACH CHERRY
R: STRAWBERRY
T: CHOCOLATE
List: VANILLA CARAMEL PEACH CHERRY STRAWBERRY CHOCOLATE

Pass 4:

Bins: Space: PEACH CHERRY
A: VANILLA CHOCOLATE
E: STRAWBERRY
L: CARAMEL
List: PEACH CHERRY VANILLA CHOCOLATE STRAWBERRY CARAMEL

Pass 5:

Bins: Space: PEACH
B: STRAWBERRY
E: CARAMEL
L: VANILLA CHOCOLATE
Y: CHERRY
List: PEACH STRAWBERRY CARAMEL VANILLA CHOCOLATE CHERRY

Pass 6:

Bins: H: PEACH
L: VANILLA
M: CARAMEL
O: CHOCOLATE
R: CHERRY
W: STRAWBERRY
List: PEACH VANILLA CARAMEL CHOCOLATE CHERRY STRAWBERRY

Pass 7:

Bins: A: CARAMEL STRAWBERRY
C: PEACH CHOCOLATE
I: VANILLA
R: CHERRY
List: CARAMEL STRAWBERRY PEACH CHOCOLATE VANILLA CHERRY

Pass 8:

Bins: A: PEACH
E: CHERRY
N: VANILLA
O: CHOCOLATE
R: CARAMEL STRAWBERRY
List: PEACH CHERRY VANILLA CHOCOLATE CARAMEL STRAWBERRY

Pass 9:

Bins: A: VANILLA CARAMEL
E: PEACH
H: CHERRY CHOCOLATE
T: STRAWBERRY

List: VANILLA CARAMEL PEACH CHERRY CHOCOLATE STRAWBERRY

Pass 10:

Bins: C: CARAMEL CHERRY CHOCOLATE
P: PEACH
S: STRAWBERRY
V: VANILLA

List: CARAMEL CHERRY CHOCOLATE PEACH STRAWBERRY VANILLA

5. An application in which the array of data items consumed all available memory would not have the space necessary to store the array of pointers.

7. Although the introduction of pointers into the bubble sort routine will not improve its $O(n^2)$ nature, there will most likely be an increase in run-time efficiency. This is because physical swapping of data is drastically reduced. If the data to be swapped were records with numerous fields of records themselves, many machine operations would be involved. But with pointers, only integers need be swapped, involving many fewer machine operations.

9. The pointer strategy would have the least effect on selection sort, because it guarantees a fewer number of data exchanges (only one per outer loop iteration) than either of the other sorts. Since the pointer sort affects the efficiency of data exchanges, and since fewer swaps are made with selection sort, less overall time is saved with selection sort than with the other two sorting algorithms; these sorting algorithms swap more often, and would therefore benefit more significantly from improved swapping efficiency.

11.
```
PROCEDURE PointerSelectionSort (N : integer;
                                VAR Pointers : IntegerArray;
                                List : SortArray);

{ Given:  Array List containing entries in locations 1 through N. }
{         Array Pointers that are integers pointing to the data   }
{         in array List.                                          }
{ Task:   Selection sort logic using pointers instead of actual   }
{         data movement.                                          }
{ Return: Array Pointers that point to the correctly arranged     }
{         data or array List.                                     }
VAR    K, J, MinPosition: integer;
       Temp: integer;

BEGIN
  FOR K := 1 TO N DO
    Pointer[K] := K;
  FOR K := 1 TO N-1 DO
    BEGIN
      MinPosition := Pointer[K];
      FOR J := K+1 TO N DO
        IF List[ Pointer[J] ].Key < List[MinPosition].Key  THEN
           MinPosition := Pointer[J];
      Temp := Pointer[K];
      Pointer[K] := Pointer[MinPosition];
      Pointer[MinPosition] := Temp
    END
END;
```

13.
```
FUNCTION Digit (Number,K: integer): SingleDigit;

{ Given:   Integers Number and K                       }
{ Task:    Determine the Kth digit of Number           }
{ Return: The Kth digit of Number                      }

VAR P,Q: integer;

        FUNCTION PowerOfTen (I: integer): integer;

         { Given:   Integer I                    }
         { Task:    Computer 10 to the I power   }
         { Return: 10 to the I power             }

          VAR Count,Total: integer;

           BEGIN
             IF I = 0 THEN PowerOfTen := 1
             ELSE
               BEGIN
                 Total := 1;
                 FOR Count := 1 TO I DO
                   Total := Total * 10;
                 PowerOfTen := Total
               END
           END;

BEGIN
  P := PowerOfTen (K);    {Determine 10 to the K power  }
  Q := PowerOfTen (K-1); {Determine 10 to the K-1 power}
  Digit := (Number - P*(Number DIV P)) DIV Q
END;
```

Section 1.5

1. Initial array with Low, High, and Middle = (High + Low) **DIV** 2. Target is 43. Found is **false** to begin.

Low				Mid					High
1	2	3	4	5	6	7	8	9	10
18	40	46	50	52	58	63	70	77	90

Low	Mid		High						
1	2	3	4	5	6	7	8	9	10
18	40	46	50	52	58	63	70	77	90

		Mid Low	High						
1	2	3	4	5	6	7	8	9	10
18	40	46	50	52	58	63	70	77	90

Since 43 < 46, High points to "2" and the search ends with Found = **false.**

3. A symbol table is a list of the identifiers that have been declared in a program and which the compiler continually searches as the program is compiled. Since the sequential search is O(n), the continual searching of the symbol table uses up too much time to be practical.

5. 21 or fewer times.

7. This version of the binary search will work correctly provided the variable N never comes in as 0 (indicating an empty list). In this situation, Middle will be computed to be 0, which will generate an array index out-of-range error.

11. Although still O(n) in its efficiency, the code for this version of the algorithm can reduce the number of comparisons by a factor of 2. This is because we need not test for the sentinel *and* the target data each time through the loop.

13. When an array is passed by value, a physical copy of that array must be generated and passed to the procedure each time it is called. When an array is passed by reference, on the other hand, only the address of the array—an integer—need be passed to the procedure. Clearly, passing an integer (which can be quickly looked up) is far more time and space efficient than passing an entire copy of an array (which must be generated on the spot).

CHAPTER 2

Section 2.1

1. Characteristics of the software engineering approach to system development are
   - Analysis of the situation (interviews, observations, research, and so on).
   - Design of a solution (beginning with a completely abstract non-physical design).
   - Construction of a model (to anticipate various construction problems).
   - Construction of actual solution.
   - Maintenance.

3.

MEMORANDUM

TO: Recalcitrant Team Member
FROM: Dedicated Software Engineer
RE: Tactful note defending software engineering principles

As a dedicated team member whose paycheck depends on "getting it done" on time, I am as committed as you to meeting the deadlines set forth for this project. At the same time, I do not care to fall prey to the unreliable, inelegant methods of our predecessors in this company, whose lack of planning often resulted in software products with serious flaws—flaws that ended up costing this company dearly. Let me offer two sound reasons why delving into the details of Pascal code without a conceptual model, as you have suggested, would spell disaster.

First, without a conceptual model, our team would not be able to work as a team. With potentially differing ideas of the system design, individual members would inevitably waste time writing pieces of the system that did not fit together. Moreover, since team members would not have laid out the system beforehand, they would not be cognizant of what basic tasks are done frequently throughout the system. Hence, many lines of redundant code would be written, thus wasting time as well as space.

Second, what if the final system we've coded turned out not to work? Flaws that we could have detected with a conceptual model would not have been discovered until the system was up and running. And by that time, all of our hours of coding would have been wasted.

In short, if it is your interest to implement a reliable, working system—and to do so on time—creating a conceptual design simply cannot be avoided. Although it may seem like a waste of time initially, it will more than pay for itself in the end by ensuring that our final system has the best design possible, and is reliable enough to deserve the trust our company will need to place in it.

Our team will meet at 9:00 A.M. tomorrow morning to begin carving out a conceptual design. We hope to see you there.

Section 2.2

3. If users of the String ADT choose not to include calls to the Create operation because they know that certain String ADT implementations do not actually require String variable initialization, they can no longer be sure that their high-level logic will be plug-compatible with all possible String ADT implementations. Having violated the principle of information hiding, they lose one of the most valuable features of ADTs: the ability to experiment with various implementations of an ADT without recoding the high-level logic.

Section 2.3

1. For the simple two-row, four-column table

```
1  2  3  4
5  6  7  8
```

the row-major implementation would be 1 2 3 4 5 6 7 8; the column-major implementation would be 1 5 2 6 3 7 4 8.

3. Any situation in which a high percentage of the cell entries are either zeros for arithmetic values or one particular Boolean value calls for a sparse table implementation.
An example would be a table listing medical patients across the top and serious illnesses down the side. If a patient had the serious illness, then a 1 is registered; otherwise a 0 indicates the patient has not had the serious illness.

5. Allowing subscripts for an arbitrary range of ordinal values, not necessarily always integers starting at one, does not cause problems in translating two-dimensional table coordinates into linear positions. It simply requires another function to translate the arbitrary range to the range the mapping function would use.
For example,

```
TYPE Rows = 3..8;
     Columns = 23..49;
     Numbers = ARRAY [Rows,Columns] OF integer;
```

would require translating the range 3..8 for Rows to 1..6, which is what the mapping function would need, and translating the range 23..49 for Columns to 1..27. Other ordinal types would need a similar translation so that the mapping function could locate the correct linear position.

7.
```
PROCEDURE Create(VAR T : TwoDTable);

  { Given:  T, a two-dimensional table in an arbitrary state.  }
  { Task:   Initialize T to be an empty sparse table.          }
  { Return: T, an initialized, empty sparse table.             }

  BEGIN
    T[1].PilotNum := HighPilotPlus1
  END;
```

11. If a table were R rows by C columns, then a row-major implementation would require R × C locations in a linear list of the table's contents.
By implementing the sparse table with a one dimensional array of records, we could in the worst case of a table absolutely full, need R × C locations to hold records, each of which contains two integer fields. Thus for a full, or nearly full table, the row-major implementation seems to be more space efficient.
But as the percentage of **false** values increases, fewer pairs are in the array of records. The break-even point seems to be roughly 50 percent. (This is a rough estimate because of system requirements to keep track of array indicies, and so on.)

13. These implementations are imperfect for at least three reasons. First, they necessarily impose a specific ordinal type—the integers—as the table index type. The two-dimensional table definition stipulates that these indices can be *any* ordinal type, and clearly a perfect two-dimensional table ADT would provide users with a way to specify the index type in the Create operation.
Second, whereas the two-dimensional table definition states that the rows and columns are each indexed by a separate contiguous range, the implementations discussed in this chapter impose a specific range on users. The definition would seem to imply that a perfect two-dimensional table implementation would allow an arbitrary index range to be specified at the time of creation, perhaps as parameters to the Create operation.
And third, whereas the formal two-dimensional table definition imposes no restriction on the data stored in the table (other than all data must be of the same type) the implementations in this chapter have restricted the data type determined by the ADT author at compile time. Again, a "perfect" implementation should allow the ADT user to determine an appropriate data type to be stored in the table; perhaps this data type could be passed as a parameter to the Create operation.

15. The radix sort requires a sparse table because approximately 90 percent of the bin capacity can be wasted. Suppose there are 100 four-digit integers to sort with the radix sort. There must be 10 bins, each bin capable of holding all 100 four-digit integers. Suppose, that, all 100 four-digit integers happened to have a "3" in the ten's place. Then the 3-bin would be filled and the other nine bins totally empty—a waste of 90 percent of the storage capability. Since so much space is unused, a sparse table would be appropriate.

Section 2.4

1. The number and type of formal parameters associated with PrintNode must exactly match the declaration of ProcessNode in TraverseInOrder's formal parameter list. In this case, the parameter Item is declared as a **VAR** parameter instead of a Value parameter. Since PrintNode's parameter list does not exactly match the declaration in TraverseInOrder's parameter list, PrintNode cannot be legally passed to TraverseInOrder. Unless PrintNodes's Item parameter is changed to a **VAR** parameter, the code as it stands will generate a syntax error.

3.
```
PROCEDURE ChangeNegToZero(VAR ITEM : ListNode);

  { Given:   A ListNode Item                                     }
  { Task:    Test OtherData field for being negative             }
  { Return:  If OtherData < 0, then Item with OtherData := 0;    }
  {          item unchanged otherwise.                           }

  BEGIN
    IF Item.OtherData < 0 THEN
      Item.OtherData := 0
  END;
```

Assuming the existence of a keyed list L, one could call TraverseInOrder as follows:

```
TraverseInOrder(L,ChangeNegToZero);
```

5. Instead of shifting all array elements from K to L.NumberRec down one slot, this modification has the disastrous effect of clobbering all data below the Kth slot (that is, in indices > K). When the (J+1)st slot is assigned the contents of the Jth slot, the corrupted value of the Jth slot (itself a copy of the datum in the Kth slot) merely "slides down" one more slot, permanently clobbering the datum previously in that slot. This chain reaction continues all the way down the array; when it's over, indices K+1 through L.NumberRec contain a copy of the datum in index K.

11.

MEMORANDUM

TO: My Supervisor
FROM: Me
RE: Keyed list implementation for zip code application

I strongly recommend that we employ a physically ordered array to implement the zip code keyed list application. You have told me that users of this application will often want to see the information associated with a particular zip code; therefore, fast retrieval time is extremely important. Using a physically ordered array, we can achieve the excellent $O(\log_2 N)$ retrieval efficiency of the binary search.

You might argue that we will pay dearly for such efficiency in the form of poor add and delete efficiency. Although the Add and Delete operations in the physically ordered array strategy require $O(N)$ comparisons and $O(N)$ data exchanges—clearly unacceptable for an array that will contain all of our nation's zip codes—I would argue that this slow efficiency really shouldn't be a factor in this application. How often does one hear about a new U.S. zip code? And how often does our postal service delete one? To my knowledge, the United States zip codes haven't changed in years.

The point is, once a record for each zip code has been added to the list, the list will remain virtually static. So while it may take a while initially to build up the list, the slow add efficiency will be only a temporary nuisance; we will begin reaping the benefits of $O(\log_2 N)$ retrievals in no time!

13. The Success Boolean parameter for the Add operation could be returned as **false** for at least two reasons. First, Success would be **false** if the list were already full. Second, Success would be **false** if the key field of the record being added were the same as the key field of a record already in the list.

CHAPTER 3

Section 3.1

3. Here is one possible way to depict the flow of information:

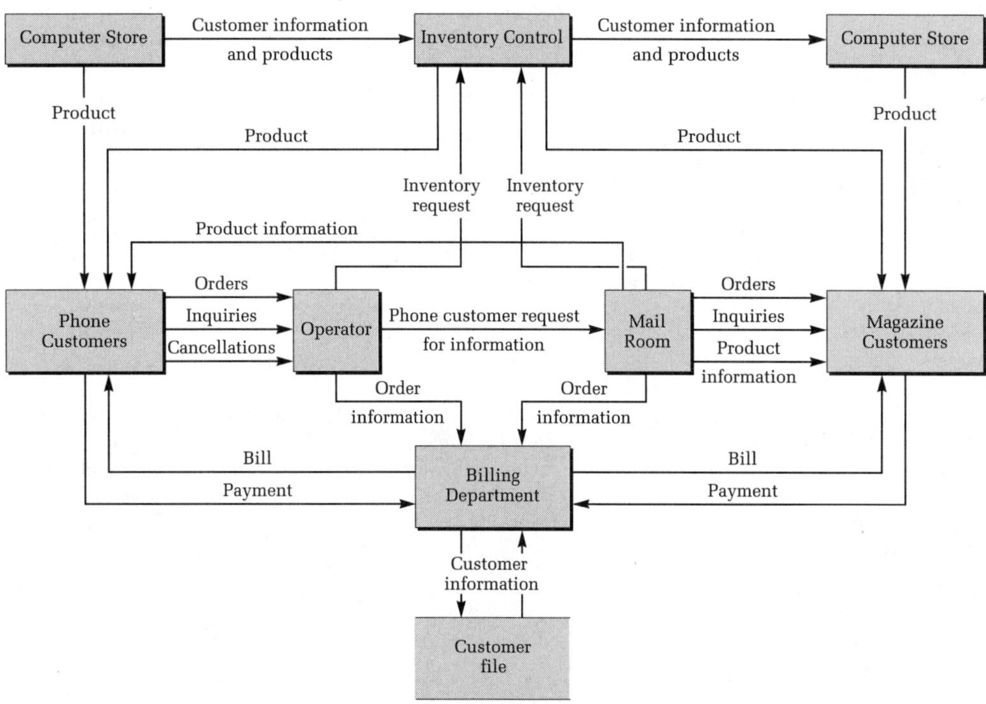

Section 3.2

1. A module that is functionally cohesive performs exactly one predefined task and does it without unexpected outcomes.

3. Since one of the modules performs two tasks, the system is not functionally cohesive. A better design would be

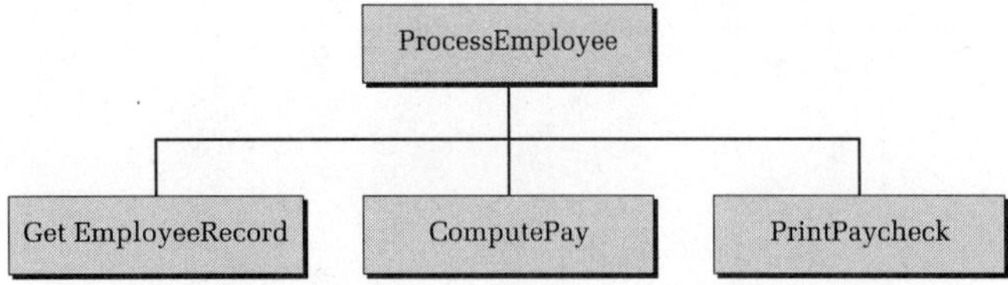

5. Using global variables is a poor strategy from a data coupling perspective because one procedure might corrupt the data needed by other procedures.

7. Data flow diagrams and modular structure charts are similar in that both are used as devices to partition the system logically into a set of subcomponents, each with a well-defined, specific task. The fundamental difference between these two modeling tools lies in the way in which each depicts the interaction among system subcomponents. Data flow diagrams present the system's subcomponents as a (more or less) linear sequence of modules through which system data flow and by which they are processed; modular structure charts present the system as a hierarchy depicting relationships among high-level (boss) and low-level (worker) modules. Thus, modular structure charts more accurately represent how the system will be designed in a computer language; they constitute the next logical refinement of the system in its evolution from abstraction to implementation.

Section 3.3

1. In the analysis phase, the system analyst, through interviews, inspections, observations, and so on reports what the user's needs are.
   In the design phase, the designer studies the analyst's report and designs a solution for the user.
   In the coding phase, the programmer codes the design provided by the design phase.
   In the testing phase, the system is checked for performance under varying conditions, especially boundary conditions in the data being used.
   In the maintenance phase, the system is modified and updated to meet changing user needs and/or to correct errors in the system.

3. A robust module is one that does not "bomb" when it receives invalid data. If every module in a system were completely robust, the system would most likely be too slow to be of practical use: too much time would be consumed by each module in checking to make certain that the data it received were valid.

7. Test data for **PROCEDURE** ReadReal could be as follows. (Note that a space is indicated by "_".)

Val	Rationale	Expected Results
_00.000	a form of 0	valid
0.0	a form of 0	valid
−0.0	a form of 0	valid
+0	a form of 0	valid
5.356	"conventional" number	valid
0.002	"conventional" number	valid
_.05	nothing left of decimal	valid
0_5_.703	spaces between digits	invalid
56	no decimal	valid
75.	unguarded decimal	valid
.	decimal only	invalid
−7	− without decimal	valid
−.5	unguarded decimal	valid
+7	+ without decimal	valid
Hi.there	test a string	invalid
−.	test no digit case	invalid
+.	test no digit case	invalid
−_5.7	test space trailing sign	valid

Note that the current algorithm would accept "−.", ".", and "+." all of which would be invalid numbers.

11.

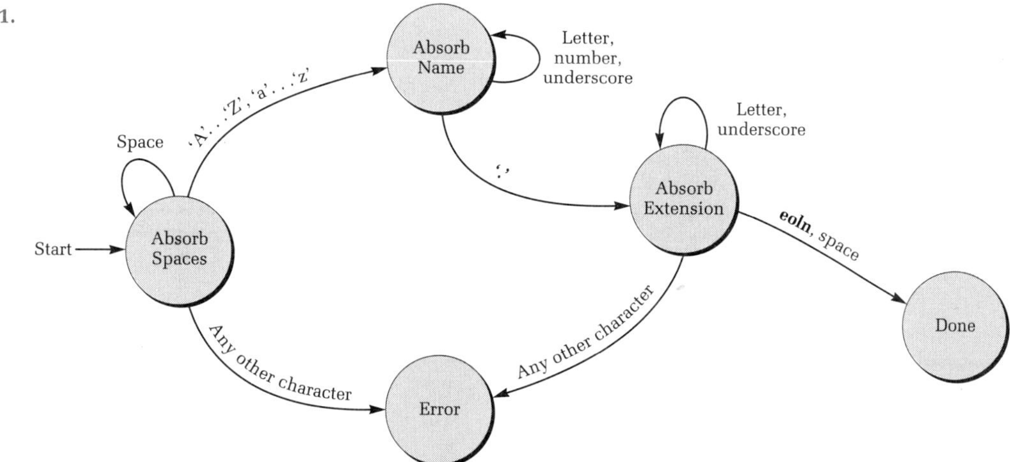

Note that this finite state machine accepts digits only in the string before the '.'; in the extension, only letters and the underscore are acceptable (including the '_' immediately following the '.'). The associated procedure follows:

```
{ Assume the following Type: }
TYPE
  FileString = PACKED ARRAY [1..MaxStringLength] OF char;

PROCEDURE ReadFileName(VAR FileName : FileString);

  { Given:  FileName a FileString.  Assume  that Chr(0) marks end of    }
  {         string, and that MaxStringLength is 1 greater than the      }
  {         length of string the user will attempt to input.            }
  { Task:   Prompt user for a valid file name until one is entered,     }
  {         employing finite state logic to verify that the input is    }
  {         valid.                                                      }
  { Return: FileName, a string containing a valid file name.            }

  TYPE
    States = (AbsorbSpaces, AbsorbName, AbsorbExtension, Error, Done);

  VAR
    S : States;
    K : integer;
    ch : char;

  BEGIN
    REPEAT
      writeln('Please enter a valid file name below:');
      K := 0;
      S := AbsorbSpaces;
      REPEAT
        read(ch);
        CASE S OF
          AbsorbSpaces:
            IF eoln THEN
              S := Error
            ELSE IF (ch IN ['A'..'Z','a'..'z']) THEN
              BEGIN
                K := K + 1;
                FileName[K] := ch;
                S := AbsorbName
              END
            ELSE IF (Ch <>' ') THEN
              S := Error;
          AbsorbName:
            .
            .
            .
          AbsorbExtension:
            .
            .
            .
          Error:
            BEGIN { Do nothing } END;
          Done:
            BEGIN { Do nothing } END
        END { CASE }
      UNTIL (S = Done) OR (S = Error);
      IF (S = Done) THEN
        FileName[K+1] := Chr(0)
      ELSE
        BEGIN
          readln;
          writeln('Invalid file name -- please reenter.')
        END
    UNTIL (S = Done)
  END;
```

Section 3.4

1. Advantages of an array implementation of a list over a random access file include cleaner code (fewer statements) and fast execution time. A disadvantage of an array is its lack of permanence.

5. Altering just one component of a sequential file requires copying all of the records in the file into a new file. This is, quite simply, impractical for large files. A random access file, in contrast, allows us to work with a single record; its contents can be modified and rewritten to the file without affecting the remainder of the file. Typical syntax is

```
seek(FileName, Position);
get(FileName);
FileName^ := UpdatedRecord;
seek(FileName,Position);
put(FileName);
```

Section 3.5

3. It could. Proofs of correctness do not take into account the limitations of a particular machine. Factors such as rounding errors in arithmetic computation, faulty user input, and exceeding the overflow and underflow cutoffs for numeric storage can all cause a "proven" algorithm to fail.

Section 3.6

1. The answer to this question would depend on the object-oriented extensions available at your institution.

CHAPTER 4

Section 4.1

1. The array involved in the PointerSort of Chapter 15 is not a linked list because its cells do not store links (to other array cells) that indicate the order in which the cells are to be traversed (the pointer array is always traversed sequentially). Instead, the pointers stored in the pointer array serve as indices to cells in a separate array (which contains the real data of interest).

3. With respect to search efficiency, both the linked list and unordered array implementations provide O(n) access to list nodes; both require a sequential search. However, whereas both implementations require O(n) comparisons to find a node, the linked list strategy requires only O(1) data exchanges actually to delete the node. Compare this to the O(n) exchanges needed by the array implementation.

   With respect to add efficiency, the linked list implementation strategy is at a disadvantage, requiring O(n) operations to find a node's rightful place in the list, and O(1) operations actually to insert it. The unordered array, on the other hand, provides O(1) add efficiency, since nodes are always added to the end of the array.

   With respect to sort efficiency, the linked list is maintained in sequential order, so no sort is required to traverse it sequentially. In contrast, the unordered array requires an O(n^2) pointer sort before it can be traversed sequentially. Here, the linked list strategy is at an advantage.

5. Merely write a procedure that receives a **real** parameter and prints this parameter only when it is positive. Then pass this procedure as the actual parameter associated with ProcessNode in LinkedTraverse.

Section 4.2

1. a.

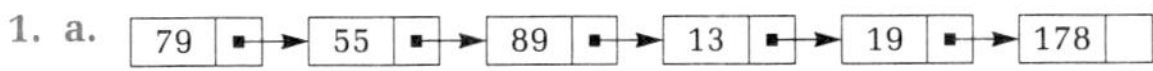

b.

	Data	Link
1	47	3
2	89	5
3	66	7
4	833	2
5	912	10
6	55	2
7	112	4
8	912	0
9	79	6
10	912	8

3.

Head: 5

	Data	Link
1	LOCKE	3
2	MILLER	3
3	SMITH	Null
4	FOSTER	1
5	ALLEN	4

(Cell 2 should be returned to the available pool of nodes.)

5.

Head: 1

	Data	Link
1	JAMES	Null

Head: 2

	Data	Link
1	JAMES	Null
2	CHILTON	1

Head: 2

	Data	Link
1	JAMES	3
2	CHILTON	1
3	SEFTON	Null

Head: 2

	Data	Link
1	JAMES	4
2	CHILTON	1
3	SEFTON	Null
4	LEE	3

Head: 1

	Data	Link
1	JAMES	4
2	CHILTON	1
3	SEFTON	Null
4	LEE	3

Head: 1

	Data	Link
1	JAMES	4
2	WAGNER	Null
3	SEFTON	2
4	LEE	3

Head: 4

	Data	Link
1	JAMES	4
2	WAGNER	Null
3	SEFTON	2
4	LEE	3

Head: 1

	Data	Link
1	AARON	4
2	WAGNER	Null
3	SEFTON	2
4	LEE	3

7.
```
PROCEDURE LinkedTraverse(VAR Head : Pointer;
                         PROCEDURE ProcessNode(VAR Item :
                                               LinkedListData));

{ Given:  Linked list reference by Head pointer.                 }
{ Task:   Traverse the list in the linear order determined by    }
{         the links, applying PROCEDURE ProcessNode to each      }
{         record in the list.                                    }
{ Return: The list referenced by Head with each node affected    }
{         by ProcessNode.                                        }

VAR
  P : Pointer;

BEGIN
  P := Head;
  WHILE (P <> NIL) DO
    BEGIN
      ProcessNode(Nodes[P].Data);
      P := Space.Nodes[P].Link
    END
 END;
```

9.
```
PROCEDURE FindNodeToDelete(VAR Head, P, Prev : Pointer;
                           DeleteData : LinkedListData;
                           VAR Found : boolean);

  { Given:  A linked list referenced by Head, and DeleteData, the data  }
  {         contained in the node to delete.                            }
  { Task:   Search linked list for node containing DeleteData.          }
  { Return: Found = true, P pointing to node containing DeleteData      }
  {         and Prev pointing to the node preceding P; or Found = false }
  {         if node with DeleteData could not be found.                 }

  BEGIN
    P := Head;
    Prev := Null;
    Found := false;
    WHILE (NOT Found) AND (P <> Null) DO
      IF (Space.Nodes[P].Data = DeleteData) THEN
        Found := true
      ELSE
        BEGIN
          Prev := P;
          P := Space.Nodes[P].Link
        END
  END;
```

13. For each of the n values we inserted into the sorted list, we would have to perform a sequential search (requiring $O(n)$ comparisons) to find its rightful place. Keep in mind that with each insertion into the sorted list, n would grow by 1, so that only the last node inserted would have a worst-case efficiency of $O(n)$; all previous nodes would have been inserted into smaller lists. Since for the linked list sort, we will have to carry out n $O(n)$ sequential searches, the efficiency of this algorithm is $O(n^2)$. As is always the case for linked lists, each of the insertions has $O(1)$ efficiency, giving us $O(n)$ total data interchanges. Compare this to the efficiencies of the other sorts we have studied: insertion sort—$O(n^2)$ comparisons and data interchanges; bubble sort—$O(n^2)$ comparisons and data interchanges; selection sort—$O(n^2)$ comparisons and $O(n)$ data interchanges; and radix sort—$O(cn)$ comparisons and $O(cn)$ data exchanges, where c = the maximum length of the data being sorted.

Section 4.3

1. a., c., f., and i. are correct.
   - b. Incorrect—cannot assign a Ptr to an integer.
   - d. Incorrect—one disposes a Ptr, not what it points to.
   - e. Incorrect—cannot dispose an integer.
   - g. Incorrect—cannot **writeln** a Ptr variable.
   - h. Incorrect—cannot **writeln** a complete record, only its fields.

3. `A^.Next^.Next := A^.Next^.Next^.Next`

effects the deletion of the third node.

5.
```
BEGIN
  B := A^.Next^.Next^.Next;
  A^.Next^.Next^.Next := NIL;
  B^.Next := A;
  A := B
END;
```

11.
```
PROCEDURE DestroyList(VAR Head : ListNodePtr);

  { Given:  Linked list referenced by Head.                       }
  { Task:   Return all dynamically allocated memory associated with }
  {         the list via dispose.                                  }
  { Return: Head, a pointer in an unreliable state.                }

  VAR
    temp : ListNodePtr;

  BEGIN
    WHILE (Head <> NIL) DO
      BEGIN
        temp := Head;
        Head := Head^.Link;
        dispose(temp)
      END
  END;
```

One couldn't dispose of the list by passing the **dispose** procedure LinkedTraverse because **dispose**'s parameter list does not exactly match that of formal parameter ProcessNode (**dispose** accepts a pointer whereas ProcessNode accepts a record).

LinkedTraverse is set up to process the current node before moving to the next node in the list. If the process were actually the **dispose** procedure, a reference to the current node would be destroyed before we advanced to the next node. With no reference to the current node, we could not access its link field, and thus we could not get to the next node in the list.

13. The array implementation of linked lists (Example 18.9) differs from the pointer variable implementation in that the method by which it allocates and deallocates pointers isn't as well encapsulated as it is in the pointer variable implementation. We can ascertain, from the declaration of the SpaceStructure record, exactly how the dynamic memory is maintained. One way we could redefine the linked list ADT to make the different implementations more consistent would be to require the linked list type to encapsulate the dynamic memory scheme it employs. In this way, users of the ADT would not have to concern themselves with the details of dynamic memory management.

15. Traversing a Pascal pointer linked list node by node while writing the data portion and the link portion to a disk file will not work. Although the data and the memory address (the link) can be written to a disk file, when the disk file is read, there is no guarantee that the data will be placed into exactly the same memory locations as when the data were originally in memory.

An alternative solution would be simply to store the structure in the file in a way that would allow a program to read it in and recapture its original form. For linked structures, this might mean storing the data nodes in the file sequentially, perhaps with special flags at the head and the tail of the list.

Section 4.4

1.

	Data	Link
0	*DUMMY	1
1	JAMES	end of list
2		3
3		4
4		5
5		6
6		7
7		8
8		end of list

Head
0

Avail
2

	Data	Link
0	*DUMMY	2
1	JAMES	end of list
2	CHILTON	1
3		4
4		5
5		6
6		7
7		8
8		end of list

Head
0

Avail
3

	Data	Link
0	*DUMMY	2
1	JAMES	3
2	CHILTON	1
3	SEFTON	end of list
4		5
5		6
6		7
7		8
8		end of list

Head
0

Avail
4

	Data	Link
0	*DUMMY	2
1	JAMES	4
2	CHILTON	1
3	SEFTON	end of list
4	LEE	3
5		6
6		7
7		8
8		end of list

Head
0

Avail
5

	Data	Link
0	*DUMMY	1
1	JAMES	4
2		5
3	SEFTON	end of list
4	LEE	3
5		6
6		7
7		8
8		end of list

Head
0

Avail
2

	Data	Link
0	*DUMMY	1
1	JAMES	4
2	WAGNER	end of list
3	SEFTON	2
4	LEE	3
5		6
6		7
7		8
8		end of list

Head
0

Avail
5

	Data	Link
0	*DUMMY	4
1		5
2	WAGNER	end of list
3	SEFTON	2
4	LEE	3
5		6
6		7
7		8
8		end of list

Head
0

Avail
1

	Data	Link
0	*DUMMY	1
1	AARON	4
2	WAGNER	end of list
3	SEFTON	2
4	LEE	3
5		6
6		7
7		8
8		end of list

Head
0

Avail
5

3.

	Data	FLink	BLink
0	*DUMMY	1	end
1	JAMES	end	0
2		3	end
3		4	2
4		5	3
5		6	4
6		7	5
7		8	6
8		end	7

Head
0

Avail
2

	Data	FLink	BLink
0	*DUMMY	2	end
1	JAMES	end	2
2	CHILTON	1	0
3		4	end
4		5	3
5		6	4
6		7	5
7		8	6
8		end	7

Head
0

Avail
3

	Data	FLink	BLink
0	*DUMMY	2	end
1	JAMES	3	2
2	CHILTON	1	0
3	SEFTON	end	1
4		5	end
5		6	4
6		7	5
7		8	6
8		end	7

Head
0

Avail
4

	Data	FLink	BLink
0	*DUMMY	2	end
1	JAMES	4	2
2	CHILTON	1	0
3	SEFTON	end	4
4	LEE	3	1
5		6	end
6		7	5
7		8	6
8		end	7

Head
0

Avail
5

	Data	FLink	BLink
0	*DUMMY	1	end
1	JAMES	4	2
2		5	end
3	SEFTON	end	4
4	LEE	3	1
5		6	2
6		7	5
7		8	6
8		end	7

Head
0

Avail
2

	Data	FLink	BLink
0	*DUMMY	1	end
1	JAMES	4	2
2	WAGNER	end	3
3	SEFTON	2	4
4	LEE	3	1
5		6	end
6		7	5
7		8	6
8		end	7

Head
0

Avail
5

	Data	FLink	BLink
0	*DUMMY	4	end
1		5	end
2	WAGNER	end	3
3	SEFTON	2	4
4	LEE	3	0
5		6	1
6		7	5
7		8	6
8		end	7

Head
0

Avail
1

	Data	FLink	BLink
0	*DUMMY	1	end
1	AARON	4	0
2	WAGNER	end	3
3	SEFTON	2	4
4	LEE	3	1
5		6	end
6		7	5
7		8	6
8		end	7

Head
0

Avail
5

5.
```
PROCEDURE InsertNodeDouble(Point1, Point2 : Pointer);

{ See Example 18.18 for Given-Task-Return documentation }

BEGIN
  Point1^.BLink := Point2^.BLink;
  Point1^.FLink := Point2;
  Point2^.BLink^.FLink := Point1;
  Point2^.BLink := Point1
END;

PROCEDURE DeleteNodeDouble(Point1 : Pointer);

{ See Example 18.19 for Given-Task-Return documentation }

BEGIN
  Point1^.BLink^.FLink := Point1^.FLink;
  Point1^.FLink^.BLink := Point1^.BLink;
  dispose(Point1)
END;
```

Section 4.5

1. The assignment strategy discussed in this section is unsafe because only one actual copy of the string exists in memory. Therefore, any change in that copy affects all string variables pointing to it—even those not directly involved in the change. The situation outlined in this problem is an excellent example. Because the Assign operation only adjusts pointers—it causes S1 and S2 to reference the same physical copy—ReadAString(S1) affects both S1 and S2. Even though only S1 was passed to ReadAString, S2 also points to what is read into S1^;WriteAString(S2),therefore,willoutputtheresultofReadAString(S1). If "Coffee" is read in for the first ReadAString and "Tea" is read in for the second, the output is "Tea."

5. b. We merely compare the efficiency of both methods' insert operation. Recall that in order to insert string T into string S, we need three pointers: (a) a pointer to the node in S after which to insert T; (b) a pointer to the first node in T; and (c) a pointer to the last node in T. The insert operations for both methods are equally efficient at obtaining (a) and (b), both requiring "Place" comparisons to get (a) and 0 comparisons to get (b). However, whereas the singly linked list method requires Length(T) comparisons to obtain (c), the doubly linked list method requires 0 comparisons. Because the doubly linked list method avoids having to walk to the end of T, it is more time efficient.

Section 4.6

5. In Example 16.14, replace the **FOR** loops in the cases for 'F' and 'P' with calls to TraverseColumn and TraverseRow respectively. Each of these calls to the traverse operations would require that you pass a procedure as a parameter. That procedure should be designed to write the pilot (for TraverseColumn) whenever it finds a **true** entry in the column of the table that is being traversed. Similarly, the procedure passed to TraverseRow should write the flight whenever it finds a **true** entry in the row that is traversed.

9. The implementation becomes space efficient only when

$$N < \frac{NRow * NCol - NRow - NCol}{5}$$

CHAPTER 5

Section 5.1

1.

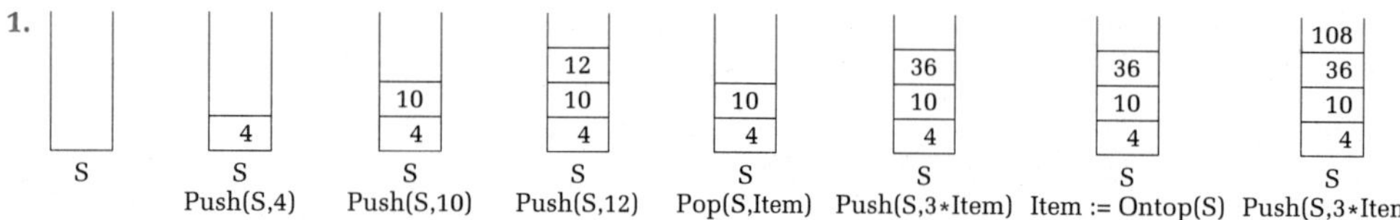

3. { Global declarations }

```
CONST
   StackSize = { Appropriate size };

TYPE
   StackType = RECORD
                 List : Array [1..StackSize] of
                        { Appropriate type };
                 Top  : integer
               END;
```

a.

```
PROCEDURE Create(Var S : StackType);

{ Given :  An array implementation of a stack. }
{ Task  :  Initialize the stack.               }
{ Return:  An initialized stack.               }

BEGIN
   S.Top := 0;
END;
```

c.

```
FUNCTION Empty(S : StackType) : boolean;

{ Given   :  An array implementation of a stack. }
{ Task    :  Test whether the stack is empty.    }
{ Return  :  true if empty; false if not empty.  }

BEGIN
   Empty := ( S.Top = 0 );
END;
```

5. The stack would grow and shrink as follows:

--	(	((	(((	((	(((	((	(	--

Section 5.2

1. Infix: A + B∗C − D/P − R
   Postfix: ABCD − PR − /∗ +
   Prefix:
   + A∗B/ − CD − PD

3.

Ch	OpStack	Postfix	Commentary
#			Push #
P			Read Ch
		P	Append Ch to Postfix
+			Read Ch
	+		Push Ch
	#		
(			Read Ch
	(		Push Ch
	+		
	#		
Q			Read Ch
		PQ	Append Ch to Postfix
−			Read Ch
	−		Push Ch
	(		
	+		
	#		
F			Read Ch
		PQF	Append Ch
)		Read Ch	
	+	PQF −	Pop and Append
	#		
/			Read Ch
	/		Push Ch
	#		
Y			Read Ch
		PQF − Y	Append Ch
#			Read Ch
		PQF − Y/ + #	Pop and Append rest of stack

7. Assume the following declarations:

```
SNptr = SNode;
SNode = RECORD
          ch : char;
          next : SNptr
        END;

PostfixString = ^StringRec;
StringRec = RECORD
              Head,
              Tail : SNptr;
            END;
```

```
PROCEDURE Append(VAR Postfix : PostfixString;
                     ch      : char);

  { Given:   Postfix String, and character ch.    }
  { Task:    Append ch to end of Postfix.          }
  { Return:  Postfix string with ch appended.      }
  { Note:    This procedure assumes that Postfix   }
  {          has been created.                     }

  VAR P : SNptr;
  BEGIN
    New(P);
    P^.ch := ch;
    P^.next := NIL;
    IF (Postfix.Head = NIL) THEN { Empty String }
      BEGIN
        Postfix.Head := P;
        Postfix.Tail := P
      END
    ELSE
      BEGIN
        Postfix.Tail^.Next := P;
        Postfix.Tail := P
      END
  END;
```

9. If operand 'A' has a stack priority that is greater than or equal to the infix priority of operand 'B,' then 'A' has equal or greater operator precedence; therefore, it is appended to the postfix string before B, and will be applied before B. Such precedence, however, can be overridden by parentheses, which force the operators between them to be unconditionally appended to the postfix string, regardless of their stack priority.

   In summary, the order in which operators are appended to the postfix string is dictated by stack priority relative to infix priority; equal or greater stack priority indicates either higher operator precedence (if the two operators being compared are different) or left-associativity, if the two operators being compared are the same.

   Hence, if we want to make the '^' operator right associative, we merely make its infix priority greater than its stack priority. Our infix and stack priority functions would then appear as follows:

Priority:	*	/	+	−	(	)	^	#
Infix	2	2	1	1	5	0	4	0
Stack	2	2	1	1	0	undefined	3	0

   The adjusted infix and stack priorities reflect both the fact that exponentiation has the highest operator precedence, and the fact that all operators except exponentiation are left-associative.

Section 5.3

3. a. Introduce an integer variable MinutesIdle, which is initialized to 0 before entering the **FOR** loop. We then add the following **ELSE** clause to the **IF** (TimeLeftOnCar = 0) AND Empty(CarQueue) clause:

```
ELSE IF (TimeLeftOnCar = 0) AND (Empty(CarQueue) THEN
  { This minute is idle }
  MinutesIdle := MinutesIdle + 1
```

b. To make this count, we merely dequeue the CarQueue until it is empty after we have exited the **FOR** loop. In Pascal, this amounts to introducing an integer variable "CarsRemaining," which we initialize to zero before dequeuing begins:

```
CarsRemaining := 0;
```

Now we are prepared to execute a **WHILE** loop:

```
WHILE NOT Empty(CarQueue) DO
  BEGIN
    Dequeue(CarQueue,Minute);
    CarsRemaining := CarsRemaining + 1
  END;
```

7.
```
PROCEDURE Create(VAR Q : Queue);

  { Given:   An arbitrary queue variable Q in an unknown state.  }
  { Task:    Initialize Q to the empty queue.                    }
  { Return: Q initialized to the empty queue.                    }

  BEGIN
    New(Q.Front);
    Q.Front^.Link := NIL;
    Q.Rear := Q.Front
  END;

FUNCTION Empty (Q : Queue) : boolean;

  { Given:   A previously created queue.                         }
  { Task:    Determine if Q is empty.                            }
  { Return: true if Q is empty; false otherwise.                 }

  BEGIN
    Empty := (Q.Front = Q.Rear)
  END;
FUNCTION Full(Q : Queue) : boolean;

  { Given:   A previously create queue.                          }
  { Task:    Determine if Q is full.                             }
  { Return: true if Q is full; false otherwise.                  }
  { Note:    Assume that the GetNode or New procedure handles    }
  {          this appropriately.                                 }
```

CHAPTER 6

Section 6.1

3. a.
```
92
6
14
```

b.
```
14
6
92
```

Note, however, that because this procedure neglects to test Head for being **NIL** before referencing Head^., a run-time "attempt to access **NIL** pointer" error will occur when the empty list is passed in for Head.

c.
```
14
6
```

Note that because this procedure neglects to test Head itself for being **NIL** before it references Head^.Link, a run-time "attempt to access **NIL** pointer" error will occur when the empty list is passed in for Head.

5. Program (a) will achieve the original intent presented. Its output is

```
MADAM
```

Program (b) will fail because it globally declares the characters being read so the recursive calls do not result in copies of the characters being pushed onto the system stack. Consequently, only the last character read is remembered and written when the recursion unwinds. Its output is

```
MMMMM
```

7. This function computes the smallest value in NumberArray within the subrange 1 . . N, where N is the value originally passed in.

11. We could insert tracer output instructions into factorial as follows:

```
FUNCTION Factorial(N : integer);

  { Given-Task-Return as in the problem statement. }

  BEGIN
    writeln('Entering Factorial with N = ',N:2);
    IF (N = 0) OR (N = 1) THEN
      BEGIN
        writeln('Computed Factorial: 1');
        Factorial := 1
      END
    ELSE
      BEGIN
        N := N - 1;
        writeln('Computing Factorial of: ',N:2, ' * ','Factorial(',N:2,');
        Factorial := N * Factorial(N)
      END
  END;
```

These tracers should clearly reveal that the factorial function is incorrectly subtracting one from N prior to the recursive call

```
Factorial := N * Factorial(N).
```

The problem, of course, is that factorial, by definition, equals

```
N * Factorial(N - 1),
```

not

```
(N - 1) * Factorial(N - 1),
```

as in the current algorithm. Hence, the problem can be easily corrected by replacing the two statements under the **ELSE** clause with the statement

```
Factorial := N * Factorial(N - 1)
```

Section 6.2

5. The output is as follows:

```
1  16
9  16
9  11
9  16
```

7. The stack frames for this function should contain three pieces of information: The current value of M, the current value of N, and the point in the program to which to return.

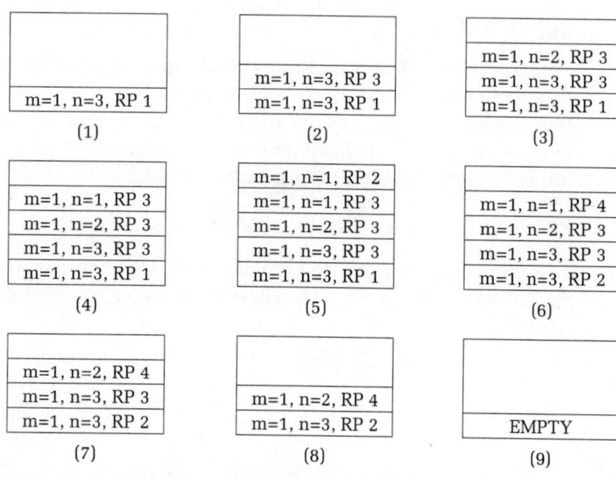

The output is as follows:

```
1  3
1  2
1  1
1  0
0  1
0  2
0  3
0  4
5
```

11. *Hint:* Consider the number of ways that M can be broken down into quarters and dimes plus the number of ways that (M − 50¢) can be broken down into half dollars, quarters, and dimes. The total of these two provide the answer in terms of quantities that are (recursively) easier to compute.

Section 6.3

5. The output is as follows:

```
12  1  2  3  4  3  3  4
 4  3  4  2  2  3  4  3
 3  4  4  3  4  3  2  3
 4  3  3  4  4  3  4  4
 2  3  4  3  3  4  4  3
 4
```

CHAPTER 7

Section 7.1

1.

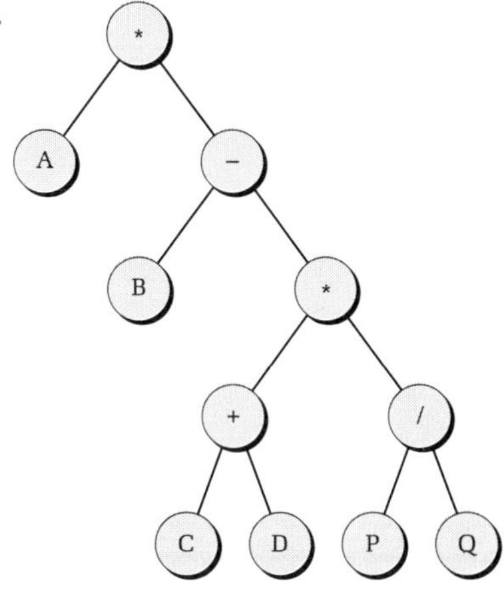

3. A tree is a hierarchically ordered data structure consisting of nodes ana links to nodes. A tree is accessed by a node called the root.

5. a. and c. are binary trees with the heap property.

   b. is not, because the node containing 35 is a subtree of the node containing 19. Similar situation for the node containing 39.

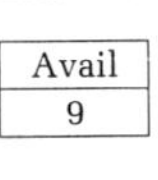

9. a.

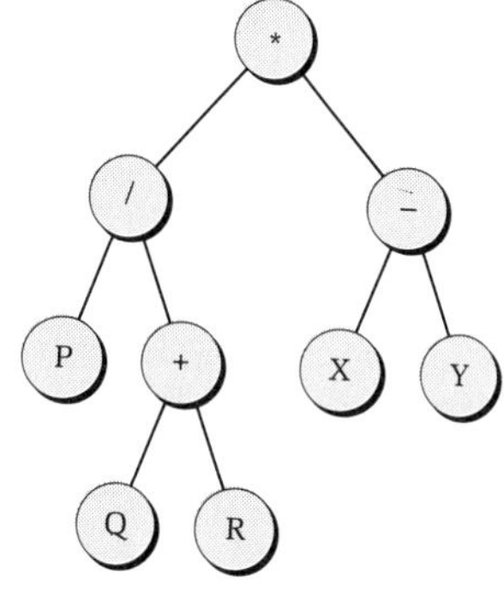

c.

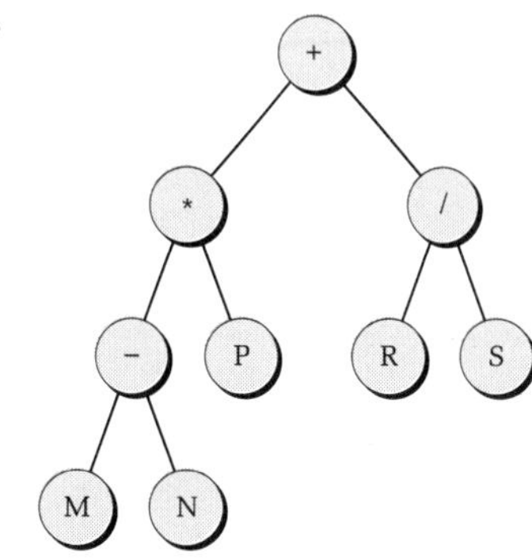

Section 7.2

1. a.

Location	Data	LeftChild	RightChild
1	C	2	–
2	R	–	3
3	G	–	–
4	F	–	–
5	X	–	4
6	Y	–	–
7	B	6	5
8	A	7	1
9		–	–

Root
8

Avail
9

b.

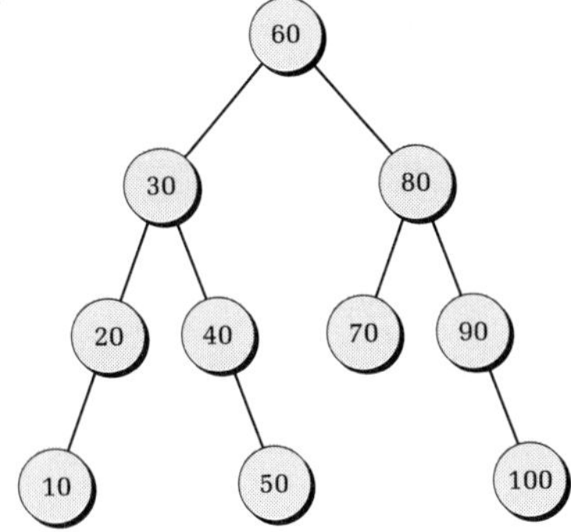

The shape of the search tree is dependent on the order in which data arrive because the first element determines the shape. The tree will give good search results if the root has a value that is the median relative to the criteria used to search the tree. If the elements added after the root alternate between the value of the root, a tree with good search results is constructed.

5. G
K
I
J
H
C
E
D
B
A

7. C
K
I
G
H
J
A
E
B
D

11.
```
PROCEDURE PostorderTrav (BT : BinaryTree;
            PROCEDURE ProcessNode (VAR Item : TreeNodeData));

   { Given:  Binary tree BT implemented using Pascal Pointer variables   }
   { Task:   Perform postorder traversal--left subtree first, then the   }
   {         right subtree, then root of BT*applying ProcessNode to      }
   {         each Item in the tree.                                      }
   { Return: Nothing.                                                    }

   BEGIN
   IF BT <> NIL THEN
     BEGIN
       PostorderTrav (BT^.LeftChild);
       PostorderTrav (BT^.RightChild);
       ProcessNode (BT^.Root)
     END
   END; { of PROCEDURE PostorderTrav }
```

15.
```
FUNCTION Eval (BT : BinaryTree) : real;

   { Given:  A nonempty algebraic expression tree.                       }
   { Task:   Evaluate the tree using a function Value to obtain          }
   {         numeric values for the operands in the tree.                }
   { Return: The value of the evaluated algebraic expression tree.       }

   { Assume a function Value is defined. }

   BEGIN
     IF BT^.Data is an operand THEN
        Eval := Value(BT^.Data)
     ELSE
        CASE BT^.Data OF
         '+' :
            Eval := Eval(BT^.LeftChild) + Eval(BT^.RightChild);
         '*' :
            Eval := Eval(BT^.LeftChild) * Eval(BT^.RightChild);
         '-' :
            Eval := Eval(BT^.LeftChild) - Eval(BT^.RightChild);
         '/' :
            Eval := Eval(BT^.LeftChild) / Eval(BT^.RightChild)
        END { of CASE statement }
   END; { of FUNCTION Eval }
```

Section 7.3

1. a. is full. b. and c. are not full.

5. b.

24
18 30
9 22 25 40

Section 7.4

1.

Item	1	2	3	4	5	6	7	8	9	10
10	10									

Item	1	2	3	4	5	6	7	8	9	10
20	20	10								

Item	1	2	3	4	5	6	7	8	9	10
30	30	10	20							

Item	1	2	3	4	5	6	7	8	9	10
40	40	30	20	10						

Item	1	2	3	4	5	6	7	8	9	10
50	50	40	20	10	30					

Item	1	2	3	4	5	6	7	8	9	10
60	60	40	50	10	30	20				

Item	1	2	3	4	5	6	7	8	9	10
70	70	40	60	10	30	20	50			

Item	1	2	3	4	5	6	7	8	9	10
80	80	70	60	40	30	20	50	10		

Item	1	2	3	4	5	6	7	8	9	10
90	90	80	60	70	30	20	50	10	40	

Item	1	2	3	4	5	6	7	8	9	10
100	100	90	60	70	80	20	50	10	40	30

3.

```
PROCEDURE PreorderTrav (BT : BinaryTree;
                   PROCEDURE ProcessNode (VAR Item: TreeDataNode));

  { Given:  Binary tree BT implemented by linear array             }
  {         representation.                                        }
  { Task:   Perform preorder traversal--root of BT, left subtree,  }
  {         then right subtree--applying ProcessNode to each Item in }
  {         the tree.                                              }
  { Return: Nothing.                                               }

  PROCEDURE PreorderTravAux (Nodelocation : integer);

  { This procedure is the behind-the-scenes recursive helper of    }
  { PreorderTrav.  The interface to PreorderTravAux is not seen    }
  { by users of the ADT.  Assumption:  Array locations which are   }
  { not presently storing data in the tree have been flagged with  }
  { an appropriate Null value.                                     }

    BEGIN
      IF NodeLocation <= MonTreeNodes THEN
        IF BT.BTData[NodeLocation] <> Null THEN
          BEGIN
            ProcessNode(BT.BTData[NodeLocation]);
            PreorderTravAux(2*NodeLocation); {  left subtree  }
            PreorderTravAux(2*NodeLocation+1); {  right subtree  }
          END
    END; { of PROCEDURE PreorderTravAux }

BEGIN
  IF BT.NumberNodes <> 0 THEN
    PreorderTravAux(1 {  location of the root of BT  })
END;  { of PROCEDURE PreorderTrav }
```

Section 7.5

1. The indentation can be obtained by increasing the indentation before traversing the left (child) subtree and decreasing the indentation again before traversing the right (sibling) subtree.

3. Preorder traversal

```
P  Q  T  U  V  C  D  E
M  N  O  W  A  G  B  H
I  J  X  K  L
```

Section 7.6

1. The order of the nodes would be Seattle, Chicago, Miami, New Orleans, Dallas, New York, Washington, Milwaukee, Phoenix, San Francisco, Los Angeles, Las Vegas, Minneapolis, Oklahoma City.

3. One way the cities could be visited is as follows: Seattle, Chicago, San Francisco, Miami, New Orleans, Las Vegas, Milwaukee, Los Angeles, Dallas, Washington, Phoenix, Minneapolis, New York City, Oklahoma City.

9. Eliminating the requirement that **TYPE** GraphNode be a subrange of an ordinal type would mean that there would not be a convenient way to index the nodes in the graph, making the normal operations more difficult to perform. One strategy to overcome that problem would be to build an indexing scheme that would make indexing the nodes very convenient.

CHAPTER 8

Section 8.1

1.
```
60  12  90  20  64   8   6
 8  12   6  20  64  90  60
 6  12   8  20  60  90  64
 6   8  12  20  60  64  90
```

3. The shell sort is named after its inventor D. L. Shell.

5. Relatively prime values of the increments are better because they insure distinct increments that will not divide evenly into each other so that data that have been compared to each other are less likely to be compared again.

7. The best case for the shell sort algorithm presented in this section would be a data set with the data already in order: each segment would be in order and no data would be swapped. The worst case would be a data set arranged in descending order because every data element would be out of order and there would be a maximum number of data swaps.

9. The body of the ShellSort procedure would be as follows:

```
 VAR
  K : integer;
BEGIN
 K := 1;
 WHILE K < N DO
   K := (3*K) + 1;
 K := K DIV 3;
 WHILE K > 0 DO
   BEGIN
     SegmentedInsertionSort(Key, N, K);  { same procedure as before }
     K := K DIV 3  { Reduce  number of segments }
   END;
END;  { of PROCEDURE ShellSort }
```

Section 8.2

1. The output would be as follows:

```
 1   7
60  12  90  30  64   8   6

 1   4
 6  12   8  30

 2   4
12   8  30

 2   2
 8

 4   4
30

 6   7
64  90

 7   7
90
```

3. The bubble sort is better than the quick sort when the data are already in order. The bubble sort can safely conclude that the data are in order after the first pass through the data; the quick sort must perform the entire sort even if the data are already in order.

5. The choice of the pivotal point will not change the overall efficiency of the quick sort; however, it does dramatically change the best and worst data sets.

9. All of the quick sort procedure would remain the same as in the book. One line in the partition procedure would change from

```
Pivot := Key[Lo];
```

to

```
{ Assume the FUNCTION median gives the median of three values. }
Pivot := Median(Key[Lo], Key[(Lo+Hi) DIV 2], Key[Hi]);
```

This variation should be more efficient because the pivot value is more likely to split the array being sorted more evenly. Quick sort is most efficient when the array is split at the midpoint.

Section 8.3

1.

```
60  12  90  30  64   8   6
60  12  90  30  64   8   6
60  64  90  30  12   8   6
 6  64  60  30  12   8  90
 8  30  60   6  12  64  90
12  30   8   6  60  64  90
 6  12   8  30  60  64  90
 8   6  12  30  60  64  90
 6   8  12  30  60  64  90
```

3. The sort derives its name from the heap structure that it uses in sorting the data.

5. The heap sort is not always as efficient as the quick sort. On average, the quick sort is slightly better than the heap sort because its big-O constant of proportionality will be smaller. However, the heap sort handles data already sorted much faster than the quick sort.

Section 8.4

1. The output for MergeSort would be

```
 1   7
60  12  90  30  64   8   6

 1   4
60  12  90  30

 1   2
60  12

 1   1
60

 2   2
60  12

 2   2
60  12
```

and so on . . .

3. **PROCEDURE** MergeSort would be more efficient if the Source parameter for the subordinate **PROCEDURE** Order were a **VAR** parameter because then the address of the array would be sent to the procedure. With Source as a value parameter, the procedure makes a local copy of the entire array upon each call. Since the procedure is recursive, many such copies may exist on the system stack at a given time. In fact, if the Source array is very large, this can lead to an overflow of the system stack and hence an execution error.

7. Heap sort, quick sort, and shell sort are unstable. Merge sort is unstable as written but can be modified so that it is stable. Bubble sort, insertion sort, and selection sort are stable.

CHAPTER 9

Section 9.1

1. a. The keys would have the following positions:

Record No.	Key
1	333
2	632
3	1090
4	459
5	379
6	238
7	
8	
9	
10	1982
11	3411

c. With the chaining method, the keys and links would be

Record No.	Key	Link
1	333	13
2	632	0
3	1090	0
4		
5		
6		
7		
8		
9		
10	1982	12
11		

Record No.	Key	Link
12	3411	14
13	459	0
14	379	15
15	238	0
16		
17		
18		
19		
20		
21		
22		

3. a. The best method to implement the card catalog in this situation would be hashing. Hashing allows for very quick searches and is fairly good at handling additions and deletions. Since the library rarely prints out an ordered list of books, the time it takes to sort the list doesn't really matter.

   c. The best method to implement the data base would be the binary search. The states are kept in order by two-letter code. All the program need do is access the record quickly, increment a field, and be able to print the list out in order. All these are handled very well by a binary search.

5. a.
```
PROCEDURE QuadraticHash (Target : KeyType;
                         SearchList : DataArray;
                         VAR InfoWanted : DataRec;
                         VAR Found : boolean);

{ This solution will search until it finds Target, finds empty location,
  or visits original hash location for a second time }

VAR
  K, J, R : integer;
  Traversed : boolean;

BEGIN
  Found := false; { Assume failure }
  Traversed := false; { Toggled to true if entire list is traversed }
  K := Hash(Target); { Call on hashing function }
  J := K;
  R := 0;
  WHILE (SearchList[J].Key <> Empty) AND NOT (Traversed OR Found) DO
    IF Target = SearchList[J].Key THEN
      BEGIN
        InfoWanted := SearchList[J];
        Found := true
      END
    ELSE
      BEGIN
        R := R + 1;
        J := ((J + R*R - 1) MOD RecordSpace) + 1; { MOD insures wraparound }
        Traversed := (J = K)
      END
 END; { OF PROCEDURE QuadraticHash }
```

Section 9.2

1. As suggested in the text, the doubly linked list is the best choice for implementing linked lists with hashing. When the order of the list is disturbed during a change of a key field or during a deletion of an item in the list, the linked list must be rebuilt. If a doubly linked list is not used, the list would have to be traversed to find the predecessor node in the linked list. The doubly linked list makes rebuilding lists more efficient.

Section 9.3

1. a. 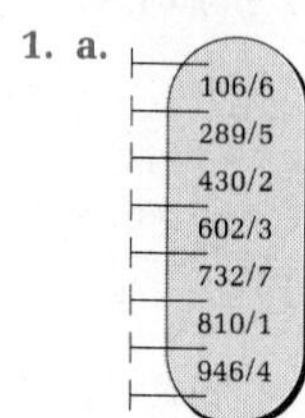

5. a. For the ISAM index, this knowledge will enable us to set the index so that the subsequent search on the disk will be more efficient.

   c. The trie is constructed the same no matter what the disk structure may be.

Index

TABLE OF ABSTRACT DATA TYPES AND THEIR IMPLEMENTATIONS